Gangster Films

For my parents,
and Jason, Chuck, Nancy,
and Debby

Gangster Films

*A Comprehensive,
Illustrated Reference to
People, Films and Terms*

by MICHAEL L. STEPHENS

McFarland & Company, Inc., Publishers
Jefferson, North Carolina, and London

British Library Cataloguing-in-Publication data are available

Library of Congress Cataloguing-in-Publication Data

Stephens, Michael L., 1961–
    Gangster films : a comprehensive, illustrated reference to people,
films and terms / by Michael L. Stephens.
      p. cm.
    Includes bibliographical references and index. ∞
    ISBN 0-7864-0046-3 (lib. bdg. : 50# alk. paper)
    1. Gangster films—Encyclopedias. 2. Detective and mystery
films—Encyclopedias. I. Title.
PN1995.9.G3S84 1996
791.43′655—dc20   95-45783
                                                    CIP

Manufactured in the United States of America

McFarland & Company, Inc., Publishers
 Box 611, Jefferson, North Carolina, 28640

Contents

Introduction

The conventions of the gangster movie have become familiar to contemporary audiences: the dizzy moll perpetually chewing gum, the well dressed gangster with the tuxedo that hides a gun, the Mafia family, the kiss of death, smokey nightclubs, tough talking dames, the burst of machine guns in the night, the incorruptible G-man triumphing against impossible criminal odds, the robbery of a small town bank and subsequent getaway, and the well planned heist gone bad. All are part of the cinematic language, the lore of the genre, as much today as in the 1930s. Substitute illegal drugs for alcohol, throw in a little nudity and graphic violence, and the films and their themes remain essentially the same. The gangster genre has provided a rich source of material for American filmmakers for over six decades, and has had a profound influence on the world's cinema.

The gangster has been part of the world's mythology for as long as anyone can remember. The highway robber was a popular character in European literature from the earliest picturesque novels. Real highway robbers terrorized the European wilderness for many centuries, and reappeared in the American west (and the mythology and literature of the Western) as the stagecoach and train robbers. However, the term "gangster"—meaning, literally, a member of a gang—did not become popular until the 1920s when it was used by American journalists to describe the Mafia and Mafia-like criminal organizations in New York and Chicago, and later applied to the rural gangsters of the early 1930s (Bonnie and Clyde, John Dillinger) who were the modern equivalent of the highway robbers.

From the early silent cinema, the contemporary gangster has been a popular figure in American movies. Early filmmakers sensed the dramatic potential of the subject and there were certainly some precedents to D. W. Griffith's *The Musketeers of Pig Alley* (Biograph, 1912), the first important gangster movie. Here one encounters the conventions of the genre while still in its infancy. Indeed, the film was made just as the big city gangs (the subject of the film) were beginning to organize themselves into the

1

modern groups, most commonly known as the Mafia. For Griffith, as for many of his antecedents, the gangster tale provided him with a ready set of characters and themes that were at once dramatic, and also the perfect vehicle for a moral or social message. Griffith later used a gangster story in his compendium *Intolerance* (Biograph, 1914), a tale of good triumphing over evil.

However, the true gangster movie did not become a reality until the 1920s during Prohibition. The gangster wars in New York and subsequent rise of real life, colorful figures like Al Capone, Mickey Cohen, Bugsy Siegel, and many others were popular subjects of the mass media. Hollywood producers, never ones to pass up a potential market, began to make gangster movies in the mid-1920s and, when these proved popular, continued to make them with increasing frequency as the decade progressed. By then, the clichés and conventions of the genre were already established, thanks both to the images perpetrated in the press and in popular pulp novels, particularly those of W. R. Burnett, who would have a profound influence on the genre in coming years. *Me, Gangster* (Fox, 1928), *The Racket* (Paramount, 1928), *Outside the Law* (Universal, 1921), and *The Big City* (MGM, 1928) are just a few of the notable gangster movies of the 1920s.

However, the finest early series of gangster movies was produced at Paramount and directed by Josef von Sternberg. Beginning with the classic *Underworld* (Paramount, 1927), and continuing through three subsequent pictures, *Docks of New York* (Paramount, 1928), *The Dragnet* (Paramount, 1928) and *Thunderbolt* (Paramount, 1929), von Sternberg, more than any other filmmaker, popularized the genre and its conventions with these four films. While still little more than contrived moral fables, the von Sternberg gangster movies emphasized style over content, and with their morally ambiguous themes and characters, and dark, expressionist style, presaged *film noir* by nearly two decades.

While the gangster drama was popular in the late silent era, the genre was not fully established until the early sound era. The genre reached its artistic zenith during this period, particularly with those gangster dramas produced at Warner Bros. in the 1930s. Under executive producer Darryl F. Zanuck, the Warner Bros. films established the genre's unsentimental, hard-boiled style. Beginning with *Little Caesar* (First National, 1931), based on W. R. Burnett's best selling novel, and directed by Mervyn LeRoy with unadorned economy (as opposed to Sternberg's labored extravagances), the genre took on renewed energy and entered its golden age. Thanks in large part to Edward G. Robinson's extraordinary performance, *Little Caesar* was a great box office success (and has been considered a classic ever since). It made Robinson, more than any of his silent predecessors, into one of the genre's first great icons.

Little Caesar was followed shortly by *Public Enemy* (Warner Bros., 1931), whose impact was just as great. Directed by William Wellman in the same hard-boiled style as *Little Caesar*, it is probably best known today as the film which made James Cagney a star, and in which he smashes a grapefruit into the face of the lingerie clad Mae Clarke.

Unlike Robinson, who was one of the few independent actors in the golden age of the studio system, Cagney was a Warner Bros. contract employee. Ripe for exploitation after this initial success, the studio subsequently cast him in ever-increasingly elaborate gangster melodramas. But the rebellious Cagney also forced the studio to put him into more heroic roles (in order to sustain his popular good guy image). The result, *G-Men* (Warner Bros., 1935), was one of the first gangster movies to feature a heroic central character, and the first to showcase police procedures.

With its remarkable group of unconventional contract players, including James Cagney, Humphrey Bogart, Ann Dvorak and Bette Davis (augmented by Edward G. Robinson's frequent appearances), and a group of writers and directors who specialized in hard-boiled subjects, Warner Bros. created the finest group of gangster movies during the genre's golden age, 1930–1940.

However, Warner Bros. was not the only studio regularly making gangster movies in the 1930s. *City Streets* (Paramount, 1931) is as hard-boiled and cynical as any of the Warner Bros. gangster movies. But Paramount relegated gangster productions mainly to its "B" units which, nevertheless, turned out an interesting series of low-budget movies starring Lloyd Nolan and Akim Tamiroff in the late 1930s.

With rare exceptions, the non–Warner gangster movies were pale imitations of the Warner style. Other studios lacked suitable personalities, while Warner Bros. had a corner on tough, cynical actors. Still, there were exceptions. Surprisingly, MGM, the home of family fare and happy endings, contributed a number of important, early gangster movies. With tough guys Clark Gable and Spencer Tracy under contract, the studio's best gangster pictures, *Manhattan Melodrama* (MGM, 1934) and *Whipsaw* (MGM, 1936), can be favorably compared to Warner's best. However, MGM's studio head, L. B. Mayer, did not appreciate the genre's hard style and realistic themes, and Gable and Tracy were most often seen in conventional action and adventure films (which Mayer believed were more suitable for a romantic lead).

Certainly the greatest of the non–Warner gangster movies from this period is *Scarface: The Shame of a Nation*, now known simply as *Scarface* (United Artists, 1932). Produced by Howard Hughes and elegantly directed by Howard Hawks, the film stars Paul Muni (ironically, borrowed from Warner Bros.), as Tony Camonte, the antihero based on Al Capone. It co-stars George Raft, whose off-screen connections with real mobsters have been well established. Making an impression as Guino Rinaldo, the coin-tossing mob underling, Raft became yet another of the genre's great male icons of the early 1930s, although in the end he made far fewer important films than his more famous (and talented) rivals.

By the late 1930s, the original gangster cycle had run its course. Robinson and Cagney were most often seen as heroes or comic villains—as in Robinson's semisatirical *Brother Orchid* (Warner Bros., 1940). Bette Davis had graduated to romantic melodramas, and Bogart, just emerging as a star, would most often appear as a flawed antihero. A decade of the Great Depression and the rise of Fascism in Europe had made Americans cynical of authority and financial institutions. The genre was revitalized during the 1940s in the more cynical, expressionistic style of *film noir*.

Perhaps the earliest of the true gangster *noirs* was *High Sierra* (Warner Bros., 1940), in which Bogart became a full fledged movie star. With its cast of antiheroes, amoral story and downbeat ending, *High Sierra* was typical of the new group of gangster movies, and its enormous financial success, along with the high box office grosses of several other contemporary releases, helped popularize the new style. Remarkably, a decade after the exploits of Bonnie and Clyde, Machine Gun Kelly and John Dillinger, it was also one of the earliest films to use the theme of the small time, rural gangster, a type of character that became more common in later films such as *They Live by Night* (RKO, 1948).

Meanwhile, in films like *Lucky Jordan* (Paramount, 1942), gangsters were enlisted in the Allied cause during World War II. Alan Ladd, the star of *Lucky Jordan*, was perhaps the most typical of the *noir* antiheroes in his 1940s movies. Invariably typecast, he first achieved popularity as a psychotic mob assassin in the classic *This Gun for Hire* (Paramount, 1942). Ladd would graduate to somewhat more heroic roles as his popularity increased, but the air of cynicism and self doubt were always qualities of his characters, particularly in the series of gangster films he starred in during the 1940s and 1950s.

Like Humphrey Bogart, Alan Ladd became a star after laboring for a decade in "B" movies and "A" supporting roles. However, the 1940s saw a new group of hard-boiled stars emerge to compete with the veterans: Kirk Douglas, Robert Mitchum and Burt Lancaster all starred in classic gangster *noirs*. The stars of the original cycle, however, also made important appearances in *films noir*: James Cagney in *White Heat* (Warner Bros., 1949) and *Kiss Tomorrow Goodbye* (Warner Bros., 1950), and Edward G. Robinson and Claire Trevor, one of the 1930s' most memorable molls, starred alongside Humphrey Bogart in the classic *Key Largo* (Warner Bros., 1948).

The 1940s also saw the first gangster biopics, in which real life mobsters were the subjects. *Roger Touhy, Gangster* (20th Century–Fox, 1944) was probably the first such biopic, but *Dillinger* (Monogram, 1944), starring

Lawrence Tierney, is the most important. A low-budget programmer, using much stock footage in its action sequences, *Dillinger* is distinguished by Tierney's powerful, visceral performance. For a time it looked like Tierney might become one of the 1940s' major new stars, but his volatile off-screen life ruined his promising career, and he was relegated mainly to negligible "B" movies.

In the 1950s, *film noir* underwent a transition from its extravagances of the previous decade, particularly in style, moving away from the shadowy, almost stagnant, films of the 1940s to a more realistic, violent style in the new decade. *The Big Heat* (Columbia, 1953) inaugurated the new style, introducing a variation on the genre, the police procedural, the most prevalent type of gangster movie from then to the present.

The 1950s also saw the production of two other, more peculiar variations on the genre, the gangster musicals *Party Girl* (MGM, 1958) and *Guys and Dolls* (MGM, 1955). However, these were not the first musicals based on gangster themes — *Casbah* (Universal, 1948) is one of the more prominent early gangster musicals — nor representative of the most common variation on the genre, the gangster satire. Beginning in the early 1930s, many gangster satires were released. The best of these, *Lady for a Day* (Columbia, 1933), *Larceny, Inc.* (Warner Bros., 1942), *A Slight Case of Murder* (Warner Bros., 1938) and *Prizzi's Honor* (20th Century–Fox, 1985) are just four of the dozen or so gangster satires.

Before the 1950s, the American gangster movie had a profound influence on international, particularly French, cinema. In the 1930s, France produced one of the first European gangster classics, *Pépé le Moko* (Paris Films, 1937), which was remade in Hollywood as the classic gangster-romance *Algiers* (United Artists, 1938). Jean Gabin, the star of the original, was a French version of Bogart or Cagney, a hard-boiled but romantic hero in the typical French fashion. Gabin starred in a number of gangster-oriented movies in his four decades as a star. However, the most important European figure in the genre was the director Jean-Pierre Melville, a man obsessed with American culture, particularly movies. He made a series of *noir*-like thrillers and gangster films over three decades, beginning in the late 1940s. Probably the best of Melville's gangster thrillers is *Le Samourai* (C.I.C.C.–Fida Cinematografica, 1967), a bizarre, moody melodrama which shows the influence of Warner Bros. gangster movies of the 1930s and 1940s *film noir*.

It is also notable that the American director Jules Dassin made two classics of the genre, *Rififi* (Miracle, 1955) and *Topkapi* (United Artists, 1964), while living in exile in France after being declared a communist during the McCarthy witchhunts of the early 1950s.

The *noir* cycle had run its course by the mid-1950s, bringing an end to the second great cycle of gangster movies. But this did not mark the end of the gangster film. Over the next three decades, a number of gangster movies of all types were released sporadically. The "B" movies of Roger Corman and American International, and the so-called blaxploitation pictures of the 1970s continued the traditions of the 1930s genre, albeit less successfully.

The Godfather (Paramount, 1972) and its sequels ushered in a new style: the gangster movie as epic art film. Certainly the first two installments in the saga are great movies, rich in detail and nuance, style, and performances, introducing a whole new group of important actors including Al Pacino, Diane Keaton and Robert Redford.

Mario Puzo's fictionalized account of the rise and fall of a Mafia family, led by the imposing godfather (Marlon Brando) was translated brilliantly to the screen by director-coscenarist Francis Ford Coppola, setting the standard by which all subsequent gangster pictures have been measured and, ultimately, have been found to fail. Coppola's *The Cotton Club* (Orion, 1983), Sergio Leone's *Once Upon a Time in America* (Warner Bros., 1984) and *Billy Bathgate* (Touchstone, 1993) have all aspired to the heights of *The Godfather* without making it.

Of the contemporary group, the best is Martin Scorsese's modern classic, *GoodFellas* (Warner Bros., 1990). Like the Godfather saga, *GoodFellas* is based on real events, but Scorsese avoided Coppola's epic scope for a more experimental narrative and interjected a dark, self-deprecating humor missing from most post–*Godfather* gangster movies.

Over the course of its sixty year history so far, the gangster movie has undergone an evolution of styles and themes. This book is an encyclopedic reference of the genre from its origins to the present. It includes entries for all the major and most of the minor gangster movies, some of the more notable off-genre pictures, and foreign films. Biographies, filmographies, listings of related subjects, and an appendix are also included, making it the most extensive single volume reference on the subject.

The Encyclopedia

Ackerman, Leonard (b. 1927)
Producer. An independent producer, Ackerman often collaborated with John H. Burrows. Together, they produced a number of low budget films in the late fifties including the ultraviolent biopic of gangster Al Capone, perhaps their most important production.
Al Capone (Allied Artists, 1959).

Across 110th Street (United Artists, 1972). 102 mins.
Executive Producers: Anthony Quinn and Barry Shear. *Producer*: Ralph Serpe. *Director*: Barry Shear. *Screenplay*: Luther Davis, based on a novel by Wally Ferris. *Music*: J. J. Johnson. *Art Director*: Perry Watkins. *Editor*: Byron Brandt.
Cast: Anthony Quinn (Capt. Frank Mattelli), Yaphet Kotto (Det. Lt. Pope), Anthony Franciosa (Nick D'Salvio), Ed Bernard (Joe Logart), Richard Ward (Doc Johnson). *With*: Norma Donaldson, Antonio Fargas, Gilbert Lewis, Marlene Warfield.
In Harlem, a gang of black thugs attempts to cut into the Mafia's stranglehold on narcotics and crime in the community. They steal $300,000 that the Mafia has gathered from their various nefarious activities. Nick D'Salvio, the Mafia's don, seeks revenge against the trio of black thieves by killing two of them and hoping to find and kill the other. Meanwhile, two cops, Frank Mattelli and Lt. Pope, are assigned to find the third man before the Mafia thugs do. Eventually, the third man is cornered in an old building. In the ensuing shootout, he is killed, as is Mattelli; but the mob is prevented from collecting its money when, at the last moment, the dying thief throws it out of the window into a busy schoolyard, where the children retrieve it.

Essentially a police procedural, *Across 110th Street* is similar in many respects to its contemporary, *Dirty Harry* (Warner Bros., 1972). However, whereas the latter is concerned with personal violence (as represented by a serial killer), this film attempts a realistic view of contemporary urban violence and organized crime. Amazingly, it manages to avoid the clichés of the blaxploitation films then so popular. Nevertheless, its attempts at realism are not totally convincing and its overwhelming sense of *noir*-like alienation and doom (the Quinn character, for example, is a crooked cop) hampers the film somewhat. Still, it is an interesting melodrama that provides a unique glimpse at the Mafia and street crime in the era of the more "nostalgic" *Godfather* sagas.

Adams, Gerald Drayson (b. 1904)
Screenwriter. A former literary agent, Adams was a successful screenwriter for three decades, beginning in the late forties. He cowrote several popular films, including two *films*

noir, Dead Reckoning (Columbia, 1947), and *The Big Steal*. The latter, an early Don Siegel movie, is an unpretentious action oriented gangster film that attempted to recapture the magic of the classic *noir, Out of the Past* (RKO, 1947), which also starred Robert Mitchum and Jane Greer. While not as successful as the earlier classic, Drayson's script, cowritten with *Out of the Past* writer Geoffrey Homes, is a rollicking adventure and a worthy addition to the *film noir* and gangster genres.

The Big Steal (RKO, 1949).

Adams, Julie (aka Julia; b. 1926)

Actress. Born Betty May Adams, Julie first used the screen name Julia. As Julia, Adams starred in *The Creature from the Black Lagoon* (Universal-International, 1954) as the menaced girl. Tall, voluptuous, and quite talented, Adams was nevertheless relegated to mostly "B" pictures. She did not have much to do in *Six Bridges to Cross*, an excellent caper drama based on a true story. Adams, the female lead, had a conventional part as the girlfriend of a cop. Unfortunately, she was never cast as a moll, a role more suitable to her seductive talents.

Six Bridges to Cross (Universal, 1955).

Adams, Nick (1931–1968)

Actor. Born Nicholas Adamschock, Adams never quite reached the big time, but left behind many memorable performances in his all too brief career. He specialized in neurotics and tough guys, and starred in the low budget gangster melodrama *Young Dillinger* as the notorious gangster. His performance is surprisingly multidimensional, and Adams manages to make the character's seething violence and psychosis almost palpable.

Young Dillinger (Allied Artists, 1965).

Adler, Jay (1899–1978)

Character actor. With his brother Luther (1903–1984) and sister Stella Adler (1895–1993), Jay was a familiar face in American movies for over three decades. His stocky build and tough visage made him a natural for sinister parts, and he most often appeared as a small time hood or gangster.

The Mob (Columbia, 1951). *My Six Convicts* (Columbia, 1952). *The Big Combo* (Allied Artists, 1955). *Illegal* (Warner Bros., 1955).

Adler, Luther (1903–1984)

Character actor. Luther, like his elder brother, specialized in tough guys, second bananas, etc. A major stage performer, he also appeared regularly in American features. He costarred in a little known but excellent "B" thriller, *Crashout*, as one of the gang of convicts who attempt unsuccessfully to escape from prison. He also had an important role in *The Brotherhood*, a minor film which, nevertheless, is an important precursor of *The Godfather* (Paramount, 1972). Adler appears as a tough old gangster, a catalyst of the story's action.

Hoodlum Empire (Republic, 1952). *The Miami Story* (Columbia, 1954). *Crashout* (Filmakers, 1955). *The Brotherhood* (Paramount, 1968).

Against All Odds (Columbia, 1984). 128 mins.

Executive Producer: Jerry Brock. *Producers*: Taylor Hackford and William S. Gilmore. *Director*: Taylor Hackford. *Screenplay*: Taylor Hackford, based on the screenplay *Out of the Past* by Daniel Mainwaring. *Music*: Michel Colombier and Larry Carlton. *Art Director*: Richard James Lawrence. *Editors*: Fredric Steinkamp and William Steinkamp.

Cast: Rachel Ward (Jessie Wyler), Jeff Bridges (Terry Brogan), James Woods (Jake Wise), Alex Karras (Hank Sully), Jane Greer (Mrs. Wyler). *With*: Richard Widmark, Dorian Harewood, Swoosie Kurtz, Saul Rubinek.

Fay Spain and Rod Steiger live it up in *Al Capone.*

Terry Brogan, an aging football star, falls in with a small-time gangster, Jake Wise, and his promiscuous girlfriend, Jessie. Jessie has disappeared after stealing some money from Jake. The down-on-his-luck Terry agrees to go to Mexico and bring her back, but instead falls for her, leading to the inevitable, tragic consequences.

Loosely based on the *film noir* classic *Out of the Past* (RKO, 1947), *Against All Odds* does not add much to the genre except some resplendent color photography and Rachel Ward's sensual performance as the amoral Jessie Wyler. Also, James Woods' performance as the bookie/gangster on the rise is very compelling.

Al Capone (Allied Artists, 1959). 105 mins.
Producers: John H. Burrows and Leonard J. Ackerman. *Director*: Richard Wilson. *Screenplay*: Malvin Wald and Henry Greenberg. *Music*: David Raksin. *Art Director*: Hilyard Brown. *Director of Photography*: Lucien Ballard. *Editor*: Walter Hannemann.

Cast: Rod Steiger (Al Capone), Fay Spain (Maureen Flannery), Murvyn Vye (Bugs Moran), James Gregory (Sergeant Schaeffer), Nehemiah Persoff (Johnny Torrio), Lewis Charles (Hymie Weiss), Joe DeSantis (Big Jim Colosimo). *With*: Martin Balsam, Louis Quinn, Raymond Bailey, Robert Gust, Peter Dane, Al Ruscio, Lewis Charles.

The Brooklyn hoodlum Al Capone arrives in Chicago in 1920 to work as a bouncer for Johnny Torrio's gambling establishment. However, the ruthless Capone is ambitious for power and soon rises to become head of the mob during Prohibition. Eventually convicted of tax evasion and sentenced to

The St. Valentine's Day Massacre reenacted in the classic "B" gangster drama *Al Capone.*

the notorious Alcatraz, Capone survives the ordeal only to die later of complications from syphilis.

Influenced by the enormous success of the television series *The Untouchables, Al Capone* was a "B" production that relied mainly on lurid violence and nonstop action. Nevertheless, despite its low budget, the film is very well written, providing some interesting psychological insights into the real life of Capone, and the performances — particularly by Rod Steiger and Fay Spain (as one of Capone's romantic interests and, not ironically, also the widow of one of his early victims) — are first rate. With its fast pace and crude direction, the film also successfully echoes the style of the genre's earliest films.

Albertson, Frank (1909–1964)

Actor. Albertson starred in a number of popular romantic comedies in the late thirties, but never quite achieved

the big time. Within a few years he had become a regular fixture in "B" movies like *Citadel of Crime*, in which he starred as a government agent fighting a gang of moonshiners.

Citadel of Crime (Republic, 1941).

Aldrich, Robert (1918–1983)

Director. A master of violent action and psychological insight (particularly portraying paranoia), Aldrich was a late master of *film noir*. *Kiss Me Deadly* is one of the finest examples of the genre, and is an interesting addition to the gangster genre. It presented a new, more deadly gang of criminals than had been portrayed before in American films. Less well known is his gangster melodrama *The Grisom Gang*, a relentlessly violent film which harks back, in theme and style, to the classics of the thirties genre.

Kiss of Death (United Artists, 1955).
The Grisom Gang (Cinerama, 1971).

Charles Boyer, as the debonair gangster Pépé le Moko, surrounded by equally debonair gangsters from *Algiers.*

Algiers (United Artists, 1938). 95 mins. *Producer*: Walter Wanger. *Director*: John Cromwell. *Screenplay*: John Howard Lawson and James M. Cain, based on the story *Pépé le Moko* by Detective Ashelbe. *Art Director*: Alexander Toluboff. *Music*: Vincent Scott and Mohammed Igorbouchen. *Director of Photography*: James Wong Howe.

Cast: Charles Boyer (Pépé le Moko), Sigrid Gurie (Ines), Hedy Lamarr (Gaby), Joseph Calleia (Slimane), Gene Lockhart (Regis), Johnny Downs (Pierrot), Alan Hale (Grandpere), Mme. Nina Koshetz (Tania). *With*: Joan Woodbury, Claudia Dell, Robert Greig, Stanley Fields, Charles D. Brown, Ben Halls.

Algiers has entered into the folklore of Hollywood, if only for Hedy Lamarr's famous line, "Come with me to the Casbah." Based on a novel which had already been adapted as a famous French film, the story centers on the exploits of the criminal Pépé le Moko. Pépé must remain in the sanctuary of the Casbah section of Algiers to avoid capture by the police; but his love for the beautiful, tempestuous Gaby eventually leads to his demise.

Algiers presents a rather romantic view of the criminal underworld, but it is also one of the first to deal somewhat realistically with the less glamorous aspects of gangster life. Charles Boyer gave one of his best performances as the doomladen jewel thief, but the film is best remembered for introducing the dark-haired, exotic Hungarian actress Hedy Lamarr to American films. The movie made her a star overnight. Unfortunately, she would never again appear in a film as successful as this.

Publicity still from *Alibi*, one of the earliest gangster talkies, showing the influence of art deco design in its set, but little of the hard-boiled realism that would emerge at Warner Bros. within two years.

Alibi (United Artists, 1929). 84 mins. *Presenter*: Joseph M. Schenck. *Producer/Director*: Roland West. *Screenplay*: C. Gardner Sullivan and Roland West, based on the play *Nightstick* by John Griffith Wray, J. C. Nugent, and Elaine S. Carrington. *Art Director*: William Cameron Menzies. *Director of Photography*: Ray June. *Editor*: Hal Kern.

Cast: Chester Morris (Chick Williams), Harry Stubbs (Buck Backman), Mae Busch (Daisy Thomas), Eleanor Griffith (Joan Manning), Irma Harrison (Totts, the Cabaret Dancer). *With*: Regis Toomey, Al Hill, James Bradbury, Jr., Elmer Ballard, Kernan Cripps, Purnell B. Pratt.

Chick Williams is a gangster who romances and marries Joan Manning, the daughter of a policeman, using her as an alibi for a robbery. His wife, of course, believes Chick is innocent, but the police have infiltrated Chick's gang via an undercover agent. When Chick discovers the deception, he has the agent killed; but his criminal life comes to an end when he is cornered and gunned down by the police in his own home.

One of the earliest gangster talkies, *Alibi* stars Chester Morris, one of the genre's first stars. Morris, a Broadway star, was brought to Hollywood in the late twenties, and immediately achieved stardom. Handsome and quite talented, he was popular throughout the thirties, but he appeared in few good films and is all but forgotten today. The film suffers from its primitive technique, but it remains interesting as one of the first gangster epics of the sound era.

Allen, Gwen (Fictional character)
Jean Harlow's elegant, but superficial moll in *Public Enemy* (Warner

Bros., 1931) is a small supporting role, the least famous in the film. She is the second moll the main character, Tom Powers (James Cagney), takes up with after abandoning his first lover, Kitty (Mae Clarke), when she provokes him to smash a grapefruit in her face during a violent argument.

Allen, Lewis (1905–1986)
Director. Allen was a fine director of "B" action films and melodramas. He had a great sense of style, and punctuated his movies with strong visuals and characterizations. Few of his movies have stood the test of time, but all of his gangster films have commendable qualities. The best of these is probably *A Bullet for Joey*, which gave strong roles to two aging icons of the genre, Edward G. Robinson and George Raft.
Desert Fury (Paramount, 1947). *A Bullet for Joey* (United Artists, 1955). *Illegal* (Warner Bros., 1955).

Allied Artists
From the late thirties to the late fifties, Allied Artists was one of the most prominent Poverty Row studios. It was the "A" half of the production company, reserving its cheaper productions for its other half, Monogram Pictures. Allied Artists hit its stride in the fifties, producing a series of gritty, realistic thrillers directed by such superior filmmakers as Don Siegel and Phil Karlson. Siegel made the great "B" prison picture *Riot in Cell Block 11* for the studio in this decade, while Karlson made the extraordinary *The Phenix City Story*. Equally brilliant are the gangster *noir The Gangster* and Joseph H. Lewis' *The Big Combo*, unquestionably one of the best "B" movies ever. In the late fifties, the studio began to concentrate on television production and its theatrical releases grew increasingly rare. The studio stopped production altogether in the late sixties, but left a legacy of fine "B" movies including a handful of important gangster movies.
1947: *The Gangster*. 1954: *Riot in*

Cell Block 11. 1955: *The Big Combo, Las Vegas Shakedown, The Phenix City Story*. 1959: *Al Capone*. 1960: *Pay or Die*. 1961: *The George Raft Story*. 1965: *Young Dillinger*.

Alonzo, John (b. 1934)
Cinematographer. A major talent who emerged in the seventies, Alonzo brought a gritty, realistic style to the films he worked on in that decade. *Bloody Mama*, an early film in his *oeuvre*, is typical of his style.
Bloody Mama (American International, 1970).

Altman, Robert (b. 1922)
Director. A darling of critics, Altman has rarely lived up to the acclaim lavished on him. His films suffer from thematic and technical pretension; and his only real success, *M.A.S.H.* (United Artists, 1970), does not stand up well to repeated viewing. His single contribution to the gangster genre, *Thieves Like Us*, pales in comparison to the original version of the same story, *They Live by Night* (RKO, 1948).
Thieves Like Us (United Artists, 1974).

Alton, John (b. 1901)
Cinematographer. After a brief apprenticeship in his native Hungary, Alton absorbed the techniques of expressionism, then immigrated to the United States in 1924 and quickly established himself as a leading Hollywood cinematographer. He did not really hit his stride, however, until nearly two decades later when, teaming with director Anthony Mann, he photographed several superior *noir* thrillers. An exceptional photographer of black and white films, he also translated the pseudoimpressionistic designs in the color classic, *An American in Paris*. His black and white films, including those listed below, are characterized by a kind of rarified expressionism: sharp contrasts between light and shadow, distorted closeups, etc.

Four gangster icons from one of the genre's classics, *The Amazing Dr. Clitterhouse* **(left to right): Humphrey Bogart, Allen Jenkins, Edward G. Robinson and Claire Trevor.**

T-Men (Eagle-Lion, 1947). *Raw Deal* (Eagle-Lion, 1948). *The Big Combo* (Allied Artists, 1955).

The Amazing Dr. Clitterhouse (Warner Bros., 1938). 83 mins.
Associate Producer: Robert Lord. *Director*: Anatole Litvak. *Screenplay*: John Wexley and John Huston, based on the play by Barre Lyndon. *Music*: Max Steiner. *Art Director*: Carl Jules Weyl. *Director of Photography*: Tony Gaudio. *Editor*: Warren Low.
Cast: Edward G. Robinson (Dr. Clitterhouse), Claire Trevor (Jo Keller), Humphrey Bogart (Rocks Valentine), Gale Page (Nurse Randolph), Donald Crisp (Inspector Lane), Allen Jenkins (Okay). *With*: Thurston Hall, John Litel, Henry O'Neill, Maxie Rosenbloom, Curt Bois, Ward Bond.
Dr. Clitterhouse, a college professor writing a study of criminal mental ability, joins the mob to study its members' psychology. He masterminds several jewel robberies for the gang led by Rocks Valentine. Clitterhouse is romantically attracted to Valentine's moll, Jo Keller. The jealous Valentine tries to get rid of Dr. Clitterhouse, but he survives; now mentally unbalanced by his connections with the mob, he decides to kill Valentine for his final chapter about homicide. He poisons Valentine and is arrested for the crime. However, he is ultimately acquitted.
Certainly one of the strangest of all gangster films, *The Amazing Dr. Clitterhouse* is, nevertheless, a compelling study of the psychology of gangsters and the allure of the underworld. Generally a satire, its qualities as such were overlooked at the time of its release. It has held up surprisingly well, thanks to a first rate cast, an excellent script, and the brisk direction of Anatole Litvak.

Ambler, Eric (b. 1909)

Novelist. One of the most popular novelists of his generation, the British born Eric Ambler specialized in thrillers set in exotic locales. Many of his novels were adapted for the screen, most notably the *films noir The Mask of Dimitrios* (Warner Bros., 1944) and Orson Welles' *Journey Into Fear* (RKO, 1944). *Topkapi*, based on his novel, and directed with great style and verve by Jules Dassin, is typical of his work. The story, about a makeshift gang of jewel thieves, is one of the most entertaining variations on this much-used theme.

Topkapi (United Artists, 1964).

American International Pictures

Independent production company founded in 1955 by Samuel Z. Arkoff and James H. Nicholson. The company thrived for nearly three decades by producing low budget exploitation pictures aimed at teenage audiences. Roger Corman emerged as one of the studio's most important directors, chiefly associated with horror films, but also directing two gangster pictures, *Machine Gun Kelly* and *Bloody Mama*. The studio provided an outlet for up-and-coming directors and writers, and one of Martin Scorsese's earliest features, the gangster melodrama *Boxcar Bertha*, was made for American International. None of American International's gangster pictures can be called classics, but all are entertaining, action oriented melodramas with just a touch of sex.

1958: *The Bonnie Parker Story*, *Machine Gun Kelly*. 1970: *Bloody Mama*, *A Bullet for Pretty Boy*. 1972: *Boxcar Bertha*. 1973: *Black Caesar*, *Dillinger*.

Amfitheotrof, Daniele (1901–1983)

Composer. A Russian born composer and arranger, Amfitheotrof immigrated to Hollywood in 1938. An expert at gloomy scores, he composed the music for a number of important thrillers and melodramas. The two scores listed below, unique additions to the gangster genre, are among his best.

The Damned Don't Cry (Warner Bros., 1950). *The Big Heat* (Columbia, 1953).

Anderson, Judith (1898–1990)

Actress. The Australian-born Anderson was a major stage star in Great Britain and the United States before settling in Los Angeles during the forties. Her dark, icy presence made her a natural for sinister roles such as the cold hearted governess in Alfred Hitchcock's *Rebecca* (RKO, 1940). In the quickie *Lady Scarface*, Anderson was perfectly cast as the sadistic head of a gang of violent criminals.

Lady Scarface (RKO, 1941).

Anderson, Maxwell (1888–1959)

Playwright. An adaptable and often quite brilliant dramatist, Maxwell Anderson's reputation has suffered somewhat since his death. Many of his plays were adapted for the screen, none more brilliantly than *Key Largo*. It is his only contribution to gangster literature, but a significant one.

Key Largo (Warner Bros., 1948).

Andrews, Dana (b. 1909)

Actor. A major star in the forties and early fifties, Dana Andrews, born Carver Daniel Andrews, gave one of his best performances in Otto Preminger's thriller *Where the Sidewalk Ends*. Andrews stars as a policeman whose father is a mobster and who, after accidentally killing a fugitive he is tracking, becomes involved in organized crime against his better judgment. Unfortunately, Andrews' malevolent qualities were not exploited in further films, although his talents would have made him an excellent portrayer of mobsters.

Where the Sidewalk Ends (20th Century–Fox, 1950).

Angels' Alley (Monogram, 1948). 64 mins.

Producer: Jan Grippo. *Director*: William Beaudine. *Screenplay*: Edward Seward, Tim Ryan, and Gerald Schniter. *Director of Photography*: Marcel LePicard. *Art Director*: Dave Milton. *Music*: Edward Kay. *Editor*: William Austin.

Cast: Leo Gorcey (Slip Mahoney), Huntz Hall (Sach), Billy Benedict (Whitey), David Gorcey (Chuck), Gabriel Dell (Ricky), Frankie Darro (Jimmy Mahoney). *With*: Nestor Paiva, Nelson Leigh, Geneva Gray, Rosemary La Planche, Mary Gordon.

Jimmy Mahoney, a recently released convict, is determined to lead a life of virtue. He moves in with his cousin Slip and Slip's mother. Unable to find work, Mahoney joins a car theft ring, but it is Slip who is caught by the police in a "sting." Although Slip takes the fall to protect Mahoney, he and his family eventually obtain information against the car theft ring, thus proving their own innocence.

The East Side Kids had "evolved" into the Bowery Boys series for the "B" studio Monogram in the late forties. Leo Gorcey and Huntz Hall were still the mainstays of the series, but it had degenerated into self parody and poor production values. *Angels' Alley* is fairly typical of the series, but it is interesting for its concentration on small-time gangsters and moral redemption. Indeed, it is one of the best of the series. Unfortunately, this formula was not repeated in further episodes.

Angels with Dirty Faces (Warner Bros., 1938). 97 mins.

Producer: Sam Bischoff. *Director*: Michael Curtiz. *Screenplay*: John Wexley and Warren Duff, *story by* Rowland Brown. *Director of Photography*: Sol Polito. *Music*: Max Steiner. *Art Director*: Robert Haas. *Editor*: Owen Marks.

Cast: James Cagney (Rocky Sullivan), Pat O'Brien (Jerry Connelly), Humphrey Bogart (James Frazier), Ann Sheridan (Laury Martin), George Bancroft (Mac Keefer), Billy Halop (Soapy). *With*: Bobby Jordan, Leo Gorcey, Bernard Punsley, Huntz Hall, William Tracy.

Two boyhood friends break into a boxcar. One escapes and grows up to become a priest, Father Jerry Connelly. Rocky, on the other hand, is captured and sentenced to reform school. He grows up to become a notorious criminal. An idol of the local East Side (New York) kids, Rocky attempts to recover $100,000 stolen from him by his crooked attorney, James Frazier. Frazier and a dishonest politician, Mac Keefer, own a nightclub together. When they refuse to return Rocky's money, Rocky kidnaps Keefer, thus forcing an uneasy alliance between himself and Frazier's gang.

Father Connelly, meanwhile, carries on a campaign to clean up the East Side from the influence of the gangsters. Frazier and Keefer plan to kill the priest, but Rocky kills them instead. Rocky is convicted and sentenced to death. When Father Connelly visits Rocky shortly before his execution, the priest tries to convince him to feign cowardice, thus dispelling the kids' heroic image of him. Initially Rocky refuses, but when confronted with the electric chair several moments later, he cries and begs for mercy.

Essentially a reworking of *Manhattan Melodrama* (MGM, 1934), combined with elements from *Dead End* (United Artists, 1937), *Angels with Dirty Faces* remains one of the most famous of all gangster films. With powerful performances by James Cagney and Humphrey Bogart at their evil best, and a fine supporting cast including George Bancroft and Pat O'Brien, the film was directed in high style by Michael Curtiz, certainly one of the best and most versatile contract directors of the era. He would later direct *Casablanca* (Warner Bros., 1942). Curtiz had a brisk, visceral style that made one forget the clichés of the plot.

Angels with Dirty Faces was also the

James Cagney and Humphrey Bogart in *Angels with Dirty Faces.*

second film in which the developing team of the East Side Kids—led by Leo Gorcey and Huntz Hall—were featured. Originally appearing in *Dead End*, the team proved so popular that they were given a series of their own. As in *Dead End*, the lives of these urban urchins were presented in an extremely disparaging light, but in the following picture, *Angels Wash Their Faces* (Warner Bros., 1938), the team's image was lightened somewhat and they increasingly became associated with tough "B" comedies. *See* East Side Kids.

Anna (Fictional character)

In *Criss Cross* (Universal, 1949), the part moll, part *femme fatale* whose avariciousness leads her ex-husband, Steve Thompson (Burt Lancaster), to join the gang of her new boyfriend, Slim Dundee (Dan Duryea) in a plan to rob an armored car. Played with under-

stated passion by the beautiful Yvonne DeCarlo, Anna is a duplicitous character, simultaneously an object of the audience's derision and their sympathy, whose weaknesses are all too human. Unfortunately, they also lead to her murder at the hands of the psychotic Dundee, who is jealous of her renewed relationship with her ex-husband. Anna is one of the most memorable female characters in the gangster and *noir* cycles.

Annakin, Ken (b. 1914)

Director. A British filmmaker, Annakin is mainly associated with a series of popular farces made in England during the sixties. *The Biggest Bundle of Them All* is a routine heist picture, notable chiefly as the last film in which Edward G. Robinson appeared as a gangster.

The Biggest Bundle of Them All (MGM, 1966).

Arkoff, Samuel (b. 1918)

Executive producer. For many years a successful show business lawyer, Samuel Z. Arkoff helped found American International Pictures in the mid-fifties, running it efficiently for many years. He is listed as executive producer on most of their releases, including three legendary lurid and violent gangster epics.

The Bonnie Parker Story (American International, 1953). *Machine Gun Kelly* (American International, 1958). *Dillinger* (American International, 1973).

Arlen, Harold (1905–1986)

Songwriter. Certainly one of the great American songwriters, Arlen was particularly active in Hollywood. He cowrote the songs for many classic musicals during the golden age of that genre. For *Casbah*, a musical adaptation of *Algiers* (United Artists, 1938), Arlen and lyricist Leo Robin composed three lush, romantic songs. They are the highlight of an otherwise disappointing film.

Casbah (Universal, 1948).

Arlen, Richard (1898–1976)

Actor. Born Cornelius van Mattemore, Arlen was a rugged and handsome man. He rose from bit parts to stardom in the mid-twenties as one of the great silent action heroes, and later became a durable leading man in "B" movies. In Josef von Sternberg's early gangster classic *Thunderbolt*, Arlen played the archetypal "good guy" opposite George Bancroft's gangster. He had an equally important role in the little known Warner gangster epic, *Let 'Em Have It*, in a typically heroic role.

Thunderbolt (Paramount, 1929). *Let 'Em Have It* (United Artists, 1935).

Armstrong, Robert (1890–1973)

Actor. Robert Armstrong will be forever remembered for his part as the foolhardy film producer in *King Kong* (RKO, 1933) and its sequels, *Son of Kong* (RKO, 1933) and *Mighty Joe Young* (RKO, 1949). Most often cast as a tough hero, he could also play criminal parts, as he did in the early gangster drama *The Racketeer* and in *Citadel of Crime*. However, perhaps because he was relegated to "B" movies, he never emerged as an important actor in the genre.

The Racketeer (Pathé, 1929). *G-Men* (First National, 1935). *Citadel of Crime* (Republic, 1941).

Arnold, Edward (1890–1956)

Character actor. Arnold, born Guenther Schnieder, was one of the great character actors in American movies for over two decades, beginning in the early thirties. The rotund, energetic Arnold was almost always seen as a big-city businessman or slightly seedy politician. He is probably best remembered for his leading roles in a series of incomparable comedies, but he could also play sinister roles. In fact, in all three of his gangster films, Arnold portrays villainous parts, making an indelible impression upon the genre in the early forties.

The Earl of Chicago (MGM, 1940), *Johnny Apollo* (20th Century–Fox, 1941). *The Glass Key* (Paramount, 1942).

Arthur, Jean (1905–1995)

Actress. Jean Arthur, born Gladys Greene, is a legendary leading lady of Hollywood's golden age. The blonde, squeaky voiced woman was a feminist heroine in a series of classic social comedies from the late thirties and early forties. Her eccentric qualities were particularly suited to romantic farce, but her urban working girl image was adaptable to all genres. She costarred in three early gangster movies, most notably John Ford's classic, *The Whole Town's Talking*. She starred in this semisatire as a typically brash newspaper woman involved in a case of mistaken identity.

Street of Chance (Paramount, 1930).

Left to right: **Sam Jaffe (Doc Riedenschneider), Jean Hagen (Doll Conovan) and Sterling Hayden (Dix Handley), a trio of hapless criminals, plan a heist doomed to fail in** *The Asphalt Jungle.*

Public Hero No. 1 (MGM, 1935). *The Whole Town's Talking* (Columbia, 1935).

Arthur, Robert (1909–1986)

Producer. A producer of mostly routine films for Universal and Columbia, Arthur did make a few prestigious films, including Fritz Lang's gangster *noir* classic, *The Big Heat.*

The Big Heat (Columbia, 1953).

The Asphalt Jungle (MGM, 1950). 112 mins.

Producer: Arthur Hornblow, Jr. *Director*: John Huston. *Screenplay*: Ben Maddow and John Huston, *story by* W. R. Burnett. *Music*: Miklos Rozsa. *Art Directors*: Cedric Gibbons and Randall Duell. *Director of Photography*: Harold Rosson. *Editor*: George Boembler.

Cast: Sterling Hayden (Dix Handley), Louis Calhern (Alonzo D. Emmerich), Jean Hagen (Doll Conovan), James Whitmore (Gus Minissi), Sam Jaffe (Dr. Erwin Riedenschneider), John McIntire (Commissioner Hardy). *With*: Marc Lawrence, Barry Kelley, Anthony Caruso, Teresa Celli, Marilyn Monroe, William Davis.

A crooked lawyer, Alonzo D. Emmerich, finances a jewel heist led by ex-con Dr. Riedenschneider, who gathers a disparate gang that manages to carry out the crime. Nevertheless, their own incompetence and greed cause their getaway to unravel, and at the end of the film, all of the criminals have been killed or captured.

Arguably the greatest of all heist films, *The Asphalt Jungle* remains one of the classics of the *film noir* and gangster genres. Its unsavory characters and gloomy premise set a new standard at the time, and the film confirmed John Huston's status as one of the great writer-directors of his generation. Indeed, the film showed most of those associated with it in their best light, and provided Marilyn Monroe with one of her best early roles as the crooked lawyer's moll.

In the early seventies, during the height of blaxploitation, *The Asphalt Jungle* was remade as *Cool Breeze* (MGM, 1972), directed by Gene Corman, with a black cast. It was popular, but ineptly made.

Astor, Mary (1906–1987)

Actress. Born Lucille Lange-Lanke, Mary Astor began acting as a juvenile during the early twenties. Despite her youth, she immediately achieved stardom and became a familiar face in American movies for over two decades. Demure and reserved, she often played romantic heroines in costume epics, but she is probably best remembered as the cynical villainess in John Huston's *The Maltese Falcon*. By contrast, in the early gangster epics *Ladies Love Brutes* and *The Little Giant*, she played stereotypical "good girls." In the little known *Desert Fury*, she starred as a madam who has turned into a casino owner involved in a deadly romantic triangle with a gangster on the lam.

Ladies Love Brutes (Paramount, 1930). *The Little Giant* (First National, 1933). *The Maltese Falcon* (Warner Bros., 1941). *Desert Fury* (Paramount, 1947).

Ayres, Lew (b. 1908)

Actor. After becoming a star in Lewis Milestone's antiwar masterpiece, *All Quiet on the Western Front* (Universal, 1930), Ayres free-lanced before signing a contract with MGM, where he starred in many of the studio's less prestigious productions during the thirties. Often cast as the "boy next door," Ayres appeared in the early Warner Bros. gangster melodrama *The Door-*

way to Hell as a big time hoodlum who controls a big-city bootleg racket. The film, however, is best remembered today for one of James Cagney's earliest appearances as a gangster.

The Doorway to Hell (Warner Bros., 1930).

Baby Face Nelson (United Artists, 1957). 85 mins.

Producer: Al Zimbalist. *Director*: Don Siegel. *Screenplay*: Daniel Mainwaring. *Director of Photography*: Hal Mohr. *Music*: Van Alexander. *Art Director*: David Milton. *Editor*: Leon Barsche.

Cast: Mickey Rooney (Lester Gillis [aka Baby Face Nelson]), Carolyn Jones (Sue), Sir Cedric Hardwicke (Doc Saunders), Chris Dark (Jerry), Ted de Corsia (Rocca), Leo Gordon (John Dillinger). *With:* Emile Meyer, Anthony Caruso, Dan Terranova.

Released from prison, Baby Face Nelson is involved in the murder of a union leader. His girlfriend, Sue, helps him escape, and he murders the man who betrayed him before he is shot and wounded during a robbery. When Nelson recovers, he joins the John Dillinger gang. During one heist, the bloodthirsty Nelson guns down six men. When Dillinger is killed, Nelson takes over the gang. The F.B.I. catches up with him, and he is critically wounded in a shootout. At his urging, his moll Sue finishes him off.

Released at the nadir of the gangster cycle, *Baby Face Nelson* was widely dismissed as imitative and artistically irrelevant. In fact, it is one of the finest films of the genre and an important one for its influence on later gangster films. Its graphic violence and action were new and exhilarating in an era of mostly unimaginative dramas and comedies. Indeed, the limited budget and shooting schedule (a mere 19 days) probably contributed to the director's gutsy style. It remains one of Don Siegel's best, if most neglected, films. It is also notable for the extraordinary performances of its three principals, Carolyn

Mickey Rooney (left), as the real life Baby Face Nelson, and his gang pull an armored car heist in *Baby Face Nelson*.

Jones, Jack Elam and, above all, Mickey Rooney in the title role.

Bacall, Lauren (b. 1924)

Actress. Born Betty Jean Perske in Brooklyn, New York, Bacall attended the American Academy of Dramatic Arts and briefly worked as a model. When director Howard Hawks saw her picture on the cover of *Harper's Bazaar*, he brought her to Hollywood, determined to make her a star. Indeed, he succeeded when he teamed her with Humphrey Bogart in the exotic romantic thriller, *To Have and Have Not* (Warner Bros., 1944). Her sultry beauty and husky voice made her a star overnight, and her subsequent romance and marriage to Bogart was celebrated on and off the screen: the lovers were teamed in three wildly popular *film noir* thrillers in the following four years. Of these, *Key Largo* might well be the most famous; it is also generally considered one of the masterpieces of the gangster genre. Bacall's role in the film is typical: tough and strong-willed, her Nora Temple is the moral center of the story.

Key Largo (Warner Bros., 1948).

Back Door to Heaven (Paramount, 1939). 81 mins.

Producer: William K. Howard. *Director*: William K. Howard. *Screenplay*: John Bright and Robert Tasker, *story by* William K. Howard. *Director of Photography*: Hal Mohr. *Music*: Erno Rapee. *Editor*: Jack Murray.

Cast: Aline MacMahon (Miss Williams), Jimmy Lydon (Frankie the Youth), Wallace Ford (Frankie the Adult), Anita Magee (Carol), William Harrigan (Mr. Rogers), Jane Seymour (Mrs. Rogers), Robert Wildhack (Rudolph Herzing). *With*: Billy Redfield,

Kenneth LeRoy, Raymond Roe, Al Webster, Joe Garry.

The movie is divided into two parts. The prologue is set during the pre-Roaring Twenties era, when Frankie, a young boy, is about to graduate from grammar school. His poverty-stricken parents are drunkards and small-time criminals, and the only person who seems to have an interest in the boy is Miss Williams, his teacher. But when Frankie steals a harmonica to play in the band on graduation day, he is sent to reform school and then to the state penitentiary.

The second part of the film, "The Play," follows Frankie as an adult recently released from prison. He returns to his small hometown and begins seeing his childhood sweetheart, Carol; but when two of his friends, also ex-convicts, rob a diner and kill the owner, Frankie is arrested and wrongly convicted of the murder. He manages to escape and return to his hometown, where he is gunned down by the police.

Back Door to Heaven, with its pessimistic screenplay and moody atmosphere, points the way to *film noir*, the offshoot genre which would emerge in the following decade. It is unusual in that the violence is less explicit than in similar films of the era. Interestingly, the film was shot at Paramount's Astoria lot in New York City (where the Marx Brothers filmed many of their early classics). This film was one of the last major productions shot there during Hollywood's golden era.

A sadly neglected film, the movie was cowritten by John Bright, who also collaborated on *Public Enemy* (Warner Bros., 1931), one of the most important gangster titles.

Bacon, Lloyd (1890–1955)

Director. If Lloyd Bacon's name is little known today, it is not for lack of talent. Like Michael Curtiz, he was a great studio craftsman, and like the Hungarian, Bacon was a mainstay at Warner Bros. during that studio's golden era. His economical style was less flashy than Curtiz's, but no less effective. Indeed, he helped define the spare style of the studio during the late thirties. He directed many of Warner's top gangster films in this era, including the classics *Invisible Stripes* and *Brother Orchid*. The latter is notable for its wry humor and excellent performance by Edward G. Robinson. By virtue of these two films alone, Lloyd Bacon remains one of the genre's important directors.

Marked Woman (Warner Bros., 1937). *San Quentin* (Warner Bros., 1937). *Racket Busters* (Warner Bros., 1938). *A Slight Case of Murder* (Warner Bros., 1938). *Invisible Stripes* (Warner Bros., 1939). *Brother Orchid* (Warner Bros., 1940). *Larceny, Inc.* (Warner Bros., 1942).

Baer, Max (1909–1959)

Character actor. A former champion boxer, Baer turned to acting in the mid-forties. In many films, he played supporting roles, generally as a tough sidekick. In his only gangster film, *The Harder They Fall*, he had a small role as a boxer.

The Harder They Fall (Columbia, 1956).

Bailey, Jeff (Fictional character)

In *Out of the Past* (RKO, 1947), Bailey, the role played by Robert Mitchum, is the most explicit example of the *film noir* antihero. A private detective, he is just as corruptible as his gangster nemesis, Whit Sterling, and ultimately his moral weakness causes his destruction. This is in marked contrast to the thirties' antigangster heroes who stood as examples of stereotypical "good guys," F.B.I. agents, district attorneys, etc.

Baldwin, Earl (1904–1978)

Screenwriter. A staff writer for Warner Bros., Baldwin specialized in action pictures and adventures. He worked on three gangster epics, the best being

Brother Orchid, one of the great satires of the genre.

The Mouthpiece (Warner Bros., 1932). *A Slight Case of Murder* (Warner Bros., 1938). *Brother Orchid* (Warner Bros., 1940).

Ballard, Lucien (b. 1908)

Cinematographer. Ballard's distinguished career began in the mid-thirties. He worked on many classic films, and his dark, shadowy style was perfectly suitable to the gloomy romanticism of American crime melodrama.

Blind Alley (Columbia, 1939). *The Killing* (United Artists, 1956). *Al Capone* (Allied Artists, 1959). *Pay or Die* (Allied Artists, 1960). *The Rise and Fall of Legs Diamond* (Warner Bros., 1960).

Bancroft, Anne (b. 1931)

Actress. Born Anna Marie Louise Italiano in the Bronx, Anne Bancroft began acting and dancing on stage at age four. She made her movie debut in 1952, but achieved her greatest success on Broadway. Dubbed "a female Brando" by New York critics, she was known for her intense performances; yet she never quite achieved screen stardom despite many good performances. In *The Naked Street*, early in her film career, she had a memorable role as the wife of a sadistic small-time gangster.

The Naked Street (United Artists, 1955).

Bancroft, George (1882–1956)

Actor. Bancroft began his performing career in minstrel shows around the turn of the century. He eventually became a major star on Broadway, and began appearing in movies in the early twenties. His large, menacing air made him a natural for villainous roles, and indeed he was the first major star of the emerging gangster genre. He was the lead in three of Josef von Sternberg's earliest masterpieces — *Underworld*, *Docks of New York*, and *Thunderbolt* — and later played supporting roles (always as a gangster) in several other important genre titles.

Underworld (Paramount, 1927). *Docks of New York* (Paramount, 1928). *Thunderbolt* (Paramount, 1929). *Ladies Love Brutes* (Paramount, 1930). *Angels with Dirty Faces* (Warner Bros., 1938). *Each Dawn I Die* (Warner Bros., 1939).

Bandello, Cesare Enrico "Rico" (Fictional character)

With this single performance as "Rico," the gangster, in *Little Caesar* (Warner Bros., 1930), Edward G. Robinson became a star overnight and created one of American cinema's legendary characters. Partly based on Al Capone, Rico is a small-town crook who moves to the big city to seek his fame and fortune. Bandello soon takes over the local mob and rules with an iron fist. He is not above personally killing his rivals. But his empire begins to crumble through a series of miscellaneous incidents. The once mighty "Little Caesar" is soon reduced to living in a flophouse, and when taunted by a story in the paper that quotes the police calling him "yellow," Rico arrogantly calls the police department to brag of his successes against them. Unfortunately, the police trace the call, and as Rico walks down the street on the way back to his residence, he is ambushed by the lawmen. As he falls down, near death, he asks aloud, "Mother of Mercy, is this the end of Rico?"

The character of Rico Bandello is a complex one, the subject of much critical debate. Some have gone so far as to suggest that he is a homosexual, but, in fact, Rico is more asexual, finding a substitute for such things in power and violence. Nevertheless, it is Edward G. Robinson's powerful performance that brings the character to life and makes *Little Caesar* still such a pleasure to watch.

Bannion, Sgt. Dave (Fictional character)

In Fritz Lang's *The Big Heat* (Columbia, 1953), the heroic Bannion (Glenn Ford) marks an important departure from the police heroes of previous gangster films. Unlike those generally flawless characters, Bannion is both susceptible to corruption (even if he does not fully succumb), and capable of cruelty and extreme violence. Innocent citizens often suffer at his hands in his one-man crusade against organized crime. The characterization of Bannion had a profound influence on later characterizations of police officers, particularly notable in films like *Dirty Harry* (Warner Bros., 1972).

Barnes, George (1893–1953)

Cinematographer. Certainly one of the most distinguished American cinematographers, George Barnes' career began in the early twenties when he photographed several notable films starring Douglas Fairbanks. He specialized in well lit adventures and comedies, but his work also shows the influence of expressionism, particularly in his work for Alfred Hitchcock on *Rebecca* (RKO, 1940) for which he won an Academy Award. The forties were a golden time for Barnes, and among the many classic films on which he served as director of photography was the gangster satire *Mr. Lucky*, a fine example of his glossy style.

Mr. Lucky (RKO, 1943).

Barrie, Wendy (1912–1978)

Actress. Born Margaret Jenkins in Hong Kong, Barrie was a veteran of British stage and film before her importation to Hollywood in the early thirties. Her fair beauty and upper-crust accent made her popular in mostly light films and costume epics, but she never quite achieved stardom. Still, she was very talented, and her performances, even in minor roles, are always striking. She was the second female lead in *Dead End* and *I Am the Law*, and the female lead in *Eyes of the Underworld*,

although she did not have much to do in any of them. She is more notable, perhaps, for her real life off-screen affair with notorious gangster Bugsy Siegel.

Dead End (United Artists, 1937). *I Am the Law* (Columbia, 1938). *Eyes of the Underworld* (Universal, 1942).

Barrow, Clyde (1910–1934)

Barrow was the Oklahoma-born gangster who, with his girlfriend Bonnie Parker (?–1934) terrorized the Southwestern United States during the early years of the Great Depression (*see also* Parker, Bonnie). Bonnie and Clyde's gang of country bumpkins robbed banks throughout Texas, Louisiana, Oklahoma and Arkansas before most of them were killed in shootouts with the police or captured. Bonnie and Clyde were ambushed by Texas Rangers in 1934. Like many rural gangsters of the thirties, however, they were popular with many Depression-era American citizens who, despite their many indiscriminate murders, saw them as modern-day Robin Hoods. The peculiar sexuality of both—they were apparently very promiscuous bisexuals (although it has also been suggested that Barrow was impotent)—has also entered the mythology and, with their exploits, has inspired many notable films: *You Only Live Once* (United Artists, 1939), *They Live by Night* (RKO, 1948), *Gun Crazy* (United Artists, 1949), *The Bonnie Parker Story* (American International, 1958), with Barrow's name changed, peculiarly, to Guy Darrow!, and of course, *Bonnie and Clyde* (Warner Bros., 1967).

Barrymore, Lionel (1878–1954)

Actor. The oldest member of the Barrymore siblings, Lionel Barrymore also had the longest film career. Unlike his handsome younger brother, John, a matinee idol on stage and in films for three decades, Lionel was a character actor, specializing in mostly sympathetic parts. His film career began before his teens, and he costarred in D. W. Griffith's important early gangster film, *The Musketeers of Pig Alley.* Confined to a wheelchair as a result of extreme arthritis, his career continued unabated nevertheless. One of his most famous performances was in the gangster classic *Key Largo* as James Temple, the brave owner of a seedy motel overrun by mobsters led by Johnny Rocco (Edward G. Robinson).

The Musketeers of Pig Alley (Biograph, 1912). *Public Hero No. 1* (MGM, 1935). *Key Largo* (Warner Bros., 1948).

Barthelmess, Richard (1895–1963)
Actor. Discovered by the great actress Alla Nazimova, Richard Barthelmess became one of silent film's greatest stars after a brief career on the stage in his native New York. With the coming of sound his popularity decreased somewhat, but he continued to play second leads until his retirement in the early forties. He played an atypically unsympathetic role in the early gangster melodrama *The Finger Points*, his only appearance in the genre.

The Finger Points (First National, 1931).

Bartlett, Eddie (Fictional character)
Although not as well known as James Cagney's most famous gangster character, Tom Powers in *Public Enemy* (Warner Bros., 1931), his gangster character in *The Roaring Twenties* (Warner Bros., 1939) is more complex and in many ways more interesting. Bartlett is a tough product of the New York streets and warfare: a veteran of the First World War, he becomes a cab driver and then a bootlegger during Prohibition. Like so many working class urbanites with little hope for the future (both then and now), the trade in illicit controlled substances and the huge sums that can be made are too great a temptation for Bartlett. He builds a criminal empire over the course of the twenties, often battling his rival George Hally (Humphrey Bogart). But

the repeal of Prohibition in the early thirties wipes out his fortune and Bartlett is soon back driving a cab. When Hally threatens a friend of his, Bartlett shoots and kills his old rival and then, like so many before him, on screen and off, Bartlett is gunned down on the street by the police.

Basevi, James
Director. Basevi was staff art director for 20th Century-Fox where he worked on many of their modest budget releases. His work is often quite imaginative, making good use of minimal resources. Basevi worked on one interesting gangster film.

Roger Touhy, Gangster (20th Century-Fox, 1944).

Baxter, Warner (1889–1951)
Actor. A legend of silent and early sound films, Baxter usually played distinguished looking heroes in action films. Although he made many movies for both Paramount and Warner Bros., he was cast, by MGM, in only a single gangster film. *Penthouse*, in which Baxter gives a fine performance as a lawyer framed by the mob, is not a particularly memorable film, but it is directed in typically swift style by W. S. Van Dyke.

Penthouse (MGM, 1933).

The Beast of the City (MGM, 1932). 74 mins.
Producer: Hunt Stromberg. *Director*: Charles Brabin. *Screenplay*: John Mahin, *story by* W. R. Burnett. *Director of Photography*: Norbert Brodine. *Art Director*: Cedric Gibbons. *Editor*: Anne Bauchens.

Cast: Walter Huston (Captain Jim Fitzpatrick), Jean Harlow (Daisy Stevens), Wallace Ford (Ed Fitzpatrick), Jean Hersholt (Sam Belmonte), Dorothy Peterson (Mary Fitzpatrick), Tully Marshall (District Attorney Michaels). *With*: John Miljan, J. Carrol Naish, Mickey Rooney, Clarence Wilson, Charles Sullivan.

Captain Jim Fitzpatrick is an honest

501-92

A familiar scene from dozens of gangster films—the mobster with a Tommy gun in a shoot-out. In this case, Warren Beatty, from *Bonnie and Clyde.*

cop determined to shut down Sam Belmonte, a dangerous racketeer. However, the city's administration is hopelessly corrupt. When Fitzpatrick makes headlines after capturing two hoodlums in a holdup, the officials are forced to appoint the hero as police commissioner. Now in a position to pursue Belmonte, Fitzpatrick sets out to arrest the mobster and close down his operations. However, his crusade is complicated by his dishonest brother, Ed, whose girlfriend, Daisy Stevens, is connected with Belmonte and his gang. However, Ed is eventually murdered by Belmonte's henchmen after he sides with Jim. In the climactic gun battle, most of the cops, including Jim Fitzpatrick, Belmonte, Daisy, and most of the gang are killed.

Released at the height of the initial surge of gangster films in the thirties, *Beast of the City* is one of the most fascinating of the early gangster classics. Unique for its uncompromising pessimism and unflinching analysis of official and criminal corruption, the film is a social criticism, but also supremely entertaining. This is primarily due to its source material—a novel by W. R. Burnett, who also wrote *Little Caesar* (1930), which became one of the early legends of the genre.

Beatty, Warren (b. 1937)

Actor, producer, and director. One of contemporary Hollywood's more complex talents, Beatty's virtues are often obscured by his public image. Born Warren Beaty in Richmond, Virginia, he is the younger brother of actress, dancer and author Shirley MacLaine. He studied acting with actress and teacher Stella Adler (whose two brothers, Luther and Jay Adler were notable character actors). He had a brief Broadway career before making a splash in the film *Splendor in the Grass* (Warner Bros., 1961). A series of less memorable roles followed until Beatty produced and starred in *Bonnie and Clyde*. The film introduced a new level of violence (and down-played the Clyde Barrow character's real life homosexuality and impotence) but is most often cited for its excellent performances by Beatty and Faye Dunaway as Bonnie Parker. Beatty returned to similar themes more than two decades later with *Bugsy*, which he produced and in which he again starred in the title role. Less distinguished than its predecessor, the film is nevertheless a compelling exploration of the real life exploits of the notorious gangster Bugsy Siegel.

Bonnie and Clyde (Warner Bros., 1967). *Bugsy* (Warner Bros., 1992).

Beaudine, William (1890–1970)

Director. Beaudine's career began as an assistant to D. W. Griffith in 1909. He began directing in 1915, and quickly became one of the most prolific directors of "B" movies, making several hundred features before retiring in 1966. Although his films are not notable for their style, Beaudine explored every genre, mostly for lesser known studios like PRC and Monogram, and his enormous filmography included two minor gangster dramas.

Those Who Dance (Warner Bros., 1930). *Angels' Alley* (Monogram, 1948).

Beery, Noah (1884–1946)

Character actor. The older brother of Wallace Beery, Noah was the silent era's most celebrated villain. With the coming of sound, his roles grew smaller, but he remained a popular personality. Large and menacing, he usually played lumbering bad guys, particularly in countless westerns. Typically, in the minor crime melodrama *Out of Singa-*

pore, he played the villain, his only appearance in a gangster film.

Out of Singapore (Goldsmith, 1932).

Beery, Wallace (1889–1949)

Character actor. Like his older brother Noah, Wallace Beery had the broken nose and scarred visage of a boxer; unlike Noah, however, Wallace most often played lead roles and was a popular star of the thirties and forties. Beginning his career in the circus, Wallace graduated to vaudeville and Broadway. He made his first film appearance in 1913, thereafter chiefly playing tough guys and villains until the advent of sound. It was then that he found his popular image—tough, ugly, slow thinking and easygoing. He was equally at home in comedies and dramas, but starred in only one gangster melodrama, *The Secret Six*, as Louis Scorpio, the menacing leader of a big-city criminal organization. His characterization of the well dressed, deceptively good natured gang boss would become familiar as the decade progressed.

The Secret Six (MGM, 1932).

Belafonte, Harry (b. 1927)

Actor. Belafonte was born in New York City. After a stint in the Navy, he studied acting at New York's Dramatic Workshop while also performing in clubs. He became a major nightclub and recording star, and made his film debut in 1953. He costarred in Robert Wise's *Odds Against Tomorrow* as one of the doomed bank robbers.

Odds Against Tomorrow (United Artists, 1959).

Belita (b. 1924)

Actress. Born Gladys Jepson-Turner in London, England, Belita was an ice skating champion before Hollywood beckoned in the early forties. She subsequently appeared in many films, particularly musicals (she was also an accomplished dancer), but she never achieved real stardom. Her exotic beauty enlivened a few good "B" movies, including the very interesting *The Gangster*, in which she played the moll of a sadistic mobster.

The Gangster (Allied Artists, 1947).

Bellamy, Ralph (1904–1993)

Actor. A versatile stage and screen actor, Bellamy was born in Chicago. After success on Broadway, Bellamy made his screen debut in the early sound gangster classic, *The Secret Six*, costarring with the formidable Jean Harlow, Wallace Beery and Clark Gable. The film was an enormous success and typed Bellamy—who played an uppercrust simpleton and sissy—as a well meaning but not wholly intelligent member of the wealthy class in many dramas and comedies over the following two decades. He costarred in three subsequent gangster films, most memorably in *Blind Alley* as a psychiatrist held hostage by a psychotic mobster.

The Secret Six (MGM, 1931). *Blind Alley* (Columbia, 1939). *Brother Orchid* (Warner Bros., 1940). *Queen of the Mob* (Paramount, 1940).

Belmondo, Jean-Paul (b. 1933)

Actor. Sexy, charming and appealingly homely, the French leading man Jean-Paul Belmondo skyrocketed to fame in Jean-Luc Godard's homage to American crime films, *Breathless* (Imperia, 1959). He subsequently became the modern European image of the hard-boiled antihero, a kind of French Bogart. He costarred with Alain Delon in *Borsalino*, an immensely popular gangster film which brought the genre back into vogue in Europe.

Borsalino (Paramount, 1970).

Bendix, William (1906–1964)

Character actor. Although he became famous for playing working-class heroes and tough guys, William Bendix was in reality the son of a conductor at New York City's Metropolitan Opera. After various jobs, Bendix ventured into theater in the mid-thirties and made his Broadway debut in 1939. His gravelly voice and boxer's face typecast him as a dense, though often good-hearted, man. He is particularly well remembered for the films in which he costarred with his real life best friend, Alan Ladd, including the classic gangster film *The Glass Key*. Indeed, as the violent gangster Jeff, Bendix provided the movie's best performance. He was equally impressive in *Race Street*, for once in a good-guy role, and as a murderous thief in Don Siegel's exhilarating gangster and chase melodrama *The Big Steal*. One of his best performances is in the little known *Crashout*, one of the finest of the prison subgenre.

The Glass Key (Paramount, 1942). *Race Street* (RKO, 1948). *The Big Steal* (RKO, 1949). *Crashout* (Filmakers, 1955).

Bening, Annette (b. 1958)

Actress. Bening made a remarkable screen debut as the sexy *femme fatale* in the modern *noir The Grifters* (Miramax, 1990). She was equally impressive in *Bugsy*, produced by her future husband Warren Beatty, in which she played the actress-moll of Bugsy Siegel.

Bugsy (Warner Bros., 1992).

Benton, Robert (b. 1932)

Screenwriter. Benton was a successful magazine writer and art director before teaming with writer David Newman in the mid-sixties. The duo had immediate success with *Bonnie and Clyde*, a compelling biopic of the notorious gangsters. The film is notable for its unsentimental violence and psychological insight, and remains Benton's and Newman's best work.

Bonnie and Clyde (Warner Bros., 1967).

Berger, Ralph (1912–1986)

Art director. Berger was an important and influential art director whose best work was done for RKO in the forties. He worked on Don Siegel's *The*

Big Steal, a fine example of his pseudo-expressionist style.

The Big Steal (RKO, 1949).

Bernstein, Leonard (1918–1989)

Composer. Arguably the most important "serious" American composer in the mid–twentieth century, Bernstein worked intermittently as a film composer. All of his work in this area is notable. His classic score for *On the Waterfront* is a typical mixture of late-romantic and jazzier styles.

On the Waterfront (Columbia, 1954).

Berry, John (b. 1917)

Director. Berry was born in New York and began work as an actor, joining Orson Welles' Mercury Theatre Company in the late thirties. His first association with film was as Billy Wilder's assistant on *Double Indemnity* (Paramount, 1944). He was promoted to director the following year and made several interesting films, including *Casbah*, the musical remake of *Algiers* (United Artists, 1938) and the *film noir* melodrama *He Ran All the Way* (United Artists, 1951). Shortly after the latter was released, Berry was blackballed by the House Un-American Activities Committee. He made several films in France before returning to Hollywood in the seventies, but he was unable to reestablish the momentum he lost in the early fifties.

Casbah (Universal, 1948).

Bezzerides, A. I. (b. 1908)

Screenwriter. Albert Isaac Bezzerides was one of the most important (if now sadly neglected) screenwriters of the forties and fifties. He specialized in the new hard-boiled style characterized by *film noir*, collaborating on several of the most important titles in that genre. He cowrote a single gangster film with the equally notable master of the hard-boiled, Geoffrey Homes.

A Bullet for Joey (United Artists, 1955).

Bickford, Charles (1889–1967)

Actor. Charles Bickford was born in Cambridge, Massachusetts, and graduated from M.I.T. After working as a civil engineer and sailor, he got into show business by way of burlesque. He made his Broadway debut in 1919 and achieved instant stardom. Lured to Hollywood by director Cecil B. DeMille in 1929, he became a star when teamed opposite Greta Garbo in *Anna Christie* (MGM, 1930). After a few years as a romantic lead, Bickford settled into the character roles that suited his craggy and intense features. In the "B" gangster drama *Gangs of New York*, he starred as both a murderous gangster and his good-guy lookalike, creating one of the genre's most unique and best performances.

Gangs of New York (Republic, 1938).

The Big City (MGM, 1928). 69 mins.

Director: Tod Browning. *Screenplay*: Waldemar Young, *titles by* Joe Farnham, *story by* Tod Browning. *Director of Photography*: Henry Sharp. *Art Director*: Cedric Gibbons. *Editor*: Harry Reynolds.

Cast: Lon Chaney (Chuck Collins), Marceline Day (Sunshine), James Murray (Curly), Betty Compson (Helen), Matthew Betz (Red). *With*: John George, Virginia Pearson, Walter Percival, Lew Short, Eddie Sturgis.

Chuck Collins operates a cabaret as a front for fencing stolen goods. His girlfriend, Helen, manages a costume shop which Chuck and his gang also use for their criminal activities. Chuck and his gang fight with a rival gang led by Red. Eventually, Helen and a friend, Sunshine, convince Chuck and his partners to go straight while Red goes to jail.

The Big City, along with the trio of Josef von Sternberg silent crime dramas, is one of the earliest true gangster films. Although its story is rather naive, and its morality decidedly Victorian, the film is surprisingly realistic and unsentimental. Tod Browning, mainly associated with horror films, here creates a film which holds its own with the technical and artistic innovations of the contemporaneous Sternberg films. Lon Chaney's performance is equally impressive.

The Big Combo (Allied Artists, 1955). 89 mins.
Producer: Sidney Harmon. *Director*: Joseph H. Lewis. *Screenplay*: Philip Yordan. *Director of Photography*: John Alton. *Music*: David Raksin. *Art Director*: Rudi Feld. *Editor*: Robert Eisen.
Cast: Cornel Wilde (Detective Lieutenant Diamond), Richard Conte (Brown), Brian Donlevy (McClure), Jean Wallace (Susan Cabot), Robert Middleton (Peterson), Lee Van Cleef (Fante), Earl Holliman (Mingo). *With*: Helen Walker, Jay Adler, Ted De Corsia, Helen Stanton, Roy Gordon, Whit Bissell, Steve Mitchell.

Susan Lowell, a beautiful young society girl, is desired by Leonard Diamond, a cop, and Brown, the head of a local mob. The rivalry between the two men leads to violence and torture, while Brown also fights for control of the rival gang. Eventually, Brown is betrayed by his wife, and in the climactic shootout in an isolated airplane hangar, he is killed by Diamond.

The Big Combo might be the greatest of all "B" movies. Considered a classic *film noir*, it is filled with an unrelenting sense of fatalism, perverse sexuality, and violence. Indeed, its violent action harks back to the gangster films of the early thirties. The director, Joseph H. Lewis, creates a misty, dark world which mirrors the ambiguities of the characters, superbly portrayed by Wilde, Conte and Wallace. If all but forgotten today, *The Big Combo* remains one of the classics of both the gangster and *film noir* genres.

The Big Heat (Columbia, 1953). 90 mins.
Producer: Robert Arthur. *Director*: Fritz Lang. *Screenplay*: Sydney Boehm, based on the novel by William P. McGivern. *Director of Photography*: Charles Lang, Jr. *Music*: Daniele Amfitheatrof. *Art Director*: Robert Peterson. *Editor*: Charles Nelson.
Cast: Glenn Ford (Sgt. Dave Bannion), Gloria Grahame (Debby Marsh), Jocelyn Brando (Katie Bannion), Alexander Scourby (Mike Lagana), Lee Marvin (Vince Stone), Jeanette Nolan (Bertha Duncan). *With*: Peter Whitney, Willis Bouchey, Robert Burton, Adam Williams, Howard Wendell.

Dave Bannion, a homicide detective investigating the sudden suicide of a police officer, is suddenly told by his superiors to lay off the case. He has discovered a connection between the dead cop and a local gangster, Mike Lagana. In fact, Lagana and his gang control the local authorities, including the police, through bribes and blackmail. Bannion, one of the few honest cops, is determined to arrest Lagana and break up his organization. Meanwhile, Vince Stone, one of Lagana's associates, believes that Bannion is having an affair with his girlfriend, Debby. During an argument Stone throws coffee in Debby's face and she turns on the gang, giving Bannion the information he needs to arrest Lagana. Debby lures Vince into a trap, and after she throws hot coffee in his face, he fatally shoots her.

Fritz Lang had explored themes of official corruption, criminal gangs, and moral ambiguity from the very beginning of his film career. *The Big Heat*, however, was his only true gangster drama in the American tradition. The film can be enjoyed for its fast-paced story of gangsters and police, but like all of Lang's films, its simple story is complicated by layers of symbolism. One of the most violent of the new breed of crime films in the fifties, its popularity bred a new group of similar films, and its influence can still be felt today in the work of directors like Martin Scorsese.

Wallace Beery (left), Robert Montgomery (center), and Karl Dane (right) from *The Big House*, **perhaps MGM's most important early gangster picture and still one of the best of the subgenre of prison pictures.**

The Big House (MGM, 1930). 86 mins.

Director: George Hill. *Screenplay*: Frances Marion, with additional dialog by Joe Farnham and Martin Flavin. *Director of Photography*: Harold Wenstrom. *Art Director*: Cedric Gibbons. *Editor*: Blanche Sewell.

Cast: Chester Morris (Morgan), Wallace Beery (Butch), Lewis Stone (Warden), Robert Montgomery (Kent), Leila Hyams (Anne). *With*: George F. Marion, J. C. Nugent, Karl Dane, DeWitt Jennings, Matthew Betz, Claire McDowell.

Morgan, a convicted forger, is sent to prison. His cell mates are Butch, a murderer, and the youthful Marlowe, who was convicted of manslaughter due to a traffic accident. Morgan escapes from prison and hides out with Anne, Marlowe's sister, with whom he falls in love. Determined to go straight, he is recaptured and sent back to prison before he and the girl can start their new life together. Here, he learns that Butch is planning an escape from the prison's terrible conditions. Marlowe, hoping for an early release, tells the authorities of the planned escape. In the ensuing riot, Morgan intervenes and helps quell the disturbance. He is paroled and rejoins Anne.

The Big House was the earliest of the prison dramas so common in the thirties. It is not, strictly speaking, a gangster film, but its unsentimental view of petty criminals and corrupt authorities is a theme common to the genre. In fact, the movie was an enormous box office success and helped kick off the initial gangster cycle in the early thirties.

The Big Operator (MGM, 1959). 90 mins.

Executive Producer: Albert Zugsmith. *Producer*: Red Doff. *Director*: Charles Haas. *Screenplay*: Robert Smith, based on a story by Paul Gallico. *Director of Photography*: Walter H. Castle. *Music*: Van Alexander. *Editor*: Ben Lewis.

Cast: Mickey Rooney (Little Joe Braun), Steve Cochran (Bill Gibson), Mamie Van Doren (Mary Gibson), Mel Torme (Fred McAfee), Ray Danton (Oscar Wetzel), Jim Backus (Cliff Heldon). *With*: Ray Anthony, Jackie Coogan, Charles Chaplin, Jr., Vampira, Billy Daniels, Ben Gage.

Little Joe Braun, a crooked union leader, is under investigation by a government committee on organized crime. When questioned, he denies knowing a mob thug who has done some strong-arm work for him. When two union members agree to testify against him, Braun threatens them, resorting to kidnapping the son of one of the men. Nevertheless, they remain resilient. With the help of other disaffected union members and the police, they help bring about Braun's downfall.

The Big Operator is not a major film, but an enjoyable one largely due to Mickey Rooney's strong performance as the evil union leader. The film also further demonstrates the new themes which distinguished gangster melodramas in the fifties. Mob infiltration of organized labor was a timely subject and a common theme in movies, perhaps most famously depicted in Elia Kazan's *On the Waterfront* (Columbia, 1954).

The Big Shot (Warner Bros., 1942). 82 mins.

Producer: Walter MacEwen. *Director*: Lewis Seiler. *Screenplay*: Bertram Millhauser, Abem Finkel, and Daniel Fuchs. *Director of Photography*: Sid Hickox. *Music*: Adolph Deutsch. *Art Director*: John Hughes. *Editor*: Jack Killifer.

Cast: Humphrey Bogart (Duke Berne), Irene Manning (Lorna Fleming), Richard Travis (George Anderson), Susan Peters (Ruth Carter), Stanley Ridges (Martin Fleming), Minor Watson (Warden Booth). *With*: Chick Chandler, Joseph Downing, Howard Da Silva, Murray Alper, Roland Drew.

Duke Berne is a three time loser who unsuccessfully tries to go straight. When he fails, he joins a holdup gang led by a crooked lawyer, Martin Fleming. When Fleming discovers that his wife, Lorna, was once Berne's mistress, he frames the ex-convict. Sentenced to prison, Berne escapes and joins Lorna in a mountain lodge. Learning that a friend is going to be convicted of a murder committed by Fleming, Berne and Lorna leave the cabin, determined to clear their friend. The police, however, have found their hideout, and in the subsequent shootout, Lorna is killed. Berne manages to get away, finds Fleming and kills him, but he, too, is fatally wounded. Before he dies, Berne gives the police the information that clears his friend.

The Big Shot is notable as the last "B" movie Humphrey Bogart made for Warner Bros. A particularly well-made "B," it features an unusually sophisticated screenplay and a surprisingly effective chemistry between Bogart and Irene Manning. Indeed, it might well be one of the most romantic of all pre–gangster *noir* movies.

The Big Steal (RKO, 1949). 71 mins.

Executive Producer: Sid Rogell. *Producer*: Jack L. Gross. *Director*: Don Siegel. *Screenplay*: Gerald Drayson Adams and Geoffrey Homes, based on the story "The Road to Carmichael's" by Richard Wormser. *Director of Photography*: Harry J. Wild. *Music*: Leigh Harline. *Art Directors*: Albert S.

D'Agostino and Ralph Berger. *Editor*: Samuel E. Beetley.

Cast: Robert Mitchum (Duke), Jane Greer (Joan), William Bendix (Blake), Patric Knowles (Fiske), Ramon Novarro (Colonel Ortega), Don Alvarado (Lieutenant Ruiz), John Qualen (Seton). *With*: Pasquel Garcia Pena, Henry Carr, Jose Logan, Primo Lopez, Frank Hagney.

Duke Haliday, an Army officer in charge of payroll, is arrested by Blake, a police detective and accused of stealing $300,000. The innocent Haliday escapes, determined to find the actual thief, with Blake hot on his trail. The chase leads to Mexico, where Haliday picks up a pretty passenger, Joan, who is searching for her ex-employer, Jim Fiske, who, she claims, has stolen $2,000 from her. The couple soon realize that they are looking for the same man, and despite their initial antipathy toward each other, they agree to work together. They track Fiske to a small Mexican town where he is to meet his boss, a mobster who also employs the crooked cop, Blake. At Fiske's hideout, a gun battle ensues and Haliday and Joan emerge victorious. Haliday, having fallen for Joan, recovers the money and clears his name.

The Big Steal was produced during the turbulence surrounding the drug-charge conviction of Robert Mitchum. Howard Hughes, then in charge of RKO, personally oversaw the film's production in an attempt to reestablish (with distributors and the public) Mitchum's reputation as the studio's leading male star. Thus, the film is essentially a vehicle for its star's amiable qualities. It is, essentially, a modest chase movie, but its quick pace, gangster and mystery elements, and ingratiating cast, all helped make the film a box office success. It also confirmed Mitchum's popularity, despite the scandal which almost ruined his career. In fact, after serving a brief sentence for drug possession, Mitchum returned to Hollywood a bigger star than ever, thanks in large part to the success of this film.

Big Town Czar (Universal, 1939). 61 mins.

Director: Arthur Lubin. *Screenplay*: Edmund L. Hartman, based on a story by Ed Sullivan. *Director of Photography*: Ellwood Bredell. *Editor*: Philip Cahn.

Cast: Barton MacLane (Phil Daley), Tom Brown (Danny Daley), Eve Arden (Susan Warren), Jack LaRue (Mike Luger). *With*: Frank Jenks, Walter Woolf King, Oscar O'Shea, Esther Daley, Horace MacMahon, Ed Sullivan.

Phil Daley is a big-time gangster who has risen above his humble beginnings to control a New York racketeering organization. When his younger brother Danny quits college to join his gang, Phil is upset. Despite having to fight a rival gang, Phil manages to set Danny on the correct path, but is arrested for murder after escaping an ambush.

Big Town Czar is a modest "B" gangster drama, notable chiefly for its source, a story by journalist Ed Sullivan, who would later become the famous television personality. The film suffers largely from poor production values and self-conscious moralizing (a curse in the era of the Production Code), but the cast, particularly Barton MacLane, is very good.

The Biggest Bundle of Them All (MGM, 1968). 105 mins.

Producer: Joseph Shaftel. *Director*: Ken Annakin. *Screenplay*: Sy Salkowitz. *Director of Photography*: Piero Portalupi. *Music*: Riz Ortolani. *Art Director*: Arrigo Equini. *Editor*: Ralph Sheldon.

Cast: Robert Wagner (Harry Price), Raquel Welch (Julianna), Godfrey Cambridge (Ben Brownstead), Vittorio de Sica (Cesare Celli), Edward G. Robinson (Professor Samuels), Davey Kaye (Davey Collins). *With*: Francesco Mule, Victor Spinetti, Yvonne Sanson, Mickey Knox, Femi Bennssi, Andrea Aureli.

A gang of ragtag novice criminals

kidnaps a mobster in Italy, demanding a ransom. When none of his underworld pals underwrite his rescue, the mobster, Celli, convinces the gang to let him train them to carry out a heist. Celli enlists "Professor" Samuels to help them; predictably, the heist eventually fails because of the gang's ineptitude.

An Italian-American coproduction, this rather routine heist melodrama is notable chiefly for the appearance of Edward G. Robinson in his last role as an underworld figure.

Billy Bathgate (Touchstone, 1993). 117 mins.
Producers: Arlene Donovan and Robert F. Colesberry. *Director*: Robert Benton. *Screenplay*: Tom Stoppard, based on the novel by E. L. Doctorow. *Director of Photography*: Nestor Almendros. *Music*: Mark Isham. *Production Designer*: Patrizia Von Brandenstein. *Editors*: Alan Klein and Robert Reitano.
Cast: Dustin Hoffman (Dutch Schultz), Nicole Kidman (Drew Preston), Loren Dean (Billy Bathgate), Bruce Willis (Bo Weinberg), Steven Hill (Otto Berman), Steve Buscemi (Irving). *With*: Bill Jaye, John Costelloe, Tim Jerome, Stanley Tuci, Moira Kelly.

Billy Bathgate is an ambitious teenager who becomes an errand boy for Dutch Schultz's gang. When Schultz kills Bo Weinberg, a rival gangster, he seduces Weinberg's mistress, the elegant but frivolous Drew Preston. Bathgate is put in charge of watching over Ms. Preston and soon has a brief but passionate affair with the moll. Eventually, she runs off with another man and Schultz is killed by rivals. Most of his gang is murdered, but Bathgate is spared when the rivals think that he knows little about Schultz's operation. Bathgate, having learned from his experiences with the gang, is now determined to return to school and lead an honest life.

Sadly, *Billy Bathgate* is a weak version of E. L. Doctorow's brilliant novel. Doctorow is a difficult writer to translate to the screen, and all that remains of his elegant style are the bare bones, particularly some of its flashback structure. The real problems with the film are the perfunctory direction and the miscast leading roles, especially Dustin Hoffman's Dutch Schultz, who comes off as an eccentric rather than a murderous lunatic.

Binyon, Claude (1905–1978)
Screenwriter. An important figure in American movies for three decades, beginning in the thirties, Binyon cowrote many interesting films, specializing in sophisticated dramas and comedies. He also directed a few titles, including a gangster film; although it is not one of the genre's classics, it is notable for its witty dialogue.
Stolen Harmony (Paramount, 1935).

Biroc, Joseph (b. 1903)
Cinematographer. Biroc's career began in the mid-forties. Although he was known for his gritty style, he was less original than many of his contemporaries.
Johnny Allegro (Columbia, 1949). *Loan Shark* (Lippert, 1952). *The F.B.I. Story* (Warner Bros., 1959). *The Grisom Gang* (Cinerama, 1971).

Bischoff, Sam (1890–1976)
Producer. Bischoff is an interesting figure from Hollywood's golden era. After a brief career as a writer and director—he directed the important early gangster-prison melodrama *The Last Mile*—he was promoted to producer at Warner Bros. in 1935 and subsequently produced some of that studio's most important titles, including five gangster movies. In the forties he joined Columbia, where he continued to demonstrate a hardboiled style. In the fifties he became an independent producer, overseeing many important releases during the next two

The ill-cast Dustin Hoffman (left) as the real life Dutch Schultz in the disappointing film version of E. L. Doctorow's classic novel, *Billy Bathgate*.

decades, including two interesting additions to the gangster genre, *A Bullet for Joey* and Phil Karlson's *The Phenix City Story*.

The Last Mile (Worldwide, 1932; director only). *Angels with Dirty Faces* (Warner Bros., 1938). *San Quentin* (Warner Bros., 1938). *You Can't Get Away with Murder* (Warner Bros., 1939). *Castle on the Hudson* (Warner Bros., 1940). *A Bullet for Joey* (United Artists, 1955). *The Phenix City Story* (Allied Artists, 1955).

Black Caesar (American International, 1973). 87 mins.

Producer: Larry Cohen. *Director and Screenplay*: Larry Cohen. *Directors of Photography*: Fenton Hamilton and James Signorelli. *Music*: James Brown. *Production Design*: Larry Lurin. *Editor*: George Folsey, Jr.

Cast: Fred Williamson (Tommy Gibbs), D'Urville Martin (Reverend Rufus), Gloria Hendry (Helen), Art Lund (John McKinney), Val Avery (Cordova). *With*: Minnie Gentry, Julius W. Harris, Phillip Royce, William Wellman, Jr., Myrna Hansen.

Tommy Gibbs grows up on the tough streets of Harlem where his life of crime begins during childhood. As an adult, he rises to become the cruel head of the local black mob. His ruthless rule comes to an end when he is gunned down by a rival.

Exploitation master Larry Cohen made this low-budget black version of *Little Caesar* (First National, 1931), one of the earliest "blaxploitation" pictures of the early seventies. Ultraviolent, it was an enormous box office success and made Fred Williamson into an important black American star in the early part of the decade. It is also notable for its borrowing of the famous grapefruit scene from *Little Caesar*.

The Black Hand (MGM, 1950). 92
    mins.
Producer: William H. Wright. *Director*: Richard Thorpe. *Screenplay*:
Luther Davis, *story by* Leo Townsend.
Director of Photography: Paul C.
Vogel. *Art Directors*: Cedric Gibbons
and Gabriel Scognamillo. *Editor*: Irving
Warburton.
    Cast: Gene Kelly (Johnny Columbo),
J. Carrol Naish (Louis Lorelli), Teresa
Celli (Isabella Gomboli), Marc Lawrence (Caesar Xavier Serpi), Frank
Puglia (Carlo Sabballera), Barry Kelley
(Captain Thompson), Peter Brocco
(Roberto Columbo). *With*: Mario
Siletti, Carl Milletaire, Eleanora
Mendelsshon, Gracia Narcisco, Burke
Symon, Bert Freed.
    In New York's "Little Italy" at the
turn of the century, Johnny Columbo
is a crusading young man who, with the
aid of veteran police detective Louis
Lorelli, tries to expel the Mafia from
his neighborhood.
    A minor addition to the genre, *The
Black Hand* is interesting for several
reasons. First, it provided Gene Kelly
with a strong dramatic role at the
height of his fame as a musical star.
Second, based on historical events, it
deals with the subject of organized
crime in a realistic fashion. Indeed, the
film holds up well today.

The Black Raven (Producers Releasing
    Corporation, 1943). 62 mins.
Producer: Sigmund Neufeld. *Director*: Sam Newfield. *Screenplay*: Fred
Myton. *Director of Photography*:
Robert Cline. *Music*: David Chudnow.
Art Director: Dave Milton. *Editor*:
Holbrook N. Todd.
    Cast: George Zucco (Amos Bradford), Wanda McKay (Lee Winfield),
Noel Madison (Mike Baroni), Bob
Randall (Allen Bentley), Byron
Foulger (Horace Weatherby). *With*:
Charles Middleton, Robert Middlemas, Glenn Strange, I. Stanford Jolley.
    Amos Bradford, "The Raven," is a
one-time gangster who runs a lonely

roadside inn called "The Black Raven."
One rainy night, a motley group of
travellers stop at the inn for shelter
from the storm. Among the guests,
which include an eloping couple and an
embezzler, is a gangster who has just
escaped from prison and is seeking revenge against the Raven. As the evening
progresses, several murders occur. Eventually, Bradford is fatally wounded, but
his assassin is also brought to justice.
    The Black Raven is a chamber piece,
set almost entirely in two or three
rooms and with a minimal cast. The
typically poor PRC production values
are offset by a taut script and strong
performances, making this "B" film an
interesting addition to the genre.

Black Tuesday (United Artists, 1954).
    80 mins.
Producer: Robert Goldstein. *Director*: Hugo Fregonese. *Screenplay*:
Sidney Boehm. *Director of Photography*: Stanley Cortez. *Music*: Paul
Dunlap. *Art Director*: Hilyard Brown.
Editor: Robert Golden.
    Cast: Edward G. Robinson (Vincent
Canelli), Peter Graves (Peter Manning),
Jean Parker (Hatti Combest), Milburn
Stone (Father Slocum), Warren Stevens
(Joey Stewart). *With*: Jack Kelly, Sylvia Findley, James Bell, Victor Perrin.
    On the day ("Black Tuesday") that
gangster Vincent Canelli is scheduled
to be executed for a murder committed
during a robbery, he escapes from
prison, aided by a guard whose daughter has been kidnapped by Canelli's
gang. Canelli, with his moll, Hatti
Combest, hides out at a warehouse
after shooting his way out of prison.
The gang holds several hostages for
ransom, but the police, who have followed the trail of blood left by Peter
Manning, one of Canelli's henchmen
who was wounded in the getaway, surround the warehouse. Canelli threatens
to kill the hostages if the police attack,
and to prove it, he kills one of the captives. Manning, however, has a change
of heart. Instead, he kills Canelli, but,

Edward G. Robinson (right) in one of his last roles as a hard-boiled gangster in *Black Tuesday*. Jean Parker (left) as his moll and Peter Graves (center) as his right hand man, are obviously startled by some off-screen threat.

as he leaves the hideout, is killed by the police.

Black Tuesday is an unrelentingly tense and uncompromising gangster thriller. Coming late in the cycle, and during an era of increased screen violence, the movie is simultaneously a throwback to the classics of the thirties and a representative of the new, bloodier era. Its screenplay, by the brilliant Sidney Boehm, is very good, and the film provided Edward G. Robinson one of his best later roles as the amoral gangster.

Blake, Johnny (Fictional character)

As played by Edward G. Robinson in *Bullets or Ballots* (First National, 1935), Blake was the first genre role in which Robinson was on the right side of the law, an honest cop who joins the mob as a secret operative in an investigation.

Blind Alley (Columbia, 1939). 61 mins.

Director: Charles Vidor. *Screenplay*: Philip MacDonald, Michael Blankfort, and Albert Duffy, based on the play by James Warwick. *Director of Photography*: Lucien Ballard. *Music*: Morris W. Stoloff. *Editor*: Otto Meyer.

Cast: Chester Morris (Hal Wilson), Ralph Bellamy (Dr. Anthony Shelby), Ann Dvorak (Mary), Joan Perry (Linda Curtis), Melville Cooper (George Curtis). *With*: Rose Stradner, John Eldredge, Ann Doran, Marc Lawrence, Scott Beckett, Milburn Stone.

Hal Wilson, a notoriously violent gangster, and his gang take over a country home while escaping from the police. The homeowner is Dr. Anthony Shelby, a psychiatrist interested in criminal pathology. Hal is more than willing to talk about his problems, and the doctor slowly unravels the history

James Cagney and Joan Blondell at their hard-boiled best as confidence tricksters in the neglected classic *Blonde Crazy.*

of the gangster's life and subsequent mental problems. Hal comes to understand his pathological behavior, but it is too late to prevent his final, deadly confrontation with the police.

Blind Alley is a surprisingly effective thriller with an interesting premise and excellent screenplay. A "B" film, it features a superb group of second string players, including Chester Morris (then in box office decline) and Ann Dvorak, who gives one of the best performances of her career as his moll. The film was later remade as the *noir* thriller *The Dark Past* (Columbia, 1949).

Blonde Crazy (Warner Bros., 1931). 74 mins.
   Producer and Director: Roy Del Ruth. *Screenplay*: Kubec Glasmon and John Bright. *Director of Photography*: Sid Hickox. *Music*: Leo F. Forbstein.

Songs: E. A. Swan, Gerald Marks and Buddy Fields; Roy Turk and Fred Ahlert. *Art Director*: Jack Okey. *Editor*: Ralph Dawon.
   Cast: James Cagney (Bert Harris), Joan Blondell (Ann Roberts), Louis Calhern (Dapper Dan Barker), Noel Francis (Helen Wilson), Guy Kibbee (A. Rupert Johnson, Jr.), Ray Milland (Joe Reynolds). *With*: Polly Walters, Charles Lane, William Burress, Peter Erkelenz, Walter Percival, Nat Pendleton.

Bert Harris, a bellhop in a resort who moonlights as a bootlegger and blackmailer, teams with Ann Roberts, the equally crooked maid. Successful in their escapades, they move west to avoid the authorities but are fleeced by Dapper Dan, a mobster. Eventually, Bert and Ann take revenge on Dapper Dan, but the excitement of their life together has worn thin. They break up and Ann marries a respectable stock broker. Bert is arrested before he can escape to Europe. When Ann learns of his misfortunes, she visits Bert in prison, tells him she is bored with her life of respectability, and says that she will await his release.

Blonde Crazy marked the third pairing of Cagney and Blondell, but it was the team's first real popular success. Essentially a satire, the film uneasily mixes comedy with music and petty thievery, but Blondell and Cagney more than compensate. Indeed, in many ways, it is one of the most entertaining of the early Warner gangster films.

Blondell, Joan (1909–1979)

Actress. Born in New York City, Joan Blondell was one of the most popular stars of the thirties. Her big, wide eyes and slightly daffy personality typecast her as a stereotypical dizzy blonde, but she also appeared in many dramatic roles. As one of Warner's top female contract players, she was often cast as the female lead or in a strong supporting role, starring in many important productions. She made memorable appearances in four gangster films for the studio during the thirties, most notably in the James Cagney vehicles *Public Enemy* and *Blonde Crazy*. She was particularly memorable as a con-woman in the latter, nearly managing the unlikely feat of upstaging Cagney.

Blonde Crazy (Warner Bros., 1931). *Public Enemy* (Warner Bros., 1931). *Three on a Match* (First National, 1932). *Bullets or Ballots* (First National, 1936).

Bloody Mama (American International, 1970). 90 mins.

Executive Producers: Samuel Z. Arkoff and James H. Nicholson. *Producer/Director*: Roger Corman. *Screenplay*: Robert Thom, *story by* Robert Thom and Don Peters. *Director of Photography*: John Alonzo. *Music*: Don Randi. *Editor*: Eve Newman.

Cast: Shelley Winters (Kate "Ma" Barker), Pat Hingle (Sam Adams Pendlebury), Don Stroud (Herman Barker), Diane Varsi (Mona Gibson), Bruce Dern (Kevin Dirkman), Clint Kimbrough (Arthur Barker), Robert De Niro (Lloyd Barker). *With*: Robert Walden, Alex Nicol, Michael Fox, Scatman Crothers, Stacy Harris, Pamela Dunlap.

The film tells the story of Ma Barker and her gang of robbers comprised of her sons and their trashy girlfriends — one of the most colorful Chicago-area gangs of the Prohibition era. Loosely based on the exploits of the real Ma Barker, it is one of director Roger Corman's best, notable for Shelley Winters' campy performance in the title role. In typical Corman fashion, violence and sex are exploited to the extreme. Still, the film's enormous success had a profound influence on the new age of crime thrillers, including big-budget films like *The Godfather* (Paramount, 1972).

Blue, Monte (1890–1963)

Character actor. Born in Indianapolis, Blue was a lumberjack and cowboy before beginning his film career in the mid-teens. Large and powerfully built, he played gangsters, strong men, and occasional heroes in the over 200 films. He starred in two early gangster silents but is all but forgotten today.

Skin Deep (Warner Bros., 1929). *Those Who Dance* (Warner Bros., 1930).

Blystone, John G. (1892–1938)

Director. Blystone was a competent craftsman who worked almost exclusively in "B" movies. He directed films in all genres, but was especially at home with comedy. He also directed one of James Cagney's lesser-known gangster films, the semisatirical *Great Guy*, but his sensibilities were ill suited to the genre.

Great Guy (Grand National, 1937).

Body and Soul (United Artists, 1947).
104 mins.
Producer/Director: Robert Rossen.
Screenplay: Abraham Polonsky. *Director of Photography*: James Wong Howe. *Music*: Hugo Friedhofer. *Art Director*: Nathan Juran. *Editor*: Francis Lyon.
Cast: John Garfield (Charlie Davis), Lilli Palmer (Peg Born), Hazel Brooks (Alice), Anne Revere (Anna Davis), William Conrad (Quinn), Joseph Pevney (Shorty Polaski), Canada Lee (Ben Chaplin). *With*: Art Smith, James Burke, Virginia Gregg, Peter Virgo, Joe Devlin.

Charlie Davis, a young street tough from New York, is a talented boxer. He rises to the top of his profession with the help of Peg Born, a kind girl from his neighborhood. Along the way, he dumps Peg for Alice, a society girl, but soon realizes that he is being used by his manager, a gangster who controls the sport. Although he is set up to "take a dive," he wins the championship. His career finished, he is at last confident he has done the right thing.

Body and Soul is one of the most famous *film noir* exposés of corruption. The subject was a timely one in a period when boxing was widely believed (and subsequently proven) to be "fixed." Indeed, boxing came to symbolize both the aspirations and corruptibility of American society in several key *noir* thrillers in the forties and fifties. *Body and Soul* is one of the best of the group, effectively combining social criticism with gangster themes.

Boehm, Sidney (b. 1908)

Screenwriter. Boehm's film career began in the late forties after many years as a journalist and pulp writer. He quickly established himself as one of the most prolific and reliable screenwriters of the fifties. Although Boehm wrote for various genres, his specialty was crime stories, and he penned many of the best "B" movies of the fifties and sixties. His best known screenplay is for Fritz Lang's *noir*-gangster classic, *The Big Heat*, but all of his screenplays are well above average.

Side Street (MGM, 1949). *The Undercover Man* (Columbia, 1949). *The Big Heat* (Columbia, 1953). *Black Tuesday* (United Artists, 1954). *Rogue Cop* (MGM, 1954). *Six Bridges to Cross* (Universal, 1955). *Violent Saturday* (20th Century–Fox, 1955). *Hell on Frisco Bay* (Warner Bros., 1956). *Seven Thieves* (20th Century–Fox, 1960; producer also).

Boetticher, Budd (b. 1916)

Director. Born Oscar Boetticher, Budd was an adventurer who, after years as a bull fighter among other things, found his way to Hollywood in the forties, working his way up to director. He helmed many "B" movies, including a superior low-budget gangster melodrama, *The Rise and Fall of Legs Diamond*, one of the best attempts to recapture the spirit of the genre's best films of the thirties.

The Rise and Fall of Legs Diamond (Warner Bros., 1960).

Bogart, Humphrey (1899–1957)

Actor. It is perhaps ironic that the man most associated with the gangster genre was the product not of tough streets but of quiet privilege. He was born Humphrey DeForest Bogart in New York City, the son of a prominent doctor and a famous illustrator. Although he would one day come to personify the common man, Bogart received a classical education. Nonetheless, he had a rebellious streak and, instead of going off to prep school as expected, joined the Navy. It was while in the Navy that Bogart was injured in an accident which permanently disfigured him, causing the slight paralysis in his upper lip which caused his distinctive lisp. After the service, he turned to acting, beginning a long if not particularly distinguished career on Broadway before achieving stardom as the psychotic gangster, Duke Mantee, in Robert Sherwood's *The Petrified Forest*. Bogart played the role in the film version as well, providing the screen with its definitive image of criminal paranoia. Although the film was a success, it did not make him into a true star. This was partly due to neglect — as a contract player for Warner Bros., he must have seemed like just another tough-guy character actor to a studio which had James Cagney and Edward G. Robinson as its main stars. Thus, Bogart was mainly relegated to "B" movies and supporting roles during the thirties. If anything, Duke Mantee typecast Bogart as the psychotic bad guy in countless movies, but he managed to shine through as several notable supporting characters in *Angels with Dirty Faces, San Quentin*, and *Dead End*.

Bogart's real stardom began with *High Sierra*, in which he starred as the doomed gangster Roy Earle. But it took his performances in *The Maltese Falcon* and *Casablanca* (Warner Bros., 1942) to break typecasting, allowing him to play heroes and good guys. Indeed, after *Casablanca*, he rarely played criminals again, and his appearances in the genre tended to be in good-guy roles. A notable exception was *The Desperate Hours*, in which he played one of his most notorious gangsters.

Of all the stars associated with gangster films, Humphrey Bogart probably remains foremost. Certainly, he and Edward G. Robinson were the only actors to appear consistently in this type of movie for over two decades, managing to bring a sense of humanity to some of the most memorable gangsters and villains in the history of American movies.

Up the River (Fox, 1930). *Three on a Match* (First National, 1932). *Bullets or Ballots* (First National, 1936). *The Petrified Forest* (Warner Bros., 1936). *Dead End* (United Artists, 1937). *Kid Galahad* (Warner Bros., 1937). *Marked Woman* (Warner Bros., 1937). *San Quentin* (Warner Bros., 1937). *The Amazing Dr. Clitterhouse* (Warner Bros., 1938). *Angels with Dirty Faces* (Warner Bros., 1938). *Racket Busters* (Warner Bros., 1938). *Invisible Stripes* (Warner Bros., 1939). *King of the Underworld* (Warner Bros., 1939). *The Roaring Twenties* (Warner Bros., 1939). *You Can't Get Away with Murder* (Warner Bros., 1939). *Brother Orchid* (Warner Bros., 1940). *High Sierra* (Warner Bros., 1941). *The Maltese Falcon* (Warner Bros., 1941). *The Big Shot* (Warner Bros., 1942). *Dead Reckoning* (Columbia, 1947). *Key Largo* (Warner Bros., 1948). *The Enforcer* (Warner Bros., 1951). *The Desperate Hours* (Paramount, 1955). *The Harder They Fall* (Columbia, 1956).

Bond, Ward (1903–1960)

Actor. Born in Denver, Ward Bond was a champion football player at the University of Southern California, where he befriended his fellow teammate, Marion Morrison, who would soon be known as John Wayne. Bond and Wayne remained lifelong friends, and both appeared in many of John Ford's best westerns. Unlike Wayne, however, Bond never achieved real stardom, except in "B" movies. His rugged features relegated him to supporting parts, although he appeared in nearly every Hollywood genre. He often played the tough second lead, as he did in the James Cagney vehicle, *Kiss Tomorrow Goodbye*, his few appearances in the gangster genre.

Night Key (Universal, 1937). *Kiss Tomorrow Goodbye* (Warner Bros., 1950).

Bonnie and Clyde (Warner Bros., 1967). 111 mins.

Producer: Warren Beatty. *Director*: Arthur Penn. *Screenplay*: David Newman and Robert Benton. *Director of Photography*: Burnett Guffey. *Music*: Lester Flatt and Earl Scruggs. *Art Director*: Dean Tavoularis. *Editor*: Dede Allen.

Recreating the real life rural gang Bonnie and Clyde and associates are, left to right, Gene Hackman, Estelle Parsons, Warren Beatty, Faye Dunaway and Michael J. Pollard.

Cast: Warren Beatty (Clyde Barrow), Faye Dunaway (Bonnie Parker), Gene Hackman (Buck Barrow), Michael J. Pollard (C. W. Moss), Estelle Parsons (Blanche), Denver Pyle (Frank Hamer), Gene Wilder (Eugene Grizzard). *With*: Dub Taylor, James Stiver, Clyde Howdy, Gary Goodgion, Ken Mayer, Martha Adcock.

The criminal life of redneck gangsters Bonnie Parker and Clyde Barrow is recalled. With Clyde's brother Buck and several others, the disparate gang terrorizes the countryside in the southwestern United States, indiscriminately robbing small-town banks and killing anyone who gets in their way. In 1933, after a year of mayhem, Buck is killed in a shootout, and the gang becomes the focus of the media and the emergent F.B.I. Eventually, the remaining trio — Bonnie, Clyde, and C. W. Moss — are ambushed and gunned down by Texas Rangers.

Immensely popular on its initial release, *Bonnie and Clyde* is a rollicking, violent exposé of the real life gangsters who became folk heroes in the early Depression years. While the film ignores some of the controversial aspects of the real characters (the homosexuality of Clyde Barrow for example), the tense style and violent action make up for its few faults. In fact, the film is important for a number of reasons, including the innovative level of violence and bloodletting. Its popularity also helped revive interest in the gangster genre, and a whole group of new films exploring these themes were made over the next several years, culminating in the artistic triumph of *The Godfather* (Paramount, 1972).

The Bonnie Parker Story (American International, 1958). 79 mins.

Executive Producers: James H. Nicholson and Samuel Z. Arkoff. *Producer*: Stanley Shpetner. *Director*: William Witney. *Screenplay*: Stanley Shpetner. *Director of Photography*: Jack Marta. *Music*: Ronald Stein. *Editor*: Frank Keller.

Cast: Dorothy Provine (Bonnie Parker), Jack Hogan (Guy Darrow), Richard Bakalyn (Duke Jefferson), Joseph Turkel (Chuck Darrow), William Stevens (Paul). *With*: Ken Lynch, Douglas Kennedy, Patti Huston, Joel Colin, Jeff Morris, Jim Beck.

The film follows the criminal exploits of the real life Bonnie Parker and Clyde Barrow—here renamed Guy Darrow. Except for the name changes of the male characters, the film remains true to the facts. Indeed, Dorothy Provine's trashier Bonnie Parker is closer to the real woman than Faye Dunaway's more glamorous portrayal a decade later. Little more than "B" exploitation, *The Bonnie Parker Story* still manages to entertain, thanks in large part to Provine's superb performance. It is also notable as one of American International's first forays into the genre.

Borgnine, Ernest (b. 1917)

Actor. Born Ermes Borgnino in Hamden, Connecticut, Borgnine's broad frame and tough visage made him a forceful character actor, and he was often typecast as a villain in films, including two gangster efforts. In *The Mob* he has a supporting role as a gang underling, while in *Pay or Die* he stars as a crusading police detective waging a war against the Mafia in New York's Little Italy.

The Mob (Columbia, 1951). *Pay or Die* (Allied Artists, 1960).

Born Reckless (20th Century–Fox, 1937). 78 mins.

Producer: Sol M. Wurtzel. *Director*: Malcolm St. Clair. *Screenplay*: John Patrick, Robert Ellis, and Helen Logan, *story by* Jack Andrews. *Director of Photography*: Daniel B. Clark. *Music*: Samuel Kaylin. *Art Director*: Chester Gore. *Editor*: Alex Troffey.

Cast: Rochelle Hudson (Sybil Roberts), Brian Donlevy (Bob "Hurry" Kane), Barton MacLane (Jim Barnes), Robert Kent (Lee Martin), Harry Carey (Dad Martin). *With*: Pauline Moore, Chick Chandler, William Pawley, Francis McDonald, George Wolcutt, Joseph Crehan.

A variation on the earlier, popular *Taxi!* (Warner Bros., 1932), *Born Reckless* tells the story of racketeers who control the taxi trade, and the honest drivers, led by Bob "Hurry" Kane, who fight against them. The film is typical of "B" films of the era, with the necessary moral ending (the cab drivers emerge triumphant). Otherwise, the only redeeming virtues of the film are its impressive cast.

Borsalino (Paramount, 1970). 126 mins.

Producer: Alain Delon. *Director*: Jacques Deray. *Screenplay*: Jean-Claude Carriere, Claude Santet, Jacques Deray, and Jean Cau. *Director of Photography*: Jean-Jacques Tarbes. *Music*: Claude Bolling. *Art Director*: Francois de Lamothe. *Editor*: Paul Cayatte.

Cast: Jean-Paul Belmondo (Capella), Alain Delon (Siffredi), Michel Bouquet (Rinaldi), Catherine Rouvel (Lola), Francoise Christophe (Mme. Escarguel). *With*: Corinne Marchand, Julian Guiomar, Arnoldo Foa, Nicole Calfan, Christian de Tiliere.

In Marseilles, France, in the early thirties, two crooks work their way up through the rackets, eventually becoming the heads of the local gang controlling the area's gambling and prostitution.

Roughly contemporaneous with *The Godfather* (Paramount, 1972), *Borsalino* was a somewhat satirical study of similar themes in France. The film was an enormous box office success in

Europe (perhaps because of its sex and violence), resurrecting the gangster genre. It was a moderate success in the United States (where it was relegated to art cinemas), but it remains an interesting adaptation of the styles and themes popularized by American movies of the thirties and forties.

Borzage, Frank (1893–1962)
Director. Although neglected today, perhaps because he favored sentimental melodramas, Frank Borzage was a superior filmmaker with a passionate, lush visual style. *Strange Cargo*, his single contribution to the gangster genre, is an interesting and rather bizarre adventure film characterized by Borzage's typically baroque style.
Strange Cargo (MGM, 1940).

Bowers, William (1916–1987)
Screenwriter. A distinguished screenwriter, Bowers wrote or cowrote a number of classic films, beginning in the early forties. He was especially adept at hard-boiled subjects, and contributed two excellent, if not particularly well known, screenplays to the gangster genre.
The Mob (Columbia, 1951). *Tight Spot* (Columbia, 1955).

Boyd, William (1895–1972)
Actor. Boyd will be forever remembered as the star of the "B" Western series *Hopalong Cassidy*. He also made a few appearances as character leads before becoming typecast as the Western hero, including a small part in the early sound gangster film, *Those Who Dance*, ironically as a mob henchman.
Those Who Dance (Warner Bros., 1930).

Boyer, Charles (1899–1978)
Actor. Leading man Charles Boyer, born in Figeac, France, was the very image of sophisticated European romance for American audiences in the thirties and forties. He was cast in many exotic romances opposite some of Hollywood's most beautiful actresses, including Hedy Lamarr in *Algiers*. Boyer's role in this film, as a doomed gangster, was atypical, and he did not return to this type again. However, the film's enormous popularity and Boyer's surprisingly humane and effective performance helped move the genre in a more contemplative direction during the forties.
Algiers (United Artists, 1938).

Boyle, Robert (b. 1910)
Art director. Boyle graduated from the University of Southern California with a degree in architecture. After several of the architectural firms he worked for went broke, he entered the film industry. He served as art director for all the major studios but is probably best known for his long association with Alfred Hitchcock. He also worked on a single gangster movie late in the genre's fifties cycle.
The Brothers Rico (Columbia, 1957).

Brabin, Charles (1883–1957)
Director. The British born Brabin had a successful career as a stage and film director in his native country before moving to Hollywood in the late twenties. He directed a number of impressive "B" movies and a few "A" films, including *The Beast of the City*, an important early gangster talkie.
The Beast of the City (MGM, 1932).

Brady, Scott (1924–1985)
Actor. Born Gerald Tierney, Scott Brady was the younger brother of tough-guy actor Lawrence Tierney, and like him, specialized in hard-boiled roles, mostly in "B" movies. He co-starred with Lawrence as one of the gangsters in the excellent "B" gangster-heist film *The Hoodlum*.
The Hoodlum (United Artists, 1951).

Brand, Neville (b. 1921)
Character actor. The heavyset, tough looking Brand began a film career in 1948 after many years in the

military—he was the fourth most decorated soldier in World War II—appearing in dozens of movies, generally as a villain. In Don Siegel's gangster-prison drama *Riot in Cell Block 11*, he starred as the leader of the rioting prisoners. He had a supporting role in the "B" classic, *Kansas City Confidential*, typically as a mob henchman. However, he made his greatest impression with his recurring role as Al Capone in the television series, *The Untouchables*, whose pilot was released as a feature film, *The Scarface Mob*, in Europe.

Kansas City Confidential (United Artists, 1952). *Riot in Cell Block 11* (Allied Artists, 1954). *The Scarface Mob* (Cari Releasing, 1960).

Brando, Jocelyn (b. 1919)
Character actress. Although not as well known as her younger brother Marlon, Jocelyn Brando has proven equally talented. After a successful stage career, she began appearing in movies during the early fifties, including supporting roles in two fifties gangster titles. In *The Big Heat*, she plays the devoted wife of a crusading detective who dies in a gangland bombing meant for her husband. In *Nightfall*, on the other hand, she plays the moll of a murderous bank robber.

The Big Heat (Columbia, 1953). *Nightfall* (Columbia, 1957).

Brando, Marlon (b. 1924)
Actor. Considered by some to be the greatest actor of his generation, Marlon Brando's screen performances often lapse into over-emoting and self-parody. He was particularly impressive early in his career, as in *On the Waterfront*, in which he starred as Terry Malloy, the boxer corrupted by gangsters. The same year, Brando also starred as a motorcycle gangster in *The Wild One*. This film's success and Brando's image had a profound influence on the emerging youth and rock 'n' roll culture of the mid-fifties. His role

in the satirical musical *Guys and Dolls* was more in the traditional gangster mode. However, his most important performance in the genre is in *The Godfather*. His mumbling, slow-moving Don Corleone has become the very image of the gangster of myth—so much so, it is said that real life mobsters have modeled themselves after Brando's character.

On the Waterfront (Columbia, 1954). *The Wild One* (Columbia, 1954). *Guys and Dolls* (MGM, 1955). *The Godfather* (Paramount, 1972).

Bredell, Elwood ("Woody")
Cinematographer. Bredell was a major pioneer in the development of *film noir* aesthetics, helping to create the dark, smokey and moody tones associated with the genre. He collaborated with director Robert Siodmak on a number of forties classics, including the *noir*-gangster classic *The Killers*.

The Killers (Universal, 1946).

Breen, Richard (1919–1967)
Screenwriter. A successful, if not particularly outstanding, screenwriter, Breen authored many popular movies beginning in the late forties. He wrote the screenplay for Jack Webb's moody "B" gangster drama, *Pete Kelly's Blues*, his only contribution to the genre.

Pete Kelly's Blues (Warner Bros., 1955).

Brent, Evelyn (1899–1975)
Actress. Born Elizabeth Mary Riggs in Tampa, Florida, and raised in Brooklyn, Evelyn Brent became one of the biggest stars of the late silent era. A dark-haired ethereal beauty, she starred in two of Joseph von Sternberg's seminal gangster classics, *The Dragnet* and *Underworld*. In the former, she made an impression as one of the earliest (and most sensual) gangster molls. In the latter, her moll was closer to the *femmes fatales* of *film noir*.

Underworld (Paramount, 1927). *The Dragnet* (Paramount, 1928).

Brent, George (1904–1979)
Actor. Born George Brent Nolan in Dublin, Ireland, Brent had a brief stage career in his homeland before fleeing during political turmoil. Continuing his stage career in the United States, he was spotted by Hollywood scouts and signed to a contract. A suave and romantic leading man, he was a popular matinee idol in the thirties. He was often cast as the romantic interest opposite a strong female lead such as Bette Davis, with whom he appeared in typically heroic fashion, in *Special Agent*. The film, however, was dominated by Davis. In the "B" gangster drama *Racket Busters*, he played the good guy opposite Humphrey Bogart's baddie.

Special Agent (Warner Bros., 1935).
Racket Busters (Warner Bros., 1938).

Bresler, Jerry (1912–1977)
Producer. An independent producer, Bresler specialized in modest-budget, high-quality films. He produced Robert Parrish's early fifties gangster picture, *The Mob*; this was Bresler's only contribution to the genre.

The Mob (Columbia, 1951).

The Bribe (MGM, 1949). 98 mins.
Producer: Pandro S. Berman. *Director*: Robert Z. Leonard. *Screenplay*: Marguerite Roberts, *story by* Frederick Nebel. *Director of Photography*: Joseph Ruttenberg. *Music*: Miklos Rozsa. *Art Directors*: Cedric Gibbons and Malcolm Brown. *Editor*: Gene Ruggiero.
Cast: Robert Taylor (Rigby), Ava Gardner (Elizabeth Hintian), Charles Laughton (J.J. Bealer), Vincent Price (Carwood), John Hodiak (Tug Hintian). *With*: Samuel S. Hinds, John Hoyt, Tito Renaldo, Martin Garralaga.
Rigby, a customs agent employed by the United States Justice Department, is sent to a small Caribbean island to investigate the illegal sales of surplus war materiel. There he encounters the suave leader of the gang, Carwood, and his loyal henchman, Bealer. Rigby's investigation is hampered by a cafe singer, Elizabeth, an employee of Carwood's, who attempts to bribe and then kill him. In the end, however, Rigby succeeds in closing Carwood's operations (after a violent, memorable fire fight) and winning the love of Elizabeth as well.

The Bribe is a typical example of MGM's approach to crime stories — filling the movie with exotic locations (here shot on the studio's back lot) and overloading the plot with romantic complications. Ava Gardner was given star billing for the first time in this rather stolid melodrama, and although never more beautiful, her scenes with Robert Taylor are predictable. Furthermore, the gangster elements (which, in fact, had some basis in reality), were suppressed in favor of the romantic subplot.

Bridges, Jeff (b. 1949)
Actor. The son of Lloyd Bridges, Jeff was born in Los Angeles and entered movies in the early seventies. He slowly rose to quasi-stardom, achieving a peak in the mid-eighties. Specializing in eccentrics, he made an impression in the cult favorite, *Thunderbolt and Lightfoot*, as a drifter and con-artist who teams with a notorious bank robber. He was less successful in *Against All Odds*, the remake of *Out of the Past* (RKO, 1947) in the role originated by Robert Mitchum.

Thunderbolt and Lightfoot (United Artists, 1974). *Against All Odds* (Columbia, 1984).

Bridges, Lloyd (b. 1913)
Actor. Lloyd Bridges is one of those actors whose screen careers never reach the heights but who are nonetheless stamped indelibly on the American consciousness. He had his greatest success on television's *Sea Hunt*, but he also made many memorable appearances in mostly "B" movies, usually

cast as the stalwart hero, occasionally as a villain. He costarred in two minor gangster dramas, playing heroic, but flawed, characters.

Hideout (Republic, 1949). *Trapped* (Eagle-Lion, 1949).

Bright, John

Screenwriter. Bright specialized in hard-boiled crime thrillers and action pictures. As a staff writer for Warner Bros. in the early thirties, he cowrote several notable films, including the gangster classics *Blonde Crazy* and *Public Enemy*. He moved to Paramount in 1938, where his style and themes underwent a slight change, but did cowrite a neglected gangster film, *Back Door to Heaven*, which contains his usual bright, sarcastic, pithy dialog.

Blonde Crazy (Warner Bros., 1931). *Public Enemy* (Warner Bros., 1931). *Back Door to Heaven* (Paramount, 1939).

The Brink's Job (Universal, 1978). 100 mins.

Executive Producer: Dino De Laurentiis. *Producer*: Ralph Serpe. *Director*: William Friedkin. *Screenplay*: Walon Green, based on the book by Noel Behn. *Art Director*: Angelo Graham. *Editors*: Bud Smith and Robert K. Lambert.

Cast: Peter Falk (Tony Pino), Peter Boyle (Joe McGinnis), Allen Goorwitz (Vinnie Costa), Warren Oates (Specs O'Keefe), Gena Rowlands (Mary Pino). *With*: Paul Sorvino, Sheldon Leonard, Gerald Murphy, Kevin O'Connor, Claudia Peluso.

A disparate group of petty criminals led by Tony Pino plan to rob the Brink's office in Boston. Carrying out the heist successfully, they then wait out the statute of limitations. However, when Specs, one of the members of the gang, is arrested for another robbery, he agrees to exchange information for a lighter sentence. The other members of the gang are arrested only two days before the statute of limitations expires.

The Brink's Job was based on real events that also inspired the better heist drama, *Six Bridges to Cross* (Universal, 1955). The director, William Friedkin, was no doubt hoping to recapture the spirit and success of his modern gangster classic *The French Connection* (20th Century–Fox, 1971), but the film wallows in self indulgence and lackluster performances, ultimately failing to live up to its promise.

Broadway (Universal, 1929). Approximately 80 mins.

Presenter: Carl Laemmle. *Producer*: Carl Laemmle, Jr. *Director*: Paul Fejos. *Screenplay*: Edward T. Lowe, Jr., Charles Furthman, Tom Reed, based on the play by Jed Harris, Philip Duning, George Abbott. *Director of Photography*: Hal Mohr. *Editors*: Robert Carlisle, Edward Cahn.

Cast: Glenn Tryon (Roy Lane), Evelyn Brent (Pearl), Merna Kennedy (Billie Moore), Thomas Jackson (Dan McCom), Robert Ellis (Steve Cradell). *With*: Otis Harlan, Paul Porcasi, Marion Lord, Fritz Feld.

Roy Lane and Billie Moore are two nightclub entertainers who become involved with mobsters when their employer is murdered by a gang. Enlisting the entertainers' aid, the nightclub owner's mistress, Pearl, kills the mob boss who murdered her lover. Roy and Billie are then free to marry and continue their careers.

An enormous stage success in 1926, *Broadway* is a rather naive, cliché ridden movie typical of its time. It is important only as one of the first successful sound gangster films. It was later remade as *Broadway* (Universal, 1942), directed by the brilliant comedy director William A. Seiter and starring George Raft and Pat O'Brien. The latter film is not, however, one of Seiter's best and quickly disappeared after its release.

Brodine, Norbert (1893–1970)

Cinematographer. One of the great cinematographers of Hollywood's golden age, Norbert Brodine's career began in the late teens and reached its zenith in the thirties. His style was straightforward and unadorned, yet also oddly expressive. He photographed some of the great comedies of the late thirties for MGM and Hal Roach. *Beast of the City* is typical of his early style. In the late forties, however, his style underwent a radical change, absorbing the highly sculptured, contrasted lighting familiar to expressionism. It was then that he photographed several of the most important early *films noir: The House on 92nd Street* (20th Century–Fox, 1945), *Boomerang* (20th Century–Fox, 1947), *Thieves Highway* (20th Century–Fox, 1949), and the *noir*-gangster classic *Kiss of Death.*

Beast of the City (MGM, 1932). *Kiss of Death* (20th Century–Fox, 1947).

Bronson, Charles (b. 1922)

Actor. Born Charles Buchinsky in Scooptown, Pennsylvania, Bronson was the son of a coal miner. After varied experience, he moved to Los Angeles in the fifties and began appearing in small roles and bit parts almost immediately. His scarred features and tough, working class demeanor typecast him as hoods and villains. As the title character in Roger Corman's low-budget gangster movie *Machine Gun Kelly*, Bronson was in his element as the brooding killer, a forerunner of the antiheroes he would play in countless action oriented crime thrillers in the seventies. In *The Mechanic*, for example, he starred as a mob assassin. However, he is probably best remembered as a kind of second string Clint Eastwood, the "good guy" who makes his own rules to enforce the law, in three of his most popular, gangster-oriented films: *The Stone Killer, The Valachi Papers*, and *Mr. Majestyk*, which is based on a novel by Elmore Leonard.

Machine Gun Kelly (American International, 1958). *The Mechanic* (United Artists, 1972). *The Valachi Papers* (Columbia, 1972). *The Stone Killer* (Columbia, 1973). *Mr. Majestyk* (United Artists, 1974).

Brook, Clive (1887–1974)

Actor. Born Clifford Brook in London, Clive Brook was an insurance salesman, journalist, and veteran of World War I before becoming an actor in the late teens. The debonair and handsome Brook was soon a popular leading man of the gentlemanly, stiff upper lip sort on stage and in film. He arrived in Hollywood in 1924, where his popularity continued unabated. He became famous as Sherlock Holmes in two films, as well as starring in two of Josef von Sternberg's early classics, including *The Shanghai Express* (Paramount, 1932). In Sternberg's seminal gangster classic *Underworld*, he co-starred as a derelict who joins a gang and quickly rises to the top of the underworld.

Underworld (Paramount, 1927).

Brooks, Phyllis (1914–1995)

Actress. Born Phyllis Weiler, the gorgeous, blonde Phyllis Brooks had a brief career as a model before Hollywood beckoned in the early thirties. Despite some talent and charisma, she never rose above "B" productions, but she was one of the most popular low-budget actresses for nearly two decades before her retirement. She mainly played light roles, with occasional dramatic parts in more prestigious films. She had a leading role in John Ford's *Up the River*, a prison-gangster film, but had little to do among its male dominated cast.

Up the River (20th Century–Fox, 1938).

Brooks, Richard (b. 1912)

Screenwriter. After gaining experience as a journalist, Richard Brooks became a leading screenwriter during the forties. He specialized in hard-boiled subjects with psychological insight, and was a key figure in the development of *film noir*. The *noir*-gangster films *Brute Force* and *Key Largo* are among his finest efforts. He later became an important director of serious, somewhat pretentious melodramas.

Brute Force (Universal, 1947). *Key Largo* (Warner Bros., 1948).

Brown, Harry (1917–1986)

Screenwriter. Briefly a journalist before serving in the military during World War II, Harry Brown cashed in on his experiences with several well received war novels. As a screenwriter, he concentrated largely on war themes, but also worked on classics like *A Place in the Sun* (Columbia, 1951). He wrote the screenplay (based on Horace McCoy's novel) for *Kiss Tomorrow Goodbye*, one of James Cagney's most unrelentingly violent, cynical gangster movies.

Kiss Tomorrow Goodbye (Warner Bros., 1950).

Brown, Harry Joe (1892–1972)

Director and producer. Harry Joe Brown was a producer for nearly all of his movie career, beginning in the silent era. Married for many years to "B" star Sally Eilers, he produced many popular "A" and "B" titles, including *The Rains Came* (20th Century–Fox, 1939), *Alexander's Ragtime Band* (20th Century–Fox, 1938), and Fritz Lang's uncharacteristic, but brilliant, Western, *Western Union* (20th Century–Fox, 1941). He also directed a number of films, almost all "B"s — primarily in the early thirties. Among these is an early, minor gangster film.

The Squealer (Columbia, 1930).

Brown, Rowland (1901–1963)

Screenwriter and director. A restless figure who had experience as a cartoonist before entering the movies, Brown was a notorious perfectionist and egomaniac whose film career, as a result, was a fitful one. He was most active during the early thirties when he wrote or directed a handful of very good films, including the neglected gangster classic *Quick Millions*. He also worked on the scripts for two later gangster classics. However, his violent temper and extreme egomania destroyed his career and he disappeared after the early forties.

Quick Millions (Fox, 1931; writer and director). *Angels with Dirty Faces* (Warner Bros., 1938; story only). *Johnny Apollo* (20th Century–Fox, 1940; cowriter only).

Browning, Tod (1881–1962)

Director. The legendary Tod Browning, who directed a variety of movies, is remembered today as a master of the macabre. His *London After Midnight* (MGM, 1927), *Dracula* (Universal, 1931), *Freaks* (MGM, 1932), and *The Devil Doll* (MGM, 1936) are all milestones of that genre. Less well known are his two gangster films, *The Big City* and *Outside the Law*. Both are well made, but the latter is best known for an early appearance by Edward G. Robinson.

The Big City (MGM, 1928). *Outside the Law* (Universal, 1930).

Bruce, Virginia (1910–1982)

Actress. Born Helen Virginia Briggs in Minneapolis, Bruce went to Los Angeles to attend college, but found her way into the movies instead. The delicate, liquid eyed blonde rose through the ranks to become one of MGM's biggest stars in the early thirties. She played conventional roles and was little more than pretty decoration in her films. She costarred in an entertaining gangster film, *Let 'Em Have It*, as the object of a gangster's kidnapping scheme.

Let 'Em Have It (United Artists, 1935).

Bryan, Jane (b. 1918)

Actress. Born Jane O'Brien, Jane

Bryan was an attractive, under appreciated leading lady of the thirties. Before her early retirement in 1940, she costarred in a number of interesting movies, all for Warner Bros. If forgotten today, she nevertheless remains an important figure in the gangster genre by virtue of her appearances in five notable films. Interestingly, she did not play molls, but often portrayed sympathetic characters, making her one of the more unique female personages in the genre.

Kid Galahad (Warner Bros., 1937). *Marked Woman* (Warner Bros., 1937). *A Slight Case of Murder* (Warner Bros., 1938). *Invisible Stripes* (Warner Bros., 1939).

Bugsy (Tristar, 1992). 120 mins. *Producers*: Mark Johnson, Barry Levinson and Warren Beatty. *Director*: Barry Levinson. *Screenplay*: James Toback. *Director of Photography*: Allen Daviau. *Music*: Ennio Morricone. *Production Designer*: Dennis Gassner. *Editor*: Stu Linder.

Cast: Warren Beatty (Bugsy Siegel), Annette Bening (Virginia Hill), Harvey Keitel (Mickey Cohen), Ben Kingsley (Meyer Lansky), Elliott Gould (Harry Greenberg), Joe Mantegna (George). *With*: Richard Sarafian, Bebe Neuwirth, Gian-Carlo Scandiuzz, Wendy Phillips, Stephanie Mason.

Bugsy Siegel, a mob underling and strong arm man, has been sent from New York to Los Angeles to head up new Mafia operations on the West Coast. Siegel's flamboyance and self absorption border on the psychotic, and he even arranges a screen test for himself through his Hollywood connections. Meanwhile, he begins an affair with Virginia Hill, an actress with aspirations of her own. Encouraged by Hill, Siegel creates a scheme to turn the sleepy town of Las Vegas, Nevada, into a gambling paradise. With funds extorted from prominent Hollywood sources and borrowed from the Mafia, he begins building the Flamingo, a casino named after his mistress. His own wife and family suffer from his absences, and the hotel-casino financial overruns eventually become an embarrassment to the mob. Part of Siegel's monetary problems stem from Virginia Hill's embezzlements, but before he can reverse his fortunes, the mob kills Siegel and takes over his operation.

Based on real life gangster Bugsy Siegel's last two years, *Bugsy* is a somewhat romanticized version of events but sticks closer to the truth than other mob biopics. It is an exceptionally well written and well directed movie with good performances, particularly by supporting players Harvey Keitel and Ben Kingsley as Siegel's real life mob associates Mickey Cohen and Meyer Lansky, and Joe Mantegna who, as in *Godfather III* (Paramount, 1990), plays a mob henchman.

Bullitt (Warner Bros./7 Arts, 1968). 114 mins. *Producer*: Philip D'Antoni. *Director*: Peter Yates. *Screenplay*: Alan R. Trustman and Harry Kleiner, based on the novel *Mute Witness* by Robert L. Pike. *Director of Photography*: William A. Fraker. *Music*: Lalo Schifrin. *Art Director*: Albert Brenner. *Editor*: Frank P. Keller.

Cast: Steve McQueen (Detective Lieutenant Frank Bullitt), Robert Vaughn (Walter Chalmers), Jacqueline Bisset (Cathy), Don Gordon (Detective Delgetti), Robert Duvall (Weisberg). *With*: Norman Fell, Simon Oakland, Stanford Brann, Justin Tarr, Carl Reindel.

An independent minded police detective, Frank Bullitt, against the orders of his superiors, hunts down and kills a Chicago thief who has been promised a deal if he testifies before a Senate committee.

An exhilarating thriller, *Bullitt* is probably best known for its extraordinary car chase. Enormously popular, it was a contemporary version of the *noir* police procedurals, best exemplified by *The Big Heat* (Columbia, 1953). Its success inspired a whole group of cop-as-antihero thrillers in the early seventies, the best of which is perhaps *Dirty Harry* (Warner Bros., 1971).

Burr, Raymond (1917–1993)

Character actor. Long before he found stardom on television as Perry Mason, Raymond Burr was one of the screen's most memorable villains. Large and menacing, he played killers of all types in both "A" and "B" productions, including perhaps his most memorable role in Alfred Hitchcock's *Rear Window* (Universal, 1954). However, his villains in *His Kind of Woman* and *Raw Deal* are no less compelling and frightening.

Raw Deal (Eagle-Lion, 1948). *His Kind of Woman* (RKO, 1951).

Before television success as good guy lawyer Perry Mason, Raymond Burr was one of the most striking villains of the forties and fifties, often appearing as a psychotic mobster.

Busch, Mae (1897–1946)

Actress. One of silent cinema's legendary leading ladies, Busch is remembered as much today for her off-screen extravagances as for her occasionally splendid performances in the films of Erich von Stroheim and her countless pairings with Laurel and Hardy. She costarred in the early sound gangster movie *Alibi*, but by then her popularity had begun to wane. However, she continued to play character parts right up to her death.

Alibi (United Artists, 1929).

Buttolph, David (b. 1902)

Composer. Buttolph was one of the busiest film composers in the thirties, forties and fifties. He was an especially gifted composer of dramatic scores for thrillers and action-oriented dramas, including two gangster movies.

Show Them No Mercy (20th Century–Fox, 1935). *The Enforcer* (Warner Bros., 1951).

C-Man (Film Classics, 1949). 76 mins.

Producer: Rex Carlton. *Director*: Joseph Lerner. *Screenplay*: Berne Giler. *Director of Photography*: Gerald Hirschfield. *Music*: Gail Kubik. *Editor*: Geraldine Lerner.

Cast: Dean Jagger (Cliff Holden), John Carradine (Doc Spencer), Lottie Elwen (Kathy), Harry Landers (Owney), Rene Paul (Matty Royal), Walter Vaughn (Inspector Brandon). *With*: Adelaide Klein, Edith Atwater, Jean Ellyn, Walter Brooke.

Cliff Holden is a United States Customs Service agent assigned to locate and break up a gang of smugglers operating in New York City. His investigation leads to kidnapping, assault and murder, but eventually he discovers that the head of the gang is a "respectable" physician, Doc Spencer. Holden manages to break up the gang and arrest Doc Spencer.

C-Man is a surprisingly well made gangster thriller. While the script suffers from the usual pitfalls of "B" movies, the movie more than makes up for them with its quick pace, violent action, and real location work.

Caan, James (b. 1939)

Actor. Born James Cahn in New York City, Caan has specialized in tough guy roles for much of his film career. Although he made his first appearance in the early sixties, he did not achieve real success until the early seventies with several riveting performances including his role as Sonny Corleone in *The Godfather*.

The Godfather (Paramount, 1972).

Cabot, Bruce (1904–1972)

Actor. Born Etienne Jacques de Bujac in Carlsbad, New Mexico, Bruce Cabot was the grandson of a French diplomat. His work experience was varied, but his film career began in the early thirties when, after meeting David O. Selznick at a Hollywood party, he convinced the producer to give him a screen test. Selznick was impressed and soon cast him as the male lead in *King Kong* (RKO, 1933). Cabot's square-jawed masculinity typecast him as a hero or villain in countless "B" movies. He was particularly memorable as the chief bad guy in *Let 'Em Have It* and in the neglected masterpiece, *Show Them No Mercy*.

Let 'Em Have It (United Artists, 1935). *Show Them No Mercy* (20th Century–Fox, 1935). *Homicide Bureau* (Columbia, 1939).

Cabot, Susan (1927–1986)

Actress. A dark-haired beauty, Susan Cabot is associated almost exclusively with "B" productions released by American International, particularly those produced and directed by Roger Corman. Among these is the neat little gangster movie, *Machine Gun Kelly*, in which she played the moll of the notorious gangster.

Machine Gun Kelly (American International, 1958).

Caged (Warner Bros., 1950). 96 mins. *Producer*: Jerry Wald. *Director*: John Cromwell. *Screenplay*: Virginia Kellogg and Bernard C. Schoenfeld. *Director of Photography*: Carl Guthrie. *Music*: Max Steiner. *Art Director*: Charles H. Clarke. *Editor*: Owen Marks.

Cast: Eleanor Parker (Marie Allen), Agnes Moorehead (Ruth Benton), Ellen Corby (Emma), Hope Emerson (Evelyn Harper), Betty Garde (Kitty), Jan Sterling (Smoochie). *With*: Lee Patrick, Olive Deering, Jane Darwell, Gertrude Michael, Queenie Smith.

Marie Allen is implicated in a robbery committed by her husband who is killed during the heist. Once behind bars, she discovers firsthand the inhumane conditions that all prisoners experience. She has a child while in prison, but hardened by her "rehabilitation," faces an uncertain future after her release.

Coscenarist Virginia Kellogg researched this project by having herself committed to several women's prisons for weeks at a time. Thus, this distaff version of the prison drama avoids some of the more sordid, exploitative elements seemingly inherent in this subgenre. It is in fact a superior piece of "B" filmmaking, bleak and unsentimental in its portrayal of women behind bars. It is highlighted by several strong performances including Hope Emerson as a sadistic prison guard, and Agnes Moorehead as the humanitarian warden dealing with the corrupt forces that make prison so dehumanizing.

Cagney, James (1899–1986)

Actor. "I'm sick of carrying guns and beating up women," James Cagney said in 1931. Try as he might, Cagney will always be remembered as one of the movies' legendary bad guys. With Edward G. Robinson, Humphrey Bogart, and George Raft, he remains one of the genre's major icons despite his comparatively few appearances as a gangster. Yet, his cocky walk, punchy personality, and physical idiosyncrasies in several classic performances endeared him to generations; he remains the very image of the big city gangster. Cagney shot to stardom in his sixth movie, *Public Enemy*, as the gangster who smashes a grapefruit in his girlfriend's face. In a film essentially considered a programmer, Cagney's swaggering, brilliant performance established him as a major star and cemented his image as an arrogant, well-dressed gangster. Although he continued to play gangsters throughout the thirties, his popularity convinced Jack Warner to allow him to vary his

Early publicity still of the youthful James Cagney with his famous smirk, just as he was becoming a star in the early thirties.

parts with the occasional good guy in films such as *Taxi!* and *G-Men*. Also as a change of pace, Cagney played a small-time con man in the little known *Blonde Crazy*, a sexy, semisatire of the genre. However, he returned to gangster parts in several important films including *Angels with Dirty Faces*, the movie in which he constantly hunches his shoulders. In the forties, Cagney refused to accept roles in gangster films, but he made two memorable returns to the genre in *White Heat* and *Kiss Tomorrow Goodbye*. The former is famous for Cagney's final scene, on a tower engulfed in flames, in which he shouts, "Look Ma, top of the world!"— certainly one of the genre's most enduring sequences.

Blonde Crazy (Warner Bros., 1931). *Public Enemy* (Warner Bros., 1931). *Smart Money* (Warner Bros., 1931). *Taxi!* (Warner Bros., 1932). *Lady Killer* (Warner Bros., 1933). *Jimmy the Gent* (Warner Bros., 1934). *G-Men* (First National, 1935). *Great Guy* (Grand National, 1936). *Angels with Dirty Faces* (Warner Bros., 1938). *Each Dawn I Die* (Warner Bros., 1939). *The Roaring Twenties* (Warner Bros., 1939). *White Heat* (Warner Bros., 1949). *Kiss Tomorrow Goodbye* (Warner Bros., 1950).

Cagney, Jeanne (1908–1984)

Character actress. James Cagney's younger sister Jeanne (born Jean) was an exceptionally talented actress who found her greatest success on the stage. She also played supporting roles in "A" movies and leads in "B" movies, but never achieved much cinematic success. She had a memorable role in *Quicksand*, as the *femme fatale* who leads Mickey Rooney's character into a life of crime and murder.

Quicksand (United Artists, 1950).

Cagney, William (b. 1902)

Producer. The younger brother of James Cagney, William Cagney was an active producer in the forties and fifties.

Among the many films he produced is *Kiss Tomorrow Goodbye*, one of his brother's best later gangster movies.

Kiss Tomorrow Goodbye (Warner Bros., 1950).

Cahn, Edward L. (1907–1963)

Director. "Fast Eddie" Cahn was, for three decades, a prolific director of "B" movies. He worked in all genres, and his films are occasionally quite good. His two gangster titles are tolerable "B" productions.

Confidential (Mascot, 1935). *Inside the Mafia* (United Artists, 1959).

Cain, James M. (1892–1977)

Novelist and screenwriter. One of the most important commercial novelists of his time, James M. Cain had a profound influence on crime fiction and the emerging genre of *film noir*: *Double Indemnity* (Paramount, 1944), *Mildred Pierce* (Warner Bros., 1945), and *The Postman Always Rings Twice* (MGM, 1946) are all adapted from his novels. He was less successful as a screenwriter, although he did cowrite the famous gangster-romance *Algiers*, and was an uncredited contributor to *Out of the Past*.

Algiers (United Artists, 1938). *Out of the Past* (RKO, 1947; uncredited co-writer).

Caine, Michael (b. 1933)

Actor. Caine was born Maurice Micklewhite, Jr., in London, England. After military experience, he turned to acting and his unabashed Cockney charm and mild manner made him popular. He starred in the modern gangster thriller *Get Carter* as a hit man who gets revenge against the mobsters who killed his honest brother.

Get Carter (MGM, 1971).

Calhern, Louis (1895–1956)

Character actor. Born Carl Henry Vogt in New York City, Louis Calhern was one of the busiest character actors in American movies for over three decades beginning in the twenties. He had supporting roles in two legendary gangster classics, *Blonde Crazy* and *The Asphalt Jungle*, playing dapper gangsters in both.

Blonde Crazy (Warner Bros., 1931). *The Asphalt Jungle* (MGM, 1950).

Calleia, Joseph (1897–1975)

Character actor. Calleia turned to acting after a career as an opera singer. His dark, slightly sinister looks made him a natural villain, and his gangster characters are all mob henchmen.

Public Hero No. 1 (MGM, 1936). *Algiers* (United Artists, 1938). *The Glass Key* (Paramount, 1942). *Cry Tough* (United Artists, 1959).

Camonte, Tony (Fictional character)

The character played by Paul Muni in *Scarface* (United Artists, 1932) was based on the real life Al Capone, here embellished with hints of an incestuous relationship with his sister and other psychological abnormalities.

Canelli, Vincent (Fictional character)

In *Black Tuesday* (United Artists, 1954), Edward G. Robinson makes one of his last appearances as a gangster, one of his most sadistic and violence-prone characterizations.

Capone, Al (1899–1947)

A second generation Italian-American, Capone grew up in the ghettos of New York. From an early age he was involved with gangs, and his face was slashed in a barroom brawl over a woman he insulted—hence his nickname "Scarface." A mob enforcer infamous for his sadism, he rose in the ranks of the New York Mafia under mob boss Frankie Yale. After Yale sent him to Chicago to take over the liquor rackets there, Capone quickly rose to lead the Mafia in the Midwest, murdering his main rival, Bugs Moran, in the infamous St. Valentine's Day Massacre. Capone also became the target of the F.B.I.'s Eliot Ness, but despite Ness's violent attempts to close Capone down, he was finally brought to justice for income tax evasion! Still, he eventually paid for his youthful vices when he contracted syphilis and died a lingering death. Capone was the basis for the characters in *Scarface* (United Artists, 1932) and *Little Caesar* (First National, 1931), and, to a lesser degree, in *Public Enemy* (Warner Bros., 1931). He also was the subject of biopics (after his death, when it was less risky) such as *Al Capone* (Allied Artists, 1959), *The Scarface Mob* (Cari Releasing, 1962) and *The St. Valentine's Day Massacre* (20th Century–Fox, 1967). *The Untouchables* (Universal, 1988) was based on the book by Eliot Ness and the popular television series (1959–62).

Carlisle, Mary (b. 1912)
Actress. A star of "B" movies in the thirties and forties, Carlisle appeared in three low budget gangster movies.
Hunted Man (Paramount, 1938). *Illegal Traffic* (Paramount, 1938). *The Tip-Off Girls* (Paramount, 1938).

Carradine, David (b. 1936)
Actor. The lanky, sad-eyed son of character actor John Carradine, David Carradine has found his greatest success on television and in "B" movies. He gave a memorable performance in Martin Scorsese's low budget gangster film, *Boxcar Bertha*, inspired by the legend of Bonnie and Clyde.
Boxcar Bertha (American International, 1972).

Carradine, John (1906–1988)
Character actor. Born Richmond Reed Carradine in New York City, John Carradine is one of the most familiar character actors in American movies. For over four decades, the tall, gaunt actor with the deep, full voice appeared in over 200 films. He acted in countless grade-Z horror films, almost always as a mad scientist, but he also had major roles in important movies including *The Grapes of Wrath* (20th

Century–Fox, 1940). In the "B" gangster thriller *C-Man*, he played the front man for a gang of jewel smugglers.
C-Man (Film Classics, 1949).

Casbah (Universal, 1948). 94 mins.
Producer: Nat G. Goldstone. *Director*: John Berry. *Screenplay*: Ladislas Bushfekete and Arnold Manoff, based on the novel *Pépé le Moko* by Detective Ashelbe. *Director of Photography*: Irving Glassbert. *Music and Songs*: Harold Arlen. *Lyrics*: Leo Robin. *Art Directors*: Bernard Herzbrun and John F. DeCuir. *Editor*: Edward Curtiss.
Cast: Yvonne De Carlo (Inez), Tony Martin (Pépé le Moko), Peter Lorre (Silmane), Marta Toren (Gaby), Hugo Haas (Omar), Thomas Gomez (Louvain), Douglas Dick (Carlo). *With*: Katherine Dunham, Herbert Rudley, Gene Walker, Curt Conway, Andre Pola.
A musical version of *Algiers* (United Artists, 1938), *Casbah* suffers from its gloss and concessions to the clichés of musicals, but it was an interesting attempt to revitalize the gangster genre (then suffering from over-exposure) in a new context. Despite its relative success, however, a similar project was not tried again until MGM released the much better *Guys and Dolls* in 1955.

Cassavetes, John (1929–1990)
Writer and director. The New York born Cassavetes first came to the movies in the mid-fifties as an actor employing the James Dean brooding style. When his acting career failed to take off, he returned to New York and made a self-financed feature, *Shadows* (Cassel, 1959), whose improvisational style influenced a whole generation of art-film directors. While making a series of similar features, he flirted with commercialism, perhaps most successfully in *Gloria*, a well received gangster thriller.
Gloria (Columbia, 1980).

Castle, William (1914–1977)
Director. Born William Schloss in

Chicago, Castle is famous for his gimmicky low budget thrillers from the fifties and sixties. Prior to specializing in campy horror, however, he was one of the most imaginative "B" directors, and both of his well-made "B" gangster films are surprisingly free of the cheap effects that characterize his later releases.

Johnny Stool Pigeon (Universal, 1949). *The Houston Story* (Columbia, 1949).

Castle on the Hudson (Warner Bros., 1940). 76 mins.
Associate Producer: Samuel Bischoff. *Director*: Anatole Litvak. *Screenplay*: Seton I. Miller, Brown Holmes, Courtenay Terrett, based on the book *20,000 Years in Sing Sing* by Warden Lewis E. Lawes. *Director of Photography*: Arthur Edeson. *Music*: Adolph Deutsch. *Editor*: Thomas Richards.
Cast: John Garfield (Tommy Gordon), Ann Sheridan (Kay Manners), Pat O'Brien (Warden Walter Long), Burgess Meredith (Steven Rockford), Jerome Cowan (Ed Crowley). *With*: Henry O'Neill, Guinn Williams, John Litel, Edward Pawley, Grant Mitchell, Margot Stevenson.
A remake of *20,000 Years in Sing Sing* (First National, 1933), this version stresses the concept of criminal as victim to an even greater degree. However, it stays close to the original with its story of a gangster and his moll (here played by John Garfield and Ann Sheridan at their gritty best) and the experiences of prison life.

Celli, Teresa (b. 1923)
Actress. Celli was briefly active in films during the late forties and early fifties, but when her career failed to take off, she quickly disappeared from the Hollywood scene. She costarred in a single gangster movie, holding her own against the formidable talents of Gene Kelly and J. Carrol Naish.
The Black Hand (MGM, 1950).

Chaney, Lon (1883–1930)
Actor. Born Leonidas Chaney, "The Man of a Thousand Faces" was the younger son of deaf parents, a skilled mime who learned his craft simply by trying to communicate with them. His older brother owned a vaudeville theater in his hometown of Colorado Springs, Colorado, and it was there that Chaney began to perform. He toured for many years as a comic mime, mixing dialog with physical action, before deciding to try his hand in the movies. He immediately put his skills as a mime and make-up artist to work, and he promptly developed into the legendary silent performer. Although he found his greatest fame as a star of horror movies, he actually played many types of roles. In *The Big City*, for example, he played a comparatively conventional role as a front for a gang of jewel thieves who decide to go straight.
The Big City (MGM, 1928).

Chaney, Lon, Jr. (1906–1973)
Character actor. Although he achieved immortality as the monster in *The Wolf Man* (Universal, 1941), Chaney (born Creighton Tull Chaney in Oklahoma City) played a wide variety of roles in his more than three decade career. Unfortunately, he did not have the talent of his father, and he was thus relegated to "B" horror films and melodramas where his bulky, menacing presence could be put to best use. In his single gangster film, *Eyes of the Underworld*, Chaney, atypically, is on the side of the law.
Eyes of the Underworld (Universal, 1942).

Charisse, Cyd (b. 1921)
Actress and dancer. Born Tula Ellice Finklea in Amarillo, Texas, the long-legged Cyd Charisse was originally a ballet dancer. Her film career began in 1943, and she subsequently appeared in over 25 movies. She married singer Tony Martin in 1948. Most active in

musicals, she costarred in the rather dour gangster musical *Party Girl*, one of the rare attempts to combine these two seemingly disparate genres.

Party Girl (MGM, 1958).

The Chase (United Artists, 1946). 86 mins.
Producer: Seymour Nebenzel. *Director*: Arthur Ripley. *Screenplay*: Philip Yordan, based on the story "The Black Path of Fear" by Cornell Woolrich. *Director of Photography*: Franz F. Planer. *Music*: Michel Michelet. *Art Director*: Robert Usher. *Editor*: Ed Mann.
Cast: Robert Cummings (Chuck Scott), Michele Morgan (Lorna Roman), Peter Lorre (Gino), Steve Cochran (Johnson), Jack Holt (Commander Davidson), Don Wilson (Fats). *With*: Alexis Minotis, Nina Koshetz, Jimmy Ames, James Westerfield, Shirley O'Hara.

When Chuck Scott, a derelict, finds and returns a wallet belonging to mobster Eddie Roman, the gangster hires him as his personal chauffeur. Soon Chuck is in love with Lorna Roman, Eddie's abused wife, who falls for the gentle chauffeur. After they run away to Cuba together, Lorna is murdered in a Havana night spot. Chuck manages to escape, but before he can prove his innocence, he is killed by Eddie and his henchmen who have followed them to the Cuban city. In the end, however, it all turns out to be a dream.

The Chase is one of the most uncompromising *films noir*. Like most of the movies in that genre, the criminal elements serve mainly as a counterpoint to the erotic and existential themes of the story. Yet, the gangster elements in this particular *noir* qualify it as a borderline gangster movie.

Chicago
When Al Capone, a mob hit man, left his native New York in the late teens to go to Chicago to help run the

rackets there, the mob was already well established in the city. But with Prohibition and Capone's succession as Chicago mob boss in the early twenties, the city's reputation as the mob capital of the United States superseded any of its virtues. Of course, the city and its officials were no more corrupt than any other in the country at that time, but Capone's publicity seeking personality attracted the attention of the media and, as a result, of the F.B.I. as well: the Bureau's director, J. Edgar Hoover, understood the value of publicity as well as anyone, and sent one of his best agents, Eliot Ness, to coordinate the law enforcement battle against the mob. The nation's newspapers eagerly covered the wars between the mob and law enforcement, but ultimately Capone's empire collapsed after he was convicted for income tax evasion.

By then, writers such as W. R. Burnett had begun to exploit the commercial potential of gangster stories, and Hollywood inevitably followed. Capone's exploits inspired *Scarface* (United Artists, 1932), *The Scarface Mob* (Cari Releasing, 1962), *The Untouchables* television series during the late fifties and early sixties, Brian DePalma's film *The Untouchables* (Paramount, 1987), and a number of "B" gangster pictures set in the city, including *Chicago Confidential* (United Artists, 1957). Also, Billy Wilder's comedy *Some Like It Hot* (United Artists, 1959) begins in Chicago on the day of the notorious St. Valentine's Day Massacre, when Capone's gang assassinated a rival gang.

Chicago Confidential (United Artists, 1957). 75 mins.
Producer: Robert E. Kent. *Director*: Sidney Salkow. *Screenplay*: Raymond T. Marcus. *Director of Photography*: Kenneth Peach, Sr. *Music*: Emil Newman. *Editor*: Grant Whytock.
Cast: Brian Keith (Jim Fremont), Beverly Garland (Laura), Dick Foran (Blane), Beverly Tyler (Sylvia), Elisha

Cook, Jr. (Candymouth), Paul Langton (Jake Parker). *With*: Tony George, Douglas Kennedy, Gavin Gordon, Jack Lambert, John Morley, Phyllis Coates.

Loosely based on real events, this "B" gangster movie follows an honest D.A., Jim Fremont, as he prosecutes a Chicago union president who was framed by gangsters. When he discovers the man is innocent, he goes after the mobsters. *Chicago Confidential* is just one of several topical "exposés" produced during the fifties when such subjects were familiar because of the Senatorial Crime Hearings that made headlines throughout the decade.

Chicago Syndicate (Columbia, 1955). 84 mins.
Director: Fred F. Sears. *Screenplay*: Joseph Hoffman, *story by* William Sackheim. *Directors of Photography*: Henry Freulich and Fred Jackman, Jr. *Music*: Ross D. Maggio. *Editor*: Viola Lawrence.
Cast: Dennis O'Keefe (Barry Amsterdam), Abbe Lane (Connie Peters), Paul Stewart (Arnie Valent), Xavier Cugat (Benny Chico), Allison Hayes (Joyce Kern), Dick Cutting (David Healey). *With*: Chris Alcaide, William Challe, John Zaremba, George Brand, Mark Hanna, Carroll McComas.

Arnie Valent, the leader of a Chicago gang, hides his criminal activities behind various legitimate businesses including a nightclub where his moll, Connie Peters, is a singer. Accountant Barry Amsterdam, a member of a citizen's group determined to close down the mobster's operations, goes to work for Valent, hoping to collect information needed to convict the mobster of tax evasion. With the help of Joyce Kern, whose father was murdered by Valent, Amsterdam uncovers information that leads to a violent confrontation in which the mobster is shot and killed by the police.

Chicago Syndicate is a surprisingly well made "B" movie. Its conventional

plot is overcome by excellent on-location filming, swift-moving action, and the musical talents of band leader Xavier Cugat and singer-actress Abbe Lane.

Chinatown After Dark (Action Pictures, 1931). 50 mins.
Producer: Ralph M. Like. *Director*: Stuart Paton. *Screenplay*: Betty Burbridge. *Director of Photography*: Jules Cronjager. *Music*: Lee Zahler. *Art Director*: Ben Dore. *Editor*: Viola Roehl.
Cast: Rex Lease (Jim Bonner), Barbara Kent (Lotus), Edmund Breese (Lee Fong), Carmel Myers (Madame Ying Su), Frank Mayo (Ralph Bonner). *With*: Billy Gilbert, Lloyd Whitlock, Laska Winter, Michael Visaroff, Charles Murphy.

During an uprising in China, a prince, Lee Fong, is rescued by an American who is subsequently killed. The prince flees to America with the man's daughter, Lotus, whom he raises in San Francisco's Chinatown. Years later, when the Chinese underworld discovers that Lee Fong is to inherit a valuable dagger, they target Fong and the girl. Eventually, however, the police close in on the gangsters and everything works out for the best.

Chinatown After Dark is a typical early sound "B" movie. Set in the exotic underworld of San Francisco's Chinatown—a popular location since the silent era—the film maintains an effective atmosphere. Unique because of its setting, it is also interesting for the performance of great character comedian Billy Gilbert as the police detective investigating the Chinese underworld.

Churchill, Marguerite (b. 1910)
Actress. The pert and pretty leading lady Marguerite Churchill was a popular star during the thirties. She appeared in a few interesting films including the early gangster movie *Quick Millions* as a society girl who snubs the leader of a violent criminal organization, and the gangster horror film, *The Walking*

Dead, a Boris Karloff vehicle directed by Michael Curtiz.

Quick Millions (Fox, 1931). *The Walking Dead* (Warner Bros., 1936).

Cianelli, Eduardo (1887-1969)

Character actor. The Italian born Cianelli had a successful Broadway career before going to Hollywood in the early thirties. His finely etched features and smooth voice made him the definitive suave villain in dozens of movies over the next three decades. In the little-known *Law of the Underworld*, his only gangster movie, he typically costarred in a villainous role.

Law of the Underworld (RKO, 1938).

Cimino, Michael (b. 1940)

Screenwriter and director. Cimino is notorious as the director of the megaflop, *Heaven's Gate* (United Artists, 1980), the extravagant western which largely caused the financier and distributor to go bankrupt. The film also virtually destroyed Cimino's career, and the writer-director of *The Deer Hunter* (United Artists, 1978) has found it difficult to reestablish his once promising career. He cowrote two important movies in the early seventies before writing and directing the well received gangster-heist drama *Thunderbolt and Lightfoot*, which was followed by the career high *The Deer Hunter* and *Heaven's Gate*. After the failure of the latter, it took him five years to get a chance to make another movie. Unfortunately *Year of the Dragon*, despite some good moments, was neither a critical nor financial success.

Thunderbolt and Lightfoot (United Artists, 1974). *Year of the Dragon* (MGM, 1985).

Citadel of Crime (Republic, 1941). 56 mins.

Associate Producer and Director: George Sherman. *Screenplay*: Don Ryan. *Director of Photography*: Ernest Miller. *Music*: Cy Feuer. *Editor*: Les Orlebeck.

Cast: Robert Armstrong (Cal Fullerton), Frank Albertson (Jim Rogers), Linda Hayes (Ellie Jackson), Russell Simpson (Jess Meekins), Skeets Gallagher (Chet). *With*: William Haade, Jay Novello, Paul Fix, Bob McKenzie, Wade Crosby, William Benedict.

Big-city gangsters devise a plan to import moonshine from rural West Virginia. They enlist the help of a country boy, Cal Fullerton, who convinces the moonshiners to join the operation, but the federal government has sent an agent, Jim Rogers, to investigate. Rogers infiltrates the moonshiners' gang in the West Virginia mountains, breaks up their alliance with the gangsters, and in the process wins the love of a local girl.

Citadel of Crime is a typical Republic "B" programmer. Directed by Western director George Sherman, the film's visual style and mood are not unlike an oater's—even the good guys versus bad guys plot recalls that genre. Still, its fast pace and excellent performances make it an enjoyable addition to the gangster genre.

City Heat (Warner Bros., 1983). 97 mins.

Producer: Fritz Manes. *Director*: Richard Benjamin. *Screenplay*: Sam O. Brown (Blake Edwards) and Joseph Stinson. *Director of Photography*: Nick McLean. *Music*: Lennie Niehaus, with songs by Harold Arlen and Ted Koehler, and George and Ira Gershwin. *Production Design*: Edward Carfagno. *Screenplay*: Jacqueline Cambas.

Cast: Clint Eastwood (Lieutenant Speer), Burt Reynolds (Mike Murphy), Jane Alexander (Addy), Madeline Kahn (Caroline Howley), Rip Torn (Primo Pitt), Irene Cara (Ginny Lee). *With*: Richard Roundtree, Nicholas Worth, Robert Davis, Jude Farese, John Hancock, Tab Thacker.

In 1933 Kansas City Police Lieutenant

Speer and his old friend, private detective Mike Murphy, find themselves involved in a gang war when Murphy's partner, Dehl Swift, steals a ledger from one gangster, hoping to sell it to his rival. Swift is murdered, his girlfriend and Murphy are kidnapped, and several others are killed before Speer manages to rescue his friends and eliminate both mob leaders.

A strange, surreal gangster picture, *City Heat* is an homage to the gangster melodramas of the thirties. Yet, it apparently started out as a satire: its original source was a screenplay by Blake Edwards, who was also set to direct it. When Richard Benjamin took over the project, he re-fashioned the screenplay along more conventional lines. The result is a passable gangster movie, notable chiefly for Clint Eastwood's superb performance.

Contemporary stars evoke the thirties as lawmen waging a war against the Kansas City Underworld in *City Heat.*

City Streets (Paramount, 1931). 82 mins.

Producer: E. Lloyd Sheldon. *Director*: Rouben Mamoulian. *Screenplay*: Oliver H. P. Garrett, Max Marcin, *story by* Dashiell Hammett. *Director of Photography*: Lee Garmes. *Music*: Sidney Cutner. *Editor*: William Shea.

Cast: Gary Cooper (The Kid), Sylvia Sidney (Nan Sooley), Paul Lukas (Big Fellow Maskal), William "Stage" Boyd (McCoy), Guy Kibbee (Pop Cooley), Stanley Fields (Blackie). *With*: Wynne Gibson, Betty Sinclair, Terry Carroll, Bob Kortman, Barbara Leonard.

Nan Sooley, the stepdaughter of Pop Sooley, a racketeer, falls in love with a carnival worker, The Kid. She encourages The Kid to join the beer-running rackets, but he refuses. When Nan is sent to prison for refusing to give the police information about a murder case that could send her stepfather to jail, The Kid joins the rackets, hoping to get some dope on the gang that will help free the girl. When Nan finally is released, she pleads with gang boss McCoy to let The Kid leave the organization. In the ensuing argument, one of McCoy's henchmen kills him. Believing Nan did it, the other gangsters plan to "take her for a ride," but she is rescued by The Kid and they flee the big city.

Released toward the end of Prohibition, *City Streets* was topical and, in the style of Dashiell Hammett, hard-boiled and uncompromisingly grim. It was also one of the earliest sound gangster movies to be shot in a self-consciously arty style. Director Rouben Mamoulian had a notoriously lush, extravagant visual style that was better suited to costume pictures and romantic comedies. Still, despite these seemingly contrasting styles — artistic prettiness and narrative realism — the film is successful due to its excellent performances and extraordinary style. One of the genre's earliest classics, *City Streets* reportedly was one of Al Capone's favorite films.

Clarke, Mae (b. 1910)

Actress. If the pert and blonde Mae Clarke is remembered at all today, it is certainly for the legendary scene in *Public Enemy* in which James Cagney smashes a grapefruit in her face. She was a key player in Warner Bros.' rise in the early thirties, starring in many of their important releases and indeed several important pictures at other studios, including *Frankenstein* (Universal, 1931). While the grapefruit scene is an enduring image of the gangster genre, Clarke also costarred in several other important crime movies. Her role in *Public Enemy* typecast her as a tough-talking, urbane dame (a kind of less refined Jean Harlow), and she played variations of this gangster moll in many of her subsequent movies. She was reteamed with Cagney in the superior *Lady Killer* and the lesser-known *Great Guy*, and was also memorable as the moll in *Penthouse*, one of MGM's attempts to cash in on Warner's success. Although remembered only by film buffs today, Clarke continued to appear in movies well into the sixties, and will no doubt be forever recognized for her role in *Public Enemy*.

Public Enemy (Warner Bros., 1931). *Lady Killer* (Warner Bros., 1933). *Penthouse* (MGM, 1933). *Great Guy* (Warner Bros., 1936).

Clarke, T. E. B. (b. 1907)

Screenwriter. A former journalist, the British screenwriter T. E. B. Clarke began writing scripts during the forties. During the forties and fifties, Clarke wrote many of Britain's great satires, most for the Ealing Studios. Among these is the classic gangster comedy *The Lavender Hill Mob*, a superior example of fifties British comedy.

The Lavender Hill Mob (J. Arthur Rank, 1951).

Clay, Johnny (Fictional character)

As an actor, Sterling Hayden did not have much range — he was best when playing stalwart characters who seem to accept their fates with little emotion. He played two very similar such characters in two classic tales of heists gone wrong: Dix Handley in *The Asphalt Jungle* (MGM, 1950) and Johnny Clay in *The Killing* (United Artists, 1956). Clay is an ex-con who plans a "final" heist. He brings together a disparate gang of thieves to rob a race track, but eventually and inevitably the plan unravels. As Clay and his moll, Fay (Coleen Gray), make a hasty attempt to flee the country, fate intervenes at the airport: the luggage full of stolen loot falls to the ground, scattering its contents in the wind and exposing Clay as one of the wanted thieves.

Cobb, Lee J. (1911–1976)

Character actor. Born Leo Jacoby in New York City, Lee J. Cobb was one of the most powerful character actors of his generation. He first achieved success on Broadway, creating the character of Willy Loman in Arthur Miller's *Death of a Salesman*, and continued to appear on stage long after his successful film career began. In Hollywood he often played menacing roles, perhaps most famously as the mob boss in *On the Waterfront*. Likewise, in *Party Girl*, he costarred as a corrupt gangster chief.

On the Waterfront (Columbia, 1954). *Party Girl* (MGM, 1958).

Cochran, Steve (1917–1965)

Actor. Born Robert Alexander Cochran, Steve Cochran was a star of "B" movies in the forties and fifties. Although physically a conventional leading man type, he specialized in heavies, appearing in four gangster movies, most notably *The Damned Don't Cry* (in a pivotal role as a small-time gangster), and *White Heat* (as one of the members of James Cagney's gang). He did not vary these characterizations in the two other "B" titles, typically playing hoodlums in both.

The Damned Don't Cry (Warner Bros., 1950). *Highway 301* (Warner Bros., 1950). *I, Mobster* (20th Century-Fox, 1959). *White Heat* (Warner Bros., 1959).

Coen, Joel (b. 1958) and **Coen, Ethan** (b. 1956)

Writers and directors. Certainly the most prominent of contemporary filmmaking teams, the Coens might also be the most successful brother team ever to work behind the camera. Their innovative, exciting style has endeared them to many critics, while others have attacked their occasionally thinly plotted screenplays. Nevertheless, *Miller's Crossing*, their homage to thirties gangster movies, manages to succeed despite the lapses in the plot. Typically showcasing their style, including bizarre humor, extravagant camera movements, and bravura performances, it might well be a modern classic.

Miller's Crossing (20th Century-Fox, 1991).

Cohn, Harry (1891–1958)

Mogul and producer. The founder of Columbia Pictures, Harry Cohn is the stereotypical Hollywood mogul: vulgar, megalomaniacal, dictatorial. He had a somewhat more active role in the production of individual movies than other moguls, particularly early in the studio's history. He is listed as producer of several thirties Columbia releases, although it is doubtful if he had much of an artistic influence on these productions which include two minor gangster movies.

The Squealer (Columbia, 1930). *The Criminal Code* (Columbia, 1931).

Colbert, Claudette (b. 1905)

Actress. Born Lily Claudette Chauchoin in France, Claudette Colbert moved with her parents to the United States while still a child. She studied to be a fashion designer, but had greater success with acting, making her Broadway debut in 1923. A major stage star, she was signed by Paramount in the late twenties and quickly developed into a leading lady, maintaining her stardom throughout the next two decades. Her whimsical, urbane qualities were best suited to sexy, sophisticated dramas and comedies. Early in her career, however, she starred in two gangster movies. *The Hole in the Wall*, notable chiefly for Edward G. Robinson's first appearance in a gangster movie, features an impressive Colbert as an embittered ex-con seeking revenge against those who sent her to prison. In *I Cover the Waterfront* she plays the innocent daughter of a mobster.

The Hole in the Wall (Paramount, 1929). *I Cover The Waterfront* (United Artists, 1933).

Collins, Kitty (Fictional character)

The quintessential *film noir femme fatale* in *The Killers* (Universal, 1946) who betrays her lover, the Swede (Burt Lancaster), Collins was memorably played by Ava Gardner at her most elegant and seductive best.

Collyer, June (1907–1968)

Actress. The pert, pretty Collyer was a popular star in the transition period from silent to sound in the late twenties through the early thirties. Mainly appearing in light romances, she also starred in the early gangster drama *Me, Gangster* as the object of a mobster's affection.

Me, Gangster (Fox, 1928).

Columbia

Founded by the two Cohn brothers, Harry and Joe, Columbia was long considered one of the "little two" (with

Universal) against the "big five" (MGM, Paramount, Warner Bros., RKO, and 20th Century–Fox). While Joe ran the business in New York City, Harry ran the studio in Hollywood, quickly gaining the (apparently well deserved) reputation of a tyrant and penny-pincher. However, with a limited budget he managed to turn out many successful movies and provided Frank Capra a home during the thirties. Capra was largely responsible for the studio's prestigious productions, even making a classic early gangster satire, *Lady for a Day*. Both Howard Hawks and John Ford also made films at the studio during the thirties, contributing classics to the genre: Hawk's *The Criminal Code*, and Ford's *The Whole Town's Talking*. For the most part, however, the truly great Columbia gangster movies are few and far between. Most of them are "B" titles, yet occasionally a remarkable and important film was made at the studio: *Gilda* and *Dead Reckoning* in the forties, *The Big Heat* and *On the Waterfront* in the fifties, and Samuel Fuller's *Underworld U.S.A.* in the sixties. All of Columbia's gangster movies are distinguished by their simple, gritty style (never encumbered by extravagant technique), unsentimental themes and violent action.

1930: *The Squealer*. 1931: *The Criminal Code*. 1933: *Lady for a Day*. 1935: *The Whole Town's Talking*. 1938: *Crime Takes a Holiday, I Am the Law, When G-Men Step In*. 1939: *Blind Alley, The Lady and the Mob, Homicide Bureau*. 1941: *The Face Behind the Mask*. 1947: *Dead Reckoning*. 1949: *Johnny Allegro, The Undercover Man*. 1950: *711 Ocean Drive*. 1951: *The Mob*. 1952: *My Six Convicts*. 1953: *The Big Heat*. 1954: *The Miami Story, On the Waterfront, The Wild One*. 1955: *Chicago Syndicate, Inside Detroit, Joe Macbeth*. 1956: *The Harder They Fall, The Houston Story, Tight Spot*. 1957: *The Brothers Rico, Nightfall*. 1961: *Underworld U.S.A.* 1972: *The Stone Killer*. 1980: *Gloria*. 1984: *Against All Odds*.

Columbo, Spats (Fictional character)

The immaculately dressed gangster played by George Raft in Billy Wilder's satire *Some Like It Hot* (United Artists, 1959), Columbo was loosely based on Al Capone and several other real life gangsters, including Bugsy Siegel, whom Raft had known.

Compson, Betty (1896–1974)

Actress. An attractive blonde, Compson first achieved fame in the mid-teens as a featured player in short comedies produced by Al Christie. Although almost completely forgotten today, she was a major star of the late silent era, and continued to play character roles into the fifties. She costarred in four important early gangster movies including Tod Browning's *The Big City* and Joseph von Sternberg's *The Docks of New York*.

The Big City (MGM, 1928). *The Docks of New York* (Paramount, 1928). *Skin Deep* (Warner Bros., 1929). *Those Who Dance* (Warner Bros., 1930).

Confidential (Mascot, 1935). 68 mins. *Director*: Edward L. Cahn. *Screenplay*: Wellyn Totman and Olive Cooper, *story by* John Rathmell and Scott Darling. *Directors of Photography*: Ernest Miller and Jack Marta. *Editor*: Ray Curtiss.

Cast: Donald Cook (Dave Elliot), Evelyn Knapp (Maxine), Warren Hymer (Midget), J. Carroll Naish (Lefty), Herbert Rawlinson (J. W. Keaton). *With*: Theodore Von Eltz, Morgan Wallace, Kane Richmond, Reed Howes.

A typical "B" gangster movie of the thirties, *Confidential* involves an undercover G-man, Dave Elliott, who has infiltrated a gang in order to find the man who murdered his partner.

In many ways, it is essentially a remake of *G-Men* (Warner Bros., 1935), but also an excellent example of thirties "B" movie making at its best, with quick pacing by director Edward L.

Cahn and a fine performance by J. Carrol Naish as a mob gunman.

Connelly, Jerry (Fictional character)

The character played by Pat O'Brien in *Angels with Dirty Faces* (Warner Bros., 1938), Connelly, a Catholic priest, represents the moral center in an environment of urban corruption. Unlike his childhood friend, Rocky Sullivan (James Cagney), Connelly manages to avoid the temptations of the street. Ultimately, he becomes Sullivan's moral nemesis, and when Sullivan is convicted of murder, Connelly tries to convince the mobster to feign terror as he is led to the electric chair, thus disillusioning the street youth who idolize him. The priest is partly successful.

Conovan, Doll (Fictional character)

Film noir introduced a new type of female character to American cinema, the *femme fatale*, but the old-fashioned gangster moll—clinging, supportive, yet often the object of abuse—remained a constant in the new genre. Doll Conovan (Jean Hagen) is one such character, but with an extra, more realistic dimension. She is neither merely the object of a gangster's desires nor just a representative of the "bad girl," but rather a beautiful woman who gives moral support to her gangster lover, Dix Handley (Sterling Hayden), and is his intellectual equal as well. Memorably, at film's end, after Handley has been shot by the police, she drives her lover into the desert and to certain doom for both: Doll Conovan is definitely not the cold-hearted gold digger of the past.

Conrad, Robert (b. 1935)

Actor. Born Conrad Robert Falk, Robert Conrad has found his greatest success on television as a tough-guy hero. In *Young Dillinger* he played real life gangster Pretty Boy Floyd.

Young Dillinger (Allied Artists, 1965).

Conrad, William (b. 1920)

Character actor. The heavy-set Conrad is probably best known as the title character in the popular television crime series *Cannon*. However, for over two decades before that, he was a useful and busy character actor, a kind of second string Raymond Burr who played unpleasant villains in mostly "B" pictures. In *The Killers*, he played one of the hired hit men. He also played a mobster in *Body and Soul*.

The Killers (Universal, 1946). *Body and Soul* (United Artists, 1947).

Constantine, Eddie (1917–1993)

Actor. The American born Eddie Constantine is almost completely unknown in his homeland. In Europe, however, he became the epitome of the hard-boiled antihero type most associated with Humphrey Bogart. He starred in many popular movies, including a few classics produced mostly in France. He specialized in amorous (and tongue-in-cheek) secret agents and raincoat clad private detectives. He also made occasional character appearances in British movies, including a brief role in the minor classic *The Long Good Friday*, typically as a tough gangster.

The Long Good Friday (Black Lion, 1980).

Conte, Richard (1911–1975)

Actor. Born Nicholas Conte, the Italian-American Richard Conte was a popular action hero in the forties and fifties. He is an important personality of the genre by virtue of his appearance (as a gangster in each) in three superb "B" gangster movies. His last big screen appearance was in *The Godfather*, in which he had a small supporting role as an aging mobster.

The Big Combo (Allied Artists, 1955). *New York Confidential* (Warner Bros., 1955). *The Brothers Rico* (Columbia, 1957). *The Godfather* (Paramount, 1972).

Cook, Donald (1900–1961)

Actor. A popular stage performer, Cook never achieved the film stardom expected of him. However, for more than two decades, beginning in the early thirties, he was the leading man in well over two dozen "B" pictures, including a single gangster movie.

Confidential (Mascot, 1935).

Cook, Elisha, Jr. (1902–1995)

Character actor. Like Peter Lorre, the diminutive Cook specialized in cowards, menacing gunsels, and occasionally a deceptively quiet hero. His career began in 1930, after stage experience, and hit its stride a decade later with his scene stealing role in *The Maltese Falcon*. He subsequently appeared in a number of classic *films noir* and a few gangster movies. Perhaps his most important role in the genre was in *The Killing* as the cowardly gang member whose sluttish, avaricious wife (Marie Windsor) is the catalyst in the unravelling of the heist-plot.

The Maltese Falcon (Warner Bros., 1940). *The Gangster* (Allied Artists, 1947). *The Killing* (United Artists, 1956). *Chicago Confidential* (United Artists, 1957). *The Outfit* (MGM, 1973).

Cooper, Gary (1901–1961)

Actor. The gentlemanly and quiet-spoken Cooper was the son of English immigrants. Born and raised in Montana, he learned to ride horses on his father's ranch. He also lived for a time in England where he attended private schools. After graduating from college with a degree in journalism, he set out to be a cartoonist; when that profession failed to work out, he found himself in Los Angeles working as an extra, mostly in westerns. By the end of the twenties he was a star, specializing in what can be described as a Hemingwayesque hero: stoic, quiet and romantic, but not afraid to use violence when necessary. Indeed, this is just the sort of part he played in the early gangster classic *City Streets*. However, his on-screen personality was ill-suited to the emerging genre, and this film contains his only gangster role.

City Streets (Paramount, 1931).

Coppola, Francis Ford (b. 1939)

Screenwriter and director. After many years as a screenwriter and director of primarily "B" movies, Coppola emerged as one of the most important American directors of the early seventies. *The Godfather* established his reputation, but he has not been able to live up to the promise of this film, largely because of his propensity for extravagance and experimentation. Both *The Godfather* and its first sequel are acknowledged classics, but the third film in the trilogy suffers largely from a weak script. After the success of the early *Godfather*s, Coppola returned to similar themes in *Cotton Club*, an evocative if not entirely successful attempt to capture the spirit of thirties gangster mythology.

The Godfather (Paramount, 1972; cowriter). *Godfather, Part II* (Paramount, 1974; cowriter). *The Cotton Club* (Orion, 1984). *Godfather III* (Paramount, 1991; cowriter).

Corey, Wendell (1914–1968)

Actor. Corey's professional career as an actor began in 1935. By 1942 he was acting on Broadway and became a full-fledged stage star a couple of years later. As a film actor he was essentially a conventional leading man, playing mainly good natured types. He played a gangster's henchman in *Desert Fury*, his screen debut, and in *I Walk Alone*, a neglected gangster *noir*.

Desert Fury (Paramount, 1947). *I Walk Alone* (Paramount, 1948).

Corleone, Don Vito (Fictional character)

Mumbling through a mouth full of cotton, Marlon Brando's character in *The Godfather* (Paramount, 1972)—

the well-dressed patriarch of a violent crime family—became the mythological symbol of the Italian-American mobster. Apparently drawing on the characteristics of certain real godfathers, Don Vito Corleone has allegedly been emulated by contemporary organized crime bosses.

Cormack, Bartlett

Playwright and screenwriter. Cormack is best known as the author of the hit play *The Racket*, which was twice adapted for the screen.

The Racket (Paramount, 1928). *The Racket* (RKO, 1951).

Corman, Roger (b. 1926)

Producer and director. As the leading director for the independent "B" production company American International, Corman made a name for himself with a series of extremely low budget exploitation pictures. Despite their virtually non-existent budgets and tight shooting schedules (many were shot in less than a week), they are all surprisingly well made, and a few are minor classics. Among the best of these are two excellent gangster pictures, *Machine Gun Kelly* and *I, Mobster*. After the extraordinary success of his Edgar Allan Poe adaptations in the sixties, Corman again returned to the genre with *The St. Valentine's Day Massacre*, which, like all of his movies, emphasizes violence and sex. After two final gangster pictures in the early seventies, he produced *Boxcar Bertha*, Martin Scorsese's second professional film. Corman then founded the production and distribution company New World Pictures, where he has helped finance features of many young directors including Jonathan Demme.

Machine Gun Kelly (American International, 1958; director only). *I, Mobster* (20th Century–Fox, 1959; producer and director). *The St. Valentine's Day Massacre* (20th Century–Fox, 1967; producer and director). *Bloody Mama* (American International, 1970; pro-

ducer and director). *Boxcar Bertha* (American International, 1972; producer only).

Cortez, Ricardo (1899–1977)

Actor. Tall, dark and handsome, Cortez was a major star of the late silent era. His screen image was that of a virile Latin in the Valentino mold; yet, in reality, he was Austrian, born Jacob Kranz in Vienna. His career went into eclipse with the coming of sound, but he continued to play character roles well into the fifties. He appeared in three gangster movies, and was the original Sam Spade in the first version of *The Maltese Falcon*.

The Maltese Falcon (Warner Bros., 1931). *Special Agent* (Warner Bros., 1935). *The Walking Dead* (Warner Bros., 1936).

Cotter, Ralph (Fictional character)

The character played by James Cagney in *Kiss Tomorrow Goodbye* (Warner Bros., 1950) is perhaps one of the most vicious gangsters portrayed in the genre's later period. Cotter, a prison escapee, flees to a small town where he exploits the citizens' naivete and vices to quickly become "boss" of the community. The cynicism of the character is leavened somewhat by Cagney's sly tongue-in-cheek performance.

The Cotton Club (Orion, 1984). 128 mins.

Producer: Robert Evans. *Director*: Francis Ford Coppola. *Screenplay*: William Kennedy, *story by* Francis Ford Coppola, Mario Puzo, and William Kennedy. *Director of Photography*: Stephen Goldblatt. *Music*: John Barry. *Art Directors*: David Chapman, Gregory Bolton. *Editors*: Barry Malin and Robert Q. Lovett.

Cast: Richard Gere (Dixie Dwyer), Gregory Hines (Delbert "Sandman" Williams), Diane Lane (Vera Cicero), Lonette McKee (Lila Rose Oliver), Bob Hoskins (Owney Madden), Nicolas

Cage (Vincent Dwyer). *With*: James Remar, Allen Garfield, Fred Gwynne, Gwen Verdon, Lisa Jane Persky, Maurice Hines.

In 1928 Harlem, musician Dixie Dwyer, after rescuing a gangster ambushed by a rival, is hired to be a companion to Vera Cicero, the gangster's girlfriend. Meanwhile, two black brothers are hired as featured dancers at the Cotton Club, a popular night spot owned by the gangster. Sandman Williams, one of the brothers, begins romancing Lila Oliver, another entertainer at the club. The complicated plot revolves around this mixed group of protagonists, and involves numbers rackets, violence among rival gangsters, racism, romance and betrayal. Eventually, after the gangster is murdered by mobsters employed by Lucky Luciano, Cicero and Dwyer are free to be together.

The Cotton Club was obviously an attempt by director Francis Ford Coppola to recapture the spirit of *The Godfather* (Paramount, 1972). It is at times a lyrical, compelling movie, but it suffers from an overly complicated plot. The film's epic scope is typical of Coppola, but it fails to live up to its promise. Still, the mixture of romantic themes and history—the gangster characters are based on actual people, and the movie's settings are real—gives it an authenticity missing from other modern attempts at recreating the genre.

Counterfeiting

An interesting crime, counterfeiting has been a popular theme in pulp fiction, most notably in the novels of Gerald Petevich and Elmore Leonard. The crime and its practitioners have figured prominently in surprisingly few gangster pictures, perhaps because of the somewhat more esoteric nature of the crime. Lloyd Nolan starred in two of these films, *T-Men* (Eagle-Lion, 1947) and *The Tip-Off Girls* (Paramount, 1938), playing an undercover man who infiltrates gangs of counter-

feiters. The little seen, but excellent "B" thriller *To Live and Die in L. A.* (MGM/United Artists, 1985) is based on one of Petevich's novels.

Crabbe, Larry "Buster" (1907–1983)

Actor. Like Johnny Weissmuller, another famous screen Tarzan, Crabbe was a gold medal winner in swimming during the 1932 Olympics. After his athletic triumphs, he entered movies and became a star of countless "B" action pictures. He had small supporting roles in four "B" gangster melodramas produced at Paramount during the late thirties.

King of the Gamblers (Paramount, 1937). *Hunted Man* (Paramount, 1938). *Illegal Traffic* (Paramount, 1938). *The Tip-Off Girls* (Paramount, 1938).

Crashout (Filmakers, 1955). 88 mins.
Producer: Hal E. Chester. *Director*: Lewis Foster. *Screenplay*: Hal E. Chester and Lewis Foster. *Director of Photography*: Russell Metty. *Music*: Leith Stevens. *Art Director*: Wiard Ihnen. *Editor*: Robert Swink.

Cast: William Bendix (Van Duff), Arthur Kennedy (Joe Quinn), Luther Adler (Pete Mendoza), William Talman (Swanee Remsen), Gene Evans (Monk Collins). *With*: Marshall Thompson, Beverly Michaels, Gloria Talbot, Adam Williams, Percy Helton, Melinda Markey.

Five prisoners, led by Van Duff, manage a daring escape from prison and take refuge in an abandoned tunnel. When they hold up a roadhouse, one of the men is wounded in a shootout with the police. They bring in a doctor to help their friend, but when they no longer have use for the medico, they kill him. Upon finding refuge in a farmhouse, one of the convicts falls in love with a girl who lives there. The prisoners eventually are all hunted down and killed except for the one who has fallen in love, who returns to prison knowing the girl will be awaiting his release.

All but forgotten, *Crashout* is a neglected minor classic of the fifties. Unrelentingly violent and cynical, the film is extremely well made despite a limited budget. Its greatest virtue is a superb cast: William Bendix as the cold-hearted leader, Luther Adler as his womanizing sidekick, Gene Evans as the dumb thug, Arthur Kennedy as the intellectual prisoner and Marshall Thompson as the young man who loves the country girl.

Crawford, Broderick (1911–1986)

Character actor. The big, fast-talking Crawford was a mainstay in American movies for over two decades beginning in the late thirties. The son of famed stage and film comedienne Helen Broderick, Crawford's large size and kicked-in-looking face typecast him as hard-bitten and usually corrupt big-city officials. He played gangster bosses in all three of his appearances in the genre.

Larceny, Inc. (Warner Bros., 1942). *The Mob* (Columbia, 1951). *New York Confidential* (Warner Bros., 1955).

Crawford, Joan (1906–1977)

Actress. Born Lucille le Sueur in San Antonio, Texas, Joan Crawford overcame her humble origins to become one of the legendary film stars of golden age Hollywood. Although she first achieved fame as a happy-go-lucky flapper during the late twenties, she did not achieve real stardom until the early thirties. As one of the key personalities of MGM in the thirties, she was the studio's sole representative of the "real" American working woman. Mainly cast in a series of romantic melodramas, she occasionally varied these parts with roles in tougher movies. She costarred in two early, although not particularly notable, gangster movies, but her roles in *Strange Cargo* and *The Damned Don't Cry* are more interesting. In the former she plays a kind of Mary Magdalene in this bizarre tale of escaped gangsters and religious redemption. Her role in *The Damned Don't Cry* is one of several *film noir* parts she played after joining Warner Bros. in the mid-forties.

Four Walls (MGM, 1928). *Hush Money* (Fox, 1931). *Strange Cargo* (MGM, 1940). *The Damned Don't Cry* (Warner Bros., 1950).

Crazy Mama (New World, 1975). 82 mins.

Producer: Julie Corman. *Director*: Jonathan Demme. *Screenplay*: Robert Thom, *story by* Francis Duel. *Director of Photography*: Bruce Logan. *Music*: Marshall Leib. *Art Director*: Peter Jamison. *Editors*: Allan Holzman and Lewis Teague.

Cast: Cloris Leachman (Melba), Stuart Whitman (Jim Bob), Ann Sothern (Sheba), Tisha Sterling (Sheba in 1932), Jim Backus (Mr. Albertson), Donny Most (Shawn). *With*: Linda Purl, Bryan England, Merle Earle, Sally Kirkland, Clint Kimbrough, Vince Barnett.

Set in the fifties, the film involves a family of car thieves led by the revengeful widow Melba, whose husband was killed by the police a quarter century earlier. The gang moves east across the United States, adding members as they go; eventually several members are killed in confrontations with police. The survivors open a deli in Miami Beach.

Crazy Mama is typical of the exploitative crime movies produced by Roger Corman (the uncredited "ghost" producer of this movie). As directed by Jonathan Demme, more than a decade before he became a critic's darling, the movie emerges as a tongue-in-cheek takeoff on *Bonnie and Clyde* (Warner Bros., 1967). Fast paced and violent, it presents the protagonists as humorous antiheroes, while the police are depicted as corrupt and villainous. As unpretentious entertainment, *Crazy Mama* remains an enjoyable homage to the great gangster movies of the thirties and forties.

Cregor, Laird (1916-1944)
Character actor. The tall, stocky Laird Cregor had a brief career that was sadly cut short by a fatal illness. In that short time, however, he emerged as one of the most talented character actors of his era, specializing in the type of vaguely noble, yet quite ridiculous and even cowardly villains that made Sydney Greenstreet famous. He was particularly notable in such a role in the classic early *noir This Gun for Hire*, as the seedy gangster who motivates the film's plot.
This Gun for Hire (Paramount, 1942).

Crichton, Charles (1910-1995)
Director. A talented filmmaker, Crichton is best known for his work at Ealing Studios during the fifties, when he directed several classic satires including, most importantly, *The Lavender Hill Mob*, perhaps the greatest of all gangster satires.
The Lavender Hill Mob (J. Arthur Rank, 1951).

Crime Takes a Holiday (Columbia, 1938). 59 mins.
Director: Lewis D. Collins. *Screenplay*: Jefferson Parker, Henry Altimus, and Charles Logue. *Director of Photography*: James S. Brown, Jr. *Editor*: Dwight Caldwell.
Cast: Jack Holt (Walter), Marcia Ralston (Peggy), Russell Hopton (Jerry Clayton), Douglass Dumbrille (J. J. Grant), Arthur Hohl (Joe). *With*: Thomas Jackson, John Wray, William Pawley, Paul Fix, Harry Woods, Joe Crehan.
To rid his town of gangsters, crusading district attorney Walter Forbes targets local underworld kingpin J. J. Grant. When he cannot get the information needed to send Grant to prison, Forbes creates a complicated scheme involving the prosecution of an innocent man accused of crimes committed by the gangster. Forbes hopes Grant will step forward to confess in order to help his innocent friend. However, the plan backfires when the man is convicted and sentenced to death, but, in the end, Grant is brought to justice and the innocent man is set free.
Jack Holt was the star of a series of "B" action movies made by Columbia during the thirties. *Crime Takes a Holiday* is typical of the series: violent, silly, clichéd, but occasionally fun. The performances are hopelessly inept, but somehow the movie survives as one of the best good guy versus bad guy "B" gangster dramas of the late thirties.

Crime Wave (Warner Bros., 1953). 73 mins.
Producer: Bryan Foy. *Director*: Andre de Toth. *Screenplay*: Crane Wilbur, based on a story by John and Ward Hawkins. *Director of Photography*: Bert Glennon. *Music*: David Buttolph. *Editor*: Thomas Reilly.
Cast: Sterling Hayden (Detective Lieutenant Sims), Gene Nelson (Steve Lacey), Phyllis Kirk (Ellen), Ted de Corsia ("Doc" Penny), Charles Bronson (Hastings), Jay Novello (Dr. Otto Hesler). *With*: James Bell, Dub Taylor, Gayle Kellogg, Mark Chandler, Richard Benjamin, Timothy Carey.
Steve Lacey is a paroled ex-con who is desperately trying to go straight. When three old friends from prison escape, they force Lacey to join their gang of bank robbers. Hard-bitten police detective Sims is hot on their trail, and he eventually manages to wipe out the escapees while helping Lacey to reform.
Crime Wave is one of several "B" crime thrillers starring Sterling Hayden made in the fifties. One of the best entries in the series, it features fast paced action and an unsentimental screenplay by Crane Wilbur, one of the most talented screenwriters of the period. In some ways its theme of the ex-con trying to reassimilate into society is similar to earlier gangster dramas, most notably *Invisible Stripes* (Warner Bros., 1939), but set apart by the concentration on

Left to right: Phyllis Kirk, Gene Nelson and Charles Bronson — later an icon of the seventies — in the superior "B" gangster thriller, *Crime Wave.*

law enforcement characters and its *noir*-like cynicism.

The Criminal (Anglo-Amalgamated, 1960). 97 mins.
Producer: Jack Greenwood. *Director*: Joseph Losey. *Screenplay*: Alan Owen, *story by* Jimmy Sangster. *Director of Photography*: Robert Krasker. *Music*: Johnny Dankworth. *Art Director*: Scott McGregor. *Editor*: Reginald Mils.
Cast: Stanley Baker (Johnny Bannion), Margit Sand (Suzanne), Sam Wanamaker (Mike Carter), Gregoire Aslan (Frank Saffron), Jill Bennett (Maggie). *With*: Laurence Naismith, Noel Willman, Patrick Magee, Edward Judd, Dorothy Bromiley.

While in prison, small-time criminal Johnny Bannion plans a race track heist. Once released, Bannion and partner Mike Carter successfully carry out the robbery. When he is later betrayed by a girl friend and arrested, Bannion refuses to tell where he hid the stolen $100,000. When Carter arranges Bannion's escape, the latter is killed by an associate before he can reveal where the money is stashed.

American expatriate director Joseph Losey, another victim of the McCarthy witchhunt, spent most of his creative life in Great Britain where, beginning in the late fifties, he made a series of extremely pretentious melodramas. *The Criminal* is not the best known of Losey's British productions, but it is a compelling, entertaining crime film which reminds one of Losey's forties *films noir*. Although it resembles many similar heist melodramas, it is unique due to its British setting and more laid back style.

The Criminal Code (Columbia, 1931). 97 mins.
Producer: Harry Cohn. *Director*:

Howard Hawks. *Screenplay*: Seton I. Miller and Fred Niblo, Jr., based on the play by Martin Flavin. *Director of Photography*: James Wong Howe and L. William O'Connell. *Art Director*: Edward Jewell. *Editor*: Edward Curtiss.

Cast: Walter Huston (Warden Brady), Phillips Holmes (Robert Graham), Constance Cummings (Mary Brady), Mary Doran (Gertrude Williams), De Witt Jennings (Captain Gleason), Boris Karloff (Gats Galloway). *With*: John Sheehan, Otto Hoffman, Clark Marshall, Arthur Hoyt, Ethel Wales.

Robert Graham, having recently moved to New York City, takes a girl to a dance. While there, he gets into an argument with another man and, to protect the girl's honor, kills him in a fight. The district attorney, Brady, railroads him into prison and later, by coincidence, becomes the warden of the institution. When a planned breakout backfires, the prisoners murder a stoolie. Only Graham knows who the killers are, but according to the criminal code he has adopted, he refuses to name the killers. He is put into solitary confinement, but when the real killer confesses, Graham is paroled.

An early prison-oriented gangster drama, *The Criminal Code* is notable chiefly for its cynical realism and superior performance by Boris Karloff as the prison trusty who becomes a cold-blooded killer. Indeed, his performance helped elevate him toward stardom and, in part, convinced director James Whale that he could play the Monster in the upcoming *Frankenstein* (Universal, 1931). The film is also notable for its screenplay cowritten by Seton I. Miller, later a master of hardboiled thrillers, and as one of the earliest successes of director Howard Hawks.

Criss Cross (Universal, 1949). 87 mins. *Producer*: Michel Kraike. *Director*: Robert Siodmak. *Screenplay*: Daniel Fuchs, based on the novel by Don Tracy. *Director of Photography*: Frank Palmer. *Music*: Miklos Rozsa. *Art Directors*: Bernard Herzbrun and Boris Leven. *Editor*: Ted J. Kent.

Cast: Burt Lancaster (Steve Thompson), Yvonne De Carlo (Anna), Dan Duryea (Slim Dundee), Stephen McNally (Pete Ramirez), Richard Long (Slade Thompson), Percy Helton (Frank). *With*: Esy Morales, Tom Pedi, Alan Napier, Griff Barnett, Meg Randall.

Steve Thompson, an employee of an armored car company, renews a relationship with his ex-wife, the exotically beautiful Anna, who, now married to violent gangster Slim Dundee, convinces Steve to join his gang. When Steve discovers that Anna and Slim are planning to blame him for an armored car robbery planned by Slim, Steve decides to double cross them. Anna, however, decides that she loves her first husband and, after the deadly robbery, joins him in a secluded hideout. Slim tracks them to the cabin, kills them both, and waits for the police, who are closing in on him.

Criss Cross is a neglected *noir* masterpiece directed by Robert Siodmak, perhaps the most underrated director of the forties. Somber and cynical, the film gave its three principals some of their best roles. Yvonne De Carlo is especially notable as the *femme fatale* catalyst for the film's tragic action.

Cromwell, John (1887–1979)
Director. Cromwell has often been described as an "A" director with "B" sensibilities. While it is true that many of his efforts are little more than exploitation films, his best movies hold up extremely well. However, because he reputedly never developed a personal style, he is usually dismissed by critics. Among his best movies are several notable crime thrillers, all of which are characterized by an odd mixture of glossy style and gritty realism.

Algiers (United Artists, 1938). *Caged*

Burt Lancaster and Yvonne De Carlo as the doomed lovers in the neglected *Criss Cross*, which contained perhaps their best performances.

(Warner Bros., 1950). *The Racket* (RKO, 1951).

Cronyn, Hume (b. 1911)

Character actor. Born Hume Cronyn Blake in Ontario, Canada, Hume Cronyn, the son of a prominent politician, made his stage debut at nineteen. He became a leading stage actor on Broadway during the thirties, and married British actress Jessica Tandy in 1942. Making his film debut in Alfred Hitchcock's *Shadow of a Doubt* (Universal, 1943), he subsequently starred in several additional movies directed by the Master of Suspense. Interestingly, despite his obvious charm, he often played vicious bad guys, none more notable than his sadistic, quasifascist prison guard in *Brute Force*.

Brute Force (Universal, 1947).

Crosby, Floyd (1899–1986)

Cinematographer. Although his career began in the early thirties, he worked only sporadically in the movies until the early fifties, when he photographed Fred Zinnemann's *High Noon* (Universal, 1952). He then became one of the most prolific directors of photography in Hollywood, working mainly for American International and Roger Corman. For Corman he photographed the gangster movie *Machine Gun Kelly*, his single contribution to the genre.

Machine Gun Kelly (American International, 1958).

Cruze, James (1884–1942)

Director. The Danish-American Cruze, born Jens Cruz Bosen in Utah, became a leading movie director of the twenties and thirties after achieving success as a popular actor of the early silent era. As a director, he specialized in unpretentious entertainments, particularly action films, including two interesting if not truly classic thirties gangster movies.

I Cover the Waterfront (United Artists, 1933). *Gangs of New York* (Republic, 1938).

Cry Tough (United Artists, 1959). 83 mins.

Producer: Harry Kleiner. *Director*: Paul Stanley. *Screenplay*: Harry Kleiner, based on the novel by Irving Shulman. *Director of Photography*: Phillip Lathrop. *Music*: Laurino Almedio. *Art Director*: Edward Carrere. *Editor*: Frederic Knudtson.

Cast: John Saxon (Miguel Estrado), Linda Cristal (Sarita), Joseph Calleia (Senor Estrada), Harry Townes (Carlos), Don Gordon (Incho), Perry Lopez (Toto). *With*: Frank Puglia, Penny Santon, Joe de Santis, Barbara Luna, Paul Clarke, John Sebastian.

Set in New York City, the movie tells the story of a Puerto Rican youth, Miguel Estrada, and his rise to the top of a gang. One of several similar movies released at that time, it concentrates on street gangs, rather than stereotypical organized crime. Cynical and tough, it is little more than a conventional "B" movie, but it achieved some notoriety for its daring nudity in the lovemaking scenes between John Saxon and Linda Cristal.

Culp, Robert (b. 1930)

Actor. Culp became a popular personality during the sixties when he costarred with Bill Cosby in the television series *I Spy*. Unfortunately, Culp was unable to capitalize on this success, but he did appear in a few notable movies during the late sixties. He also directed and costarred with Cosby in *Hickey and Boggs*, a tough-minded crime thriller with gangster overtones.

Hickey and Boggs (United Artists, 1972).

Cummings, Robert (1908–1991)

Actor. After many years as a minor star in Hollywood, beginning in the mid-thirties, Cummings achieved real popularity on television in the fifties. His easy charm and effervescent personality made him a natural comic actor, but he also occasionally played tougher characters, perhaps most memorably in Alfred Hitchcock's *Saboteur* (Universal, 1942) and *Dial M for Murder* (Warner Bros., 1954). He also starred in the undeservedly forgotten gangster *noir The Chase*, a minor classic of the genre.

The Chase (United Artists, 1946).

Cummins, Peggy (b. 1925)

Actress. Born in England, Cummins was a juvenile star in her native country during the thirties and early forties. After moving to the United States during the mid-forties, she did not become, as expected, a major star, despite being one of the sexiest personalities on the screen. She did appear in a number of "B" movies, most importantly *Gun Crazy*, as the psychotic carnival performer turned robber and murderess. Despite this extraordinary performance, she did not catch on with American audiences, and, during the fifties, she returned to England, where she continued to appear in movies and on television well into the seventies.

Gun Crazy (United Artists, 1950).

Curtis, Tony (b. 1925)

Actor. Born Bernard Schwartz in New York City, Tony Curtis rose from abject poverty to become a leading star of the fifties. After experience on Broadway, he was signed by Universal in 1949. Following several years in small parts, he graduated to leads and seemed for a time to be destined for major stardom. In retrospect, however, he was little more than a conventional leading man who had the good fortune to be cast in a few great movies. Most often cast in heroic or romantic/ swashbuckling roles, he also appeared in a few contemporary crime movies. He had a small part in the late gangster movie *Johnny Stool Pigeon*, and then starred in the minor *noir* gangster epic *Forbidden* and the unjustly forgotten *Six Bridges to Cross*, a superior heist drama based on a real Brinks armored car robbery. However, his best known appearance in the gangster genre is in Billy Wilder's classic satire *Some Like It Hot*, as one of the two musicians hiding out from the mob.

Johnny Stool Pigeon (Universal, 1949). *Forbidden* (Universal, 1953). *Six Bridges to Cross* (Universal, 1955). *Some Like It Hot* (United Artists, 1959).

Curtiz, Michael (1888–1962)

Director. The Hungarian born Mihaly Kertesz, who changed his name after moving to the United States during the mid-twenties, will be forever remembered as the director of *Casablanca* (Warner Bros., 1942). After success in Europe, Curtiz was hired by Jack Warner and became one of the most prolific directors in Hollywood for over three decades. During that time, he managed to create a number of classic movies, including *Doctor X* (First National, 1932), *The Adventures of Robin Hood* (Warner Bros., 1938), *Yankee Doodle Dandy* (Warner Bros., 1942), and *Mildred Pierce* (Warner Bros., 1945). An enthusiastic filmmaker, he was also a technical genius who used his camera better than just about any other director before or since. All of his gangster movies are classics, and each is typical of his style, featuring fluid camera movements, moody lighting techniques (borrowed from German expressionism), and taut, hard-boiled performances.

20,000 Years in Sing Sing (First National, 1933). *Jimmy the Gent* (Warner Bros., 1934). *The Walking Dead* (Warner Bros., 1936). *Kid Galahad* (Warner Bros., 1937). *Angels with Dirty Faces* (Warner Bros., 1938).

D'Agostino, Albert S. (1893–1970)

Art director. One of the great Hollywood art directors of the golden age, D'Agostino was to RKO what Cedric Gibbons was to MGM. D'Agostino worked for RKO from 1936 to 1958, and is largely responsible for that studio's art deco style. He also designed the sets for their best gangster and *noir* movies.

Mr. Lucky (RKO, 1943). *Out of the Past* (RKO, 1947). *Race Street* (RKO, 1948). *They Live by Night* (RKO, 1948). *The Big Steal* (RKO, 1949). *His Kind of Woman* (RKO, 1951). *The Racket* (RKO, 1951). *The Narrow Margin* (RKO, 1952).

Damn Citizen (Universal, 1958). 88 mins.

Producer: Herman Webber. *Director*: Robert Gordon. *Screenplay*: Stirling Silliphant. *Director of Photography*: Ellis W. Carter. *Music*: Henry Mancini. *Editor*: Patrick McCormack.

Cast: Keith Andes (Col. Francis C. Grevemberg), Maggie Hayes (Dorothy Grevemberg), Gene Evans (Major Al Arthur), Lynn Bari (Pat Noble), Jeffery Stone (Paul Musso), Edward C. Platt (Joseph Kosta). *With*: Ann Robinson, Sam Buffington, Clegg Hoyt, Kendall Clark, Rusty Lane.

Damn Citizen recounts the true life story of World War II hero Francis C. Grevemberg, who joined the Louisiana state police and carried on a campaign against organized crime. A minor late gangster movie told from the viewpoint of law enforcement, it is notable chiefly for its pseudodocumentary technique and location shooting in New Orleans.

The Damned Don't Cry (Warner Bros., 1950). 103 mins.

Producer: Jerry Wald. *Director*: Vincent Sherman. *Screenplay*: Jerome Weidman and Harold Medford, *story*

by Gertrude Walker. *Music*: Daniele
Amfitheotroff. *Art Director*: Robert
Haas. *Editor*: Clarence Kolster.

Cast: Joan Crawford (Ethel White-
head), David Brian (George Castle-
man), Steve Cochran (Nick Prenta),
Kent Smith (Martin Blackford), Hugh
Sanders (Grady), Selena Royle (Patricia
Longworth). *With*: Jacqueline de Wit,
Morris Ankrum, Sara Perry, Richard
Egan, Jimmy Moss, Edith Evanson.

After the tragic death of her only
child in a traffic accident, Ethel Whitehead leaves her staid husband and seeks
out a new life in the big city, becoming
a model and high class call girl. En-
couraging the career of a male friend,
Martin Blackford, who has become in-
fatuated with her, Ethel introduces him
to George Castleman, a mob kingpin,
and he becomes the gangster's accountant. Ethel is the mistress of Castleman, and indeed does love him, but
grows to despise the way he uses her,
particularly in a set-up to kill a rival.
When she falls for the rival, Castleman
personally murders him and plans to
kill Ethel as well. She flees to her old
hometown, and Castleman is killed by
her old suitor, Martin Blackford, who
becomes a wanted man while Ethel
returns for her unhappy existence.

The Damned Don't Cry is a fabulous
example of the blending of styles and
themes that occurred during the late
forties. With its heavy gangster overtones, it manages to fit into the genre,
but the conventional "woman's movie"
melodrama and expressionist style
make it differ from the gangster movies
of the thirties. Indeed, its themes of
moral ambiguity and personal corruption are familiar to fans of *film noir*,
the genre to which this gangster movie
actually belongs.

Dangerous to Know (Paramount, 1938).
70 mins.
Producer and Director: Robert
Florey. *Screenplay*: William R. Lippmann and Horace McCoy, based on
the novel and play *On the Spot* by

Edgar Wallace. *Director of Photography*: Theodor Sparkuhl. *Art Director*:
Hans Drier. *Editor*: Arthur Schmidt.

Cast: Anna May Wong (Madame
Lan Ying), Akim Tamiroff (Stephen
Recka), Gail Patrick (Margaret Van
Kase), Lloyd Nolan (Inspector Bran-
don), Harvey Stephens (Philip Easton).
With: Anthony Quinn, Roscoe Karns,
Porter Hall, Barlowe Borland, Hedda
Hopper, Hugh Sothern.

Stephen Recka is the cultured head
of a gang of racketeers. Despite his cultural refinements, he is absolutely ruthless and sends his men to kill his enemies with no remorse. His growing love
for a wealthy society girl, Margaret Van
Kase, leads to his ultimate downfall.

Dangerous to Know is nothing more
than a routine programmer which attempted to cash in on the then-current
popularity of the thirties gangster
genre. In the thirties, Akim Tamiroff, a
popular star of "B" movies, was generally cast as a hulking bad guy in the
Edward G. Robinson mode. *Dangerous to Know* is one of several films to
star him in this type of role, and,
although he is quite effective, the best
scenes belong to Anna May Wong, the
sensual Chinese-American actress who
plays Tamiroff's mistress. There is a
particularly memorable scene where
she disembowels herself to the strains
of Tchaikovsky, an action typical of
the film's director, Robert Florey, a
French expressionist who specialized in
horror films.

Daniels, William (1895–1970)

Cinematographer. Unquestionably
one of the great American cinematographers, Daniels helped define the look
of Hollywood movies during the golden
age of the studio system. His glossy,
dreamy style (later refined by elements
of expressionism and gritty realism), is
pseudonymous with the romantic
melodramas of MGM, the studio at
which he worked for over two decades,
beginning in the early twenties. He is
mainly associated with romances and

comedies, particularly those starring Greta Garbo. Although not as inventive as some of his contemporaries, William Daniels was certainly one of the most original, and his work, whatever the overall quality of the movies, is never less than exemplary.

The Last Gangster (MGM, 1937). *Brute Force* (Universal, 1947). *Forbidden* (Universal, 1953). *Six Bridges to Cross* (Universal, 1955).

Danton, Ray (b. 1931)

Actor. Despite consistently excellent performances and obvious charisma, Danton never achieved real stardom. Still, he was outstanding as the title character in *The Rise and Fall of Legs Diamond* and *The George Raft Story*. During the mid-sixties he moved to Europe, where he starred in a few well received action movies, but his best work was probably in his two late fifties gangster movies.

The Rise and Fall of Legs Diamond (Warner Bros., 1960). *The George Raft Story* (Allied Artists, 1961).

Dark City (Paramount, 1950). 88 mins.
Producer: Hal B. Wallis. *Director*: William Dieterle. *Screenplay*: Leonardo Bercovici and John Meredyth Lucas, based on the story *No Escape* by Larry Marcus. *Director of Photography*: Victor Milner. *Music*: Franz Waxman. *Art Director*: Franz Bachelin. *Editor*: Warren Low.

Cast: Charlton Heston (Danny Haley), Lizabeth Scott (Fran), Viveca Lindfors (Victoria), Dean Jagger (Captain Garvey), Don De Fore (Arthur Winant), Jack Webb (Augie), Ed Begley (Barney). *With*: Harry Morgan, Walter Sande, Mark Keuning, Mike Mazurki, Stanley Prager, Walter Burke.

Danny Haley, a cardsharp and leader of a gang of gamblers and con men, fleeces a victim. When the victim commits suicide, his crazed brother vows revenge and stalks the gang. Haley is helped by Fran, the former girlfriend of the suicide victim, and Captain Garvey, who believes the man was actually murdered. Eventually Garvey cracks the case and the madman is arrested.

Dark City is typical of the high budget *noirs* produced at Paramount during the late forties and early fifties. As directed by German emigré William Dieterle, this gangster melodrama has all the requisite rain-swept, fog shrouded sets familiar to the genre. The cast is adequate, but the film suffers from a confusing, improbable screenplay. It is probably best known as Charlton Heston's film debut.

Dark Streets (First National, 1929). 55 mins.
Producer: Ned Marin. *Director*: Frank Lloyd. *Adaptor-dialog*: Bradley King, *story by* Richard Connell. *Director of Photography*: Ernest Waller. *Editor*: Edward Schroeder.

Cast: Jack Mulhall (Pat McGlone/Danny McGlone), Lila Lee (Katie Dean), Aggie Herring (Mrs. Dean), Earl Pingree (Cuneo), Will Walling (Police Captain). *With*: E. H. Calvert, Maurice Black, Lucien Littlefield, Pat Harmon.

Twin brothers Pat McGlone, an honest cop, and Danny McGlone, a leader of a gang of small-time thieves, are in love with the same girl, Katie Dean. When Danny's gang robs a whorehouse, Pat witnesses the crime. The gang plans to kill Pat, but in a case of mistaken identity, accidentally kills its leader instead.

With its dated, improbable plot, *Dark Streets* conforms to the clichés of "B" movies. However, as one of the early sound gangster movies produced by First National, it is an important, if minor, movie. Its primitive style and screenplay would be refined by the studio over the following two or three years as the genre matured.

Da Silva, Howard (1909–1986)

Character actor. Born Harold Silverblatt in Cleveland, Ohio, Da Silva gained experience as a steel worker and stage actor before settling in Hollywood during the thirties. Tough looking, Da Silva specialized in hard-boiled supporting roles, playing a violent escaped convict in the classic forties gangster *noir They Live by Night*, oddly his only appearance in the genre.

They Live by Night (RKO, 1948).

Dassin, Jules (1911–1992)

Director. Dassin was one of the prominent figures whose career was destroyed by the McCarthy witchhunt of the late forties. After years of experience as a director of short films and as a radio writer and actor, Dassin began directing features in 1942. He hit his artistic stride four years later with his brutal gangster prison drama *Brute Force*, for which he was instantly recognized as an important talent. He followed this success with three equally brilliant *films noir*: *Naked City* (Universal, 1948), *Thieves Highway* (20th Century–Fox, 1949), and *Night and the City* (20th Century–Fox, 1950). His political troubles began while he was directing the latter films, and he retreated to Europe where his career continued unabated, if less interesting. Nevertheless, he did direct two of the better heist dramas, *Rififi* and *Topkapi*.

Brute Force (Universal, 1947). *Rififi* (United Artists, 1954). *Topkapi* (United Artists, 1964).

Daves, Delmar (1904–1977)

Screenwriter. After varied experience as a writer and journalist, Daves was hired as a staff writer for MGM in 1933. He immediately established himself as a successful screenwriter and moved to Warner Bros. a few years later. For Warner he wrote or cowrote important movies, including the gangster classic *The Petrified Forest*. In fact, he was so successful that, in 1943, Warner allowed him to direct, thus making him one of the earliest staff writers to move to filming his own

screenplays. He subsequently cowrote and directed many excellent movies, including the *film noir* classic *Dark Passage* (Warner Bros., 1947).

The Petrified Forest (Warner Bros., 1946; cowriter).

Davis, Bette (1908–1992)

Actress. Born Ruth Elizabeth Davis in Lowell, Massachusetts, Bette Davis began acting in summer stock as a child. She made her Broadway debut in 1929 and was in Hollywood by 1930. At first, despite her obvious talent, producers had no idea what to do with her. Her unconventional looks confused studio executives, but her fiery performances immediately established her as a compelling new talent. Signed by Warner Bros., she became the notoriously macho studio's leading female star, specializing in bad girls or bitches, but also playing the occasional tragic heroine. She was surprisingly active in gangster movies, costarring in nine features, teamed with James Cagney in several during the thirties. Probably her best known performance in the genre, however, was in the classic *The Petrified Forest*, in which she stars as the brave diner waitress who stands up against the violent gangster Duke Mantee (Humphrey Bogart).

Three on a Match (First National, 1932). *20,000 Years in Sing Sing* (First National, 1933). *The Big Shakedown* (First National, 1934). *Fog Over Frisco* (First National, 1934). *Jimmy the Gent* (Warner Bros., 1934). *Special Agent* (Warner Bros., 1935). *The Petrified Forest* (Warner Bros., 1936). *Kid Galahad* (Warner Bros., 1937). *Marked Woman* (Warner Bros., 1937).

Davis, Charlie (Fictional character)

In *film noir*, sports figures were often used as symbols of the violence and senselessness of modern society. They were also often grossly exploited in real life by crooked managers, team owners, and promoters, particularly in the case of professional boxers. In *Body*

Humphrey Bogart as the dashing, psychotic gangster Baby Face Martin, surrounded by the Dead End Kids from the classic *Dead End*. **Leo Gorcey is seen at bottom left.**

and Soul (United Artists, 1947), Charlie Davis is the quintessential mob-exploited boxer. In one of John Garfield's best performances, he brings to life the plight of this hapless and unfortunate character who rises to fame, abandons his loyal girlfriend, and finally double-crosses the mobsters who have been using him by winning a match he is supposed to lose. Garfield was nominated for an Academy Award for his powerful and touching performance as Charlie Davis, the archetype of several similar characters in subsequent *films noir*.

Davis, James "Brick" (Fictional character)

The enormous popularity of the gangster pictures of the early thirties caused a typically kneejerk reaction by conservatives in the government and elsewhere. The theory was that the films glorified violence, immorality and challenges to authority. There was even talk of an outright ban by certain narrow-minded public officials. As silly as the arguments were, this small but very vocal minority did have at least one effect: Warner Bros. decided to make a film with their number one star of gangster pictures, James Cagney, in the role of a mob-fighting hero, James "Brick" Davis. The result, *G-Men* (Warner Bros., 1935), was one of the most entertaining and, interestingly, *violent* additions to the genre. The film was officially endorsed by the F.B.I. and was later used as a training film! Cagney's performance was typically energetic, and the film's box office success inspired a whole series of mostly inferior imitations.

Dawn, Gaye (Fictional character)

Claire Trevor always managed to imbue her characters, no matter how big or small the part, with a certain dignity and humanity that brought them to life. This is certainly the case with *Key Largo*'s Gaye Dawn, probably her most important role as a moll in the gangster genre, and one of the most touching characterizations of its type. Gaye is the mistress of Johnny Rocco (Edward G. Robinson), a sadistic mobster on the run from the law. Rocco and his gang take over a small dilapidated Florida resort hotel to wait out a storm before fleeing to Cuba. Rocco is soon engaged in a battle of wills with Frank McCloud (Humphrey Bogart), one of the hostages, while also using every other moment to humiliate his mistress. Gaye was once a promising singer, but after years of Rocco's abuse, has become a lush. At one point he forces her to sing a salacious song; but his abuse of his girlfriend backfires: it forces McCloud to take action and eventually kill Rocco.

Day, Laraine (b. 1917)

Actress. Born in Roosevelt, Utah, Laraine Day appeared with the Long Beach Players and made her screen debut in *Stella Dallas* (Paramount, 1937). Although talented and attractive, she never achieved real stardom, but costarred in the engaging gangster satire *Mr. Lucky* opposite Cary Grant.

Mr. Lucky (RKO, 1943).

Day, Richard (1894–1972)

Art director. A fascinating figure who led a varied, adventurous life, Day was a prominent art director in Hollywood for over four decades, beginning in the twenties. Mainly employed by 20th Century–Fox, he was the set designer (often in collaboration) for many classic films including two excellent gangster movies.

Dead End (United Artists, 1938). *On the Waterfront* (Columbia, 1954).

Dead End (United Artists, 1937). 93 mins.

Producer: Samuel Goldwyn. *Director*: William Wyler. *Screenplay*: Lillian Hellman, based on the play by Sidney Kingsley. *Director of Photography*: Gregg Toland. *Music Director*: Alfred Newman. *Art Director*: Richard Day. *Editor*: Daniell Mandell.

Cast: Joel McCrea (Dave Connell), Sylvia Sidney (Drina Gordon), Humphrey Bogart (Joe "Baby Face" Martin/ Marty Johnson), Allen Jenkins (Hunk), Wendy Barrie (Kay Burton), Claire Trevor (Francey), Gabriel Dell (T. B.). *With*: Billy Halop, Huntz Hall, Leo Gorcey, Minor Watson, Charles Peck, James Burke, Marjorie Main.

Dead End, set amidst New York's notorious East Side tenements, tells the intertwined stories of several residents. Baby Face Martin, a murdering mobster admired by local youth, has returned to his birthplace to see his mother and find his ex-girlfriend, Francey. Dave Connell, a frustrated architect who cannot find work in Depression-era New York, takes care of two young women, Drina and Kay. Drina's impressionable brother Tommy falls in with a group of local teenage thugs and, in a moment of frustrated confusion, is responsible for the knifing of a wealthy man. Meanwhile, Baby Face Martin is rejected by his mother and discovers that Francey has become a cheap hooker. He decides to kidnap a local rich kid, but his plans backfire, and he is killed by Dave Connell, who decides to use his reward money to help defend Tommy Gordon.

Based on a successful play, *Dead End* is typically stagy and, at times, static and predictable. Yet, because of strong performances and William Wyler's excellent direction, the film manages to satisfy, successfully conveying the desperation and futility of slum life at the height of the Great Depression. It is also memorable for providing Humphrey Bogart with one of his best gangster roles of the thirties, for Claire Trevor's supporting performance as the hardened streetwalker

James Cagney and Pat O'Brien surrounded by the Dead End Kids in the classic, *Angels with Dirty Faces.*

(she would later become one of *film noir*'s most important *femmes fatales*), and for introducing the Dead End Kids. Although not strictly a gangster movie, *Dead End* did provide the genre with a compelling, realistic view of the conditions that lead some individuals into a life of crime.

Dead End Kids

Leo Gorcey and Huntz Hall were cast as street toughs in the immensely successful *Dead End* (United Artists, 1937). Their starmaking parts made them popular with audiences, and they were subsequently reteamed in *Angels with Dirty Faces* (Warner Bros., 1938). At this point the team also included Billy Halop, among others, who was reteamed with Gorcey and Hall in *Angels Wash Their Faces* (Warner Bros., 1939), a less satisfying movie which lightens their characters and

stresses comedy. The group then splintered into the Little Tough Guys and the East Side Kids, groups that interlapped in increasingly inferior "B" movies produced at Warner Bros. during the early forties. Eventually Gorcey and Hall joined Poverty Row studio Monogram as the leaders of the Bowery Boys in countless "B" movies made from 1946 to 1958.

DeCarlo, Yvonne (b. 1922)

Actress. Born Peggy Yvonne Middleton in Vancouver, Ontario, DeCarlo was originally a dancer in nightclubs. Signed to Paramount as a contract player in the early forties, and after the usual buildup in supporting roles, she was promoted to leads during the mid-forties. A dark-haired, sensual actress, she somehow never achieved real stardom, although she enlivened many good "B" movies with her exotic beauty.

She appeared in three gangster movies, most notably Robert Siodmak's underrated *Criss Cross*, in which she plays one of the forties' most memorable *femmes fatales*.

Brute Force (Universal, 1947). *Casbah* (Universal, 1949). *Criss Cross* (Universal, 1949).

DeCorsia, Ted (1904–1973)

Character actor. A native New Yorker, DeCorsia is best remembered as a hulking villain. He was always cast as a mob henchman in his gangster movies.

The Enforcer (Warner Bros., 1951). *Crime Wave* (Warner Bros., 1953). *The Big Combo* (Allied Artists, 1955). *Baby Face Nelson* (United Artists, 1957). *Inside the Mafia* (United Artists, 1959).

DeCuir, John F. (b. 1918)

Art director. DeCuir is an important art director from the late golden age of the Hollywood studios. Employed by Universal in the forties, he designed the productions for many important films including the classic gangster prison epic *Brute Force*. His most original, vigorous designs were created for Universal, but his best known work, created for 20th Century–Fox during the fifties, includes many legendary technicolor musicals and comedies.

Brute Force (Universal, 1947).

Dekker, Albert (1904–1968)

Character actor. Born Albert van Dekker in Brooklyn, the large framed Dutch-American actor had a successful stage career in the twenties and thirties, making his film debut in 1937. He specialized in eccentric villains, most famously as the title character in the sci-fi horror classic *Dr. Cyclops* (Paramount, 1940). His performance as Moll, the evil escapee, in *Strange Cargo* set the standard for his subsequent gangster film appearances. Of these, probably the most famous is his thug Colfax in the gangster *noir* classic *The Killers*.

Strange Cargo (MGM, 1940). *Buy Me That Town* (Paramount, 1941). *The Killers* (Universal, 1946). *Illegal* (Warner Bros., 1955).

Delon, Alain (b. 1935)

Actor and producer. A popular modern French matinee idol, Alain Delon has been a romantic leading man in European movies since the late fifties. He often played conventional heroes or heroic bad guys with a sense of humor, as in *Borsalino*, which he also produced. A huge box office hit in Europe, *Borsalino* is a kind of French *Godfather* (Paramount, 1972), and like the American gangster movie, inspired several sequels. Delon also played a gangster in *The Sicilian Clan*, a less successful precursor to the later hit.

The Sicilian Clan (20th Century–Fox, 1968). *Borsalino* (Paramount, 1970).

Del Ruth, Roy (1895–1961)

Director. Like so many American directors of his generation, Del Ruth began his movie career as a writer and gag man for comedy producer Mack Sennett. During the twenties, he directed comedy shorts for Ben Turpin, Billy Bevan, and Harry Langdon (for whom Frank Capra also worked). Del Ruth joined Warner Bros. at the beginning of the sound era, and his simple, hard-boiled techniques were perfectly suitable to the style emerging at the studio during that period. He directed many of the studio's most important early gangster movies, including the original version of *The Maltese Falcon* and the James Cagney classics *Blonde Crazy*, *Taxi!*, and *Lady Killer*. He also helmed several notable musicals and comedies during the thirties. A dependable technician, Del Ruth never developed a personal style to set him apart from equally successful studio hacks of the thirties and forties. Nevertheless, he is unquestionably an important director of the early gangster cycle.

The Maltese Falcon (Warner Bros.,

1921). *Blonde Crazy* (Warner Bros., 1931). *Taxi!* (Warner Bros., 1932). *The Little Giant* (First National, 1933). *Lady Killer* (Warner Bros., 1933).

Demarest, William (1892–1983)
Character actor. Famous as the gruff Uncle Charlie on television's *My Three Sons*, Demarest's career began in vaudeville in the teens, and he entered movies during the late twenties. He played a variety of parts, usually variations of his gruff comic type, and was particularly memorable in the series of great screwball comedies directed by Preston Sturges. He also played an honest cop in *Hell on Frisco Bay*, his only appearance in the gangster genre.
Hell on Frisco Bay (Warner Bros., 1956).

Demme, Jonathan (b. 1944)
Director. Yet another graduate of Roger Corman's "school" of low budget, high quality productions, Demme made a name for himself in the seventies with the exploitation gangster movie *Crazy Mama*. The box office and critical success of this movie did not immediately effect Demme, and it took more than a decade for his career to really take off. It was during this period that he directed his second gangster picture, *Married to the Mob*. Both films are notable for their vigorous performances and tongue-in-cheek approach.
Crazy Mama (New World, 1975). *Married to the Mob* (Paramount, 1991).

De Niro, Robert (b. 1943)
Actor. For two decades, beginning in the early seventies, Robert De Niro has epitomized motion picture acting. Discovered by Martin Scorsese, De Niro has achieved his greatest success in this director's movies. Like other method actors, he seems to inhabit his characters, to literally become them, but he mostly avoids the excessive mumbling, emoting style of the method performers. He has been particularly effective in villainous or bad guy roles, most notably in Scorsese's modern gangster classic *GoodFellas*, in which De Niro plays a mob hit man. However, from the very beginning of his career he has played street thugs and toughs, and early on, made a name for himself in Roger Corman's "B" movie *Bloody Mama* as one of Ma Barker's murderous sons. Another of his early pre-star roles was in Scorsese's *Mean Streets*, a melodrama with gangster overtones. His starmaking performance came a year later in *The Godfather II*, the successful sequel to the original hit. De Niro dared to play Vito Corleone as a young man, the role Marlon Brando had played as the mature mob boss in *The Godfather* (Paramount, 1972). De Niro more than held his own, impressing critics and the public alike. Although

Robert De Niro, gangster icon of the contemporary American cinema, in one of his earliest gangster roles in *Godfather II*.

identified with such roles, he has only rarely returned to gangster roles. Less well known is his performance in Sergio Leone's gangster epic *Once Upon a Time in America*. Altogether, Robert De Niro has become a contemporary version of Humphrey Bogart and James Cagney—whatever the variety of roles he plays, he is almost exclusively identified by the public with his gangster parts.

Bloody Mama (American International, 1970). *Mean Streets* (Warner Bros., 1973). *The Godfather, Part II* (Paramount, 1974). *Once Upon a Time in America* (Warner Bros., 1984). *GoodFellas* (Warner Bros., 1991).

DePalma, Brian (b. 1940)

Director. DePalma emerged with the group of filmmakers that includes Francis Ford Coppola, Martin Scorsese, Steven Spielberg, and George Lucas. All of them were college trained, but each developed his own style. With the exception of Scorsese, DePalma might well be the most talented of the group. He has been attacked by certain critics for his appropriation of styles—particularly Alfred Hitchcock's—but he has consistently demonstrated an ability to use and reinvent these styles in new and exciting ways. Like Scorsese, DePalma is a great technician, but he is also less pretentious and more commercial. His contribution to the genre, *The Untouchables*, is a typical mixture of generic conventions and exhilarating, violent action.

The Untouchables (Paramount, 1988).

Deray, Jacques (b. 1927)

Director. A commercial filmmaker, the French Deray has been making popular movies since the late fifties. He has little individual style, but has made a number of good movies including the enormously successful *Borsalino*, whose themes and popularity (in Europe) presaged the better-known American gangster movie, *The Godfather* (Paramount, 1972).

Borsalino (Paramount, 1970).

Desert Fury (Paramount, 1947). 94 mins.

Producer: Hal Wallis. *Director*: Lewis Allen. *Screenplay*: Robert Rossen, based on the novel by Ramona Stewart. *Directors of Photography*: Charles Lang and Edward Cronjager. *Music*: Miklos Rozsa. *Art Director*: Perry Ferguson. *Editor*: Warren Low.

Cast: John Hodiak (Eddie Bendix), Lizabeth Scott (Paula Haller), Burt Lancaster (Tom Hansen), Wendell Corey (Johnny Ryan), Mary Astor (Fritzie Haller), Kristine Miller (Claire Lindquist). *With*: William Harrigan, James Flavin, Jane Novak, Ana Camargo.

Fritzie Haller, a one time madam in New York, has opened a small gambling casino in Nevada. Her beautiful daughter Paula is rebellious and wants to get away from the quiet life in the desert town where they live. Eddie Bendix, a gangster on the lam with his bodyguard Johnny Ryan, takes a cabin near Haller's casino and renews his acquaintance with former flame Fritzie. However, he finds himself very attracted to her daughter, who is dating Tom Hansen, a local lawman. Hansen grows suspicious of Bendix and when he confronts him, a fight breaks out. Bendix is killed and Hansen is reunited with Paula.

Desert Fury is an interesting, obscure *noir* melodrama from the genre's great early period. It is full of *noir* icons, and is directed in fine style by Lewis Allen. The convoluted screenplay, by the usually reliable Robert Rossen, is redeemed by excellent performances, particularly Mary Astor's glamorous, earthy ex-madam.

The Desperate Hours (Paramount, 1955). 112 mins.

Producer and Director: William Wyler. *Screenplay*: Joseph Hayes, based

11573-58

Fredric March (left) and Humphrey Bogart (right) in _Desperate Hours_, a taut thriller that marked Bogart's last appearance as a gangster and one of his most vicious.

on his novel. _Director of Photography_: Lee Garmes. _Music_: Gail Kubik. _Art Directors_: Hal Pereira and Joseph M. Johnson. _Editor_: Robert Swink.

Cast: Humphrey Bogart (Glenn Griffin), Fredric March (Dan Hilliard), Arthur Kennedy (Jesse Bard), Martha Scott (Eleanor Hilliard), Dewey Martin (Hal Griffin), Gig Young (Chuck). _With_: Mary Murphy, Richard Eyer, Robert Middleton, Alan Reed, Don Haggerty, Whit Bissell, Ray Collins.

A quiet suburban home is invaded by three escaped convicts who plan to use the house as a temporary hideout. The three mobsters, led by the psychotic Glenn Griffin, terrorize the family until the neighbors, suspicious of the new "friends," call the police. All three convicts are killed.

Hardly original—the theme had been used in several earlier movies including the classic _film noir The_

Dark Past (Columbia, 1949)—_The Desperate Hours_ is still a taut thriller in the style of thirties gangster movies. It is best known as the last movie in which Humphrey Bogart starred as a gangster.

De Toth, Andre (b. 1912)

Director. Born Endre Toth in Hungary, De Toth had a brief but successful career in his native country during the late thirties and early forties before he immigrated to the United States at the beginning of World War II. For the next two decades, he worked in Hollywood, where he made a number of excellent "B" movies including the _film noir The Pitfall_ (United Artists, 1948), _House of Wax_ (Warner Bros., 1953), the first 3D production by a major studio, and a superior gangster crime thriller, _Crime Wave_.

Crime Wave (Warner Bros., 1954).

Deutsch, Adolph (1897–1980)
Composer. During the thirties and forties, Deutsch was employed at Warner Bros., where he composed the scores for several important movies including *The Maltese Falcon* and *High Sierra*. He later worked for Billy Wilder on his classic gangster satire *Some Like It Hot*.

High Sierra (Warner Bros., 1940). *The Maltese Falcon* (Warner Bros., 1941). *The Big Shot* (Warner Bros., 1942). *Some Like It Hot* (United Artists, 1959).

Diamond, I. A. L. (1915–1991)
Screenwriter. Born Itek Dommnici in New York City, Diamond had experience as a journalist before entering movies as a writer during the mid-forties. He cowrote many movies, few of any merit, until he teamed with writer/director Billy Wilder during the late fifties. Their first collaboration, *Some Like It Hot*, is a classic. Diamond subsequently worked exclusively with Wilder.

Some Like It Hot (United Artists, 1959).

Dickinson, Angie (b. 1931)
Actress. Success in a beauty pageant brought the former Angeline Brown of Kulm, North Dakota, to Hollywood in 1954. At first she was given the usual blonde bombshell roles, but she proved to have some talent which became particularly evident on television during the seventies. In Don Siegel's remake of *The Killers* she made an impression as the deadly *femme fatale*.

The Killers (Universal, 1964).

Dieterle, William (1893–1972)
Director. The German born Dieterle began directing in Berlin after a brief career as an actor. He moved to the United States in the early thirties and subsequently proved to be one of the most brilliant studio contract directors in Hollywood. Mostly employed by Paramount, he helped establish that studio's highly expressionist style of the thirties. He directed three gangster pictures including the classic *Dr. Socrates* and the gangster *noir Dark City*. Whatever their faults, both are typical of his extravagant style.

Fog Over Frisco (First National, 1943). *Dr. Socrates* (Warner Bros., 1935). *Dark City* (Paramount, 1950).

Dillinger (Monogram, 1945). 74 mins.
Producers: Maurice King and Frank King. *Director*: Max Nosseck. *Screenplay*: Phil Yordan. *Music*: Dimitri Tiompkin. *Art Director*: Dave Milton. *Editor*: Edward Mann.

Cast: Edmund Lowe (Specs), Anne Jeffreys (Helen), Lawrence Tierney (Dillinger), Eduardo Cianelli (Murph), Marc Lawrence (Doc), Elisha Cook, Jr. (Kirk). *With*: Ralph Lewis, Ludwig Stossel, Else Jannsen, Hugo Prosser, Dewey Robinson, Bob Perry.

After robbing a grocery store to impress a girlfriend, John Dillinger is caught and sent to prison. There, he meets Specks, a small-time hood who has his own gang. After being paroled, Dillinger helps Specks and several other convicts break out of prison. The gang embarks on a series of crimes and the charismatic Dillinger soon gains control of the group. Dillinger then meets Helen, a girl who had worked at a movie box office booth he had once robbed. They begin an affair and she encourages his life of crime. Specks is jealous of Dillinger, and when he double crosses the violent mobster, he is killed. Helen, however, having grown tired of her life with the notorious criminal, betrays him to the police. Setting him up in front of a movie theater, she wears red to let the F.B.I. agents know whom to gun down.

Only loosely based on fact, *Dillinger* claims to tell the real life story of thirties gangster John Dillinger. It omits much of the truth, but Philip Yordan's script more than compensates. Indeed, Yordan was nominated for an Academy Award for his work. Max Nosseck's direction (which economically used stock footage from earlier gangster pictures), is spare and equally dynamic. Tough-guy actor Lawrence Tierney gives one of his best performances, and the film's tremendous box office success helped make him a popular star before self destruction ruined his career a few years later. Indeed, Monogram's *Dillinger* is arguably one of the best "B" movies ever made, and it provided a career boost for many of those associated with it, including producers Maurice and Frank King, whose previous productions were cheap and only moderately successful. *Dillinger*'s success helped establish them as one of the leading teams of "B" producers during the forties and fifties.

Dillinger (American International, 1973). 107 mins.
Executive Producers: Samuel Z. Arkoff and Lawrence A. Gordon. *Producer*: Buzz Feitshans. *Director and Screenplay*: John Milius. *Director of Photography*: Jules Brenner. *Music*: Barry Devorzon. *Art Director*: Trevor Williams. *Editor*: Fred Feitshans, Jr.
Cast: Warren Oates (John Dillinger), Ben Johnson (Melvin Purvis), Michelle Phillips (Billie Frechette), Cloris Leachman (Anna Sagel, aka The Woman in Red), Harry Dean Stanton (Homer Van Meter), Steve Kanaly ("Pretty Boy" Floyd). *With:* Richard Dreyfuss, Geoffrey Lewis, John Ryan, Roy Jensen, John Martino, Read Morgan, Frank McRae.
Sticking a little closer to the facts than its predecessor, this second "B" version of the life of John Dillinger is a dynamic, violent exploitation picture which marked the directorial debut of screenwriter John Milius. Milius concentrates as much on the law enforcement officials led by Melvin Purvis as he does on the exploits of Dillinger and his gang. Milius cuts between Purvis and Dillinger, following each to the inevitable confrontation in front of Chicago's Biograph Theatre, where

Dillinger was gunned down by federal agents. The film concentrates on violence and action, but it provided Warren Oates with one of his best roles as the rural Midwestern gangster whose career paralleled those of the equally legendary Bonnie and Clyde.

Dillon, John Francis (1887–1934)
Director. Dillon's promising career was cut short by his tragic early demise. He had considerable success as a director of silent dramas during the mid-twenties, and made several good sound movies before his untimely death. Among these is the seminal gangster movie *The Finger Points*, a minor but important early addition to the genre.
The Finger Points (First National, 1931).

Disbarred (Paramount, 1939). 58 mins.
Associate Producer: Stuart Walker. *Director*: Robert Florey. *Screenplay*: Lillie Hayward and Robert Presnell, *story by* Harry Sauber. *Director of Photography*: Harry Fischbeck. *Music Director*: Boris Morros. *Art Directors*: Hans Dreier and William Flannery. *Editor*: Arthur Schmidt.
Cast: Gail Patrick (Joan Carroll), Robert Preston (Bradley Kent), Otto Kruger (Tyler Cradon), Sidney Toler ("Hardy" Mardsen), Edward Marr (Harp Harrigan). *With*: Charles D. Brown, Helen MacKeller, Clay Clement, Frank M. Thomas, Virginia Dabney.
Joan Carroll, a country lawyer, is brought to the big city by Tyler Cradon to defend his friend, Harp Harrigan, who has been accused of pointing a lethal weapon at a state's witness. At first she believes her client is innocent, but due to the friendship of a young district attorney, Bradley Kent, she soon realizes that both Harrigan and Cradon are mobsters. With Kent's help, Joan sends her clients to prison.
A low budget late thirties gangster "B" movie, *Disbarred* has a surprising amount of top talent associated with it.

Director Robert Florey made several superior "B" movies in the thirties and forties, including a couple of classic horror movies. Likewise, actors Robert Preston, Gail Patrick, and Otto Kruger were all very popular, if not really first rate stars. However, *Disbarred* is a cheap, rather static programmer that seems to have been made by its cast and crew to kill time between more important projects.

Diskant, George E. (1907–1965)
Cinematographer. Diskant had his greatest success in the late forties and early fifties, when he photographed several excellent *films noir* including the gangster *noirs The Narrow Margin, They Live by Night*, and *The Racket*. His style epitomizes the extravagant height of *noir* style, characterized by sharp contrasts between light and shadow, and fog and rainswept sets.
They Live by Night (RKO, 1948). *The Racket* (RKO, 1951), *The Narrow Margin* (RKO, 1951). *Kansas City Confidential* (United Artists, 1952).

Dix, Richard (1894–1949)
Actor. Born Ernest Brimmer in New York City, Richard Dix was one of the most popular leading men of the twenties. Although his career went into decline during the thirties, he continued to be popular in "B" movies, usually in heroic or good guy roles, as in *Eyes of the Underworld*, his only gangster movie.
Eyes of the Underworld (Universal, 1942).

The Docks of New York (Paramount, 1928). Approx. 90 mins.
Associate Producer: J. G. Bachmann. *Director*: Josef von Sternberg. *Screenplay*: Jules Furthman, *story by* John Monk Saunders. *Titles*: Julian Johnson. *Director of Photography*: Harold Rosson. *Art Director*: Hans Dreier. *Editor*: Helen Lewis.
Cast: George Bancroft (Bill Roberts), Betty Compson (Sadie), Olga Baclanova (Lou), Clyde Cook (Sugar Steve), Mitchell Lewis (3rd Engineer). *With*: Gustav von Seyffertitz, Guy Oliver, May Foster, Lillian Worth.

Ship's stoker Bill Roberts saves waterfront tramp Sadie from suicide and, later, while drunk, marries her. The following day he returns to his ship, where an engineer tries to seduce Sadie. The lecher is killed by his wife, Lou, and Sadie is charged with the crime. Lou later confesses and Sadie is released, but is charged with stealing clothes. Bill, realizing that he loves Sadie, jumps ship and returns just in time to save her from being sentenced. He confesses to stealing the clothes and is sent to jail, but promises to return to Sadie after serving his time.

Essentially a romantic melodrama, *The Docks of New York* is one of the important late silent movies which had influence on the emerging gangster genre. To a lesser degree its style could still be seen in *film noir* nearly two decades later. Filming entirely in the studio, Josef von Sternberg conjured up a foggy, shadowy New York underworld, but his greatest achievement (and that of the scenarist) is the realistic, unsentimental portrayal of the characters and situations. It is not merely a morality tale, but one about the ambiguities of good and evil people, a key theme of the early gangster genre (in which cops are often as corrupt as the gangsters) and of later *film noir*.

Dr. Mabuse, der Spieler (UFA, 1922). 122 mins.
Director: Fritz Lang. *Screenplay*: Fritz Lang and Thea Von Harbou, based on the novel by Norbert Jacques. *Director of Photography*: Carl Hoffmann. *Art Directors*: Carl Starl Urach, Otto Hunte, Erich Kettlehut, Karl Vollbrecht.
Cast: Rudolph Klein-Rogge (Dr. Mabuse), Gertrude Weicker (Countess Stolst), Aud Egede-Nissen (Cara), Alfred Abel (Count Told), Bernhard

Goetzke (Wenk), Paul Richter (Edgar Hull).

Based on Norbert Jacques' 1921 novel *Dr. Mabuse, der Spieler* (Dr. Mabuse, the Gambler), the film recounts the tale of the rise and fall of the diabolical Dr. Mabuse, who controls an underworld mob from his casino. His gang is involved in counterfeiting, extortion and bombing. Hunted by Wenk, a Berlin prosecutor, he eventually goes mad and is shipped off to a mental hospital.

One of Fritz Lang's great silent films, *Dr. Mabuse, der Spieler* was originally released in two parts (both running a little over an hour). It marked a break with contemporary German cinema by eschewing expressionistic sets for realistic designs, costumes, and even some location shooting. Indeed, it has a famous chase sequence shot partly in the sewers of Berlin which later was largely recreated in *The Third Man* (United Artists, 1948). Adapted by Lang and his wife Thea Von Harbou, it was the first and remains the greatest German gangster movie. Internationally popular, it had a profound influence, particularly on Josef von Sternberg, whose American gangster movies of the late twenties owe an enormous debt to Lang's great film. Lang made a well received sequel to the movie, *The Testament of Dr. Mabuse* (Nero Films, 1933), which recounts the mobster's escape from the mental institution, his attempts to go straight, and his eventual death at the hands of his ex-cohorts. Rarely seen in the United States and initially repressed by the Nazis, it was Lang's last German film before fleeing the regime of Adolf Hitler.

Doctor Socrates (Warner Bros., 1935). 69 mins.

Producer: Robert Lord. *Director*: William Dieterle. *Screenplay*: Robert Lord and Mary C. McCall. *Story*: W. R. Burnett. *Director of Photography*: Tony Gaudio. *Music Director*: Leo Forbstein. *Editor*: Ralph Dawson.

Cast: Paul Muni (Dr. Lee Caldwell), Ann Dvorak (Josephine Gray), Barton MacLane (Red Bastian), Raymond Brown (Ben Suggs), Ralph Remley (Bill Payne), Hal K. Dawson (Mel Towne). *With*: Marc Lawrence, Sam Wren, Hobart Cavanaugh, Henry O'Neil, Mayo Methot, Carl Stockdale.

A gang of thieves breaks into wealthy Dr. Caldwell's house. One of them is injured, however, and they force the doctor to operate on him while they take refuge there. Caldwell also shelters Josephine Gray, a female hitchhiker, who suspicious neighbors believe is the gangster's moll. In fact, Gray is being held against her will by the dangerous gang. Neighbors, meanwhile, contact the police, but before they arrive, Dr. Caldwell convinces the gangsters they have been infected with deadly yellow fever. (He actually injects them with a "serum" that puts them to sleep.) Finding the gang unconscious, the G-Men haul them off to jail, and the doctor and young girl are free to pursue their growing passion for one another.

With its wildly improbable plot, the oddly titled *Dr. Socrates* is one of the more bizarre entries in the distinguished group of gangster movies produced during the thirties. However, it is notable for the excellent direction by William Dieterle, and good performances by genre icons Paul Muni and Ann Dvorak, here in a decidedly less important movie than *Scarface* (United Artists, 1932), their first teaming. *Dr. Socrates* was a minor box office success and was remade as a "B" picture, *King of the Underworld*, with Humphrey Bogart as the main gangster, by Warner Bros. in 1939.

Doctorow, E. L. (b. 1931)

Novelist. Doctorow's novels mix real events and characters with fiction. His novel *Ragtime* was successfully adapted, providing James Cagney with his final screen role. Less successful was the disappointing adaptation of his novel *Billy Bathgate*, a historical romance partly based on the lives of real life gangsters.

Billy Bathgate (Universal, 1992).

The Don Is Dead (Universal, 1973). 117 mins.

Producer: Hal B. Wallis. *Director*: Richard Fleischer. *Screenplay*: Marvin H. Albert, adapted from his novel by Christopher Trumbo and Michael Butler. *Director of Photography*: Richard H. Kline. *Music*: Jerry Goldsmith. *Art Director*: Preston Ames. *Editor*: Edward A. Biery.

Cast: Anthony Quinn (Don Angelo Dimorra), Frederic Forrest (Tony Fargo), Robert Forster (Frank Regabulto), Al Lettieri (Vince Fargo), Angel Tompkins (Ruby Dunne), Charles Cioffi (Luigi Orlando). *With*: Jo Anne Meredith, J. Duke Russo, Louis Zorich, Anthony Charnota, Ina Balin.

A feud erupts among a Mafia family after the death of their Don. Angelo Dimorra is given half of the old Don's New York territory, while Luigi Orlando controls the other half. The feud is complicated by the obligatory moll, Ruby Dunne, who is loved by both mob bosses. Eventually, the violent clashes between the gangs lead to Luigi's death, and Dimorra is reduced to a hopeless cripple. Yet another gangster steps in and becomes the new boss of both territories.

The Don Is Dead, an exploitation picture released shortly after *The Godfather* (Paramount, 1972), brought distinguished producer Hal B. Wallis' career to a virtual end. The talent behind the camera was especially good — director Richard Fleischer is a neglected talent — and Anthony Quinn is typically compelling. However, the screenplay relies too heavily on the clichés of the genre, and the film emerges as little more than a "B" version of *The Godfather*.

Donlevy, Brian (1889–1972)

Character actor. The Irish-born Donlevy moved to the United States with his parents as a young boy. After an adventurous youth, he joined Pershing's Mexican Expedition as a teenager and served as a pilot during World War I. Beginning his acting career in the early twenties, he had success on Broadway and then found popularity in Hollywood as a character lead, usually playing toughs or villains. His roles in four gangster movies are evenly split between mobsters and good guys — the former in *Born Reckless* and *The Glass Key*, and the latter in *Kiss of Death* and *Hoodlum Empire*.

Born Reckless (20th Century–Fox, 1937). *The Glass Key* (Paramount, 1942). *Kiss of Death* (20th Century–Fox, 1947). *Hoodlum Empire* (Republic, 1952).

The Doorway to Hell (Warner Bros., 1930). 78 mins.

Director: Archie Mayo. *Screenplay*: George Rosener, based on the story "A Handful of Clouds" by Rowland Brown. *Director of Photography*: Barney McGill. *Music Director*: Leo F. Forbstein. *Editor*: Robert Crandall.

Cast: Lew Ayres (Louis Ricarno), Charles Judels (Sam Marconi), Dorothy Mathews (Doris), Leon Janney (Jackie Lamar), James Cagney (Steve Mileway). *With*: Robert Elliott, Kenneth Thompson, Jerry Mandy, Noel Madison, Bernard Granville, Fred Angus, Dwight Frye.

Louis Ricarno is a big-time hoodlum who controls the bootleg racket in a big city. Although he controls the racket with an iron hand, he relinquishes control to his lieutenant, Steve Mileway, in order to get married. After his wife Doris betrays him and his brother is killed by rivals, he decides to give up the straight life to seek revenge, but instead is killed by members of his former gang.

One of the earliest sound gangster movies, *The Doorway to Hell* is rather stolid and slow going. Lew Ayres was miscast as a bad guy, and today the film remains of interest only as James Cagney's first gangster movie.

Doran, Ann (b. 1914)

Character actress. Born in Amarillo, Texas, Ann Doran began her film career in the early thirties not long after moving to Los Angeles, where she had a brief career as a model. She became one of the busiest character actresses in American movies, appearing in literally dozens of films over the next three decades. She most often played the friend of the heroine or appeared in small walk-on roles. In *Blind Alley*, she plays one of the hostages held in a house by a group of gangsters on the lam.

Blind Alley (Columbia, 1939).

Dorn, Dolores (b. 1935)

Actress. Born Dolores Dorn-Heft, Dorn had a brief, moderately successful stage career in the fifties before starring in a series of "B" movies. A sexy blonde, she often played bad girls or morally ambiguous characters. She is probably best known as the complex heroine of Sam Fuller's underrated *Underworld U.S.A.* After her momentary flirtation with Hollywood, she had great success on the stage, beginning in the early sixties.

Underworld U.S.A. (Columbia, 1961).

Douglas, Gordon (b. 1909)

Director. Douglas was one of the most prolific "B" directors of the forties, fifties, and sixties. He made many successful movies, but he was little more than a very competent craftsman. He was at his best with unpretentious action pictures (particularly Westerns) and he made two superb gangster pictures. Of these, *Kiss Tomorrow Goodbye* is an acknowledged classic, thanks mainly to James Cagney's charismatic performance as a vicious gangster.

San Quentin (RKO, 1946). *Kiss Tomorrow Goodbye* (United Artists, 1950).

Douglas, Kirk (b. 1916)

Actor. Douglas was born Issur Danielovitch (which later was changed to Isidore Demsky) in Amsterdam, New York, to Russian Jewish parents who had immigrated to the United States in 1910. After graduating from St. Lawrence University, Douglas studied at the American Academy of Dramatic Art in New York while supporting himself with a series of odd jobs. After serving in the Navy during World War II, he returned to New York, where his intense presence and rugged good looks (famous for the deep chin cleft) made him a success on Broadway. Douglas was a natural performer and his stage success led naturally to Hollywood, where he made his movie debut in the *film noir* classic *The Strange Love of Martha Ivers* (Paramount, 1946). His early career was devoted to playing second leads, generally morally ambiguous characters, weaklings, or outright villains. He played gangsters in two of his early movies, *I Walk Alone* and *Out of the Past*, and his Whit Sterling in the latter is one of *film noir*'s enduring criminal characterizations. He did not become a full-fledged leading man until *Champion* (United Artists, 1949), in which he stars as a boxer who becomes a victim of his own greed and the corrupt underworld of sports. From then on, he generally played sympathetic roles or heroes. He returned to a villainous role in the "B" gangster drama *The Brotherhood*, which predated the much better *The Godfather* (Paramount, 1972). It is for his performance in *Out of the Past* and to a lesser degree, *I Walk Alone*, that Douglas remains one of the great gangster villains of the late forties.

Out of the Past (RKO, 1947). *I Walk Alone* (Paramount, 1948). *The Brotherhood* (Paramount, 1968).

Douglas, Paul (1907–1959)

Character actor. Douglas was a professional football player and radio sportscaster before becoming an actor in the mid-thirties. He appeared in many productions before achieving stardom in the enormously successful comedy, *Born Yesterday*. A large, rather imposing and bombastic performer, he found his greatest screen success in comedies. His unsympathetic role in the little-known "B" gangster movie *Joe Macbeth* is uncharacteristic, remaining one of his finest performances.

Joe Macbeth (Columbia, 1955).

Doyle, Jimmy "Popeye"

The real life New York police detective who carried out a one man war against French drug dealers and had a successful movie, *The French Connection* (20th Century–Fox, 1971), made about his adventures. The film's sequel, *French Connection II* (20th Century–Fox, 1975), on the other hand, is wholly a work of fiction.

The Dragnet (Paramount, 1928). Approx. 90 mins.

Producer and Director: Josef von Sternberg. *Screenplay*: Jules Furthman and Charles Furthman, *story by* Oliver H. P. Garrett. *Titles*: Herman Mankiewicz. *Director of Photography*: Harold Rosson. *Art Director*: Hans Dreier. *Editor*: Helen Lewis.

Cast: George Bancroft (Two-Gun Nolan), Evelyn Brent (The Magpie), William Powell (Dapper Frank Trent), Fred Kohler ("Gabby" Steve), Francis McDonald (Sniper Dawson), Leslie Fenton (Shakespeare).

When his partner is killed by two bootleggers, police detective Two-Gun Nolan, blaming himself for his partner's death, turns to the bottle and is thrown off the force. When he later meets the Magpie, the moll of mob leader Dapper Frank Trent, she falls for him and informs on her gangster lover. Nolan straightens out and tries to bring Trent to justice, but when Trent shoots the girl for betraying him, Nolan kills him in a shootout. The girl lives and Nolan marries her before rejoining the force.

An enormous box office success at the time of its release, *The Dragnet* is considered one of the most important "lost" movies of the late silent era. Certainly not as great as Josef von Sternberg's predecessor, *Underworld* (Paramount, 1927), *The Dragnet* is more conventional but ironically had an even greater influence on the emerging gangster genre.

Drake, Frances (b. 1908)

Actress. Almost completely unknown today, Drake was a popular star in the thirties. She appeared in a number of good movies, including *Mad Love* (MGM, 1935), but appeared mainly in second rate "B" movies including the minor gangster drama *Midnight Taxi*.

Midnight Taxi (20th Century–Fox, 1937).

Dreier, Hans (1884–1966)

Art director. Like so many of the great Hollywood art directors, the German-born Dreier was originally an architect. After becoming a stage designer during the mid-teens, he began designing movie productions in the early twenties and was quickly established as one of German cinema's leading art directors. He was hired by the fledgling American studio, Paramount, in 1923. As supervising art director until his retirement in 1950, he was largely responsible for the studio's elegant, art deco influenced style. He designed the sets for many of director Ernst Lubitsch's classic comedies, as well as Josef von Sternberg's melodramas, including several seminal gangster movies. Like many art directors, Dreier's career has been neglected by historians, but there can be little question that, as an arbiter of style and taste, he is one of the most important figures of Hollywood's golden age.

Underworld (Paramount, 1927). *The Docks of New York* (Paramount, 1928). *The Dragnet* (Paramount, 1928). *Thunderbolt* (Paramount, 1929). *Stolen Harmony* (Paramount, 1935). *King of Alcatraz* (Paramount, 1936).

King of Gamblers (Paramount, 1937).
King of Chinatown (Paramount, 1938).
The Tip-Off Girls (Paramount, 1938).
You and Me (Paramount, 1938). *Disbarred* (Paramount, 1939). *Queen of the Mob* (Paramount, 1940). *Buy Me That Town* (Paramount, 1941). *The Glass Key* (Paramount, 1942). *Lucky Jordan* (Paramount, 1942). *This Gun for Hire* (Paramount, 1942). *I Walk Alone* (Paramount, 1948).

Dru, Joanne (b. 1923)
Actress. Born Joanne la Coque in Logan, West Virginia, the sexy, dark-haired Dru was a model and showgirl before entering movies during the mid-forties. She found her greatest success in several classic westerns directed by Howard Hawks and John Ford during the late forties. She also costarred in three gangster movies, most notably as a moll in *711 Ocean Drive*.
711 Ocean Drive (Columbia, 1950). *Forbidden* (Universal, 1953). *Hell on Frisco Bay* (Warner Bros., 1956).

Duell, Randall (b. 1916)
Art director. Duell was employed by MGM for many years beginning in the forties. He collaborated with Cedric Gibbons on many productions including the influential *noir*-gangster drama, *The Asphalt Jungle*, whose realistic sets broke with the glittery, romantic traditions of the studio.
The Asphalt Jungle (MGM, 1950).

Duff, Howard (b. 1917)
Actor. Duff first achieved fame as detective Sam Spade on a popular radio series. As a film actor, he specialized in toughs or heroes, mostly in "B" movies, and had a small supporting role in the gangster prison classic *Brute Force*. In *Johnny Stool Pigeon*, one of the early gangster movies to deal with drug smugglers, he starred as an undercover G-man who joins a gang.
Brute Force (Universal, 1947). *Johnny Stool Pigeon* (Universal, 1949).

Duff, Warren (1904–1979)
Screenwriter and producer. As a contract writer for Warner Bros. during the thirties, Duff wrote or cowrote a number of important movies, including two classic gangster films, *Angels with Dirty Faces* and *Invisible Stripes*. He later became a staff producer for RKO, where he made many movies including the classic gangster *noir Out of the Past*.
Heat Lightning (Warner Bros., 1934). *Angels with Dirty Faces* (Warner Bros., 1938). *Invisible Stripes* (Warner Bros., 1939). *Out of the Past* (RKO, 1947; producer only).

Dunaway, Faye (b. 1941)
Actress. With her high cheekbones, green eyes, and chic style, Dunaway was both one of the loveliest and talented actresses of her generation. Born in Florida, she appeared in a few Off Broadway plays before going to Hollywood in 1967. In that year alone, she appeared in three movies, including the gangster classic *Bonnie and Clyde*. Her portrayal of a real life rural gangster is perhaps a little too glamorous, but she manages to capture the psychological intensity and violence of Bonnie Parker.
Bonnie and Clyde (Warner Bros., 1967).

Dundee, Slim (Fictional character)
One of *film noir*'s most memorably psychotic and cold-blooded gangsters, played by Dan Duryea in *Criss Cross* (Universal, 1949), Slim Dundee is a dandy obsessed with the superficial, his appearance in particular, who favors extravagant clothing financed by his criminal activities. Exceedingly vain, he is prone to violent outbursts. Dundee is the boss of a local mob which carries out an armored car robbery and kills two armed guards in the process. Later, at his hideout in the country, he murders his moll and an accomplice when he discovers they are having an affair — as fate would have it, just as the

police are arriving and surrounding the hideout. Dundee, perhaps in shock from the brutal act he has just committed and knowing he must face the inevitable, quietly exits the hideout as the approaching police car sirens grow louder and louder.

Duning, George (b. 1908)

Composer. Duning's film career began in the early forties. He was employed mainly at Columbia, for whom he composed many good, if not particularly inspired, scores, including those for three gangster movies produced during the forties and fifties.

Johnny Allegro (Columbia, 1949). *The Brothers Rico* (Columbia, 1957). *Nightfall* (Columbia, 1957).

Dunlap, Paul

Composer. Dunlap was most active in the fifties, composing incidental music for a number of movies including the gangster drama *Black Tuesday*.

Black Tuesday (United Artists, 1954).

Dunne, Phillip (b. 1908)

Screenwriter. Dunne's successful film career began in the early thirties after his experience as a journalist in his native New York City. He specialized in epic adventures, although he also wrote a few comedies and romantic dramas. His single contribution to the gangster genre, *Johnny Apollo* (cowritten with Rowland Brown), is a classic.

Johnny Apollo (20th Century–Fox, 1940).

Duryea, Dan (1907–1968)

Actor. Tall, blonde, charismatic Duryea was usually typecast as a whining, sneering villain. He played gangsters in all three of his genre films, including the neglected classic *Criss Cross*, in which he stars as one of the forties' most memorable criminals.

Criss Cross (Universal, 1949). *Johnny Stool Pigeon* (Universal, 1949). *Manhandled* (Paramount, 1949).

Duvivier, Julien (1896–1967)

Director. Duvivier was one of the great directors in his native France during the thirties. He made many classics in various genres, but specialized in lush, romantic melodramas. His internationally successful *Pépé le Moko* had an influence on late thirties gangster movies throughout the world and was remade in Hollywood as *Algiers* (United Artists, 1938). The original, with its rougher style, is closer in spirit to the American gangster movies of the early thirties, and remains a classic European crime movie of the prewar era.

Pépé le Moko (Paris Films, 1937).

Dvorak, Ann (1912–1979)

Actress. Born Anna McKim into a New York City theatrical family, Dvorak entered silent films as a child. As an adult, she developed into one of the most sensual actresses of her time. Dark and exotically beautiful, she was most often seen in intelligent roles. She became a star via her performance in *Scarface*, in which she played Cesca Camonte, the sister of gangster Tony Camonte and the object of his bizarre affections. She subsequently became one of the genre's first female icons and costarred in six other gangster pictures. Her most important roles were in *G-Men*, *Dr. Socrates* and *Blind Alley*, in which she plays a moll.

Scarface (United Artists, 1932). *Three on a Match* (First National, 1932). *Heat Lightning* (Warner Bros., 1934). *Dr. Socrates* (Warner Bros., 1935). *G-Men* (First National, 1935). *Gangs of New York* (Republic, 1938). *Blind Alley* (Columbia, 1939).

Dwan, Allan (1885–1981)

Director. The extremely prolific Joseph Aloysius Dwan became a filmmaker in 1914, directing many silent shorts and features over the next fifteen years. Indeed, he remained a very active director throughout his career, averaging three films a year between

1929 and 1950, when he retired. The consummate professional director, he made movies of all types for both major and minor studios. His best is the great war picture *Sands of Iwo Jima* (Republic, 1949), an excellent example of his spare but visceral style (which many have compared to John Ford's). He directed a single gangster movie, the highly entertaining *Human Cargo*.

Human Cargo (20th Century–Fox, 1936).

Each Dawn I Die (Warner Bros., 1939). 92 mins.

Associate Producer: David Lewis. *Director*: William Keighley. *Screenplay*: Norman Reilly Raine, Warren Duff, and Charles Perry, based on the novel by Jerome Odlum. *Director of Photography*: Arthur Edeson. *Music*: Max Steiner. *Art Director*: Max Parker. *Editor*: Thomas Richards.

Cast: James Cagney (Frank Ross), George Raft ("Hood" Stacey), Jane Bryan (Joyce Conover), George Bancroft (Warden John Armstrong), Maxie Rosenbloom (Fargo Red), Stanley Ridges (Muller), Alan Baxter (Polecat Carlisle), *With*: Victor Jory, Willard Robertson, Paul Hurst, John Wray, Louis Jean Heydt, Ed Pawley.

Reporter Frank Ross discovers that the local district attorney has been concealing information about a crooked construction company. The D.A. frames Ross on a drunk driving charge and he is sentenced to prison. While behind bars, Frank befriends "Hood" Stacey, a notorious gangster. Ross plans a daring courtroom escape, but when it fails, Stacey believes Ross has squealed. Eventually Stacey discovers that he was betrayed by another associate. In the concluding riot between prisoners and prison guards, Stacey is killed, but Ross somehow manages to survive and helps bring reform to the justice system.

Arguably the greatest of all prison gangster pictures, *Each Dawn I Die* is a powerful melodrama with fiery performances by James Cagney and George Raft. The film manages to repress the seemingly inherent preaching of prison dramas in favor of action. However, it also shows the violence, paranoia, and extreme boredom of day to day existence in prison.

Eagle-Lion

Originally known as Producers Releasing Corporation, the company became known as Eagle-Lion when it was purchased by a European concern in the late forties. Its product, however, remained essentially the same: very cheap "B" movies, made quickly (usually in a matter of days) and with little merit. However, some of the studio's *films noir* of the late forties, including three excellent gangster thrillers, are very good. Of these, the best are the two rugged, uncompromisingly violent thrillers *Raw Deal* and *T-Men*, both directed by Anthony Mann.

1947: *T-Men*. 1948: *Raw Deal*. 1949: *Trapped*.

The Earl of Chicago (MGM, 1940). 85 mins.

Producer: Victor Saville. *Director*: Richard Thorpe. *Screenplay*: Lesser Samuels, *story by* Brock Williams, Charles de Grancourt, and Gene Fowler. *Director of Photography*: Ray June. *Music*: Werner R. Heymann. *Art Director*: Cedric Gibbons. *Editor*: Fred Sullivan.

Cast: Robert Montgomery (Silky Kilmount), Edward Arnold (Don Ramsey), Edmund Gwenn (Muncie), Reginald Owen (Gervase Gonwell), E. E. Clive (Redwood). *With*: Frederic Worlock, Miles Mander, William Stack, Norma Varden, Kenneth Hunter.

Silky Kilmount, an American gangster, discovers he is descended from British nobility. He journeys to England to collect an inheritance, but discovers he likes the quiet British way of life. Eventually, he falls back into his criminal way of life, kills a man, and is sentenced to a long term in

British prison. With its ludicrous plot, the "B" *Earl of Chicago* is a campy, entertaining gangster movie that came toward the end of the initial cycle. It is decidedly minor, but Robert Montgomery as the dapper gangster manages to pull off the part without looking ridiculous.

Earle, Roy (Fictional character)

The doomed gangster character in *High Sierra* (Warner Bros., 1941) helped make Humphrey Bogart a full fledged star. Earle is typical of the thirties gangster, and one of the earliest examples of the *noir* antihero. Caught in circumstances beyond his control, Earle hurls toward his inevitable doom with cynical resignation. Allegedly based on real life gangster John Dillinger, Earle was one of the few movie villains of the era to achieve audience empathy, due to Bogart's sensitive portrayal.

Eastwood, Clint (b. 1930)

Actor. Eastwood is one of the few contemporary stars who can be favorably compared to stars of the past. He is a bona fide superstar whose name alone can ensure box office success. Generally specializing in heroes (however flawed), he has also played the occasional unsympathetic role. He has made two appearances in the genre. In the cult favorite *Thunderbolt and Lightfoot*, he is one of the two luckless bank robbers. Less interesting is *City Heat*, although Eastwood's performance in this failed attempt at a modern gangster movie is compelling.

Thunderbolt and Lightfoot (United Artists, 1974). *City Heat* (Warner Bros., 1983).

Edeson, Arthur (1891–1970)

Cinematographer. Edeson is one of the great American cinematographers, having photographed a number of classics including *All Quiet on the Western Front* (Universal, 1930), *Frankenstein* (Universal, 1931), *The*

Invisible Man (Universal, 1933), and *Casablanca* (Warner Bros., 1942). His style can be described as a kind of modified expressionism. His work on six gangster movies is never less than exemplary regardless of the overall quality of the movies.

Me, Gangster (Fox, 1928). *The Last Mile* (World Wide, 1932). *Racket Busters* (Warner Bros., 1938). *Each Dawn I Die* (Warner Bros., 1939). *Castle on the Hudson* (Warner Bros., 1940). *The Maltese Falcon* (Warner Bros., 1941).

Egan, Richard (1921–1987)

Actor. Tall, rugged, and virile, Egan was once touted as a likely successor to Clark Gable. He never achieved that degree of stardom, of course, but he gave some memorable performances in his three decades in the movies. Unfortunately, his part in *Violent Saturday*, his only gangster film, was not well written and did not give him much to do.

Violent Saturday (20th Century-Fox, 1955).

Elam, Jack (b. 1916)

Character actor. Laconic, swarthy, and lean, Elam was one of the most familiar faces in American movies for over three decades, beginning in 1950. Often playing comic roles, Elam, who has a prosthetic right eye, has also played menacing villains. In Phil Karlson's great "B" gangster movie *Kansas City Confidential*, Elam played a vicious gangster who participates in a doomed heist.

Kansas City Confidential (United Artists, 1952).

Emerson, Faye (1917–1983)

Actress. Born in Elizabeth, Louisiana, the cool, ethereal, and beautiful Faye Emerson enjoyed considerable popularity in the thirties and forties. She almost always played socialites, but was effectively cast against type in *Lady Gangster* as a small town girl who

moves to the big city and becomes involved with gangsters.
Lady Gangster (Warner Bros., 1942).

The Enforcer (Warner Bros., 1951). 87 mins.
Producer: Milton Sperling. *Director*: Bretaigne Windust (uncredited, Raoul Walsh). *Screenplay*: Martin Rackin. *Director of Photography*: Robert Burks. *Music*: David Buttolph. *Art Director*: Charles H. Clarke. *Editor*: Fred Allen.
Cast: Humphrey Bogart (Martin Ferguson), Zero Mostel (Big Babe Lazich), Ted De Corsia (Albert Mendoza), Everett Sloane (Ivan Mendoza), Roy Roberts (Captain Frank Nelson). *With*: Lawrence Tolan, King Donovan, Bob Steele, Adelaide Klein, Don Beddoe, Tito Vuolo, John Kellogg.
Martin Ferguson, a district attorney, is determined to send the head of Murder, Inc., the group of mob assassins, to prison. Albert Mendoza, the leader of the gangsters, awaits trial for murder, but the main witness against him is "accidentally" killed. However, one of the other assassins testifies against Mendoza. Ferguson, protecting another witness, guns down her would-be assassin. The girl also testifies, and Mendoza is convicted and sentenced to death, thus bringing down the criminal organization.
Told in semi-documentary fashion, *The Enforcer* was loosely based on the notorious and all too real Murder, Inc. In one of his last gangster movies, Humphrey Bogart, for a nice change of pace, plays a man on the right side of the law. If not quite a classic, *The Enforcer* almost qualifies, remaining one of the better minor entries in the genre.

Enright, Ray (1896–1965)
Director. For almost all of his three decade career, beginning in the late twenties, Enright was a contract director for Warner Bros. He specialized in high quality "B" action pictures, but he also directed the classic musical *Dames* (Warner Bros., 1934). It remains his best known work, although many of his movies have much to recommend them. He also directed *Skin Deep*, one of Warner Bros.' earliest gangster movies.
Skin Deep (Warner Bros., 1929).

Essex, Harry (b. 1910)
Screenwriter. Essex cowrote many superior "B" movies beginning in the forties. Among these are the *films noir He Walked by Night* (Eagle-Lion, 1948) and *The Killer That Stalked New York* (Eagle-Lion, 1950), and the sci-fi classic *It Came from Outer Space* (Universal, 1953). He also cowrote Phil Karlson's *Kansas City Confidential*, one of the best "B" gangster movies of the fifties.
Kansas City Confidential (United Artists, 1952).

Every Little Crook and Nanny (MGM, 1972). 95 mins.
Producer: Leonard J. Ackerman. *Director*: Cy Howard. *Screenplay*: Cy Howard, Jonathan Axelrod and Robert Klane, based on the novel by Ed McBain. *Director of Photography*: Philip Lathrop. *Music*: Fred Karlin. *Art Director*: Philip Jefferies. *Editor*: Henry Berman.
Cast: Lynn Redgrave (Nanny/Miss Poole), Victor Mature (Carmine), Paul Sand (Benny), Maggie Blye (Stella), Austin Pendleton (Luther). *With*: Dom DeLuise, Louise Sorel, Philip Graves, Lou Cutell, Leopold Trieste.
Carmine, an underworld leader, becomes a soft drink manufacturer. When he and his wife go to Europe for a vacation, they leave their young son in the care of a proper English nanny. However, the boy is kidnapped and a ransom is demanded. The nanny, Miss Poole, fearful of what Carmine might do to her once he learns of his son's kidnapping, enlists the help of two bungling hoodlums to help rescue the little boy. After many complications, the

boy is rescued just in time, as his parents return from their vacation.

Only mildly amusing, this gangster satire is notable mainly for *noir* icon Victor Mature's last appearance in the genre. He gives a surprisingly adept comic performance as the mob boss who has gone straight.

Eyes of the Underworld (Universal, 1942). 61 mins.

Associate Producer: Ben Pivar. *Director*: Roy William Neill. *Screenplay*: Michael L. Simmons and Arthur Stawn, *story by* Maxwell Shane. *Director of Photography*: George Robinson. *Editor*: Frank Gross.

Cast: Richard Dix (Police Chief Richard Bryant), Wendy Barrie (Betty Standing), Lon Chaney (Benny), Lloyd Corrigan (J. C. Thomas), Edward Pauley (Lance Merlin), Don Porter (Edward Jason). *With*: Billy Lee, Marc Lawrence, Joseph Crehan, Wade Boteler, Steve Pendleton.

When automobiles and tires are stolen due to wartime rations, local police chief Richard Bryant orders his lieutenant to put a stop to the crimes. However, the lieutenant is actually one of the members of the gang led by Lance Merlin. An undercover G-man, Edward Jason, has infiltrated the gang, and with his help, the gangsters are tracked down and arrested.

A "B" gangster movie, *Eyes of the Underworld* is notable chiefly for its timely plot device: cars and rubber tires were a precious commodity because of wartime rations, and indeed the subject of some underworld activity.

Face Behind the Mask (Columbia, 1941). 69 mins.

Producer: Wallace McDonald. *Director*: Robert Florey. *Screenplay*: Allen Vincent and Paul Jarrico, based on the radio play by Thomas Edward O'Connell. *Director of Photography*: Franz A. Planer. *Music Director*: Morris W. Stoloff. *Editor*: Charles Nelson.

Cast: Peter Lorre (Janos Szaby), Evelyn Keyes (Helen Williams), Don Beddoe (Jim O'Hara), George E. Stone (Dinky), John Tyrrell (Watts). *With*: Stanley Brown, Al Seymour, James Seay, Warren Ashe, Charles Wilson, George McKay.

A Hungarian immigrant, Janos Szaby, is horribly burned in a tenement fire. Plastic surgery fails to restore his face, but a kindly doctor makes him a lifelike mask. Bitter and unable to find work, Janos drifts into a life of crime and eventually becomes the head of a local gang. He falls in love with a blind girl, Helen Williams, who perceives his good nature. But his fellow gangsters believe that their leader's girlfriend has betrayed them to the police, and they murder her. Szaby gets revenge by killing the members of his gang one by one, eventually being killed himself in a climactic shoot out.

An uneasy mix of the horror and gangster genres, *Face Behind the Mask* manages nevertheless to be one of the most interesting "B" movies of the early forties. Director Robert Florey was at his best with this sort of grim material. He created an almost surreal atmosphere out of dramatic lighting and extravagant camera work. However, the film really belongs to Peter Lorre, whose compassionate performance is one of his best.

Fairbanks, Douglas, Jr. (b. 1909)

Actor. The conventionally debonair and handsome leading man, Fairbanks was an attractive, popular star in the thirties. Like his father, he often starred in swashbucklers, but he was perhaps more at home in drawing-room comedies. He received second billing behind Edward G. Robinson in the gangster classic *Little Caesar*, in which he played a dancer who fronts for a gang led by his friend Cesare Bandello (Robinson). It is his only appearance in a gangster movie.

Little Caesar (First National, 1930).

Farrell, Charles (b. 1901)

Actor. After stage experience, Farrell entered movies in the early twenties and quickly became a major star of the late silent era. He managed to survive the transition to sound, and remained popular until the mid-thirties when he began to play leads in "B" movies and character roles in "A" productions. He starred in the minor gangster movie *The Big Shakedown* just as his career was on the descent, while costar Bette Davis' career was on the rise. His talents, however, were ill suited to the genre.

The Big Shakedown (First National, 1934).

Farrell, Glenda (1904–1971)

Actress. The Oklahoma born Farrell was a popular star of the thirties. Contracted to Warner Bros., she acted in many of their top productions. In *Little Caesar* she was the romantic interest in this otherwise male dominated gangster classic.

Little Caesar (First National, 1931).

Farrow, John (1904–1963)

Director. John Farrow is one of cinema's more neglected figures. A great visual stylist, he created some of forties' best *films noir*: *The Big Clock* (Paramount, 1948), *The Night Has a Thousand Eyes* (Paramount, 1948), and *Where Danger Lives* (RKO, 1950). *His Kind of Woman*, a *noir* with gangster themes, is a neglected classic with superior performances by Robert Mitchum, Jane Russell, and Raymond Burr.

His Kind of Woman (RKO, 1951).

The F.B.I. and G-men

Established in 1924 by executive turned law enforcement officer J. Edgar Hoover (1895–1972), the Federal Bureau of Investigation was set up initially to help enforce Prohibition. Despite some highly questionable techniques including beating, torture and various other illegal activities, the Bureau was quickly established as an heroic American police force. Although almost completely ineffective in preventing crime, the force was somewhat more successful in creating and improving investigative techniques. Under the dictatorial Hoover, the Bureau was widely promoted for its "all American" values, particularly in the press (while Hoover led a double life as a transvestite and homosexual). In the mid-thirties, after years of popular gangster movies featuring criminals as protagonists, Hoover pressured Hollywood into making new films with G-men (as F.B.I. agents were commonly called) as heroes. Thus, James Cagney portrayed a gang-busting F.B.I. agent in *G-Men* (First National, 1935), an immensely popular entertainment that helped promote the image of the F.B.I. in the thirties and forties, and indeed, to the present. The enormous success of this film inspired a number of others featuring F.B.I. agents battling gangsters: *Special Agent* (Warner Bros., 1935), *The Tip-Off Girls* (Paramount, 1938), *When G-Men Step In* (Columbia, 1938), the serial *Gang Busters* (Universal, 1942), and *The Undercover Man* (Columbia, 1942). The propagandistic *The F.B.I.* (Warner Bros., 1959) gave some insight into the Bureau's war against real gangsters of the thirties. Meanwhile, on television, the exploits of real life F.B.I. agent Eliot Ness inspired a series, *The Untouchables* (1959–1962), based on his attempts to close down Al Capone's operations in Chicago. The series' pilot episode was released in Europe as *The Scarface Mob* (Cari Releasing, 1962). Other G-men also occasionally appeared on screen. In *C-Man* (Film Classics, 1949) the main character is a customs investigator, while in *T-Men* (Eagle-Lion, 1947) and the contemporary *To Live and Die in L.A.* (United Artists, 1986), the undercover agents work for the Treasury Department.

The F.B.I. Story (Warner Bros., 1959). 149 mins.
Producer and Director: Mervyn LeRoy. *Screenplay*: Richard L. Breen and John Twist, based on the book by Don Whitehead. *Director of Photography*: Joseph Biroc. *Music*: Max Steiner. *Art Director*: John Beckman. *Editor*: Philip W. Anderson.
Cast: James Stewart (Chip Hardesty), Vera Miles (Lucy Hardesty), Murray Hamilton (Sam Crandall), Larry Pennell (George Crandall), Nick Adams (Jack Graham), Diane Jergens (Jennie). *With*: Jean Willes, Joyce Taylor, Victor Millan, Parley Baer, Fay Roope, Ed Prentiss.

The professional and private life of would-be lawyer turned F.B.I. agent Chip Hardesty is followed from the time he joins the Bureau to his retirement.

Really nothing more than propaganda supporting J. Edgar Hoover (who oversaw the film's production) and the agency he ran with an iron fist, *The F.B.I. Story* is interesting mainly for its insights into the criminal underworld of the twenties and thirties. The real life exploits of bootleggers and rural criminals Baby Face Nelson and John Dillinger are recounted. However, the film's too cautious approach and self-aggrandizing celebration of the Federal Bureau of Investigation hamper its impact and overall enjoyment.

Feathers (Fictional character)
Evelyn Brent's prototypical moll in *Underworld* (Paramount, 1927), cool and elegantly beautiful, is a kind of human trophy for her unsophisticated gangster lover, Bull Weed (George Bancroft). She in turn is attracted to his power and is willing to put up with his abuse because of the status and monetary compensation that her relationship with him provides.

Fegte, Ernest (1900–1976)
Art director. The German born

Fegte was a leading art director in German cinema before moving to Hollywood in 1933, the year Adolf Hitler became chancellor. He worked for RKO, Republic, United Artists, and Sam Goldwyn, but his best work was for Paramount. In collaboration with Hans Dreier, he worked on many classics, including three gangster movies, in the thirties and forties.
You and Me (Paramount, 1938).
Queen of the Mob (Paramount, 1940).
Lucky Jordan (Paramount, 1942).

Femme fatale
This was a new type of female character introduced in the *film noir* crime pictures of the forties — the fatal woman who is just as immoral, greedy and murderous as her villainous male counterparts. Such women in *film noir* were no longer the victims of men, but the victimizers. *Film noir*, of course, is a genre unto itself which generally ignored the subject of conventional mobsters and crime, but there were a few notable exceptions in which the *femme fatale* was a central character. In *Out of the Past* (RKO, 1947), Kathie Moffatt (Jane Greer), both a moll and a *femme fatale*, brings about her own and several men's demises through her own greed. In *The Killing* (United Artists, 1956), Sherry Peatly (Marie Windsor) helps bring about the downfall of a makeshift gang after a heist. And in *The Gangster* (Allied Artists, 1947), Nancy Starr (Belita) betrays her mob boss lover to the police, resulting in his downfall.

Fenton, Frank (1916–1987)
Screenwriter. Briefly active in the late forties and early fifties, Fenton worked exclusively for RKO. He was an uncredited cowriter of *Out of the Past* (RKO, 1947), and also wrote John Farrow's neglected classic *His Kind of Woman*, one of the fifties' best gangster movies.
His Kind of Woman (RKO, 1951).

Fenton, Leslie (1902–1978)

Character actor. The British born Fenton moved to Hollywood in the early thirties and acted in many movies over the next decade, generally as an uppercrust type. He played small supporting roles in James Cagney's starring vehicles *Public Enemy* and *Lady Killer*. In the late thirties he retired from acting and became a leading director of "B" movies.

Public Enemy (Warner Bros., 1931). *Lady Killer* (Warner Bros., 1933).

Ferraro, Nick (Fictional character)

Before *Perry Mason*, Raymond Burr played a whole host of villains in more than a dozen movies, perhaps most famously as the white-haired murderer in Alfred Hitchcock's *Rear Window* (Paramount, 1953). One of his best such performances, however, is in *His Kind of Woman* (RKO, 1951) as mob boss Nick Ferraro. Ferraro is a man without a country—he has been kicked out of the United States—but with a plan: anchored off the coast of Mexico on his luxurious yacht, Ferraro plans to kill a small-time American adventurer, Dan Milner (Robert Mitchum), assume his identity and reenter the United States to take over his gang, the leadership of which has been usurped by a rival. But his elaborate scheme goes awry through the intervention of a motley crew of heroes including a vain actor on a Mexican holiday (Vincent Price in one of his best performances). Burr is both menacing and witty as the psychotic Ferraro.

Film noir

A rather nebulous term referring principally to a group of American crime thrillers made between 1944 and 1956. Influenced by German expressionist cinema, hard-boiled literature (via Raymond Chandler, Dashiell Hammett, and James M. Cain) and, to a lesser degree, the gangster movies of the thirties, the cycle is distinguished by its cynicism, antiheroes, the *femme fatale* and often an extravagant style. Sometimes mislabeled as mere style, *film noir* is a true genre with its own set of themes and preoccupations. The shadowy style so identified with the cycle is evident only in the early films. Later it evolved into a less extravagant, documentary-like style, and the use of black and white photography (a lucky coincidence in an era when nearly all films were made in black and white) was also brilliantly translated into a handful of color films. The genre concentrated mainly on petty thieves and crimes of passion, but gangsters made important appearances, perhaps most notably in *Out of the Past* (RKO, 1947). Indeed, this movie features an intriguing combination of *noir* characters, including a private detective antihero (Robert Mitchum) and an old style gangster (Kirk Douglas). *The Gangster* (Allied Artists, 1947) is an equally brilliant "B" gangster *noir* distinguished from its thirties predecessors by its cynicism and unique view point. The genre is also important for introducing the heist drama as an important subgenre most distinguished by *The Asphalt Jungle* (MGM, 1950).

Other important *films noir* with gangsters as central characters include *The Big Heat* (Columbia, 1953), *The Big Steal* (RKO, 1949), *The Bribe* (MGM, 1949), *Forbidden* (Universal, 1953), *The Hoodlum* (United Artists, 1951), *Kansas City Confidential* (1952), *The Narrow Margin* (RKO, 1952), *Odds Against Tomorrow* (United Artists, 1959), *The Set-Up* (RKO, 1949), *The Big Combo* (Allied Artists, 1955), *Body and Soul* (United Artists, 1947), *Brute Force* (Universal, 1947), *His Kind of Woman* (RKO, 1951), *Kiss of Death* (20th Century–Fox, 1947), *The Phenix City Story* (Allied Artists, 1955), *Raw Deal* (Eagle-Lion, 1948), *They Live by Night* (RKO, 1948), *The Undercover Man* (Columbia, 1949), and *White Heat* (Warner Bros., 1949).

The Finger Points (First National, 1931). 88 mins.

Director: John Francis Dillon. *Screenplay*: Robert Lord, *dialog by* John Monk Saunders, *story by* John Monk Saunders and W. R. Burnett. *Director of Photography*: Ernest Haller. *Editor*: Leroy Stone.

Cast: Richard Barthelmess (Breckenridge Lee), Fay Wray (Marcia Collins), Regis Toomey (Breezy Russell), Clark Gable (Louis Blanco), Richard Elliott (City Editor). *With*: Oscar Apfel, Robert Glecker, Mickey Bennett, Herman Krumpfel, J. Carrol Naish.

Breckenridge Lee, a small town boy who has come to the big city to find his fame and fortune, goes to work for a newspaper as a reporter. However, he soon discovers he can make more money taking bribes from gangsters who want their activities kept quiet. His fellow reporter, Marcia Collins, has fallen in love with him, and when she discovers his association with the mob, she tries to encourage him to get out. But he is too deeply immersed, and when a story about a murder by the mob leader, Louis Blanco, is accidentally printed, Blanco has the young reporter killed.

The Finger Points came early in the developing gangster cycle and is surprisingly devoid of the clichés of some of the other early genre movies. Disarmingly cynical, it is not quite a classic, but is nevertheless an important early gangster movie, perhaps best remembered for providing Clark Gable with one of his few unsympathetic roles.

First National

Founded in 1917, First National was a prominent production and distribution studio until 1929, responsible for many popular films by stars like Charlie Chaplin, Mary Pickford and Richard Barthelmess. However, it could never quite make the big time, and in 1929 was purchased by Warner Bros. In fact, Warner Bros. moved to First National's lot over the course of the early thirties. Until 1936, First National continued to exist in name only, and a number of Warner's pictures were released under that banner. Generally, the First National titles were even grittier and more violent than the Warner Bros. films. Several of the gangster genre's classic films were released as First National pictures including *Little Caesar*, the film which kicked off the initial cycle in the thirties.

1929: *Dark Streets*. 1931: *The Finger Points, Little Caesar*. 1932: *Three on a Match*. 1933: *The Little Giant, 20,000 Years in Sing-Sing*. 1934: *The Big Shakedown, Fog Over Frisco*. 1935: *G-Men*. 1936: *Bullets or Ballots*.

Fishbeck, Harry (1896–1984)

Cinematographer. Fishbeck's career began in the late teens. Almost exclusively associated with "B" movies, his style was rather flat and conventional. He photographed two minor gangster movies.

Ladies Love Brutes (Paramount, 1930). *Stolen Harmony* (Paramount, 1935).

Fisher, Steve

Screenwriter. With Sydney Boehm, Oliver H. P. Garrett, William McGivern, Crane Wilbur, and Philip Yordan, Steve Fisher was one of the most important hard-boiled screenwriters of the forties and fifties. Originally a mystery novelist, his popular *I Wake Up Screaming* became one of the earliest true *films noir* when adapted for the screen in 1941. On the basis of this success, Fisher was hired to work for several studios, and over the course of the next decade, he wrote or cowrote a number of important crime thrillers including *Lady in the Lake* (MGM, 1947) and *Johnny Angel* (RKO, 1945). He wrote three gangster movies including the classic Bogart film *Dead Reckoning*.

Dead Reckoning (Columbia, 1947). *Las Vegas Shakedown* (Allied Artists, 1955). *I, Mobster* (20th Century–Fox, 1959).

Fitzgerald, Edward (1899–1968)
Cinematographer. Fitzgerald worked mainly in "B" movies. His style is unimaginative, but his work on *New York Confidential* shows a *noir* influence.
New York Confidential (Warner Bros., 1955).

Fitzpatrick, Captain Jim (Fictional character)
Fitzpatrick, played by Walter Huston in *Beast of the City* (MGM, 1932), was one of the earliest examples of the self-righteous cop who obeys only his own laws to bring criminals to justice. When he makes headlines by capturing two holdup men, Jim Fitzpatrick, one of the only honest policemen on his force, is appointed the head of the police department by a reform commission. He sets out to crush the organization of mob boss Sam Belmonte (Jean Hersholt), but only succeeds in angering the violent gangster and the city officials on his payroll. Fitzpatrick's situation is further complicated by the fact that his younger brother Ed (Wallace Ford) is also a member of Belmonte's gang. Fitzpatrick, however, is determined to bring Belmonte to justice and stops at nothing to do so. Eventually, he leads a group of honest cops to Belmonte's headquarters, where, in the climactic battle, nearly all of them are killed, as well as most of Belmonte's gang, including the leader, Daisy, Ed's girlfriend who is also a member of the gang, and Ed himself, who has sided with his brother to bring the gangster to justice.

Captain Jim Fitzpatrick became the model for many similar characters in years to come, most notably Sergeant Dave Bannion in *The Big Heat* (Columbia, 1953) and Lieutenant Harry Callahan in the non-gangster thriller *Dirty Harry* (Warner Bros., 1971).

Fleisher, Richard (b. 1916)
Director. The son of the great animator Max Fleisher, Richard Fleisher is an under-appreciated talent whose four-decade career began in 1947. His best works are his early "B" movies which include the classic gangster *noir* *The Narrow Margin*, probably his finest movie.
Trapped (Eagle-Lion, 1949). *The Narrow Margin* (RKO, 1951). *Mr. Majestyk* (United Artists, 1974).

Flippen, J. C. (1898–1971)
Character actor. A native of Little Rock, Arkansas, Flippen was one of the busiest character actors in American movies. His career began in the early thirties and he remained active right up to his death. Large and rather menacing, Flippen almost always played mob henchmen in his gangster movies.
They Live by Night (RKO, 1948). *The Wild One* (Columbia, 1954). *Six Bridges to Cross* (Universal, 1955).

Florey, Robert (1900–1979)
Director. Florey has been called "the French expressionist," and indeed his visual style is close to that of William Dieterle and Robert Siodmak. His career began in Paris, where he worked his way up to editorial assistant and assistant producer and director. He moved to Hollywood in 1921 and immediately began directing. Successful, he returned to France in the early thirties for a few years (where he directed several important movies) before permanently settling in the United States. He is probably best known as the director of the Marx Brothers' first movie, *The Coconuts* (Paramount, 1929), and two classic horror films, *Murders in the Rue Morgue* (Universal, 1932) and *The Beast with Five Fingers* (Warner Bros., 1946). However, most of his career was devoted to "B" movies, few of which are of any merit except for Florey's extravagant visuals. Among these are a number of gangster movies and, indeed, Florey might have been the most active director in the genre. His best gangster effort is *Dangerous to Know*,

a superior "B" movie. *Face Behind the Mask* is also excellent, with a good performance by Peter Lorre.

King of Gamblers (Paramount, 1937). *Dangerous to Know* (Paramount, 1938). *King of Alcatraz* (Paramount, 1938). *Disbarred* (Paramount, 1939). *Face Behind the Mask* (Columbia, 1941). *Lady Gangster* (Warner Bros., 1942). *Roger Touhy, Gangster* (20th Century-Fox, 1944).

Foch, Nina (b. 1924)

Actress. The cool, blonde Nina Foch was one of the most sensual and attractive personalities of the forties and fifties. Born Nina Fock in Leyden, Holland, and raised in the United States, Foch starred in several good films, but never quite achieved first rank stardom. Nevertheless, her performances were always compelling, particularly in seductive roles, as in *Johnny Allegro*. Probably her best role in the genre, however, is in *Illegal* as the wife of a gangster who kills her husband in self defense.

Johnny Allegro (Columbia, 1949). *The Undercover Man* (Columbia, 1949). *Illegal* (Warner Bros., 1955).

Fog Over Frisco (First National, 1934). 68 mins.

Producer: Robert Lord. *Director*: William Dieterle. *Screenplay*: Robert N. Lee and Eugene Solow, *story by* George Dyer. *Director of Photography*: Tony Gaudio. *Editor*: Hal McLernon.

Cast: Bette Davis (Arlene Bradford), Donald Woods (Tony Stirling), Margaret Lindsay (Valkyr Bradford), Lyle Talbot (Spencer Carleton), Arthur Byron (Everett Bradford), Hugh Herbert (Izzy Wright). *With*: Irving Pichel, Gordon Wescott, Henry O'Neill, William B. Davidson, Alan Hale.

Valkyr Bradford discovers her stepsister, Arlene, is cavorting in the underworld. Meanwhile, Arlene's father, Arthur, believes that she has persuaded her fiancé, Spencer Carleton, to sell stolen securities. Everett Bradford convinces his daughter, who is under the influence of the local mob boss, to go straight. But when Arlene testifies against a mobster, Valkyr is kidnapped. The gang demands that valuable evidence be turned over in exchange for her return. However, they are traced to their waterfront hideout and, in a gun battle, Valkyr is rescued. The mastermind of the gang is then unmasked and arrested.

Bette Davis' career was just beginning when she starred in this "B" gangster drama. Despite its unambitious origins as a double-bill feature, it is in fact very well made with a good script and superior direction by William Dieterle. However, it is Davis' performance which really saves this film from being just another run of the mill programmer.

Fonda, Henry (1905–1982)

Actor. Beginning in 1935, Henry Fonda was cinema's perennial American boy-next-door for over three decades. Whatever the genre, Fonda almost always played the honest, hard working good-guy who achieves success. In Fritz Lang's *You Only Live Once*, he played a variation on the type as a basically honest man who falls into a life of crime that ultimately leads to his demise. It is one of Fonda's best early performances.

You Only Live Once (United Artists, 1937).

Forbidden (Universal, 1953). 84 mins.

Producer: Ted Richmond. *Director*: Rudolph Maté. *Screenplay*: William Sackheim and Gil Doud. *Director of Photography*: William Daniels. *Music*: Frank Skinner. *Art Directors*: Bernard Herzbrun and Richard Riedel. *Editor*: Edward Curtiss.

Cast: Tony Curtis (Eddie Darrow), Joanne Dru (Christine), Lyle Bettiger (Justin Keit), Marvin Miller (Chalmer), Victor Sen Yung (Allan), Peter J. Mamakos (Sam), Mae Tai Sing (Soo Lee). *With*: Howard Chuman, Weaver

Levy, Harold Fong, David Sharpe, Aen Ling Chow, Alan Dexter.

Eddie Darrow, a mob underling, is sent to Macao to retrieve Christine, the beautiful widow of a racketeer, together with the incriminating evidence she carries with her. In the process, and after much antagonism between the two, Darrow and Christine eventually fall in love and manage to escape, eliminating the assassins sent to kill them.

Forbidden is a minor gangster *noir* that promises great things but never manages to rise above its predictable script or "B" production values. As a routine thriller, however, it is enjoyable.

Ford, John (1895–1973)

Director. Arguably cinema's greatest filmmaker, John Ford was at his best when directing roving, brawling, sprawling outdoor epics tinged with a bit of romantic sentimentalism. He directed a single gangster movie, *The Whole Town's Talking*, a great satire of the genre which features one of Edward G. Robinson's best performances.

The Whole Town's Talking (Columbia, 1935).

Ford, Philip (1900–1976)

Director. John Ford's nephew Philip spent his entire career, which began in 1945 and ended in 1952, as a house director at Republic pictures. Extremely talented, he has been ignored by most critics because his filmography mainly consists of "B" westerns. Nevertheless, he made films in several genres, including two gangster movies, both of which are quite good.

The Last Crooked Mile (Republic, 1946). *Hideout* (Republic, 1949).

Ford, Wallace (1897–1966)

Character actor. Born Sam Grundy in London, England, Ford had brief success on the British stage and in films before moving to Hollywood in the early thirties. He subsequently appeared

in dozens of movies, playing everything from butlers and businessmen to well dressed criminals.

T-Men (Eagle-Lion, 1947).

Forde, Eugene (1898–1987)

Director. Born in Providence, Rhode Island, Forde was a child actor who appeared in plays with Blanche Sweet, William S. Hart and Mary Pickford. In his teens, he played juvenile leads in silent shorts, but soon began directing. He developed into a competent, if not particularly inventive, director of mostly "B" movies for 20th Century-Fox. He directed a single, minor gangster picture for Fox.

Midnight Taxi (20th Century–Fox, 1937).

Forrest, Steve (b. 1924)

Actor. Born in Huntsville, Texas, Forrest had radio and television experience before entering movies in the early fifties. Born William Forrest Andrews, he is the younger brother of Dana Andrews. Although he is a competent actor who has appeared in a few good movies, he never achieved the first rank, playing tough heroes in mostly "B" movies and television shows.

Rogue Cop (MGM, 1954).

Forte, Fabian (b. 1942)

Singer and actor. As a pop star in the early sixties, Fabian was a momentary heartthrob for teenage girls. He also acted in a few films, one of the best being the low budget *A Bullet for Pretty Boy*, in which he played real life gangster Pretty Boy Floyd.

A Bullet for Pretty Boy (American International, 1970).

Foster, Dianne (b. 1928)

Actress. Born Dianne Laruska in Canada, Foster was briefly popular in the fifties. She appeared in mostly "B" productions, including the excellent *The Brothers Rico*, in which she played the wife of a reformed mobster who is pulled back into the organization.

Although her role was perfunctory, her performance is quite good.
The Brothers Rico (Columbia, 1957).

Foster, Lewis (1900–1974)
Director and screenwriter. Foster started out with Hal Roach as a writer and occasional director of comedy shorts. He had his greatest success as a screenwriter, collaborating on many classic films, including Frank Capra's *Mr. Smith Goes to Washington* (Columbia, 1939). He also worked occasionally as an associate producer for his friend, director George Stevens. Foster's varied career also included a stint as writer and director of unpretentious but generally very well made commercial productions. He made two gangster movies. *Manhandled* is a rather conventional *noir* thriller, but *Crashout* is a superior prison escape drama, certainly one of the best "B" movies of the fifties.
Manhandled (Paramount, 1949).
Crashout (Filmakers, 1955).

Foster, Preston (1901–1970)
Actor. In the thirties, the tall, imposing, square-jawed Preston Foster was the leading star of action films. He almost always played heroes, but occasionally accepted villainous roles. He costarred in four minor gangster movies, including two prison dramas, *Up the River* and *The Last Mile*. In the latter he played one of his few villains, a murderer sentenced to death row.
The Last Mile (World Wide, 1932).
Heat Lightning (Warner Bros., 1934).
Up the River (20th Century–Fox, 1938). *Roger Touhy, Gangster* (20th Century–Fox, 1944).

Four Walls (MGM, 1928). Approximately 90 mins.
Director: William Nigh. *Screenplay*: Joe Farnham and Alice Miller, based on the play by George Abbott and Dand Burnett. *Director of Photography*: James Wong Howe. *Editor*: Harry Reynolds.

Cast: John Gilbert (Benny), Joan Crawford (Frieda), Vera Gordon (Mrs. Horowitz), Carmel Myers (Bertha), Robert Emmett O'Connor (Sullivan), Louis Natheaux (Monk), Jack Byron (Duke).

Gang boss Benny, convicted of murdering a rival, is sent to prison. While behind bars he decides to go straight. His gang is taken over by a rival who also moves in on Benny's old moll, Frieda. After he is released from prison, Benny avoids his old gang until he is forced into action during a bar brawl. He takes command of the gang, defeats his rival, and escapes with Frieda. His pursuer falls to his death during the chase, and Benny returns to his old ways.

Released during the late silent era, *Four Walls* was a rather silly gangster movie saved by the considerable charisma of stars John Gilbert (then at the height of his popularity) and Joan Crawford.

Foy, Bryan (1895–1977)
Producer. As one of vaudevillian Eddie Foy's "Seven Little Foys," Bryan Foy was the eldest of the sons who found fame on American stages in the early years of this century. As an adult, Foy first found success as a songwriter before becoming a director in the late twenties. He was reasonably successful as a director, but he had his greatest success as a producer for Warner Bros. Indeed, Foy supervised all of their "B" productions from the mid-thirties to the early fifties, often personally producing as many as ten or more features a year. In his own way, Foy was a major influence on Warner Bros.' hardboiled style that emerged in the thirties and reached its artistic heights in the forties with *Casablanca* (Warner Bros., 1942) and several classic *films noir*. Foy produced a handful of gangster movies, all very well made "B" productions.
Hell's Kitchen (Warner Bros., 1939). *King of the Underworld* (Warner Bros., 1939). *Highway 301* (Warner

Bros., 1950). *Crime Wave* (Warner Bros., 1953).

Francey (Fictional character)

Claire Trevor's small supporting role in *Dead End* (United Artists, 1937) is also one of her best. Francey is a beautiful young woman who has been beaten down by her life in the slums and the lack of opportunities during the Great Depression. She has become a prostitute, a symbol of the compromises one must make to survive in poverty. Her meeting with her childhood boyfriend, Joe Martin, now a notorious gangster known as "Baby Face," becomes a catalyst for the mobster's demise at the hands of another slum resident, one who refuses to compromise his morals in order to escape his poverty.

Franciosa, Anthony (b. 1928)

Actor. Born Anthony Papelo in New York, Franciosa first attracted attention as a stage actor before making his film debut in the mid-fifties. He has often been typecast as a hot-blooded Italian, and in *Across 110th Street*, he played a Mafia don.

Across 110th Street (United Artists, 1972).

Francis, Anne (b. 1930)

Actress. The beautiful, blonde Anne Francis was a child model and radio personality before she became an actress. Tall and voluptuous, she was a very competent actress, although she never made the big time, perhaps because of "competition" Marilyn Monroe's domination of good female starring roles during the fifties. A popular star of "B" movies, Francis played her most famous role in *Forbidden Planet* (MGM, 1956). She had a supporting role in *Rogue Cop*, a superior "B" gangster thriller.

Rogue Cop (MGM, 1954).

Francis, Kay (1899–1968)

Actress. Born Katherine Gibbs in Oklahoma, the cool, dark-haired beauty Kay Francis was one of the thirties' biggest female stars. She was at her best in romantic melodramas, suffering at the hands of cads, but she also demonstrated a comedic side in Ernst Lubitsch's classic *Trouble in Paradise* (Paramount, 1932). Her sophisticated image was not well suited to the hard-boiled world of the gangster genre, but she costarred in two minor gangster movies. In *Street of Chance*, she played the wife of a gambler mixed up with the New York underworld. In the "B" drama *King of the Underworld*, she starred as a physician seeking revenge against a gangster played by Humphrey Bogart, whose fame was on the rise while hers was diminishing.

Street of Chance (Paramount, 1930). *King of the Underworld* (Warner Bros., 1939).

Frankenheimer, John (b. 1930)

Director. Before his career began to falter in the late sixties, Frankenheimer seemed set to become one of the most important directors of his generation. After his extraordinary early success with great movies like *The Manchurian Candidate* (United Artists, 1962) and *The Birdman of Alcatraz* (United Artists, 1961), Frankenheimer found it difficult to find the right projects and his career was eclipsed by the group of slightly younger directors, including Francis Ford Coppola, that emerged in the early seventies. When *French Connection II* was released, he was at a critical low point and, indeed, despite some good moments, the film is eclipsed by its predecessor, directed by William Friedkin.

French Connection II (20th Century-Fox, 1975).

Frazier, James (Fictional character)

Humphrey Bogart's character in *Angels with Dirty Faces* (Warner Bros., 1938), one of a long line of hoodlums he played during his career, is a typically dandified gangster who, like the two leading characters in the film, Rocky Sullivan (James Cagney) and Father Jerry Connelly (Pat O'Brien), is a product of the tough Irish ghetto in New York City. His plans to eliminate Father Connelly, who is leading a campaign to rid the city of gangsters, ultimately leads to his murder at the hands of Connelly's childhood friend, Sullivan. A small role effectively and memorably performed by Bogart, it did not convince either audiences or Warner's executives that he could carry a film like Cagney, and he continued to play similar characters for several more years before he rose to full-fledged stardom.

The French Connection (20th Century-Fox, 1971). 104 mins.
Producer: Philip D'Anton. *Director*: William Friedkin. *Screenplay*: Ernest Tidyman, based on the book by Robin Moore. *Director of Photography*: Owen Roizman. *Music*: Don Ellis. *Art Director*: Ben Kazaskow. *Editor*: Jerry Greenberg.
Cast: Gene Hackman (Jimmy "Popeye" Doyle), Fernando Rey (Alain Charnier), Roy Scheider (Buddy Russo), Tony Lo Bianco (Sal Boca), Marcel Bozzuffi (Pierre Nicoli), Frederic de Pasquale (Devereaux). *With*: Bill Hickman, Ann Rebbot, Harold Gary, Arlene Farber, Eddie Egan.

Popeye Doyle, a New York City police detective, and his partner, Buddy Russo, investigate a heroin smuggling ring. Through violent and questionable methods which sometimes violate the law, they eventually discover that the head of the drug smuggling ring is the suave French criminal, Alain Charnier. However, in the end, they fail to capture Charnier, who escapes to France.
The French Connection was one of the earliest of the new breed of crime thrillers that emerged during the late sixties and early seventies: excessively violent films in which the good guys often rely on methods usually used only by villains — torture, threats, bribes, etc. However, here the actions of the protagonists are given some credence by the plot and characters based on the real life exploits of New York policemen Eddie Egan, who played a minor roll in the film, and Sonny Grosso. In retrospect, *The French Connection* is not nearly as revolutionary or extraordinary as it appeared at the time. It suffers somewhat from Gene Hackman's hammy performance and director William Friedkin's reliance on television techniques, not the least of which is his annoying use of quick zooms. However, it is overall an entertaining addition to the group of seventies gangster crime thrillers, and its famous chase scene remains exciting.

French Connection II (20th Century-Fox, 1975). 119 mins.
Producer: Robert L. Rosen. *Director*: John Frankenheimer. *Screenplay*: Robert and Laurie Dillon. *Director of Photography*: Claude Renoir. *Music*: Don Ellis. *Art Directors*: Gerard Viard and Georges Glon. *Editor*: Tom Rolf.
Cast: Gene Hackman (Popeye Doyle), Fernando Rey (Alain Charnier), Bernard Fresson (Inspector Barthelemy), Jean Pierre Castaldi and Charles Millot (Aides of Barthelemy), Cathleen Nesbitt (Mrs. Charnier). *With*: Pierre Collet, Alexandre Fabre, Philippe Leotard, Ed Lauter, Jacques Dynam.

Gene Hackman returns in his Academy Award winning role as New York cop Popeye Doyle, here tracing drug king pin Alain Charnier to France. Doyle does not get much cooperation from the local authorities in Marseilles, but eventually, with the help of Inspector Barthelemy, an honest cop, he confronts and kills the gangster in a climactic shootout.
Unlike its predecessor, *French Connection II* is wholly fictional. Its improbable plot is overshadowed by

violent action and lurid scenes of the French underworld. Director John Frankenheimer does not do much with the material, but the film is not really bad, either. Ultimately it is nothing more than a slickly made, routine thriller.

Freund, Karl (1890–1969)
Cinematographer. The Czech-born Freund was one of the most important cinematographers in German silent movies. Freund helped develop the extravagant expressionist style which influenced Hollywood films in the thirties and forties. After moving to the United States, Freund worked on several important productions, including the classic horror movie *The Mummy* (Universal, 1932), which he directed. Among the later American films he photographed, *Key Largo* is unquestionably one of the most important.
Key Largo (Warner Bros., 1948).

Friedhofer, Hugo (1902–1981)
Composer. Although not as well known as some of his great contemporaries — Bernard Herrmann and Victor Young, for example — Friedhofer is worthy of praise. His best known score was for the classic *The Best Years of Our Lives* (United Artists, 1946), but his score for the great gangster *noir Body and Soul*, is equally impressive.
Body and Soul (United Artists, 1947).

Friedkin, William (b. 1939)
Director. Briefly successful in the seventies, Friedkin was at his best with unpretentious action oriented pictures. Unfortunately, after the incredible success of *The French Connection* and *The Exorcist* (Warner Bros., 1973), his career went into decline. His visceral, kinetic style, influenced by his early career in television, is best demonstrated in *The French Connection*, his finest movie.

The French Connection (20th Century–Fox, 1971).

Friedman, Seymour (b. 1917)
Director. Hoping to pursue a career as a doctor after graduating with a Bachelor of Science from Cambridge College, Friedman was convinced by his father, a Hollywood studio executive, to try his hand in the movies. For many years he worked as an assistant director before he was given the chance to direct in 1948. His entire career was spent making "B" movies, mostly for Columbia. *Loan Shark*, his only gangster movie, is probably his best film, although it is far from distinguished. Nevertheless, it gave George Raft one of his better later roles.
Loan Shark (Lippert, 1952).

Friendly, Johnny (Fictional character)
In *On the Waterfront* (Columbia, 1954), the ironically named character played by Lee J. Cobb is a sleazy mobster who controls the waterfront and its workers. But when he orders the murder of a dock worker who plans to testify before a government committee, Friendly finds himself in conflict with a hardened ex-boxer and dock worker, Terry Malloy (Marlon Brando), who is not so easily swayed. Eventually, he meets Malloy on the docks, where they engage in a fistfight. Malloy and Friendly are both badly beaten, but Malloy has a moral victory when his fellow dock workers side with him.
Lee J. Cobb's performance as the mobster, while overshadowed by Brando's performance, is no less intense or brilliant.

The Friends of Eddie Coyle (Paramount, 1973). 103 mins.
Producer: Paul Monash. *Director*: Peter Yates. *Screenplay*: Paul Monash, based on the novel by George V. Higgins. *Director of Photography*: Victor J. Kemper. *Music*: Dave Grusin. *Art Director*: Gene Callahan. *Editor*: Pat Jaffe.

Cast: Robert Mitchum (Eddie Coyle), Peter Boyle (Dillon), Richard Jordan (Dave Foley), Steven Keats (Jackie), Alex Rocco (Scalise), Joe Santos (Artie Van), Mitchell Ryan (Waters). *With*: Peter MacLean, Kevin O'Morrison, Marvin Licherman, Carolyn Pickman, James Tolkan, Margaret Ladd.

After some recent convictions, two time loser Eddie Coyle makes a deal with the authorities to help reduce his prison sentence. Agreeing to inform on the local mob, he infiltrates a gang planning a bank robbery. After the leader is arrested, the mob believes that Coyle betrayed them. In fact, the leader's arrest was actually caused by another informant, Dillon, a psychotic hitman. Ironically, Dillon is ordered to assassinate Coyle, which he carries out in his usual efficient manner.

The Friends of Eddie Coyle can be described as hyper-realism, with its dour subject, realistically told without sentimentalism not meant for wide scale box office success but offering an interesting, insightful portrait of small time gangsters. Robert Mitchum's performance as the desperate criminal sacrificed by the petty aspirations of government officials is superb as always, but the film's depressing subject matter does not make for enjoyable entertainment.

Fuchs, Daniel (1903–1978)
Screenwriter. Fuchs worked as a scenarist in Hollywood in the forties. Almost always associated with hardboiled subjects, he wrote three gangster pictures, all of very high quality, including the classic *noir Criss Cross*.
The Big Shot (Warner Bros., 1942). *The Gangster* (Allied Artists, 1947). *Criss Cross* (Universal, 1949).

Fuller, Leland (1899–1986)
Art director. Originally an architect, Fuller began working in films in the thirties. He is most often associated with the highly imaginative designs for

Otto Preminger's *films noir* in the late forties. He spent most of his career at 20th Century-Fox, where, in collaboration with Lyle Wheeler, he helped design the productions for many classic movies, including *Kiss of Death*, one of the great gangster *noirs* of the late forties.
Kiss of Death (20th Century-Fox, 1947).

Fuller, Sam (b. 1912)
Director and screenwriter. Fuller was one of the earliest "B" directors to be recognized as an important artist. Indeed, his movies are the equivalent of great pulp literature. Sometimes infuriatingly silly and contrived, they are often quite profound. Like novelists Dashiell Hammett and Raymond Chandler, Fuller used the milieu of the fictional crime genres to explore complicated themes of contemporary man's place in the modern world. His work has been described as that of action and ideas, and the best of his movies are now recognized classics. He began his film career, after varied experience, as a screenwriter, contributing to a number of "B" movies, including the gangster thriller *Gangs of New York*. He did not begin directing until a decade later. Nearly all of his best movies are crime thrillers, but only *Underworld U.S.A.* can be described as a gangster movie. Made late in his career, it is typical of his work — violent, paranoid, and very erotic. It is one of the finest examples of the later period of the gangster genre.
Gangs of New York (Republic, 1938; cowriter only). *Underworld U.S.A.* (Columbia, 1961; cowriter, producer and director).

Furthman, Charles (1894–1969)
Screenwriter. The younger brother of Jules Furthman, one of the great screenwriters of Hollywood's golden age, Charles Furthman was most active in the late twenties and early thirties. His best work, including two famous early gangster dramas, was for director

James Cagney with three similarly well dressed, but hard-boiled characters in *G-Men*, one of his few heroic roles in the genre.

Josef von Sternberg during the late silent era.

Underworld (Paramount, 1927). *Thunderbolt* (Paramount, 1929).

Furthman, Jules (1888–1966)

Screenwriter. For over three decades, beginning in the early twenties, Jules Furthman was one of the most consistently brilliant American screenwriters. He specialized in hard-boiled but romantic melodrama, as personified by Josef von Sternberg's exotic movies of the early thirties. However, his greatest collaboration was with his friend Howard Hawks, with whom he wrote many classics (Hawks, incidentally, never took credit for his collaborations with Furthman). Among these collaborations are two Sternberg movies from the late silent era, *The Docks of New York* and *The Dragnet*,

and it is now difficult to determine who did what in their collaborations, since only Furthman received credit for these two pictures. Furthman also worked on Sternberg's *Thunderbolt* in collaboration with a number of other credited writers, including his brother Charles Furthman.

The Docks of New York (Paramount, 1928). *The Dragnet* (Paramount, 1928). *Thunderbolt* (Paramount, 1929).

G-Men (Warner Bros., 1935). 85 mins. *Director*: William Keighley. *Screenplay*: Seton I. Miller, based on the book *Public Enemy No. 1* by Gregory Rogers. *Director of Photography*: Sol Polito. *Music Director*: Leo F. Forbstein. *Song*: Sammy Fain and Irving Kahal. *Art Director*: John J. Hughes. *Editor*: Jack Killifer.

Cast: James Cagney ("Brick" Davis), Ann Dvorak (Jean Morgan), Margaret Lindsay (Kay McCord), Robert Armstrong (Jeff McCord), Barton MacLane (Brad Collins), Lloyd Nolan (Hugh Farrell), William Harrigan (McKay). *With*: Edward Pawley, Russell Hopton, Noel Madison, Regis Toomey, Addison Richards, Raymond Hatton, Adrian Morris.

"Brick" Davis, a poor slum boy, is taken under the wing of a local racketeer who helps raise him and pays for his education. Davis becomes a G-man and investigates the gangland murder of a fellow agent. Because of his unusual youth, he has many connections with the underworld, and many of his fellow officers believe he is a traitor. An old girlfriend, Jean Morgan, now married to a gang member, tells Davis where the gang hideout is located. Davis, who is surprised to discover that his old mentor is head of the murderous gang, has a shootout with the gangsters and arrests the survivors. Disillusioned, Davis almost resigns, but after rescuing his boss' sister from another mob, he decides to remain a law officer.

In the early thirties, following the incredible success and impact of the early gangster movies, the studios came under attack by religious and other groups for "glamorizing" gangsters. *G-Men* was Warner Bros.' response to the criticism. In fact, it was the most prominent early gangster film to concentrate on the activities of government law enforcement agents, and it had the advantage of starring James Cagney, here cast for the first time on the side of the law. Essentially little more than propaganda for the F.B.I. — J. Edgar Hoover was the unofficial advisor on the film — its classic status is assured because of James Cagney's typically dynamic performance.

G-Men Never Forget (Republic, 1948). 12 Chapters.
Associate Producer: Mike Franko-vich. *Directors*: Fred Brannon and Yakima Canutt. *Screenplay*: Franklin Adreon, Basil Dickey, Jesse Duffy, Sol Shor. *Director of Photography*: John MacBurnie. *Music*: Mort Glickman.

Cast: Clayton Moore (Ted O'Hara), Roy Barcroft (Murkland/Cameron), Ramsay Ames (Frances Blake), Drew Allen (Duke), Tom Steele (Parker), *With*: Jack O'Shea, Edmund Cobb, Barry Brooks, Stanley Price, Dale Van Sickel.

Murkland is a gangster who runs a protection racket. When he is broken out of jail by a henchman, a plastic surgeon makes him look like the police commissioner, Cameron. The real life Cameron is kidnapped while Murkland, in disguise, runs his criminal organization from the local police headquarters. Meanwhile, two detectives, Ted O'Hara and Frances Blake, begin to investigate the rise of crime in their city. Murkland's various violent attempts to get rid of the two honest policemen backfire. Eventually O'Hara and Blake expose Murkland and, after a violent confrontation, the criminal mastermind is arrested, the kidnapped commissioner is set free, and the city returns to normal.

Coming near the end of the golden age of Republic's serials, *G-Men Never Forget* is typical of the studio's best cliffhangers, full of violent action, hair raising stunts, and murderous villains. The cast is superb, including Clayton Moore as one of the honest G-men. Moore, of course, would later achieve fame as television's Lone Ranger.

Gabin, Jean (1904–1976)
Actor. Born Alexis Moncourge, the stock, virile, world weary Jean Gabin was one of France's biggest male stars beginning in the early thirties. He most often played doomed romantic leads, as in the influential *Pépé le Moko*, the most important of his two gangster movies. In the popular *The Sicilian Clan*, he played the elderly mafioso.

Pépé le Moko (United Artists, 1938).

Paris Touchez Pas au Grisbi (Corona, 1953). *The Sicilian Clan* (Fox–Europa/ Les Films du Siecle, 1968)

Gable, Clark (1901–1960)

Actor. Although he will be forever remembered as Rhett Butler in *Gone with the Wind* (MGM, 1939), Clark Gable's movie career began in 1924 and, over a thirty-six year period, included many excellent performances. Before his screen image jelled in the mid-thirties — as the ideal of the slightly roguish, masculine American male — Gable played as many bad guys as romantic heroes. In the two early gangster movies *The Finger Points* and *Manhattan Melodrama*, he was surprisingly convincing as a murderous gangster. The latter is his most important performance in the genre, but he also starred in the curious prison escape drama *Strange Cargo* as an escapee from Devil's Island whose adventures are filled with Biblical metaphors.

The Finger Points (First National, 1931). *Manhattan Melodrama* (MGM, 1934). *Strange Cargo* (MGM, 1940).

Gaby (Fictional character)

The heroine of *Pépé le Moko* (Paris Films, 1937), *Algiers* (United Artists, 1938) and *Casbah* (Universal, 1948) is part moll, part *femme fatale*, a sophisticate from Paris who, on a trip to North Africa, has a brief affair with the gangster Pépé le Moko, to whom she is attracted largely because of his reputation within the criminal underworld. But when she callously abandons him to return to Paris, Pépé risks leaving the Arab Quarter, is turned over to the police by an informer, and then commits suicide as Gaby's ship sails out of sight. Memorably portrayed, respectively in the films above, by Mirelle Balin, Hedy Lamarr and Marta Toren.

Gallagher, Blackie (Fictional character)

With the success of *Gone with the Wind* (MGM, 1939), and countless adventure films having established his amiable heroic image, it is difficult for contemporary audiences to imagine Clark Gable as a villain but, in fact, he played many villainous roles early in his film career. In *Manhattan Melodrama* (MGM, 1934), he played his most famous gangster, Blackie Gallagher. Gallagher, however, is not wholly amoral: when his ex-moll marries a rising district attorney who becomes the victim of a blackmailer, Blackie murders the blackmailer. Blackie is sentenced to death and bravely goes to meet his fate to save the reputation and career of his ex-moll's new husband.

Gang Busters (Universal Serial, 1942). 13 Chapters.

Associate Producer: Ford Beebe. *Directors*: Ray Taylor and Noel Smith. *Screenplay*: Morgan Cox, Al Martin, Vic McLeod, George Plympton, based on the radio serial by Phillips H. Lord. *Director of Photography*: William Sickner and John Boyle. No editor credited.

Cast: Kent Taylor (Detective Lt. Bill Bannister), Irene Hervey (Vicki Logan), Ralph Morgan (Professor Mortis), Robert Armstrong (Detective Tim Nolan), Richard Davies (Happy Haskins), Joseph Crehan (Chief Martin O'Brien). *With*: Ralf Harolde, John Gallaudet, George Watts, William Haade, George Lewis, Victor Zimmerman.

Based on a popular radio series, *Gang Busters* recounts the adventures of undercover cop Bill Bannister and his attempts to track down a gang of terrorists and criminals who hold a city in the grip of fear. Like all serials, the emphasis is on action and violence as the mystery unravels and the heroes barely manage to escape from a series of hair-raising dangers as they track down the leader of the dangerous gang. *Gang Busters* is unpretentious and fun and something of a rarity, since gang activities were not usually the subject of serials. Of course, it is not exactly realistic, but it is exhilarating entertainment, and at the time, a huge success.

Gangs of Chicago (Republic, 1940). 66 mins.
Associate Producer: Robert North. *Director*: Arthur Lubin. *Screenplay*: Karl Brown. *Director of Photography*: Elwood Bredell. *Music*: Cy Feuer. *Art Director*: John Victor Mackay. *Editors*: Murray Seldeen and Lester Orlebeck.
Cast: Lloyd Nolan (Matty Burns), Barton MacLane (Ramsey), Lola Lane (June), Ray Middleton (Bill Whitaker), Astrid Allwyn (Virginia). *With*: Horace McMahon, Howard Hickman, Leona Roberts, Charles Halton, Addison Richards, John Harmen, Dwight Frye.

While in law school, the young Matty Burns befriends a youthful gang leader, Ramsey. He offers Ramsey advice on how to circumvent the law, and after graduating, helps Ramsey recruit members. Meanwhile, the F.B.I. recruits Bill Whitaker, Burns' former friend and fellow lawyer, to use his relationship with Burns to help close down Ramsey's operations. Eventually, when Burns feels guilty for his actions, he confronts Ramsey and, in the ensuing argument, kills the gang leader. He is arrested, knowing that he faces either life in prison or the death sentence for the murder.

Gangs of Chicago is a typical low budget gangster movie from the tail end of the initial cycle. However, it is surprisingly well made despite its clichéd plot, helped enormously by Lloyd Nolan and Barton MacLane's energetic performances.

Gangs of New York (Republic, 1938). 67 mins.
Director: James Cruze. *Screenplay*: Wellyn Totman, Sam Fuller, Charles F. Royal, with additional dialog by Jack Townley, based on a story by Herbert Asbury and Sam Fuller. *Director of Photography*: Ernest Miller.

Music Director: Alberto Colombo. *Editor*: William Morgan.
Cast: Charles Bickford (Rocky Thorpe/John Franklin), Ann Dvorak (Connie), Alan Baxter (Dancer), Wynne Gibson (Orchid), Harold Huber (Pantella). *With*: Willard Robertson, Maxie Rosenbloom, Charles Trowbridge, John Wray, Jonathan Hale, Fred Kohler.

When Rocky Thorpe, the leader of a violent gang, is about to be released from prison, his place is taken by John Franklin, a law enforcement agent who looks exactly like the gangster. Franklin uncovers evidence to keep Thorpe in prison and, along the way, begins a romance with Connie, a gang associate.

Gangs of New York might well be the best of Republic's gangster movies. James Cruze's direction is very good, and the performances are first rate. Ann Dvorak is particularly good, here playing, for a change, a good girl opposite Wynne Gibson's moll. The movie's enormous box office success inspired a marginal sequel, *Gangs of Chicago* (Republic, 1940) which, although not nearly as good as its predecessor, is equally entertaining.

The Gangster (Allied Artists, 1947). 84 mins.
Producers: Frank and Maurice King. *Director*: Gordon Wiles. *Screenplay*: Daniel Fuchs, based on his novel *Low Company*. *Director of Photography*: Paul Ivano. *Music*: Louis Gruenberg. *Art Director*: F. Paul Sylos. *Editor*: Walter Thompson.
Cast: Barry Sullivan (Shubunka), Belita (Nancy Starr), Joan Lorring (Dorothy), Akim Tamiroff (Nick), Henry ("Harry") Morgan (Shorty), John Ireland (Karty), Sheldon Leonard (Cornell). *With*: Charles McGraw, John Kellogg, Elisha Cook, Jr., Jeff Corey, Ted Hecht, Clancy Cooper.

A neurotic gangster, Shubunka, has reached a crossroads in his life. Cornell, a rival, is attempting to take over

Akim Tamiroff, minor gangster icon from the thirties, reappeared in the genre in a supporting role as a mobster in the superior "B" gangster-*noir*, *The Gangster*. He is seen here with Joan Lorring in a brief respite from the violence and paranoia in the film.

Shubunka's gang. Shubunka, however, is giving all his attention to his mistress, Nancy. An associate sells out Shubunka to his rival, and after alienating Nancy because of his intense jealousy, Shubanka is shot down by Cornell's men on a rainy street.

Following the enormous box office success of *Dillinger* (Monogram, 1945), the King Brothers produced this gangster movie in the hopes of repeating that early success. While not as popular as its predecessor, *The Gangster* did well and, in fact, is a better film. Its relentless pessimism qualifies it as one of the most important "B" *films noir*. It is very well made despite the low budget, with a superior screenplay by Daniel Fuchs, and fine performances by a superior cast including aging "B" gangster icon Akim Tamiroff as one of the gangsters and Sheldon Leonard as the upstart mobster.

The Gangsters of New York (Reliance-Mutual, 1914). Four reels approx. 65 mins.

Director and Writer: James Kirkwood.

Cast: Henry B. Walthall (Porkey Dugan), Jack Dillon (Biff Dugan), Master O. Child (Jimmie Dugan), Fred Herzog (The District Attorney). *With*: A. Horine, Consuelo Bailey, R. Reiley, C. Lambert, Ralph Lewis.

One of the earliest true gangster movies, *The Gangsters of New York* recounts the adventures of the Dugan brothers, tenement youths who join a gang. Released only two years after D. W. Griffith's *The Musketeers of Pig Alley* (Biograph, 1912), the seminal gangster drama, *The Gangsters of New York* is interesting for its portrait of petty criminals during the years just after the turn of the century, a period when the mafia was beginning to emerge.

Gardner, Ava (1922–1991)

Actress. The extraordinarily beautiful Ava Gardner was Hollywood's leading sex symbol and glamor queen between the end of World War II and the rise of Marilyn Monroe in the early fifties. She played in many films during the mid-forties, before her appearance in the *film noir* classic *The Killers* made her a superstar. This film established her dark and exotic sensual screen image, and she remains one of *noir's* most important, alluring *femmes fatales* for this one performance alone. She was equally compelling in *The Bribe*, but the film did not have the impact of the earlier success.

The Killers (Universal, 1947). *The Bribe* (MGM, 1949).

Garfield, John (1913–1952)

Actor. Born Julius Garfinkle, the

John Garfield, seen here from a publicity still from the late thirties, became one of the new *noir* era's most cynical antiheroes in a series of gangster movies and thrillers in the forties. He was later one of the most prominent targets of Senator Joseph McCarthy as an alleged communist.

future John Garfield grew up in the Jewish slums of New York City. He knew the mean streets of New York and the city's tough guys. Politically, he would always champion the downtrodden (and as a result, became a target of Joseph McCarthy in the early fifties), and he most often played gangsters and criminals in the movies. Indeed, Garfield became one of the most important hard-boiled actors of the forties but, unlike James Cagney, Humphrey Bogart, and Edward G. Robinson, who played similar roles in the thirties, Garfield's characters were often morally ambivalent. Thus, he is one of the key figures in *film noir*. Although his most enduring screen role was in the *noir* thriller *The Postman Always Rings Twice* (MGM, 1947), he also starred in two important, authentic gangster movies. His starmaking performance in *They Made Me a Criminal* (RKO, 1939), an off-genre movie, firmly established his screen image as the alienated victim of circumstance, a variation of which he would play in his two true gangster movies, *Castle on the Hudson* and *Body and Soul*. His performance in the latter is certainly one of his best: his portrayal of boxer Charlie Davis, a victim of personal greed and the mob's corruption of the sport, is the archetype of several similar *films noir* which followed.

Castle on the Hudson (Warner Bros., 1940). *Body and Soul* (United Artists, 1947).

Garland, Beverly (b. 1926)

Actress. Born Beverly Fessenden in Santa Cruz, California, the attractive Garland was a popular leading lady in "B" movies during the late forties and early fifties, usually playing a tough dame. She costarred in the classic *film noir D.O.A.* (United Artists, 1949), and played a moll in the excellent "B" gangster drama *The Miami Story*, her only appearance in the genre.

The Miami Story (Columbia, 1954).

Garmes, Lee (1897–1978)

Cinematographer. One of the world's great cinematographers, Garmes is best known for his glittering black and white photography, and particularly for his collaboration with director Josef von Sternberg on several of the master's greatest movies. Indeed, soft focus, romantic, rainswept, and exotic images—the very picture of classic, glamorous Hollywood in the thirties and forties—can largely be attributed to Garmes. His work was always glamorous, and he was at his best when photographing beautiful women, but he also worked on a surprising number of gritty, realistic dramas, including three gangster movies. Among these is one of the genre's most important classics, *Scarface: Shame of a Nation*, in which his extravagant style was only slightly repressed.

City Streets (MGM, 1931). *Scarface: Shame of a Nation* (United Artists, 1932). *The Desperate Hours* (Paramount, 1955).

Garr, Teri (b. 1952)

Actress. Throughout the seventies and eighties, the blonde, attractive Garr always seemed just on the verge of real stardom, but never really quite made it. She was at her best in comedy, but she is also a capable dramatic actress. Her comedic and sexual qualities were exploited to good advantage in *The Sting II*, in which she starred as a con woman mixed up in a complicated scam.

The Sting II (Universal, 1982).

Garrett, Oliver H. P. (1897–1952)

Screenwriter. For nearly three decades, beginning in the late twenties, Garrett was one of the most consistently successful screenwriters in American movies. Like too many of his fellow screenwriters, Garrett's career has been ignored by historians, but there can be little question of his importance, particularly as a writer of hard-boiled subjects. He had his greatest success in the thirties, working on three important early gangster movies, *Street of Chance, City Streets*, and *Manhattan Melodrama*. He also contributed the original story for Josef von Sternberg's *The Dragnet*, an influential late silent gangster movie. Of his later work as a screenwriter, the script for *Dead Reckoning* (which provided Humphrey Bogart with one of his best roles) is certainly one of his best.

The Dragnet (Paramount, 1928). *Street of Chance* (Paramount, 1930). *City Streets* (Paramount, 1931). *Manhattan Melodrama* (MGM, 1934). *Dead Reckoning* (Columbia, 1947).

Garson, Marie (Fictional character)

One of the most underrated film actresses of her time, Ida Lupino always brought an extra dimension to her characters that brought them to life. Such is the case with Marie Garson, the moll she played in *High Sierra* (Warner Bros., 1940). Garson is the physically abused girlfriend of a small-time hood who falls for the only man who has really ever cared for her, Roy Earle (Humphrey Bogart). Earle has been sprung from prison by her boyfriend to help lead the heist of a remote California resort. He takes pity on her, treating her with kindness, and Garson quickly abandons her old boyfriend for him. Likewise, she is one of the few women who has ever understood him. After completing the heist, they flee into the Sierra Nevada Mountains, but when the police close in on them, Earle abandons their car to try to escape by foot into the mountains. He is cornered among the rocks like a savage animal. As he tries to get away, he is shot and killed in front of his lover, and Marie collapses onto the ground, weeping uncontrollably. She has lost the only person she has ever loved.

Along with one or two of Claire Trevor's moll performances, Ida Lupino's performance is one of the genre's greatest female characterizations, and Marie Garson remains one of the genre's quintessential molls.

Gaudio, Tony (1885–1951)

Cinematographer. The Italian-born Gaudio was one of the most important Hollywood directors of photography during the thirties. Although his style was not particularly original, he used the techniques developed by others to great advantage. Under contract to Warner Bros., he contributed the cinematography to several of their most important films, including *Anthony Adverse* (1936), *The Life of Emile Zola* (1937), and the great color film *The Adventures of Robin Hood* (1938). Gaudio is one of the most important cinematographers of the gangster genre, having worked on many of Warner Bros.' most important crime titles during the thirties and forties.

Little Caesar (First National, 1931). *Lady Killer* (Warner Bros., 1933). *Fog Over Frisco* (First National, 1934). *Dr. Socrates* (Warner Bros., 1935). *Kid Galahad* (Warner Bros., 1937). *The Amazing Dr. Clitterhouse* (Warner Bros., 1938). *Brother Orchid* (Warner Bros., 1940). *High Sierra* (Warner Bros., 1941). *Larceny, Inc.* (Warner Bros., 1942).

The George Raft Story (Allied Artists, 1961). 105 mins.

Producer: Ben Schwalb. *Director*: Joseph M. Newman. *Screenplay*: Crane Wilbur, based on the life of George Raft. *Director of Photography*: Carl Guthrie. *Music*: Jeff Alexander. *Art Director*: David Milton. *Editor*: George White.

Cast: Ray Danton (George Raft), Jayne Mansfield (Lisa Lang), Julie London (Sheila Patton), Barrie Chase (June), Barbara Nichols (Texas Guinan), Brad Dexter (Benny "Bugsy" Siegel), Neville Brand (Al Capone). *With*: Frank Gorshin, Herschel Bernardi, Joe De Santis, Robert Straus, Jack Lambert.

Very loosely based on his real life, this feature recounts the rise of George Raft from his humble beginnings in New York's Hell's Kitchen slums to his fame as a motion picture star. Along the way he meets and befriends a number of underworld figures, including Bugsy Siegel and Al Capone.

George Raft's friendships with real life gangsters were widely rumored in Hollywood, where the details were occasionally reported (naturally with some circumspection) by gossip columnists. Raft himself finally wrote of his mob connections in a series of articles for the *Saturday Evening Post* during the mid-fifties, but the series, like this movie, omitted many realistic details. In fact, *The George Raft Story* is really entirely fictional, with only the bare outline of Raft's life (and mob connections) intact.

Gertsman, Maury (b. 1910)

Cinematographer. Gertsman's work is utilitarian, but he photographed a number of good films. His cinematography in *Johnny Stool Pigeon* is typical of his rather flat, uninventive style.

Johnny Stool Pigeon (Universal, 1949).

Get Carter (MGM, 1971). 110 mins.

Producer: Michael Klinger. *Director*: Mike Hodges. *Screenplay*: Mike Hodges, based on the novel *Jack's Return Home* by Ted Lewis. *Director of Photography*: Wolfgang Suschitzky. *Music*: Roy Budd. *Art Director*: Roger King. *Editor*: John Trumper.

Cast: Michael Caine (Jack Carter), Ian Hendry (Eric), Britt Eklund (Anna), John Osborne (Kinnear), Tony Beckley (Peter). *With*: Geraldine Moffatt, Dorothy White, Rosemarie Dunham, Petra Markham, Alun Armstrong, Bryan Mosley, Bernard Hepton.

Mob hit man Jack Carter, one of a London based gang's most efficient killers, returns to Newcastle, his hometown, for the funeral of his brother, an honest businessman who was murdered by the mob. Enraged, Carter seeks revenge by systematically tracking down and killing those responsible for his brother's death.

Although it is not exactly pleasant viewing, *Get Carter* is one of the most prominent near-contemporary gangster movies. Unique for its British setting, the film recalls several elements and themes of classic American gangster movies and, in its pessimistic view of the protagonist and the British underworld, even has something in common with *film noir*. Very well made and a big success, its best feature is Michael Caine's performance as the efficient, cold blooded mob killer.

Gibbons, Cedric (1893–1960)

Art director. A graduate of the Art Students League in New York, Gibbons worked for his father's architectural firm before entering films in 1915. He made a name for himself as an art director for producer Sam Goldwyn before joining the fledgling Metro-Goldwyn-Mayer studio in 1924. As supervising art director for MGM for the next 32 years, Gibbons was largely responsible for the design department of that studio's glossy style, and is thus arguably the most important of the great Hollywood art directors. Either alone or in collaboration, Gibbons worked on many classic films. However, his tastes were geared toward the almost surreal and gaudily romantic, which were perfectly suitable to MGM's house style but not necessarily to more realistic subjects. Gangster movies were rarely made at MGM, whose bosses preferred fantasy and happier subjects, and Gibbons' designs for the few that were made by the studio demonstrate the conflicts created by his glittering style on one hand and the subject's naturalistic, hard-boiled themes on the other.

The Big City (MGM, 1928). *Four Walls* (MGM, 1928). *The Big House* (MGM, 1930). *The Last Gangster* (MGM, 1937). *The Earl of Chicago* (MGM, 1940). *The Asphalt Jungle* (MGM, 1950). *The Black Hand* (MGM, 1950).

Gilbert, John (1895–1936)

Actor. Born into a show business family, the handsome Gilbert became one of the legendary stars of the silent screen. Well liked with both female and male fans, he was at his best in costume and romantic melodramas, particularly those costarring his real life lover Greta Garbo. In the early gangster drama *Four Walls*, he starred as the tough leader of a street gang. Not entirely convincing in the role, the film was, nevertheless, a big hit thanks to Gilbert's enormous popularity.

Four Walls (MGM, 1928).

Gilda (Columbia, 1946). 110 mins. *Producer*: Virginia Van Upp. *Director*: Charles Vidor. *Screenplay*: Marion Parsonnet, adapted by Jo Eisinger from a story by E. A. Ellington. *Director of Photography*: Rudolph Maté. *Music*: Morris Stoloff. *Songs*: "Put the Blame on Mame" and "Amado Mio" by Doris Fisher and Allan Roberts. *Art Directors*: Stephen Goosson and Van Nest Polglase. *Editor*: Charles Nelson. *Cast*: Rita Hayworth (Gilda), Glenn Ford (Johnny Farrell), George Macready (Ballin Mundson), Joseph Calleia (Obregon), Steven Geray (Uncle Pio). *With*: Joe Sawyer, Gerald Mohr, Robert Scott, Lionel Royce, S. Z. Martel.

Johnny Farrell, a two bit con man and gambler, is accosted on an Argentine waterfront by hoodlums and rescued by Ballin Mundson. Mundson, who owns a popular local night spot, hires the grateful Farrell, who, through his tenacity and loyalty, soon rises to become Mundson's second in command. Mundson's activities include gambling and other assorted illegal activities. The tranquility of these mobsters' lives is broken by the sudden arrival of Gilda, a beautiful woman whom Mundson marries. Unknown to Mundson, Farrell and Gilda, a nightclub singer, were once lovers. He begins to suspect that they did know each other previously—partly because of their extreme antagonism – and grows jealous. When Mundson's criminal activities catch up with him, he fakes his death in a plane crash. Farrell takes over the business, and he and Gilda become lovers again. When Mundson returns, there is the inevitable confrontation, during which Farrell kills his former boss. Gilda and Farrell decide to give up the nightclub and start a new life together.

The archetypal *film noir*, *Gilda* has just enough gangster elements to qualify it for this genre as well. Of course, as is true in all *films noir*, the real story is not the rather superficial and silly crime story, but the underlying themes of moral corruption, doomed romanticism, and overt pessimism. The film is atypical, due to its homosexual undertones, but its greatest virtue is Rita Hayworth's erotically charged performance. The film's box office success was phenomenal and made Hayworth one of the biggest stars of the late forties.

Gish, Lillian (1896–1993)

Actress. With her sister, Dorothy, Lillian Gish was one of cinema's first real stars. Her waif-like personality is one of silent movies' most enduring images. A protégée of director D. W. Griffith, she starred in his *The Musketeers of Pig Alley*, one of the earliest true gangster movies, as a young wife attracted to a local hoodlum.

The Musketeers of Pig Alley (Biograph, 1912).

The Glass Alibi (Republic, 1946). 68 mins.

Producer and Director: W. Lee Wilder. *Screenplay*: Mindret Lord. *Director of Photography*: Henry Sharp. *Music Director*: Alexander Laszlo. *Production Design*: Frank Welch. *Editors*: Asa Clark and John F. Link.

Cast: Paul Kelly (Max Anderson), Douglas Fowley (Joe Eikner), Anne Gwynne (Belle Marlin), Maris Wrixon (Linda Vale), Jack Conrad (Benny

Bradini), Cy Kendall (Red Hogan). *With*: Cyril Thurston, Selmer Jackson, Vic Potel, Phyllis Adair, George Chandler.

Red Hogan, a notorious gangster wanted by the authorities, takes refuge in the house of Malibu socialite Linda Vale. He calls his moll, Belle Marlin, not knowing that she is in the arms of her lover, newspaperman Joe Eikner. Eikner leads the police to the beach house and Hogan is arrested. Coincidentally, Eikner discovers that Vale is stricken with a fatal illness and has only six months to live. With Belle's help, he seduces and marries the wealthy woman, but when she does not die as expected, he decides to kill her. He shoots his wife, but Linda actually dies of a heart attack and, although the police suspect him, they do not expect to get a conviction. Ironically, Hogan escapes from prison and murders his ex-lover, Belle Marlin. Eikner's fingerprints are all over the crime scene and, despite his protestations of innocence, he is convicted of the crime and sentenced to death.

W. Lee Wilder, Billy Wilder's older brother, had an even more bleak and cynical world view than Billy did. Although he did not become a major director, he did make a number of fine "B" movies, of which *The Glass Alibi* is probably the best. The gangster elements are minor, but the film is an interesting example of the new type of crime thriller that emerged from the gangster genre during the forties.

The Glass Key (Paramount, 1935). 80 mins.

Producer: E. Lloyd Sheldon. *Director*: Frank Tuttle. *Screenplay*: Kathryn Scola, Harry Ruskin, Kubec Glasmon, based on the novel by Dashiell Hammett. *Director of Photography*: Henry Sharp. *Art Director*: Hans Dreier. *Editor*: Hugh Bennett.

Cast: George Raft (Ed Beaumont), Edward Arnold (Paul Madvig), Claire Dodd (Janet Henry), Rosalind Keith

(Opal Madvig), Charles Richmond (Senator Henry). *With*: Ray Milland, Emma Dunn, Guinn Williams, Tammany Young, Charles C. Wilson, Patrick Moriarity, Ann Sheridan.

This first version of Dashiell Hammett's best seller is a rather conventional, minor gangster movie from the genre's heyday. It is notable largely for George Raft's appearance as the mob henchman, one of his least-known but best performances. The plot of this film and that of its remake are identical, following the novel closely.

The Glass Key (Paramount, 1942). 85 mins.
Producer: Fred Kohlmar. *Director*: Stuart Heisler. *Screenplay*: Jonathan Latimer, based on the novel by Dashiell Hammett. *Director of Photography*: Theodor Sparkuhl. *Music*: Victor Young. *Art Directors*: Hans Dreier and Haldane Douglas. *Editor*: Achie Marshek.
Cast: Brian Donlevy (Paul Madvig), Veronica Lake (Janet Henry), Alan Ladd (Ed Beaumont), Bonita Granville (Opal Madvig), Richard Denning (Taylor Henry), Joseph Calleia (Nick Varna), William Bendix (Jeff). *With*: Frances Gifford, Donald MacBride, Margaret Hayes, Moroni Olson, Eddie Marr, Arthur Loft, Pat O'Malley.

Ed Beaumont is the cold-hearted, dedicated henchman of political boss Paul Madvig. When Madvig becomes the target of a blackmail scheme by a rival, Beaumont must find the culprit. Despite complications, including a romantic liaison with the sexy Janet Henry, and confrontations with Jeff, a pugnacious, near psychopathic thug hired by his boss to stop the investigation, Beaumont eventually discovers that a ruthless gambler, Nick Varda, is behind the scheme.

One of the earliest true *films noir*, *The Glass Key* was also one of the last gangster movies in the initial cycle. A familiar story of political corruption, this second version differs from the original in several important ways. First, the romance between Ed Beaumont and Janet Henry is given greater emphasis, and several scenes are notably erotic. Secondly, the underlying themes of personal moral corruption and mindless violence (prominent themes in *film noir*) are also more greatly emphasized.

The film is also notable as the second teaming of Veronica Lake and Alan Ladd, who became a formidable box office duo during the early to midforties. While their scenes together are conspicuously sexual, the film's best performance belongs to William Bendix as Ed Beaumont's murderous foil.

Gleason, Jackie (1916–1987)
Actor. A veteran of vaudeville and burlesque, Gleason achieved immortality as the star of the classic television comedy *The Honeymooners*. Although an immensely talented comedian, much of his film career was devoted to dramatic roles, at which he proved very effective. In *The Sting II*, he costarred as a thirties con man involved in a complicated scheme to swindle millions. Gleason's performance is very good, but the film is a pale imitation of its predecessor.
The Sting II (Universal, 1982).

Glennon, Bert (1893–1967)
Cinematographer. One of Hollywood's most distinguished cinematographers, Glennon specialized in outdoor epics. He photographed many classic westerns and war dramas, and two interesting, if not really important, gangster dramas.
Show Them No Mercy (20th Century-Fox, 1935). *Crime Wave* (Warner Bros., 1953).

Gloria (Columbia, 1980). 120 mins.
Producer, Director and Screenplay: John Cassavetes. *Director of Photography*: Fred Schuler. *Production Designer*: Rene D'Auriac. *Editor*: Jack McSweeney.

Gena Rowlands as the tough ex-gun moll Gloria Swenson on the run from the mob in John
Cassavetes' *Gloria.*

Cast: Gena Rowlands (Gloria Swenson), Juan Adames (Philip Dawn), Julie Cameron (Jeri Dawn), Lupe Garnica (Margarita Vargas), Jessica Castillo (Joan Dawn). *With*: Basilio Franchina, Tom Noonan, Tony Kensich, Ronnie Maccone, Philomena Spagnole, Ralph Dolman, Gary Klarr.

Gloria Swenson is an aging gangster's moll who has decided to break with the past. She witnesses the gangland slaying of Jack Dawn and his wife, who were stealing money from Gloria's former lover, a gang boss. She rescues the couple's young son, Phil, and together they flee the mob henchmen. Despite some close calls, they manage to escape from New York to seek a new life in Pittsburgh.

Gloria is John Cassavetes least pretentious, most commercial movie. Despite this, its screenplay is very uneven, and the film was neither a commercial nor critical success. Still, the dynamic performance of Cassavetes' wife, Gena Rowlands, in the title performance is riveting and helps make the film a noticeable recent gangster thriller.

The Godfather (Paramount, 1972). 175 mins.

Producer: Albert S. Ruddy. *Director*: Francis Ford Coppola. *Screenplay*: Mario Puzo and F. F. Coppola, based on the novel by Mario Puzo. *Director of Photography*: Gordon Willis. *Music*: Nino Rota. *Art Director*: Warren Clymer. *Editors*: William Reynolds, Peter Zinner, Marc Laub, Murray Solomon.

Cast: Marlon Brando (Don Vito Corleone), Al Pacino (Michael Corleone), James Caan (Sonny Corleone), Richard Castellano (Clemenza), Robert Duvall (Tom Hagen), Sterling Hayden (McCluskey), Richard Conte (Barzini), Diane Keaton (Kay Adams). *With*:

John Marley, Al Lettieri, Abe Vigoda, Talia Shire, Gianni Russo, John Cozale, Rudy Bond, Al Martino, Alex Rocco. The movie which raised the gangster drama to epic proportions, *The Godfather* tells the complicated and involved story of Don Vito Corleone, the patriarch of the New York Mafia, their battles with rivals, the police, and even each other. Some critics decried the allegedly romantic glow the film casts over its bloodthirsty criminals (to say nothing of the extremely graphic violence), but few could deny its dramatic strength, its ability to rivet attention for an incredible three hours of Mafia power plays, and sheer bravura style. Mario Puzo's novel was loosely based on the activities of real Sicilian-American gangsters, but it also allegedly had an effect on real life mobsters: Marlon Brando's performance is said to have inspired certain Mafiosi, and his acting is certainly notable, but the less hammy performances are at least as interesting: Al Pacino as the son who tries to avoid joining the mob, but fails due to personal greed; James Caan as the henchman gunned down by rivals (he won a best supporting actor Academy Award for the role); Diane Keaton as the girl who loves Michael Corleone and tries to keep him out of the family business; and many others, including Abe Vigoda as a mob lieutenant, and brief roles for Sterling Hayden and Richard Conte, two veterans of tough guy and gangster

Al Pacino as the youthful gangster Michael Corleone from the classic *The Godfather II*.

parts. The film won a number of Academy Awards: best picture, best actor (Brando), best screenplay (Puzo and Francis Ford Coppola), and best director (Coppola). All were deserved, and the film remains a classic.

The Godfather Part II (Paramount, 1974). 200 mins.

Producer and Director: Francis Ford Coppola. *Screenplay*: F. F. Coppola and Mario Puzo, based on the novel *The Godfather* by Mario Ruzo. *Director of Photography*: Gordon Willis. *Music*: Nino Rota. *Art Director*: Angelo Graham. *Editors*: Peter Zinner, Barry Malkin, Richard Marks.

Cast: Al Pacino (Michael Corleone), Robert Duvall (Tom Hagen), Diane Keaton (Kay), Robert De Niro (Vito Corleone), John Cazale (Fredo

Corleone), Talia Shire (Connie Corleone), Lee Strasberg (Hyman Roth). *With*: Michael V. Gazzo, Richard Bright, Gaston Moschin, G. D. Spradlin, Tom Rosqui, Frank Svero.

The Godfather II acts as both a sequel and preface to its successful predecessor. It traces the early life of Vito Corleone as a child orphaned by murder in Sicily and as a young immigrant learning the rackets in turn of the century New York. This story is intercut with the contemporary story of Vito's heir, Michael Corleone, his forays into Las Vegas and Cuba, and his power struggles with rivals and family members—events consistently punctuated by explicitly violent killings.

At least as rich and dynamic as the original, this sequel was equally successful at the box office, won several Academy Awards (including one for best picture) and provided important parts for the "New Brando," Robert De Niro, Diane Keaton, Robert Duvall, and Al Pacino as the brooding heir to his father's rackets.

Godfather III (Paramount, 1991). 189 mins.

Producer and Director: Francis Ford Coppola. *Screenplay*: F. F. Coppola and Mario Puzo. *Director of Photography*: Gordon Willis. *Music*: Carmine Coppola. *Production Designer*: Dean Tavoularis. *Editors*: Barry Malkin, Lisa Fruchtman and Walter Murch.

Cast: Al Pacino (Michael Corleone), Diane Keaton (Meg Adams), Talia Shire (Connie Corleone Pizzi), Andy Garcia (Vincent Mancini), Eli Wallach (Don Allabella), Sofia Coppola (Mary Corleone). *With*: Joe Mantegna, Bridget Fonda, Raf Vallone, Franc D'Ambrosio, Richard Bright, Donal Donnelly, Helmut Berger.

The finale to the original saga begins in 1979 as Michael Corleone is trying to go straight and reunite with his family. However, a power struggle within the mafia and the Vatican pull him back into a life of crime, with tragic results: an assassination attempt on his life culminates with the death of his beloved daughter. Corleone then retires unhappily to an estate in Sicily.

While it is a poor imitation of the originals, *Godfather III* does contain some of the creative sparks of the first two films. Particularly notable is the extravagantly staged assassination sequence set during the performance of an opera, with scenes intercut between the Corleones watching the opera, and the assassins backstage maneuvering to kill the family. The film suffers, however, from a weak script. Still, Coppola and Puzo demonstrated a willingness to take on controversial themes in their subplot involving the Vatican's ties to the Mafia, and conservatives within the church murdering the liberal Pope John Paul I—both of which have been alleged in several best sellers.

Goldstone, Nat G.

Producer. A staff producer for Universal, Goldstone produced many movies for the studio, beginning in the late thirties. Mostly producing "B" movies, he also produced a few prestigious movies including *Casbah* and the musical remake of *Algiers* (United Artists, 1938).

Casbah (Universal, 1948).

Goldwyn, Samuel (1882-1974)

Producer. The former Samuel Goldfish, son of Polish immigrant, Sam Goldwyn was one of the original movie moguls. After various work experiences, he began producing movies in the early teens, and quickly became one of the leading figures of the emerging film industry. He was one of the earliest producers to regularly make movies in Los Angeles (before 1915, nearly all of the American movies were made in New York or Florida) and one of the most powerful independent producers of Hollywood's golden age. He founded the original Goldwyn Company, which merged with the Metro and Mayer studios in the early twenties (consequently he had no connection with the studio). He thereafter produced his films on his own lot, releasing them through United Artists. Goldwyn specialized in highly commercial family films, but occasionally tackled tougher subjects. Of these, *Dead End* is certainly one of the most prestigious: a powerful evocation of slum life in New York City and its deleterious effects on its inhabitants, a life that Goldwyn knew something about, having grown up on the mean streets of New York just before the turn of the century. He also produced the glossy gangster musical *Guys and Dolls* toward the end of his career.

Dead End (United Artists, 1937). *Guys and Dolls* (United Artists, 1955).

Golitzen, Alexander (b. 1907)
Art director. After studying architecture, Golitzen entered movies in the early thirties, first making a name for himself with producer Samuel Goldwyn. He subsequently worked for several of the major studios and as an independent. In 1954 he became the supervising art director at Universal and worked on a single good, if not particularly well known, gangster drama the following year.

Six Bridges to Cross (Universal, 1955).

Gomez, Thomas (1905–1971)
Character actor. After many years on the stage, Gomez began acting in movies during the early forties. Tall, heavy set, and rather menacing, he appeared, generally as a villain, in a number of classic *films noir*, including *Force of Evil* (MGM, 1948), which touches on gangster themes. In *Key Largo*, he played one of the mob henchmen who terrorize lodgers at a Florida motel.

Key Largo (Warner Bros., 1948).

GoodFellas (Warner Bros., 1991). 146 mins.
Executive Producer: Barbara DeFina. *Producer*: Irwin Winkler. *Director*: Martin Scorsese. *Screenplay*: Nicholas Pileggi and Martin Scorsese, based on the book *Wiseguy* by Nicholas Pileggi. *Director of Photography*: Michael Ballhaus. *Production Designer*: Kristi Zea. *Editor*: Thelma Schoomaker.

Cast: Robert De Niro (James Conway), Ray Liotta (Henry Hill), Joe Pesci (Tommy De Vito), Lorraine Bracco (Karen Hill), Paul Sorvino (Paul Cicero). *With*: Frank Sivero, Tony Darrow, Mike Starr, Frank Vincent, Chuck Low, Frank Dileo.

Henry Hill is an impressionable, ambitious and immoral Irish-American who joins the New York mob as a teenager and rises to prominence in the Mafia. Along the way he befriends James Conway, a fellow Irishman, and the psychotic Tommy De Vito, a mob hit man who kills people indiscriminately. During the late seventies, after twenty years in the Mafia, Hill is caught up in a gang war that eventually costs the lives of many of his acquaintances, including De Vito. He decides to cooperate with federal authorities by testifying against his old friends. With his wife, Karen, he goes into hiding as one of the most infamous people in the Federal Witness Protection Program.

Based on Nicholas Pileggi's biography of Henry Hill, *GoodFellas* is Martin Scorsese's most ambitious film, a complicated narrative (including flashbacks and foreshadowings), that might well be his masterpiece. It is full of rich, real life characters performed brilliantly by a superb cast including Joe Pesci (as Tommy De Vito), who won a best supporting actor Academy Award. With his excellent cast, Scorsese created an extraordinary portrait of Mafia life in the fifties, sixties and seventies that is aided by Thelma Schoomaker's innovative editing and a soundtrack of pop tunes which immediately pinpoint the period of the scene and underscore the dramatic intensity. Altogether, *Good-Fellas* is a great film which transcends its genre origins to emerge as a modern classic.

Goosson, Stephen (1889–1973)
Art director. Yet another ex-architect turned art director, Goosson's film career began in the mid-teens. In the early thirties, he joined Columbia Pictures as supervising art director, and remained with the studio for the rest of his career. Goosson was extremely important to the studio, able to work wonders with miniscule budgets. He added a great deal to the look of Frank Capra's classic thirties films, and also had a profound influence on *film noir*, working on, among others, the classic *Gilda*.
Gilda (Columbia, 1946). *Dead Reckoning* (Columbia, 1947).

Gorcey, Leo (1915–1969)
Actor. The son of a vaudeville performer, the diminutive, tough-talking Gorcey began acting as a teenager, achieving fame in the original Broadway production of *Dead End* in 1936. The following year, he was brought to Hollywood to appear in the film version produced by Samuel Goldwyn and directed by William Wyler, and he made an immediate impression as the leader of the gang of street youths. With Huntz Hall, Gorcey became a starring member of the Dead End Kids and was signed by Warner Bros. The two actors subsequently appeared in the immensely successful *Angels with Dirty Faces*, an equally brilliant social drama disguised as a gangster movie. The Dead End Kids series quickly deteriorated at Warner Bros., briefly becoming the East Side Kids series before both Hall and Gorcey signed with poverty row studio Monogram, where the team was renamed the Bowery Boys during the mid-forties. The Bowery Boys, who lasted for more than a decade, appeared in a cheaply produced series of pseudo-comedies,

few of any merit. Of the series, *Angels' Alley* comes closest to recapturing the spirit of the earlier Dead End Kids gangster movies.
Dead End (United Artists, 1937). *Angels with Dirty Faces* (Warner Bros., 1938). *Angels' Alley* (Monogram, 1948).

Gordon, Robert (1895–1971)
Director. Gordon was a "B" movie director who was most active during the fifties. He directed the classic sci-fi movie *It Came from Outer Space* (Columbia, 1955) and a single, undistinguished gangster movie.
Damn Citizen (Universal, 1958).

Grahame, Gloria (1925–1981)
Actress. The unusual looking Grahame was one of the most sensual actresses of the forties and fifties, a performer whose sultry persona was exploited to good effect in several *films noir*, including the gangster-oriented thriller *The Big Heat*. She mainly played cheap, amoral women who lead vulnerable men astray, with a few conventional roles in between, but she was at her best in bad girl roles. In *Odds Against Tomorrow*, made toward the end of her popularity, she played a nymphomaniac who contributes to the downfall of a gang of bank robbers.
The Big Heat (Columbia, 1953). *Odds Against Tomorrow* (United Artists, 1959).

Grand Slam (Paramount, 1968). 121 mins.
Producers: Harry Colombo and George Papi. *Director*: Giuliano Montaldo. *Screenplay*: Mino Roli, Marcello Fondato, Antonio De La Loma. *Director of Photography*: Antonio Macasoli. *Music*: Ennio Morricone. *Art Directors*: Alberto Boccianti and Juan Alberto Soler. *Editor*: Nino Baragli
Cast: Janet Leigh (Mary Ann), Robert Hoffman (Juan-Paul Audry), Edward G. Robinson (Professor James Anders), Adolfo Celi (Mark Muilford), Klaus Kinski (Erich Weiss).

With: Riccardo Cucciolla, Jussara, Miguel Del Castillo.

James Anders is an elderly, mild mannered professor who retires from his university job in Rio de Janiero and returns to his home in New York City, where he seeks out an old friend, Mark Muilford, who is now a powerful mobster. Anders proposes a plan to rob a company safe in Rio which contains $10 million in diamonds, and Muilford agrees. Anders assembles a group of four specialists, and they work undercover at the city's famous carnival. The heist is carried out, but the police almost bring it to an end, killing two of the thieves. When the third criminal returns to New York, he discovers that the case thought to be full of diamonds is empty. In fact the heist has all been part of an elaborate scheme devised by the professor and his beautiful colleague, Mary Ann, who both have escaped to Rome with all the diamonds. In the end, however, they are left empty-handed when, by coincidence, the bag of diamonds is snatched by a petty thief on a motorcycle.

Grand Slam, an Italian production with a largely American cast, provided one of Edward G. Robinson's last film appearances. A competent heist drama, it was enormously successful but otherwise of little importance and, today, is a dated melodrama in the sixties tradition. Nevertheless, it is interesting for Robinson's unique portrayal of an intellectual thief.

Granger, Farley (b. 1925)

Actor. Granger was a major star from the late forties through the early fifties. He often played flawed pretty boys, most famously in Alfred Hitchcock's *Rope* (Universal, 1949) and *Strangers on a Train* (RKO, 1951). One of his best roles was in *They Live by Night*, one of the earliest treatments of the Bonnie and Clyde story, in which Granger played the Clyde Barrow–like role. He played a more conventional big-city gangster in *The Naked Street*.

In the little-known but very interesting *Side Street*, he played a mailman who inadvertently becomes the target of mobsters when he steals some "hot" money.

Side Street (MGM, 1949). *They Live by Night* (RKO, 1949). *The Naked Street* (United Artists, 1955).

Grant, Cary (1904–1986)

Actor. Although the public preferred to see the former Archibald Leach as well-dressed romantic leads, particularly in screwball comedies, he also played a few tougher roles. Among these is the unusual gangster in the semisatirical *Mr. Lucky*, one of the more interesting variations on gangster themes.

Mr. Lucky (RKO, 1943).

Grant, Katherine (b. 1933)

Actress. An attractive brunette, Grant had a brief period of popularity in "B" movies during the fifties before retiring to marry Bing Crosby. She costarred in two good "B" gangster movies, but was little more than decoration in each.

The Phenix City Story (Allied Artists, 1955). *The Brothers Rico* (Columbia, 1957).

Graves, Peter (b. 1925)

Actor. Born Peter Aurness in Minneapolis, Minnesota, Graves is the brother of actor James Arness. Best known as the gray-haired star of the television series *Mission Impossible*, Graves made his film debut in 1950, and found a niche as a second lead and character actor, mostly in "B" movies. In *Black Tuesday*, he costarred as a henchman to Edward G. Robinson's sadistic gang leader.

Black Tuesday (United Artists, 1954).

Gray, Colleen (b. 1922)

Actress. Although nearly forgotten today, Gray was a popular leading lady during the forties and fifties. Born

Doris Jensen in Staplehurst, Nebraska, the strikingly beautiful brunette first began performing in local theaters before moving to Hollywood during the mid-forties. Although she appeared in many "A" productions, she found her greatest success in "B" movies. She appeared in five gangster movies, the most important of which are *Kiss of Death* and *The Killing*. One of the genre's most attractive female icons, she was not the typical moll, generally appearing as the girlfriend of the hero or as a victim, but she made a memorable moll in Stanley Kubrick's classic heist film *The Killing*. Her role in this film, however, was not as strong as Marie Windsor's *femme fatale*, the catalyst of the heist's ultimate failure.

Kiss of Death (20th Century–Fox, 1947). *Lucky Nick Cain* (20th Century–Fox, 1951). *Kansas City Confidential* (United Artists, 1952). *Las Vegas Shakedown* (Allied Artists, 1955). *The Killing* (United Artists, 1956).

Green, Alfred E. (1889–1960)

Director. Green's film career began in 1917. The consummate professional, his visual style is always at the service of the narrative. Nearly as prolific as director Michael Curtiz (and like Curtiz, he was mostly employed by Warner Bros.–First National) he made all types of films. One of his best films is the early gangster drama *Smart Money*, which stars two of the genre's greatest icons, Edward G. Robinson and James Cagney, in their only film together.

Smart Money (Warner Bros., 1931).

Green, Clarence (b. 1918) & **Rouse, Russel** (b. 1916)

Screenwriters, producers and directors. Although they did work separately, Greene and Rouse generally collaborated, beginning as screenwriters during the mid-forties. They subsequently wrote screenplays for some popular movies, few of which are outstanding. However, in the fifties, they began to produce and direct (Green

usually produced, with Rouse directing) their own films, including an excellent "B" gangster thriller, *New York Confidential*.

New York Confidential (Warner Bros., 1955).

Greenstreet, Sydney (1879–1954)

Character actor. For several decades, the British-born Greenstreet was a popular stage actor in Great Britain and the United States. He made his screen debut at the age of sixty-one as the Fat Man in John Huston's classic *The Maltese Falcon* and instantly became a star. Ironically, the peaceful, well-mannered Englishman became one of the forties' most memorable Hollywood villains, bringing a sly wit to each of his characterizations.

The Maltese Falcon (Warner Bros., 1941).

Greer, Jane (b. 1924)

Actress. Born Bettyjane Greer in Washington, D. C., the diminutive Jane Greer was one of the most attractive screen personalities of the late forties. As Kathie Moffatt in *Out of the Past*, she was one of *film noir*'s deadliest and most memorable *femmes fatales*. This film's enormous box office success led to her reteaming with Robert Mitchum in *The Big Steal*, in which Greer's character is much more sympathetic. Retiring in the mid-fifties to raise a family, she has returned to the screen in a handful of cameos and small parts, most notably in the remake of *Out of the Past*, *Against All Odds*, and a good modern gangster movie, *The Outfit*.

Out of the Past (RKO, 1947). *The Big Steal* (RKO, 1949). *The Outfit* (MGM, 1973). *Against All Odds* (Columbia, 1984).

Grey, Virginia (b. 1917)

Actress. The daughter of a silent film director, Virginia Grey literally grew up in the movie industry. Blonde and very attractive, she played leads in "B" movies and second female leads in major productions during the thirties and forties. Toward the end of her career, she costarred in the minor "B" gangster movie *Highway 301* as the moll of a dimwitted gangster.

Highway 301 (Warner Bros., 1950).

Griffin, Glenn (Fictional character)

Humphrey Bogart's final gangster character, in *The Desperate Hours* (Paramount, 1955), is one of three escaped convicts who holds a family hostage and is eventually outwitted by them.

Griffith, D. W. (1874–1948)

Director. David Wark Griffith, the first acknowledged great movie director, is usually associated with Victorian melodramas, but in fact he made movies of all types, including slapstick comedies and, in one notable case, a gangster movie. Certainly one of the earliest gangster movies, the enormously popular *The Musketeers of Pig Alley*, shot on location in New York, is a landmark in the history of screen realism.

The Musketeers of Pig Alley (Biograph, 1912).

Griffith, Raymond (1894–1937)

Producer. Griffith is a fascinating but nearly forgotten figure of American popular cinema. In the mid-twenties, after many years as a comedy writer for producer Mack Sennett, among others, Griffith signed with Paramount as a comic actor and immediately became a major star. Indeed, certain critics have called several of his comedy features from this era masterpieces of the genre, comparing them favorably to the best work of Charles Chaplin, Buster Keaton, and Harold Lloyd. Unfortunately, a mysterious accident in his youth had rendered him virtually speechless. After a well-received cameo as the dying soldier in *All Quiet on the Western Front* (Paramount, 1930), Griffith signed with Fox

as a staff producer, a job he held until his untimely death. For Fox and 20th Century-Fox, Griffith produced a variety of films especially some good screwball comedies and a single, superior gangster thriller.

Show Them No Mercy (20th Century-Fox, 1935).

Grinde, Nick (1891–1979)

Director. Grinde was a prolific "B" director who specialized in action oriented thrillers, including two minor gangster movies.

Public Enemy's Wife (Warner Bros., 1936). *King of Chinatown* (Paramount, 1938).

Guffey, Burnett (1905–1983)

Cinematographer. One of the great American cinematographers of his generation, Guffey's distinguished career began in the early forties. He worked on several *films noir*, including *The Reckless Moment* (Columbia, 1948) and *In a Lonely Place* (Columbia, 1950), both known for their extravagant visual styles. However, his best known work is probably in *From Here to Eternity* (Columbia, 1953), and he was the director of photography for a number of gangster pictures during this period. Unlike many of his contemporaries, Guffey easily adapted to color, and he created the shimmering, Academy Award-winning cinematography for *Bonnie and Clyde*, which is as good as any of his black and white work.

The Undercover Man (Columbia, 1949). *Tight Spot* (Columbia, 1955). *The Harder They Fall* (Columbia, 1956). *The Brothers Rico* (Columbia, 1957). *Nightfall* (Columbia, 1957). *Bonnie and Clyde* (Warner Bros.-7 Arts, 1967) — Academy Award for Best Cinematography.

Guinness, Alec (b. 1914)

Actor. A veteran stage actor, Guinness began his spectacular film career during the late forties. Before becoming a familiar face as a character actor in international films, beginning in the late fifties, he starred in several classic British comedies. He was one of the most familiar faces in the inventive Ealing comedies, the product of a small but resourceful British studio that released through the J. Arthur Rank Corporation. He most often played gentle characters who become the hapless victims of their own or other's bizarre schemes. In the classic *The Lavender Hill Mob*, he played such a character, the mild-mannered clerk who engineers a doomed heist. It remains one of his finest performances.

The Lavender Hill Mob (J. Arthur Rank, 1951).

Gun Crazy (United Artists, 1950). 87 mins.
Producer: Frank and Maurice King. *Director*: Joseph H. Lewis. *Screenplay*: Mackinley Kantor and Millard Kaufman. *Director of Photography*: Russell Harlan. *Music*: Victor Young. *Art Director*: Gordon Wiles. *Editor*: Harry Gerstad.
Cast: Peggy Cummins (Annie Laurie Starr), John Dall (Bart Tare), Berry Kroeger (Packett), Morris Carnovsky (Judge Willoughby), Anabel Shaw (Roby Tare), Harry Lewis (Clyde Boston). *With*: Nedrick Young, Trevor Bardette, Mickey Little, Rusty Tamblyn, Paul Frison, Dave Bair.

Bart Tare's obsession with guns always leads him to trouble. As a youth, he breaks into a store to steal a treasured rifle and, as a result, spends many years in a reformatory. After his release, he returns to the small town where he grew up. With two friends, he attends a traveling carnival that is passing through town. He is fascinated by the side show performer Annie Starr, a.k.a. "Annie Oakley," a trick shooter, and when he proves to be as adept with guns as she is, he is invited to join the carnival. Bart and Annie's affair leads to marriage, but they are fired by the carnival's jealous manager. Their money quickly disappears and, in an act of desperation, they turn to a life of crime. They begin by robbing gas stations and liquor stores, then graduating to banks. Although Bart abhors violence, his beautiful wife seems almost sexually excited by violence and murder, and his own sexual obsession with Annie leads Bart into acts of extreme violence. Eventually they temporarily "retire," taking jobs at a meat packing plant and planning to carry out one final robbery by stealing the plant's payroll. During the robbery, Annie kills two of the plant's employees. Chased by the police, they eventually find themselves surrounded in an overgrown field. Confused and desperate, Bart murders Annie just as the police shoot him. Their bodies fall together in a final, lifeless embrace.

Loosely based on the life and carrier of Bonnie and Clyde, *Gun Crazy* is an erotic, dour thriller often considered one of the greatest of all "B" movies. It is directed with superb skill by Joseph H. Lewis, and superbly acted by John Dall and Peggy Cummins as the doomed couple. The robbery and action scenes are brilliantly executed and truly suspenseful. The film is a classic and, despite its inevitably gloomy outlook, one of the most entertaining of its time.

Guys and Dolls (MGM, 1955). 158 mins.
Producer: Sam Goldwyn. *Director*: Joseph L. Mankiewicz. *Screenplay*: Joseph L. Mankiewicz, based on the musical by Jo Swerling and Abe Burrows, from a story by Damon Runyon. *Director of Photography*: Harry Stradling. *Songs*: Frank Loesser. *Art Director*: Cedric Gibbons. *Editor*: Daniel Mandell.
Cast: Marlon Brando (Sky Masterson), Jean Simmons (Sarah Brown), Frank Sinatra (Nathan Detroit), Vivian Blaine (Adelaide), Robert Keith (Lieutenant Brannigan), Stubby Kaye (Nicely-Nicely Johnson), Sheldon Leonard (Harry the Horse). *With*:

Marlon Brando as the cheerful gangster Nathan Detroit and Vivian Blaine in one of the few successful gangster musicals, *Guys and Dolls*.

Frank Sinatra and Vivian Blaine (center) surrounded by dapper mobsters in *Guy and Dolls*.

Johnny Silver, B. S. Pully, Dan Dayton, Regis Toomey, Katherine Givney, Veda Ann Borg.

While combining gangster themes with the musical might seem incongruous, there have been several notable attempts. Of the gangster musicals, *Guys and Dolls* is certainly the most successful. Based on one of humorist Damon Runyon's best short stories, the film recounts the amorous adventures of gambler Sky Masterson, gangster Nathan Detroit, their molls, Sarah Brown and Adelaide, and how they are reformed by the Salvation Army. Originally a hit stage musical, the film version suffers from the miscast leads, but the excellent supporting cast gives generally energetic performances. Its greatest asset, however, is the highly imaginative art direction (including purposely surreal, garish sets) and superior songs by Frank Loesser.

Gwynne, Fred (1926–1993)

Character actor. Tall and lanky, Gwynne was most famous as a lugubrious comic actor on television, memorably as Herman Munster in the series *The Munsters* (1964–65). On the big screen, he played mob henchmen in *On the Waterfront* and *The Cotton Club*.

On the Waterfront (Columbia, 1954). *The Cotton Club* (Orion, 1984).

Haas, Hugo (1901–1968)

Character actor. The Czech-born Haas had a prominent stage and screen career in Europe before moving to Hollywood in the late thirties. The heavy-set actor was usually typecast as a thick-accented villain or henchman. In *Casbah*, his role was somewhat similar to Sydney Greenstreet's in *Casablanca* (Warner Bros., 1942) — the vaguely sinister bar owner of the exotic underworld of Algiers. Haas later produced, directed, wrote, and starred in a series of strange, masochistic melodramas which have a devoted following.

Casbah (Universal, 1948).

Haas, Robert (1887–1962)

Art director. Haas studied architecture at the University of Pennsylvania and practiced from 1912 to 1920 before entering movies. He worked for several studios before joining Warner Bros. in 1929, remaining with them until his retirement in 1950. He was the art director for several of Warner's important gangster movies.

Three on a Match (First National, 1932). *The Little Giant* (First National, 1933). *Angels with Dirty Faces* (Warner Bros., 1938). *The Maltese Falcon* (Warner Bros., 1941). *The Damned Don't Cry* (Warner Bros., 1950).

Hackford, Taylor (b. 1946)

Director. Hackford attracted considerable critical attention for his first feature *The Idolmaker* (United Artists, 1980), an evocative portrait of early rock and roll impresarios. He followed this with the enormously successful *An Officer and a Gentleman* (Paramount, 1982). Unfortunately, his next film, *Against All Odds* was a tepid remake of the classic gangster *noir Out of the Past* (RKO, 1947), and it was neither a box office nor a critical success.

Against All Odds (Columbia, 1984).

Hackman, Gene (b. 1930)

Actor. Certainly one of the most charismatic actors of his generation, Gene Hackman began appearing on stage during the mid-fifties and in the movies during the early sixties. For many years he worked as a character actor and first achieved widespread acclaim as Buck, Clyde Barrow's equally violent brother, in *Bonnie and Clyde*. He achieved real fame, however, as Popeye Doyle in *The French Connection* and its sequel, *French Connection II*.

Bonnie and Clyde (Warner Bros.–7 Arts, 1967). *The French Connection* (20th Century–Fox, 1971). *French Connection II* (20th Century–Fox, 1975).

Hagen, Jean (1923–1977)

Actress. After stage experience, the talented Hagen began appearing in films during the late forties. Blonde and very attractive, she had a spotty movie career, the highlight of which is probably her moll in John Huston's classic *The Asphalt Jungle.*

The Asphalt Jungle (MGM, 1950).

Hall, Al (1894–1968)

Director. Hall, a Broadway actor and director, was a competent if not particularly inventive studio director, working almost exclusively for Paramount during the thirties and Columbia during the forties. He was at his best with light comedy and drama, but he also directed three minor gangster movies.

Madame Racketeer (Paramount, 1932). *Limehouse Blues* (Paramount, 1934). *I Am the Law* (Columbia, 1938).

Hall, Huntz (b. 1920)

Actor. As a teenager, Hall, a native New Yorker, performed on stage, most notably in *Dead End*, Sydney Kingsley's gangster drama. Like Leo Gorcey, he went to Hollywood to appear in the film version and was subsequently reteamed with Gorcey and several other "Dead End Kids" in *Angels with Dirty Faces*. His early, sinister image became more comical over time, particularly when the team became the Bowery Boys at Monogram Pictures, where he always played the put-upon sidekick to Leo Gorcey's gang leader.

Dead End (United Artists, 1937). *Angels with Dirty Faces* (Warner Bros., 1938). *Angels' Alley* (Monogram, 1948).

Haller, Ernest (1896–1970)

Cinematographer. One of the most important cinematographers of the thirties and forties, Haller is best known for his work on *Gone with the Wind* (MGM, 1939) and the great *film noir Mildred Pierce* (Warner Bros., 1945). He photographed several important gangster movies during the genre's heyday, and was largely responsible for the gritty, unadorned visual style of Warner Bros.' gangster movies of the thirties.

The Finger Points (First National, 1931). *Night After Night* (Paramount, 1932). *Invisible Stripes* (Warner Bros., 1939). *The Roaring Twenties* (Warner Bros., 1939).

Hally, George (Fictional character)

One of Humphrey Bogart's last supporting roles as a gangster was in *The Roaring Twenties* (Warner Bros., 1939), which starred James Cagney. As George Hally, Bogart played one of his most cowardly and simpering villains, a veteran of the First World War who becomes a murderous big-city mobster. Never less than immaculately dressed, Hally is the fierce rival of Cagney's Eddie Bartlett, a bootlegger, who eventually kills him in a memorably violent gun battle. A year later, Bogart would star in *High Sierra* (Warner Bros., 1940), directed by Raoul Walsh, the director of *The Roaring Twenties*, and the film that would help make him into a full-fledged star.

Hammett, Dashiell (1894–1961)

Novelist and screenwriter. Despite his sparse output (four novels and two collections of short stories), Hammett had a profound influence on pulp literature and popular culture in general. His spare style, which is similar to Hemingway's, has been copied, but it was his hard-boiled themes and characters which had the greatest impact. The whole detective genre in popular literature would be all but unimaginable without his models. Best known as the creator of the archetypal private detective Sam Spade, the hero of *The Maltese Falcon*, he also wrote many stories in the vein of W. R. Burnett. Of these, the novel *The Glass Key* is the most prominent and, like *The Maltese Falcon*, was twice made as a film. In both cases, the second versions are the classics. He also contributed the screenplay for the important early gangster movie *City Streets*, one of his few original scripts.

City Streets (Paramount, 1931; screenwriter). *The Maltese Falcon* (Warner Bros., 1931). *The Glass Key* (Paramount, 1935). *The Maltese Falcon* (Warner Bros., 1941). *The Glass Key* (Paramount, 1942).

Handley, Dix (Fictional character)

A new kind of antihero was introduced in *film noir*, and Dix Handley is one of the most famous examples. In *The Asphalt Jungle* (MGM, 1950), Handley (Sterling Hayden) is a typical small-time *noir* criminal, not a true mobster or Mafioso of old, and doomed, inevitably, to tragedy and failure. Despite his tough facade, Handley is a jumble of neuroses who perhaps senses his own failure to come. That failure is the result of a botched heist which he helps plan. Shot by the police, who have arrested or killed the other members of Handley's makeshift gang, the film ends as he escapes with his moll, Doll Conovan. His ultimate fate, however, is sealed. Hayden's stone-faced, typically bland performance perfectly captures the peculiar duality of Handley's personality.

Hard Guy (Producers Releasing Corp., 1941). 67 mins.

Producers: George Merrick and Arthur Alexander. *Director*: Elmer Clifton. *Screenplay*: Olive Drake. *Director of Photography*: Eddie Linden. *Editor*: Charles Henkel.

Cast: Jack LaRue (Vic), Mary Healy (Julie), Kane Richmond (Steve), Iris Adrian (Goldie), Gayle Mellott (Doris), Jack Mulhall (Cassidy). *With*: Howard Banks, Ben Taggart, Montague Shaw, Ina Guest, Arthur Gardner.

Vic is a nightclub owner and small-time racketeer who forces his female employees to marry rich young men and then extort money from their spouses' unhappy parents for a quick annulment. When one of the girls refuses to carry out his plan, Vic kills her. Her sister, Julie, then gets a job at the club to gather evidence against the slimy, cold-blooded racketeer. She is aided by Steve, and together they help ring the downfall of the killer.

A typical PRC programmer, *Hard Guy* is a cheaply produced gangster movie with a minimal cast and even more minimal settings — almost all of the action takes place in the nightclub. Nevertheless, it is a taut, watchable thriller, due in large part to Jack LaRue's performance. LaRue, a perennial bad guy in mostly "B" movies, had some of the same, intense qualities of George Raft and James Cagney, but never became a full-fledged star. His performance in this film, as the murderous pimp and racketeer, is one of his most memorable.

The Harder They Fall (Columbia, 1956). 109 mins.

Producer: Philip Yordan. *Director*: Mark Robson. *Screenplay*: Philip Yordan, based on the novel by Budd Schulberg. *Director of Photography*: Burnett Guffey. *Music*: Lionel Newman. *Art Director*: William Flannery. *Editor*: Jerome Thoms.

Cast: Humphrey Bogart (Eddie Willis), Rod Steiger (Nick Benko), Jan Sterling (Beth Willis), Mike Lane (Toro Moreno), Max Baer (Buddy Brannen), Jersey Joe Walcott (George). *With*: Edward Andrews, Harold J. Stone, Carlos Montalban, Nehemiah Persoff, Felice Orlandi, Herbie Faye.

Eddie Willis, a has-been sports journalist, is down on his luck until he is hired by Nick Benko, the head of a boxing syndicate, to help promote a bumbling fighter, Toro Moreno. Moreno is large and imposing, but also an inept boxer. When he wins a series of fixed fights, he is given a shot at the championship. When his opponent in another fight collapses and dies, Moreno blames himself. When Willis informs Toro that the fights he won were fixed and that the other boxed died of a hemorrhage caused by a beating by another boxer, Moreno is determined to fight the champion on his own terms. Moreno is badly beaten and, in disgust, Willis gives him his share of the earnings from the fixed fights and sends him home to Argentina. Although he receives physical threats, Willis sets out to write a series of articles exposing the boxing racket.

The Harder They Fall is the most uncompromising and cynical of the boxing oriented *films noir*. Brutally realistic, it was based on Budd Schulberg's exposé of the then-contemporary boxing syndicates and their corrupt manipulation of the sport. It gave Rod Steiger yet another gangster role in a Schulberg based film—the other being *On the Waterfront* (Columbia, 1954)—and provided Humphrey Bogart with his last screen role, ironically as the good guy in the genre in which he once was the quintessential villain.

Harlan, Russell (1903–1974)

Cinematographer. Harlan began his film career as, of all things, a stuntman before switching to cinematography during the mid-thirties. His style was simple and direct.

Riot in Cell Block 11 (Allied Artists, 1954).

Harline, Leigh (1907–1969)

Composer. A prolific and versatile composer, Harline wrote the scores for a variety of films. When composing for thrillers, his style was vaguely similar to Max Steiner's: piquant, yet oddly melodic and dramatically intense when necessary.

They Live by Night (RKO, 1948).

Harlow, Jean (1911–1937)

Actress. In the thirties, Harlow was the perfect American sex symbol: tough, flamboyant, irreverent, and unimpressed by her importance, her characters seemed to epitomize the American spirit during the Great Depression. Born Harlean Carpenter in Kansas City, Missouri, she married a wealthy young businessman when she was sixteen and moved with him and her mother-manager to Hollywood. She began appearing in small parts in a variety of films (most notably as a foil for Laurel and Hardy) during the late twenties before she was discovered by Howard Hughes, who cast her in *Hell's Angels* (United Artists, 1930). At nineteen, she became a major star overnight. Her platinum blonde hair and forthright, sensual screen image became an indelible symbol of the thirties. Her fame was consolidated with *Public Enemy*, as a gangster moll opposite James Cagney. She also played a moll in the equally hard-boiled *The Beast of the City* and *The Secret Six* but, like Marilyn Monroe, she was at her best in comedy. Unlike MGM's other female stars, Harlow was all American and proletarian, and her few roles as an upperclass dame were apparently difficult for her to pull off. Also like Monroe, Harlow was a victim of the media, which delighted in revealing details of her allegedly sordid private life. She died at the height of her fame (of an untreated ailment), but remains American movies' most interesting and, with the possible exception of Marilyn Monroe, most talented sex symbol.

Public Enemy (Warner Bros., 1931). *The Secret Six* (MGM, 1931). *Beast of the City* (MGM, 1932).

Hart, Dorothy (b. 1923)

Actress. A pretty brunette, Hart generally played second leads and leads in "B" movies. She costarred in a single minor gangster movie.

Loan Shark (Lippert, 1952).

Haskin, Byron (1899–1984)

Director. A respected cinematographer for most of his career, Haskin began directing in the late forties, specializing in high quality and low budget sci-fi dramas. His first film as a director, *I Walk Alone*, is very much in the tradition of Paramount's *films noir*: dark, moody, and psychologically intense.

I Walk Alone (Paramount, 1947).

Hathaway, Henry (1898–1985)

Director. Even if Henry Hathaway's reputation has diminished in recent years, there can be little doubt about the overall quality of his films. Indeed, he made more than his share of classic movies, and he remains the greatest director of hard-boiled themes. *The Lives of a Bengal Lancer* (Paramount, 1935), *The House on 92nd Street* (20th Century-Fox, 1945), *Call Northside 777* (20th Century-Fox, 1948), and *Niagara* (20th Century-Fox, 1953) are just a few of his classics. Equally at home with Westerns and contemporary settings, Hathaway directed three superior gangster dramas. Of these, *Kiss of Death* is probably the best known, but all are characterized by his visceral style and almost irreverent approach.

Johnny Apollo (20th Century-Fox, 1940). *Kiss of Death* (20th Century-Fox, 1947). *Seven Thieves* (20th Century-Fox, 1960).

Hawks, Howard (1896–1977)

Director. Of the great American film directors, Howard Hawks was the most versatile, moving effortlessly between genres and making at least one classic in each. His Westerns and screwball comedies are incomparable, but he also directed one of the most important and influential early gangster dramas, *Scarface*. Although less well known, he also made one of the best prison dramas, *The Criminal Code*, a much more realistic movie than *The Big House* (MGM, 1930). Both of these Hawks films (on which he collaborated without taking credit on the scenarios) are characterized by an economy of style and a fast pace which is deceptively simple.

The Criminal Code (Columbia, 1931). *Scarface: The Shame of a Nation* (United Artists, 1932).

Hayden, Sterling (1917–1986)

Actor. Born Sterling Walter Relyea in Montclair, New Jersey, the handsome, rangy Sterling Hayden came to epitomize the stoic antihero in American movies during the forties and fifties. From the cycle of crime thrillers he starred in during these two decades, the best known is certainly *The Asphalt Jungle*, in which he plays one of the doomed jewel robbers. He played a similar role in Stanley Kubrick's equally fatalistic *The Killing*. In *Manhandled*, he played a tough insurance investigator tracing jewel robberies. One of his best, but least known, performances was in *Crime Wave*, in which he plays a relentless cop hunting down a group of bank robbers.

Manhandled (Paramount, 1949). *The Asphalt Jungle* (MGM, 1950). *Crime Wave* (Warner Bros., 1953). *The Killing* (United Artists, 1956).

Hayworth, Rita (1918–1987)

Actress. Hayworth was *the* sex symbol of the forties — the epitome of Hollywood glamour and smoldering sensuality. Off camera, she was shy and reserved and she was only an adequate actress; but the camera loved her, and her on-screen charisma is undeniable. Born Margarite Carmer Cansino in Brooklyn, her father was a famous ballroom dancer. He groomed his daughter for stardom and, as a teenager, she was his main dancing partner, appearing in vaudeville and in nightclubs throughout the country. Her life was difficult — among other things, her father allegedly sexually abused her — but eventually she ended up in Hollywood under contract to Columbia. Although unquestionably attractive, her dark, ethnic beauty made her difficult to cast in an era of such overt bigotry, and it was felt that audiences in middle America would not accept her in lead roles. Nevertheless, she stuck it out, got better roles as the thirties progressed, and underwent some minor plastic surgery, mainly electrolysis to raise her hairline to make her more acceptable. As her popularity increased during the early forties, she was cast in lead roles, mostly in musicals (she was one of Fred Astaire's favorite partners), but she will probably be best remembered as the title character in the classic *film noir Gilda*. Generally cast in lighter fare as a star, she appeared in a wide variety of films. Among these is a minor gangster drama from the late thirties, made just as her star began to ascend.

Homicide Bureau (Columbia, 1939). *Gilda* (Columbia, 1946).

Heat Lightning (Warner Bros., 1934). 63 mins.
Producer and Director: Mervyn LeRoy. *Screenplay*: Brown Holmes and Warren Duff, based on the play by George Abbott and Leon Abrams. *Director of Photography*: Sid Hickox. *Editor*: Howard Bretherton.
Cast: Aline MacMahon (Olga), Ann Dvorak (Myra), Preston Foster (George), Lyle Talbot (Jeff), Glenda Farrell ("Feathers"/Mrs. Rifton), Frank McHugh (Chauffer). *With*: Ruth Donnelly, Williard Robertson, Edgar Kennedy, Theodore Newton, Jane Darwell, Muriel Evans.
George and Jeff, two hoodlums on the run, stop at a Southwestern filling station and restaurant run by George's ex-moll, Olga. Jeff seduces the pretty, vulnerable Myra, Olga's younger sister. Meanwhile, two wealthy divorcées have also stopped at the restaurant. George and Jeff plan to rob the two rich women, but they are foiled by Olga who, upon learning of Myra's seduction, kills the two gangsters before the police arrive.
Predating *The Petrified Forest* (Warner Bros., 1936), *Heat Lightning* is a passable melodrama with essentially the same plot. Although not a classic,

it holds up very well. Its greatest virtue is Ann Dvorak's performance as the not so innocent girl seduced by the roguish gangster. Its slight comic relief, in the form of the eccentric divorcées, is also a nice touch in an otherwise cynical screenplay, quite typical of its cowriter, Warren Duff. Indeed, although not as well known as many of its contemporaries, *Heat Lightning* is one of the best early Warner Bros.' gangster movies.

Hecht, Ben (1894–1964)
Screenwriter. An underrated talent, Hecht was a novelist, short story writer, poet, playwright, screenwriter and film director. Originally a journalist in his native Chicago during the late teens and early twenties (just as the city's underworld emerged), Hecht spent time in Berlin during the midtwenties, working as a correspondent and writing excellent short stories. Aligned with the Dadaists, he was really always just a highly imaginative commercial writer. He found film the perfect medium to express himself, first working for director Josef von Sternberg after his return from Germany in the late twenties. Although probably best known for the biting wit of his stage and movie satires, he was also a master of hard-boiled subjects and thrillers. Indeed, his screenplay for Sternberg's seminal gangster movie, *Underworld*, predates his classic stage farces, *The Front Page* and *The Twentieth Century*, both written with Charles MacArthur several years later. Hecht wrote or cowrote many crime and psychological thrillers, including several of Alfred Hitchcock's best films of the forties and several important gangster movies: the classics *Scarface* and *Kiss of Death*, and the less well known Otto Preminger thriller, *Where the Sidewalk Ends*. All are distinguished by their piquant dialog, fast pace, and unsentimental approach.
Underworld (Paramount, 1929). *Scarface* (United Artists, 1932). *Kiss of*

Death (20th Century-Fox, 1947). *Where the Sidewalk Ends* (20th Century-Fox, 1950).

Hedrick, Earl (1896–1984)

Art director. Long employed at Paramount, Hedrick was one of Hans Dreier's chief collaborators during the forties. His style was somewhat more subdued than Dreier's, best demonstrated in Preston Sturges' comedies during the forties. His work with Dreier on the "B" prison drama *The King of Alcatraz* is also typical, a strange mixture of realism and art deco designs.

King of Alcatraz (Paramount, 1938).

Heffron, Richard (b. 1930)

Director. Mainly working in television, Heffron has also directed a few features, including a near-contemporary gangster drama, *Newman's Law*, which attracted some critical attention at the time of its release. It remains Heffron's most important film.

Newman's Law (Universal, 1974).

Heisler, Stuart (1894–1979)

Director. A good, if uninventive, director of "B" movies, Heisler also made a few prestigious films. Of these, the most important is *The Glass Key*, a gangster drama which, with its semi-expressionist style and leading actors (Veronica Lake and Alan Ladd), is a notable early *film noir*.

The Glass Key (Paramount, 1942).

Heists

This subgenre found its greatest expression and maturity in *film noir*, but it was an element in certain pulp novels during the thirties and at least one non-*noir* gangster movie, *I Stole a Million* (Universal, 1939). *The Asphalt Jungle* (MGM, 1950) was the first great heist drama and established the formula for the group of films which followed. In each, a group of disparate criminals comes together to carry out a heist. The heist is planned in great detail, carried off successfully, but falls apart because of the gangsters mistakes, jealousies, and bad luck. *The Killing* (United Artists, 1956), *Six Bridges to Cross* (Universal, 1955), *The Brinks Job* (Universal, 1978), which was based on a real heist, *Seven Thieves* (20th Century-Fox, 1960), and *The Sicilian Clan* (Fox-Europa/Les Films du Siecle, 1968) all follow this formula. The first, directed by Stanley Kubrick, is a classic. The last is one of France's most successful films. Edward G. Robinson starred in two European productions, *The Biggest Bundle of Them All* (MGM, 1968) and *Grand Slam* (Paramount, 1968), as an aging gangster planning one last heist. Neither are particularly important. Much more interesting are two heist dramas directed by Jules Dassin, *Rififi* (Miracle, 1955) and *Topkapi* (United Artists, 1964). Both are classics of the subgenre, made in Europe while Dassin was in exile in France after the communist witch hunt of the fifties. *Kansas City Confidential* (United Artists, 1952), a great "B" movie, varies the formula somewhat by following the mobsters after the heist as one of them attempts to kill the others and keep the money for himself. The film foreshadows the modern heist drama *Reservoir Dogs* (Live American, 1993), which has a similar theme, but a much bloodier outcome in the modern style.

Hell on Frisco Bay (Warner Bros., 1956). 98 mins.

Associate Producer: George Bertholon. *Director*: Frank Tuttle. *Screenplay*: Sydney Boehm and Martin Rackin, based on the novel by William P. McGivern. *Music*: Max Steiner. *Art Director*: John Beckman. *Editor*: Folmar Blangsted.

Cast: Alan Ladd (Steve Rollins), Edward G. Robinson (Victor Amato), Joanne Dru (Marcia Rollins), William Demarest (Dan Bianco), Paul Stewart (Joe Lye), Fay Wray (Kay Stanley). *With*: Perry Lopez, Renata Vanni,

Nestor Paiva, Stanley Adams, Willis Bouchey, Peter Hanson.

Steve Rollins, an ex-cop, is released from prison after five years, determined to discover who framed him on a manslaughter charge. Rejecting the help of his faithless ex-wife, Marcia, and his boss, Dan Bianco, he learns that a local racketeer, Victor Amato, is the culprit. He refuses to join Victor's gang. With the help of Kay Stanley, the moll of one of Victor's rivals whom he has had killed, Rollins proves his innocence, and the racketeer is captured by the police while trying to escape.

More than twenty years after their initial gangster cycle, Warner Bros. still managed to put out crime dramas that were comparable in quality to their early thirties thrillers. While not quite a classic, *Hell on Frisco Bay* holds up very well, thanks to its hard-boiled, unsentimental screenplay, and excellent performances, particularly by Edward G. Robinson as yet another cold-blooded gangster.

Hellinger, Mark (1903–1947)

Screenwriter and producer. A prominent New York–based journalist during the late twenties and early thirties, Hellinger moved to Hollywood during the late thirties. For many years he was a useful screenwriter, working on a number of successful films. He provided the story for the classic gangster movie *The Roaring Twenties*. As a producer, he joined Universal, where he created his greatest legacy during the mid-forties. Hellinger was a kind of Val Lewton–like producer whose work shows a definite artistic vision, particularly in bleak, cynical urban melodramas. Of the classics he produced during this period, the best is the gangster thriller *The Killers*, based on Ernest Hemingway's short story. He also produced and narrated the classic *film noir The Naked City* (Universal, 1948), released shortly after his untimely death. Had he lived, he might well have

become a producer-auteur as important as Val Lewton.

The Roaring Twenties (Warner Bros., 1939; story only). *The Killers* (Universal, 1946; producer only).

Hellman, Lillian (1905–1984)

Screenwriter. An important playwright, Hellman was also Dashiell Hammett's lover and a successful screenwriter. She adapted Sydney Kingley's play *Dead End*, one of her most important screenplays.

Dead End (United Artists, 1937).

Hell's Kitchen (Warner Bros., 1939). 81 mins.

Producers: Mark Hellinger and Bryan Foy. *Directors*: Lewis Seiler and E. A. Dupont. *Screenplay*: Crane Wilbur and Fred Niblo, Jr. *Story*: Crane Wilbur. *Director of Photography*: Charles Rosher. *Editor*: Howard Bretherton.

Cast: Billy Halop (Tony), Bobby Jordan (Joey), Leo Gorcey (Gyp), Huntz Hall (Ace), Gabriel Dell (Bingo), Bernard Punsley (Ouch), Frankie Burke (Soap), Ronald Reagan (Jim). *With*: Margaret Lindsay, Stanley Fields, Fred Tozere, Grant Mitchell, Arthur Loft, Vera Lewis.

The last of the Dead End Kid's vehicles, *Hell's Kitchen* is typical of the deteriorating quality of the series during the late thirties. Its plot is only serviceable: a misunderstood ex-con who runs a shelter is mistakenly identified as a criminal, and the kids have to run it while he temporarily hides out. However, it is still a serious movie (unlike the later Bowery Boys series), and presents an unsentimental view of street gang life during the late years of the Great Depression. It is also notable for two additional reasons. First, its screenplay was written by Crane Wilbur, one of the masters of hard-boiled themes during the forties. Secondly, it was one of Mark Hellinger's earliest films as a producer. During the late forties, Hellinger would achieve notoriety as one of Universal's top producers with *The Killers* (1946) and several other important *films noir*.

Herbert, F. Hugh (1897–1957)
Screenwriter. Herbert is an interesting if nearly forgotten screenwriter. Generally considered a second string screenwriter even while working in Hollywood, he nevertheless wrote a number of superior films, generally cynical romantic comedies. His film career began in the late twenties after experience as a playwright. He continued to write successful plays, many of which were adapted for the screen, throughout his nearly thirty-year film career. He wrote the screenplay for the important early gangster drama *Lights of New York*.
Lights of New York (Warner Bros., 1928).

Hershey, Barbara (b. 1948)
Actress. The attractive, talented Hershey has been a critical and popular success since the late sixties. Born Barbara Herzstein in New York City, she acted on stage before beginning her successful and varied film career in 1968. One of her best early performances was in Martin Scorsese's *Boxcar Bertha*, a film inspired by the life of Bonnie Parker.
Boxcar Bertha (American International, 1972).

Herzbrun, Bernard (1891–1978)
Art director. Yet another ex-architect, Herzbrun was a leading art director, beginning in the thirties. He did his best work for Universal, creating the designs for many important productions, including the classic prison drama *Brute Force* and Robert Siodmak's great *film noir Criss Cross*.
Stolen Harmony (Paramount, 1935). *Up the River* (20th Century-Fox, 1938). *Brute Force* (Universal, 1947). *Criss Cross* (Universal, 1949). *Johnny Stool Pigeon* (Universal, 1949). *Forbidden* (Universal, 1953).

Heston, Charlton (b. 1923)
Actor. Born John Charlton Carter in Evanston, Illinois, the tall, muscular, strong-jawed Heston played a succession of bigger than life characters in a variety of historical epics. He also played a few more humane, flawed characters, most memorably as a crooked gambler investigating a series of murders in *Dark City*, his only gangster film.
Dark City (Paramount, 1950).

Hickey and Boggs (United Artists, 1972). 111 mins.
Executive Producer: Richard L. O'Connor. *Producer*: Fouad Said. *Director*: Robert Culp. *Screenplay*: Walter Hill. *Director of Photography*: Wilmer Butler. *Music*: Ted Ashford. *Editor*: David Barlatsky.
Cast: Bill Cosby (Al Hickey), Robert Culp (Frank Boggs), Rosalind Cash (Nyona), Carmen (Mary Jane), Louis Moreno (Quemando), Ron Henrique (Quemando's Brother). *With*: Robert Mandan, Michael Moriarty, Lester Fletcher, Sil Words, Bernie Schwartz, Vincent Gardenia.
In the tradition of gangster movies that chronicle the adventures of police against the underworld, *Hickey and Boggs* follows the two title characters, Los Angeles police detectives, in their attempts to recover money taken in a heist. The conventional plot is updated with graphic violence and a racial integration sub-theme. Walter Hill's screenplay is very good, cutting expertly between the two cops and the curious underworld figures who are also seeking the pilfered fortune. A moderate success at the time of its release, the film is much better in retrospect. Bill Cosby and Robert Culp had previously costarred in the immensely popular television series *I Spy*, and the film was an attempt to carry that popularity to the big screen. If it was not entirely successful at making them into full-fledged movie stars, it did prove that they were a compelling team with their

own peculiar brand of charisma. It also proved that Culp had the talent to direct, and it is unfortunate that he did not have the opportunity to make more films like this one.

Hickox, Sid (b. 1895)
Cinematographer. Long employed by Warner Bros., Hickox was vitally important to the studio's image during the thirties and forties. Hickox refined the studio's unadorned, realistic photography so favored in the thirties, giving it extra luster and emphasizing shadowy effects. He was the director of photography for many classic films, including two Howard Hawks movies, *To Have and Have Not* (Warner Bros., 1944) and *The Big Sleep* (Warner Bros., 1945), the *film noir* classic *Dark Passage* (Warner Bros., 1947), and many excellent gangster movies. Indeed, Hickox is one of the genre's most important cinematographers, and his best work remains some of the most imaginative in popular movies.
Those Who Dare (Warner Bros., 1930). *Blonde Crazy* (Warner Bros., 1931). *The Little Giant* (First National, 1933). *The Big Shakedown* (First National, 1934). *Heat Lightning* (Warner Bros., 1934). *Special Agent* (Warner Bros., 1935). *San Quentin* (Warner Bros., 1937). *A Slight Case of Murder* (Warner Bros., 1938). *King of the Underworld* (Warner Bros., 1939). *The Big Shot* (Warner Bros., 1942). *White Heat* (Warner Bros., 1949).

Hideout (MGM, 1934). 82 mins.
Director: W. S. Van Dyke. *Screenplay*: Frances Goodrich and Albert Hackett. *Story by* Mauri Grashin. *Cinematography*: Ray June and Sidney Wagner. *Editor*: Basil Wrangel.
Cast: Robert Montgomery (Lucky Wilson), Maureen O'Sullivan (Pauline), Edward Arnold (MacCarthy), Elizabeth Patterson (Mrs. Miller), Whitford Kane (Mr. Miller), Mickey Rooney (Willie). *With*: C. Henry Gordon, Henry Armetta, Murial Evans,

Edward Brophy, Herman Bing, Louise Henry, Harold Huber.
Lucky Wilson is the second in command in an extortion protection racket run by Tony Berrelli. In a run-in with the police, Wilson is shot in the hand and flees to the country. He takes refuge with a farmer and his family, telling them he was injured by hoodlums. Under the influence of rural life and his growing love for the farmer's daughter, Pauline, he begins to see the error of his ways. He returns to the big city to face the consequences of his crimes while Pauline agrees to await his return.
For years, MGM had an unofficial "B" unit, producing low cost, high yield program pictures to meet their release quota. *Hideout* is one of those pictures, and it suffers from the usual curses of a "B" production, including a hackneyed screenplay and poor production values. Robert Montgomery was badly cast as a tough gangster, but the film does have some good moments, many played by Mickey Rooney as Pauline's annoying younger brother.

Higgin, Howard (1893–1938)
Director. Higgin's film career began in the early twenties. By the latter part of the decade, Higgin was a leading talent, but his career went into a slight decline after the arrival of sound. Still, he directed a number of interesting films before his untimely death. His movies are tough and unsentimental, not unlike Warner Bros.' movies of the early thirties. Among these is a superior early gangster drama, *The Racketeer*, typical of his fast paced, realistic style.
The Racketeer (Pathé, 1929).

Higgins, John C.
Screenwriter. Higgins wrote a number of good "B" movies, beginning in the late forties. Of these, *T-Men* is probably the best and most typical: a tough, unsentimental cop thriller with a resilient hero who manages to overcome

Left to right: Alan Curtis, Arthur Kennedy, Humphrey Bogart, Barton MacLane and Ida Lupino—the gang in *High Sierra* plans their heist.

murderous odds, and in the end, wins a victory over a gang of counterfeiters. *T-Men* (Eagle-Lion, 1948).

High Sierra (Warner Bros., 1941). 100 mins.
Executive Producer: Hal B. Wallis. *Director*: Raoul Walsh. *Screenplay*: John Huston and W. R. Burnett, based on the novel by W. R. Burnett. *Director of Photography*: Tony Gaudio. *Music*: Adolph Deutsch. *Art Director*: Ted Smith. *Editor*: Jack Killifer.
Cast: Humphrey Bogart (Roy Earle), Ida Lupino (Marie Garson), Alan Curtis (Babe Kozak), Arthur Kennedy (Red Hattery), Joan Leslie (Velma), Henry Hull ("Doc" Banton), Barton MacLane (Jake Kranmer). *With*: Henry Travers, Elisabeth Risdon, Cornel Wilde, Minna Gombell, Paul Harvey, Donald MacBride, Jerome Cowan.

Roy "Mad Dog" Earle is sprung from jail by a gang planning to rob a resort hotel. Earle and his younger cohorts plan the crime carefully, waiting for just the right moment to pull off the heist. Earle, however, falls in love with Marie, the much put-upon and violated moll and, when he befriends a blind girl, his tender, more human side is exposed. The heist is carried out, and Earle gives his share to the family of the blind girl so that she can have an expensive operation to restore her sight. He then tries to flee to Mexico with Marie, but meets his end when the police corner him in the Sierra Madre mountains.

When George Raft turned down the role of "Mad Dog" Earle, Bogart got the part. Previously a character actor and lead for Warner Bros., Bogart shot to stardom in *High Sierra*. His charisma, so long repressed by the studio, was irresistible, and he played the doomed character to the hilt. John Huston and W. R. Burnett's taut and unsentimental screenplay, based on Burnett's best-selling novel, presaged the new style of gangster yarns that emerged in the forties. The direction and performances are very good making *High Sierra* one of the genre's greatest films.

A remake, *I Died a Thousand Times* (Warner Bros., 1955), directed by Stewart Heisler, starred Jack Palance as Roy Earle and Shelley Winters as Marie. It is an efficient entertainment, but pales in comparison to the original.

Highway 301 (Warner Bros., 1950). 83 mins.
Producer: Bryan Foy. *Director and Screenplay*: Andrew Stone. *Director of Photography*: Carl Guthrie. *Music*: William Lava. *Editor*: Owen Marks.
Cast: Steve Cochran (George), Virginia Grey (Mary), Gaby Andre (Lee), Edmon Ryan (Truscott), Robert Webber (William Phillips). *With*: Wally Cassell, Aline Towne, Richard Evan, Edward Norris.
Highway 301 is a typical, conventional "B" gangster movie of the early fifties. In a semi-documentary style expertly rendered by Andrew Stone, it recounts the rise and fall of a southern gang based in Virginia. What the film lacks in plot it makes up in violent action. "B" actor Steve Cochran is very good as the gang leader who, while trying to escape the pursuing police, meets a gory end under a speeding train.

Hill, George (1895-1934)
Director. Hill, born in Douglass, Kansas, was just one of more than a dozen protégés of D. W. Griffith who became a successful Hollywood director. Under contract to MGM, beginning in the early twenties, Hill was a top director of commercial features. He had a considerable critical reputation in the early thirties, thanks to many excellent films, including the

seminal gangster prison drama *The Big House*, an atypical MGM movie because of its unglamorous portrayal of prison life. His mysterious suicide cut short one of the most promising talents of the early sound era.
The Big House (MGM, 1930).

Hill, George Roy (b. 1922)
Director. A successful stage director for many years, Hill began directing movies during the early sixties. He has a talent for epic, glossy entertainment, best personified by his modern gangster drama-satire *The Sting*, for which he won an Academy Award as best director.
The Sting (Universal, 1973).

Hill, Walter (b. 1942)
Screenwriter. As a screenwriter, and later as a writer and director, Hill has specialized in tough, uncompromisingly cynical thrillers which often are compromised by their pretensions. *Hickey and Boggs*, a gangster and cop thriller, is typical of his work.
Hickey and Boggs (United Artists, 1972).

His Kind of Woman (RKO, 1951). 120 mins.
Executive Producer: Howard Hughes. *Associate Producer*: Robert Sparks. *Director*: John Farrow. *Screenplay*: Frank Fenton, *story by* Frank Fenton and Jack Leonard. *Director of Photography*: Harry J. Wild. *Music*: Constantin Bakaleinikoff. *Art Director*: Albert S. D'Agostino. *Editor*: Eda Warren.
Cast: Robert Mitchum (Dan Milner), Jane Russell (Leonore Brent), Vincent Price (Mark Cardigan), Tim Holt (Bill Lusk), Charles McGraw (Thompson), Raymond Burr (Nick Ferraro). *With*: Marjorie Reynolds, Leslye Banning, Jim Backus, Philip Van Zandt, John Mylong, Erno Verebes.
One night, Dan Milner, a down on his luck gambler, is accosted by two

hoodlums. After roughing him up, they offer him $500 if he will stay at a Mexican resort. Although the offer is out of the ordinary, Miller knows he does not really have another choice. In Mexico, he befriends singer Lenore Brent and an egocentric movie actor, Mark Cardigan, who is pursuing an affair with Brent. Through the help of F.B.I. agent Bill Lusk, Milner discovers that a deported gangster, Nick Ferraro, is planning to have him killed so he may assume his identity and reenter the United States. When Ferraro kidnaps Milner and holds him on his yacht, Lusk gathers together a makeshift posse among his rich friends to rescue Milner. Ferraro is killed in the confrontation, Milner is reunited with Lenore, and Lusk reluctantly becomes a celebrated hero.

One of *film noir*'s neglected classics, *His Kind of Woman* is a typical RKO feature produced by Howard Hughes. Featuring his protégée Jane Russell, and his favorite male employee, Robert Mitchum—a pair later teamed in the Hughes-produced *Macao* (RKO, 1952)—it features several songs performed by Russell, exotic settings, tough dialog, and plenty of double entendré. The whole thing is wildly entertaining, thanks to its superb cast, including Vincent Price as a vain movie star and Raymond Burr at his despicable best, and the expert direction of John Farrow.

Hodiak, John (1914–1955)
Actor. Hodiak was born in Pittsburgh to a Polish-Ukrainian family. He went to Hollywood via stage and radio success, and became a star in the absence of other leading men during World War II. He did not serve in the military because of hypertension, an ailment which would eventually kill him. His somber, sensitive demeanor was perfectly suited to the cynical forties, and he played a variety of antiheroes. He was especially good in the neglected gangster melodrama *Desert*

Fury as a tough hoodlum on the lam. He also had a supporting role in *The Bribe*. His screen career went into decline during the late forties, and he returned successfully to a stage career before his death.
Desert Fury (Paramount, 1947). *The Bribe* (MGM, 1949).

Hoffman, Dustin (b. 1937)
Actor. Unquestionably one of the leading actors of his generation, Hoffman specializes in character leads, generally intense eccentrics of the type he played in the immensely popular *Tootsie* (Universal, 1983). His screen image is that of a gentle, thoughtful character and was thus a poor choice to play the psychotic, murderous real life gangster Dutch Schultz in *Billy Bathgate*. He is therefore not believable in the role, his only performance in the genre.
Billy Bathgate (Touchstone, 1993).

Hogan, James (1891–1943)
Director. Hogan's career as a director began in the early twenties. With the arrival of sound, he became an efficient if unimaginative director of "B" movies for Paramount and Columbia. *Queen of the Mob*, a "B" gangster drama coscripted by Horace McCoy, is one of Hogan's best films.
Queen of the Mob (Paramount, 1940).

Holden, William (1918–1981)
Actor. Before Billy Wilder cast him in *Sunset Boulevard* (Paramount, 1949), William Holden's film career was rather spotty. Born William Franklin Beedle in Illinois, he was spotted by a movie talent agent while acting at Pasadena Junior College. He became a star overnight with his first movie, *Golden Boy* (Paramount, 1939), but his low key, natural style was alien to American movies in the thirties and forties. *Invisible Stripes* was his second film, and he holds his own against some formidable talent including Humphrey Bogart. Holden plays the kid brother

of a gangster (George Raft) who manages to stay out of the gang which ultimately destroys his brother's life.

Invisible Stripes (Warner Bros., 1939).

The Hole in the Wall (Paramount, 1929). 73 mins.

Director: Robert Florey. *Screenplay*: Pierre Collings, based on the play by Fred Jackson. *Director of Photography*: George Folsey. *Editor*: Morton Blumenstock.

Cast: Claudette Colbert (Jean Oliver), Edward G. Robinson ("The Fox"), David Newell (Gordon Grant), Nelly Savage (Madame Mystera), Donald Meek (Goofy), Louise Closser Hale (Mrs. Ramsey). *With*: Alan Brooks, Katherine Emmett, Marcia Kagno, Barry Macollum.

Edward G. Robinson plays "The Fox," a gangster in love with Jean Oliver, who was sent to prison on false charges and now seeks revenge against those who framed her. The Fox kidnaps the granddaughter of ring leader Mrs. Ramsey, allowing Jean time to recognize the error of her ways. She then runs away with her boyfriend, Gordon Grant, a newspaperman who was helping her.

Rather typical of the early gangster pictures in its uneasy mix of Victorian melodrama and contemporary crime themes, *The Hole in the Wall* is notable only for Edward G. Robinson's first appearance as a gangster. However, Robert Florey's style, although primitive, is admirable.

Holt, Jack (1888–1951)

Actor. Charles John Holt II was born in Winchester, Virginia. He began working in silent movies as a stuntman and became a popular strong-jawed hero of action pictures. In the sound era he played character roles and leads in "B" movies. He played a gang leader in the early gangster movie *The Squealer*, but was on the other side of the law in *Crime Takes a Holiday*. His son Tim Holt was also a successful actor.

The Squealer (Columbia, 1930). *Crime Takes a Holiday* (Columbia, 1938).

Homes, Geoffrey

Screenwriter and novelist. Geoffrey Homes was the pseudonym of screenwriter Daniel Mainwaring. Under the Homes nom de plume, Mainwaring wrote several best-selling pulp novels, including *Build My Gallows High*, which he adapted as *Out of the Past*. He wrote several other screenplays, including two additional gangster dramas, under this pseudonym. He also wrote many films, including a single gangster movie, under his real name. (*See* Mainwaring, Daniel).

Out of the Past (RKO, 1947). *The Big Steal* (RKO, 1949). *A Bullet for Joey* (United Artists, 1955).

Homicide Bureau (Columbia, 1939). 56 mins.

Producer: Jack Fier. *Director*: C. C. Coleman, Jr. *Screenplay*: Earle Snell. *Director of Photography*: Benjamin Kline. *Music*: Morris Stoloff. *Editor*: James Sweeney.

Cast: Bruce Cabot (Jim Logan), Rita Hayworth (J. G. Bliss), Marc Lawrence (Chuck Brown), Richard Fiske (Hank), Moroni Olsen (Captain Haines), Norman Willis (Briggs). *With*: Lee Prather, Gene Morgan, Robert Paige, Eddie Featherston, Stanley Andrews, John Tyrell.

Bruce Cabot, most famous for his role in *King Kong* (RKO, 1933), was also a familiar face in "B" pictures, usually cast as a tough guy on either side of the law. In *Homicide Bureau* he plays a police detective who is investigating a series of murders carried out by a racket selling stolen scrap iron. Rita Hayworth's brief appearance enlivens an otherwise dreary, poorly made "B" gangster picture.

The Hoodlum (United Artists, 1951). 61 mins.

Executive Producer: Jack Schwartz. *Producer*: Maurice Kosloff. *Director*: Max Nosseck. *Screenplay*: Sam Neuman and Nat Tanchuck. *Director of Photography*: Clark Ramsey. *Art Director*: Fred Preble. *Editor*: Jack Killifer.

Cast: Lawrence Tierney (Vincent Lubeck), Allene Roberts (Rosa), Edward Tierney,k a.k.a. Scott Brady (Johnny Lubeck), Lisa Golm (Mrs. Lubeck), Marjorie Riordan (Eileen). *With*: Stuart Randall, Ann Zika, John DeSimone, Tom Hubbard, Eddie Foster.

Vincent Lubeck, a hardened criminal, is released after years behind bars when his mother pleads for mercy to the parole board. Lubeck convinces the board that he has changed his ways, when in fact he has not. He begins working for his brother's gas station, while secretly planning an armored car robbery and putting together the gang to carry out the heist. The gangsters commit the caper, but plans go awry and, in the end, they are all either apprehended or killed.

Lawrence Tierney was briefly elevated to stardom with the success of the classic "B" movie *Dillinger* (Monogram, 1945). He was cast in some "A" pictures, most notably the classic *film noir Born to Kill* (RKO, 1948), but his unpredictable, volatile, and self destructive personality got him into trouble, and nervous studio chiefs refused to hire him. He soon found himself back in "B" pictures, from which he would never emerge. *The Hoodlum* is one of the best of these, a taut, brittle, and cynical thriller that, like *Dillinger*, was directed by Max Nosseck in typically dark style.

Hoodlum Empire (Republic, 1952). 98 mins.
Producer: Herbert J. Yates. *Director*: Joseph Kane. *Screenplay*: Bruce Manning and Bob Considine, *story by* Bob Considine. *Director of Photography*: Reggie Lanning. *Music*:

Nathan Scott. *Art Director*: Frank Arrigo. *Editor*: Richard Van Enger.
Cast: Brian Donlevy (Senator Bill Stephens), Claire Trevor (Connie Williams), Forrest Tucker (Charlie Fignatalli), Vera Ralston (Marte Dufour), Luther Adler (Nicki Mancani), John Russell (Joe Gray). *With*: Gene Lockhart, Grant Withers, Taylor Holmes, Roy Bancroft, William Murphy, Richard Jaeckel.

After joining the Army and serving in World War II, former gangster Joe Gray returns home, determined to go straight. He opens a service station, which is successful, but then becomes the target of his former gang mates, who are jealous of his success in a legitimate business. They then use his name in a series of crimes. Eventually, however, the G-men, led by Senator Bill Stephens, close in on the operation and shut it down.

Hoodlum Empire is a rather poor gangster movie, despite an excellent cast including Luther Adler as the mob leader and Claire Trevor as yet another moll. The film is rather typical of Republic's output. Despite its modest budget, it suffers from poor production values and a lame script.

Hoover, J. Edgar (1895–1972)
Director of the Federal Bureau of Investigation. After experience in business and law enforcement, Hoover took over the F.B.I. in 1924 in response to President Warren G. Harding's call for a federal force to fight the rise of organized crime during Prohibition. He cleaned up the corrupt bureau and molded it into a force to fight crime. Despite some successes, the F.B.I. was not particularly effective against big city gangsters. It had somewhat better luck against rural gangsters, most notably John Dillinger who was killed in an F.B.I. ambush. Hoover's greatest talent was probably his ability to use the media to his and the bureau's advantage; and early on, Hollywood succumbed to his peculiar charms.

Under his influence, Warner Bros. made *G-Men* (1935), a propaganda film including a white bread portrayal of the bureau that features James Cagney playing his first good-guy role in the gangster genre. Several similar films followed. Many were inspired by Hoover's articles and memoirs, *Persons in Hiding*, which gives some insight into the F.B.I.'s war against gangsters during the thirties and forties.

Hornblow, Arthur (1893–1976)
Producer. After Broadway experience, Hornblow moved to Hollywood in 1926 and quickly became a leading producer, mainly for Paramount. He produced John Huston's *The Asphalt Jungle* after becoming an independent producer during the late forties.
The Asphalt Jungle (MGM, 1950).

Hoskins, Bob (b. 1942)
Actor. The short, stocky, bald Hoskins is a dynamic and charismatic performer who first came to attention in Great Britain as a character actor on television and in films. His extraordinary performance in the British gangster movie *The Long Good Friday*, as a particularly murderous gang leader, helped make him into one of the most unlikely stars of contemporary movies. He also had a supporting role in the American gangster movie *The Cotton Club*, as a henchman with a convincing American accent.
The Long Good Friday (Black Lion, 1980). *The Cotton Club* (Orion, 1984).

Houseman, John (1902–1991)
Producer. Born Jacques Houseman to German immigrants in England, Houseman immigrated to the United States as a young adult and made a fortune in the stock market. When the market crashed in 1929, he turned to a career in the theater, at first as a playwright and then as a producer. He discovered the young Orson Welles several years later, and with him formed the Mercury Theatre. He followed Welles to Hollywood, but the two had a falling out and, after returning to New York for several years, he once again moved to Hollywood where he quickly became an established producer during the mid-forties. He worked mainly for Paramount and MGM, usually producing commercial films with a message. He produced the classic gangster *noir*, *They Live by Night*, one of his many prestigious productions. After retiring during the early sixties, he reluctantly returned to acting and became an unexpected star in his seventies.
They Live by Night (RKO, 1948).

The Houston Story (Columbia, 1956). 79 mins.
Producer: Sam Katzman. *Director*: William Castle. *Screenplay*: James B. Gordon. *Director of Photography*: Henry Freulich. *Art Director*: Paul Palmentola. *Editor*: Edwin Bryant.
Cast: Gene Barry (Frank Duncan), Barbara Hale (Zoe Crane), Edward Arnold (Paul Atlas), Paul Richards (Gordie Shay), Jeanne Cooper (Madge), Frank Jenks (Louie). *With*: John Zaremba, Chris Alcaide, Paul Levitt, Pete Kellett, Leslie Hunt, Claudia Bryar.
Notorious "B" horror director William Castle directed this minor gangster yarn built around a story of crooked politicians, oil millionaires, and a gang of thieves who steal gasoline and resell it on the black market. Lurid and at times rather silly, it is nevertheless an entertaining thriller, due to the performances of Barbara Hale as a ritzy moll and Edward Arnold as the leader of the local mob.

Howard, Leslie (1890–1943)
Actor. Born Leslie Stainer to Hungarian parents in Great Britain, the tall, light-haired Howard had a considerable stage career in London before entering movies at the age of forty. The personification of the intellectual sex

symbol, he is most identified with his romantic role as Ashley Wilkes in *Gone with the Wind* (MGM, 1939). He occasionally varied romantic roles with stronger parts in tougher films, perhaps most famously in the classic gangster melodrama *The Petrified Forest*. Howard originated the role of Alan Squire, the writer whose philosophical beliefs are put to the test in a violent encounter with an homicidal gangster, on Broadway. When he was signed by Warner Bros. to reprise the role, he insisted his costar from the stage production, Humphrey Bogart, be signed to play Duke Mantee, the gangster. This act might well be his most important contribution to the genre.

The Petrified Forest (Warner Bros., 1936).

Howard, William K. (1899–1954)

Director. Howard's career began in the silent era and came to an end during the mid-forties. He was essentially a "B" director, but he also directed a few "A" productions. One of his best films is the minor gangster classic *Back Door to Heaven*, an interesting, almost experimental movie.

Back Door to Heaven (Paramount, 1939).

Howe, James Wong (1899–1976)

Cinematographer. The Chinese-American Howe, born Wong Tung Jim, was one of the great cinematographers of his time. His style was less extravagant than many of his equally great contemporaries (William Daniels, for example), and combined both gritty realism and glossy romanticism. He photographed a number of gangster movies, including several classics.

Four Walls (MGM, 1928). *The Criminal Code* (Columbia, 1931). *Manhattan Melodrama* (MGM, 1934). *Whipsaw* (MGM, 1935). *Algiers* (United Artists, 1938). *Body and Soul* (United Artists, 1947).

Hoyt, John (b. 1905)

Character actor. Although nearly forgotten today, Hoyt was an incisive, talented character actor who specialized in smooth criminals. In the superior "B" gangster movie *Trapped*, he costarred as the dapper head of the Treasury Department who infiltrates a gang of counterfeiters.

Trapped (Eagle-Lion, 1949).

Hubbard, Lucien (1888–1971)

Screenwriter. Hubbard is a typical example of the consummate professional screenwriter who worked in Hollywood during the golden age of the studio system: he took whatever assignments he was given with enthusiasm and carried them out with efficiency. For Warner Bros.–First National, he wrote two minor gangster movies.

The Star Witness (Warner Bros., 1931). *Three on a Match* (First National, 1932).

Hudson, Rochelle (1914–1972)

Actress. After grooming by the studios, and a number of roles as an ingenue in some popular movies during the thirties, Hudson landed more hard-boiled roles during the late thirties. In *Show Them No Mercy*, she played a typical early role as an innocent woman held hostage, with her husband and baby, by a violent gang.

Show Them No Mercy (20th Century–Fox, 1935).

Hughes, Howard (1905–1976)

Producer and studio chief. Hughes built his fortune from a considerable inheritance. He was essentially an enthusiastic amateur filmmaker, and he dabbled in the movies, beginning in the late twenties. In 1948 he purchased the perennially floundering RKO, finally becoming the owner of a studio (as he had long dreamed), and then proceeded to destroy it. His megalomania ensured that he interfered and tried to control every production and even his employees' private lives. As a result, many of the political liberals left the studio (Hughes was a notorious arch-conservative who supported Joseph McCarthy), thus creating a "brain drain" at what had formally been one of the more experimental and daring studios. By the mid-fifties, the studio was bankrupt. Yet, Hughes had his supporters, and he did personally oversee several important productions during his tenure at RKO: the *film noir* *Macao* (RKO, 1952) and the gangster movie *His Kind of Woman* (both featuring his protégée, actress Jane Russell). However, his most important contribution to the gangster genre is certainly his production of *Scarface.*

Scarface (United Artists, 1932). *His Kind of Woman* (RKO, 1951). *The Racket* (RKO, 1951).

Hughes, Ken (b. 1922)
Director. The British-born Hughes has worked in Hollywood and Great Britain. His single gangster movie, *Joe Macbeth*, is one of the fifties most creative, equating Shakespeare's tragedy with a gang leader's life.

Joe Macbeth (Columbia, 1955).

Human Cargo (20th Century-Fox, 1936). 65 mins.
Producer: Sol M. Wurtzel. *Director*: Allan Dwan. *Screenplay*: Jefferson Parker and Doris Malloy, based on the novel *I Will Be Faithful* by Kathleen Shepard. *Director of Photography*: Daniel B. Clark. *Art Director*: Duncan Cramer. *Editor*: Louis Loeffler.
Cast: Claire Trevor (Bonnie Brew-ster), Brian Donlevy (Packy Camp-bell), Alan Dinehart (Lionel Crocker), Ralph Morgan (District Attorney Carey), Helen Troy (Susie), Rita Can-sino, aka Rita Hayworth (Carmen). *With*: Morgan Wallace, Herman Bing, John McGuire, Ralf Harolde, Wade Boteler, Harry Wood.
A Los Angeles district attorney is determined to close down a dangerous alien smuggling ring. The gang has

murdered a number of those willing to testify against them, and thus it has been difficult to gather evidence. However, Packy Campbell, a news-paper reporter, and his rival at another paper, Bonnie Brewster, investigate the case. Eventually they team up and find an illegal alien, Carmen, who is willing to testify against the gang. In the pro-cess, the two reporters fall in love.

A "B" production, *Human Cargo* is an interesting variation on popular gangster themes, loosely based on real incidents. Claire Trevor, best known for her molls and *femmes fatales*, is here on the side of the law. Rita Hay-worth, billed under her real name, Can-sino, also makes a brief appearance, several years before dying her hair red and reemerging as one of the forties greatest sex symbols.

Hunted Man (Paramount, 1932). 63 mins.
Producer: Stuart Walker. *Director*: Louis King. *Screenplay*: Horace McCoy and William R. Lippmann, based on the play by Alfred Duffy and Marian Grant. *Director of Photography*: Vic-tor Milner. *Musical Director*: Boris Morros. *Art Director*: Hans Dreier. *Editor*: Ann Bauchans.
Cast: Lloyd Nolan (Joe Albany), Mary Carlisle (Jane Harris), Lynne Overman (Peter Harris), J. Carrol Naish (Morton Rice), Anthony Quinn (Mac), Buster Crabbe (James Flowers). *With*: Johnny Downs, Dorothy Peter-son, Delmer Watson, Regis Toomey, Louis Miller, George Davis.
With admirable directness and brevity, *Hunted Men*, a "B" picture, tells much the same story as *The Desperate Hours* (Paramount, 1955) does at nearly twice the length. Joe Albany, a gangster who runs from the police after murdering a rival, takes refuge in an ordinary suburban house. He takes the family hostage but, gradually mellowing under their calm-ing influence, he is finally persuaded by the patriarch to give himself up.

Lloyd Nolan, who gives a vivid performance as the murderous gangster, is supported by a superior cast, including the blonde, exotically beautiful Mary Carlisle as his moll.

Hush Money (Fox, 1931). 68 mins. *Director*: Sidney Lanfield. *Story and Screenplay*: Philip Klein and Courtney Terrett, *additional dialog*: Dudley Nichols. *Director of Photography*: John Seitz. *Editor*: John Canfield.

Cast: Joan Bennett (Janet Gordon), Hardie Albright (Stuart Elliott), Owen Moore (Steve Pelton), Myrna Loy (Flo Curtis). *With*: C. Henry Gordon, Douglas Cosgrove, George Raft, Hugh White.

An impressionable young woman, Janet Gordon, has an affair with Steve Pelton, a notorious gangster. When Pelton's gang is caught in an extortion scheme, Janet is sentenced to a year in prison. After her release, she befriends a kind policeman and marries a millionaire. When Pelton is released, he attempts to blackmail Janet, but the policeman turns the tables on him, informing his former colleagues that it was Pelton who informed on them. Pelton is then murdered by the gang.

A taut gangster programmer, *Hush Money* is an interesting melodrama typical of the genre's early years. Short on action, it relies on a streamlined plot and strong performances. The film's star, Joan Bennett, would later become a major icon of *film noir*. For most of her youth, however, she was in the shadow of her older sister, Constance Bennett, and like her, dyed her hair platinum blonde. She was relegated mainly to programmers like *Hush Money* until the early forties, when she restored her dark hair and became a full-fledged star "overnight."

Huston, Angelica (b. 1952)
Actress. Tall, dark, and exotically attractive, Angelica Huston is the daughter of director John Huston. Always a welcome addition to any film, she made her greatest impression as the gang leader's daughter in her father's *Prizzi's Honor*, for which she won an

The elegant Angelica Huston from the contemporary gangster classic *Prizzi's Honor*, directed by her father, John Huston.

Paul Muni (center) as James Allen in *I Am a Fugitive from a Chain Gang* **suffers at the hands of brutal prison guards.**

Academy Award for best supporting actress.

Prizzi's Honor (20th Century-Fox, 1985).

Huston, John (1906–1987)

Director. The son of character actor Walter Huston, and father of actress Angelica Huston, John Huston is one of the legendary figures of Hollywood's golden age. After an extraordinarily adventurous youth, he settled in Hollywood and became a leading screenwriter. He specialized in hard-boiled subjects, epitomized by his screenplay for the classic gangster movie *High Sierra*, which presaged his own films as director in theme and style. Huston's best films as director are those which explore slightly existential, Hemingway-like themes: the individual caught in a corrupt and often violent system, unable to escape, but facing his inevitable end with stoic bravery. Technically, his style as a director is similar to that of Raoul Walsh and John Ford: unadorned, simple, and again, hard-boiled. Although his best work was created in his first decade as a film-maker, he seemed to be artistically revitalized in the years shortly before his death when he again made several brilliant films, including his gangster satire *Prizzi's Honor*.

The Amazing Dr. Clitterhouse (Warner Bros., 1938; cowriter only).

Paul Muni in a publicity still from *I Am a Fugitive from a Chain Gang*, **one of Warner Bros.'**
most brutally realistic, hard-boiled gangster movies of the early thirties.

High Sierra (Warner Bros., 1940; cowriter only). *The Maltese Falcon* (Warner Bros., 1941; director and screenplay). *Key Largo* (Warner Bros., 1948; director and cowriter). *The Asphalt Jungle* (Warner Bros., 1950; director and cowriter). *Prizzi's Honor* (20th Century–Fox, 1985; director only).

Huston, Walter (1884–1950)
    Character actor. After many years on the stage, Huston, father of John and grandfather of Angelica, went to Hollywood in his mid-forties and quickly became one of the most respected character actors in American movies. A charismatic and intense actor, he often outshone the starring actors, even when his roles were small. He was best as a rogue or eccentric, but he also played occasional leads, and

starred in three early, important gangster movies. Of these, the most interesting is *The Beast of the City*, in which he starred as an honest cop fighting the underworld and a corrupt political machine. With its pessimistic theme, the film is one of the more notable precursors to *film noir*.
    The Criminal Code (Columbia, 1931). *The Star Witness* (Warner Bros., 1931). *The Beast of the City* (MGM, 1931).

I Am a Fugitive from a Chain Gang
    (Warner Bros., 1932). 93 mins.
    Executive Producer: Darryl F. Zanuck. *Producer*: Hal Wallis. *Director*: Mervyn LeRoy. *Screenplay*: Howard J. Greene and Brown Holmes, based on Robert E. Burns' autobiography *I Am a Fugitive from a Georgia Chain Gang*. *Director of Photography*:

Sol Polito. *Art Director*: Jack Okey. *Editor*: William Holmes.

Cast: Paul Muni (James Allen), Glenda Farrell (Marie Woods), Helen Vinson (Helen), Preston Foster (Pete), Allen Jenkins (Barney), Edward Ellis (Bomber Wells). *With*: John Wray, Hale Hamilton, Harry Woods, David Landau, Edward J. McNamara.

James Allen, a hero returning from World War I, finds his life in rural Georgia dull and stupefying. Taking to the road to find a new life, he befriends the wrong man and is implicated in a robbery and murder. Allen is convicted and sent to a brutal southern prison farm. Eventually he escapes, flees to the North, changes his name, and becomes a respected engineer. He marries a vulgar bar girl who becomes an embarrassment, and later falls in love with a beautiful society girl, Helen. She convinces him to return to Georgia and turn himself in, believing that his success and new position in life will make the authorities pardon him; but the pardon does not come through and he is sent back to prison with a very long sentence. He manages to escape again, but he has become embittered. He returns north and again sees Helen. Before disappearing into the shadows, he answers Helen's question about how he lives by saying, "I Steal."

Robert E. Burns' harrowing memoir, *I Am a Fugitive from a Georgia Chain Gang* became one of the most important Warner Bros. productions of the early thirties. Unlike its more entertaining contemporaries, the film presented a cynical picture of life in the United States during the Great Depression. This was not escapist fare but real life drama told in uncompromisingly gritty style. It also provided Paul Muni with one of his best roles, and remains a classic American film.

I Am the Law (Columbia, 1938). 83 mins.

Producer: Everett Riskin. *Director*: Al Hall. *Screenplay*: Jo Swerling, based on a series of articles by Fred Allhoff. *Director of Photography*: Henry Freulich. *Musical Director*: Morris Stoloff. *Editor*: Viola Lawrence.

Cast: Edward G. Robinson (John Lindsay), Barbara O'Neil (Jerry Lindsay), John Beal (Paul Ferguson), Arthur Loft (Tom Ross), Marc Lawrence (Eddie Girard), Douglas Wood (Berry), Wendy Barrie (Frankie Ballou), Otto Kruger (Eugene Ferguson). *With*: Robert Middlemass, Ivan Miller, Charles Halton, Louis Jean Heydt, Emory Parnell.

John Lindsay, a law professor, is hired by a small town to clear out gangsters. He employs a young man, Paul Ferguson, to help him, but when it proves difficult to gather sufficient evidence against the gang, impatient officials fire him. However, with Ferguson and reporter Frankie Ballou, Lindsay continues to investigate the gang. He pits gang members against each other and eventually he discovers that the real culprit is Eugene Ferguson, Paul's father, the man who originally hired him. Ferguson commits suicide but, convinced by Lindsay that crime does not pay, wills his fortune to crime prevention.

Wildly improbable, *I Am the Law* veers between satire and seriousness. Its somewhat didactic plot is tinged with comic elements, particularly Robinson's broad performance as the rather inept professor. The film is notable, however, for providing Robinson with one of his few heroic roles in the genre.

I Cover the Underworld (Republic, 1955). 70 mins.

Producer: William J. O'Sullivan. *Director*: R. G. Springsteen. *Screenplay*: John K. Butler. *Director of Photography*: Reggie Lanning. *Music*: R. Dale Butts. *Director*: Tony Martinelli.

Cast: Sean McClory ("Gunner" and John O'Hara), Joanne Jordan (Joan Marlowe), Ray Middleton (Police Chief), Jaclynne Greene (Gilda), Lee Van Cleef (Flash Logan). *With*: James Griffith,

Hugh Sanders, Roy Roberts, Peter Mamakos, Robert Crosson.

John O'Hara, a divinity student, convinces the police to allow him to infiltrate his twin brother's (Gunner) gang shortly before Gunner's parole. With the aid of Gunner's moll, Gilda, John gathers enough evidence to break up the gang, but not soon enough to save his brother, who is gunned down by his own men soon after his release.

I Cover the Underworld is a typical "B" crime thriller from the fifties. It is saved from being merely routine largely by Lee Van Cleef's performance as the defacto leader of the gang during Gunner O'Hara's absence.

I Cover the Waterfront (United Artists, 1933). 72 mins.
Director: James Cruze. *Screenplay*: Wells Root, *additional dialog by* Jack Jerne, based on the book by Max Miller. *Director of Photography*: Ray June. *Songs*: Edward Heyman and Johnny Green. *Editor*: Grant Whytock.
Cast: Claudette Colbert (Julie Kirk), Ben Lyon (Joseph Miller), Ernest Torrence (Eli Kirk), Hobart Cavanaugh (McCoy), Maurice Black (Ortegus). *With*: Harry Bereford, Purnell Pratt, George Humbert, Rosita Marstina, Wildred Lucas.

Newspaper reporter Joseph Miller romances Julie Kirk, the daughter of Eli Kirk, a man suspected of running a murderous illegal alien smuggling racket. When Julie discovers that she is being used by Miller to gather information against her father, she rejects him but she also rejects her father when she discovers his real nature. By then, Miller has gathered enough information to help the police put Kirk behind bars.

A very modest early gangster picture, *I Cover the Waterfront* is best known as one of Claudette Colbert's early features. It has little to recommend it except for her sensual performance and Ernest Torrence's turn as the outwardly kind but inwardly cruel smuggler of human cargo.

I, Mobster (20th Century–Fox, 1959). 82 mins.
Producers: Roger Corman and Gene Corman. *Director*: Roger Corman. *Screenplay*: Steve Fisher, based on the novel by Joseph Hilton Smyth. *Director of Photography*: Floyd Crosby. *Music*: Gerald Fried and Edward L. Alperson. *Art Director*: Daniel Haller. *Editor*: William B. Murphy.
Cast: Steve Cochran (Joe Sante), Lita Milan (Teresa Porter), Robert Strauss (Black Frankie), Celia Lovsky (Mrs. Sante), Lili St. Cyr (Herself), John Brinkley (Ernie Porter). *With*: Yvette Vickers, Jeri Southern, Grant Withers, John Mylong, Wally Cassell.

Testifying before a Senate crime committee, Joe Sante recounts his life of crime, culminating in his murder of national crime boss Paul Moran (Grant Withers).

When he was not busy churning out horror films or teen exploitation pictures, Roger Corman made crime melodramas. *I, Mobster* is typical of all of his productions: cheap, violent, sexy, and exploitative. However, it does have a decent screenplay by veteran writer Steve Fisher, an important *film noir* figure, which sets it apart from his other fifties productions.

I Stole a Million (Universal, 1939). 80 mins.
Associate Producer: Burt Kelly. *Director*: Frank Tuttle. *Screenplay*: Nathanael West, *story by* Lester Cole. *Director of Photography*: Milton Krasner. *Editor*: Edward Curtiss.
Cast: George Raft (Joe Laurik/ Harris), Claire Trevor (Laura Benson), Dick Foran (Paul Carver), Henry Armetta (Nick), Victor Jory (Pation), Joseph Sawyer (Billings). *With*: Irving Bacon, Stanley Ridges, Jerry Marlowe, Edmund MacDonald, Ben Taggert.

After he is cheated by the company he works for, cab driver Joe Laurik takes up a life of crime. Using the alias "Harris," he joins a gang and eventually heads it during a bank robbery.

After the crime is successfully carried off, he flees to California to start a new life. He meets and marries a young woman, Laura Benson, who, after discovering his past, urges him to turn himself in. She tells him shè will be waiting for him after his release.

I Stole a Million is a modest gangster picture with a decent screenplay by the great novelist Nathaniel West. Echoing the socially relevant theme of Raft's *Invisible Stripes*, it is less downbeat and, as a result, less effective. However, it provided Claire Trevor with an excellent role, one of her few good girls in the genre.

I Walk Alone (Paramount, 1948). 97 mins.
Producer: Hal B. Wallis. *Director*: Byron Haskin. *Screenplay*: Charles Schnee, based on the play *Beggars Are Coming to Town* by Theodore Reeves. *Director of Photography*: Leo Tover. *Music*: Victor Young. *Art Directors*: Hans Dreier and Franz Bachelin. *Editor*: Arthur Schmidt.
Cast: Burt Lancaster (Frankie Madison), Lizabeth Scott (Kay Lawrence), Kirk Douglas (Noll Turner), Wendell Corey (Dave), Kristine Miller (Mrs. Richardson), George Rigaurd (Maurice). *With*: Mike Mazurki, Marc Lawrence, Mickey Knox, John Bishop, Roger Henry, Bruce Lester.

After his release from prison, ex–rum runner Frankie Madison cannot adjust to life and is bitter about the fourteen years he spent in jail. He seeks revenge against Noll Turner, his ex-partner, for whom he had taken the fall. In the intervening years, Turner had used the profits from the illegal smuggling to open a successful nightclub. Turner has also moved in on Madison's girlfriend, Kay Lawrence, a singer in the club. Turner's days, however, are numbered and, after a gun battle with Madison, he is finished off by the cops. Madison and Lawrence decide to start a new life together.

Not quite a classic, mainly because of a weak screenplay, *I Walk Alone* is a notable gangster *noir* produced by Paramount. The production values and performances are first rate, but somehow the film fails to satisfy.

Illegal (Warner Bros., 1955). 88 mins.
Producer: Frank P. Rosenberg. *Director*: Lewis Allen. *Screenplay*: W. R. Burnett and James R. Webb, based on the play *The Mouthpiece* by Frank J. Collins. *Director of Photography*: Peverell Marley. *Music*: Max Steiner. *Art Director*: Stanley Fleischer. *Editor*: Thomas Reilly.
Cast: Edward G. Robinson (Victor Scott), Nina Foch (Ellen Miles), Hugh Marlowe (Ray Borden), Robert Ellenstein (Joe Knight), De Forrest Kelley (Edward Clary), Jay Adler (Joseph Carter), Albert Dekker (Frank Garland). *With*: James McCallion, Edward Platt, Jan Merlin, Ellen Corby, Jayne Mansfield.

Victor Scott is a district attorney with a reputation for toughness, but when he sends the wrong man to the electric chair, he quits and becomes a defense lawyer. When Ellen Miles, the wife of an ex-employee, kills her husband in self defense after she discovers he is an informer for the mob, Scott begins to believe she is the mob informer. Although Scott believes she killed her husband to cover up her crimes, he agrees to defend her. The mob boss, Frank Garland, tries to assassinate Scott, but only succeeds in wounding him. With the help of Garland's ex-moll, Scott proves Ellen's innocence and sends Garland to prison.

Twenty-five years after the success of *Little Caesar* (Warner Bros., 1930) had kicked off the initial gangster cycle, Edward G. Robinson was still one of the genre's active icons. His roles on the right side of the law were comparatively rare and generally confined to minor films. This is certainly true of *Illegal*, which was cowritten by *Little Caesar* author W. R. Burnett. It is not a bad film, but rather weak and, in the fashion of the time, relies on graphic violence rather than character or plot development. Robinson's performance is as good as always, and Jayne Mansfield does well as the moll.

Illegal Traffic (Paramount, 1938). 73 mins.
Associate Producer and Director: Louis King. *Screenplay*: Robert Yost, Lewis Foster, and Stuart Anthony. *Director of Photography*: Henry Sharpe. *Music*: Borris Morros. *Art Directors*: Hans Dreier and Robert Odell. *Editor*: Harvey Johnstone.
Cast: J. Carrol Naish (Lewis Zomar), Mary Carlisle (Carol Butler), Robert Preston (Bent Martin), Pierre Watkin (Jigger), Larry "Buster" Crabbe (Steve). *With*: George Mckay, Richard Denning, Philip Warren, Sheila Darcy, Dolores Casey, Regis Toomey.

Ambitious G-man Bent Martin is assigned to go undercover and join a racket led by supposedly honest businessmen, Lewis Zomar and Jigger, whose transport company is a front for spiriting away gangsters from the scenes of their crimes. Martin discovers the true nature of their business and, when he confronts the two men, a shootout ensues in which Zomar is killed.

With its fast pace and no-nonsense action, *Illegal Traffic* resembles the best of Republic's serials. This "B" gangster picture is one of Paramount's best, thanks to its good script, swift pace (courtesy of director Louis King), and better than average cast.

Ince, Ralph (1882–1937)
Character actor. Ince was a prominent stage actor whose film career began during the late teens. In the twenties he was a second-string star. With the coming of sound, he began to play second leads and character parts, including a rival gangster to Edward G. Robinson's Rico in *Little Caesar* and a gang leader in *The Star Witness*. Ince was also a director and, in the mid-

thirties, he moved to Great Britain, where he helmed a number of quota quickies.
Little Caesar (Warner Bros., 1930).
The Star Witness (Warner Bros., 1931).

Inside Detroit (Columbia). 80 mins.
Cast: Dennis O'Keefe (Blair Vickers), Pat O'Brien (Gus Linden), Mark Damon (Gregg Linden), Larry Blake (Max Harkness), Ken Christy (Ben Macauley). *With*: Joseph Turkel, Paul Bryar, Robert E. Griffin, Guy Kingsford, Dick Rich, Norman Leavitt.

In the fifties, a series of "B" gangster pictures emerged that exposed alleged corruption and criminal activity in particular cities. Epitomized by Phil Karlson's superior *The Phenix City Story* (Allied Artists, 1955) and *Kansas City Confidential* (United Artists, 1952), they were all based, however loosely, on real events or topical subjects, and all used semi-documentary techniques to tell their stories. *Inside Detroit* is typical of the group, focusing on Gus Linden, a dishonest union boss who tries to wrest control of the union from Blair Vickers, an honest man. With the help of his mob cronies, Linden attempts to assassinate Vickers. Eventually, however, he is caught and sent to prison.

The plot is loosely based on a then-contemporary story, and it is a moderate success in conveying mob corruption in the automobile unions. It is saved from being merely routine by the strong performances of Dennis O'Keefe and Pat O'Brien.

Inside the Mafia (United Artists, 1959). 72 mins.
Producer: Robert E. Kent. *Director*: Edward L. Cahn. *Screenplay*: Orville H. Hampton. *Director of Photography*: Maury Gertsman. *Art Director*: Bill Glasgow. *Editor*: Grant Why.
Cast: Cameron Mitchell (Tony Ledo), Elaine Edwards (Anne Balcom), Robert Strauss (Sam Galey), Jim L. Brown (Doug Blair), Ted De Corsia

George Raft (center) and Humphrey Bogart (right) from *Invisible Stripes*.

(Augie Martello). *With*: Grant Richards, Richard Karlan, Frank Gerstle, Sid Clute, Louis Jean Heydt, Steve Roberts.

Yet another group of fifties crime exposes, *Inside the Mafia* is unique for its portrayal of the real mafia and, as such, is a precursor to the *Godfather* series of the seventies. Even its plot resembles the later series in its recounting of a battle among members for control of the mob. However, with its "B" production values, streamlined plot, and reliance on violent action, it is clearly a product of its time.

Intolerance (Wark Distributing, 1916). 210 mins.

Director and Screenplay: D. W. Griffith. *Director of Photography*: G. W. Bitzer and Karl Brown.

Cast (Modern Story): Mae Marsh (Girl), Fred Turner (Iter Father), Robert Harron (Boy), Sam de Grasse (Jenkins), Lillian Gish (Girl who rocks the cradle). *With*: Tom Wilson, Walter Long, Lloyd Ingraham, Monte Blue, Lucille Brown.

The great director and film pioneer D. W. Griffith had already explored the growing menace of modern gangsterism in his seminal *The Musketeers of Pig Alley* (Biograph, 1912) when he made his epic masterpiece *Intolerance*. Although unwieldy and confusing, *Intolerance* contrasts four historical tableuxs in a tale of morality versus immorality throughout the ages. The modern story, intercut with the others, tells of the trials and tribulations of street gangsters, corrupt big business, and the effects of poverty on crime: in other words, the very social conditions which would influence the rise of organized crime in America throughout the twentieth century. For that, it remains a powerful indictment of the economic conditions which are still largely responsible for crime in the United States.

Invisible Stripes (Warner Bros., 1939). 82 mins.
Executive Producer: Hal B. Wallis. *Director*: Lloyd Bacon. *Screenplay*: Warren Duff, based on the book by Warden Lewis E. Lawes. *Director of Photography*: Ernest Haller. *Music*: Heinz Roehmheld. *Art Director*: Max Parker. *Editor*: James Gibbons.

Cast: George Raft (Cliff Taylor), Jane Bryan (Peggy), William Holden (Tim Taylor), Humphrey Bogart (Chuck Martin), Flora Robson (Mrs. Taylor), Paul Kelly (Ed Kruger), Lee Patrick (Molly Daniels). *With*: Henry O'Neill, Frankie Thomas, Moroni Olsen, Margot Stevenson, Marc Lawrence, William Haade, Joseph Downing.

After his release from prison, Cliff Taylor discovers that he wears "invisible stripes," the stigma of an ex-con that follows him everywhere. The only work he can find is menial, when he can find work, and he is constantly hassled by the police. His younger brother, Tim, desperate to help support his wife, Peggy, decides that crime may be the only available course. To help Tim, Cliff joins a local gang of bank robbers who carry off a series of heists. Now with a great deal of money, he opens a gas station with his brother. But when the gang believes that he has betrayed them to the police, Cliff is gunned down.

One of Warner Bros.' classic gangster pictures from the latter part of the initial cycle, *Invisible Stripes*, is interesting for its blend of conventional melodrama and a relevant social theme. With a fine screenplay by Warren Duff and brisk direction by Lloyd Bacon, it is arguably George Raft's best vehicle in the genre.

Ireland, John (b. 1914)
Actor. Born on Vancouver, British Columbia, Ireland played in Shakespeare on Broadway before moving to Hollywood during the mid-forties. He specialized in introspective, stoic heroes in action pictures and costume romances while playing the occasional antihero. He played supporting roles in two late gangster movies, most notably as a mob henchman in the superior "B" movie *Raw Deal*.

Raw Deal (Eagle-Lion, 1948). *Party Girl* (MGM, 1958).

Ivano, Paul (1900–1984)
Cinematographer. Ivano's work is rather conventional, with the notable exception of *The Shanghai Gesture* (United Artists, 1941), the seminal *film noir*. However, it is debatable whether Ivano or the film's codirector, Josef von Sternberg, is really responsible for its inventive photography. Ivano also photographed the classic "B" gangster movie *The Gangster*, which also displays some inventive techniques.

The Gangster (Allied Artists, 1947).

Jaffe, Sam (1893–1984)
Character actor. Short, wiry, and with an eccentric hair style reminiscent of cartoon character Woody Woodpecker, Jaffe was certainly one of the most interesting character actors of his time. He split his career between the stage and screen, thus appearing in a relatively small number of movies. Yet, he was always excellent in each of his film performances. In John Huston's *The Asphalt Jungle*, he gave one of his best performances as Doc Riedenschneider, the mastermind behind the failed jewel heist.

The Asphalt Jungle (MGM, 1950).

Jagger, Dean (1903–1982)
Actor. Born Dean Jeffries in Lima, Ohio, Jagger performed in vaudeville and on Broadway. Sturdy and strong featured, Jagger played tough heroes and villains in many popular movies. In his single gangster movie, *C-Man*, Jagger starred as a customs agent

investigating a group of smugglers in New York City.
C-Man (Film Classics, 1949).

Jarrett, Arthur Cody (Fictional character)

After a decade of playing sympathetic and heroic characters, James Cagney's popularity began to wane and he eagerly returned to familiar ground when he played the mob boss Cody Jarrett in the classic *White Heat* (Warner Bros., 1949). Directed by Raoul Walsh, *White Heat* brought back all the violent flavor of the gangster pictures of the previous decade and provided Cagney with one of his best roles. Jarrett, however, is a protagonist of the *noir* school, linked irrevocably to a tragic destiny. A cold-blooded killer and sexual sadist, Cody Jarrett is also peculiarly close to his beloved mother. After his gang carries out a botched and violent train heist, Jarrett is cornered in a chemical plant by the police. As he climbs a gas tower during the shoot out with the authorities, the tower's tank is ignited and Jarrett is consumed in the flames, but not before uttering perhaps the most famous line in the gangster and *noir* genres, "Look Ma! Top of the World!"

Jeffries, Ann (b. 1923)

Actress. The former Anne Carmichael, Jeffries (also spelled Jeffreys), an opera singer turned actress, was popular in "B" movies during the forties. In *Dillinger*, the classic "B" gangster movie, she played the luscious Lady in Red who leads the gangster to his death.

Dillinger (Monogram, 1945).

Jenkins, Allen (1900–1974)

Character actor. Specializing in tough, wisecracking supporting roles, Jenkins was a key figure in Warner Bros. pictures during the thirties. Born Alfred McGonegal in New York, he had extensive Broadway experience before his film career began in the early

thirties. His characters have been described as "illiterate, illogical, but illuminating mugs," and he appeared in more than two hundred movies.

I Am a Fugitive from a Chain Gang (Warner Bros., 1932). *The Big Shakedown* (First National, 1934). *Jimmy the Gent* (Warner Bros., 1934). *The Amazing Dr. Clitterhouse* (Warner Bros., 1938). *Racket Busters* (Warner Bros., 1938). *A Slight Case of Murder* (Warner Bros., 1938).

Jergens, Adele (b. 1922)

Actress. Born in Brooklyn, the platinum blonde Jergens was a chorus girl on Broadway before winning a beauty contest that took her to Hollywood. She was a popular performer in "B" movies, playing a variety of saucy dames, gangster's molls, and temptresses. She costarred in a single, minor gangster movie, typically as a moll.

The Miami Story (Columbia, 1954).

Jewell, Edward C.

Art director. Jewell's career began in the silent era, when he worked on a number of major productions. Many years later, after the arrival of sound, he worked mainly for Poverty Row studios like Producers Releasing Corporation and Monogram, but he also did some work for Columbia. Because of his tendency to combine Germanic with more conventional designs, he has been described as the Hans Dreier of Poverty Row.

The Racketeer (Pathe, 1929). *The Squealer* (Columbia, 1930). *The Criminal Code* (Columbia, 1931). *T-Men* (Eagle-Lion, 1947).

Jimmy the Gent (Warner Bros., 1934). 67 mins.

Executive Producer: Jack L. Warner. *Director*: Michael Curtiz. *Screenplay*: Ray Nazarro and Laird Doyle. *Director of Photography*: Ira Morgan. *Music*: Leo R. Forbstein. *Editor*: Thomas Richards.

Icons Betty Davis and James Cagney in *Jimmy the Gent*, their most entertaining film.

Cast: James Cagney (Jimmy Corrigan), Bette Davis (Joan Martin), Alice White (Mabel), Allen Jenkins (Louis), Alan Dinehart (Charles Wallingham), Mayo Methot (Gladys Farrell). *With*: Hobart Cavanaugh, Philip Faversham, Philip Reed, Ralf Harolde, Arthur Hohl.

Jimmy Corrigan is a crooked genealogist: he uncovers heirs to unclaimed fortunes and then cons them out of their money. When his girlfriend, Joan Martin, discovers his occupation, she joins the firm of a rival genealogist, Charles Wallingham, believing that his practice is legitimate. Jealous, Jimmy takes on the air of a refined gentleman to impress Joan, while also exposing Wallingham as an even greater crook than he is. Chagrined, Joan returns to Jimmy.

A hard-boiled comedy, *Jimmy the Gent* marked the first pairing of James Cagney and Bette Davis. They proved a formidable team, intense, likeable, and immensely charismatic. A swift paced, tough little movie, it remains one of the genre's oddest films because of its uncharacteristic message: crime, it seems, occasionally does pay!

Joe Macbeth (Columbia, 1955). 90 mins.

Producer: Mike Frankovich. *Director*: Ken Hughes. *Screenplay*: Philip Yordan. *Director of Photography*: Basil Emmett. *Musical Director*: Richard Taylor. *Art Director*: Alan Harris. *Editor*: Peter Rolfe Johnson.

Cast: Paul Douglas (Joe Macbeth), Ruth Roman (Lily Macbeth), Bonar Colleano (Lennie), Gregoire Aslan (Duncan), Sidney James (Banky), Harry Green (Big Dutch). *With*: Teresa Thorne, Minerva Pious, Nicholas Stuart, Robert Arden, Bill Nagy.

At the urging of his shrewish wife, Lily, and an opportunistic fortune ame similar to the char-

teller, Joe Macbeth rises from hench-men to gang leader through violence and murder. Once at the top, however, he soon finds himself the target of equally ruthless rivals who eventually kill him.

With its screenplay derived from Shakespeare's tragedy, Joe Macbeth is certainly one of the more atypical gangster movies. Philip Yordan, a master of hard-boiled screenplays, here crafted one of his niftiest screenplays. The Shakespearean elements are kept to a minimum in favor of violent action and suspense. Paul Douglas' fierce per-formance is superb, and the film re-mains one of the genre's best "B" pictures.

Johnny Allegro (Columbia, 1949). 81 mins.
Producer: Irving Stone. *Director*: Ted Tetzlaff. *Screenplay*: Karen DeWolf and Guy Endore, *story by* James Edward Grant. *Director of Photography*: Joseph Biroc. *Music*: George Duning. *Art Director*: Perry Smith. *Editor*: Jerome Thoms.
Cast: George Raft (Johnny Allegro), Nina Foch (Glenda Chapman), George Macready (Morgan Vallin), Will Geer (Shultzy), Gloria Henry (Addie), Harry Antrim (Pudgy). *With*: Ivan Triesault, Bill Phillips, Walter Rode, Paul E. Burns, Fred Sears, Thomas Browne.

Johnny Allegro, a former gangster, is now employed by the Treasury Department. He is sent to a Caribbean island to gather evidence against Morgan Vallin, a neo-fascist who is try-ing to overthrow the American govern-ment by flooding the market with counterfeit money. He discovers that Vallin is a psychopath who gets his kicks by hunting down people in the jungle like big game. Allegro's mission is complicated by Glenda Chapman, Vallin's moll, but together they even-tually bring the madman to justice.

An uninspired attempt to recreate the exotic, mysterious, sensual world

of *Gilda* (Columbia, 1946), the film was nevertheless a popular success, thanks largely to the scenery and Nina Foch's erotic presence. Interestingly, Macready's character, Morgan Vallin, even had a name similar to the char-acter he played in *Gilda*, Ballin Munsen. In any case, whereas the former is a classic, the latter film is just a run of the mill mystery.

Johnny Apollo (20th Century–Fox, 1940). 93 mins.
Producer: Darryl F. Zanuck. *Asso-ciate Producer*: Harry Joe Brown. *Director*: Henry Hathaway. *Screen-play*: Philip Dunne and Rowland Brown, *story by* Samuel G. Engel and Hal Long. *Director of Photography*: Arthur Miller. *Music and Songs*: Frank Loesser and Lionel Newman. *Editor*: Robert Bischoff.
Cast: Tyrone Power (Bob Cain), Dorothy Lamour ("Lucky" Dubarry), Edward Arnold (Robert Cain, Sr.), Lloyd Nolan (Nickey Dwyer), Charles Grapewin (Judge Emmett F. Brennan), Lionel Atwill (Jim McLaughlin), Marc Lawrence (Bates). *With*: Jonathan Hale, Russell Hicks, Fuzzy Knight, Charles Lane, Selmer Jackson, Charles Trowbridge.

When his father is involved in a bank failure, Bob Cain is disillusioned by wealthy society's rejection of him. Cain turns his back on the upper class of his youth and becomes the right hand man of Nicky Dwyer, the head of the local mob. He has an affair with Dwyer's dizzy moll, "Lucky" Dubarry; but when he is sent to prison, he is reunited with his father who is serving time for the fraud involved in the bank failure. Away from the corrupting influence of Dwyer and Dubarry, he realizes his mistake and reforms.

A rather silly melodrama, *Johnny Apollo* was a big hit at the time of its release. It is interesting for its insights into wealthy people's fascination with gangsters, but Tyrone Power is not really believable in the lead role. The sexy Dorothy Lamour, however, steals the film as the harebrained moll.

Johnny Dangerously (20th Century-Fox, 1984). 92 mins.
Producer: Michael Hertzberg. *Director*: Amy Heckerling. *Screenplay*: Norman Steinberg, Bernie Kukoff, Harry Colomby, and Jeff Harris. *Production Design*: Joseph R. Jennings. *Director of Photography*: David M. Walsh. *Music*: John Morris. *Editor*: Perm Herring.
Cast: Michael Keaton (Johnny Dangerously), Joe Piscopo (Vermin), Marilu Henner (Lil), Maureen Stapleton (Mom), Peter Boyle (Dundee), Griffin Dunne (Tommy). *With*: Richard Dimitri, Glynnis O'Connor, Byron Thames, Danny DeVito, Dom DeLuise.

In the thirties a young boy joins the rackets to help pay for his ailing mother's hospital bills. He grows up to become Johnny Dangerously, a notorious gangster. With his friend, Dundee, he forms an alliance against fellow mobster Vermin and an honest district attorney, Tommy, but eventually their illegal activities catch up with them and Dangerously is sent to prison.

After his initial burst of fame, and before the *Batman* series of movies carried him to superstardom, Michael Keaton starred in several box office failures, including *Johnny Dangerously*. A rather lame and uninteresting satire, it has a superior cast and excellent art direction, which perfectly captures the feel of thirties gangster movies.

Johnny Stool Pigeon (Universal, 1949). 76 mins.
Producer: Aaron Rosenberg. *Director*: William Castle. *Screenplay*: Robert L. Richards, *story by* Henry Jordan. *Director of Photography*: Maury Gertsman. *Music*: Milton Schwartzwald. *Art Directors*: Bernard Herzbrun and Emrich Nicholson. *Editor*: Ted J. Kent.

Cast: Howard Duff (George Morton), Shelley Winters (Terry), Dan Duryea (Johnny Evans), Tony Curtis (Joey Hyatt), John McIntire (Avery), Gar Moore (Sam Harrison). *With*: Leif Erickson, Barry Kelley, Hugh Reilly, Wally Maher, Gregg Barton, Charles Drake.

Johnny Evans, a gangster serving time in prison, agrees to help a G-man, George Morton. After his wife dies of drug abuse, Morton wants to infiltrate a dope ring and, with Evans' help, is able to do so. He travels with the ring all over the western United States, Canada, and Mexico before the operation is busted by intrepid narcotics agents.

Before his success as a horror film producer and director in the sixties, William Castle had a prominent career directing "B" crime thrillers. *Johnny Stool Pigeon* is one of the best, with a good, if rather simplistic, screenplay and an excellent cast. Particularly notable is Shelley Winters' performance as the saucy moll who comes to the aid of federal agent Morton.

Jones, Carolyn (1933–1983)
Actress. Born in Amarillo, Texas, the small, dark-haired Carolyn Jones is best known for her role on the cult television series *The Addams Family*. Her unconventional beauty typecast her in offbeat roles, but she also played the moll of gangster Baby Face Nelson, one of her best starring performances, in the 1957 film of that title.
Baby Face Nelson (United Artists, 1957).

Jory, Victor (1902–1982)
Character actor. The tough, imposing air Jory displayed on film was not a pose: while serving in the Navy, he became a champion amateur boxer. After studying acting and moving to California during the early twenties, he began appearing in movies. His robust physique, saturnine features, and lugubrious voice typecast him as a heavy,

usually in action pictures. He played a gangster in the minor film *I Stole a Million*.

I Stole a Million (Universal, 1939).

June, Ray (1898–1958)
Cinematographer. June worked mainly on minor productions. His style was conventional, rather flat and impersonal—thus, he was the perfect cinematographer for commercial films in black and white or color.

Alibi (United Artists, 1929).

Juran, Nathan (b. 1907)
Art director. A graduate of M.I.T. in architecture, Juran entered the movies in 1937 after practicing in New York for several years. Most of his career was spent at 20th Century–Fox, where he often collaborated with Richard Day. In the fifties, Juran also directed several successful science fiction movies. He was the art director for the influential gangster *noir Body and Soul*, his only contribution to the genre.

Body and Soul (United Artists, 1947).

Kane, Joseph (1894–1975)
Director. Kane was one of Republic's most prolific staff directors, making literally dozens of movies between 1935 and 1958. The vast majority of these were Westerns. He occasionally directed a movie with a contemporary theme. Among these is a gangster movie, *Hoodlum Empire*. Although entertaining and often competently made, none of his movies are important in any way.

Hoodlum Empire (Republic, 1952).

Kansas City Confidential (United Artists, 1952). 98 mins.
Producer: Edward Small. *Director*: Phil Karlson. *Screenplay*: George Bruce and Harry Essex, *story by* Harold R. Greene and Rowland Brown. *Director of Photography*: George Diskant. *Music*: Paul Sawtell.

Art Director: Edward L. Ilou. *Editor*: Buddy Small.
Cast: John Payne (Joe Rolfe), Coleen Gray (Helen), Preston Foster (Tim Foster), Dona Drake (Teresa), Jack Elam (Harris), Neville Brand (Kane). *With*: Lee Van Cleef, Mario Seletti, Howard Negley, Ted Ryan, George Wallace, Vivi Janiss.

When his pension proves inadequate, retired Kansas City police captain Timothy Foster devises an elaborate armored car robbery. The plan is carried out, but an innocent ex-con, Joe Rolfe, is arrested. Although released due to insufficient evidence, he vows revenge against the real culprits. With the aid of Helen, Foster's daughter, he discovers that Foster is planning to double-cross his colleagues. Foster kills a couple of his confederates before Rolfe confronts him. After a shootout, Rolfe kills Foster, collects a reward, and wins the love of Helen.

Kansas City Confidential is a classic "B" movie, superbly directed by Phil Karlson in his usual kinetic style. The performances are all first rate, particularly those of the aging Preston Foster and his trio of robbers: Lee Van Cleef, Neville Brand, and Jack Elam.

Karloff, Boris (1887–1969)
Character actor. Born William Henry Pratt in London, Karloff began acting in Canada in 1910 before moving to the United States several years later. His film career began in 1919 and he subsequently played a variety of villains in countless obscure movies until he portrayed the creature in *Frankenstein* (Universal, 1931). The movie's success typecast him in horror films, despite his gentle, refined off-screen nature. He appeared in several early gangster pictures, often as a mob boss, henchman or killer. His finest genre performance is in Howard Hawks' *The Criminal Code*, in which he plays the maniacal murderer.

The Criminal Code (Columbia, 1931). *Smart Money* (Warner Bros.,

1931). *The Guilty Generation* (Columbia, 1931). *Graft* (Universal, 1931). *Scarface* (United Artists, 1932). *Behind the Mask* (Columbia, 1932). *The Miracle Man* (Paramount, 1932). *Night World* (Universal, 1932). *The Walking Dead* (Warner Bros., 1936). *Black Friday* (Universal, 1940).

Karlson, Phil (b. 1908)
Director. Born Philip Karlstein, Karlson studied law before entering the movies in the mid-thirties. By 1944, he had worked his way up from prop boy to director. Over the next eight years he directed a variety of films, mostly for the Poverty Row studio Monogram, before finding his voice in the *noir* thriller *Scandal Sheet* (Columbia, 1952). Karlson went on to consolidate his reputation as a director with a series of tightly budgeted, brutally violent crime thrillers. His style was graceful yet kinetic and never flinched in the face of cruelty. His gangster pictures are some of the great "B" movies of the genre. Particularly admirable are *Kansas City Confidential* and *The Scarface Mob*, the theatrical release of the pilot for the hit television series *The Untouchables*. He also directed the Elvis Presley vehicle *Kid Galahad*, perhaps the weirdest gangster musical of them all.
Kansas City Confidential (United Artists, 1952). *The Phenix City Story* (Allied Artists, 1955). *The Brothers Rico* (Columbia, 1957). *The Scarface Mob* (Cari Releasing, 1962). *Kid Galahad* (United Artists, 1961).

Kaufman, Boris (1906–1980)
Cinematographer. The Polish-born Kaufman was a leading cinematographer in Europe before moving to Hollywood in 1942. He was the director of photography on many American movies, but he was one of the least prolific of the great cinematographers. His entire filmography consists of only thirty-three titles. His style, first established in Europe, is lush, inventive, and often romantically inclined, and he was a master of diffuse lighting and soft focus. He won an Academy Award for best cinematography for his work on the classic *On the Waterfront*, his only gangster movie.
On the Waterfront (Columbia, 1954).

Kazan, Elia (b. 1909)
Director. A prominent stage actor and director, Kazan, born Kazanjoglous of Greek and Turkish descent, began his film career as a director during the mid-forties. A prominent member of New York's leftist Group Theatre during the thirties, he specialized in topical and social themes and had a notable lush, almost European style somewhat influenced by German expressionism. *On the Waterfront*, arguably his masterpiece, is a typical example of his attempts to combine serious themes in a commercial format; he succeeded quite admirably and it is far less pretentious than his subsequent movies. It remains one of the genre's classics.
On the Waterfront (Columbia, 1954).

Keaton, Diane (b. 1946)
Actress. Although she will probably be remembered for her eccentric portrayals in Woody Allen's comedies, Keaton also costarred in all the *Godfather* films. She played a wife who tries unsuccessfully to keep her husband, Michael Corleone (Al Pacino), from taking over the mob after the death of his father (Marlon Brando).
The Godfather (Paramount, 1972). *Godfather Part II* (Paramount, 1974).

Keaton, Michael (b. 1951)
Actor. Prior to achieving phenomenal success in the *Batman* features, Keaton was originally known for his comic performances. He played the title role in *Johnny Dangerously*, a failed attempt to satirize the gangster genre.
Johnny Dangerously (20th Century-Fox, 1984).

Keighley, William (1893–1984)
Director. As one of Warner Bros.' chief house directors beginning in the early thirties, William Keighley made many of the studio's important productions. Thus, he directed a number of key gangster films, including the superior James Cagney vehicles *G-Men* and *Each Dawn I Die*. His style is typical of Warner Bros. in its simplicity and unpretentiuosness.

G-Men (Warner Bros., 1935). *Bullets or Ballots* (First National, 1936). *Each Dawn I Die* (Warner Bros., 1939).

Keitel, Harvey (b. 1947)
Character actor. The husky, craggy-faced Keitel first came to attention in the films of Martin Scorsese during the seventies. He costarred in the low budget *Mean Streets* as a young Italian-American with family connections to the Mafia. He also played one of the murderous gangsters in Scorsese's *GoodFellas* and one of the hapless thieves in the Scorsese influenced *Reservoir Dogs*.

Mean Streets (Warner Bros., 1975). *GoodFellas* (Warner Bros., 1990). *Reservoir Dogs* (Live America, 1993).

Keith, Brian (b. 1921)
Character actor. Although he is a forceful actor who has played a variety of roles in many movies, Brian Keith will probably be remembered as the understanding uncle in the television series *Family Affair*. Yet, he was also an effective villain and hero. He appeared in two minor gangster movies, playing the hero in both, during the fifties.

Tight Spot (Columbia, 1955). *Chicago Confidential* (United Artists, 1957).

Keller, Walter E.
Art director. Keller's film career began in the early twenties, but he did his best work, always in collaboration with Albert S. D'Agostino, at RKO during the forties. He helped design the productions for Val Lewton's series of classic "B" horror films, including *Cat People* (RKO, 1942), *I Walked with a Zombie* (RKO, 1943), and *The Body Snatcher* (RKO, 1945), as well as some great *films noir*. His work on the minor gangster picture *Race Street* is exemplary.

Race Street (RKO, 1948).

Kelly, Barry (1907–1989)
Character actor. Large and imposing, Kelly played villainous supporting roles in many movies throughout the forties and fifties. He played mob henchmen in three gangster movies.

The Undercover Man (Columbia, 1949). *The Black Hand* (MGM, 1950). *711 Ocean Drive* (Columbia, 1950).

Kelly, Gene (1912–1996)
Actor. Best known for his athletic dancing in many MGM classics, Kelly also played, less effectively, a few dramatic roles during his career. One of his best non-musical performances is in *The Black Hand*, in which he plays a crusader against organized crime in turn of the century New York City.

The Black Hand (MGM, 1950).

Kelly, Paul (1899–1956)
Actor. Kelly was born in Brooklyn and as a juvenile appeared on stage and then in movies. His career came to a halt when he murdered the abusive husband of his lover in 1927. After spending two years in prison for manslaughter, he married the woman of his obsessions, Dorothy MacKaye, and returned to the stage and screen. A well regarded stage actor, the tall, steely actor's film career was relegated mainly to "B" movies but continued unabated until his death. He played supporting roles in two gangster pictures and starred in *The Glass Alibi*, one of Republic's best gangster films.

Queen of the Mob (Paramount, 1940). *The Glass Alibi* (Republic, 1946). *Side Street* (MGM, 1949).

Real life husband and wife Humphrey Bogart and Lauren Bacall in *Key Largo*, **perhaps their most fondly remembered joint appearance.**

Kennedy, Arthur (1914–1995)

Character actor. John Arthur Kennedy was born in Worcester, Massachusetts, and began performing on stage during the mid-thirties. James Cagney discovered the fair-haired young actor and brought him to Hollywood to play his brother in the boxing picture *City for Conquest* (Columbia, 1940). Kennedy subsequently played one of the gangsters in the classic *High Sierra* before serving in World War II. He resumed his film career after service and during the fifties was one of the busiest character actors in American movies. He played a variety of professional types as well as a few bad guys. He appeared in two additional gangster movies. In *Crashout*, a superior "B" picture, he played one of the doomed escaped convicts. In *The Desperate Hours* he played a neighbor who comes to believe the family next door is being held hostage by a gang of escaped convicts.

High Sierra (Warner Bros., 1941). *Crashout* (Filmakers, 1955). *The Desperate Hours* (Paramount, 1955).

Kent, Robert E.

Screenwriter and producer. Kent worked mainly as a screenwriter on hard-boiled "B" pictures during the fifties. He wrote the screenplay for *The Miami Story*, a "B" gangster picture. He also produced a few movies, including yet another "B" gangster movie, *Chicago Confidential*. He later worked extensively on television.

The Miami Story (Columbia, 1954). *Chicago Confidential* (United Artists, 1957).

Key Largo (Warner Bros., 1948). 100 mins.

Humphrey Bogart and Edward G. Robinson in *Key Largo*, their finest film together.

Producer: Jerry Wald. *Director*: John Huston. *Screenplay*: Richard Brooks and John Huston, based on the play by Maxwell Anderson. *Director of Photography*: Karl Freund. *Music*: Max Steiner. *Art Director*: Leo K. Kuter. *Editor*: Rudi Fehr.

Cast: Humphrey Bogart (Frank McCloud), Edward G. Robinson (Johnny Rocco), Lauren Bacall (Nora Temple), Lionel Barrymore (James Temple), Claire Trevor (Gaye Dawn), Thomas Gomez (Curley). *With*: Harry Lewis, John Rodney, Marc Lawrence, Dan Seymour, Monte Blue.

Off the Florida coast, on the remote island Key Largo, the crippled James Temple and his widowed daughter-in-law, Nora, run a small hotel. They are visited by Frank McCloud, a friend of Nora's husband who served with him in World War II. McCloud, deeply affected

by his friends' deaths in the war, has become a committed pacifist. He finds his beliefs challenged, however, when the hotel is overrun by Johnny Rocco and his gang. Rocco, a notorious gangster wanted by the police, plans to escape to Cuba. Eventually, Frank agrees to fly Rocco, his moll, Gaye, and the rest of the gang to Cuba, but he manages to overpower the gang and kill Rocco. He returns to Nora a different man.

Maxwell Anderson's original play was a verse drama. Richard Brooks' adaptation retains much of the original action, adding mainly the final confrontation. Indeed, the film features the ambiance of a drama, but is saved from tedium by the assured direction of John Huston and one of the best casts ever assembled. The genre's great icons, Humphrey Bogart and Edward

G. Robinson, are here at their very best, supported by the likes of the formidable Thomas Gomez (as one of the hoodlums), Claire Trevor, and Lauren Bacall. Trevor, as Rocco's abused moll, won an Academy Award for best supporting actress. The film remains one of the most entertaining of the entire genre.

Keyes, Evelyn (b. 1919)
Actress. The petite, fair-haired Keyes will be forever remembered as Scarlett O'Hara's younger sister in *Gone with the Wind* (MGM, 1939). Her substantial talent could not overcome the burden of this film's success, but she was a popular leading lady of mostly "B" pictures during the forties. She gave some of her best performances in several interesting minor *films noir*, including *The Killer That Stalked New York* (United Artists, 1950). She costarred opposite Peter Lorre in the unusual gangster movie *Face Behind the Mask* as a blind girl who falls in love with a disfigured killer.
Face Behind the Mask (Columbia, 1941).

Kid Galahad (Warner Bros., 1937). 101 mins.
Associate Producer: Samuel Bischoff. *Director*: Michael Curtiz. *Screenplay*: Seton I. Miller, based on the novel by Francis Wallace. *Director of Photography*: Tony Gaudio. *Music*: Heinz Roemheld and Max Steiner. *Art Director*: Carl Jules Weyl. *Editor*: George Amy.
Cast: Edward G. Robinson (Nick Donati), Bette Davis (Louise "Fluff" Phillips), Humphrey Bogart (Turkey Morgan), Wayne Morris (Kid Galahad), Jane Bryan (Marie Donati), Ben Weldon (Buzz Stevens). *With*: Harry Carey, William Haade, Joe Cunningham, Soledad Jimenez, Veda Ann Borg.
A down and out fight manager, Nick Donati, discovers a young man in a street scuffle and believes he has found

a champion. Dubbed "Kid Galahad" by Louise Phillips, Nick's mistress, the boy begins his training and climb in the boxing world. When Nick discovers that his mistress and sister, Marie, are both attracted to the Kid, he decides to get even. He arranges a fight between the Kid and the champion, even though he is not ready to fight the more experienced boxer. He further fixes the fight with a crooked gangster and promoter, Turkey Morgan. During the fight, however, the two girls convince Nick to give the Kid the proper instructions to win the fight. Angry at the doublecross, Turkey confronts Nick and, in the ensuing gun battle, both are killed. The Kid wins the title, but quits the game to marry Marie.

In many ways, *Kid Galahad* resembles a Frank Capra movie. Much more cynical than any of Capra's movies, however, *Kid Galahad* also presages *film noir* with its theme of moral corruption and greed in the boxing world. Indeed, it is a classic of its era, with powerful performances all around, and the usual kinetic style of Michael Curtiz, arguably the most underrated director of Hollywood's golden age.

Phil Karlson directed a remake (released by United Artists in 1963) with Elvis Presley in the title role. As a vehicle for Presley, it is an odd choice, and it suffers from the usual weaknesses of his movies, although Karlson's direction is good.

Kiley, Richard (b. 1922)
Character actor. Stage and broadcast veteran Richard Kiley is known for his deep, sonorous voice and smooth villainy in his many movie appearances. He played in two gangster movies early in his career. He played a mob henchman in *The Mob*. In *The Phenix City Story* he starred as a returning G.I. who battles the local mob after he becomes a prosecutor.
The Mob (Columbia, 1951). *The Phenix City Story* (Allied Artists, 1955).

"Killer Mannion" (a.k.a. Arthur Ferguson Jones) (Fictional character) Off camera, Edward G. Robinson was a quiet, gentle man who was active in liberal politics and a collector of fine art. In real life, he despised guns and hated gunfire. He also was a very talented actor who quickly realized that his extraordinary performance in *Little Caesar* (Warner Bros., 1930) had typecast him. Of the triumvirate of actors most associated with gangster roles — Robinson, James Cagney and Humphrey Bogart — Robinson had the most difficulty escaping his on-screen image. However, from the beginning of his stardom, after the success of *Little Caesar*, Robinson tried to play a variety of characters and was not above making fun of his on-screen image. Perhaps his best such role was as the timid hardware clerk, Arthur Ferguson Jones, who is constantly confused with the mobster "Killer Mannion" whom he resembles exactly (both roles were played by Robinson). With his identity mistaken by both the police and Mannion's gang, Jones is able to infiltrate the latter and eventually bring about the downfall of the notorious mob leader, despite his apparent timidity. As the two characters, Robinson's dual performance is both menacing and hilarious.

The Killers (Universal, 1946). 105 mins.
Producer: Mark Hellinger. Robert Siodmak. *Screenplay*: Anthony Veiller, based on the story by Ernest Hemingway. *Director of Photography*: Woody Bredell. *Music*: Miklos Rosza. *Art Directors*: Jack Otterson and Martin Obzina. *Editor*: Arthur Hilton.
Cast: Edmond O'Brien (Riordan), Ava Gardner (Kitty), Burt Lancaster (Swede), Albert Dekker (Colfaz), Sam Levene (Lubinsky), Charles McGraw (Al), William Conrad (Max). *With*: John Miljan, Virginia Christine, Vince Barnett, Charles D. Brown, Queenie Smith.
A pair of hired killers enter a small town searching for their target, Swede. They find him waiting silently in a darkened room, and he offers no resistance. Riordan, an insurance investigator working on another case, becomes obsessed with the crime and carries out his own investigation. He learns that Swede was involved with a gang of thieves and had been double-crossed by an amoral woman, Kitty Collins. Riordan now helps recover the money stolen by the gang and sets himself up to help the police catch the criminals.

After several years as a minor screenwriter and producer, Mark Hellinger burst into the limelight with this production. Only the first half hour of the film is based on Ernest Hemingway's story; the rest was devised by screenwriter Anthony Veiller. Veiller constructed a spare, cynical, hard-boiled scenario that perfectly meshes with Hemingway's style and themes. To portray Swede, Hellinger wisely chose newcomer Burt Lancaster, who shot to prominence with this film. However, more than anyone, the film really belongs to director Robert Siodmak, whose bravura style was influenced by German expressionism. *The Killers* firmly established the new style of crime thriller — *film noir* — that had emerged in the mid-forties, and it remains one of the genre's greatest films.

The Killers (Universal, 1964). 93 mins.
Producer and Director: Donald Siegel. *Screenplay*: Gene L. Coon, based on the story by Ernest Hemingway. *Director of Photography*: Richard L. Rawlings. *Music*: Johnny Williams. *Art Directors*: Frank Arrigo and George Chan. *Editor*: Richard Belding.
Cast: Lee Marvin (Charlie), Angie Dickinson (Sheila Farr), John Cassavetes (Johnny North), Ronald Reagan (Browning), Clu Gulager (Lee), Claude Akins (Earl). *With*: Norman Fell, Virginia Christine, Can Haggerty, Robert Phillips, Kathleen O'Malley, Ted Jacques.

Plot-wise, Don Siegel's remake of the classic 1946 *film noir* differs in some minor aspects, emphasizing violence and action. It remains essentially the same, however, in that John Cassavetes plays the role of the doomed man who joins a gang of bank robbers and is then double-crossed by the *femme fatale* (Angie Dickinson). Interestingly, this version was originally made for television, but when it proved too violent for broadcast, it was released as a feature. If not quite a classic, it remains a fine example of Siegel at his violent best.

The Killing (United Artists, 1956). 83 mins.
Producer: James B. Harris. *Director*: Stanley Kubrick. *Screenplay*: Stanley Kubrick, with additional dialog by Jim Thompson, based on the novel *Clean Break* by Lionel White. *Director of Photography*: Lucien Ballard. *Music*: Gerald Fried. *Art Director*: Ruth Sobotka Kubrick. *Editor*: Betty Steinberg.
Cast: Sterling Hayden (Johnny Clay), Coleen Gray (Fay), Vince Edwards (Bal Cannon), Jay C. Flippen (Marvin Unger), Marie Windsor (Sherry Petty), Elisha Cook, Jr. (George Petty), Ted De Corsia (Randy Kennan), Joe Sawyer (Mike O'Reilly). *With*: Tim Carey, Jay Adler, Joseph Turkel, Maurice Oboukhoff, James Edwards.

Ex-convict Johnny Clay, a small-time criminal, plans a daring racetrack robbery with a disparate group of amateur criminals: Randy Kennan, a corrupt cop; Mike O'Reilly, the track bartender; George Petty, the betting window teller; and several others. The robbery is carried out successfully, but begins to fall apart shortly thereafter. Sherry Petty, the avaricious wife of George, learns of the plot and informs her boyfriend. The boyfriend and several others try to rob the crooks at their hideout but are wiped out in the ensuing gun battle. Mortally wounded, George staggers home and kills his wife. Clay attempts to leave the country but is apprehended at the airport when the money-laden suitcase falls off a baggage cart and scatters the bills into the wind.

The Killing was released at the end of the *noir* cycle and seems to sum up the themes and style of the genre. Unrelentingly bleak, there are really no redeeming characters in the film. The film is shot in a raw, nervy style which captures both the exhilarating pace and downbeat theme of the story.

King, Louis (1898–1962)
Director. Louis King had a long and productive career in Hollywood, beginning in the late twenties. He specialized in unpretentious action pictures, and many of his movies are quite good. He made a trio of "B" gangster pictures for Paramount in 1938, the best of which is *Tip-Off Girls*, a very well made movie of its kind.
Hunted Men (Paramount, 1938). *Illegal Traffic* (Paramount, 1938). *Tip-Off Girls* (Paramount, 1938).

King, Maurice and **King, Frank**
Producers. The King brothers were independent producers in the forties and fifties who specialized in low budget exploitation pictures. They produced three "B" gangster pictures, all of them outstanding.
Dillinger (Monogram, 1945). *The Gangster* (Allied Artists, 1947). *Gun Crazy* (United Artists, 1950).

King of Alcatraz (Paramount, 1938). 56 mins.
Associate Producer: William C. Thomas. *Director*: Robert Florey. *Screenplay*: Irving Reis. *Director of Photography*: Harry Fischbeck. *Music*: Borris Morros. *Art Directors*: Hans Dreier and Earl Hedrick. *Editor*: Eda Warren.
Cast: Gail Patrick (Dale Borden), Lloyd Nolan (Raymond Grayson), Harry Carey (Captain Glennon), J. Carrol Naish (Steve Murkil), Robert

Preston (Robert MacArthur), Anthony Quinn (Lou Gedney). *With*: Dennis Morgan, Virginia Dabney, Emory Parnell, Nora Cecil, Dorothy Howe.

After a daring heist, Steve Murkil and his gang attempt to escape on a cruise ship. When one of the gangsters becomes ill, Dale Durden, a nurse, performs an operation (via instructions over the radio) which saves the gangster's life. The gang almost manages to escape but, by a twist of fate, is captured in the end.

A good, if rather short, "B" gangster picture, the misleadingly titled *King of Alcatraz* is one of Robert Florey's best in the genre. It also contains one of J. Carrol Naish's most prominent roles, the suave gangster Steve Murkil.

King of Chinatown (Paramount, 1938). 54 mins.

Associate Producer: Stuart Walker. *Director*: Nick Grinde. *Screenplay*: Lillie Hayward and Irving Reis, *story by* Herbert Biberman. *Director of Photography*: Leo Tover. *Music*: Borris Morros. *Art Directors*: Hans Dreier and Robert Odell. *Editor*: Eda Warren.

Cast: Anna May Wong (Dr. Mary Ling), Akim Tamiroff (Frank Baturin), J. Carrol Naish (The Professor), Sidney Toler (Dr. Chang Ling), Philip Ahn (Bob Li). *With*: Anthony Quinn, Bernadene Hayes, Roscoe Karns, Ray Mayer, Richard Denning.

The Professor, gang boss Frank Baturin's second in command, guns down his boss and takes over the gang. Unbeknown to him, however, Baturin has survived and is nursed back to health by a doctor, Mary Ling. When he is healthy enough to confront the Professor, a shootout ensues in which both are fatally wounded. Baturin lives long enough, however, to ensure that Dr. Ling and her father, also a physician, have sufficient funds for an ambulance unit to operate in Chinatown.

One of several "B" gangster pictures starring Akim Tamiroff made by Paramount in the late thirties, *King of*

Chinatown is an unpretentious, swift-moving action picture. Its best virtue is the excellent cast, including minor icons Tamiroff, J. Carrol Naish, and Anthony Quinn (as one of the gangsters).

King of Gamblers (Paramount, 1937). 79 mins.

Director: Robert Florey. *Screenplay*: Doris Anderson, *story by* Tiffany Thayer. *Director of Photography*: Harry Fischbeck. *Musical Director*: Borris Morros. *Art Directors*: Hans Dreier and Robert Odell. *Editor*: Harvey Johnstone.

Cast: Claire Trevor (Dixie), Lloyd Nolan (Jim), Akim Tamiroff (Steve Kalkas), Larry "Buster" Crabbe (Eddie), Helen Burgess (Jackie Nolan), Porter Hall (George Kramer). *With*: Harvey Stephens, Barlowe Borland, Purnell Pratt, Colin Tapley, Paul Fix, Cecil Cunningham.

In the late thirties, Paramount was known for the best "B" pictures in the business, and *King of Gamblers* shows why. While the plot is flimsy — a crooked gambler (Akim Tamiroff) is undone by a nightclub singer (Claire Trevor) and an investigative reporter (Lloyd Nolan) — it is directed with such great style and zip, and its performances are so intense that it manages to overcome its faults. *King of Gamblers* is not an important movie, but it is one of the most entertaining of the early "B" gangster movies.

King of the Underworld (Warner Bros., 1939). 69 mins.

Associate Producer: Bryan Foy. *Director*: Lewis Seiler. *Screenplay*: George Bricker and Vincent Sherman, based on the novel *Dr. Socrates* by W. R. Burnett. *Director of Photography*: Sid Hickox. *Music*: Heinz Roemheld. *Art Director*: Charles Novi. *Editor*: Frank Dewar.

Cast: Humphrey Bogart (Joe Gurney), Kay Francis (Carole Nelson), James Stephenson (Bill Forrest), John

Eldredge (Niles Nelson), Jessie Busley (Aunt Margaret). *With*: Arthur Aylesworth, Raymond Brown, Harland Tucker, Charles Foy, Ralph Remley, Murray Alper.

With some minor changes, *King of the Underworld* is a remake of *Dr. Socrates* (Warner Bros., 1935). Warner Bros. were masters of remaking their "A" pictures as "B" productions, and *King of the Underworld* is a classic example of that marketing ploy. What this version lacks in subtlety, it makes up in action and violence. It was released at a time in Bogart's career when he looked destined to be permanently employed in "B" pictures; yet within months he would be cast as Roy Earle in *High Sierra* (Warner Bros., 1940) and his career would take a decidedly different turn.

Kingsley, Sidney (b. 1906)
Playwright. A leading American playwright during the thirties, Kingsley's most important play is *Dead End*, which was adapted successfully by Lillian Hellmann and has become a classic.
Dead End (United Artists, 1937).

Kirk, Phyllis (b. 1926)
Actress. Born Phyllis Kirkegaard, Miss Kirk was a leading lady of many "B" pictures during the forties and fifties. She was the original Lois Lane, her most famous role, in the *Superman* serial and television series. She costarred in a single minor gangster picture.
Crime Wave (Warner Bros., 1953).

Kiss of Death (20th Century–Fox, 1947). 98 mins.
Producer: Fred Kohlmar. *Director*: Henry Hathaway. *Screenplay*: Ben Hecht and Charles Lederer, *story by* Eleazar Lipsky. *Director of Photography*: Norbert Brodine. *Music*: David Buttolph. *Art Directors*: Leland Fuller and Lyle Wheeler. *Editor*: J. Watson Webb, Jr.

Cast: Victor Mature (Nick Bianco), Brian Donlevy (D'Angelo), Coleen Gray (Nettie), Richard Widmark (Tom Udo), Taylor Holmes (Earl Howser), Howard Smith (Warden), Karl Malden (Sergeant William Cullen). *With*: Anthony Ross, Mildred Dunnock, Milliard Mitchell, Temple Texas, J. Scott Smart, Wendell Phillips.

After he is wounded in a shootout during a botched robbery, Nick Bianco is offered a deal by District Attorney D'Angelo. D'Angelo agrees to reduce his sentence if Nick will inform on other criminals. Nick refuses, but he begins to consider the offer in prison after his letters to his wife are returned unopened. He soon learns that, after having an affair with a gangster named Rizzo, his wife recently committed suicide. Concerned about his children, and wanting revenge against Rizzo, Nick finally agrees to help D'Angelo. Nick is released and gathers information against the gangsters. D'Angelo then implicates Rizzo as the informer, and he is killed by his confederates. Nick remarries but, when his testimony against a sadistic killer, Tommy Udo, fails to send the hit man to prison, Nick and his family become Udo's target of revenge. Sending his family away, Nick hunts down Udo, but he is ambushed and repeatedly shot before Udo is killed by the police. An ambulance carries the critically wounded Nick to the hospital, leaving the viewer to believe that he will survive and begin a new life with his family.

The brilliant and talented director Henry Hathaway was one of the most widely praised American filmmakers of his time, and *Kiss of Death* demonstrates why. Combining documentary-like techniques with the more stylized technique of *noir* expressionism, Hathaway creates a world of lurking danger and madness. The film was shot largely on location in New York (then a novel idea) from a superb screenplay by Ben Hecht and Charles Lederer. It was enormously popular and made Richard

Barbara Payton seeks revenge against her lover, James Cagney, in *Kiss Tomorrow Goodbye*, **certainly the most sadistic and violent of Cagney's gangster movies.**

Widmark a star. His edgy performance as Tommy Udo, with his hyena laugh and penchant for pushing wheelchair bound old ladies down stairways, is one of the great screen performances of the forties. Altogether, *Kiss of Death* further demonstrates that Hathaway is now one of the most neglected major directors of his time.

Kiss Tomorrow Goodbye (Warner Bros., 1950). 102 mins.
  Producer: William Cagney. *Director*: Gordon Douglas. *Screenplay*: Harry

Brown, based on the novel by Horace McCoy. *Director of Photography*: Peverell Marley. *Music*: Carmen Dragon. *Art Director*: Wiard Ihnen. *Editors*: Truman Wood and Walter Hannemann.

Cast: James Cagney (Ralph Cotter), Barbara Payton (Holiday Carleton), Helena Carter (Margaret Dobson), Ward Bond (Inspector Weber), Luther Adler (Cherokee Mandon), Barton MacLane (Reece). *With*: Steve Brodie, Rhys Williams, Herbert Heyes, John Litel, William Frawley, Robert Karnes, Kenneth Tobey.

After escaping from a prison farm, Ralph Cotter and a fellow inmate find refuge in a corrupt, out of the way small town. Cotter soon discovers which officials can be bribed and blackmailed and quickly gains control of the town, but when he seduces a politician's daughter, it proves to be his undoing. His mistress, Holiday, kills him rather than give him up.

Based on one of Horace McCoy's most cynical hard-boiled novels, *Kiss Tomorrow Goodbye* is one of the most disparaging of all crime movies. Following *White Heat* (Warner Bros., 1949), James Cagney played a villain even more psychotic and destructive than his character in the previous film. Directed by Gordon Douglas, *Kiss Tomorrow Goodbye* emphasizes violence and sadistic brutality. It does not make for pleasant viewing, but Cagney is typically electrifying in his last genre role.

Kitty (Fictional character)

Mae Clarke's small supporting role in *Public Enemy* (Warner Bros., 1931) is one of the most famous female characters in the gangster genre. Kitty is the archetypal gangster's moll, veracious, wisecracking, and as much the object of her lover's wrath as his affection: in a famous scene, her mobster boyfriend, Tom Powers (James Cagney), smashes a grapefruit in her face. Soon afterward, he unceremoni- ously dumps Kitty for an equally super- ficial but more elegant moll, Gwen Allen (Jean Harlow).

Kleiner, Harry (b. 1916)

Screenwriter and producer. Kleiner is a prolific screenwriter whose best work was created in the forties and fifties. He wrote several notable *films noir*, and wrote and produced the "B" gangster movie *Cry Tough*, a well made, traditional gangster picture. His superb *policier Bullit*, with its gangster elements and cop as vigilante charac- ter, was immensely influential.

Cry Tough (United Artists, 1959; producer and screenplay). *Bullit* (Warner Bros., 1968; screenplay only).

Knapp, Evelyn (1908–1981)

Actress. A leading lady, Knapp starred in two or three dozen "B" pic- tures during the thirties and forties, and several serials, including the re- make of *The Perils of Pauline* (Univer- sal, 1934). Of her two gangster movies, the most important is *Smart Money*, one of James Cagney's lesser films in the genre.

Smart Money (Warner Bros., 1931). *Confidential* (Mascot, 1935).

Knowles, Patric (b. 1911)

Character actor. Born Reginald Knowles in Great Britain, Patric had a prominent stage and screen career in his native country before moving to Hollywood in 1936. For over forty years, he was one of Hollywood's most welcome character actors, specializing, as in *The Big Steal*, in smooth villains. *The Big Steal* (RKO, 1949).

Koch, Howard W. (b. 1916)

Director. In the fifties, Koch directed a number of interesting "B" pictures, including a very good *film noir*, *Shield for Murder* (United Artists, 1954), and the remake of the prison drama *The Last Mile*, whose greatest asset is Mickey Rooney's strong performance as a condemned killer. Koch later became a prominent producer and studio executive.

The Last Mile (United Artists, 1959).

Kohler, Fred (1889–1938)
Character actor. The scraggly featured Kohler was most often seen in Westerns as a bad guy. He costarred in an early gangster picture, *Roadhouse Nights*, as a heavy. It is his only appearance in the genre.

Roadhouse Nights (Paramount, 1930).

Kohlmar, Fred (1905–1969)
Producer. Kohlmar had an interesting career, producing many notable and a few classic movies, including two gangster *noirs*. *The Lady and the Mob* is a minor addition to the gangster genre.

The Lady and the Mob (Columbia, 1939). *The Glass Key* (Paramount, 1942). *Kiss of Death* (20th Century-Fox, 1947).

Kramer, Stanley (b. 1913)
Producer. As a producer, and later as a producer and director, Kramer was concerned chiefly with presenting social themes in a commercial setting. *My Six Convicts*, for example, depicts the psychology and pathology of criminals. *The Wild One*, his most important contribution to the genre, explored the new and growing phenomenon of motorcycle gangs and youth culture.

My Six Convicts (Columbia, 1952). *The Wild One* (Columbia, 1954).

Krasner, Milton (b. 1901)
Cinematographer. Certainly one of the most important American cinematographers of the forties and fifties, Krasner had an elegant sense of style, whether photographing inexpensive black and white movies or expensive color extravaganzas. He is one of the leading *film noir* cinematographers, borrowing from and refining the German expressionist style of the twenties.

Among the cycle of classic *films noir* he photographed in the forties is *The Set-Up*, a perfect example of the genre's early technique at its extravagant best. His work on two other gangster pictures, while not as important as his *noirs*, is no less exemplary.

I Stole a Million (Universal, 1939). *The Set-Up* (RKO, 1949). *The St. Valentine's Day Massacre* (20th Century-Fox, 1967).

Kruger, Otto (1885–1974)
Character actor. Born in Toledo, Ohio, Kruger was a matinee idol in the twenties. After some silent movies, he moved permanently to Hollywood in the early thirties and remained active for three decades. His wavy hair, trim mustache, and suave manner became a Hollywood trademark. Although he played a few romantic roles, he is best known as an elegant cad, and he played mobsters in his three gangster movies.

I Am the Law (Columbia, 1938). *Disbarred* (Paramount, 1939). *711 Ocean Drive* (Columbia, 1950).

Kubrick, Stanley (b. 1928)
Writer and director. After experience as a photojournalist, mainly for *Life* magazine, Kubrick began his career as a film director by making an independent movie on a shoestring budget. From the very beginning he demonstrated great visual style. His third film, *The Killing*, is one of the great late *films noir*, a masterful blend of style and story.

The Killing (United Artists, 1956; director and cowriter).

Ladd, Alan (1913–1964)
Actor. Pint-sized, fair-haired Alan Ladd was the perfect hero for the forties: brooding and stoic, he could either be quietly menacing or heroic and, as such, came to represent the image of the *film noir* protagonist. Born in Hot Springs, Arkansas, Ladd had icy looks and a fine resonant voice, but his lack of expression doomed him to small

Film noir icons Veronica Lake and Alan Ladd, gangster stars of the cynical forties.

roles for much of his early career until he played the cold, heartless killer in *This Gun for Hire*. This seminal *noir* thriller was an enormous box office success and made Ladd and his costar Veronica Lake into major stars. Although neither was a particularly gifted actor, they both had enormous charisma, particularly together, and they were subsequently reteamed in several notable movies, including the gangster *noir The Glass Key*. While his hired killer in *This Gun for Hire* is a classic antihero, Ladd's other roles in the gangster genre are more conventionally heroic.

The Glass Key (Paramount, 1942). *Lucky Jordan* (Paramount, 1942). *This Gun for Hire* (Paramount, 1942). *Hell on Frisco Bay* (Warner Bros., 1956).

Ladies Love Brutes (Paramount, 1930). 83 mins.

Director: Rowland V. Lee. *Screenplay*: Waldemar Young and Herman J. Mankiewicz, based on the play *Pardon My Glove* by Zoe Akins. *Director of Photography*: Harry Fischbeck. *Art Director*: Hans Dreier. *Editor*: Eda Warren.

Cast: George Bancroft (Joe Froziati), Mary Astor (Mimi Howell), Fredric March (Dwight Howell), Margaret Quimby (Lucille Gates), Stanley Fields (Mike Mendino). *With*: Ben Hendricks, Jr., Freddie Burke, David Durand, Lawford Davidson, Ferike Boros.

Joe Froziati, a crooked building contractor, falls in love with an unhappy society girl, Mimi Howell, whose marriage is on the rocks. When she rejects him, he plans to kidnap her child. Rival gangsters interfere, however, by kidnapping Mimi's children and Joe's children. Joe rescues the children, but he does not win the love of Mimi.

Based on a successful semisatirical play, *Ladies Love Brutes* is a minor gangster picture, notable mainly as one of the series starring George Bancroft, who had shot to stardom in Josef von Sternberg's gangster pictures during the late twenties.

The Lady and the Mob (Columbia, 1939). 65 mins.

Producer: Fred Kohlmar. *Director*: Ben Stoloff. *Screenplay*: Richard Maibaum and Gertrude Purcell, based on a story by George Bradshaw and Price Day. *Director of Photography*: John Stumar. *Editor*: Otto Meyer.

Cast: Fay Bainter (Hattie Leonard), Ida Lupino (Lila Thorpe), Lee Bowman (Fred Leonard), Henry Armetta (Zambrogio), Warren Hymer (Frankie O'Fallon). *With*: Harold Huber, Forbes Murray, Joseph Sawyer, Tom Dugan, Joseph Caits, Jim Toney.

When Hattie Leonard, the matronly head of a bank, finds herself trapped by a protection racket, she forms a rival gang and puts the other gangsters in their place.

A "B" gangster comedy, *The Lady and the Mob* is a minor but enjoyable movie with a good performance by film veteran Fay Bainter as the matronly gang boss.

Lady for a Day (Columbia, 1933). 95 mins.

Director: Frank Capra. *Screenplay*: Robert Riskin, based on the story "Madame la Gimp" by Damon Runyon. *Director of Photography*: Joseph Walker. *Editor*: Gene Havlick.

Cast: Warren William (Dave the Dude), May Robson (Apple Annie), Guy Kibbee (Judge Blake), Glenda Farrell (Missouri Martin), Ned Sparks (Happy), Louise Parker (Louise). *With*: Walter Connolly, Nat Pendleton, Robert Emmett O'Connor, Wallis Clark, Hobart Bosworth.

Apple Annie, a New York street peddler of produce, has a daughter, Louise, who was raised in foster homes and at boarding schools. When Annie learns that her daughter and fiancé, a wealthy Spanish nobleman, are coming to visit, she is panicked: for years, she has written her daughter that she is a wealthy woman. Appealing to Dave the Dude, a big time gambler, and his gangster friends, she is set up in a mansion for a week to fool her daughter. Eventually the ruse is discovered, but Louise, rather than reject her mother, asks her to live with her new family.

With its mixture of comedy and sentimentality, *Lady for a Day* is a typical Frank Capra film from the thirties. Indeed, it was the first of his social comedies upon which his considerable reputation now rests. Based on one of Damon Runyon's most popular short stories, it is full of Runyonesque gangsters, semicorrupt officials, and colorful dialog. A unique addition to the genre, with its good-natured, nonviolent gangsters, it remains a minor classic. Capra's remake, *Pocketful of Miracles* (Columbia, 1961), as with other musical gangster films, is an artistic disaster, lacking much of the punch and charm of the original. It was also Capra's last film.

Lady Gangster (Warner Bros., 1942). 62 mins.
Director: Florian Roberts (Robert Florey). *Screenplay*: Anthony Coldeway, based on the play by Dorothy Mackaye and Charles Miles. *Director of Photography*: Arthur Todd. *Art Director*: Ted Smith. *Editor*: Harold McLernon.
Cast: Faye Emerson (Dot Barton), Frank Wilcox (Kenneth Phillips), Julie Bishop (Myrtle Reed), Roland Drew (Candy Wells), Jackie Gleason (Wilson), Dorothy Vaughn (Jenkins). *With*: Dorothy Adams, Vera Lewis, Bill Hopper, Herbert Rawlinson, Charles Wilson, Peggy Diggins.

Dot Barton, a small-town girl, moves to the big city and promptly falls in with the wrong crowd. She is arrested and sent to prison, and upon release decides to seek revenge against radio commentator Kenneth Phillips, a friend from her childhood who had inadvertently implicated her in the crime for which she was convicted. However, she soon discovers she is in love with Phillips and they plan to get married.

Another of the series of "B" gangster movies directed by Robert Florey, *Lady Gangster* is notable mainly for his elegant style.

Lady Killer (Warner Bros., 1933). 67 mins.
Director: Roy Del Ruth. *Screenplay*: Ben Markson and Lillie Hayward, based on the story "The Finger Man" by Rosalind Keating Shaffer. *Director of Photography*: Tony Gaudio. *Art Director*: Robert Haas. *Editor*: George Amy.
Cast: James Cagney (Dan), Mae Clarke (Myra), Leslie Fenton (Duke), Margaret Lindsay (Lois), Henry O'Neill (Ramick), Willard Robertson (Conroy), Douglas Cosgrove (Jones).

With: Russell Hopton, Raymond Hatton, William Davidson, John Marston, Majorie Gateson.

Dan Quigley, a fast-talking theater usher, loves movies. He also joins a gang and quickly becomes a top mobster. When things get too hot with the police, Quigley flees to California. By chance he is given a small part in a movie and becomes an overnight star when it is released. His old gang arrives, complete with his moll, Myra. Like him, Myra has reformed and together they help the police round up his old comrades.

Lady Killer is the lightest early Cagney gangster picture, and it reunites him with his *Public Enemy* costars Mae Clarke and Leslie Fenton. The ludicrous plot is played straight and is all the better for it. Extremely entertaining, it is directed with great verve by Roy Del Ruth in his unabashedly hard-boiled style.

Lady Scarface (RKO, 1941). 69 mins.
Producer: Cliff Reid. *Director*: Frank Woodruff. *Screenplay*: Arnaud D'Usseau and Richard Collins. *Director of Photography*: Nicholas Musuraca. *Music*: Constantin Bakaleinikoff. *Art Directors*: Albert S. D'Agostino and Carroll Clark. *Editor*: Harry Marker.
Cast: Dennis O'Keefe (Lieutenant Mason), Judith Anderson (Slade), Frances Neal (Ann Rogers), Mildred Coles (Mary Powell), Eric Blore (Mr. Hartford), Marc Lawrence (Lefty). *With*: Damian O'Flynn, Marion Martin, Rand Brooks, Andrew Tombes, Arthur Shields, Lee Bonnell.

Judith Anderson stars as a mysterious gang leader known to authorities as Slade and believed by them to be responsible for a series of sensational robberies and murders. The police do not know that Slade is a woman, but eventually a tough cop, Lt. Mason, unmasks the dangerous gangster and brings her to justice.

A very minor "B" gangster picture,

Lady Scarface is notable mainly for Judith Anderson's intense performance as the woman who turns master criminal as a result of her bitterness over a hideous scar which disfigures her face!

Lagana, Mike (Fictional character)
Lagana is the perverse gangster of *The Big Heat* (Columbia, 1953) who holds a whole city in the grips of terror and becomes the target of an honest cop, Sergeant Dave Bannion. Lagana (Alexander Scourby) and Bannion's (Glenn Ford) private war results in the deaths of several innocent people, including Bannion's wife (Jocelyn Brando), who inadvertently triggers a bomb in her husband's car which has been set by Lagana's henchmen to kill the cop. Eventually, however, the moll of Bannion's hit man, Vince Stone (Lee Marvin), informs on the hit man's illegal activities. He is arrested along with a number of his cronies, including Stone, who has murdered the moll before Bannion can save her.

Lake, Veronica (1919–1973)
Actress. For a time in the early to mid-forties, no one was a bigger star than Veronica Lake. Her famous "peek-a-boo" hair style was copied by female fans around the world, and she was the very personification of Hollywood glamour during the war years. Born Constance Ockleman in Brooklyn, Lake, a former teenage model, first appeared on screen in the late thirties as Constance Keene. Signed to Paramount, she became a huge star in the aviation picture *I Wanted Wings* (Paramount, 1941), and consolidated her popularity in several subsequent successes, including the gangster *noir* *This Gun for Hire* with Alan Ladd. Although not a very good actress, one cannot deny her smoldering sensuality and incredible charisma. The diminutive blonde's cool on-screen image was perfectly matched to Alan Ladd's stoic heroism, and they were reteamed in

several subsequent successes, including *The Glass Key*, perhaps their least memorable pairing.
The Glass Key (Paramount, 1942).
This Gun for Hire (Paramount, 1942).

Lamarr, Hedy (b. 1913)
Actress. Dark-haired and exquisitely beautiful, Lamarr was born Hedy Kaisler in Vienna, Austria. Coldly mysterious on-screen, she was one of Hollywood's great glamour queens during the late thirties and forties. Probably best known today for her nude scenes in the sensual art house classic *Extase* (U.S. title: *Ecstasy*) (Czechoslovakia, 1933), she came to personify exotic beauty in many minor Hollywood movies. Certainly her most important Hollywood role was in *Algiers*, in which her thick accent did not seem out of place.
Algiers (United Artists, 1938).

Lancaster, Burt (1913–1995)
Actor. Tall, strong-jawed, and athletically built, Lancaster was also one of the most intelligent stars of the forties and fifties. After his noticeable performance in a forgettable Broadway play won the attention of talent scouts, he was signed to Universal and appeared in what was to be a routine thriller, *The Killers*. Far from routine, the film was instantly recognized as a classic, and Lancaster became a star overnight. He had come along at the perfect time, and quickly emerged as one of the brightest of the new breed of more naturalistic actors who would define the era. Indeed, his role in *The Killers* was typical of his early roles in a series of classic gangster *noirs* in which he always played the stoic antihero at the mercy of exterior forces (particularly female) and occasionally of his own greed and faults. Of the films in the series, *Criss Cross* contains one of his best performances, as the basically honest man who falls prey to a *femme fatale*, joins a gang of armored car robbers, and eventually

meets his doom at the hands of the gang boss.

The Killers (Universal, 1946). *Brute Force* (Universal, 1947). *Desert Fury* (Paramount, 1947). *I Walk Alone* (Paramount, 1948). *Criss Cross* (Universal, 1949).

Landers, Lew (1901–1962)
Director. An extremely prolific director of "B" movies, Landers made a few films under his real name, Louis Friedlander, and more than fifty as Lew Landers. He directed mainly for RKO and Columbia, but also worked briefly for several other studios. Many of his films, including his single gangster picture, *Law of the Underworld*, are very good. As this film demonstrates, he was a master of fast cutting and exhilarating action sequences.

Law of the Underworld (RKO, 1936).

Lane, Lola (1909–1981)
Actress. Born Dorothy Mullican in Macy, Indiana, Lola Lane was the older sister of actress Priscilla Lane. She began appearing in movies during the late twenties, and starred in several popular family comedies with her sisters Priscilla and Rosemary during the late thirties. Although she never became a full-fledged star, she was a mainstay in "B" movies during the thirties and forties and costarred in a single, minor gangster movie.

Gangs of Chicago (Republic, 1940).

Lane, Priscilla (1917–1995)
Actress. Born Priscilla Mullican in Indianola, Iowa, Priscilla was the youngest of five sisters who had success in Hollywood during the thirties and forties. Originally a singer, the pretty, blonde Priscilla had the longest career of the sisters, starring mainly in "B" thrillers. One of her most important roles was in the classic gangster picture *The Roaring Twenties*.

The Roaring Twenties (Warner Bros., 1939).

Lanfield, Sidney (1898–1972)
Director. Educated at the University of Chicago, Sidney Lanfield played in a jazz band during the late teens and early twenties, and later worked as a comedian in vaudeville. In the twenties Lanfield worked for Fox as a comedy writer before turning to directing in 1930. He is known mainly for his light entertainments and his 1939 screen version of Conan Doyle's *The Hound of the Baskervilles*. He also directed a good minor gangster picture, *Hush Money*, best known as one of George Raft's early appearances in the genre.

Hush Money (Fox, 1931).

Lang, Charles, Jr. (b. 1902)
Cinematographer. A distinguished cinematographer, Lang's career began in the mid-twenties and continued until the mid-seventies. Although his style was somewhat conventional, he demonstrated the shadowy influence of German expressionist cinema in several notable films, including *Desert Fury*. His long, fruitful collaboration with Billy Wilder resulted in several classic films, including the gangster satire *Some Like It Hot*.

Street of Chance (Paramount, 1930). *Desert Fury* (Paramount, 1947). *The Big Heat* (Columbia, 1953). *Some Like It Hot* (United Artists, 1959).

Lang, Fritz (1890–1976)
Director. Lang was a rising star in the art world of post–World War I Germany when he abandoned painting for the new art form, motion pictures. It was a fateful choice, as he quickly became a leading filmmaker during the early twenties. He brought a painter's vision to his great silent epics, which demonstrated expressionist style and themes of political corruption and personal alienation. His leftist sympathies were always evident, but never overwhelmed the unadulterated commercialism of his productions. Among his silent classics is *Dr. Mabuse, the Gambler*, a mythic gangster adventure

which was enormously popular throughout the world. One of his early sound features was the sequel, *The Testament of Dr. Mabuse*. After immigrating to the United States after the rise of Adolf Hitler (his wife and collaborator, Thea Von Harbou, remained behind to become a major figure in Hitler's propaganda machine), Lang's movies became more modest, although, thematically, remained just as ambitious. His second American feature, *You Only Live Once*, an off-genre gangster picture, is important for its influence on contemporary crime dramas and as a precursor to *film noir*. Lang's *You and Me* is a minor, but compelling addition to the genre. Of Lang's gangster movies, probably the best known is *The Big Heat*, a classic thriller which has had a profound influence on similar movies. Although more important for his *films noir* and cynical espionage thrillers, Fritz Lang is a major director of gangster films, thanks to a handful of influential releases.

Dr. Mabuse, the Gambler (Nero Films, 1923). *The Testament of Dr. Mabuse* (Nero Films, 1932). *You Only Live Once* (United Artists, 1937). *You and Me* (Paramount, 1938). *The Big Heat* (Columbia, 1953).

Lansky, Meyer (1898–1953)

Lansky was a Jewish mobster who rose to a powerful position in the New York underworld and the Italian Mafia. As the Mafia grew in power during the twenties, gangsters from the Irish and Jewish mobs were assimilated and often achieved great power in the Italian dominated gangs. Lansky is one of the best examples of the urban gangster, with his pretensions to elegance and sophistication—he was rarely seen in public in anything but the latest fashions—which masked a deep-seated paranoia, inferiority complex and murderous tendencies. He was kicked out of the United States after World War II (he had helped the war effort,

however, by insisting that the corrupt waterfront dock workers cooperate with the government) and settled in Sicily. He was assassinated by rivals there while planning a return to the United States. A few years before that, he had ordered the assassination of Bugsy Siegel, his former enforcer, whom he had sent to Hollywood to set up operations there; but Siegel had wasted too much of the mob's money in Las Vegas, which he was trying to establish as a gambling center. Lansky and his cronies provided examples for many of the urban gangsters portrayed in American cinema. He was played by Ben Kingsley in *Bugsy* (Tristar, 1992).

Larceny, Inc. (Warner Bros., 1942). 95 mins.

Producer: Hal B. Wallis. *Director*: Lloyd Bacon. *Screenplay*: Everett Freeman and Edwin Gilbert, based on the play *The Night Before Christmas* by Laura and S. J. Perelman. *Director of Photography*: Tony Gaudio. *Art Director*: Edward Jewell. *Editor*: Ralph Dawson.

Cast: Edward G. Robinson (Pressure Maxwell), Jane Wyman (Denny Costello), Broderick Crawford (Jug Martin), Jack Carson (Jeff Randolph), Anthony Quinn (Leo Dexter), Edward Brophy (Weepy Davis). *With*: John Qualen, Barbara Jo Allen, Harry Davenport, Grant Mitchell, Jackie Gleason.

Pressure Maxwell and Jug Martin are two gangsters who are released from prison and asked by former colleagues to participate in a bank robbery. They refuse, planning their own caper instead. They open a luggage store next door to a bank. They plan to tunnel into the bank, but their plot is complicated by Denny Costello, Pressure's daughter, who falls in love with one of their legitimate store employees, and by an incompetent compatriot who, while trying to blow a hole in the wall between the two establishments, succeeds only in destroying the luggage store. Pressure and Jug are then left with their business in splinters, but determined to go straight.

A wild comedy-drama, *Larceny, Inc.* marked Edward G. Robinson's return to Warner Bros. after a prolonged absence. Here he plays a comic variation on his early roles, although Anthony Quinn steals the picture as the incompetent gangster.

LaRue, Jack (1903–1984)

Actor. Born Gaspare Biondolillo in New York, LaRue entered sound films in the early thirties, after a Broadway career. Intense, wiry, and menacing, he was most often seen in villainous roles in "A" and "B" pictures. He was a prominent "B" star, appearing in dozens of low budget productions in his more than thirty years in the movies. His performance in the gangster movie *Hard Guy* can be favorably compared to James Cagney's best performances in the genre.

Hard Guy (Producers Releasing Corp., 1941).

Las Vegas Shakedown (Allied Artists, 1955). 76 mins.

Producer: William F. Broidy. *Director*: Sidney Salkow. *Screenplay*: Steve Fisher. *Director of Photography*: John Martin. *Music*: Edward J. Kay. *Editor*: Chandler House.

Cast: Dennis O'Keefe (Joe Barnes), Coleen Gray (Julie Rae), Charles Winninger (Mr. Raff), Thomas Gomez (Sirago), Dorothy Patrick (Dorothy Reid), Mary Beth Hughes (Mabel). *With*: Elizabeth Patterson, James Millican, Robert Armstrong, Joseph Downing, Lewis Martin, Mara McAfee.

Sirago, a notorious gangster, wants to take over the Las Vegas gambling establishment owned by Joe Barnes. Sirago plans to kill Barnes, using two thugs to carry out the job. Barnes, meanwhile, has fallen in love with a young school teacher, Julie Rae, who is writing a treatise on the evils of gambling. They barely manage to escape Sirago's thugs, and the mad gangster resorts to several murders while hunting them down. Eventually, Barnes and Rae turn the tables on Sirago, who is killed by his own men.

A standard "B" melodrama, *Las Vegas Shakedown* is better than most, largely because of its excellent location shooting (when the resort was still little more than a few small, quaint hotels), and Coleen Gray's sensual presence.

LaShelle, Joseph (b. 1903)

Cinematographer. LaShelle demonstrated a great sense of style with the seminal *film noir Laura* (20th Century-Fox, 1944), for which he won an Academy Award. With few exceptions, none of his other films demonstrated the originality of this classic. In the sixties he replaced Charles Lang, Jr., as Billy Wilder's favorite director of photography.

Where the Sidewalk Ends (20th Century–Fox, 1950).

The Last Crooked Mile (Republic, 1946). 67 mins.

Associate Producer: Rudolph E. Abel. *Director*: Philip Ford. *Screenplay*: Jerry Sackheim, based on the radio drama by Robert L. Richards. *Director of Photography*: Alfred Keller. *Music Director*: Richard Cherurn. *Art Director*: Frank Hotaling. *Editor*: William P. Thompson.

Cast: Donald Barry (Tom Dwyer), Ann Savage (Sheila Kennedy), Adele Mara (Bonnie), Tom Powers (Floyd Sorelson), Sheldon Leonard (Ed McGuire), Nestor Paiva (Farrar). *With*: Harry Shannon, Ben Weldon, John Miljan, Charles D. Brown, John Dehner, Anthony Caruso.

A group of bank robbers pull off a heist in a small town, but are killed by police at a roadblock while trying to flee. The insurance company hires a private detective, Tom Dwyer, to retrieve the stolen money which mysteriously disappeared between the robbery and the roadblock killing. With the aid of an ex-flame, Bonnie, Dwyer tracks the stolen money to a local gangster, Ed McGuire, and his sultry mistress, Sheila Kennedy.

The Last Crooked Mile is "B" film-making at its best: tough, gritty, and cynical. Philip Ford's direction is superior, as are the performances and screenplay. Ann Savage is particularly notable as the seductive moll. She played the murderous *femme fatale* in the "B" *noir* classic *Detour* (Producers Releasing Corporation, 1946), and is equally compelling in this movie. *The Last Crooked Mile* still shows up on television late shows and is well worth viewing.

The Last Gangster (MGM, 1937). 81 mins.

Director: Edward Ludwig. *Screenplay*: John Lee Mahin, *story by* William Wellman and Robert Carson. *Director of Photography*: William Daniels. *Editor*: Ben Lewis.

Cast: Edward G. Robinson (Joe Krozac), James Stewart (Paul North), Rose Stradner (Talya Krozac), Lionel Stander (Curly), Douglas Scott (Paul North, Jr.), John Carradine (Casper). *With*: Alan Baxter, Sidney Blackmer, Edward Brophy, Edward Marr, Grant Mitchell.

Returning from a European vacation and honeymoon, gang boss Joe Krozac discovers that another mobster has taken his place. After his attempt at revenge fails, he is sent to prison. His wife divorces him and marries Paul North, a successful journalist, who adopts Krozac's son as his own. When Krozac is released a decade later, he heads east to seek revenge against his ex-wife and her husband, but is kidnapped by members of his old gang who force him to reveal where a long lost treasure is hidden. Later, when he sees that his young son is better off with his stepfather, he decides against seeking vengeance. He is then killed by a rival hoodlum.

A minor gangster picture, *The Last Gangster* does have an interesting screenplay by MGM staff writer John Lee Mahin. Its portrayal of Joe Krozac's inability to deal with the outside world after he is released from prison is very convincing. However, the glossy, expensive production (typical of the studio) almost swamps the gritty realism of the screenplay. Still, it is one of Edward G. Robinson's better minor vehicles.

The Last Mile (World Wide, 1932). 84 mins.

Producer: E. W. Hammons. *Director*: Sam Bischoff. *Screenplay*: Seton I. Miller, based on the play by John Wexley. *Director of Photography*: Arthur Edeson. *Musical Director*: Val Burton. *Editors*: Martin Cohn and Rose Loewinger.

Cast: Preston Foster (Killer Mears), Howard Phillips (Richard Walters), George E. Stone (Berg), Noel Madison (D'Amaro), Alan Roscoe (Kirby). *With*: Paul Fix, Al Hill, Daniel L. Haynes, Frank Sheridan, Alec B. Francis, Edward Van Sloan.

Preston Foster stars as Killer Mears, a hardened criminal who has been sentenced to death. Ironically, the tough murderer suffers at the hands of sadistic guards and fellow prisoners. He plans an escape with several other prisoners, but it ultimately fails and Mears is killed.

Based on real life events, *The Last Mile* was originally a successful Broadway play starring Spencer Tracy. Fledgling company World Wild Pictures acquired the rights and Samuel Bischoff directed the motion picture version. The result was an extremely violent, action packed melodrama that was also quite effective. One of the best gangster prison pictures, it was very successful but did not help the production company, which folded shortly thereafter.

The Last Mile (United Artists, 1959). 81 mins.

Producers: Max J. Rosenberg and Milton Subotsky. *Director*: Howard W. Koch. *Screenplay*: Milton Subotsky and Seton I. Miller, based on the play by John Wexley. *Director of Photography*: Joseph Brun. *Music*: Van Alexander. *Editors*: Robert Brockman and Patricia Jaffe.

Cast: Mickey Rooney (Killer Mears), Alan Bunce (Warden), Frank Conroy (O'Flaherty), Leon Janney (Callahan), Frank Overton (Father O'Connors). *With*: Clifford David, Harry Millard, John McCurry, Ford Rainey, John Seven.

The remake of *The Last Mile* is like its predecessor—a superior "B" movie. It remains just as savage, violent and uncompromisingly cynical as the earlier version. Mickey Rooney's performance as Killer Mears is one of his best, and the film holds up quite well today. Its social message against the harshness of prison life is still relevant.

Laszlo, Ernest (1905–1984)

Cinematographer. The Hungarian-born Laszlo was a leading cinematographer for more than three decades. He photographed a few minor *films noir*, but his brightly lit style was opposed to expressionist style. He was at his best with conventional subjects. He was the director of photography for a minor but interesting gangster *noir*.

Manhandled (Paramount, 1949).

Latimer, Jonathan (1906–1984)

Screenwriter. Latimer specialized in hard-boiled action pictures and thrillers. A good screenwriter, he wrote the screenplay for *The Glass Key*, the classic *noir* version based on Dashiell Hammett's novel.

The Glass Key (Paramount, 1942).

The Lavender Hill Mob (J. Arthur Rank, 1951). 82 mins.

Producer: Michael Balcon. *Director*: Charles Crichton. *Screenplay*: T. E. B. Clarke. *Director of Photography*: Douglas Slocombe. *Music*: Georges Auric. *Art Director*: William Killner. *Editor*: Seth Holt.

Cast: Alec Guinness (Holland), Stanley Holloway (Pendlebury), Sidney James (Lackery), Alfie Bass (Shorty), Marjorie Fielding (Mrs. Chalk), Edie Martin (Miss Evesham). *With*: John Salen, Ronald Adam, Arthur Hambling, Gibb McLaughlin, John Gregson, Clive Morton.

Holland, a mild-mannered clerk, works for a company that handles gold bullion and distributes it to British banks. Bored with his quiet life, Holland creates a scheme to steal some of the bullion and make himself instantly rich. With the help of a loudmouthed metalsmith, Pendlebury, he steals the bullion and then melts it down and shapes it into little models of the Eiffel Tower, thus making it easier to smuggle out of the country. However, the gold Eiffel Towers are mixed up with a batch of Eiffel Tower toys, complicating the thievery and ultimately leading to the failure of the scheme.

The Lavender Hill Mob is *the* classic heist satire. One of the earliest of the great comedies made at Britain's Ealing Studios during the fifties, the film was created by the team who made most of their classics: producer Michael Balcon, screenwriter T. E. B. Clarke, and director Charles Crichton, as well as actor Alec Guinness. With its mixture of classic farce and slapstick, *The Lavender Hill Mob* remains one of the best comic variations on the gangster genre.

Law of the Underworld (RKO, 1938). 58 mins.

Producer: Robert Sisk. *Director*: Lew Landers. *Screenplay*: Bert Granet and Edward L. Hatmann, based on the play by John B. Hymer and Samuel Shipman. *Director of Photography*: Nicholas Musuraca. *Music*: Roy Webb. *Art Director*: Albert S. D'Agostino. *Editor*: Ted Chusman.

Cast: Chester Morris (Gene Filmore),

Anne Shirley (Annabelle), Eduardo Cianelli (Rocky), Walter Abel (Rogers), Richard Bond (Tommy), Lee Patrick (Dorothy). *With*: Paul Guilfoyle, Frank M. Thomas, Eddie Acuff, Jack Arnold, Jack Carson.

Law of the Underworld is a lukewarm remake of *The Pay-Off* (RKO, 1930), a minor early gangster movie. The plot, adapted from a moderately successful stage play, centers on gentlemanly gang boss Gene Filmore, who sacrifices his life for the freedom of two innocent young lovers, Annabelle and Tommy, who are caught up in underworld activities. Despite a good cast, the film is merely a sappy, sentimental melodrama.

Lawson, John Howard (1886–1972)

Screenwriter. For many years a notable screenwriter, Lawson's career came to an end when he was blackballed for his Marxist affiliations during the early fifties. At his best with hard-boiled subjects, particularly war movies and psychological thrillers, he cowrote *Algiers*, the adaptation of *Pépé le Moko*, with James M. Cain.

Algiers (United Artists, 1938).

Leachman, Cloris (b. 1926)

Actress. A runner-up in the Miss America contest, Leachman made her screen debut in Robert Aldrich's classic *film noir Kiss Me Deadly* (United Artists, 1953). She subsequently played glamorous supporting roles in movies and on television until, in her midforties, she achieved stardom as Phyllis on the hit television series *The Mary Tyler Moore Show* during the early seventies. She subsequently costarred in many movies, generally cast as an eccentric. Probably her best-known lead role was as the matriarch of a gang of thieves in Roger Corman's *Crazy Mama*. She also had a supporting role in Corman's *Dillinger* as "The Lady in Red" who lures the notorious gangster into an ambush by G-men.

Dillinger (American International, 1973). *Crazy Mama* (New World, 1975).

Leavitt, Sam (1917–1984)

Cinematographer. Leavitt was a leading cinematographer of the conventional school. Eschewing expressionism and innovative lighting schemes, Leavitt preferred bright, flat lighting, moving easily between black and white and color. He photographed one gangster picture.

Seven Thieves (20th Century–Fox, 1960).

Le Baron, William (1886–1949)

Producer and studio executive. For a time in the late twenties and early thirties, Le Baron was head of production at RKO. He later was a staff producer at Paramount, for whom he produced the minor but interesting *Night After Night*.

Night After Night (Paramount, 1932).

Lederer, Charles (1906–1976)

Screenwriter and director. For three decades, beginning in the early thirties, Lederer was a leading screenwriter of hard-boiled comedies and thrillers. Of the latter, *Kiss of Death*, the classic gangster *noir* cowritten with Ben Hecht, is the most important. Lederer also wrote and directed *Never Steal Anything Small*, James Cagney's last gangster film, and one of both men's least interesting works.

Kiss of Death (20th Century–Fox, 1947; cowriter only). *Never Steal Anything Small* (Universal, 1959).

Lee, Lila (1902–1973)

Actress. Born Augusta Apel in New York, Lila Lee began her career as a child actress in vaudeville. The diminutive, dark-haired actress was a major star of the twenties. She starred in *Dark Street*, a seminal Warner Bros.–First National gangster picture.

Dark Streets (First National, 1929).

Lee, Rowland V. (1891–1975)
Director. The son of actor parents, Lee grew up in the theater. He began acting as a child, continuing to perform until he was drafted during World War I. On his return, Lee, who had been acting in movies since 1915, accepted more roles before becoming a film director in 1921. He directed many successful silent pictures and "B" sound movies. Probably his best-known films are the horror classics *Son of Frankenstein* (Universal, 1939) and *Tower of London* (Universal, 1939). Most of his movies, however, are action pictures and adventures. He directed a single, early sound gangster picture, but it is not particularly notable.
Ladies Love Brutes (Paramount, 1930).

Lee-Kirk, Mark
Art director. A fine craftsman, Lee-Kirk (also known as Mark-Lee Kirk) was a leading art director for 20th Century–Fox and RKO. Best known for his collaborations with Richard Day on a number of John Ford's classics, he is also the man who designed the production for Orson Welles' masterpiece, *The Magnificent Ambersons* (RKO, 1942). His set designs and art direction for the gangster fantasy *Mr. Lucky* are superb.
Mr. Lucky (RKO, 1943).

Leigh, Janet (b. 1927)
Actress. Born Janet Morrison in Merced, California, Leigh was a college student with no previous performing experience when she was spotted by a talent scout and signed to a contract. At first she played the typical ingenue roles, but the voluptuous blonde played more mature roles during the mid-fifties. She costarred in three minor gangster pictures, the best of which is *Rogue Cop*, but will be forever remembered as the woman who is murdered in the shower in Alfred Hitchcock's *Psycho* (Universal, 1960).

Rogue Cop (MGM, 1954). *Pete Kelly's Blues* (Warner Bros., 1955). *Grand Slam* (Paramount, 1968).

Leonard, Elmore (b. 1925)
Novelist. A former advertising executive, Leonard began writing Western novels in the fifties. His *3:10 to Yuma* became a classic when it was adapted for the screen by director Delmar Daves and Columbia in 1957. In the sixties Leonard turned increasingly to contemporary crime thrillers, of which he is now the acknowledged living master. Surprisingly few of his novels have been adapted, despite their cinematic possibilities. *Mr. Majestyk*, while not a classic, is proof that Leonard's visceral, violent melodramas are perfect sources for contemporary action and crime thrillers.
Mr. Majestyk (United Artists, 1974).

Leonard, Robert Z. (1889–1968)
Director. Former stage and screen actor Robert Z. Leonard began working in the film business in 1907. He worked his way up to director in 1914, and joined the fledgling Metro-Goldwyn-Mayer during the mid-twenties. He remained at MGM until 1955, becoming one of their most reliable, if not particularly inventive, house directors. His early reputation was established via several popular melodramas, but in fact he directed films of all types. One of the more interesting is the gangster *noir The Bribe*, which, while not a classic, does have some excellent moments.
The Bribe (MGM, 1949).

Leonard, Sheldon (b. 1907)
Character actor. The tall, stoic, and rather sinister Leonard is a New York native who specialized in lurking mobsters, villains, and tough guys in many movies, beginning in the late thirties. Of his four gangster movies, *Lucky Jordan* provided his best role, typically a tough gangster. Leonard later became a major television executive.

Lucky Jordan (Paramount, 1942). *The Last Crooked Mile* (Republic, 1946). *The Gangster* (Allied Artists, 1947). *Guys and Dolls* (MGM, 1955).

Leone, Sergio (1921–1989)

Director. The Italian Leone came to the fore in the sixties with his spaghetti westerns, usually starring Clint Eastwood. Leone had an obsession with American themes, and it was inevitable that he would make a gangster movie. The result, *Once Upon a Time in America*, is an overlong and confusing epic, but it also has some exhilarating moments, particularly in its explicit and violent action scenes.

Once Upon a Time in America (Warner Bros., 1984).

Le Roy, Mervyn (1900–1987)

Director. A small, lively, dynamic workhorse of a man, Le Roy was a child actor on stage before breaking into films as a bit player during the early twenties. He soon became a leading gag man and script writer for comedies and dramas before graduating to directing features in the late twenties. Employed by First National, he soon found himself working for Warner Bros. when the latter took over the former at the beginning of the sound era. It was then that Le Roy emerged as an important filmmaker. Under the auspices of the youthful Darryl F. Zanuck, Le Roy achieved great fame with the punchy, hard-hitting *Little Caesar* and several notable films which followed. All are gritty, topical, often quite cynical, and unsentimental. In retrospect, *Little Caesar* suffers somewhat from its static style, but its performances are dynamic. It established Edward G. Robinson as a major star, Le Roy as a major director, and Warner Bros. as a major studio. It also kicked off the initial cycle of gangster movies in what would become the genre's golden decade. Of Le Roy's gangster pictures that followed, the most important is

I Am a Fugitive from a Chain Gang. Rightly known as the most uncompromising of all the early Warner Bros. gangster pictures, it also marked an advance in Le Roy's technique, as he left the studio soundstages behind for some very effective location shooting.

As Zanuck's favorite director, Le Roy was given almost complete artistic control of his movies, perhaps because he thought like a producer: undeniably a great craftsman, Le Roy was also a prolific director of quality entertainment. Indeed, for a time in the late thirties, he even gave up directing and joined MGM as a house producer, coordinating the production of, among other films, the classic *Wizard of Oz* (1939). However, he found he was happiest as a director and, during the early forties, returned to directing. In whatever genre he worked, Le Roy was at his best with small scale, personal films in which the story and characters were more important than a flashy style. His deceptively simple style is almost subversive, and it had a profound influence on later directors, particularly hard-boiled filmmakers like Raoul Walsh and John Huston. Although he made only two classics in the genre, there can be little doubt that Mervyn Le Roy was one of the most important directors of gangster movies.

Little Caesar (First National, 1930). *I Am a Fugitive from a Chain Gang* (Warner Bros., 1932). *Three on a Match* (First National, 1932). *Heat Lightning* (Warner Bros., 1934). *The F.B.I. Story* (Warner Bros., 1959).

Let 'Em Have It (United Artists, 1955). 90 mins.

Producer: Edward Small. *Director*: Sam Wood. *Screenplay*: Joseph Moncure March and Elmer Harris. *Director of Photography*: J. Peverell Marley and Robert Planck. *Editor*: Grant Whytock.

Cast: Richard Arlen (Mal Stevens), Virginia Bruce (Eleanor Spencer),

Alice Brady (Aunt Ethel), Bruce Cabot (Joe Keefer), Harvey Stephens (Van Rensseler), Eric Linden (Buddy Spencer). *With*: Joyce Compton, Gordon Jones, J. Farrell MacDonald, Paul Stanton, Bodil Rosing.

Although Eleanor Spencer, a wealthy girl, is warned that her brutish chauffeur, Joe Keefer, plans to kidnap her, she ignores the warning. Keefer is tied to organized crime and is sentenced to prison for his involvement in gang activities; but Eleanor believes he is a victim of circumstance, and she arranges for him to be paroled. However, once out, he helps the other members of the gang escape to embark on a crime spree. Meanwhile, Eleanor's younger brother, Buddy, joins the G-men and is later killed by Keefer's men. The other G-men agree to bring the gang to justice, while Eleanor realizes she was wrong to believe that all criminals can be reformed.

Although a minor entry in the genre, *Let 'Em Have It* is one of the more uncompromisingly realistic of the early gangster pictures. It also has an interesting Fritz Langian symbolic touch: after helping his gang break out of prison, Keefer undergoes plastic surgery. Unfortunately, the surgeon has carved his initials into his face, permanently branding him.

Levinson, Barry (b. 1932)

Screenwriter and director. Levinson is best known for his witty human comedies set in his hometown of Baltimore. He has a highly developed sense of visual style that is glossy and elegant, but his films are usually nothing more than slick entertainments. This is certainly true of *Bugsy*, a very slick, entertaining biopic of the notorious real life gangster which, nevertheless, lacks the necessary personal attachment which makes a real work of art.

Bugsy (Tristar, 1993).

Lewis, Joseph H. (b. 1900)

Director. Arguably the greatest "B"

director, Joseph H. Lewis had a baroque style comparable to Max Ophuls and Michael Curtiz at their extravagant best. He was at his best with contemporary thrillers featuring a strongly erotic or psychological theme. His *films noir* are classics of the genre and include three gangster pictures: *The Undercover Man*, *Gun Crazy*, and *The Big Combo*. Of the three, *Gun Crazy* is the best known, a brilliant variation of the Bonnie and Clyde story. However, *The Big Combo* is equally noteworthy, and contains some of his typically pyrotechnical style. *The Undercover Man*, a rather conventional police thriller, is also well above average. Lewis is a fascinating figure who has been neglected too long.

The Undercover Man (Columbia, 1949). *Gun Crazy* (United Artists, 1949). *The Big Combo* (Allied Artists, 1955).

Lights of New York (Warner Bros., 1928). Approximately 90 mins.
Producer and Director: Bryan Foy. *Screenplay*: Hugh Herbert and Murray Roth. *Director of Photography*: Ed Du Par. *Editor*: Jack Killifer.
Cast: Helene Costello (Kitty Lewis), Cullen Landis (Eddie Morgan), Gladys (Molly Thompson), Mary Carr (Mrs. Morgan), Wheeler Oakman (Hawk Miller). *With*: Eugene Pallette, Robert Elliott, Tom Dugan, Tom McGuire, Guy Dennery.

Lights of New York is notable chiefly as the first "all talking" feature. Its style is typically primitive, and the story contrived: a pair of barbers get mixed up with gangsters. It is an important footnote for the genre, however, for its line, spoken by a gangster, concerning a victim: "Take him for a ride."

Limehouse Blues (Paramount, 1934). 66 mins.
Director: Alexander Hall. *Screenplay*: Arthur Phillips, Cyril Hume and Grover Jones. *Director of Photography*:

Edward G. Robinson as the dapper "Little Caesar" meets a violent end in the classic gangster drama *Little Caesar*.

Harry Fischbeck. *Songs:* Sam Coslow. *Art Director:* Hans Dreier.

Cast: George Raft (Harry Young), Jean Parker (Toni), Anna May Wong (Tu Tuan), Kent Taylor (Eric Benton), Montagu Love (Pug Talbot). *With:* Billy Bevan, John Rogers, Robert Lorrainne, E. Alyn Warren, Wyndham Standing.

One of a select group of gangster pictures set in the Chinatowns of various cities, *Limehouse Blues* stars George Raft as a half-caste Chinese man, Harry Young, who leaves New York City and becomes a major underworld figure in London. His downfall comes about when he falls in love with a prostitute, much to the chagrin of his mistress, Tu Tuan, who turns him into the police.

The contrived plot and poor performances in this movie (with the exception of the exotically beautiful Anna May Wong) do not rise above its "B" origins, despite some good production values.

Lindsay, Margaret (1910–1981)

Actress. Born Margaret Kies in Dubuque, Iowa, Lindsay had a brief stage career before moving to Hollywood in 1933. Despite her talent and engaging screen presence, her career never really took off, and she spent her time in "B" movies and supporting roles in "A" pictures. She starred in a single "B" gangster picture.

Public Enemy's Wife (Warner Bros., 1936).

Liotta, Ray (b. 1958)

Actor. An intense, talented performer, Ray Liotta seems set to become one of the major American movie stars of the nineties. He had the lead role in Martin Scorsese's modern gangster classic *GoodFellas*, but was overshadowed by costar Joe Pesci's flashier supporting role in the film. *GoodFellas* (Warner Bros., 1990).

Little Caesar (First National, 1930). 77 mins.
Executive Producer: Darryl F. Zanuck. *Director*: Mervyn Le Roy. *Screenplay*: Francis Faragoh, based on the novel by W. R. Burnett. *Director of Photography*: Tony Gaudio. *Art Director*: Jack Okey. *Editor*: William Holmes.
Cast: Edward G. Robinson (Cesare "Rico" Bandello), Douglas Fairbanks, Jr. (Joe Massara), Glenda Farrell (Olga Strassoff), William "Buster" Collier, Jr. (Tony Passa), Ralph Ince (Diamond Pete Montana), George E. Stone (Otero). *With*: Thomas Jackson, Stanley Fields, Armand Kaliz, Sidney Blackmer, Landers Stevens.

Cesare Bandello, known as "Rico" to his friends, and Joe Massara are small-town criminals who set out to make their fortune in the big city. Joe is a part time dancer who falls in love with a beautiful and classy vaudeville hoofer, Olga Strassoff. With Olga, Joe begins a vaudeville act and leaves his criminal life behind. Bandello, however, eagerly enters the dangerous world of big city organized crime. Through murder and intimidation, he quickly rises to the top of the mob, earning the nickname "Little Caesar." Eventually only the "Big Boy" stands in his way. When Joe refuses to join the gang as his right hand man, Rico threatens to kill Olga. However, Rico's empire has begun to crumble, as much of his gang is either captured by police or killed by rivals and Rico goes into hiding. But taunted by newspaper stories accusing him of cowardice, he calls the police. The police trace the call, swarm to capture him and, when they spot him walking down the street, ambush him from behind a billboard ironically advertising Joe and Olga's act. In the shootout, the

police gun down Rico and, as he lies in the gutter near death, he asks aloud, "Mother of Mercy, is this the end of Rico?"

Little Caesar's enormous box office success kicked off the gangster cycle of the thirties, and made Edward G. Robinson into a major star. Ironically, the Jewish, refined, and gentle natured actor would be forever identified with this prototypical Italian-American mobster. W. R. Burnett's best selling novel was ably adapted by screenwriter Francis Faragoh and director Mervyn Le Roy in typically hard-boiled Warner Bros. style, and sentimentality is nearly nonexistent. Visually exciting, due in part to Edward G. Robinson's mesmerizing performance, *Little Caesar* deserves its classic status, remaining one of the genre's finest films.

The Little Giant (First National, 1933). 74 mins.
Producer: Darryl F. Zanuck. *Director*: Roy Del Ruth. *Screenplay*: Robert Lord and Wilson Mizner, *story by* Robert Lord. *Director of Photography*: Sid Hickox. *Music*: Leo F. Forbstein. *Art Director*: Robert Haas. *Editor*: George Marks.
Cast: Edward G. Robinson (James Francis "Bugs" Ahearn), Helen Vinson (Polly Cass), Mary Astor (Ruth Wayburn), Kenneth Thomson (John Stanley), Russell Hopton (Al Daniels), Shirley Grey (Edith). *With*: Donald Dillaway, Louise Mackintosh, Berton Churchill, Helen Mann, Selmer Jackson.

"Bugs" Ahearn, a notorious gangster, has had a run of bad luck at the end of Prohibition; namely, his livelihood (smuggling and selling liquor) has been legalized, thus eliminating his income. He decides it is time to find a new way to fame and fortune, and thus crashes polite society in Southern California. He finds that polite society, however, is not all that polite, and he becomes the victim of a fraud scheme by his glamorous girlfriend, Polly Cass, and her relatives. Eventually, with the help of his old gang, he manages to retrieve his money and ultimately takes up with the less glamorous, but more honest, Ruth Wayburn.

The Little Giant is one of the earliest gangster satires, with a popular Depression era theme of the wealthy being more crooked than criminals. The film succeeds on all counts, thanks to superior direction, script, and performances. The title, incidentally, was both a tongue in cheek reference to, and an attempt to cash in on, the enormously successful *Little Caesar* (First National, 1931).

Litvak, Anatole (1901–1974)

Director. The Russian-born Litvak was attracted to the theater as a teenager, working as a stagehand before going to college and earning a degree in philosophy. In the early twenties he joined Nordkino, the leading Russian production company, for whom he directed a single picture. He moved to Germany in 1925 and worked as an assistant director until 1930, when he began directing movies for UFA, the company that also employed Fritz Lang, among others. His commercial productions in Germany, and later France, show the influence of expressionism. His French movies during the late thirties were popular, and he was brought to the United States in 1937. He quickly established himself as an imaginative director of stylish melodramas. His single gangster picture, *The Amazing Dr. Clitterhouse*, is atypical among his films, but it is equally stylish and generally acknowledged as one of the genre's minor classics.

The Amazing Dr. Clitterhouse (Warner Bros., 1938).

Loan Shark (Lippert, 1952). 79 mins.
Producer: Bernard Luber. *Director*: Seymour Friedman. *Screenplay*: Martin Rackin and Eugene Ling. *Director of Photography*: Joseph Biroc. *Art Director*: Field Gray. *Editor*: Al Joseph.
Cast: George Raft (Joe Gargen), Dorothy Hart (Ann Nelson), Paul Stewart (Donelli), Helen Westcott (Martha), John Hoyt (Phillips). *With*: Henry Slate, William Phipps, Russell Johnson, Benny Baker, Larry Dobkin, Charles Meredith.

Released from prison, Joe Gargen moves in with his sister and her family. Not long after, his honest, hardworking brother-in-law is murdered by a loan shark racket, and Joe vows revenge. He infiltrates the racket, exposing its leader, Phillips, and in the inevitable showdown, kills him.

By the early fifties, George Raft's popularity was on the demise and he was reduced to starring in "B" thrillers like *Loan Shark*. The film is primarily distinguished by Paul Stewart as mob henchman Donelli, John Hoyt as gang boss Phillips, and its evocative, *noir* style.

Lombard, Carole (1908–1942)

Actress. The blonde and vivacious Lombard, wife of Clark Gable, was at her best in screwball comedies, but she played a variety of dramatic roles early in her career, even appearing as a moll in a weird, early gangster movie, *The Racketeer*.

The Racketeer (Pathé, 1929).

The Long Good Friday (Black Lion Films, 1980). 105 mins.
Producer: Barry Hanson. *Director*: John MacKenzie. *Screenplay*: Barrie Keefe. *Director of Photography*: Phil Meheux. *Music*: Francis Monkman. *Art Director*: Vic Symonds. *Editor*: Mike Taylor.
Cast: Bob Hoskins (Harold), Helen Mirren (Victoria), Dave King (Parky), Brian Hall (Alan), Eddie Constantine (Charlie), Stephen Davies (Tony). *With*: Derek Thompson, Bryan Marshall, P. H. Moriarty, Paul Freeman, Charles Cork.

With a mob associate, Charlie, mob boss Harold plans a building project for the 1988 Olympics, to be held in England. However, when things begin to go awry, including bombings which kill his henchmen and destroy his projects, Harold discovers that the Irish Republican Army is responsible. He unleashes his own army of criminals against the terrorist army; but in the end, it is the terrorists who are successful and Harold is killed.

Highly praised at the time of its release, *The Long Good Friday* was an international success and helped make Bob Hoskins into a star. The film is well made, with an intense performance by Hoskins and the always

Peter Lorre in a publicity shot from the late thirties, is one of the gangster genre's most memorable minor icons.

sensual Helen Mirren as his clinging (and equally crooked) wife. It is also notable for its political underpinnings, as it attacks both the British government and the vile IRA, both of which are depicted as equally corrupt and corrupting. *The Long Good Friday*, in fact, is one of the best near-contemporary gangster pictures to be made in Europe or, for that matter, the world.

Lord, Robert (1900–1976)

Screenwriter and producer. Lord had a long, successful career at Warner Bros.-First National, beginning as a screenwriter in the mid-twenties. He wrote or cowrote many important features, including two gangster pictures, *The Finger Points* and *The Little Giant*, for the company during the late twenties and early thirties. However, it

is as a producer that he achieved his greatest success. He produced a number of classic films for the studio, including several more gangster pictures. In the fifties he formed an independent production company with Humphrey Bogart, coproducing many of the actor's last movies.

The Finger Points (First National, 1931; screenwriter only). *The Little Giant* (First National, 1933; screenwriter only). *20,000 Years in Sing Sing* (First National, 1933; associate producer and cowriter). *Fog Over Frisco* (First National, 1934; producer only). *Dr. Socrates* (Warner Bros., 1935; producer only). *The Amazing Dr. Clitterhouse* (Warner Bros., 1938; producer only).

Lorre, Peter (1904–1964)

Character actor. Born Ladislav Loewenstein in Roszahegy, Hungary (later Rosenberg, Czechoslovakia), Lorre was originally a bank clerk. After taking acting lessons in Vienna, he made his stage debut in Zurich, but after performing for several years in Switzerland, Austria, and Germany, he looked to the cinema for better opportunities. His rolling eyes, timid manner and mysterious personality could adapt to either sympathetic or sinister roles, but he is probably best remembered for his villainous characterizations. He became a major star as the serial killer in Fritz Lang's *M* (UFA, 1930), and subsequently played a variety of madmen and villains in Germany, Great Britain and the United States. Off camera, his adventurous personality endeared him to some of Hollywood's legendary "wild men," including John Barrymore, Humphrey Bogart, and Errol Flynn, who made sure that he was given small but important roles in many of their films, particularly Bogart's. Thus, in *The Maltese Falcon*, he played Joel Cairo, one of the murderous gang seeking the valuable jewel encrusted Falcon. Lorre starred in many "B" movies, including a superior psychological gangster thriller, *The Face Behind the Mask*. He also played small but key roles in several other gangster pictures.

Strange Cargo (MGM, 1940). *The Face Behind the Mask* (Paramount, 1941). *The Maltese Falcon* (Warner Bros., 1941). *The Chase* (United Artists, 1946). *Casbah* (Universal, 1948).

Losey, Joseph (1909–1984)

Director. In the late forties and early fifties, Losey was one of the most promising American directors. He directed several memorable "B" *films noir*, but his career was interrupted by accusations that he was a communist. Moving to Great Britain, he reestablished himself and proved to be a major director during the sixties with a series of extremely pretentious, existential melodramas. His single gangster film,

The Criminal, predates this era, however, and is one of his more watchable European films. It proves that Losey was at his best with violent character driven thrillers.

The Criminal (Anglo-Amalgamated, 1960).

Love, Montague (1877–1943)

Character actor. Born in Portsmouth, England, Love was a veteran stage actor when he moved to the United States in 1913 to become one of the leading villains of silent movies. Later, in dozens of talkies, he played a variety of well spoken villains, generals, and monarchs. He costarred in a single, minor gangster picture, portraying one of his few sympathetic roles.

Out of Singapore (Goldsmith, 1932).

Lowe, Edmond (1890–1971)

Actor. After Broadway experience, the smooth, mustachioed Lowe began his film career in 1919 and was almost always seen in rather typical and conventional romantic roles. With the coming of sound, Lowe increasingly played supporting roles in "A" pictures and leads in "B" pictures. In *Dillinger* he played Specs, one of the gang members who briefly and unsuccessfully challenges Dillinger as leader of the notorious gang.

Dillinger (Monogram, 1945).

Loy, Myrna (1905–1993)

Actress. Loy was born Myrna Williams in Raidersburg, Montana, and moved to Los Angeles with her family when she was a young girl. A trained dancer, she began acting in movies during the mid-twenties and appeared in more than sixty movies before becoming a full-fledged star during the early thirties. Interestingly, this most American of women often played exotic (particularly Oriental) roles early in her career, largely because of her own rather unusual beauty. In the mid-thirties, however, she became an American archetype, deeply sensual, extremely intelligent, witty, and motherly. Her best performances were in MGM's screwball comedies, particularly the *Thin Man* series, but she also appeared in a number of gangster movies, most notably *Manhattan Melodrama*, perhaps MGM's best crime film.

Hush Money (Fox, 1931). *Penthouse* (MGM, 1933). *Manhattan Melodrama* (MGM, 1934). *Whipsaw* (MGM, 1935).

Lubin, Arthur (b. 1901)
Director. Lubin was a prolific director of "B" movies, mainly for Universal. He directed a variety of pictures, including several of Abbott and Costello's earliest comedies, but also some thrillers, action pictures and two gangster movies.

Big Town Czar (Universal, 1939). *Gangs of Chicago* (Republic, 1940).

Lucky Jordan (Paramount, 1942). 84 mins.
Associate Producer: Fred Kohlmar. *Director*: Frank Tuttle. *Screenplay*: Darrell Ware and Karl Tunberg, *story by* Charles Leonard. *Director of Photography*: John Seitz. *Music*: Victor Young. *Art Directors*: Hans Dreier and Haldane Douglas. *Editor*: Archie Marshek.
Cast: Alan Ladd (Lucky Jordan), Helen Walker (Jill Evans), Sheldon Leonard (Slip Moran), Mabel Paige (Annie), Marie McDonald (Pear), Lloyd "Crash" Corrigan (Ernest Higgins). *With*: Russell Hoyt, Dave Willock, Miles Mander, John Wengraf, Charles Cane, George F. Meador.
Released during the year Alan Ladd achieved stardom in *The Glass Key* (Paramount, 1942) and *This Gun for Hire* (Paramount, 1942), *Lucky Jordan* was his third starring role in eight months and his first as a top-billed actor. Ladd stars as a con man and mob killer who joins the Army and outwits a Nazi spy ring.

Less distinguished than its predecessors, *Lucky Jordan* did confirm Ladd's box office popularity. Its gangster elements were repressed in favor of a topical wartime theme but it remains a pleasant seriocomedy.

Lucky Luciano (Avco-Embassy, 1974). 116 mins.
Producer: Franco Cristaldi. *Director*: Francesco Rosi. *Screenplay*: Lino Junnuzzi, Tonino Guerra, and Francesco Rosi. *Director of Photography*: Pasqualino DeSantis. *Music*: Piero Piccioni. *Editor*: Ruggero Mastroianni.
Cast: Gian-Maria Volonte (Lucky Luciano), Rod Steiger (Gene Gianini), Edmond O'Brien (Harry J. Anslinger), Charles Siragusa (Himself), Vincent Gardina (American Colonel). *With*: Silverio Blasi, Charles Cioffi, Magda Konopka, Larry Gates, Jacques Monod.
The career of real life Mafia boss Lucky Luciano is recounted from his beginnings in New York City to his demise (by an assassin's bullets) in Italy after being deported by the United States government. Luciano was, in fact, one of the most notorious figures in the rise of the Mafia in the United States, and he controlled the mob with an iron fist for much of his life. Absolutely ruthless, his protégés Bugsy Siegel and Al Capone carried his legacy of violence and corruption into the American heartland. The United States government found it as difficult to prosecute Luciano as it did Capone, but eventually he was convicted of income tax evasion (like Capone). After several years in prison, he was released to help the American effort during World War II and then was deported to his native Sicily. He remained in charge of the American mob, however, until his assassination by rivals in the fifties.
An Italian production, *Lucky Luciano* is firmly in the tradition of the new breed of violent, neo-realistic gangster

pictures that emerged during the seventies. However, it fails to live up to its promise and is only a minor entry in the genre.

Lucky Nick Cain (20th Century–Fox, 1951). 87 mins.
Producer: Joseph Kaufman. *Director*: Joseph M. Newman. *Screenplay*: George Callahan and William Rose, based on the novel *I'll Get You for This* by James Hadley Chase. *Director of Photography*: Otto Heller. *Music*: Walter Goehr. *Art Director*: Ralph Brinton. *Editor*: Russell Lloyd.

Cast: George Raft (Nick Cain), Coleen Gray (Kay Wonderly), Enzio Staiola (Toni), Charles Goldner (Massini), Walter Rilla (Mueller), Martin Benson (Sperazza). *With*: Peter Illing, Hugh French, Peter Bull, Elwyn Brook-Jones, Constance Smith.

While vacationing in Europe, gambler Nick Cain is framed for the murder of a U. S. treasury agent who was investigating a counterfeit ring. With the aid of the beautiful Kay Wonderly, a nightclub singer, Cain sets out to clear his name. He eventually discovers that Mueller is the leader of the gang and, with the local authorities, helps bring the mobster to justice.

A decidedly minor "B" gangster movie, *Lucky Nick Cain* is notable mainly for its Italian location shooting and the always compelling presence of the sensual Colleen Gray.

Ludwig, Edward T. (1895–1960)
Director. The Russian-born Ludwig came to the United States as a child. Starting in films as an actor during the silent era, he turned to writing and directing during the twenties. He directed many "B" movies, some of which are above average, from 1932 until his death. He directed one of Edward G. Robinson's minor gangster pictures, his only contribution to the genre in the late thirties.
The Last Gangster (MGM, 1937).

Lukas, Paul (1894–1971)
Character actor. Born Paul Lukacs in Hungary, Lukas first came to the fore as a stage and screen actor in Central Europe. Lukas was signed to Paramount in 1927, subsequently appearing in more than thirty movies in a variety of roles, particularly as a suave Nazi in several movies during the forties. He played a mob boss in the seminal gangster movie *City Streets*.
City Streets (Paramount, 1931).

Lupino, Ida (b. 1918)
Actress. The British-born Lupino was from a long line of English performers that included her father, Stanley Lupino, a famous comic actor. After success in Britain on stage and in movies, she moved to the United States in 1934. The diminutive, fair-haired actress was a mainstay in American movies for the next two decades, always giving strong performances, even in minor movies. Interestingly, she became an icon of hard-boiled Americana, particularly *film noir*, starring in, writing, and directing several notable titles in that genre. She starred in two gangster movies, most importantly in *High Sierra* as the moll with a heart of gold.
The Lady and the Mob (Columbia, 1939). *High Sierra* (Warner Bros., 1941).

Lyon, Ben (1901–1979)
Actor. Born and raised in Atlanta, Lyon first achieved fame as a stage actor during the twenties. Dark, rugged and handsome, Lyon went to Hollywood in the late twenties, starring in a number of successful movies. However, he never became a full-fledged star, despite some talent. He married Bebe Daniels (one of the twenties most sensual stars, and a notable second lead during the thirties), and surprisingly became a huge star of radio in Great Britain during the late thirties. Indeed, the couple's popularity in Britain is

comparable to that of Lucille Ball and Desi Arnez in the fifties, and they also starred together in a popular television series and a few movies. Early in his film career, Lyon starred in a minor gangster picture, *I Cover the Waterfront*, his only appearance in the genre.

I Cover the Waterfront (United Artists, 1933).

McCloud, Frank (Fictional character)

While Humphrey Bogart appeared in a number of films with James Cagney, he only costarred once with the other great male icon of the genre, Edward G. Robinson, in *Key Largo* (Warner Bros., 1948), but, of course, it is one of the great gangster films. In it, Bogart plays Frank McCloud, a veteran turned pacifist who has come to a small Florida resort to visit the family of a wartime buddy who was killed in action. With the others, McCloud is held hostage by Johnny Rocco (Edward G. Robinson) and his gang as they wait out a storm in the hotel. When McCloud shrinks from a confrontation with the gangster, he is accused of cowardice by his friend's widow (Lauren Bacall). When he does stand up to Rocco after he humiliates his moll (Claire Trevor), McCloud is beaten up by Rocco's thugs. The beating, however, reawakens McCloud's sense of duty, and when Rocco tries to escape the island resort in a small boat, he sneaks aboard and eliminates Rocco's gang one by one and finally Rocco himself.

Frank McCloud is in part a symbolic figure. The film was based on Maxwell Anderson's terse drama, a symbolic play about the role of violence in establishing and maintaining freedom. For Anderson, McCloud represents the "peace at all costs" liberal who at last comes to his senses and reacts violently against the conservative repression and mindless violence represented by Johnny Rocco.

In any case, few reviewers make note of the political didacticism of the film, perhaps missed because Bogart's performance, as well as the rest of the cast, is so powerful it subverts the moralizing message.

McCord, Ted (1898–1976)

Cinematographer. A distinguished cinematographer, McCord began his career in the mid-twenties and came to an end in the late sixties. He occasionally displayed an innovative, lush style, particularly for director John Huston. One of his best films, in the most extravagant early *noir* style, is *The Damned Don't Cry*.

The Damned Don't Cry (Warner Bros., 1950).

McCoy, Horace

Novelist and screenwriter. Of the major hard-boiled crime novelists of his time, McCoy used themes that were closest to those of W. R. Burnett. Like Burnett, McCoy concentrated on organized crime and the effects of indiscriminate violence. A few of his novels were adapted in the forties (as *noirs*). McCoy also worked as a screenwriter, mainly as a contract writer for Paramount in the late thirties. He cowrote several interesting, minor gangster movies.

Great Guy (Grand National, 1936). *Dangerous to Know* (Paramount, 1938). *Hunted Man* (Paramount, 1938). *Queen of the Mob* (Paramount, 1940).

McCrea, Joel (1905–1990)

Actor. The tall, good looking McCrea proved to be one of the most durable of Hollywood leading men without ever becoming a full-fledged star. Although probably best remembered as a star of high quality "B" westerns, he was also a very good comic actor and starred in many classic romantic and screwball comedies in the late thirties and early forties. He starred in a single gangster picture, *Dead End*, but was

overshadowed by his more charismatic costars.
Dead End (United Artists, 1937).

MacDonald, Philip (1896–1987)
Novelist, short story writer and screenwriter. The British-born Mac-Donald is best known for his highly imaginative short stories and novels which were adapted for the screen. He worked occasionally as a screenwriter, and cowrote *Blind Alley*, an influential psychological gangster thriller.
Blind Alley (Columbia, 1939).

McGill, Barney (1889–1941)
Cinematographer. McGill's career began in the late teens. He mainly worked for Warner Bros., for whom he photographed two gangster pictures, the most important being the prison drama *20,000 Years in Sing Sing*.
The Doorway to Hell (Warner Bros., 1930). *20,000 Years in Sing Sing* (First National, 1933).

McGivern, William P. (1924–1983)
Novelist and screenwriter. As a hard-boiled writer, McGivern achieved prominence in the early fifties for his new breed of crime novels: cynical, violent and unsentimental, they generally featured a rogue cop at the center of the story, as in his most famous work, *The Big Heat*. Many of his novels were adapted for the screen, but McGivern, unlike many of his contemporaries and predecessors, did not work in Hollywood.
The Big Heat (Columbia, 1953). *Rogue Cop* (MGM, 1954). *Hell on Frisco Bay* (Warner Bros., 1956). *Odds Against Tomorrow* (United Artists, 1959).

McGraw, Charles (1914–1980)
Actor. The heavyset, strong-jawed McGraw was a prominent tough-guy character actor in "A" pictures who often played leads in "B" pictures. He appeared in four gangster movies. In *The Killers*, he played one of his few villainous roles as an hired assassin. He most often played good guy roles, however, as in the *noir* classic *The Narrow Margin*.
The Killers (Universal, 1946). *T-Men* (Eagle-Lion, 1947). *His Kind of Woman* (RKO, 1951). *The Narrow Margin* (RKO, 1952).

Machine Gun Kelly (American International, 1958). 84 mins.
Executive Producers: James H. Nicholson and Samuel Z. Arkoff. *Producer and Director*: Roger Corman. *Screenplay*: R. Wright Campbell. *Director of Photography*: Floyd Crosby. *Music*: Gerald Fried. *Art Director*: Dan Haller. *Editor*: Ronald Sinclair.
Cast: Charles Bronson (Machine Gun Kelly), Susan Cabot (Flo), Morey Amsterdam (Fandango), Jack Lambert (Howard), Wally Campo (Maize). *With*: Bob Griffin, Barboura Morris, Richard Devon, Ted Thorp, Mitzi McCall, Frank De Kova.
The real life "Machine Gun Kelly" (George R. Kelly, 1897–1954), was a notoriously violent small-time rural gangster who, for a time, terrorized the Midwest during the thirties. This film, departing from the facts, does at least adhere to the outline of his life in its account of his career, beginning as a bootlegger in the twenties to his eventual capture as a bank robber and subsequent long prison sentence. It is a typically cheap Roger Corman production redeemed (barely) by Charles Bronson's intense performance as the brooding robber and murderer.

McHugh, Frank (1899–1981)
Character actor. McHugh, a vaudeville veteran, was one of the busiest Hollywood character actors, appearing in more than 150 movies in his nearly forty years in pictures, beginning in 1929. He almost always played Irish characters as comic relief in dramatic movies, as in his two gangster pictures.

Heat Lightning (Warner Bros., 1934). *Bullets or Ballots* (First National, 1936).

McIntire, John (b. 1907)
Character actor. Tough, square-jawed McIntire, after Broadway experience, played a variety of cops, mob henchmen, and occasional villains in films. He appeared in two gangster pictures, including Phil Karlson's excellent "B" *The Phenix City Story*, in which he played an honest political candidate murdered by mobsters.
Johnny Stool Pigeon (Universal, 1949). *The Phenix City Story* (Allied Artists, 1955).

McLaglen, Victor (1883–1959)
Character actor. The burly, good natured character actor Victor McLaglen was born in Tunbridge Wells, England. After stage experience, he starred in a number of silent films in Great Britain. He moved to Hollywood in the early thirties, specializing in happy go lucky characters, most notably for director John Ford. He played a gangster in his only appearance in the genre.
Roger Touhy, Gangster (20th Century-Fox, 1944).

MacLane, Barton (1902–1969)
Character actor. Former college football star MacLane was discovered while in school and offered a Hollywood contract. He also acted on Broadway. Tall and burly, he almost always played hulking villains, tough guys, and dimwitted mobsters in both "A" and "B" productions and is one of the gangster genre's icons.
Dr. Socrates (Warner Bros., 1935). *G-Men* (First National, 1935). *Bullets or Ballots* (First National, 1936). *Born Reckless* (20th Century-Fox, 1937). *San Quentin* (Warner Bros., 1937). *You and Me* (Paramount, 1938). *You Only Live Once* (United Artists, 1938). *Big Town Czar* (Universal, 1939). *Gangs of Chicago* (Republic, 1940).

High Sierra (Warner Bros., 1941). *The Maltese Falcon* (Warner Bros., 1941). *Kiss Tomorrow Goodbye* (Warner Bros., 1950).

MacMahon, Aline (b. 1899)
Character actress. A prominent stage actress, MacMahon was a popular second lead during the thirties and forties. With her sad eyes and gentle manner, she usually played melancholy, sensitive women. She starred in three minor gangster pictures, always as the good girl.
The Mouthpiece (Warner Bros., 1932). *Heat Lightning* (Warner Bros., 1934). *Back Door to Heaven* (Paramount, 1939).

McQueen, Steve (1930–1980)
Actor. The unconventional, brooding McQueen became one of the icons of the sixties and seventies. He is best known for his quiet tough guys in action pictures. In *Bullitt* he gave one of his finest performances as the cop who brings a mobster to "justice" (by killing him), and he influenced a number of later similar characters including, most importantly, Clint Eastwood's Dirty Harry.
Bullitt (Warner Bros.–7 Arts, 1968).

Macready, George (1909–1973)
Character actor. Born in Providence, Rhode Island, Macready had a long Broadway career before coming to the screen during the early forties. His scarred face and rather sinister presence made him a notable villain of the era, perhaps most famously in the classic *film noir Gilda*. He played a similar role in the later gangster picture *Johnny Allegro*, almost stealing the film from its nominal stars Nina Foch and George Raft.
Gilda (Columbia, 1946). *Johnny Allegro* (Columbia, 1949).

Madame Racketeer (Paramount, 1932).
72 mins.
Directors: Alexander Hall and Harry

Wagstaff Gribble. *Screenplay*: Malcolm Stuart Boylan and Harvey Gates. *Director of Photography*: Henry Sharp. *Art Director*: Hans Dreier. *Editor*: Tom Miranda.

Cast: Alison Skipworth (Countess von Claudwig/Martha Hicks), Richard Bennett (Elmer Hicks), George Raft (Jack Houston), John Breeded (David Butterworth). *With*: Evelyn Knapp, Gertrude Messinger, Robert McWade, J. Farrell MacDonald, Walter Walker.

An elderly con woman, Martha Hicks, comes to America and marries a *hotelier*. She plans to con him out of his fortune so that she and her two daughters can live in the style they were accustomed to in Europe. She tries to marry off her daughters to wealthy men, but eventually her criminal activities catch up with her. She is sent to prison, where she regales her fellow prisoners with her adventurous tales.

A minor gangster picture, *Madame Racketeer* is a rather silly tale of con artists and, in typical Depression style, of the gullible rich. Matronly Alison Skipworth is good as the con woman, and George Raft makes a brief appearance as a mobster mixed up with one of the daughters.

Maddow, Ben

Screenwriter. Maddow was an efficient if not particularly inventive screenwriter active during the fifties and sixties. His most prominent screenplay is *The Asphalt Jungle*, which he adapted with John Huston from W. R. Burnett's best seller.

The Asphalt Jungle (MGM, 1950).

The Mafia

The Italian Mafia ("Family") had its roots in Sicily during the Middle Ages. Many Italian immigrants settled in the ghettos in New York City, beginning in the late nineteenth century. Many of them joined street gangs, preying chiefly on their fellow immigrants, and specializing in petty crimes, extortion, and prostitution. Known as the Black Hands, the Italian mob was one of three ethnic street gangs in competition during the early twentieth century (the other two were run by Jewish and Irish immigrants, respectively). The Irish gang, known as the White Hands, was the most powerful until a bloody gang war erupted in the early twenties, during which the Mafia emerged triumphant. Although there has been some crossing over — Meyer Lansky, one of the most powerful Mafia chieftains for over three decades, beginning in the twenties, was Jewish — the Mafia refers mainly to the Italian mob. Finding incredible resources in bootlegged liquor during Prohibition, the Mafia fanned out of New York City into other lucrative markets, most notably Chicago, where the murderous Al Capone set up his operations. By the end of 1933, with the repeal of the 18th Amendment, the Mafia had become a powerful organization centered around several "families" and involved in both legal and illegal operations. They are, of course, the subject of numerous films covering a whole range of activities and real life figures: *The Black Hand* (MGM, 1950), *Al Capone* (Allied Artists, 1959), *The Brotherhood* (Paramount, 1968), *The Don Is Dead* (Universal, 1973), *The French Connection* (20th Century–Fox, 1971), *The George Raft Story* (Allied Artists, 1961), *The Killers* (Universal, 1946), *Little Caesar* (First National, 1931), *Lucky Luciano* (Avco-Embassy, 1974), *On the Waterfront* (Columbia, 1954), *Public Enemy* (Warner Bros., 1931), *The Roaring Twenties* (Warner Bros., 1939), *The St. Valentine's Day Massacre* (20th Century–Fox, 1961), *Scarface* (United Artists, 1932), *Some Like It Hot* (United Artists, 1959), *The Cotton Club* (Orion, 1984), and *Prizzi's Honor* (20th Century–Fox, 1985) among others. However, certainly the most famous and greatest explorations of Mafia life are Francis

Ford Coppola's *Godfather* films: *The Godfather* (Paramount, 1972), *The Godfather Part II* (Paramount, 1974), and *The Godfather III* (Paramount, 1992).

Mahin, John Lee (1902–1984)

Screenwriter. All but forgotten today, Mahin was one of the most prominent screenwriters of his generation. As a contract writer for MGM, beginning in the early thirties, he wrote the screenplays for many classic movies. He specialized in hard-boiled action movies and adventures. Of his three gangster pictures, *Scarface* (written in collaboration with Ben Hecht and Seton I. Miller) is his most prominent, but *The Beast of the City* is a neglected classic of the genre.

The Beast of the City (MGM, 1932). *Scarface* (United Artists, 1932). *The Last Gangster* (MGM, 1937).

Mainwaring, Daniel

Screenwriter and novelist. As Geoffrey Homes, Mainwaring published pulp fiction and adapted his most successful pulp novel, *Build My Gallows High* (with uncredited contributions by Frank Fenton and James M. Cain) as the gangster *noir* classic, *Out of the Past*. Both as Homes and Mainwaring, he wrote many screenplays, including those for two notable "B" gangster pictures, during the late forties and fifties.

The Phenix City Story (Allied Artists, 1955). *Baby Face Nelson* (United Artists, 1957).

Malden, Karl (b. 1913)

Character actor. Born Malden Sekulovich in Gary, Indiana, Malden made his mark as in intense stage actor, beginning in the thirties. His congenial, homely face and husky build made him a natural working-class character actor, generally projecting innocence and moral strength, as in his two gangster pictures.

Where the Sidewalk Ends (20th Cen-

tury–Fox, 1950). *On the Waterfront* (Columbia, 1954).

Malloy, Terry (Fictional character)

In *On the Waterfront* (Columbia, 1954), the character played by Marlon Brando who speaks the immortal line, "I could a been a contender...," Malloy is a one-time boxer whose career is ruined when he takes a fall for a mob payoff. He is reduced to working on the decks as a day laborer, while his brother, a mob functionary, exploits his fellow workers. After he is tricked into helping mobsters kill a dock worker who talks too much, Malloy befriends the victim's widow and, with the urging of a kind hearted priest, he is convinced to help expose the mob. Eventually he engages in a fistfight with the leading gangster, Johnny Friendly (Lee J. Cobb), on the waterfront. Beaten, but not defeated, he has earned the respect of his fellow workers, who now believe they might have a future without the mob.

Terry Malloy is a typical Brando character from his early film career: working class, violent, not terribly bright, but honest with good intentions.

The Maltese Falcon (Warner Bros., 1931). 75 mins.

Director: Roy Del Ruth. *Screenplay*: Maude Fulton, Lucien Hubbard and Brown Holmes, based on the novel by Dashiell Hammett. *Director of Photography*: William Rees. *Editor*: George Marks.

Cast: Bebe Daniels (Ruth Wonderly), Ricardo Cortez (Sam Spade), Dudley Digges (Gutman), Una Merkel (Effie), Robert Elliott (Detective Dundy). *With*: J. Farrell MacDonald, Otto Maticsen, Morgan Wallace, Walter Long, Dwight Frye.

The original version of Dashiell Hammett's classic detective novel was a "B" production and suffers greatly in comparison to John Huston's version. Ricardo Cortez, a second string

Valentino, was no Humphrey Bogart, and Roy Del Ruth's direction was lackluster and unimaginative. However, the film is important for introducing the mythological private detective to the American screen.

The Maltese Falcon (Warner Bros., 1941). 100 mins. *Executive Producer*: Hal B. Wallis. *Associate Producer*: Henry Blanke. *Director*: John Huston. *Screenplay*: John Huston, based on the novel by Dashiell Hammett. *Director of Photography*: Arthur Edeson. *Music*: Adolph Deutsch. *Art Director*: Robert Haas. *Editor*: Thomas Richards.

Cast: Humphrey Bogart (Sam Spade), Mary Astor (Brigid O'Shaughnessy), Gladys George (Iva Archer), Peter Lorre (Joe Cairo), Sydney Greenstreet (Gutman), Elisha Cook, Jr. (Wilmer). *With*: Barton Mac-Lane, Lee Patrick, Ward Bond, James Burke, Murray Alper, John Hamilton.

After his partner, Miles Archer, is killed while shadowing a man named Thursby for a mysterious client, Miss Wonderly, private detective Sam Spade sets out to find the murderer. He confronts Miss Wonderly, who admits her real name is Brigid O'Shaughnessy and that she, too, is targeted for murder. Spade is attracted to her and agrees to help her. His investigation leads to a sinister trio: Joe Cairo, Kasper "Fatman" Gutman, and Wilmer, Gutman's inept gunsel. He learns that they are all after a valuable, jewel-encrusted statuette, the Maltese Falcon. He also discovers that Brigid is a psychotic liar who killed Miles in an attempt to frame his murder on her partner, Thursby. Although she pleads with Spade not to turn her over to the police, he coldly dismisses her advances and calls the authorities. Gutman's gang, meanwhile, is also rounded up by the police.

The Maltese Falcon, with its cynical lead character, *femme fatale*, and shadowy style, is one of the original true *films noir*. Like the original, John Huston's version sticks close to the novel, but it is distinguished by its superb cast, here at their very best. It was a new kind of gangster oriented thriller, a break with its predecessors of the thirties, yet oddly, also firmly in the tradition of the genre. Its villains were certainly a new breed, being neither street toughs nor Mafiosi.

Despite some unimaginatively staged scenes and a tendency toward staginess (at times the film resembles a talky theatrical drama), it remains a classic of both the *noir* and gangster genres.

Maltz, Albert (1908–1985)
Screenwriter. Maltz's career began in the early thirties, but he did not hit his stride until the forties, when he cowrote the classic *This Gun for Hire*. He subsequently worked on a number of other important movies, including the *film noir* classic *Naked City* (Universal, 1948), but his career came to an end when he was targeted as a communist by Senator Joseph McCarthy's committee.

This Gun for Hire (Paramount, 1942).

Mamoulian, Rouben (1897–1987)
Director. An innovative stage director, Mamoulian was brought to Hollywood at the beginning of the sound era, when, for a time, it seemed as if he might become one of the great American filmmakers. Indeed, he did make a number of classics, including the important gangster movie *City Streets* and the horror masterpiece *Dr. Jekyll and Mr. Hyde* (Paramount, 1932), but he seemed to run out of ideas in the mid-thirties. At his best, he had a fluid, elegant style that relied as much on expressionist technique as it did on realism.

City Streets (Paramount, 1931).

Mancini, Henry (1924–1994)
Composer. A leading composer of

his time, Mancini's music often bordered on schmaltz and tended to draw too much attention to itself. His score for the "B" gangster picture *Damned Citizen*, while not one of his best known, is one of his finest early scores.

Damned Citizen (Universal, 1958).

Manhandled (Paramount, 1949). 98 mins.
Producers: William H. Pine and William C. Thomas. *Director*: Lewis R. Foster. *Screenplay*: Lewis R. Foster and Whitman Chambers, based on the novel *The Man Who Stole a Dream* by L. S. Goldsmith. *Director of Photography*: Ernest Laszlo. *Music*: Darryl Claker. *Art Director*: Howard Pine. *Editor*: Howard Smith.
Cast: Dorothy Lamour (Merl Kramer), Sterling Hayden (Joe Cooper), Dan Duryea (Karl Benson), Irene Hervey (Mrs. Alton Bennet), Philip Reed (Guy Bayard), Harold Vermilyea (Dr. Redman). *With*: Alan Napier, Art Smith, Irving Bacon, Philip Reed, Benny Baker.
A complicated plot involves a crooked private detective, Karl Benson, an unscrupulous psychiatrist, Dr. Redman, a beautiful girl, Merl Kramer, and a jewelry robbery and murder. Merl, Dr. Redman's secretary, is framed by her boyfriend, Karl, for the murder and robbery of one of Dr. Redman's patients. But the psychiatrist is the real murderer who stole the patient's valuable jewels. Karl Benson, in turn, robs and murders the doctor. Eventually, however, the police discover that Benson has killed the doctor and arrive just in time, as Benson prepares to murder Merl before she can turn him in.
Manhandled is really more of a *film noir* than a gangster picture, although it is occasionally listed as the latter in some anthologies. Its characters are clearly in the *noir* canon of cynical, corrupt people, but its jewel robbery theme is one that crops up in both

genres. Either way, it is a minor film distinguished chiefly by Dan Duryea's intense performance as the corrupt private detective.

Manhattan Melodrama (MGM, 1934). 98 mins.
Producer: David O. Selznick. *Director*: W. S. Van Dyke. *Screenplay*: Oliver H. P. Garrett and Joseph L. Mankiewicz, *story by* Arthur Caesar. *Director of Photography*: James Wong Howe. *Songs*: Richard Rodgers and Lorenz Hart. *Art Director*: Cedric Gibbons. *Editor*: Ben Lewis.
Cast: Clark Gable (Blackie Gallagher), William Powell (Jim Wade), Myrna Loy (Eleanor Packer), Leo Carrillo (Father Pat), Nat Pendleton (Spud), George Sidney (Poppa Rosen), Isabel Jewell (Annabelle). *With*: Claudelle Kaye, Muriel Evans, Frank Conroy, Jimmy Butler, Mickey Rooney, Landers Stevens.
Three New York City youths grow apart as they grow older. Jim Wade becomes a politician, Pat becomes a priest, and Blackie Gallagher becomes a notorious gangster. Blackie's mistress, Eleanor, wants him to give up his criminal life, and when he refuses, her amorous attentions are then centered on Jim Wade. Wade has become the New York District Attorney, but is targeted by a crooked politician who tries to blackmail him. Blackie comes to his old friend's rescue and murders the blackmailer. Blackie is convicted of murder and sentenced to die in the electric chair. When Eleanor tells Wade why Blackie killed the man, Wade offers to testify in his behalf, but Blackie refuses, believing it would ruin Wade's chances to win the race for governor. With Father Pat at his side, he walks off to meet his fate.
Arguably the best of MGM's gangster pictures, *Manhattan Melodrama* was one of David O. Selznick's most important productions during his short tenure as a staff producer at the studio

during the mid-thirties. Clark Gable was still playing bad guys even at this juncture in his career, but his Blackie Gallagher is one of the most sympathetic gangster characters of the initial cycle, and the film's enormous success helped establish him as a romantic lead. The script is also notable for its premise, later reused in countless gangster pictures, perhaps most notably *Angels with Dirty Faces* (Warner Bros., 1938). It also firmly established William Powell and Myrna Loy as a viable team, perhaps best remembered in the *Thin Man* series of the thirties and forties.

Mankiewicz, Herman J. (1897–1953)
Screenwriter. The consummate professional screenwriter, Herman J. Mankiewicz was the older brother of writer, producer and director Joseph L. Mankiewicz. Herman was originally a second string New York drama critic before moving to Hollywood at the beginning of the sound era. For many years he was one of the most respected and highly paid American screenwriters, but in retrospect his talent was for rather superficial entertainment, and few of his films are now considered important. One notable exception is *Citizen Kane* (RKO, 1941), which he cowrote with Orson Welles and (uncredited) John Houseman. He cowrote three early gangster pictures, including two important films directed by Josef von Sternberg.
The Dragnet (Paramount, 1928). *Thunderbolt* (Paramount, 1929). *Ladies Love Brutes* (Paramount, 1930).

Mankiewicz, Joseph L. (1909–1993)
Writer, producer and director. An urbane and extremely talented man, Joseph L. Mankiewicz had an interesting, varied career in Hollywood. His older brother, Herman, helped him secure a contract at Paramount in 1929 after he had brief experience as a journalist. Mankiewicz's talents were immediately apparent, and he cowrote a

number of interesting movies. Young and charming, he also became something of a womanizer, and was romantically involved with Joan Crawford, Frances Dee, Judy Garland, and Linda Darnell, among others. He joined MGM as a staff producer in 1935 (while only twenty-four) and became one of the studio's most respected producers: *Fury* (1936), *The Philadelphia Story* (1940) and *Woman of the Year* (1941) are among the classics he produced for the studio over the course of ten years. His affair with Judy Garland caused him to be fired by MGM, and he then joined 20th Century-Fox. At that time, he began his longest period as a writer and director, making a number of classics, including *All About Eve* (20th Century–Fox, 1950). He wrote and directed the gangster musical *Guys and Dolls*, which, although highly enjoyable, failed to capture the vitality of the original stage production.
Guys and Dolls (Goldwyn-MGM, 1955).

Mann, Anthony (1906–1967)
Director. An immensely talented but critically neglected director, Anthony Mann is best known for the superb group of Westerns he made in the fifties. However, his early "B" thrillers are also praiseworthy and include three excellent gangster *noirs*.
T-Men (Eagle-Lion, 1947). *Raw Deal* (Eagle-Lion, 1948). *Side Street* (MGM, 1949).

Manning, Irene (b. 1917)
Actress. A veteran of vaudeville and operetta, Irene Manning was born Inez Harvout in Cincinatti, Ohio. Her film career began in the early forties, and she generally starred in "B" musicals to exploit her talents as a singer. She costarred with Humphrey Bogart in his last "B" picture, *The Big Shot*, in one of her more notable dramatic roles.
The Big Shot (Warner Bros., 1942).

Mansfield, Jayne (1933–1967)

Actress. Mansfield was born Vera Jane Palmer in Bryn Mawr, Pennsylvania. Tall, voluptuous, and flamboyant on screen and off, she was the most successful of the Marilyn Monroe imitators of the fifties and sixties. Despite her much publicized intelligence, she was never really a good performer, but she always commanded attention while on screen. She appeared almost exclusively in "B" pictures, including the less than truthful "biopic" *The George Raft Story*, her only appearance in the genre.

The George Raft Story (Allied Artists, 1961).

Mantee, Duke (Fictional character)

Humphrey Bogart first achieved fame as a stage actor in the twenties and early thirties. In 1934 he starred on Broadway in Robert Sherwood's drama *The Petrified Forest* as the gangster Duke Mantee, a role he repeated in the film adaptation (Warner Bros., 1936), but only after the insistence of costar Leslie Howard. Until then, Bogart's film career had been a minor one at best, but his extraordinary performance as Mantee helped make him into a successful character actor and established his screen image as the premier tough guy in American cinema.

Duke Mantee and his gang of nomadic criminals — modeled on the famous rural gangsters of the twenties and thirties (including John Dillinger and Clyde Barrow) — hide out at the Black Mesa Barbeque Cafe and Gas Station near an arid desert and petrified forest. Like Maxwell Anderson's similar drama, *Key Largo* (1938), which followed Sherwood's play four years later, but was not made into a movie until a decade after the film adaptation of *The Petrified Forest*, the characters are, in large part, symbolic. Anderson's didacticism was political — liberal versus conservative use of violence — while Sherwood's is more esoteric: the mind-less, primitive violence of Duke Mantee versus the cool intellectualism of Alan Squire (Leslie Howard), one of Mantee's hostages. However, the police shootout at the film's end, in which Mantee is killed, leaves open the question of which will triumph.

Mantegna, Joe

Actor. The Latin-American Mantegna has, since the mid-eighties, seemed to be just on the edge of real stardom, yet has never quite made it, despite his undeniable charm and talents. He has mainly played second leads, including mobsters in two contemporary gangster pictures.

The Godfather III (Paramount, 1990). *Bugsy* (Tristar, 1993).

March, Fredric (1897–1975)

Actor. Born Ernest Frederick McIntyre Bickel in Racine, Wisconsin, March was originally a banker. He quickly gave up that more steady profession for his real love, the theater. He became one of the great actors of his generation and had a substantial film career. Unlike his somewhat less talented contemporaries, however, March did not develop a recognizable screen persona, and thus is less well known today. Nevertheless, his performances were always exemplary. He starred in two gangster movies, most notably opposite Humphrey Bogart in *The Desperate Hours* as the heroic nemesis of Bogart's psychotic gangster.

Ladies Love Brutes (Paramount, 1930). *The Desperate Hours* (Paramount, 1955).

Marin, Edward L. (1899–1951)

Director. Although not exactly the most inspired of filmmakers, Marin was a competent director of "B" entertainments for Universal, MGM and RKO during the thirties and forties. His single gangster picture, *Race Street*, is a well made thriller in the famous RKO *noir* style.

Race Street (RKO, 1948).

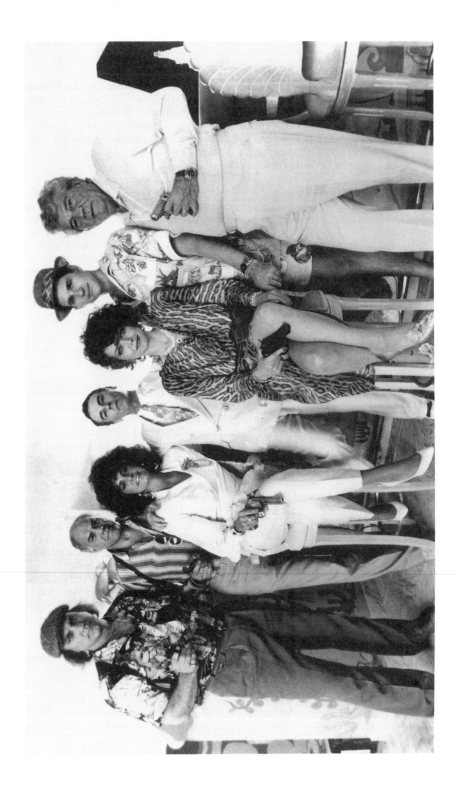

Marion, Frances (1888–1973)
Screenwriter. Marion began her career as a scenarist for silent movies during the teens. She joined MGM in the mid-twenties, and became one of the studio's most important staff writers during the thirties. She was responsible for several of Greta Garbo's classic silent melodramas, but also was a capable handler of more realistic subjects. Her gangster-prison melodrama *The Big House* is one of her most important screenplays. She also wrote *The Secret Six*, a minor early gangster picture.
The Big House (MGM, 1930). *The Secret Six* (MGM, 1931).

Marked Woman (Warner Bros., 1937). 96 mins.
Producer: Lou Edelman. *Director*: Lloyd Bacon. *Screenplay*: Robert Rosson and Abem Finkel, *additional dialog by* Seton I. Miller. *Director of Photography*: George Barnes. *Music*: Bernard Kaum and Heinz Roemheld. *Art Director*: Robert Haas. *Editor*: Jack Killifer.
Cast: Bette Davis (Mary Dwight/ Strauber), Humphrey Bogart (Prosecutor David Graham), Jane Bryan (Betty Strauber), Eduardo Cianelli (Johnny Vanning), Isabel Jewel (Emmy Lou Egan). *With*: Allen Jenkins, Mayo Methot, Lola Lane, Ben Welden, Henry O'Neill, Rosalind Marquis.
Mary Strauber, alias Dwight, is the associate of mobster Johnny Vanning. When Vanning has a man killed, Mary is brought in as a witness, but her conflicting testimony helps set Vanning free. Later, some of Vanning's henchmen kill Mary's younger sister, Betty, when she resists the advances of one of the mobsters. Mary decides to turn evidence over to the Special Prosecutor, although her face is badly scarred as a warning. Vanning is convicted, and Mary, despite her marked face, is ready to begin a new life.

Marked Woman is an atypical gangster picture, with its main character being a female mobster. A strong, well made, if ultimately minor gangster movie, *Marked Woman* is also atypical for providing Humphrey Bogart with one of his few non-gangster roles.

Marley, J. Peverell (1899–1964)
Cinematographer. If he was not the most inventive director of photography, Marley did bring a sense of elegant yet simple style to the films he photographed. Of the two gangster pictures he worked on, the most important is the James Cagney vehicle *Kiss Tomorrow Goodbye*, which displays the influence of *film noir*.
Let 'Em Have It (United Artists, 1935). *Kiss Tomorrow Goodbye* (Warner Bros., 1950).

Married to the Mob (Orion, 1988). 104 mins.
Producers: Kenneth Utt and Edward Saxon. *Director*: Jonathan Demme. *Screenplay*: Barry Strugatz and Mark R. Burns. *Director of Photography*: Tak Fugimoto. *Music*: David Byrne. *Production Designer*: Kristi Zea. *Editor*: Craig McKay.
Cast: Michelle Pfeiffer (Angela de Marco), Alec Baldwin (Frank de Marco), Matthew Modine (Mike Downey), Mercedes Ruehl (Connie Russo), Joan Cusack (Rose), Dean Stockwell (Tony "The Tiger" Russo). *With*: Ellen Foley, Marlene Willoughby, Jason Allen, Anthony J. Nili, Frank Gio, Frank Ferrara.
After her hit man husband, Frank, is murdered by Tony "The Tiger" Russo, a rival gangster, Angela de Marco goes into hiding in the colorful New York lower middle class neighborhoods. She is determined to start a new life as a hair dresser, but soon finds herself hunted by the amorous Tony the Tiger

Opposite: **Michelle Pfeiffer (third from right) as a brunette ex-gangster moll in** *Married to the Mob,* **a decidedly less glamorous role than her blonde moll in** *Scarface.*

and a handsome young F.B.I. agent, Mike Downey. Eventually, in a violent confrontation, Downey helps rescue Angela from the love struck gangster, and then decides to start a new life with the eccentric ex-moll.

Technically speaking, Jonathan Demme is the least imaginative major contemporary American director; his films all look like glossy television dramas and are really little more than commercial films with serious aspirations. Nevertheless, he often works with superior screenwriters and actors, and sometimes can rise above his limitations as a filmmaker. This is certainly true of *Married to the Mob*, which has a quirky, fast moving screenplay and excellent performances by Michelle Pfeiffer and Dean Stockwell. A modern gangster satire that can be compared favorably with its predecessors from the thirties and forties, the film's success can be attributed largely to Pfeiffer's charisma.

Marsh, Debby (Fictional character)
The moll who is physically abused by her gangster lover is a common character in the genre, but it is relatively rare that such a character enacts her own justice and causes the downfall of her lover. This is not the case with Debby Marsh (Gloria Grahame) in *The Big Heat* (Columbia, 1953). Marsh is the moll of Vince Stone (Lee Marvin), a psychotic mob henchman who treats her very badly. When he sees her with Sergeant Dave Bannion, the cop carrying on a one-man crusade against Mike Lagana (Alexander Scourby), Vince's boss, he throws scalding coffee into Debby's face, horribly disfiguring her. Seeking revenge, she informs on Vince and Lagana and then lures Vince to her apartment. She throws scalding coffee into his face, but he fatally wounds her. Bannion arrives shortly thereafter and arrests Vince for Debby's murder.

Marshall, George (1891–1975)
Director. The extremely prolific

Marshall began his career as a film director in the late teens and hit his zenith during the forties and fifties. He was at his best with comedies, directing features for Laurel and Hardy, Bob Hope, and Martin and Lewis. He also directed a few thrillers and action pictures. Of these, the best is certainly the *film noir* classic *The Blue Dahlia* (Paramount, 1946). He directed a single gangster picture, the neglected minor classic *Show Them No Mercy*.
Show Them No Mercy (20th Century–Fox, 1935).

Marshall, Tully (1864–1943)
Character actor. Born William Phillips in Nevada City, California, Marshall was a well established stage actor when he began his film career in 1914. He was one of the busiest character actors in American movies until his death. In *This Gun for Hire* he played one of his most memorable villains, the invalid industrialist who initiates the action that leads to his demise at the hands of his hired assassin. He also played a gangster in Josef von Sternberg's *Thunderbolt*.
Thunderbolt (Paramount, 1928).
This Gun for Hire (Paramount, 1941).

Martin, Joe "Baby Face" (Fictional character)
For most of the first decade of his film career, Humphrey Bogart played many different gangsters, some more memorable than others. In the classic drama *Dead End* (United Artists, 1937), based on Sidney Kingsley's play, Bogart played one of his most famous gangster characters, Joe "Baby Face" Martin. Baby Face Martin is a gangster on the lam who has returned to his hometown, New York City, for one last visit before fleeing the country. A product of the streets and tenements of the city, he is rejected by his beloved mother who hates the compromises he has made to "rise" above the poverty of his youth, and

discovers that his one-time girlfriend Francey (Claire Trevor) has become a prostitute. Martin meanwhile, plans to kidnap a rich boy, but is shot and killed by another resident of the slums. Bogart's characterization is both stereotypical — Martin is a self-centered dandy — and oddly touching.

Martin, Tony (b. 1912)
   Actor and singer. Born Alvin Morris in San Francisco, Martin was a popular crooner and band leader during the thirties and forties. His film career began in 1936, and he subsequently starred in numerous light musicals. In *Casbah*, the musical remake of *Algiers* (United Artists, 1938), he starred as the gangster Pépé le Moko.
   Casbah (Universal, 1948).

Marvin, Lee (1924–1987)
   Actor. Marvin, like Humphrey Bogart (to whom he is often compared), has come to represent an American masculinity that is hard-boiled, stoic and rugged. He played both heroes and villains, but is most memorable as the latter. He made a striking early appearance in Fritz Lang's classic *The Big Heat* as the vicious gangster and assassin who tosses boiling coffee in Gloria Grahame's face. He played a similar role in Don Siegel's remake of *The Killers*. He also played one of the motorcycle gang members in *The Wild One*.
   The Big Heat (Columbia, 1953). *The Wild One* (Columbia, 1954). *Violent Saturday* (20th Century–Fox, 1955). *The Killers* (Universal, 1964).

Maté, Rudolph (1898–1964)
   Director. Born Rudolf Matéh in Poland, Maté was an important cinematographer in Germany and Hollywood, contributing to the dark, shadowy expressionist style. He began directing at the age of forty-nine, but his career as a director is less impressive than his work as a cinematographer. Nevertheless, he did direct the *noir* classic *D.O.A.* (United Artists, 1949). His

gangster thriller *Forbidden* is less impressive.
   Forbidden (Universal, 1953).

Mature, Victor (b. 1916)
   Actor. In the forties and fifties, the tall, muscular, dark Mature was the very image of male virility, hence his nickname "the Hunk." Critics ridiculed his wooden acting, and he never seemed to take his career very seriously; yet, he was immensely popular and proved every now and then that he could act. One of his finest performances was in the *noir* thriller *Kiss of Death* as a former gangster who turns on his friends. Less well known is *Violent Saturday*, a minor but well made movie in which Mature is very good.
   Kiss of Death (20th Century–Fox, 1947). *Violent Saturday* (20th Century–Fox, 1955).

Maxwell, Marilyn (1922–1972)
   Actress. After dramatic studies, the voluptuous, statuesque, blonde Maxwell entered movies in the early forties after dramatic studies and was quickly typecast as a sexy blonde of the Marilyn Monroe type — a type, in fact, that she predated by several years. She played leads in two minor gangster thrillers.
   Race Street (RKO, 1948). *New York Confidential* (Warner Bros., 1955).

Mayo, Archie (1891–1968)
   Director. Mayo was a prolific and competent director of hard-boiled action thrillers. As a staff director at Warner Bros. during the thirties, he was an important part of the team of filmmakers who created the studio's hard-boiled style. Of his three gangster pictures, the most important is *The Petrified Forest*, a brilliant version of Robert E. Sherwood's play.
   The Doorway to Hell (Warner Bros., 1930). *Night After Night* (Paramount, 1932). *The Petrified Forest* (Warner Bros., 1936).

Mayo, Virginia (b. 1920)
Actress. Born Virginia Jones in St. Louis, Missouri, Mayo was a showgirl when she was discovered by producer Sam Goldwyn. A stunning and slightly earthy blonde, her dramatic gifts were limited, but she was popular for a time, particularly in the musical comedies starring Danny Kaye and produced by Goldwyn. She played a few dramatic roles, most notably in the classic gangster *noir White Heat*, in which she portrayed a moll.

White Heat (Warner Bros., 1949).

Me, Gangster (Fox, 1928). Approximately 90 mins.
Producer: William Fox. *Director*: Raoul Walsh. *Screenplay*: Charles Francis Coe and Raoul Walsh, based on the book by Charles Francis Coe. *Titles*: William Kernell. *Director of Photography*: Arthur Edeson. *Editor*: Louis Loeffler.
Cast: June Collyer (Mary Regan), Don Terry (Jimmy Williams), Anders Randolf (Russ Williams), Stella Adams (Lizzie Williams), Burt McIntosh (Bill Lane). *With*: Walter James, Gustav Von Seyffertitz, Al Hill, Herbert Ashton, Bob Perry.
A young street hoodlum, Jimmy Williams, organizes the robbery of $50,000. He is caught and sentenced to prison but has hidden the money. Upon his release, he decides to turn it in, but his old gang wants the money and tries to stop him. Eventually, however, he does manage to return the stolen money and redeem himself with his family.
Raoul Walsh, the great action director who later made the classic *High Sierra*, helmed this late silent gangster picture. Like so many of its era, the film suffers from its Victorian moralizing, but it is a notable early gangster movie distinguished mainly by Arthur Edeson's superior camera work.

Mean Streets (Warner Bros., 1973). 110 mins.

Producer: Johnathon T. Taplin. *Director*: Martin Scorsese. *Screenplay*: Martin Scorsese and Mardick Martin. *Director of Photography*: Kent Wakeford. *Editor*: Sid Levin.
Cast: Robert De Niro (Johnny Boy), Harvey Keitel (Charlie), David Proval (Tonly), Amy Robinson (Teresa), Richard Romanus (Michael). *With*: Cesare Danova, Victor Argo, George Memmoli, Martin Scorsese.
Johnny Boy, Charlie and Tony are three second generation Italian-Americans who have grown up in the ghettos in New York. Now in their mid-twenties, with their lives unfocused, they roam the streets in search of broads and adventure. They are, however, at a crossroads, as Johnny Boy gets into debt with a local loan shark (and nearly loses his life before paying off the debt), Tony finds steady work as a bartender, and Charlie, who is romancing Johnny's cousin Teresa, prepares to take over the restaurant run by a Mafioso uncle.
Shot on location in New York City on a low budget, *Mean Streets* is a meandering exposé of the aimless lives of three young men who have a tenuous connection with the Mafia. Fascinating and also infuriating, it is a violent melodrama which provides an insight into the environment that produces organized crime, but also suffers from the improvisational extremes that would pervade Scorsese's later films. Nevertheless, its performances are first rate, and the film's success on the festival circuit made De Niro, Keitel, and Scorsese's professional futures secure.

The Mechanic (United Artists, 1972). 100 mins.
Producers: Irwin Winkler and Robert Chartoff. *Director*: Michael Winner. *Screenplay*: Lewis John Carlino. *Directors of Photography*: Richard Kline and Robert Paynter. *Music*: Jerry Fielding. *Art Directors*: Roger E. Maus and Herbert Westbrook. *Editor*: Freddie Wilson.

Cast: Charles Bronson (Arthur Bishop), Jan-Michael Vincent (Steve McKenna), Kenan Wynn (Harry McKenna), Jill Ireland (Prostitute), Linda Ridgeway (Louise), Frank DeKova (The Man). *With*: Lindsay H. Crosby, Takayuki Kubota, Martin Gordon, James Davidson, Steve Cory.

Arthur Bishop, a hired assassin, is an expert at making his murders look like accidents. He befriends a youthful mob associate, Steve McKenna, who convinces Bishop to hire him as an assistant. McKenna, however, is actually the son of one of Bishop's victims and is seeking revenge against his father's killer. Bishop slowly realizes that McKenna has been hired by the organization to kill him. McKenna, in fact, succeeds in poisoning Bishop but is also killed by his booby-trapped car, rigged by Bishop.

One of the earliest in the series of action oriented movies that made Charles Bronson a star during the seventies, *The Mechanic* is less a study of the motivations of a hired killer and more of an excuse for extremely violent action. Nevertheless, on that level, it manages to be an entertaining modern gangster thriller.

Meeker, Ralph (b. 1920)

Actor. Meeker was born Ralph Rathgeber in Minneapolis, Minnesota. He acted in the theater during the forties, taking over the role of Stanley Kowalski in the Broadway production of *A Streetcar Named Desire*. He had a busy film career but never achieved real stardom, despite some good performances. His most famous role was as Mike Hammer in the *noir* classic *Kiss Me Deadly* (United Artists, 1955). He had a supporting role in Roger Corman's *The St. Valentine's Day Massacre* as gang boss "Bugs" Moran, who was gunned down by Al Capone's men.

The St. Valentine's Day Massacre (20th Century–Fox, 1967).

Meighan, Thomas (1879–1936)

Character actor. A Broadway star for many years, the Irish-American Meighan was also a major action hero of silent movies. His popularity peeked in the early twenties, but he continued to play supporting roles right up to his death. He starred in the original version of *The Racket*, an important early gangster drama.

The Racket (Paramount, 1928).

Melville, Jean-Pierre (1917–1973)

Director. Born Jean-Pierre Grumback in Paris, Melville was obsessed with Americana, taking his last name from his favorite author, Herman Melville. Apparently living in a loft filled with American items, Melville was most of all obsessed with American popular cinema. As a director, he often chose to make crime thrillers, which immediately set him apart from his contemporaries. Made on low budgets and shot on location, his underworld thrillers show the influence of the American *film noir* and gangster genres, while still retaining a Gallic flavor. *Le Samourai*, probably the best known of Melville's films, was seen throughout the world and has developed a cult among young American directors, particularly Quentin Tarantino (see *Reservoir Dogs*).

Le Samourai (CICC/Fida Cinematografica, 1967).

Menzies, William Cameron (1896–1957)

Art director. Although he had a varied career as both a film director and art director in Hollywood, it is certainly as the latter that he achieved his greatest success. Indeed, he was one of the most imaginative of Hollywood's great art directors, creating the sets and designs for many classic films, including *Gone with the Wind* (Selznick-MGM, 1939) and *Foreign Correspondent* (United Artists, 1940), as well as the British-made *Things to Come* (London Films, 1936), which he also directed. His work on the seminal gangster picture *Alibi* demonstrates his effective use of studio sets and impressionistic skylines.

Alibi (United Artists, 1929).

Meredith, Burgess (b. 1908)

Actor. Born George Burgess, Meredith was a member of the leftist-oriented Group Theater during the thirties. His enthusiastically eccentric style never really caught on, and after a decade of leading roles in marginally successful movies, he began playing character parts. He had an effective supporting role in *Castle on the Hudson* as a suicidal convict.

Castle on the Hudson (Warner Bros., 1940).

Metro-Goldwyn-Mayer

Under the aegis of Louis B. Mayer (as Vice President in Charge of Production) and his underling, Irving Thalberg, MGM quickly became the leading Hollywood studio in the years immediately following the studio's formation in 1924. Thalberg, the "Boy Genius," was the guiding influence on the studio, producing most of MGM's best films and, through various subordinates, overseeing the creation of others. Mayer also had a profound influence on the studio's style, which developed into glossy family entertainment, versions of literary classics, and patriotic epics. Thalberg and Mayer thus avoided more hard-boiled subjects, but the popularity of Josef von Sternberg's gangster pictures made for Paramount during the late twenties and Warner Bros.' gangster pictures in the early thirties could not be ignored by the two moguls. During their administration, there were several attempts to make gangster movies, beginning with *Four Walls* in 1928. However, MGM's early gangster pictures suffer somewhat from big budgets and overblown sets. Still, there were some notable contributions to the genre, including *The Big House*, *The Beast of the City*, and *Manhattan Melodrama*. After Thalberg's death in

1936, Mayer all but abandoned hard-boiled subjects, and the few gangster movies that were made tended to be "B" productions. The exception is John Huston's *The Asphalt Jungle*, which was clearly influenced by his years at Warner Bros. After Mayer lost control of the studio in 1952, the studio's new bosses began to make more hard-boiled movies, of which *Rogue Cop* is probably the best. The gangster genre was also combined with the musical in two moderately satisfying movies, *Guys and Dolls* and *Party Girl*. Since the golden age of the studio system, MGM has released a handful of gangster thrillers, but none of them are as important as the earlier titles.

1928: *The Big City, Four Walls*. 1930: *The Big House*. 1931: *The Secret Six*. 1932: *Beast of the City*. 1933: *Penthouse*. 1934: *Manhattan Melodrama*. 1935: *Public Hero #1, Whipsaw*. 1937: *The Last Gangster*. 1940: *The Earl of Chicago, Strange Cargo*. 1949: *The Bribe, Side Street*. 1950: *The Asphalt Jungle, The Black Hand*. 1954: *Rogue Cop*. 1955: *Guys and Dolls*. 1958: *Party Girl*. 1959: *The Big Operative*. 1968: *The Biggest Bundle of Them All*. 1971: *Get Carter*. 1973: *The Outfit*. 1985: *To Live and Die in L.A., Year of the Dragon*.

Metty, Russell (1906–1978)

Cinematographer. Metty's film career began in the mid-thirties. He was a brilliant, inventive director of photography, working well in both black and white and color: *Bringing Up Baby* (RKO, 1938), *The Stranger* (RKO, 1945), *Magnificent Obsession* (Universal, 1954), and *Spartacus* (Universal, 1960) are all fine examples of his work. He was also the director of photography for a superior "B" movie, *Crashout*, in which he demonstrated some semi-*noir* photography.

Crashout (Filmakers, 1955).

The Miami Story (Columbia, 1954). 75 mins.

Producer: Sam Katzman. *Director*: Fred F. Sears. *Screenplay*: Robert E. Kent. *Director of Photography*: Henry Freulich. *Art Director*: Paul Palmentola. *Editor*: Viola Lawrence.

Cast: Barry Sullivan (Mick Flagg), Luther Adler (Tony Brill), John Baer (Tel Delacorte), Adele Jergens (Gwen Abbott), Beverly Garland (Holly Abbott). *With*: Dan Riss, Damian O'Flynn, Christopher Alcaide, Gene D'Arcy, George E. Stone, David Kasday.

After his release from prison, former gangster Mick Flagg teams with the police to bring his former colleagues to justice.

The Miami Story relies on a conventional story line, but it is a very well made, action oriented "B" thriller that relies on its action to move the plot along. The cast is quite good, particularly the delectable Beverly Garland as a moll who falls for Barry Sullivan's tough ex-con character. The film, typical of the time, also uses a semidocumentary technique and some excellent location settings.

Midnight Taxi (20th Century–Fox, 1937). 69 mins.
Producer: Milton H. Feld. *Director*: Eugene Forde. *Screenplay*: John Patrick and Lou Breslow, *story by* Borden Chase. *Director of Photography*: Barney McGill. *Editor*: Al DeGaetano.

Cast: Brian Donlevy (Chick Gardner), Frances Drake (Gilda Lee), Alan Dinehart (Philip Strickland), Sig Rumann (John Rudd), Gilbert Roland (Flash Dillon). *With*: Harold Huber, Paul Stanton, Lon Chaney, Jr., Russell Hicks.

F.B.I. agent Chick Gardner investigates the counterfeiting ring led by Flash Dillon and Lucky Todd. Gardner joins the gang and falls for Todd's moll, Gilda Lee. The mobsters discover his true identity and plan to kill him, but Lee warns him, and with the help of his colleagues, he manages to bring the gang to justice.

A minor "B" gangster picture from the later period of the genre's initial cycle, *Midnight Taxi* does have an excellent second string cast but is otherwise of little interest.

Milestone, Lewis (1895–1980)
Director. Born Levis Milstein in New York, Milestone was a major director for over two decades, beginning in the mid-twenties. He had an almost exaggerated visual style, so much so, in fact, that his films' stories were often secondary. Unlike the similarly baroque Josef von Sternberg, however, Milestone did have a strong dramatic sense, and he rarely strayed from commercial themes. His masterpiece is certainly *All Quiet on the Western Front* (Universal, 1930), but many of his other films are equally fine. He directed the original version of *The Racket*, a seminal gangster movie that demonstrates his extravagant style.

The Racket (Paramount, 1928).

Milius, John (b. 1944)
Screenwriter and director. Milius is famous for his ultraconservative sentiments and his attraction to violent subjects. After many years as a leading scenarist, mostly of thrillers, he was given the chance to direct one of his own screenplays. The result, *Dillinger*, based on the real life gangster, is a low budget but exceptionally well made modern gangster movie.

Dillinger (American International, 1973).

Milland, Ray (1905–1986)
Actor. Born Reginald Truscott-Jones in Wales, Milland had a prominent stage career in Great Britain before moving to Hollywood during the thirties. There he became one of American film's busiest, most reliable leading men until the sixties. Indeed, he, along with Robert Montgomery and Robert Taylor, was one of the finest examples of the classic Hollywood leading man: rather conven-

tionally handsome, he specialized in contemporary characters, usually romantic leads in films which depended more on the over-all production than the star. However, he was also a fine actor, as he so ably demonstrated in Billy Wilder's *The Lost Weekend* (Paramount, 1945). He had supporting roles in two early gangster pictures, but his strong European personality was ill suited to the genre.

Blonde Crazy (Warner Bros., 1931). *The Glass Key* (Paramount, 1935).

Miller, Arthur (1894–1971)

Cinematographer. Miller was one of the most important cinematographers of his time. His style was comparatively conventional, as he preferred simple lighting schemes and camera movements. His greatest work was created in the forties, twenty years after his career began. His work on *Johnny Apollo*, while not as notable as some of his work from the same period, is no less exemplary.

Johnny Apollo (20th Century–Fox, 1940).

Miller's Crossing: (20th Century–Fox, 1990). 115 mins.

Producer: Ethan Coen. *Director*: Joel Coen. *Screenplay*: Ethan and Joel Coen. *Director of Photography*: Barry Sonnenfeld. *Music*: Carter Burwall. *Production Design*: Dennis Gassner. *Editor*: Michael Miller.

Cast: Gabriel Byrne (Tom Reagan), Marcia Gay Harden (Verna), John Turturro (Bernie Bernbaum), John Polito (John Casper), J.R. Freeman (Eddie Dane), Albert Finney (Leo). *With*: Mike Starr, Al Mancini, Richard Woods, Thomas Toner, Steve Buscemi, Mario Todisco.

Leo is a benevolent Irish gangster and political boss who rules an unnamed Eastern city with the help of Tom Reagan, his trusted lieutenant and counselor. Their control of the city is threatened by a minor Italian boss, John Casper, and his ruthless hench-

men. Meanwhile, Leo and Tom have a falling out when Tom seduces (or is seduced by) Verna, Leo's mistress. Tom is caught in a complex web of violence and murder in the gang war that ensues, but ultimately he manages to barely escape with his life.

Joel and Ethan Coen created both an homage and a wholly modern addition to the gangster genre with *Miller's Crossing*. Whatever their faults—chiefly a reliance on unintentionally obscure symbolism and weak plots—the Coen brothers make up for them in enthusiasm, attention to detail, and dark humor, all qualities one finds in *Miller's Crossing*. More than anything, they are master technicians who know how to use the camera better than any other contemporary American filmmakers except, perhaps, Martin Scorsese, and *Miller's Crossing* demonstrates the brothers' talents at their very best.

Milner, Victor (1893–1989)

Cinematographer. In the thirties, Milner's cinematography exemplified Hollywood style at its best. As director Ernst Lubitsch's collaborator, he photographed the classic romantic comedies *The Love Parade* (Paramount, 1929), *Monte Carlo* (Paramount, 1930), and *Trouble in Paradise* (Paramount, 1932). As demonstrated by these and his work on Cecil B. DeMille's *Cleopatra* (Paramount, 1934) and Lewis Milestone's *The General Died at Dawn* (Paramount, 1936), Milner had a lush, sensual style that emphasized shadowy effects and glossy close-ups. Indeed, he was one of Paramount's most important, if neglected, artisans, and he worked at the studio for most of his career. Of his two gangster movies, the most important is *Dark City*, a fine example of his use of night scenes and rainswept sets.

Hunted Man (Paramount, 1938). *Dark City* (Paramount, 1950).

Milton, David

Art director. Milton has been called

Cary Grant, in a surprising role as admittedly a rather dapper gangster, in the classic satire *Mr. Lucky*, here tries to talk Gladys Cooper out of some money while the incredulous Laraine Day watches.

the Cedric Gibbons of Monogram, because of his pervasive influence on the studio's style. He made the best of meager resources, and his designs and sets are often quite inventive. Of the three gangster movies on which he worked, the most interesting is Don Siegel's *Riot in Cell Block 11*, for which he created some appropriately menacing and claustrophobic sets. (Allied Artists, incidentally, was Monogram's later name.)

Angels' Alley (Monogram, 1948). *Riot in Cell Block 11* (Allied Artists, 1954). *The George Raft Story* (Allied Artists, 1961).

Mr. Lucky (RKO, 1943). 100 mins. *Producer*: David Hempstead. *Director*: H. C. Potter. *Screenplay*: Milton Holmes and Adrian Scott, based on the story "Bundles for Freedom" by Milton Holmes. *Director of Photography*: George Barnes. *Music*: Roy Webb. *Art Directors*: Albert S. D'Agostino and Mark Lee-Kirk. *Editor*: Theron Warth.

Cast: Cary Grant (Joe Adams), Laraine Day (Dorothy Bryant), Charles Bickford (Hard Swede), Gladys Cooper (Captain Steadman), Paul Stewart (Zepp), Alan Carney (Crunk). *With*: Henry Stephenson, Kay Johnson, Erford Gage, J. M. Kerrigan, Walter Kingsford, Edward Fielding.

Joe Adams, an ice-cold con artist and gambler determined to duck the draft and scrape up enough cash to launch his gambling ship, decides to fleece the American War Relief Society to raise the necessary bankroll. His plans, however, are thwarted by the beautiful and honest Dorothy Bryant, who eventually breaks through his icy exterior. She convinces him to use his vessel as a transporter of medical supplies.

Mr. Lucky is certainly one of the most charming of the gangster satires, thanks in large part to the refreshing performances of Cary Grant and Laraine Day. The two leads are supported by an excellent group of character actors and a fine screenplay cowritten by Adrian Scott, later an important producer of RKO's early *films noir*. The director of the film, H. C. Potter, was a master of light comedy, and here he created one of his most enjoyable films. It was an enormous box office success and later inspired a short-run television series (1959–1960) starring John Vivyan, a Cary Grant look-alike discovered by the show's creator, Blake Edwards.

Mr. Majestyk (United Artists, 1974). 104 mins.
Producer: Walter Mirisch. *Director*: Richard Fleischer. *Screenplay*: Elmore Leonard, based on his novel. *Director of Photography*: Richard H. Kline. *Music*: Charles Bernstein. *Editor*: Ralph E. Winters.
Cast: Charles Bronson (Vince Majestyk), Al Lettieri (Frank Renda), Linda Cristal (Nancy Chavez), Lee Purcell (Wiley), Paul Koslo (Bobby). *With*: Taylor Lacher, Frank Maxwell, Alejandro Rey, Gordon Rhodes.

Vince Majestyk, a melon farmer in Colorado, is convicted of trumped up charges after he hires migrant workers to pick his crop instead of members of a local labor syndicate. Majestyk is handcuffed to mob boss Frank Renda as the two are sent to prison to serve their sentences. However, Renda's gang ambushes the prison truck and sets them free. Renda offers to pay Majestyk to drive him to Mexico, but

Majestyk refuses and instead tells the police where they can find him. They fail to arrest him, and Renda vows revenge against Majestyk. Majestyk realizes that the police cannot help him and decides to protect himself against the wrath of the mobsters by killing them. He hides in the Colorado mountains and lures them into the wilderness to either kill or capture them.

Mr. Majestyk, based on Elmore Leonard's best seller, is probably the best of Charles Bronson's gangster action thrillers. It is directed in typical gut wrenching style by veteran action *noir* director Richard Fleischer, who makes good use of the expansive exteriors and the violent elements in the story, rendering them in high style.

Mitchell, Cameron (1918–1994)
Character actor. Born Cameron Mizell in Dallastown, Pennsylvania, Mitchell began acting while in college and, for many years, had a career both in film and on the stage. He is often seen as a burly hero or villain, particularly in action pictures. He starred in the "B" movie *Inside the Mafia* as a murderous gang boss.
Inside the Mafia (United Artists, 1959).

Mitchell, Millard (1900–1953)
Character actor. The rangy, nasal voiced Mitchell was a busy and popular character actor who usually played seriocomic parts during the forties and fifties. He played a jailed safecracker in the semisatirical *My Six Convicts*, his only appearance in the genre.
My Six Convicts (Columbia, 1952).

Mitchum, Robert (b. 1917)
Actor. After widely varied experience, Robert Mitchum settled in Los Angeles while in his early twenties and naturally gravitated to acting in the movies. For much of the early forties, he played small roles in "A" pictures and large roles in "B" pictures, but his popularity remained relatively small

until after his service in the Army during World War II. He suddenly became a major star, and he still is one of the key icons of the era. Husky, sleepy-eyed and lethargic, he looks as if he could not give a damn and in fact that is not far from the truth. Yet, his performances were always good, even in bad films. He seemed to represent a new kind of hero for many Americans during the post-war years; cynical, tough, and stoic, he was almost always the individual struggling against stronger centers of power. Indeed, this image was so powerful that even his conviction on marijuana charges could not dim his stardom or hurt his image as the little guy battling against corrupt officials.

It was his role in the *film noir* classic *Out of the Past* that firmly established Mitchum as a star. His character, the basically honest but corruptible private detective Jeff Bailey, remains an archetype of the genre, and it was a type he played in several subsequent *noir* thrillers, including *His Kind of Woman*, *The Big Steal* and *The Racket*, all important gangster *noirs*.

Mitchum reappeared in two gangster pictures later in his career. *The Friends of Eddie Coyle*, in which he played the title role, is one of the most effective (and downbeat) gangster movies of its time. *The Yakuza*, on the other hand, is a conventional police procedural saved by the unique theme of Americans fighting against the Japanese Mafia. For his performances in the genre during the late forties and early fifties, Robert Mitchum is as important as Edward G. Robinson and James Cagney were to the initial cycle.

Out of the Past (RKO, 1947). *The Big Steal* (RKO, 1949). *His Kind of Woman* (RKO, 1951). *The Racket* (RKO, 1951). *The Friends of Eddie Coyle* (Paramount, 1973). *The Yakuza* (Warner Bros., 1975). *Thunder Road* (United Artists, 1958).

The Mob (Columbia, 1951). 87 mins.

Producer: Jerry Bresler. *Director*: Robert Parish. *Screenplay*: William Bowers, based on the story "Waterfront" by Ferguson Findley. *Director of Photography*: Joseph Walker. *Musical Director*: Morris Stoloff. *Art Director*: Cary Odell. *Editor*: Charles Nelson.

Cast: Broderick Crawford (Johnny Damico), Betty Buehler (Mary Kiernan), Richard Kiley (Thomas Clancy), Otto Hulett (Lieutenant Banks), Neville Brand (Gunner). *With*: Ernest Borgnine, Matt Crowley, Walter Klavun, Lynn Baggett, Jean Alexander, Ralph Dumke.

Johnny Damico, a police detective, goes undercover to infiltrate the racket controlling the waterfront. With the aid of another detective, Tom Clancy, Damico sets out to gather evidence against the mysterious Smoothie, the leader of the mob. Eventually they discover the real identity of the mob leader, and he dies in a shootout with the police when they attempt to arrest him.

Broderick Crawford from the underrated gangster *noir*, *The Mob*.

The Mob was the second feature directed by former editor (and child actor) Robert Parish. Like its predecessor, it is a *noir* thriller shot on a modest budget. It relies on violent action to move its routine plot along, but it is a very well made, effective little thriller. In the *noir* style, even the heroes are vulgar and corrupt (resorting to physical violence to get information), thus creating a more realistic picture of the sometimes muddied motivations of law enforcement in their attempts to stop organized crime.

Mobsters (Universal, 1992). 110 mins. *Producer*: Steve Roth. *Director*: Michael Karbelnikoff. *Screenplay*: Nicholas Kazan and Michael Mahern. *Director of Photography*: Lajos Koltai. *Music*: Michael Small. *Production Design*: Richard Sylbert. *Editors*: Scott Smith and Joe D'Augustine.

Cast: Christian Slater (Charley "Lucky" Luciano), Richard Grieco (Benjamin "Bugsy" Siegel), Costas Mandylor (Frank Costello), Patrick Dempsey (Meyer Lansky), Lara Flynn Boyle (Mara Motes), Bianca Rossini (Rosalie Luciano). *With*: Rodney Eastman, Christopher Penn, Anthony Quinn, Traci Swenson, Trish Steele, F. Murray Abraham.

In the twenties, a group of brash street punks rise to the top of the New York underworld.

Despite its promise, with a screenplay cowritten by the brilliant Nicholas Kazan (Elia Kazan's son), *Mobsters* turned out to be a mediocre gangster picture submerged by incompetent direction and poor performances by its trendy cast. Only Lara Flynn Boyle, as a show girl who gets romantically involved with one of the gangsters, gives a decent performance in a leading role. Allegedly based on the early lives of real gangsters, it is in fact a piece of speculative fiction, but its production values, recreating New York in the early part of the twentieth century, are superior.

Moffet, Kathie (Fictional character)

An archetypal *film noir femme fatale* played by Jane Greer in *Out of the Past* (RKO, 1947), Moffet is also a moll, but her amoral character and her callous manipulation of men is more strongly in the new tradition of female characters that emerged in American cinema during the forties. The character is one of the most complex and interesting female characters in the gangster and *noir* genres.

Mohr, Hal (1894–1974)

Cinematographer. One of the most respected craftsmen of his time, Mohr was a prolific and gifted cinematographer. His best work is gritty, realistic and less stylized than some of his contemporaries.

Bullets or Ballots (First National, 1936). *The Wild One* (Columbia, 1954). *Baby Face Nelson* (United Artists, 1957). *Underworld USA* (Columbia, 1961).

Molls

The moll is the most common female character type in the gangster genre. It would be incorrect to dismiss the moll as mere decoration in a genre dominated by male characters. In fact, the moll is rarely just an object of sexual desire (for either the films' gangster or the movie audience), but rather a somewhat symbolic figure who embodies virtue corrupted by greed: whether gold digger or good girl, she is often the victim of the gangster's ill will and her own cowardice for not leaving him. Her beauty is also more often a status symbol for the gangster and the power he has attained. Yet, the best portrayals of such characters have also added an extra dimension of humanity that makes them sympathetic and not merely pathetic. In *Key Largo* (Warner Bros., 1948), for example, Claire Trevor plays Gaye Dawn, the humiliated and abused moll of Johnny Rocco (Edward G. Robinson) who clearly endures her lover's wrath because she simply loves him and tries to escape his mistreatment by staying drunk. Trevor's tender performance in this film won her an Academy Award for best supporting actress and it remains the genre's best female performance.

The moll is a figure from the earliest gangster pictures. In Josef von Sternberg's *Underworld* (Paramount, 1927), Evelyn Brent plays Feathers, a typically elegant yet amoral gold digging moll; her relationship with Bull Weed (George Bancroft), is motivated largely by her own greed. Subsequent molls have included Kitty (Mae Clarke) and Gwen Allen (Jean Harlow) in *Public Enemy* (Warner Bros., 1931), Jo Keller (Claire Trevor) in *The Amazing Dr. Clitterhouse* (Warner Bros., 1938), Marie Garson (Ida Lupino) in *High Sierra* (Warner Bros., 1941), Kathie Moffatt (Jane Greer) in *Out of the Past* (RKO, 1947), Nancy Starr (Belita) in *The Gangster* (Allied Artists, 1947), Annie Laurie Starr (Peggy Cummins) in *Gun Crazy* (United Artists, 1949), Doll Conovan (Jean Hagen) in *The Asphalt Jungle* (MGM, 1950) and Debby Marsh (Gloria Grahame) in *The Big Heat* (Columbia, 1953). *Film noir* in the forties introduced the *femme fatale*, a new type of female character in crime pictures perhaps best characterized by Jane Greer's Kathie Moffatt in the aforementioned *Out of the Past*.

Monogram Pictures

A subsidiary Studio of Allied Artists Corporation, Monogram was a "B" studio's "B" studio. It was mainly the home for the East Side Kids, the Bowery Boys (whose *Angel's Alley*, a gangster movie, was made at the studio) and Bela Lugosi during the forties. However, occasionally the studio stumbled onto a more prestigious film, such as the surprising *Dillinger*. Made on an extremely low budget, *Dillinger* was a major hit and remains a minor classic of the genre.

1945: *Dillinger*. 1948: *Angels' Alley*.

Monroe, Marilyn (1926–1962)

Actress. Monroe was one of the last great stars of the studio system and represents both the glamor of its heyday and a metaphor for its demise.

Although she desperately wanted to be a serious actress, to the point of self destruction, she was best suited to comedic roles. She played small dramatic parts early in her career, however, most memorably in the classic *The Asphalt Jungle*, in which she portrayed the moll of a gang boss. Her performance is quite good and full of both sensuality and pathos. In the classic *Some Like It Hot*, she was at her comedic best as the gorgeous singer lusted after by Tony Curtis (in drag).

The Asphalt Jungle (MGM, 1950). *Some Like It Hot* (United Artists, 1959).

Montgomery, Robert (1904–1981)

Actor. Montgomery, born Henry Montgomery, was a rather typical MGM leading man during the thirties. Tall, dark-haired, smooth and conventionally handsome, he was almost always seen as the object of the leading lady's desire. However, he did play tougher roles, most notably in *The Big House* and the odd gangster melodrama *The Earl of Chicago*. He later directed and starred in several hardboiled *films noir*, most importantly *The Lady in the Lake* (MGM, 1946), in which he played private detective Philip Marlowe.

The Big House (MGM, 1930). *The Earl of Chicago* (MGM, 1940).

Moore, Constance (b. 1919)

Actress. Popular on stage and radio, Moore was both a singer and actress. Her film career began in the late thirties, but she never achieved the expected stardom and later appeared in many "B" movies. She starred in a single, minor gangster picture.

Buy Me That Town (Paramount, 1941).

Morgan, Harry (aka Henry; b. 1915)

Character actor. Morgan was born Harry Bratsburg in Detroit. After stage experience, he made his film debut in *To the Shores of Tripoli* (20th Century-Fox, 1942) and subsequently played a variety of roles, including good guys, cops, businessmen and mob henchmen. His greatest success was on television in the series *Dragnet* (opposite long time friend and occasional fellow character actor Jack Webb) and *M.A.S.H.* as the kindly colonel. He played smooth criminals in all four of his gangster pictures.

Roger Toughy, Gangster (20th Century-Fox, 1944). *The Gangster* (Allied Artists, 1947). *Race Street* (RKO, 1948). *My Six Convicts* (Columbia, 1952).

Morgan, Helen (1900–1941)

Actress and singer. Born Helen Riggins in Danville, Illinois, Morgan was a dynamic personality on Broadway and in nightclubs during the twenties. She achieved fame as one of the first torch singers, but her attempts at film stardom were not successful and she ultimately died of alcoholism. She starred in the minor picture *Roadhouse Nights*, a rather typical early sound gangster movie.

Roadhouse Nights (Paramount, 1930).

Morgan, Michele (b. 1920)

Actress. Born Simone Roussel in Nevilly-sur-Siene, France, Morgan achieved instant stardom at eighteen in Marcel Carne's masterpiece *Quai des Brumes* (France, 1938). She was an unconventional star, noted for her aloof, quiet performances and wonderful expressive eyes. Yet, despite her diminutive size and waif-like figure, she was also one of the most sensual actresses of her time. Her popularity in Europe won her a contract with Warner Bros., who did not know what to do with her. She missed her chance at real American stardom when she lost the lead in *Casablanca* (Warner Bros., 1943) to Ingrid Bergman. However, she did give a number of good performances in some interesting minor American movies, including the gangster thriller *The Chase*. Shortly thereafter, she returned to France, where she was immediately re-established as a major star. Indeed, for many Frenchmen, she is an icon comparable only to Hollywood's biggest female stars, Greta Garbo, Joan Crawford and Bette Davis.

The Chase (United Artists, 1948).

Morris, Chester (1901–1970)

Actor. Born John Chester Brooks Morris to a theatrical family, Morris was a veteran of the stage when he became an overnight star in *Alibi*, one of the most successful of the early sound gangster movies. The hulking, rather sinister actor was then typecast in gangster roles. Indeed he was one of the first stars of the genre. Unfortunately, he is all but forgotten today, largely because he was relegated to minor movies after 1930, when his popularity proved fleeting. His most important performance in the genre was in *The Big House*, in which he starred as the forger who is dehumanized by his experiences in prison. Of his other gangster pictures, the most interesting is *Blind Alley*, in which he played a gangster who holds a family hostage, slowly realizing his psychological motivations while under the influence of one of his hostages, a psychiatrist. Morris' performance is very good. He is one of the genre's most interesting minor icons.

Alibi (United Artists, 1929). *The Big House* (MGM, 1930). *Public Hero #1* (MGM, 1935). *Law of the Underworld* (RKO, 1938). *Blind Alley* (Columbia, 1939).

Morrow, Vic (1932–1982)

Actor. Vic Morrow is probably best known as the accident victim of the *Twilight Zone: The Movie* tragedy, and as the father of actress Jennifer Jason

Leigh. Born in the Bronx, he made his screen debut as one of the young toughs in *The Blackboard Jungle* (MGM, 1955). He was most often seen as a street tough or criminal. In *Portrait of a Mobster*, he makes his only appearance in the gangster genre.

Portrait of a Mobster (Warner Bros., 1961).

Mostel, Zero (1915–1977)

Character actor. One of the most talented comic actors of his time, Mostel was the son of a rabbi. Originally a painter, he was attracted to acting during the thirties, and first made a name for himself as a standup comic. His film career began in the early forties, when he generally played supporting comic parts in musicals and comedies. His film career was interrupted by service during World War II, after which he returned to screen work and proved to be an intense dramatic actor, even playing villains in several movies. He played a gang boss in the Humphrey Bogart vehicle *The Enforcer*. His career was cut short during the McCarthy witch hunt and subsequent blacklist of the early fifties, when Mostel was accused of being a communist.

The Enforcer (Warner Bros., 1951).

The Mouthpiece (Warner Bros., 1932). 90 mins.

Directors: James Flood and Elliott Nugent. *Screenplay*: Earl Baldwin, *story by* Frank Collins. *Director of Photography*: Barney McGill. *Editor*: George Amy.

Cast: Warren William (Vincent Day), Sidney Fox (Celia), Aline Mac-Mahon (Miss Hickey), William Janney (John), John Wray (Barton). *With*: Polly Walters, Ralph Ince, J. Carrol Naish, Morgan Wallace, Noel Francis.

Vincent Day was once a successful district attorney until he sent an innocent man to his death via the executioner. He becomes a defense lawyer specializing in mob cases, but his initial good intentions are hampered by his greed. He often uses questionable techniques and even bribes to defend his clients. He falls for a beautiful young typist, Celia, who spurns his advances. Eventually, when one of his mob clients is sent to prison, his associates kill him as an act of revenge.

Loosely based on the life and career of New York attorney William J. Fallon, *The Mouthpiece* is an interesting variation on the gangster themes of the early thirties. The film stars Warren William, a dapper, competent actor who was briefly popular as a romantic lead during the early thirties. A modest success, it was later remade as *Illegal* with Edward G. Robinson as the dishonest attorney.

Mulhall, Jack (1888–1979)

Actor. Born in Wappingers Falls, New York, Mulhall was a stage actor before entering the movies in 1913. Tall and handsome, he played lead roles into the mid-twenties and character parts until the late fifties. He starred in the minor early gangster picture *Dark Streets*, in a unique dual role as two brothers, one an honest cop, the other a violent gangster.

Dark Streets (First National, 1929).

Muni, Paul (1896–1967)

Actor. Born Muni Weisenfreund in Lemberg, Poland, Paul Muni was the son of a theatrical family. He first appeared on stage in New York's thriving Yiddish theaters, where he proved a charismatic performer. He made his film debut in 1928, and, in his fourth film, *I Am a Fugitive from a Chain Gang*, Muni gave a sensitive portrayal of a man driven to crime by a ruthless society. He was nominated for an Academy Award for his performance in that role. He also starred as the physically and psychologically scarred gangster Tony Camonte (based on the real life Al Capone) in the classic

Scarface. His final contribution to the genre was in the minor *Doctor Socrates*, as a physician who becomes involved with gangsters after they break into his home.

I Am a Fugitive from a Chain Gang (Warner Bros., 1932). *Scarface* (United Artists, 1932). *Doctor Socrates* (Warner Bros., 1935).

Munsey, Captain (Fictional character)

For a number of reasons, prison has been the setting for a number of gangster pictures. In *Brute Force* (Universal, 1947), the reason was partly didactic: the film's director, Jules Dassin, was interested in exposing the inhumane conditions of America's prisons. That inhumanity was memorably embodied in Captain Munsey (Hume Cronyn), a prison guard who preys on the inmates, exploiting them, torturing and even killing those who do not do as he wishes. Eventually, during a prisoner breakout, Munsey is killed by angry prisoners.

Captain Munsey is a fairly remarkable character in Hollywood's golden age; authorities were very rarely portrayed as corrupt, and he represented a new, and sadly, more honest portrait of the police and government officials that emerged in the *films noir* of the forties and fifties.

The Musketeers of Pig Alley (Biograph, 1912). Approx. 15 mins.

Scenarist and Director: D. W. Griffith.

Cast: Lillian Gish, Walter Miller, Harry Carey, Elmer Booth, Lionel Barrymore, Jack Dillon.

A young girl (Lillian Gish) is attracted to a handsome hoodlum (Elmer Booth) but remains faithful to her husband (Walter Miller). When the husband gets mixed up with the law, the hoodlum helps him out of his scrape, and he is happily reunited with his wife.

The Musketeers of Pig Alley, a one-reel short, is important as the first

contemporary gangster movie. Using an effective documentary style, director D. W. Griffith used real locations to create a crisp, timely melodrama. It is interesting also as a historical document of the developing criminal underworld, then mainly consisting of loose bands of street thugs who were forming the organized gangs that would soon develop into the Italian, Irish and Jewish gangs—the "Mafia," as the Italians were called—that still dominate organized crime in the United States.

Musuraca, Nicholas (1895–1993)

Cinematographer. A veteran cinematographer whose film career began in the early twenties, Musuraca did not demonstrate any extraordinarily inventive style until the forties. As a contract cinematographer at RKO, he became a protégé of producer Val Lewton, who encouraged his experimentation, and Musuraca emerged as one of the great craftsmen of the era. His work for Lewton on the horror classics *Cat People* (RKO, 1942), *The Seventh Victim* (RKO, 1943) and *Curse of the Cat People* (RKO, 1944) had a profound influence on his contemporaries. His moody lighting, rainswept sets, and night scenes are both sensual and menacing, and epitomize the early *film noir* style. Musuraca is one of the genre's greatest talents, and his work on films like *Out of the Past* has never been surpassed. Both *Law of the Underworld* and *Lady Scarface* predate this great period, but both demonstrate Musuraca's mature, expressionist influenced style in individual scenes.

Law of the Underworld (RKO, 1938). *Lady Scarface* (RKO, 1941). *Out of the Past* (RKO, 1947).

My Six Convicts (Columbia, 1952). 104 mins.

Producer: Stanley Kramer. *Director*: Hugo Fregonese. *Screenplay*: Michael Blankfort, *story by* Donald Powell

Wilson. *Director of Photography*: Guy Roe. *Music*: Dimitri Tiomkin. *Art Director*: Edward Ilou. *Editor*: Gene Havlick.

Cast: Millard Mitchell (James Connie), Gilbert Roland (Punch Pinero), John Beal (Doc), Marshall Thompson (Blivens Scott), Henry Morgan (Dawson). *With*: Alf Kjellin, Jay Adler, Regis Toomey, Fay Roope, John Marley.

Doc, a young prison psychologist, recounts his experiences treating inmates in a high security prison. With the aid of James Connie, a hardened criminal and safecracker who befriends him, Doc gains the confidence of several other convicts and helps rehabilitate them.

A modest movie, *My Six Convicts* differs from similar gangster prison movies with its decidedly humorous, compassionate, and thoughtful approach to the subject. In the mode of producer Stanley Kramer, there was a liberal lesson involved; in this case, that convicts can be rehabilitated under the right circumstances.

Naish, J. Carrol (1900–1973)

Character actor. The seemingly perennial Naish was a veteran stage actor when his film career began in 1926. For the next four decades he was one of the busiest character actors in American movies, playing characters of all nationalities, generally in small roles. His handful of roles in gangster pictures were always as gang henchmen.

King of Alcatraz (Paramount, 1938). *The Black Hand* (MGM, 1950). *New York Confidential* (Warner Bros., 1955).

The Naked Street (United Artists, 1955). 84 mins.

Producer: Edward Small. *Director*: Maxwell Shane. *Screenplay*: Maxwell Shane and Leo Katcher. *Director of Photography*: Floyd Crosby. *Music*: Emil Newman. *Art Director*: Ted Haworth. *Editor*: Grant Whytock.

Cast: Farley Granger (Nicky Bradna), Anthony Quinn (Phil Regal), Anne Bancroft (Rosalie Regalzyk), Peter Graves (Joe McFarland), Else Neft (Mrs. Regalzyk). *With*: Jerry Paris, Frank Sully, John Dennis, Angela Stevens, Joe Terry, Mario Siletti.

Phil Regal, a gang boss, engineers the release from prison of an underling, Nicky Bradna, when Bradna's girlfriend (and Regal's sister) proves to be pregnant. Bradna marries the girl, but the baby dies and he proves to be a sadistic husband. Regal frames Bradna for murder, and he is convicted and sentenced to die. As an act of revenge, Bradna tells the authorities and the press about Regal's activities, eventually bringing about the gangster's downfall.

Although it is not a particularly important film, *The Naked Street* is well made, notable chiefly for its strong performance by Anthony Quinn. The film's writer and director, Maxwell Shane, was a veteran screenwriter of hard-boiled "B" thrillers, a kind of second string Phillip Yordan.

The Narrow Margin (RKO, 1952). 71 mins.

Producer: Stanley Rubin. *Director*: Richard Fleischer. *Screenplay*: Earl Felton, *story by* Martin Goldsmith and Jack Leonard. *Director of Photography*: George E. Diskant. *Art Directors*: Albert S. D'Agostino and Jack Okey. *Editor*: Robert Swink.

Cast: Charles McGraw (Walter Brown), Marie Windsor (Mrs. Neil), Jacqueline White (Ann Sinclair), Gordon Gebert (Tommy Sinclair), Queenie Leonard (Mrs. Troil), Don Beddoe (Guy Forbes). *With*: David Clarke, Peter Virgo, Paul Maxey, Harry Harvey.

Detective Walter Brown and his partner, Gus Forbes, are assigned to escort Mrs. Neil, a racketeer's widow, by train to appear as a witness against organized crime. Forbes is immediately killed by gangsters. Brown feels nothing but contempt for the woman, but feels compelled by professional duty to protect her. While on the train he befriends Ann Sinclair, a refined woman, who is traveling with her son. It is only after Mrs. Neil is assassinated by the gangsters that he is informed by his superiors (who were not sure if he was corrupt or not) that Sinclair is the real gangster's widow and government witness. He manages to deliver her safely to her destination.

The Narrow Margin deserves its reputation as one of the best "B" *noirs*. Its plot is only serviceable, but it unfolds at a rapid pace, interspersed with violent action. It gave Marie Windsor and Charles McGraw good roles, and director Richard Fleischer created a taut, exciting gangster versus cop thriller. It remains a minor classic with a devoted cult following.

Nebenzal, Seymour (1899–1951)

Producer. Nebenzal was one of the most prominent producers in Germany during the twenties and early thirties, producing some of Fritz Lang's most important films of that era. His Hollywood career was disappointing, devoted exclusively to "B" movies. The gangster *noir The Chase* is one of his more interesting productions.

The Chase (United Artists, 1946).

Neill, Roy William (1890–1946)

Director. Neill, a veteran of the film business who began his career in 1915 as an assistant to producer and director Thomas Ince (a rival of D. W. Griffith), was a very good director of "B" movies. His single gangster picture, *Eyes of the Underworld*, is a well made thriller in his simple, visceral style.

Eyes of the Underworld (Universal, 1942).

Never Steal Anything Small (Universal, 1959). 94 mins.

Producer: Aaron Rosenberg. *Director*: Charles Lederer. *Screenplay*: Charles Lederer, based on the play

Devil's Hornpipe by Maxwell Anderson and Rouben Mamoulian. *Director of Photography*: Harold Lipstein. *Music*: Allie Wrubel. *Art Director*: Alexander Golitzen. *Editor*: Russ Schoengarth.

Cast: James Cagney (Jake MacIlaney), Shirley Jones (Linda Cabot), Roger Smith (Dan Cabot), Cara Williams (Winnipeg), Nehemiah Persoff (Finelli). *With*: Horace McMahon, Virginia Vincent, Jack Albertson, Royal Dano, Robert J. Wilkie.

Jake MacIlaney, a tough stevedore, desires another man's wife, Linda Cabot, and tries to have a false corruption charge placed on her husband, Dan. Meanwhile, he rises to head the local dock worker's union through bribes, intimidation, and perjury. Eventually, however, his schemes are defeated and he is brought to justice.

Written and directed by Charles Lederer, one of the most important screenwriters of Hollywood's golden age, *Never Steal Anything Small* was a less ambitious version of *On the Waterfront* (Columbia, 1954). Unfortunately it was not one of Lederer's more inspired works, and Cagney's performance is lackluster, marking a disappointing finale to his work in the genre.

New York City

As the entry point for most of the immigrants who came to the United States, beginning in the mid–nineteenth century, New York City attracted a diverse group of people, mostly European, and their traditions. Inevitably, criminals accompanied the true economic and political refugees, finding prey among their fellow immigrants and the citizens of their new country.

While many immigrants quickly moved out of the city, New York became the permanent home for quite a number, and they congregated with people from their own countries or of similar backgrounds. Thus, tenements and whole communities were built around Jewish, Irish, Chinese and Italian immigrants, and these populations have remained largely exclusive to these various cultures until today. Likewise, organized gangs formed in these communities, at first staying within their own borders and committing mostly petty crimes—usually extortion. But as the population of the city grew, so did the opportunities for crime. The street gangs also grew, becoming more sophisticated and expanding their territories into other neighborhoods. By the first part of the twentieth century, the Irish mob was the strongest in the city, but several violent wars with the Italian Mafia weakened them considerably. As a result much of the city's organized crime since the early twenties has been controlled by the Italian Mafia.

By the early twentieth century, organized crime in New York City had already become part of national myth. Their exploits had been recounted in countless short stories, novels, plays and even movies. D. W. Griffith's *The Musketeers of Pig Alley* (Biograph, 1912), one of the very first gangster pictures, gives an interesting portrait of the New York mobster at that time. While most of the mob related headlines of the twenties centered around Chicago's gang wars and its mob chieftain Al Capone (a native New Yorker), the various gangs in New York went discreetly (relatively speaking) about their business, while continuing to inspire innumerable gangster films, beginning most notably with Josef von Sternberg's seminal *Underworld* (Paramount, 1927). Other notable films with New York settings include *The Docks of New York* (Paramount, 1928), *I Cover the Waterfront* (United Artists, 1933), *Dead End* (United Artists, 1937), *Angels with Dirty Faces* (Warner Bros., 1938), *The Roaring Twenties* (Warner Bros., 1939), *Body and Soul* (United Artists, 1947), *The Black Hand*

(MGM, 1950), *On the Waterfront* (Columbia, 1954), *The French Connection* (20th Century-Fox, 1971), *Across 120th Street* (United Artists, 1972), *The Godfather* (Paramount, 1972) and its sequel *The Godfather Part II* (Paramount, 1974), *The Brink's Job* (Universal, 1978) and *The Cotton Club* (Orion, 1984).

New York Confidential (Warner Bros., 1955). 87 mins.

Producer: Clarence Greene. *Director*: Russell Rouse. *Screenplay*: Clarence Greene and Russell Rouse. *Director of Photography*: Edward Fitzgerald. *Music*: Joseph Mullendore. *Editor*: Grant Whytock.

Cast: Broderick Crawford (Charles Lupo), Richard Conte (Nick Magellan), Marilyn Maxwell (Iris Palmer), Anne Bancroft (Katherine Lupo), J. Carrol Naish (Ben Dagajanian), Onslow Stevens (Johnny Achilles). *With*: Barry Kelley, Celia Lovsky, Herbert Heyes, Steven Geray, Bill Phillips, Henry Kulky.

Charles Lupo rises to head a New York City crime syndicate. He is dominated by his mother and obsessed with his daughter, Katherine. When he tries to marry Katherine off to his sadistic lieutenant, Nick Magellan, she commits suicide. His empire begins to crumble, and when his fellow mobsters believe he is endangering their operations by his increasing carelessness, they have him murdered.

A minor gangster picture, *New York Confidential* brings together two of the genre's icons, Broderick Crawford and Richard Conte, into a neatly packaged melodrama. The performances are good all around, but the film lacks real power and substance.

Newfield, Sam (1899–1964)

Director. Newfield, born Neufeld, was one of the most prolific film directors in Hollywood history. He directed several dozen features for Republic and Producers Releasing Corporation, whose head, Sigmund Neufeld, was his older brother. Few of his movies, the vast majority of which are quicky Westerns, have any artistic merit. His single gangster picture, *The Black Raven*, is a typical PRC production featuring a single, shadowy set to hide its cheapness and a brisk pace to cover its poorly written screenplay. Yet, it can be claimed as one of the best of the studio's then contemporary thrillers, which should give some indication how truly atrocious the majority of PRC's films are.

The Black Raven (Producers Releasing Corporation, 1943).

Newman, Alfred (1901–1970)

Composer. Newman, a former child prodigy, was one of the most prolific and brilliant Hollywood composers and arrangers. He won seven Academy Awards for his scores for such classics as *Gunga Din* (RKO, 1939), *Tin Pan Alley* (20th Century–Fox, 1940) and *The Song of Bernadette* (20th Century–Fox, 1943). His score for *Dead End* is equally superb.

Dead End (United Artists, 1937).

Newman, Joseph M. (b. 1909)

Director. Newman was a competent director of "B" movies of all types. Probably his best known film is *This Island Earth* (Universal, 1955), an interesting science-fiction movie with an antiwar theme. *The George Raft Story*, his penultimate film, is an alleged biography of the actor and his underworld connections, but it is more fantasy than truth, and has little to reveal about the world of organized crime in the mid–twentieth century.

The George Raft Story (Allied Artists, 1961).

Newman, Paul (b. 1925)

Actor. The laconic, blue-eyed Newman was compared to Marlon Brando early in his career, although in retrospect he had neither the intensity nor the charisma of Brando. Still, he slowly developed his own style that was understated and reserved. At the height of his popularity during the late sixties and early seventies, he was successfully teamed with the equally photogenic Robert Redford in two films, *Butch Cassidy and the Sundance Kid* (20th Century–Fox, 1969) and *The Sting*, both directed by George Roy Hill. The latter is famous as a tongue-in-cheek heist picture with a Damon Runyon-esque flavor, starring Newman and Redford as the perpetrators of an elaborate con job.

The Sting (Universal, 1973).

Newman's Law (Universal, 1974). 92 mins.

Producer: Richard Irving. *Director*: Richard Heffron. *Screenplay*: Anthony Wilson. *Director of Photography*: Vilis Lapenieks. *Music*: Robert Prince. *Art Director*: Alexander A. Mayer. *Editor*: John Duman.

Cast: George Peppard (Vince Newman), Roger Robinson (Garry), Eugene Roche (Reardon), Gordon Pinsent (Eastman), Abe Vigoda (Dellanzia). *With*: Louis Zorich, Michael Lerner, Victor Campos, Mel Stewart, Jack Murdock, David Spielberg.

Two police detectives, Vince Newman and Garry, his black partner, arrest a drug pusher. The arrest helps expose a drug ring. Newman, however, is framed for drug possession and realizing he cannot rely on the rules of law because the police are as corrupt as the gangsters who have bribed them, he and his partner use their own methods to break up the gang of drug pushers.

A police procedural in the style of *The French Connection* (20th Century–Fox, 1971), *Newman's Law* combines the detective and gangster genres. While it is not a classic, it is an entertaining, violent thriller, with an especially good performance by George Peppard as the Dirty Harry–like police detective.

Niblo, Fred, Jr. (1903-1973)
Screenwriter. Niblo's father, Fred Sr., was a leading silent film director. The younger Niblo was sporadically active as a screenwriter, generally of "B" thrillers. One of his most important screenplays was the prison-gangster melodrama *The Criminal Code*, cowritten with Seton I. Miller and directed by Howard Hawks. He also cowrote a minor gangster picture, *Hell's Kitchen*, one of the more obscure of the Dead End Kids programmers.
The Criminal Code (Columbia, 1931). *Hell's Kitchen* (Warner Bros., 1939).

Nichols, Dudley (1895-1960)
Screenwriter. After experience as a journalist and critic, Nichols began a distinguished career as a screenwriter in the late twenties. For more than two decades he was one of the most important screenwriters, writing or cowriting a number of classic movies. He is probably best known as one of John Ford's key collaborators of the thirties, generally adapting semipoetic but tough novels and short stories: *The Lost Patrol* (RKO, 1934), *The Informer* (RKO, 1935) and *Stagecoach* (United Artists, 1939). He worked on a single gangster movie, *Hush Money*, but his talents were better served by pseudo-literary subjects.
Hush Money (Fox, 1931).

Nicholson, Jack (b. 1937)
Actor. A charismatic actor in the Brando style, Nicholson might be as famous for his off screen antics as his on screen performances. He had experience as a stage and television actor in the late fifties, but his idiosyncratic style typecast him as an eccentric in mostly minor movies until *Easy Rider* (Columbia, 1969) made him a star. He subsequently starred in some of the best movies of the seventies and eighties. In the brilliant satire *Prizzi's Honor*, directed by his friend John Huston, Nicholson gave one of his best

performances as a dense hit man who meets his match in a pretty hit woman.
Prizzi's Honor (20th Century-Fox, 1985).

Nigh, William (1881-1955)
Director. Although his directing career began at MGM in the late twenties, he spent most of his two decades as a director making "B" movies for Republic, Monogram and Producers Releasing Corporation. He specialized in unambitious Westerns. His style was utilitarian but occasionally inspired. His *Four Walls* is one of the earliest prison-gangster films and is quite good despite the usual technical limitations of early sound movies.
Four Walls (MGM, 1928).

Night After Night (Paramount, 1932). 70 mins.
Producer: William Le Baron. *Director*: Archie Mayo. *Screenplay*: Vincent Lawrence, based on the novel *Single Night* by Louis Bromfield. *Director of Photography*: Ernest Haller. *Art Director*: Hans Dreier.
Cast: George Raft (Joe Anton), Constance Cummings (Jerry Healy), Wynne Gibson (Iris), Mae West (Maudie Triplett), Alison Skipworth (Mrs. Mabel Jellyman), Roscoe Karns (Leo). *With*: Al Hill, Louis Calhern, Harry Wallace, Dink Templeton.
Joe Anton, an ex-prizefighter, and his valet, Leo, run a successful night club during the Prohibition era. When his affair with a floozy, Iris Dawn, ends badly, he hires a teacher, Mrs. Jellyman, to instruct him in the ways of proper society. He then begins seeing Jerry Healy, a society girl. When a rival and fellow gangster causes him to lose his club, he discovers that Jerry loves him for himself and not his money.
Probably best known as the picture which introduced Mae West—as a society dame with a past and a sharp tongue—*Night After Night* also made George Raft a star after he had labored in several notable supporting roles,

Anne Bancroft comforts Aldo Ray in Jacques Tourneur's unjustly neglected gangster thriller, *Nightfall.*

including the coin tossing gangster in *Scarface* (United Artists, 1932). This movie is a modest romantic melodrama with gangster overtones, but it succeeds because of an excellent, witty screenplay and the charisma of a good cast at their best.

Nightfall (Columbia, 1957). 78 mins. *Producer*: Ted Richmond. *Director*: Jacques Tourneur. *Screenplay*: Stirling Silliphant, based on the novel by David Goodis. *Director of Photography*: Burnett Guffey. *Music*: George Duning. *Art Director*: Ross Bellah. *Editor*: William A. Lyon.

Cast: Aldo Ray (James Vanning), Brian Keith (John), Anne Bancroft (Marie Gardner), Jocelyn Brando (Laura Fraser), James Gregory (Ben Fraser), Rudy Bond (Red). *With*: Frank Albertson, George Cisar, Eddie

McLean, Lillian Culver, Maya Van Horn.

In flashback, the misadventures of Jim Vanning are recalled. While on a hunting trip, he and his best friend, a doctor, encounter a traffic accident on a mountain road. Stopping to help, they are taken hostage by the two occupants of the car, John and Red, who crashed while escaping from a robbery. They shoot and kill the doctor and wound Vanning. Believing he is dead, they steal his car and accidentally take the doctor's black bag, leaving the bag full of money behind. Vanning crawls to safety, hides the bag of money in a snow bank, and goes into hiding, fearing he will be accused of killing the doctor, whose wife had publicly made advances toward him. He is soon pursued by John and Red and an insurance investigator, Ben Fraser. Now in the present, Vanning teams with a barmaid he falls in love with, and together they follow Fraser, John and Red to a ghost town after the two criminals have recovered the bag of stolen money. Red kills his partner while arguing over the money. Vanning and the gangster fight, and Red climbs aboard a snowplow to try and run over Fraser and Marie, but Vanning pulls him from the cab. Red falls under the snowplow and dies screaming.

Highly regarded by fans of director Jacques Tourneur, who directed *Out of the Past* (RKO, 1947), *Nightfall* is a superior *noir* thriller. Based on a novel by hard-boiled writer David Goodis, it is directed with some of the same flair as Tourneur's earlier masterpiece. The flashback technique was also an element of the earlier film. If it has a fault, this minor classic suffers mainly from a "B" cast. Otherwise, it is an overlooked gem that deserves renewed interest.

Nitti, Walter Frank

The real life right-hand man of Al Capone, Nitti was an enforcer (i.e., hit man) who assassinated Capone's enemies. Nitti was a thorn in the side of F.B.I. agent Eliot Ness during the twenties. Contrary to the version of events portrayed in Brian DePalma's *The Untouchables* (Paramount, 1986), Nitti was not killed by Ness, but in fact inherited leadership of the Chicago mob when Capone was sent to prison for income tax evasion. Nitti also went to prison for a while on a similar conviction and later retired from his criminal activities. He was played with great glee by Bruce Gordon in *The Scarface Mob* (Cari Releasing, 1962) and *The Untouchables* television series, and by Billy Draco in DePalma's film.

Nixon, Marion (1904–1983)

Actress. An attractive, diminutive woman, Nixon was a moderately popular star of the twenties and, like so many stars of the silent era, found it difficult to make the transition to sound. Her career came to an end in 1933, but not before she starred in a few early sound films, including the minor gangster movie *The Pay Off*.

The Pay Off (RKO, 1930).

Nolan, Lloyd (1902–1986)

Actor. Born in San Francisco, Nolan was a seaman before he began acting on the stage in 1927. A diminutive, fairhaired man, Nolan was also a charismatic and intense actor of the hardboiled type. He played supporting roles in "A" pictures and leads in "B" movies. He is one of the genre's minor icons, appearing in more gangster movies (nearly all "B" titles) than any other actor. He was also popular in a series of crime thrillers during the thirties, generally playing heroes.

G-Men (First National, 1935). *Stolen Harmony* (Paramount, 1937). *King of Gamblers* (Paramount, 1937). *Dangerous to Know* (Paramount, 1938). *Hunted Man* (Paramount, 1938). *King of Alcatraz* (Paramount, 1938). *The Tip-Off Girls* (Paramount, 1938). *Gangs of Chicago* (Republic, 1940). *Johnny Apollo* (20th Century–Fox, 1940). *Buy Me That Town* (Paramount, 1941).

Nolan, Mary (1905–1948)

Actress. Born Mary Imogene Robertson in New York, Nolan first achieved popularity as a Ziegfeld girl in the mid-twenties. She was a popular personality of the early sound era, but her career faltered in the mid-thirties due to severe drug addiction. She costarred opposite Edward G. Robinson in the minor *Outside the Law*, released just before his breakthrough in *Little Caesar* (First National, 1930).

Outside the Law (Universal, 1930).

Nosseck, Max (1902–1972)

Director. Nosseck was another refugee from Hitler's Germany. Already an established director in his native country, he spent most of the thirties making features in Portugal, France and Spain before moving to Hollywood in 1940. Over the next twenty years, he directed a handful of "B" movies, generally in an excessively pseudo-expressionist style. Two of his best American films are gangster movies. Of these, the most important is *Dillinger*, a dynamic thriller shot on a very low budget and appropriating robbery footage from Fritz Lang's *You Only Live Once* (United Artists, 1937). The less well known *The Hoodlum* is equally worthy of praise, although in the final analysis, both are minor films.

Dillinger (Monogram, 1945). *The Hoodlum* (United Artists, 1951).

Nugent, Elliott (1899–1980)
Director. In the twenties, Nugent was a well known and respected Broadway personality as an actor, producer and playwright. However, he found his greatest success as a film director, beginning in the late twenties and continuing successfully until the mid-fifties. His gangster picture, *The Mouthpiece*, is atypical, as Nugent was really an expert comedy director, making a number of classics in that genre.

The Mouthpiece (Warner Bros., 1932; codirector).

Oates, Warren (1928–1982)
Character actor. The dynamic, talented Oates was born in Depoy, Kentucky, and moved to New York in the fifties to try his hand at acting. Eventually he became an established actor, appearing on television and in films. His hardened features made him a natural villain. He starred as John Dillinger in the second film based on the notorious gangster's life. He also played real life gangster Eddie Diamond, brother of Jack "Legs" Diamond in the "B" picture *The Rise and Fall of Legs Diamond*.

The Rise and Fall of Legs Diamond (Warner Bros., 1960). *Dillinger* (American International, 1973).

O'Brien, Edmond (1915–1985)
Actor. Originally a stage actor, O'Brien first achieved popularity as one of the members of Orson Welles' Mercury Theatre troup. He left the group for a film career in 1939 and, although he never became a full-fledged star, he was a good actor and gave many excellent performances in a variety of movies. He was most often seen as a second lead or in supporting roles during the forties and fifties, generally as a gangster. Of his five gangster movies, the most important are *The Killers* and *White Heat*. In the former he had his most unique role in the genre, as an insurance investigator who unravels a mystery surrounding a mob assassination.

The Killers (Universal, 1946). *White Heat* (Warner Bros., 1949). *711 Ocean Drive* (Columbia, 1950). *Pete Kelly's Blues* (Warner Bros., 1955). *Lucky Luciano* (Avco-Embassy, 1974).

O'Brien, Pat (1899–1983)
Character actor. The archetypal Irishman in American movies, O'Brien was born in Wisconsin to an Irish Catholic family and is probably best remembered today for his numerous portrayals of Catholic priests. He played a priest in *Angels with Dirty Faces*, one of his best performances. He played a variety of good and bad guys in his other gangster movies, all "B" pictures.

Public Enemy's Wife (Warner Bros., 1936). *Angels with Dirty Faces* (Warner Bros., 1938). *San Quentin* (Warner Bros., 1938). *Castle on the Hudson* (Warner Bros., 1940). *Inside Detroit* (Columbia, 1955).

Obzina, Martin
Art director. Former architect Obzina joined Universal in the late thirties and became one of the studio's leading art directors in the forties. He had a style that was influenced by gothic horror (he worked on many of Universal's best horror films of the

forties) and expressionism. His work on *The Killers* is among the most imaginative of the era.

The Killers (Universal, 1946).

Odds Against Tomorrow (United Artists, 1959). 96 mins.
Producer and Director: Robert Wise. *Screenplay*: John O. Killens, based on the novel by William P. McGivern. *Director of Photography*: Joseph Brun. *Music*: John Lewis. *Art Director*: Leo Kerz. *Editor*: Dede Allen.

Cast: Harry Belafonte (Johnny Ingram), Robert Ryan (Earl Slater), Shelley Winters (Lorry), Ed Begley (Dave Burke), Gloria Grahame (Helen), Will Kuluva (Bacco), Richard Bright (Coco). *With*: Lou Gallo, Fred J. Scollay, Carmen DeLavalade, Mae Barnes.

Earl Slater, a racist ex-con, is asked by Dave Burke, a cop who has been dismissed from the force for corruption, to join in his plan to rob a small-town bank in upstate New York. Johnny Ingram, a black singer, reluctantly joins the gang when his girlfriend is threatened by a gangster for an unpaid debt. The robbery fails from the beginning. Burke is killed. Earl and Johnny, bound together by fate despite their antagonisms, try to escape but the police chase them into an oil storage area. When they get into an argument, the two robbers start shooting at each other, accidentally igniting the oil tanks. The next day, someone sorting through the wreckage finds the two charred bodies. "Which is which?" he asks. "Take your pick," another person replies.

Sometimes listed as the last *film noir* of the initial cycle, *Odds Against Tomorrow* is a didactic thriller with racial overtones. While its theme was topical, the film is still a well made, suspenseful gangster thriller, distinguished by some taut direction and fine performances.

Odell, Cary
Art director. Long associated with Columbia, Odell worked on some of the studio's best films. His work is imaginative, composed of everything from *film noir* to science fiction. His set designs for *The Mob* are appropriately claustrophobic and menacing.

The Mob (Columbia, 1951).

Odell, Robert (1896–1979)
Art director. Born in Los Angeles, Odell studied architecture before entering films in 1919. He worked for a number of studios before joining Paramount in the thirties. He specialized in costume dramas and adventures but also worked on contemporary films, including a single gangster drama in collaboration with Hans Dreier.

King of Gamblers (Paramount, 1937).

O'Donnell, Cathy (1923–1970)
Actress. Born Ann Steely in Siluria, Alabama, O'Donnell was a delicate, conventional beauty, probably best known as the sweet natured Wilma Cameron, the girlfriend of a disabled war veteran in William Wyler's classic *The Best Years of Our Lives* (United Artists, 1946). However, her best performance was in the classic gangster *noir They Live by Night*, as the character based on Bonnie Parker. Although a talented actress, O'Donnell did not become a major star and is all but forgotten today.

They Live by Night (RKO, 1948).

O'Keefe, Dennis (1908–1968)
Character actor. Born Edward Flanagan in Iowa, O'Keefe was a vaudevillian as a child and juvenile and later worked briefly as a scriptwriter, mainly on Hal Roach's *Our Gang* shorts. He also played small parts in movies until 1937 when Clark Gable helped him get a contract at MGM. He subsequently played tough but sympathetic heroes and second leads in "B" movies. He is one of the genre's minor icons.

Lady Scarface (RKO, 1941). *T-Men*

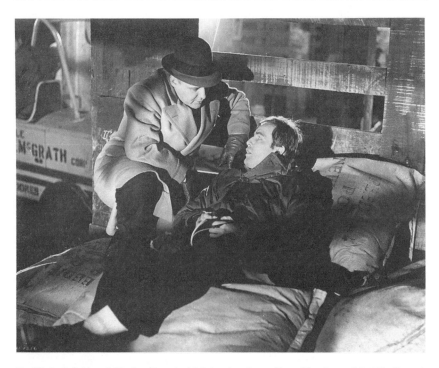

Rod Steiger (left) and Marlon Brando (right) as brothers affected by the mob in Elia Kazan's moody classic *On the Waterfront*.

(Eagle-Lion, 1947). *Raw Deal* (Eagle-Lion, 1948). *Chicago Syndicate* (Columbia, 1955). *Inside Detroit* (Columbia, 1955). *Las Vegas Shakedown* (Allied Artists, 1955).

Okey, Jack

Art director. A formidable talent, Okey worked for Warner Bros.–First National in the thirties and RKO in the forties. An important figure in the developing hard-boiled style at Warner Bros. during the early thirties, he worked on only one of the studio's gangster movies, but it is a classic: *I Am a Fugitive from a Chain Gang*. His influence at RKO was even more profound, and he was responsible for the designs of many of the studio's classic *films noir*, including the additional two listed below.

I Am a Fugitive from a Chain Gang

(First National, 1932). *Out of the Past* (RKO, 1947). *The Racket* (RKO, 1951).

On the Waterfront (Columbia, 1954). 108 mins.

Producer: Sam Spiegel. *Director*: Elia Kazan. *Screenplay*: Budd Schulberg, based on articles by Malcolm Johnson. *Director of Photography*: Boris Kaufmann. *Music*: Leonard Bernstein. *Art Director*: Richard Day. *Editor*: Gene Mildord.

Cast: Marlon Brando (Terry Malloy), Karl Malden (Father Barry), Lee J. Cobb (Johnny Friendly), Rod Steiger (Charley Malloy), Pat Henning (Kayo Dugan), Eva Marie Saint (Edie Doyle). *With*: Leif Erickson, James Westerfield, Tony Galento, Tami Mauriello, John Hamilton.

Terry Malloy, a dock worker, dreams of being a champion boxer. Although

A happy moment before the violence in Sergio Leone's epic *Once Upon a Time in America*. The smiling gangsters are, left to right, James Woods, Robert De Niro, Bill Forsythe and Burt Young.

he has the talent to fulfill that wish, fate intervenes and he never achieves his goal. His older brother Charley is a corrupt lawyer, owned by crooked union bosses. The union is controlled by a gangster, Johnny Friendly, who takes an interest in Terry. He sets up the dimwitted boxer in the murder of an anti-union dock worker. Through his affair with the dead man's sister, Edie, Terry learns of the insidious control the racketeers have on the union and its members. Through Edie's influence and that of Father Barry, Terry agrees to help expose the corrupt union bosses. Charley Malloy is killed by the mobsters when he cannot control Terry. Terry agrees to testify at the Crime Commission, but not before confronting Friendly. In the ensuing fisticuffs on the docks, Terry almost meets his match, but he succeeds in beating up the syndicate boss and earns the respect of his fellow workers.

Probably most famous for its "I coulda been a contender" scene between Marlon Brando and Rod Steiger, *On the Waterfront* is a classic exposé of union rackets, a favorite theme of the fifties. The film's didactic theme is tempered somewhat by its high style (reminiscent of *film noir*) and by its extraordinary performances. It is quite effective and moving, and sadly its topic remains relevant even today.

Once Upon a Time in America (Warner Bros., 1984). 135 mins.
    Producer: Arnon Milchan. *Director*: Sergio Leone. *Screenplay*: Leonardo Benvenuti, Piero De Bernardo, Erico Medioli, Franco Arcalli, Franco Ferrini and Sergio Leone, based on the novel *The Hoods* by Harry Grey. *Director of Photography*: Tonino Delli Colli. *Music*: Ennio Morricone. *Art Director*: Carlo Simi. *Editor*: Nino Baragli.
    Cast: Robert De Niro (Noodles),

James Woods (Max), Elizabeth McGovern (Deborah), Treat Williams (Jimmy O'Donnell), Tuesday Weld (Carol), Burt Young (Joe). *With*: Joe Pesci, William Forsythe, James Hayden, Darlanne Fleugel, Larry Rapp.

A complicated narrative centers around "Noodles" Aaronson, a small-time criminal, and his group of friends as they rise and fall in the criminal underworld during the twenties and thirties. A rivalry develops between Noodles and his loyal lieutenant, Max, which continues until the late sixties when, as heads of different gangs, their disputes result in a gang war and both men's deaths.

While its intentions were good, *Once Upon a Time in America* became an excessive, overblown and complicated attempt at a grand gangster film. Suffering from its great length, even in an edited version, the film was then one of the most expensive ever made. Sergio Leone was certainly one of the most imaginative filmmakers of his time, best known for his great Westerns, but he occasionally lapsed into elephantine excess. This is certainly true of this film. Nevertheless, it can be enjoyed for many fine sequences, particularly its extremely violent action scenes, and some good performances.

Out of Singapore (Goldsmith, 1932). 61 mins.
Producer: Ken Goldsmith. *Director*: Charles Hutchison. *Screenplay*: John S. Nattleford, *story by* Fred Chapin. *Director of Photography*: Edward S. Kull. *Editor*: S. Roy Luby.
Cast: Noah Beery (Woolf Barstow), Dorothy Burgess (Concha), Miriam Seegar (Mary Carroll), Montague Love (Scar Murray), George Walsh (Steve). *With*: James Aubrey, William Moran, Olin Francis, Ethan Laidlaw, Leon Wong.

Woolf Barstow and his associate,

Scar Murray, sign on as officers aboard a cargo ship. Barstow falls for Mary, the pretty daughter of the ship's captain, whom he slowly poisons. In Singapore, Barstow culminates a deal with a Chinese gangster to take on a bogus cargo and then sink the ship at sea for insurance money. Once at sea, however, his scheme begins to unravel, thanks to a stowaway, Concha (who seeks revenge against him), and several other complications. Eventually several of the good guys manage to escape, and the ship blows up at sea, killing all aboard.

A typical "B" picture of the early thirties produced by a fly-by-night company, *Out of Singapore* has a ridiculous plot saved only by Noah Beery and Montague Love as the gangsters. When Poverty Row studio Astor Pictures acquired the rights to the film in the early forties, it was re-released as *Gangster of the Sea*.

Out of the Past (RKO, 1947). 97 mins.
Producer: Warren Duff. *Director*: Jacques Tourneur. *Screenplay*: Geoffrey Homes, based on his novel *Build My Gallows High*. *Director of Photography*: Nicholas Musuraca. *Music*: Roy Webb. *Art Directors*: Albert S. D'Agostino and Jack Okey. *Editor*: Samuel E. Beetley.
Cast: Robert Mitchum (Jeff Bailey/Markham), Jane Greer (Kathie Moffet), Kirk Douglas (Whit Sterling), Rhonda Fleming (Meta Carson), Steve Brodie (Fisher), Virginia Huston (Ann). *With*: Richard Webb, Paul Valentine, Dickie Moore, Ken Niles, Lee Elson, Frank Wilcox.

In a small California town, Jeff Bailey runs a gas station with the assistance of a deaf and mute boy. Bailey courts the pretty Ann, but his tranquil life is interrupted when an old acquaintance arrives in town to tell him that Whit Sterling, a racketeer, wants

Opposite: Sergio Leone's classic evocation of the rain-swept *film noir* scenes from his less than classic modern gangster drama *Once Upon a Time in America*.

to see him. As they drive to Sterling's Tahoe mansion, Bailey relates his story to Ann. In flashback, Bailey is a private detective named Jeff Markham. He is hired by Whit Sterling to find Sterling's mistress, Kathie Moffet, who has shot Sterling and left him for dead. She disappeared with $40,000 of Sterling's money. Bailey/Markham traces her to Mexico and falls in love with her. They move to San Francisco and live anonymously until Fisher, Bailey's detective partner, finds them. He plans to blackmail them but in a fight Kathie shoots and kills Fisher. She flees, leaving behind evidence that she stole money from Sterling, although she told Bailey she had not. Disillusioned, he moves to the small town to start a new life. Back in the present, Bailey is surprised to find Kathie again living with Sterling. Sterling tells Bailey that he will turn him into the police as Fisher's murderer, unless Bailey agrees to help him steal tax records from an accountant who is a renegade from Sterling's gang. Bailey agrees but discovers that he is the patsy in a scheme to murder the accountant. Hunted by the police, he flees to the small town and finds that Ann still believes in him. Realizing he is in an inescapable position, he decides to confront Sterling and convinces him to turn Kathie in as the killer. Kathie, however, kills Sterling, ending Bailey's last chance to prove his innocence. Kathie tells Bailey that they belong together and should escape the country. Bailey agrees but he secretly calls the police to tell them of their escape route. At a roadblock, both are shot and killed. Back in the small town, the deaf and mute boy communicates to Ann that Jeff was really in love with Kathie so that Ann can reject Jeff's memory and free herself from the past to build a new life.

An archetypal *film noir*, *Out of the Past* has all the classic elements of the genre: a *femme fatale*, an overbearing sense of corruption and paranoia, a cynical world view, and a shadowy,

expressionistic style. It demonstrates how far the gangster genre had changed in the forties. *Film noir*, of course, is a separate genre, but the world of the gangster comes up now and again, generally as a metaphor for society's corruption and post-war malaise, one of *noir's* main themes. *Out of the Past* is one of the most prominent of the gangster *noirs*, and it remains as fresh today as it did when first released. This is largely due to the strong performances, particularly Robert Mitchum's star-making turn as Jeff Bailey and Jacques Tourneur's fluid direction.

The Outfit (MGM, 1973). 102 mins.
Producer: Carter De Haven. *Director*: John Flynn. *Screenplay*: John Flynn, based on the novel by Richard Stark. *Director of Photography*: Bruce Surtees. *Music*: Jerry Fielding. *Art Director*: Tambi Larsen. *Editor*: Ralph E. Winters.

Cast: Robert Duvall (Earl Macklin), Karen Black (Betty Harrow), Joe Don Baker (Cody), Robert Ryan (Mailer), Timothy Carey (Menner). *With*: Richard Jaeckel, Sheree North, Marie Windsor, Jane Greer, Joanna Cassidy, Henry Jones.

A professional thief, Earl Macklin, is released from prison to find his brother has been murdered by the syndicate. Macklin learns that he and his friend, Cody, have been targeted by the mob for inadvertently robbing a syndicate owned bank. With Cody, Macklin seeks his own brand of justice against the mob by robbing their illegal gambling and bookie joints. In a shootout, Macklin and Cody kill several mob hoodlums, but Macklin's girl, Betty, is also killed. Macklin traces the leader of the syndicate, Mailer, to his well guarded mansion. Both Macklin and Cody manage to breach part of the elaborate electronic security system and chase Mailer through the house, killing him in a shootout. Macklin and Cody, who is wounded, set off a bomb and manage to escape the arriving police

Al Pacino as cocaine-addicted mobster Tony and the beautiful Michelle Pfeiffer as his icy moll Elvira in Brian De Palma's remake of *Scarface*.

and rescue units (summoned by the house's silent alarms) in the confusion.

Loosely based on Richard Stark's novel, *The Outfit* harkens back to the cynical gangster thrillers of the forties. Excessively violent, it moves at a rapid pace and manages to entertain action fans. Note several cameos by *noir* icons, including Jane Greer.

Outside the Law (Universal, 1930). 70 mins.
Director: Tod Browning. *Screenplay*: Tod Browning and Garrett Fort. *Director of Photography*: Roy Overbaugh. *Editor*: Milton Carruth.
Cast: Edward G. Robinson (Cobra Collins), Mary Nolan (Connie), Owen Moore ("Fingers" O'Dell), Edwin Sturgis (Jake), John George (Humpy). *With*: Delmar Watson, DeWitt Jennings, Rockliffe Fellowes, Frank Burke, Sydney Bracey.

"Fingers" O'Dell plans a robbery, but is extorted by local gang boss, Cobra Collins, who wants a share of the stolen money. Fingers' moll, Connie, gives Cobra the wrong date for the robbery, and Fingers manages to escape with the loot. Later, Cobra is killed by the police during another robbery. Fingers and Connie are then captured by the authorities.

Directed by horror expert Tod Browning, *Outside the Law* is a primitive early sound film, notable mainly for Edward G. Robinson's early appearance as a gangster.

Pacino, Al (b. 1939)
Actor. Born Alfredo Pacino into a working class Sicilian-American family in New York City, Pacino is famous for bringing both an intensity and psychological depth to his characters. He began as an actor Off Broadway and in supporting roles in a few minor films before being cast as Michael Corleone in *The Godfather*. Pacino proved he could hold his own against the respectable Marlon Brando and the other cast members, and the film made him

a star. He played the character in two subsequent films, showing the development from an honest man into hardened Mafia boss in the course of the three movies.

The Godfather (Paramount, 1971). *The Godfather Part II* (Paramount, 1974). *The Godfather III* (Paramount, 1991).

Page, Gale (1911–1983)

Actress. The attractive, dark-haired Page was born Sally Rutter in Spokane, Washington. She was a popular leading lady of the late thirties and forties, almost always seen as a wholesome girl. She played this type of role in her two gangster pictures.

The Amazing Dr. Clitterhouse (Warner Bros., 1938). *You Can't Get Away with Murder* (Warner Bros., 1939).

Palmer, Lilli (1914–1986)

Actress. Born Lilli Peiser in Austria, Palmer became a star as a juvenile on the Berlin stage in the early thirties. She fled with her family after the rise of Hitler and moved to Great Britain where she met and married Rex Harrison and first appeared in movies. She went to Hollywood in the forties, starring in a few American films. Of these, one of the best is *Body and Soul*, in which she played the good girl abandoned by a boxer (John Garfield) on the rise.

Body and Soul (United Artists, 1947).

Paramount

Basically the creation of Adolph Zukor, a former Nickelodean operator who formed the production company Famous Players in 1912 and then merged it with Paramount Pictures in 1914. Zukor remained the president of the studio for well over four decades, but it was a succession of executives under Zukor who were responsible for the actual production of individual films. By the mid-twenties, a recognizable style had emerged that would dominate the studio's films for two decades: a sophisticated blend of European art design (by Hans Dreier and his underlings), expressive technique, and a surprisingly frank attitude toward sex. All of these are evident in the remarkable group of crime thrillers that were created by director Josef von Sternberg in the late twenties: *Underworld, The Dragnet, Docks of New York,* and *Thunderbolt*. They were all enormously popular and, in the case of the first and third films, classics. It can also be said that both the gangster and *film noir* genres began with these four films. With the exception of *City Streets* in 1931, no other classics in the gangster genre were made at Paramount during the peak decade of the genre, but the studio's "B" producers continued to create gangster films throughout the thirties. Robert Florey directed a number of these films, often starring Akim Tamiroff or Lloyd Nolan. During the forties, however, the company found an authentic hard-boiled star in the diminutive and brooding Alan Ladd. First achieving stardom as a mob hit man in the classic *This Gun for Hire*, Ladd was one of the first of the new breed of antiheroes (including Burt Lancaster and Kirk Douglas) that emerged in the forties and proved perfect for the new, cynical style of the decade. The forties and fifties saw the creation of several classic gangster *noirs*, including *The Glass Key* (a remake of the imperfect 1935 original), *Dark City, I Walk Alone,* and *The Desperate Hours,* the latter starring archetypal Warner Bros. hard-boiled actor, Humphrey Bogart. Since the fifties, Paramount has released a few gangster movies, none more important than the first two *Godfather* films, which helped kick off a miniature cycle of its own during the seventies.

1927: *Underworld*. 1928: *Docks of New York, The Dragnet, The Racket*. 1929: *The Hole in the Wall, Thunderbolt*. 1930: *Ladies Love Brutes,*

Roadhouse Nights, Street of Chance.
1931: *City Streets.* 1932: *Madame
Racketeer, Night After Night.* 1934:
Limehouse Blues. 1935: *The Glass Key,
Stolen Harmony.* 1937: *King of Gamblers.* 1938: *Hunted Man, Illegal
Traffic, King of Chinatown, The Tip-
Off Girls, Dangerous to Know, King of
Alcatraz, You and Me.* 1939: *Back
Door to Heaven, Disbarred.* 1940:
Queen of the Mob. 1941: *Buy That
Town.* 1942: *The Glass Key, Lucky Jordan, This Gun for Hire.* 1947: *Desert
Fury.* 1948: *I Walk Alone.* 1949:
Manhandled. 1950: *Dark City.* 1955:
The Desperate Hours. 1968: *Grand
Slam, The Brotherhood.* 1970: *Borsalino.* 1972: *The Godfather.* 1973: *The
Friends of Eddie Coyle.* 1974: *The
Godfather Part II.* 1991: *The Godfather, Part III.*

Paris Touchez Pas au Grisbi aka *Grisbi*
(Corona, 1953). 88 mins.
Producer: Robert Dorfmann. *Director*: Jacques Becker. *Screenplay*:
Jacques Becker, based on the novel by
Albert Aimonin.
Cast: Jean Gabin (Max), Dery
(Riton), Paul Frankeur (Pierrot), Lino
Ventura (Angelo), Vittorio Sangoli
(Ramon), Jeanne Moreau (Joay).
Max, an aging gangster close to
retirement, decides to leave the proceeds of a heist to his partner, Riton.
Riton is kidnapped by a rival gangster,
Angelo, who wants the loot for himself. A gang war ensues during which
both Riton and Angelo are killed, and
the treasure is captured by the police.
An arthouse hit in the United
States—released as *Grisbi* and *Hands
Off the Loot—Paris Touchez Pas au
Grisbi* is an example of the occasional
French gangster picture. In fact, director Jean-Pierre Melville made a series
of similar, if more esoteric, crime and
gangster thrillers which have had a profound influence (via video releases) on
contemporary directors John Woo and
Quentin Tarantino; but *Grisbi's* unpretentious style and themes were influenced by American movies of the
thirties. An enormous success, it has
become a cultural symbol for the
French who hold it as a classic equal to
Scarface (United Artists, 1932), *The
Roaring Twenties* (Warner Bros., 1939)
and *Out of the Past* (RKO, 1947).

Parker, Bonnie (?–1934)
The real life rural gangster and moll
of Clyde Barrow (1910–1934) who, with
their gang, terrorized the Southwest
during the early Depression before being gunned down by Texas Rangers.
Parker was a poor Texas girl and a
teenager when she fell in love with Barrow and joined his fledgling gang of
bank robbers. Their murderous exploits and bizarre sexuality inspired
many songs, books and movies (*see
also* Barrow, Clyde). *The Bonnie
Parker Story* (American International,
1958) is a very imaginary recounting of
Parker's life in which Barrow's name
was oddly changed to Guy Darrow.

Parker, Jean (b. 1912)
Actress. Born Lois Mae Greene in
Butte, Montana, Parker was spotted in
a high school photograph by a talent
agent and signed to MGM. Typecast as
an ingenue and girl next door, she
showed some willingness to try riskier
roles, as she did in *Limehouse Blues* as
a prostitute. She later played hard-boiled roles, and appeared as the moll
in *Black Tuesday.*
Limehouse Blues (Paramount, 1934).
Black Tuesday (United Artists, 1954).

Parrish, Robert (b. 1916)
Director. Parrish is a veteran of
Hollywood who starred as a child actor
and later achieved considerable success
as an editor before becoming a director
in the early fifties. If ultimately a minor
director, he has demonstrated a greater
range than most. His second film, *The
Mob*, is a superior thriller that pointed
the way to the more visceral, violent
style that emerged during the fifties.
The Mob (Columbia, 1951).

Party Girl (MGM, 1958). 99 mins. *Producer*: Joe Pasternak. *Director*: Nicholas Ray. *Screenplay*: George Wells, *story by* Leo Katcher. *Director of Photography*: Robert Bronner. *Music*: Jeff Alexander. *Songs*: Nicholas Brodszky and Sammy Cahn. *Art Directors*: William A. Horning and Randall Duell. *Editor*: John McSweeney, Jr.

Cast: Robert Taylor (Thomas Farrell), Cyd Charisse (Vicki Gaye), Lee J. Cobb (Rico Angelo), John Ireland (Louis Canetto), Kent Smith (Prosecutor Jeffrey Stewart), Claire Kelly (Genevieve). *With*: Corey Allen, Lewis Charles, David Opatoshu, Patrick McVey, Ken Dobbs, Barbara Lang.

In the thirties in Chicago, Thomas Farrell is a crippled but ambitious lawyer who serves as a mouthpiece for the mob run by Rico Angelo. Farrell is in love with Vicki Gaye, a nightclub singer and dancer. When Gaye's relationship with the mobsters deteriorates, and they become fearful that she will squeal on them, they target her for assassination. Farrell sees the light and in order to protect her, rats on his mob associates. A gang war erupts and Angelo is eventually brought down.

A curious oddity, *Party Girl* is a semimusical with dance sequences that take advantage of the long-legged Cyd Charisse's talents. Well directed by Nicholas Ray—a talented filmmaker responsible for several important *films noir*, including *They Live by Night* (RKO, 1949)—the film borders on parody. It also suffers from its glossy treatment and inadequate leads. However, the supporting cast is superb, particularly Lee J. Cobb as the mob boss.

Pasternak, Joe (b. 1901)

Producer. After establishing a reputation as the creator of superior musicals at Universal during the thirties, Pasternak joined MGM during the mid-forties. An important producer during MGM's golden age of musicals, he had a famous rivalry with fellow MGM producer Arthur Freed. In fact, Pasternak was responsible for the studio's more modest musicals (particularly those starring Esther Williams), and few are now acknowledged classics. Among his later productions for MGM is the modest gangster musical *Party Girl*.

Party Girl (MGM, 1958).

Patrick, Gail (1911–1980)

Actress. Born Margaret Fitzpatrick in Birmingham, Alabama, the dark-haired, pretty Gail Patrick studied law and worked as a model before being discovered as a singer by Paramount. Never a major star, she was a popular leading lady in "B" movies and played second leads in "A" productions. She starred in several minor gangster movies, even playing a lawyer in *Disbarred*.

Dangerous to Know (Paramount, 1938). *King of Alcatraz* (Paramount, 1938). *Disbarred* (Paramount, 1939).

Patrick, John (b. 1905)

Screenwriter. Born John Patrick Goggan, Patrick was a prominent commercial playwright whose work is all but forgotten: *The Hasty Heart* and *The Teahouse of the August Moon* are still occasionally performed. He was also a busy screenwriter, working on many successful if lightweight movies. Among these is a minor gangster movie.

Born Reckless (20th Century-Fox, 1937).

Paxton, John (1911–1985)

Screenwriter. In the forties and early fifties, Paxton was a major screenwriter, best known for a series of great *films noir* released by RKO during the mid-forties. He also wrote the screenplay for *The Wild One*, a unique variation on the gangster genre which helped make Marlon Brando a major star of the fifties.

The Wild One (Columbia, 1954).

The Pay Off (RKO, 1930). 65 mins.
Director: Lowell Sherman. *Screenplay*: Jane Murfin, *story by* Samuel Shipman. *Director of Photography*: J. Roy Hunt. *Art Director*: Max Ree. *Editor*: Rose Smith.

Cast: Lowell Sherman (Gene Fenmore), Marion Nixon (Annabelle), Hugh Trevor (Rocky), William Janney (Tommy), Helen Millard (Dot). *With*: George F. Marion, Walter McGrail, Robert McWade, Alan Roscoe, Lita Chevret.

When a young couple, Annabelle and Tommy, are robbed, they set out to find the culprits. Tommy recognizes one of the thieves, and the crooks kidnap them. The mob boss, Gene Fenmore, offers to hire them as members of the gang. They reluctantly agree. Later, when the gang robs a store and kills the proprietor, the young couple is arrested. Fenmore, not wanting the couple to be tried and convicted, turns in his lieutenant, Rocky, the real culprit; and as a result, his gang kills him.

An early gangster picture (and RKO feature), *The Pay Off* is a rather typical "B" film of the period. Poorly made, it suffers from wooden performances, a pitfall of early sound movies. It is interesting for its old style and well mannered, debonair gangster, a stereotype which would soon change with the release of Warner Bros.' first great gangster picture (*Public Enemy*) a year later.

Pay or Die (Allied Artists, 1960). 111 mins.
Producer and Director: Richard Wilson. *Screenplay*: Richard Collins and Bertram Millhauser, based on the life of Lieutenant Joseph Petrosino. *Director of Photography*: Lucien Ballard. *Music*: David Raksin. *Art Director*: Fernando Carrere. *Editor*: Walter Hannemann.

Cast: Ernest Borgnine (Lt. Joseph Petrosino), Zohra Lampert (Adelina Saulino), Alan Austin (Johnny Viscardi), Renata Vanni (Mama Saulino).

With: Bruno Della Santina, Franco Corsaro, Robert F. Simon, Robert Ellenstein, Howard Caine.

Based on the real life experiences of police lieutenant Joseph Petrosino, *Pay or Die* recounts his adventures fighting against the Mafia in New York's Little Italy. His crusade against the mob eventually leads to his murder, but also brings down the mob boss.

Pay or Die is a well made "B" movie that was directed by Richard Wilson, the man responsible for *Al Capone* (Allied Artists, 1959). It is notable mainly for predating the rash of police procedurals that emerged during the late sixties and early seventies.

Payton, Barbara (1927–1967)
Actress. Born in Cloquet, Minnesota, Payton was a sexy blonde leading lady of "B" movies during the fifties. Apparently something of a *femme fatale* off camera, she made headlines for her affairs with actors Franchot Tone and Tom Neal. More often than not, she played the bad girl, as she does in *Kiss Tomorrow Goodbye*.

Kiss Tomorrow Goodbye (Warner Bros., 1950).

Penn, Arthur (b. 1922)
Director. After coming to the fore via television, Penn was briefly fashionable during the late sixties. Certainly his most important film is *Bonnie and Clyde*, which he directed with great if somewhat detached style. He has never equalled this early success, either artistically or financially.

Bonnie and Clyde (Warner Bros.-7 Arts, 1967).

Penthouse (MGM, 1933). 90 mins.
Associate Producer: Hunt Stromberg. *Director*: W. S. Van Dyke. *Screenplay*: Frances Goodrich and Albert Hackett, based on the novel by Arthur Somers Roche. *Director of Photography*: Lucien Andriot and Harold Rosson. *Music*: William Axt. *Editor*: Robert J. Kern.

Cast: Warner Baxter (Jackson Durant), Myrna Loy (Gertie Waxted), Charles Butterworth (Layton), Mae Clarke (Mimi Montagne), Phillips Holmes (Tom Siddell), C. Henry Gordon (Jim Crelliman). *With*: Martha Sleeper, Nat Pendleton, George E. Stone.

Jackson Durant, a lawyer who defends underworld clients, is framed by the mob for a crime committed by them. Because he helped her friend in a similar case, society girl Gertie Waxted agrees to help Durant by pretending to romance mob boss Jim Crelliman, and thus gain evidence against the mob. When Crelliman realizes what she is up to, he plans to kill her, but in a shootout, both criminals are killed. The young couple are free to continue their romance.

Penthouse continues the minor theme of respectable society mixing with vulgar gangsters, a popular genre variation during the early thirties. It is notable mainly for Myrna Loy's typically sensual performance.

Pépé le Moko (Paris Films, 1937). 90 mins.

Director: Julian Duvivier. *Screenplay*: Julian Duvivier, based on the novel by M. Ashelbe. *Director of Photography*: Marc Frossard.

Cast: Jean Gabin (Pépé le Moko), Mirelle Balin (Gaby), Line Noro (Ines), Lucas Girdoux (Slimane), Gabriel Gabrio (Carlos), Saturnin Fabre (Grandfather), Charpin (Regis).

Wanted by the police in his beloved Paris, small-time gangster and thief Pépé le Moko takes refuge in the Casbah, a seedy quarter of Casablanca. Because the police rarely enter this section of the city, Pépé is free to live as he pleases, but he is also a prisoner of the area, unable to leave without being arrested. He has an affair with Ines, an underworld associate. However, he falls in love with Gaby, an exotically beautiful Parisian tourist. At first she is annoyed by him, but eventually succumbs

to his charms and has a brief fling with him. When she leaves Casablanca and Pépé returns to Paris, Pépé is inconsolable. He leaves the Casbah, but is turned in by an informer and arrested. As Ines' ship sails away, Pépé stabs himself and dies.

Mixing romantic tragedy with a gangster theme was a unique combination in the late thirties, and it took the French to create the subgenre. *Pépé le Moko* was the first such film (but hardly the last), and its enormous popularity had an influence throughout the world. It also made Jean Gabin into a superstar in Europe, although he would not become a star in the United States. While it was playing as a box office hit in Europe, director and actor Erich Von Stroheim saw the film and convinced MGM to buy the remake rights. The great director Julien Duvivier was brought to Hollywood to prepare the project, but Gabin refused to come over, and the studio eventually sold it to independent producer Walter Wanger. The remake, *Algiers* (United Artists, 1938) had its own success (although some of the cynicism was toned down), and it subsequently was turned into the musical—*Casbah* (Universal, 1948), although less effectively.

Pereira, Hal (1905–1983)

Art director. Pereira first made a name for himself as a set designer in the theater during the thirties. He joined Paramount in the early forties, collaborating on many important productions during the next two decades. He worked on a single gangster movie, but it does not contain his most imaginative designs.

The Desperate Hours (Paramount, 1955).

Perelman, S. J. (1904–1979)

Screenwriter. One of America's premier humorists during the mid-twentieth century, Perelman worked sporadically in Hollywood. His greatest legacy are his screenplays written in collaboration with the Marx Brothers. The gangster satire *Larceny, Inc.* is based on a play coauthored by Perelman.

Larceny, Inc (Warner Bros., 1942).

Pesci, Joe (b. 1943)
Character actor. The diminutive Pesci is an unlikely star but has become a major contemporary personality largely because of his performances in Martin Scorsese's films. Despite an annoying habit of overplaying his parts, Pesci has given some strong performances. He was at his best in Scorsese's *GoodFellas* as the psychotic mobster Tommy De Vito, a role made for overacting. Pesci won a best supporting actor Academy Award for his performance in the film.

GoodFellas (Warner Bros., 1990).

Pete Kelly's Blues (Warner Bros., 1955). 95 mins.
Producer and Director: Jack Webb. *Screenplay*: Richard L. Breen. *Director of Photography*: Hal Rosson. *Songs*: Ray Heindorf and Sammy Cahn, and Arthur Hamilton. *Art Director*: Feild Gray. *Editor*: Robert M. Leeds.
Cast: Jack Webb (Pete Kelly), Janet Leigh (Ivy Conrad), Edmond O'Brien (Fran McCarg), Peggy Lee (Rose Hopkins), Andy Devine (George Tenell), Lee Marvin (Al Gannaway). *With*: Ella Fitzgerald, Martin Milner, Thann Wyenn, Herb Ellis, Jayne Mansfield.
Pete Kelly is a strait-laced trumpet player who opposes the drive to move bootlegging into jazz nightclubs. His opposition eventually leads to a confrontation and a shootout with the underworld figures, but the mob's activities are temporarily stopped.
Told in the same matter-of-fact, documentary-like style of Jack Webb's "Dragnet," *Pete Kelly's Blues* is set in Prohibition-era Kansas City, a hot bed of jazz and underworld crime during the late twenties. A moody, dark film, it is not particularly important, but it is

enjoyable thanks to its superior score and several songs performed by Peggy Lee.

Peterson, Robert
Art director. As a key set designer at Columbia during *film noir*'s great period, Peterson worked on several of the genre's major movies. His designs for *The Big Heat*, the classic gangster *noir*, are perfectly suited to the largely studio-bound production, creating an appropriately sinister atmosphere.

The Big Heat (Columbia, 1953).

The Petrified Forest (Warner Bros., 1936). 83 mins.
Associate Producer: Henry Blanke. *Director*: Archie Mayo. *Screenplay*: Charles Kenyon and Delmar Daves, based on the play by Robert E. Sherwood. *Director of Photography*: Sol Polito. *Music*: Bernhard Kaun. *Art Director*: John Hughes. *Editor*: Owen Marks.
Cast: Leslie Howard (Alan Squire), Bette Davis (Gabrielle Maple), Genevieve Tobin (Mrs. Chisholm), Dick Foran (Boze Hertzlinger), Humphrey Bogart (Duke Mantee), Joe Sawyer (Jackie), *With*: Porter Hall, Charley Grapewin, Paul Harvey, Eddie Acuff, Adrian Morris, Nina Campana.
Alan Squire, a writer and gigolo, expounds on his philosophy that nature is fighting back at man, causing chaos. As an example, he points to Duke Mantee, a sadistic gangster who is holding a group of hostages, including Squire, at a small roadside cafe, somewhere in the West. Mantee, representing the brute force of nature, and Squire, representing human intellectualism, are immediately in conflict. Mantee is waiting at the cafe for his girlfriend so that he and his gang can escape to Mexico. Squire's taunts drive Mantee crazy, endangering the other hostages, including the lonely but sensual Gabrielle, the daughter of the cafe owner. Eventually the conflict between the two men results in a final confrontation. Mantee shoots

Humphrey Bogart (right) as the psychotic gangster Duke Mantee in *The Petrified Forest*, holds the patrons of a roadside diner hostage, including Bette Davis and Leslie Howard.

and kills Squire, but is himself killed by the police as he tries to flee the cafe.

Squire's philosophy was also essentially that of playwright Robert Sherwood, upon whose play the film was based. The struggle between the forces of nature and intellectual man was then a hot topic (and an ingredient in both Nazi and communist philosophies), about which Sherwood had an apparently cynical outlook. Indeed, Warner Bros. shot two versions, one in which Squire lives and the other in which he dies. The latter, downbeat ending (the one in the play), was kept when preview audiences reacted favorably to it. In any case, *The Petrified Forest* is a classic American film, and one of the gangster genre's great movies. Set almost entirely in the Black Mesa Barbecue Cafe and gas station near the atmospheric Petrified Forest (yet another literary symbol), the film's rather static pace is overcome by its

phenomenal performances. As most film buff's know, Warner Bros. wanted Edward G. Robinson to play Mantee, but Leslie Howard insisted that his friend Humphrey Bogart (who had originated the stage role) be given the role. Bogart's performance is electrifying, as are the performances of Howard (in a low key part) and Bette Davis. With its theatrical origins, *The Petrified Forest* transcends mere entertainment and remains a thought-provoking meditation about modern man's place in the world.

Pevney, Joseph (b. 1920)

Director. Pevney was an undistinguished director of "B" movies and indifferent "A" movies. His only film of distinction is the biopic *Man of a Thousand Faces* (Warner Bros., 1957). Of his two gangster pictures, the most interesting is *Six Bridges to Cross*, a neglected, if minor, heist picture with

an excellent screenplay by Sydney Boehm.
Six Bridges to Cross (Universal, 1955). *Portrait of a Mobster* (Warner Bros., 1961).

Pfeiffer, Michelle (b. 1957)
Actress. An exquisitely beautiful blonde actress, Pfeiffer was born in Santa Ana, California. After television experience, she began her film career at twenty-five, playing a teenager in the sappy *Grease II* (Paramount, 1982). She made an early, impressive appearance as the cold-hearted moll in *Scarface*.
Scarface (Universal, 1983). *Married to the Mob* (Orion, 1988).

The Phenix City Story (Allied Artists, 1955). 100 mins.
Producers: Samuel Bischoff and David Diamond. *Director*: Phil Karlson. *Screenplay*: Crane Wilbur and Daniel Mainwaring. *Director of Photography*: Harry Neumann. *Music*: Harry Sukman. *Editor*: George White.
Cast: John McIntire (Albert Patterson), Richard Kiley (John Patterson), Kathryn Grant (Ellie), Edward Andrews (Rhett Tanner), Lenka Paterson (Mary Jo Patterson). *With*: Biff McGuire, Truman Smith, Jean Carson, John Larch, James Edwards, Otto Hulett.

John Patterson returns from service in the Army during the Korean War to his birthplace, Phenix City, Alabama. He discovers that his politician father has been murdered, and as a result, he agrees to accept the post of attorney general to help bring about the end of mob corruption of his hometown. He eventually discovers that Rhett Tanner is the local mob boss, and launches a war against him, resulting in the town's cleanup.

The script for *The Phenix City Story* was written by two masters of the hardboiled, Crane Wilbur and Daniel Mainwaring. It was based on real events and shot in semidocumentary style by Phil

Karlson. Full of action and violence, it recreated the gangster war in vivid detail. Its fine cast is headed by a minor icon of the genre, John McIntire, and altogether manages to be a satisfactory entry in the genre.

Phinlay, Angela (Fictional character)
Hired at the last minute, Marilyn Monroe played the sexy, lubricious moll of the heist gang's financier in *The Asphalt Jungle* (MGM, 1950). Monroe's performance went a long way to making her a full-fledged star, and although she appears only briefly on screen, is one of the gangster genre's most memorable molls.

Pichel, Irving (1891–1954)
Director. While attending Harvard, Pichel began drifting through various jobs before becoming an actor during the mid-teens. After many years on the stage, he entered movies during the late twenties as a script clerk, but continued to play small supporting roles well into the thirties. He began directing in the early thirties and proved to be a reliable handler of action films. One of his finest films is *Quicksand*, an underrated study of the psychology of criminals.
Quicksand (United Artists, 1950).

Pine, William H. (1896–1955)
Producer. Known as "the Dollar Bills" because of their economic productions, Pine and his partner, producer William C. Thomas produced scores of "B" pictures and modest "A" films for Paramount, beginning in the late thirties. One of these, *Manhandled*, has been called a *film noir* and a gangster picture, but it is a minor (if entertaining) movie in either case.
Manhandled (Paramount, 1949).

Planer, Franz (1894–1963)
Cinematographer. The German-born Planer was one of the most important cinematographers of his time. He was a key figure in the development of expressionism in German popular

cinema during the twenties (and would have a profound influence on American movies over the next two decades), but Planer modified some of the harshness of this art form into a personal style distinguished by lush, sensual visuals. Thus, his greatest films tend to be romantic melodramas. However, he did photograph three gangster *noirs*. Of these, the most impressive is Robert Siodmak's neglected classic *Criss Cross*, whose tragic romantic theme seems to have inspired some of his finest subsequent work.

The Chase (United Artists, 1946). *Criss Cross* (Universal, 1949). *711 Ocean Drive* (Columbia, 1950).

Polito, Eugene (b. 1930)
Cinematographer. The son of Sol Polito, Eugene (also known as Gene) is associated exclusively with minor movies. He recreated little of his father's genius.

Portrait of a Mobster (Warner Bros., 1961).

Polito, Sol (1892–1960)
Cinematographer. Long associated with Warner Bros., Polito was a key figure in the development of that studio's gritty urban style during the thirties, photographing many important movies: *I Am a Fugitive from a Chain Gang*, *Forty-Second Street* (1932), *The Petrified Forest*, *The Charge of the Light Brigade* (1936), among others. Although his career went into eclipse during the forties, he continued to work until the fifties. His work in the thirties is his most important and includes several of Warner Bros.' most important gangster movies.

I Am a Fugitive from a Chain Gang (Warner Bros., 1932). *Three on a Match* (First National, 1932). *G-Men* (First National, 1935). *The Petrified Forest* (Warner Bros., 1936). *Angels with Dirty Faces* (Warner Bros., 1938).

Pollack, Sydney (b. 1934)
Director. Pollack made a name for himself as a television director in the early sixties. He began directing features in 1965. He has shown a tendency to pretension and self importance. In fact, the little-known thriller *The Yakuza* is one of his finest movies, a taut, suspenseful thriller that was one of the first to expose the Asian underworld.

The Yakuza (Warner Bros., 1975).

Polonsky, Abraham (b. 1910)
Screenwriter. Polonsky's promising career was cut short by the McCarthy anticommunist witch hunt during the early fifties, but not before he wrote and directed several important films. His exposé of the corrupt boxing world is one of his most important contributions.

Body and Soul (United Artists, 1947).

Portrait of a Mobster (Warner Bros., 1961). 108 mins.
Director: Joseph Pevney. *Screenplay*: Howard Browne, based on the book by Harry Grey. *Director of Photography*: Eugene Polito. *Music*: Max Steiner. *Art Director*: Jack Poplin. *Editor*: Leo H. Shreve.
Cast: Vic Morrow (Dutch Schultz), Leslie Parrish (Iris Murphy), Peter Breck (Frank Brennan), Ray Danton (Legs Diamond), Norman Alden (Bo Wetzel). *With*: Robert McQueeny, Ken Lynch, Frank de Kova, Stephen Roberts, Evan McCord, Arthur Tenen.

The career of real life mobster Arthur "Dutch" Flegenheimer (1902–1935), also known as Dutch Schultz, is recalled. From his humble beginnings to his years as a gang boss, his life was filled with violence that led to his early death. Schultz initiated the first full-scale gang wars in New York during Prohibition, when his former lieutenant, Legs Diamond, started his own bootlegging operation to compete with him. Eventually, Diamond's men killed Schultz.

A low budget picture, *Portrait of a*

Mobster concentrated on violent action to disguise its cheap sets and poor production values. It is notable largely as one of the early gangster biopics released in the wake of the successful television series "The Untouchables."

Potter, H. C. (1904–1977)

Director. After stage experience, Potter signed with RKO in 1935. He proved to be a brilliant handler of comic material, and several of his movies are classics: *Hellzapoppin'* (Universal, 1941), *The Farmer's Daughter* (RKO, 1947) and *Mr. Blandings Builds His Dream House* (RKO, 1948). His curious gangster satire *Mr. Lucky* is also a classic. Like so many comedy directors whose films are generally dismissed as frivolous, Potter has suffered from critical neglect, yet there can be little question that he was one of the most talented American directors of the forties.

Mr. Lucky (RKO, 1943).

Powell, William (1892–1984)

Actor. A suave, handsome leading man of the old school, Powell was a mainstay at MGM for more than three decades. Unlike other MGM leading men, Powell was distinguished by real talent and a self-deprecating, tongue-in-cheek approach. Most famous as Nick Charles in the *Thin Man* series, he played a variety of characters, including the occasional well dressed gangster.

The Dragnet (Paramount, 1928). *Street of Chance* (Paramount, 1930). *Manhattan Melodrama* (MGM, 1934).

Power, Tyrone (1913–1958)

Actor. Power was the son of well respected stage actor Tyrone Power, Sr. The younger Power had brief stage experience before beginning a film career in the early thirties. He became a major star in the late thirties, playing smooth romantic heroes in mostly routine movies. His only appearance in the gangster genre was in the odd *Johnny Apollo*, which came at the end of the initial cycle. Power's performance is typically low key and not altogether convincing. He was better suited to more conventional fare.

Johnny Apollo (20th Century–Fox, 1940).

Powers, Tom (Fictional character)

In *Public Enemy* (Warner Bros., 1931), Powers is the wisecracking gangster played by James Cagney, the role that made him into a star. Powers is a street punk who, through brutal force and violence, rises to become a leading gangster in New York City. His brother, a veteran of the First World War, refuses to join the rackets, preferring to toil in poverty rather than commit crimes. As Powers gains power, he loses touch with reality, having his enemies eliminated indiscriminately, while also exchanging one moll for another. Arrogant and sadistic, Powers treats his women violently—in one famous scene, he smashes a grapefruit into the face of his moll, Kitty (Mae Clarke), when she complains that he does not pay enough attention to her. Eventually, however, Powers becomes the target of rival gangsters. They murder him and then call his beloved mother to say he is coming home. When his brother opens the door to let him in, Power's bullet-ridden body, wrapped like a mummy, falls to the floor. Tom Powers' demise is one of the most memorable in all of cinema.

Preminger, Otto (1906–1986)

Director. The Austrian-born Preminger was a successful stage director and actor who emigrated to the United States in the mid-thirties after the rise of Hitler. After several false starts, he made a name for himself "overnight" with the classic *film noir, Laura* (20th Century-Fox, 1944). His cynical romantic approach was particularly well suited to *noir*. Of his five *noirs, Where the Sidewalk Ends* is unusual for its gangster theme and rather conventional

suspense plot. However, it is very well done and is a minor classic.
Where the Sidewalk Ends (20th Century-Fox, 1950).

Presnell, Robert (1894–1988)
Screenwriter. A professional screenwriter, Presnell worked quietly and without recognition for over three decades in Hollywood. He collaborated on several classics, and cowrote a single, minor gangster picture.
Disbarred (Paramount, 1939).

Preston, Robert (1918–1987)
Actor. Born Robert Preston Merservy in Newton, Massachusetts, Preston began his screen career, after stage experience, in the late thirties. For most of his career he played second leads and villains in many popular movies. He starred in *This Gun for Hire* as a policeman involved in a complicated investigation, but he was submerged by the charisma of Alan Ladd and Veronica Lake who stole the film.
This Gun for Hire (Paramount, 1942).

Pretty Boy Floyd (Continental, 1960). 96 mins.
Producer: Monroe Sachson. *Director and Screenplay*: Herbert J. Leder. *Director of Photography*: Chuck Austin. *Music*: Del Sirino. *Editor*: Ralph Rosenblum.
Cast: John Ericson (Pretty Boy Floyd), Barry Newman (Al Riccardo), Joan Harvey (Lil Courtney), Herbert Evers (Blackie Faulkner), Carl Yuck (Curly). *With*: Roy Fant, Shirley Smith, Phil Kenneally, Norman Burton, Charles Bradswell.
Charles Arthur Floyd, known as "Pretty Boy" Floyd because of his good looks, returns to Oklahoma after being rejected for an honest job, to find his father has been murdered by a local thug. He avenges his father's murder, and then robs a local bank. He gives some of the stolen money to local farmers (local newspapers refer to him as the "sagebrush Robin Hood") and then flees to Kansas City. There, he takes up with Lil Harvey, a harlot who becomes his moll, and puts together a gang. The gang terrorizes the rural communities in Kansas, culminating in the Kansas City Massacre in which five policemen were killed. However, his gang is hunted down, arrested or killed, until Pretty Boy himself meets his own violent end when shot dead by F.B.I. agents while hiding out on a farm in Ohio.
Yet another of the gangster biopics released in the wake of the success of "The Untouchables," *Pretty Boy Floyd* typically romanticizes the real life gangster and concentrates on violent action to disguise its low budget. The real life Pretty Boy Floyd was one of the group of rural gangsters who terrorized America during the thirties. Here played by "B" actor John Ericson, he emerges as a kind of Robin Hood gone awry, corrupted by greed.

Price, Vincent (1911–1993)
Character actor. Price earned art degrees at Yale University and the University of London before he took to the London stage, becoming a star at twenty-three. He returned to the United States and continued to act alternately on the stage and in film into the early fifties. He was seen most often as a fop, cad, or villain, often in horror films. He had prominent roles in two gangster *noirs*. In *The Bribe* he played a sadistic gangster. However, his best performance was in *His Kind of Woman*, as a vain movie star who finds himself entangled in a complicated plot engineered by a murderous mobster, and who redeems himself in the end by an atypical act of bravery.
The Bribe (MGM, 1949). *His Kind of Woman* (RKO, 1951).

Prison
Prison and the life of convicts has long intrigued writers and dramatists,

and no less so with filmmakers. From the earliest years of the gangster genre, prison was the subject of numerous films, developing into a subgenre with its own set of themes, characters, and clichés. *Four Walls* (MGM, 1928) is probably the first gangster prison film, set partly behind bars and featuring gangsters as main characters. However, the film which established this subgenre as legitimate is *The Big House* (MGM, 1930), where one first encounters the theme common throughout this minicycle: good and bad prisoners pitted against the corrupt, violent authorities. This formula was repeated in several notable films: *Castle on the Hudson* (Warner Bros., 1940), *The Criminal Code* (Columbia, 1931), *The Last Mile* (Worldwide, 1932, and the remake by United Artists, 1959), *San Quentin* (Warner Bros., 1937), *20,000 Years in Sing Sing* (First National, 1933), *Each Dawn I Die* (Warner Bros., 1939), and *Riot in Cell Block 11* (Allied Artists, 1954). *Caged* (Warner Bros., 1950) was the first of a new subgenre of "women behind bars" films that would grow increasingly exploitative over the next two decades. In *My Six Convicts* (Columbia, 1952), the genre was varied somewhat by a strongly sociological theme. The most interesting variation on the prison theme, however, is *Invisible Stripes* (Warner Bros., 1939), which investigates the stigma society attaches to ex-prisoners and the effects of prison experience on ex-convicts in the real world.

Prizzi's Honor (20th Century–Fox, 1985). 129 mins.
Producer: John Foreman. *Director*: John Huston. *Screenplay*: Richard Condon and Janet Roach, based on Richard Condon's novel. *Director of Photography*: Andrzej Bartkowiak. *Music*: Alex North. *Art Directors*: Michael Helmy and Tracy Bousman. *Editors*: Rudi Fehr and Kanja Fehr.
Cast: Jack Nicholson (Charley Partanna), Kathleen Turner (Irene Walker), Robert Loggia (Eduardo Prizzi), John Randolph ("Pop" Partanna), William Hickey (Don Corrado Prizzi), Angelica Huston (Maerose Prizzi). *With*: Lee Richardson, Michael Lombard, George Santopietro, Lawrence Tierney, Ann Selepegno.

Don Corrado is the aging, senile head of the Prizzi clan, a powerful mob family. His godson Charley Partanna, despite being somewhat dimwitted, is one of the family's best hit men. At the wedding of Don Corrado's daughter, Charley meets the beautiful Irene Walker, a tax consultant. Charley's girlfriend, Maerose, is Corrado's older daughter who has disgraced the family by her adulterous affair with another man. She now looks forward to her wedding to Charley so that she will once again be in the good graces of her relatives. Charley, meanwhile, is ordered to kill a man who has embezzled money from one of the family's casinos, but after successfully carrying out his assignment, he discovers that half the money is missing. Furthermore, his sultry lover, Irene, is the dead man's widow. She claims that she does not know anything about the missing money and that she did not really love her husband anyway. To further complicate matters, Charley learns that Irene is really a hit woman who also works for Don Corrado. Charley marries Irene, and later they are directed to kidnap a bank executive who has embezzled money from the gang. They plan to extort a ransom from the victim to recover the money he has stolen, but the plan begins to fall apart when Irene kills a witness. Don Corrado also discovers that she has indeed taken half of the money her husband stole. She flees, and Don Corrado orders Charley to kill her. Realizing that his loyalty is to the mob, he agrees. At their confrontation, Irene tries to shoot Charley, but he kills her with a stiletto. He is now free to marry Maerose Corrado, whose jealous machinations are partly responsible for Irene's downfall.

James Cagney as audiences wanted to see him – tough, mean and arrogant – in *Public Enemy* with Eddie Woods during a liquor heist.

A rich comic film, *Prizzi's Honor* was made in the twilight of John Huston's life and career, but it looks and feels like a young man's film. It provides a detailed look at the Mafia underworld, but is also a satire about America during the greedy Reagan years. It can be seen as an indictment of the selfishness of corporate America, but its didacticism is mild and comic. More importantly, it provided a perfect vehicle for a fine cast at their best. Particularly brilliant is Angelica Huston's portrayal of Maerose Prizzi, and she was honored with an Academy Award for best supporting actress.

Prohibition

The Eighteenth Amendment, passed in 1919 and in effect until 1933, prohibited the sale and importation of alcohol in the United States. As a kind of last act of Puritanism at its strongest, Prohibition had unforeseen consequences, not the least of which was the war between the Black Hands (the Italian Mafia) and the White Hands (the Irish Mob) from 1920 to 1925 to control the sale of illegal liquor and the subsequent rise of the Mafia. During the early twenties, Al Capone, a mob underling in New York City, was sent by his superiors to Chicago, where he built an empire from the illegal profits of liquor sales. Prohibition was the subject of several notable gangster movies, including *Little Caesar* (First National, 1931), *Public Enemy* (Warner Bros., 1931), *Scarface* (United Artists, 1932), *The Roaring Twenties* (Warner Bros., 1939), *Al Capone* (Allied Artists, 1959), *Some Like It Hot* (United Artists, 1959) and the *Godfather* saga (Paramount, 1972, 1974 and 1992).

Perhaps the most memorable image in the genre's history from *Public Enemy*: James Cagney smashing a grapefruit in moll Mae Clarke's face.

Interestingly, the lessons of the original Prohibition were ignored by later conservatives, and the prohibition against drugs has had the same effect, contributing to the rise of new international gangs, and both directly and indirectly, causing violence in the streets. The modern prohibition is the subject of several contemporary gangster movies, including, most notably, *The French Connection* (20th Century–Fox, 1971) and Brian De Palma's remake of *Scarface* (Universal, 1983).

Provine, Dorothy (b. 1937)
Actress. Born in Deadwood, South Dakota, the beautiful, voluptuous, blonde Provine began singing and dancing during her teens. She made a striking appearance during her first year in the movies, as the title character in *The Bonnie Parker Story*. She

subsequently played a variety of sexpots in many popular movies during the sixties.
The Bonnie Parker Story (American International, 1958).

Public Enemy (Warner Bros., 1931). 83 mins.
Director: William A Wellman. *Screenplay*: Kubec Glasmon, John Bright and Harvey Thew, based on the story "Beer and Blood" by John Bright. *Director of Photography*: Dev Jennings. *Musical Director*: David Mendoza. *Art Director*: Max Parker. *Editor*: Ed McCormick.
Cast: James Cagney (Tom Powers), Jean Harlow (Gwen Allen), Edward Woods (Matt Doyle), Joan Blondell (Mamie), Donald Cook (Mike Powers), Mae Clarke (Kitty). *With*: Beryl Mercer, Mia Marvin, Leslie Fenton, Rita

Flynn, Robert Emmett O'Connor, Murray Kinnell. Tom Powers and Matt Doyle are poor youths who grow up on the mean streets of Chicago. As adults they kill a cop while committing a robbery, then go to work for bootleggers as truck drivers. They rise to prominence in the gang, but Powers' older brother, a war veteran, does not join the rackets. Powers has a series of blonde mistresses, including Kitty, whom he smashes in the face with a grapefruit during an argument. He then takes up with the equally trashy Gwen Allen. Powers is cold blooded, and he kills rivals without compunction. However, eventually a rival gang catches up with them, kills Matt and wounds Tom in a shootout. As he is recuperating in the hospital, the rivals kidnap him, then call his mother to tell her he is coming home. When his brother opens the door to let him in, the bullet-ridden body, grotesquely wrapped like a mummy, falls to the floor.

Without a doubt, *Public Enemy* is one of the great films of the gangster genre. The violent tale of the rise and fall of a gangster is told in spare, linear style by director William Wellman. Completely unsentimental, it holds up particularly well when compared to many of the initial cycle's films. Much of the credit must be given to James Cagney, whose performance as the sadistic, pugnacious Tom Powers is mesmerizing. However, Jean Harlow and Mae Clarke are equally compelling as his slutty girlfriends—released two years before the Production Code, their sexuality was forthright in a way that would not be seen on American screens for more than three decades afterward.

Public Enemy's Wife (Warner Bros., 1936). 65 mins.
Director: Nick Grinde. *Screenplay*: Aben Finkle and Harold Buckley. *Director of Photography*: Ernest Haller. *Editor*: Thomas Pratt.

Cast: Pat O'Brien (Lee Laird), Margaret Lindsay (Judith Maroc/Roberts), Robert Armstrong (Gene Ferguson), Cesar Romero (Gene Maroc), Dick Foran (Tom McKay). *With*: Joseph King, Dick Purcell, Addison Richards, Paul Graetz, Selmar Jackson, Hal K. Dawson.

Gene Maroc, a convicted thief, says he will kill any man who tries to marry his wife, Judith, while he is in prison. After she is released from prison for a crime she did not commit, Judith divorces her husband and announces her engagement to Tom McKay, a wealthy playboy. Morac manages to escape with the help of his underworld cronies. G-man Lee Laird takes McKay's place, but Maroc manages to kidnap his ex-wife. The F.B.I. discovers his hideout, and Maroc is killed in a shoot out. Judith realizes that she is really in love with Laird.

A "B" gangster movie, *Public Enemy's Wife* suffers from a poor script and promises more than it delivers. Nevertheless, Cesar Romero is very good as the gangster.

Public Hero #1 (MGM, 1935). 89 mins.
Producer: Lucien Hubbard. *Director*: J. Walter Ruben. *Screenplay*: Wells Root, *story by* Wells Root and J. Walter Ruben. *Director of Photography*: Gregg Toland. *Editor*: Frank Sullivan.

Cast: Chester Morris (Jeff Crane), Jean Arthur (Theresa O'Reilly), Lionel Barrymore (Dr. Glass), Paul Kelly (Duff), Lewis Stone (Warden Alcott), Joseph Calleia (Sonny). *With*: Paul Hurst, John Kelly, Selmer Jackson, Larry Wheat, Cora Sue Collins.

While the Dillinger-like Sonny Black is in prison, F.B.I. agent Jeff Crane is assigned as his cellmate in an undercover operation to find out where his notorious Purple Gang is holding out. They escape from prison, but Sonny's sister, Theresa, tries to seduce Crane, upsetting the overprotective Sonny. Eventually, the gang is tracked down and the F.B.I. shoots Sonny while he is leaving a movie theater.

Obviously influenced by the life of John Dillinger, *Public Hero #1* was a modest, tongue-in-cheek gangster film. Essentially a "B" movie, it provided minor gangster icon Chester Morris with a rare heroic role, with Jean Arthur supporting him as the randy sister. Character actor Joseph Calleia had his most prominent role in the genre as Sonny Black , whose demise, of course, was exactly like Dillinger's.

Puzo, Mario (b. 1920)

Novelist and screenwriter. An Italian-American, Puzo caused a sensation when his novel *The Godfather* was published in 1969. He then adapted the epic novel with Francis Ford Coppola, who directed two films based on the book. Puzo has also cowritten several other films, including the third entry in the *Godfather* trilogy, a major disappointment compared to the two earlier classics.

The Godfather (Paramount, 1972). *The Godfather Part Two* (Paramount, 1974). *The Godfather III* (Paramount, 1991).

Queen of the Mob (Paramount, 1940). 61 mins.

Director: James Hogan. *Screenplay*: Horace McCoy and William R. Lippman. *Director of Photography*: Theodor Sparkuhl. *Art Directors*: Hans Dreier and Ernest Fegte. *Editor*: Arthur Schmidt.

Cast: Ralph Bellamy (Scott Langham), Jack Carson (Ross Waring), Blance Yurka (Ma Webster), Richard Denning (Charlie Webster), James Seay (Eddie Webster), Paul Kelly (Tom Webster), William Henry (Bert Webster). *With*: Jeanne Cagney, J. Carol Naish, Hedda Hopper, Pierre Watkin, Billy Gilbert, John Harmon.

Ma Webster is the matriarch of a murderous gang of bank robbers comprised of her three sons. They terrorize the countryside, and eventually the F.B.I. hunts the gang down, killing or arresting them.

Loosely based on the exploits of the real life Ma Barker and her gang and J. Edgar Hoover's memoirs, *Queen of the Mob* is a swift moving "B" combination of the gangster genre and the police procedural. Ralph Bellamy stars as the F.B.I. agent with Jeanne Cagney, James' sister, playing the wife of one of Ma Webster's non-criminal sons. Although not a major film, it was well written by Horace McCoy and William R. Lippman, and well acted.

Quick Millions (Fox, 1931). 72 mins.

Director: Rowland Brown. *Screenplay*: Courtney Terrett and Rowland Brown. *Director of Photography*: Joseph August. *Art Director*: Duncan Cramer.

Cast: Spencer Tracy (Bugs Raymond), Marguerite Churchill (Dorothy Stone), Sally Eilers (Daisy), Robert Burns (Arkansas Smith), John Wray (Kenneth Stone). *With*: Warner Richmond, George Raft, John Swor.

Bugs Raymond, a small-time mobster, forms a protection racket and becomes powerful. He meets and wants to marry Dorothy Stone, a beautiful young society girl, but she rejects him. so he decides to kidnap her on her wedding day. Before he can, however, his gang turns on him and kills him.

With the charismatic Spencer Tracy, loaned out by MGM, *Quick Millions* is an entertaining early "B" gangster drama. Cowritten and directed by the enigmatic Rowland Brown, its style is in the Warner's hard-boiled tradition, but its rather conventional, simplistic plot and moralizing hurt its overall quality.

Quicksand (United Artists, 1950). 79 mins.

Producer: Mort Brisken. *Director*: Irving Pichel. Robert Smith. *Director of Photography*: Lionel Lindon. *Music*: Louis Gruenberg. *Art Director*: Emil Newman. *Editor*: Walter Thompson.

Cast: Mickey Rooney (Dan), Jeanne Cagney (Vera), Barbara Bates (Helen), Peter Lorre (Nick), Taylor Holmes (Harvey), Art Smith (Mackey). *With*: Wally Cassel, John Galludet, Minerva Urecal, Patsy O'Connor.

On a lonely highway, two hitchhikers, Dan and Helen, are picked up by Harvey. Dan pulls a gun and forces Harvey to drive toward Mexico. By coincidence, Harvey is a lawyer and asks Dan to relate how he and his girlfriend got into trouble. Dan's troubles began with his obsession with the sultry, cold-hearted Vera. Dan is a mechanic, and in order to take out Vera, he steals from his employer. Although he intends to pay the money back, this act causes a chain of events, with Dan descending into an inescapable hell. Eventually realizing he cannot get out of the trouble he is in, he tries to get away with Helen, a "good girl." The lawyer convinces Dan to give himself up, but before he can, he is shot by the police. Dan's injuries, however, are not fatal, and Harvey agrees to defend him.

Epitomizing "B" *film noir* with its cynical plot and a helpless character caught in circumstances partly of his own making, *Quicksand* is also interesting as an example of the evolution of the gangster melodrama that had occurred by the fifties. With antecedents in Fritz Lang's *Fury* (MGM, 1935) and *You Only Live Once* (United Artists, 1937), it was also clearly influenced by the new breed of crime thrillers that emerged during the mid-forties. It is distinguished by the superior performances of Mickey Rooney and Jeanne Cagney as the *femme fatale*.

Quinn, Anthony (b. 1915)

Actor. Born in Chihuahua, Mexico, the virile, good-looking Quinn began acting in films in his early twenties. For many years he played character roles, generally as the bad guy's sidekick or a mob henchman, but was always a welcome and popular performer. His frequent appearances in the gangster genre are devoted mostly to mobsters. Had he appeared in better films, he might have become a major icon of the genre.

Hunted Man (Paramount, 1938). *King of Alcatraz* (Paramount, 1938). *King of Chinatown* (Paramount, 1938). *Larceny, Inc.* (Warner Bros., 1942). *Roger Touhy, Gangster* (20th Century-Fox, 1944). *The Naked Street* (United Artists, 1955). *Across 110th Street* (United Artists, 1972). *The Don Is Dead* (Universal, 1973).

Race Street (RKO, 1948). 79 mins.

Producer: Nat Holt. *Director*: Edwin L. Marin. *Screenplay*: Martin Rackin, based on the story "The Twisted Road" by Maurice Davis. *Director of Photography*: J. Roy Hunt. *Music*: Roy Webb. *Art Directors*: Albert S. D'Agostino and Walter Keller. *Editor*: Sam E. Beetley.

Cast: George Raft (Dan Gannin), William Bendix (Runson), Marilyn Maxwell (Robbie), Frank Faylen (Phil Dickson), Harry Morgan (Hal Towers). *With*: Gale Robbins, Cully Richards, Mack Gray, Russell Hicks, Tom Keene, William Forrest, Jim Nolan.

Dan Gannin is a bookie who decides to go straight when he begins a romantic liaison with Robbie, the widow of a war veteran. Simultaneously, his partner is killed by an extortionist gang. Vowing revenge, Gannin hunts down the gang's members and with the assistance of Runson, a boyhood friend, brings the leader, Phil Dickson, to justice.

With a somewhat bigger budget than was usual for "B" pictures, *Race Street* has some excellent production values. It suffers, however, from a weak screenplay and relies on action and violence. Still, it is entertaining and remains one of George Raft's better gangster movies.

The Racket (Paramount, 1928). Approximately 70 mins.

Robert Ryan, gangster icon from the era of *film noir* from one of the classics of that age, *Racket*, a remake of the golden era gangster picture.

Presenter: Howard Hughes. *Director*: Lewis Milestone. *Screenplay*: Harry Behn and Del Andrews, based on the play by Bartlett Cormack. *Director of Photography*: Tony Gaudio. *Editor*: Tom Miranda.

Cast: Thomas Meighan (Captain McQuigg), Marie Provost (Helen Hayes), Louis Wolheim (Nick Scarsi), George E. Stone (Joe Scarsi), John Darrow (Ames the Reporter). *With*: Skeets Gallagher, Lee Moran, Lucien Prival, Tony Mario, Henry Sedley.

A silent adaptation of Bartlett Cormack's 1927 play, this first version has been described as a forerunner of *film noir* because of its expressionistic visual style. It is also, more importantly, a contemporary of Joseph von Sternberg's silent gangster movies. A sensational exposé of big city crime, it is one of the important late silent crime movies that helped kick off the initial cycle of gangster dramas in the early thirties.

The Racket (RKO, 1951). 89 mins.
Executive Producer: Howard Hughes. *Producer*: Edmund Grainger. *Director*: John Cromwell. *Screenplay*: W. W. Haines and W. R. Burnett, based on the play by Bartlett Cormack. *Director of Photography*: George E. Diskant. *Music Director*: Mischa Bakaleinikoff. *Art Directors*: Albert S. D'Agostino and Jack Okey. *Editor*: Sherman Todd.

Cast: Robert Mitchum (Capt. Tom McQuigg), Lizabeth Scott (Irene Hayes), Robert Ryan (Nick Scanlon), William Talman (Johnson), Ray Collins (Welch), Joyce McKenzie (Mary McQuigg). *With*: Virginia Huston, Robert Hutton, William Conrad, Walter Sande, Less Tremayne.

Based on Bartlett Cormack's slightly dated 1927 play, *The Racket* picked up box office momentum from a contemporaneous war on American organized crime by Chairman Estes Kefauver and his Senate Crime Investigating

Committee. Its plot centered on an incorruptible police officer, Captain Tom McQuigg, battling a gang boss, Nick Scanlon. Torn between them is the sultry nightclub singer, Irene Hayes. In the end, Scanlon's battles with McQuigg and a fellow mobster result in his death; but the city's corrupt officials remain in power, and a sadistic lieutenant takes Scanlon's place.

Howard Hughes, who produced the original version of Cormack's play, was always attuned to the commercial potential of underworld stories. He also produced *Scarface* (United Artists, 1932), and while *The Racket* is not as good, it was successful. Part of the film's box office success was due to its superior cast (including Robert Mitchum in his first good guy role in the *noir* genre, and the brilliant Robert Ryan), and its strong style. However, as either a straight gangster movie or as a *film noir*, it is still a minor film.

Racket Busters (Warner Bros., 1938). 71 mins.
   Associate Producer: Samuel Bischoff. *Director*: Lloyd Bacon. *Screenplay*: Robert Rossen and Leonardo Bercovici. *Director of Photography*: Arthur Edeson. *Music*: Adolph Deutsch. *Art Director*: Esdras Hartley. *Editor*: James Gibson.
   Cast: George Brent (Denny Jordan), Humphrey Bogart (John "Czar" Martin), Gloria Dickson (Nora Jordan), Allen Jenkins (Skeets Wilson), Walter Abel (Hugh Allison). *With*: Penny Singleton, Henry O'Neill, Oscar O'Shea, Elliott Sullivan, Fay Helm.
   John Martin, a gang boss, tries to take over a trucking company, but he is opposed by Hugh Allison, a crusading prosecutor, and Denny Jordan, an honest truck driver. Desperate for money after his wife becomes pregnant, Denny robs the truck company's office. However, the police allow him to go free if he will join the racketeers as an undercover agent. He agrees, helps gather information against the

gang boss and then leads a revolt against the racketeers. In the ensuing fight, Denny beats up Martin, and the gangster is arrested by the police.
   A mild diversion, *Racket Busters* is a rather typical "B" production, distinguished mainly by Humphrey Bogart's performance as gangster "Czar" Martin.

The Racketeer (Pathé, 1929). Approximately 75 mins.
   Associate Producer: Ralph Block. *Director*: Howard Higgin. *Screenplay*: Paul Gangelin. *Director of Photography*: David Abel. *Art Director*: Edward Jewell. *Editor*: Doane Harrison.
   Cast: Robert Armstrong (Keene), Carole Lombard (Rhoda), Roland Drew (Tony), Jeanette Loff (Millie), John Loder (Jack). *With*: Paul Hurst, Winter Hall, Winifred Harris, Kit Guard, Al Hill, Bobby Dunn.
   A mediocre melodrama, *The Racketeer* improbably centers on a gangster, Keene, who tries to reform Tony, a concert violinist gone astray, because Keene is in love with Tony's girlfriend, Rhoda, a society girl. Of course, Keene's criminal activities ultimately catch up with him and he is gunned down by a rival.
   Silly and contrite, *The Racketeer's* one saving grace is Carole Lombard in an early performance.

Rackin, Martin (1918–1976)
   Screenwriter. Rackin was a fine, talented commercial screenwriter. He specialized in action films with Hemingway-like themes of the individual confronting his own bravery and morality in the face of corrupt power. He wrote a few crime films, including several gangster pictures. None of these is particularly important or even very ambitious, but within their limitations, all are very well written.
   Buy Me That Town (Paramount, 1941). *Race Street* (RKO, 1948). *Loan Shark* (Lippert, 1952). *Hell on Frisco*

Bay (Warner Bros., 1956). *The F.B.I. Story* (Warner Bros., 1959).

Raft, George (1895–1980)

Actor. With Edgar G. Robinson, James Cagney and Humphrey Bogart, George Raft symbolizes the gangster genre as one of its great icons. Unlike the others, however, Raft allegedly had firsthand knowledge of the gangster underworld. Like Cagney, he grew up on the streets of New York City, and his childhood friends included many later criminals and gangsters. Raft himself was a street hustler, gambler, gigolo and vaudeville dancer before moving to Hollywood in the late twenties. He played small supporting roles until his part as the coin-tossing mobster in *Scarface* made him into a star. Ironically, his off-screen friendship with real life gangsters including Bugsy Siegel was widely reported in scandal sheets throughout his career and helped typecast his on screen image. He was very prolific, appearing in more films in the genre than any of the other major icons. However, his own talents were limited, and he starred in few real classics. Among the morass of indifferent and bad films in which he starred are some good movies, including the two prison dramas, *Each Dawn I Die* and *Invisible Stripes*, and *Night After Night*, *Race Street* and *Rogue Cop*. He varied his gangster roles with more sympathetic parts, but his poor choice of movies—he turned down *The Maltese Falcon* (Warner Bros., 1941) and *Casablanca* (Warner Bros., 1943), among others—assured that his career went into eclipse during the forties, when he was relegated to mostly "B" movies. Perhaps realizing he was a prisoner of his image, he accepted roles in whatever films came his way (almost always playing a variation of his thirties persona) and eventually played a parody of his screen image (that of the tuxedoed gangster) in Billy Wilder's great satire *Some Like It Hot*.

Hush Money (Fox, 1931). *Madame*

Racketeer (Paramount, 1932). *Night After Night* (Paramount, 1932). *Scarface* (United Artists, 1932). *Limehouse Blues* (Paramount, 1934). *The Glass Key* (Paramount, 1935). *Stolen Harmony* (Paramount, 1935). *You and Me* (Paramount, 1938). *Each Dawn I Die* (Warner Bros., 1939). *I Stole a Million* (Universal, 1939). *Invisible Stripes* (Warner Bros., 1939). *Race Street* (RKO, 1948). *Johnny Allegro* (Columbia, 1949). *Lucky Nick Cain* (20th Century-Fox, 1951). *Loan Shark* (Lippert, 1952). *Rogue Cop* (MGM, 1954). *A Bullet for Joey* (United Artists, 1955). *Some Like It Hot* (United Artists, 1959).

Raines, Ella (b. 1921)

Actress. Born Ella Raubes in Snoqualmie Falls, Washington, Raines was discovered by Howard Hawks, who cast her in *Corvette K-225* (Columbia, 1943). A pretty, thin brunette in the style of his other female discoveries, particularly Lauren Bacall, Raines never rose to the heights of Bacall, but she did star in many excellent "B" movies during the forties and fifties. She had a supporting role in *Brute Force* as one of the wives of the convicts planning an escape.

Brute Force (Universal, 1948).

Raksin, David (b. 1912)

Composer. Raksin is best known for his lush, melodic, romantic scores for melodramas, epitomized by his popular music for *Laura* (20th Century-Fox, 1944). He composed the music for four minor gangster movies.

San Quentin (Warner Bros., 1937). *The Big Combo* (Allied Artists, 1955). *Al Capone* (Allied Artists, 1959). *Pay or Die* (Allied Artists, 1960).

Raven, Philip (Fictional character)

In *This Gun for Hire* (Paramount, 1942), based on Grahame Green's novel, a new type of protagonist was introduced into the world of the gangster picture, the *film noir* antihero.

Alan Ladd played the stone-faced, soulless mob hit man who gets involved with a gang of thieves who are selling poison gas to the Japanese. He eventually exposes the gang and kills the leader before he is gunned down. Raven is typical of the *noir* protagonist, caught up in a web of danger partly of his own creation and from which he finds it impossible to escape.

Raw Deal (Eagle-Lion, 1948). 79 mins. *Producer*: Edward Small. *Director*: Anthony Mann. *Screenplay*: Leopold Atlas and John C. Higgins, *story by* Arnold B. Armstrong and Audrey Ashley. *Director of Photography*: John Alton. *Music*: Paul Sawtell. *Editor*: Alfred De Gaetano.

Cast: Dennis O'Keefe (Joe Sullivan), Claire Trevor (Pat), Marsha Hunt (Ann Martin), John Ireland (Fantail), Raymond Burr (Rick Coyle). *With*: Curt Conway, Chill Wills.

Pat, the faithful moll of gangster Joe Sullivan, helps him escape from prison. On their way to meet mob boss Rick Coyle they kidnap Ann, a social worker. Joe begins to fall for the pretty Ann, and does not realize that Coyle plans to doublecross his old associate. In the final confrontation, both Joe and Rick are killed, and Pat is left alone.

One of several low budget thrillers directed by Anthony Mann in the late forties, *Raw Deal* is a taut melodrama, distinguished by Claire Trevor's touching performance as the betrayed moll.

Ray, Aldo (b. 1926)
Actor. Born Aldo de Re in Pen Argyl, Pennsylvania, Ray was discovered by John Wayne. Beefy, with a voice like a foghorn, Ray was cast mainly in minor action pictures, with supporting roles in major productions. He starred in Jacques Tourneur's brilliant "B" *noir* *Nightfall* as the central character mixed up with two very dangerous bank robbers. Although not very well known, it does contain one of Ray's finest performances.
Nightfall (Columbia, 1956).

Ray, Nicholas (1911–1979)
Director. Born Raymond N. Kienzle, Ray studied architecture at the University of Chicago (under Frank Lloyd Wright), acted on the stage (directed by Elia Kazan), and first came to the attention of Hollywood as a writer and director for radio. Producer John Houseman hired him to direct *They Live by Night* for RKO. It was an auspicious debut, a widely praised and very successful version of the Bonnie and Clyde legend. Like Elia Kazan, Ray proved to be a sympathetic handler of actors and had a strong visual style. He subsequently directed a number of the important *films noir*. He also directed the disappointing semimusical gangster picture, *Party Girl*.
They Live by Night (RKO, 1948).
Party Girl, (MGM, 1958).

Reagan, Ronald (b. 1911)
Actor. Born in Tampico, Illinois, Reagan graduated from Eureka College in 1932 and worked for five years as a sports announcer before coming to the attention of Hollywood talent scouts in the late thirties. Signed to Warner Bros., he made his film debut in 1937. While he never became a full-fledged star — nor a very competent actor — he was popular throughout the forties and fifties in a series of modest action and romantic adventures. Late in his acting career he appeared in Don Siegel's *The Killers* as the businessman who arranges a mail truck robbery. It was his last film performance before he pursued a political career.
The Killers (Universal, 1964).

Redford, Robert (b. 1936)
Actor. Born Charles Redford in Santa Monica, California, Redford wanted to be an artist and traveled in Europe as a transient painter. Back in New York, when he found it difficult to make a

living as a painter, he turned to acting. He made his Broadway debut in 1963 and began appearing in movies around the same time. His blonde, striking good looks threatened to typecast him as a bland all–American type before he was cast opposite Paul Newman in *Butch Cassidy and the Sundance Kid* (Universal, 1969). The film was an enormous success and made Redford into a superstar. Redford and Newman, with director George Roy Hill, were subsequently reteamed for *The Sting*. Redford and Newman starred as the well dressed criminals involved in a complicated con job. Like its predecessor, it was an effective re-creation of a bygone era (in this case, twenties Chicago) told in a bright and witty manner. The film's enormous success helped cement Redford as one of the most charismatic stars of his generation.

The Sting (Universal, 1973).

Reis, Irving (1906–1953)

Screenwriter. Reis was a successful radio writer and worked as a screenwriter during the late thirties. He signed with RKO in 1940 as a director and made most of his best films for that studio. Among these is a superior *film noir*, *Crack-Up* (RKO, 1946), and the romantic comedy *The Bachelor and the Bobby Soxer* (RKO, 1947). His work as a director is more important than his screenplays. However, he was an adequate screenwriter. He wrote two minor "B" gangster pictures for Paramount in the late thirties.

King of Alcatraz (Paramount, 1938).
King of Chinatown (Paramount, 1938).

Republic Pictures Corporation

A small Hollywood production and distribution company founded in 1936 by former tobacco executive Herbert J. Yates, Republic was essentially a rich man's playground; yet, it managed to compete against the larger studios by churning out cheap but skillfully made second features and serials. The studio was the home of John Wayne and Roy Rogers, among others, and is best known for their Westerns. However, major directors like John Ford and Raoul Walsh made films for Republic. The studio produced a relatively small number of gangster pictures. None of them are classics, but all are competently made, particularly *The Last Crooked Mile* and *The Glass Alibi*, two of the more entertaining "B" gangster pictures.

1938: *Gangs of New York*. 1941: *Citadel of Crime*. 1946: *The Glass Alibi, The Last Crooked Mile*. 1952: *Hoodlum Empire*. 1955: *I Cover the Underworld*. 1956: *When Gangland Strikes*.

Reservoir Dogs (Live America, 1993).

120 mins.
Producers: Harvey Keitel and Lawrence Bender. *Director and Screenplay*: Quentin Tarantino. *Director of Photography*: Andrezej Sekula. *Music Supervisor*: Karyn Rachtman. *Production Designer*: David Wasco. *Editor*: Sally Menke.

Cast: Harvey Keitel (Mr. White/ Larry), Tim Roth (Mr. Orange/ Freddy), Michael Madsen (Mr. Blonde/Vic), Chris Penn (Nice Guy Eddie), Steve Buscemi (Mr. Pink), Lawrence Tierney (Joe Cabot). *With*: Randy Brooks, Kirk Baltz, Eddie Bunker, Quentin Tarantino, Rich Turner, David Steen.

In flashback and flash-forward, a heist, planned by Joe Cabot, has a bloody, tragic conclusion as the criminals turn on each other, torture a kidnapped cop, and murder several other cops and innocent bystanders.

Before this extraordinary debut, writer, director and actor Quentin Tarantino worked in a video store as a clerk and free-lanced as a screenwriter. He planned to shoot *Reservoir Dogs* as an art film on his earnings from one of his screenplays; Harvey Keitel, having read the script, offered to help produce and star in it, and the film was made for $2 million. An enormous critical success, it has given Tarantino an extraordinary boost. The film itself follows the typical heist plot, but is set apart by its innovative structure and extreme bloodletting (influenced by Martin Scorsese and John Woo).

Richmond, Ted (b. 1912)
Producer. A former screenwriter of mostly "B" pictures, Richmond began producing in the mid-forties. He produced many pictures, a few of which are outstanding, well into the seventies. Of the two gangster *noirs* he produced, the most important is *Nightfall*, an underrated thriller directed by Jacques Tourneur.
Forbidden (Universal, 1953). *Nightfall* (Columbia, 1957).

Riedenschneider, Erwin "Doc" (Fictional character)
In *The Asphalt Jungle* (MGM, 1950), Riedenschneider is the brains behind the jewelry heist that eventually and inevitably goes wrong. Played by Sam Jaffe, Doc Riedenschneider is an aging criminal who joins the makeshift gang of jewel thieves to help plan and execute the robbery—planned to be his last before retirement. But his cool intelligence and confidence masks some deep-seated psychological problems, not the least of which is a predilection for teenage girls. It is just this personality quirk which causes the downfall of his gang; after committing the robbery, and on the way out of town, Riedenschneider stops at a roadside cafe where he becomes entranced by a teenage girl who is dancing to a tune on the jukebox. Against his better judgment, he stays to watch her, unaware that the police are hot on his trail. The authorities capture him there before he can escape, and eventually the other gang members are also apprehended.

Rififi (United Artists/Miracle, 1955). 113 mins.
Director: Jules Dassin. *Screenplay*: Rene Wheeler, Jules Dassin and Auguste le Breton, based on the novel *Du Rififi Chez des Hommes*. *Director of Photography*: Phillipe Agostini. *Music*: Georges Auric. *Art Director*: Auguste Capelier. *Editor*: Roger Dwyre.
Cast: Jean Servais (Tony Le Stephanois), Carl Mohner (Jo Le Suedois), Robert Manuel (Mario), Perlo Vito (Cesar), Megali Moel (Viviane). *With*: Marie Sobouret, Janine Darcy, Pierre Grasset, Robert Hossein, Marcel Lupovici, Dominique Maurin.
Tony Le Stephanois and his gang plan and execute the robbery of a jewelry shop. The heist is successfully pulled off but immediately begins to fall apart when the gang becomes the target of a rival gang and the police.
Perhaps the greatest crime movie made in Paris, *Rififi* was directed by the American expatriate Jules Dassin. While inevitably compared to *The Asphalt Jungle* (MGM, 1950), *Rififi* has its own excellent qualities, not the least of which is a brilliantly staged robbery sequence. Gritty and realistic, the film is very entertaining and was enormously popular. Cast member Perlo Vita, incidentally, is in fact Jules Dassin playing one of the gang members. The film's great success inspired several sequels that were popular in France during the late fifties and early sixties.

Riot in Cell Block 11 (Allied Artists, 1954). 80 mins.
Producer: Walter Wanger. *Director*: Don Siegel. *Screenplay*: Richard Collins. *Director of Photography*: Russell Harlan. *Music*: Herschell Gilbert. *Art Director*: David Milton. *Editor*: Bruce Pierce.
Cast: Neville Brand (Dunn), Emile Meyer (The Warden), Frank Faylen (Haskel), Leo Gordon (Carnie), Robert Osterloh (The Colonel), Paul Frees (Monroe). *With*: Don Kefer, Alvy Moore, Dabbs Greer, Whit Bissell, James Acton, Carleton Young.
A group of prisoners led by Dunn takes several guards hostage to demand

better treatment. Some of the prisoners go berserk in a violent riot, attacking each other and tearing up the prison. Eventually, the warden signs a document listing the prisoners' demands, ending the riot and vindicating Dunn.

Shot on location at Folsom Prison, *Riot in Cell Block 11* is a taut, grim thriller loosely based on real events. It is an important movie for several reasons, including its accurate portrayal of prison life (and the corruption and sadism of the guards), and for showing the "bad guys" as the winners in their confrontation with the authorities—a risky element in the era of authoritarian figures like Joseph McCarthy. Indeed, it is one of the best prison gangster movies, a recognized classic of the genre.

Ripley, Arthur (1895–1961)

Director. Ripley is an enigma. He was a screenwriter, assistant director and associate producer before directing his first film in 1938. He subsequently directed four other films over the next twenty years, apparently suffering from mental problems and chemical dependencies. He directed two interesting if minor gangster thrillers. *The Chase* is a strange *noir* melodrama. *Thunder Road*, made at the behest of star and producer Robert Mitchum, is a unique addition the genre—the tragic tale of backwoods moonshiners. Ripley's style was flat and documentary-like.

The Chase (United Artists, 1946). *Thunder Road* (United Artists, 1958).

The Rise and Fall of Legs Diamond (Warner Bros., 1960). 103 mins.

Producer: Milton Sperling. *Director*: Budd Boetticher. *Screenplay*: Joseph Landon. *Director of Photography*: Lucien Ballard. *Art Director*: Jack Poplin. *Editor*: Folmar Blangsted.

Cast: Ray Danton ("Legs" Diamond), Karen Steele (Alice Shiffer), Elaine Stewart (Monica), Jesse White (Leo), Simon Oakland (Lieutenant Moody), Robert Lowery (Arnold Rothstein). *With*: Judson Pratt, Warren Oates, Dyan Cannon, Frank de Kova, Gordon Jones.

Jack "Legs" Diamond is a vaudeville hoofer (hence his nickname) and petty thief who joins the mob and eventually becomes the bodyguard for the mob boss. Entangled in mob politics and with the law, his life is further complicated by his involvement with two molls, Alice and Monica. He leaves the country to let things cool down, but is betrayed after his return by his jealous ex-flame, Monica. As he lays in a drunken daze in his hotel room, he is assassinated by fellow mobsters who believe he is trying to take over the gang.

While not entirely historically accurate, *The Rise and Fall of Legs Diamond* does give an entertaining portrait of one of the most colorful gangsters of the mid–twentieth century. Directed by Budd Boetticher, mainly known for his excellent "B" Westerns starring Randolph Scott, the film is typically violent and lurid.

Riskin, Robert (1897–1955)

Screenwriter. Riskin, formally a New York based journalist, moved to Hollywood in the early thirties and became a prominent screenwriter. He is probably best known for his collaborations with director Frank Capra on several classic seriocomedies: *It Happened One Night* (Columbia, 1934), *Mr. Deeds Goes to Town* (Columbia, 1936), *You Can't Take It with You* (Columbia, 1938), and *Mr. Smith Goes to Washington* (Columbia, 1939). He also wrote the screenplay for John Ford's witty gangster satire, *The Whole Town's Talking*, based on a novel by W. R. Burnett.

The Whole Town's Talking (Columbia, 1935).

Ritt, Martin (b. 1919)

Director. With experience in the theater and television, Ritt began directing

James Cagney as the former gangster temporarily gone straight, as a taxi driver, from the classic *The Roaring Twenties.*

features in the mid-fifties. He has directed a few critically praised films in the style of Elia Kazan. His single gangster movie, *The Brotherhood*, is well made, but not particularly important. *The Brotherhood* (Paramount, 1968).

RKO

Founded in the late twenties as a joint enterprise of the Radio Corporation of America and the Keith-Orpheum cinema theater circuit to exploit the new sound technologies, the studio had great financial difficulties compounded by the Great Depression, yet managed to survive for three decades under a succession of administrations. Despite its varied leadership, the studio also developed its own unique house style, characterized during the thirties by its art deco style and sexual comedies. During the forties, a more cynical style emerged, characterized by expressionism. It was during this period that RKO produced the majority

of its gangster films, all *films noir*. Of these, probably the best known is the classic *Out of the Past*, a prototypical example of the genre at its best. Following the success of *Out of the Past*, RKO released some of the great gangster *noirs* of the late forties: *They Live by Night* (based on the Bonnie and Clyde legend), *His Kind of Woman*, *The Big Steal*, *The Narrow Margin*, and others. In 1948 Howard Hughes purchased the studio, and his eccentric reign saw the creation of some great films, and also a tendency toward conservative politics. By 1953 the studio had virtually been run into the ground by his poor business decisions and was sold to the Desilu television company; by 1957 it had ceased production altogether. However, despite its relatively small output, RKO contributed some of the most important and influential gangster movies of the *noir* style that were produced from the early forties until the mid-fifties.

Humphrey Bogart about to be shot by James Cagney in the bloody climax of *The Roaring Twenties.*

1930: *The Pay-Off.* 1938: *Law of the Underworld.* 1943: *Mr. Lucky.* 1947: *Out of the Past.* 1948: *Race Street, They Live by Night.* 1949: *The Big Steal, The Set-Up.* 1951: *His Kind of Woman, The Racket.* 1952: *The Narrow Margin.*

Roadhouse Nights (Paramount, 1930). 71 mins.
Director: Hobart Henley. *Screenplay*: Garrett Fort, *story by* Ben Hecht. *Director of Photography*: William Steiner. *Songs*: E. Y. Harburg and Jay Gorney; Eddie Jackson and Lou Clayton; and Jimmy Durant. *Editor*: Helene Turner.
Cast: Helen Morgan (Lola Fagen), Charles Ruggles (Willie), Fred Kohler (Sam Horner), Jimmy Durante (Daffy), Fuller Melish, Jr. (Hogan). *With*: Leo Donnelly, Tammany Young, Joe King, Lou Clayton, Eddie Jackson.

When a reporter is murdered by a small-town gangster, Willie Bindbugel, a fellow reporter from the same paper, is sent to find out who the killer is.

Willie discovers a town corrupted by a bootlegger, Sam Horner, and his gang. At Horner's headquarters, a roadhouse, Willie is surprised to find that Lola, the singer, is an old flame and Horner's mistress. They renew their romance and she leads him away from Horner's hit men just before the timely arrival of the authorities.

Despite the contrived and melodramatic plot, *Roadhouse Nights* is tawdry entertainment thanks to the half-clad roadhouse dancers, the smokey nightclubs, and Helen Morgan's performance of several torch songs. Jimmy Durante appears as Daffy, a nightclub comedian who befriends the reporter, played by comic actor Charles Ruggles. Altogether a strange mixture, but a compelling one nevertheless.

The Roaring Twenties (Warner Bros., 1939). 106 mins.
Executive Producer: Hal B. Wallis. *Associate Producer*: Samuel Bischoff.

Directors: Raoul Walsh and Anatole Litvak. *Screenplay*: Jerry Wald, Richard Macaulay, Robert Rossen, *story by* Mark Hellinger. *Director of Photography*: Ernest Haller. *Music*: Heinz Roemheld and Ray Heindorf. *Art Director*: Max Parker. *Editor*: Jack Killifer.

Cast: James Cagney (Eddie Bartlett), Priscilla Lane (Jean Sherman), Humphrey Bogart (George Hally), Jeffrey Lynn (Lloyd Hart), Gladys George (Panama Smith), Frank McHugh (Danny Green). *With*: Paul Kelly, Elizabeth Risdon, Ed Keane, Joseph Sawyer, Abner Biberman, John Deering, Ray Cooke.

Three veterans of World War I return to New York City and pursue very different careers. Lloyd Hart becomes a lawyer, Eddie Bartlett a taxi driver, and George Hally a bootlegger. Eddie later starts his own bootlegging business and joins George. A gang war erupts when Eddie hijacks a rival's cache of liquor, and eventually George and Eddie go their separate ways. With the stock market crash in 1929 and then the repeal of Prohibition several years later, Eddie's empire collapses. He is left with a single taxi. He agrees to come to the aid of his old friend, Lloyd, whose life has been threatened by George. Eddie kills his old partner, but is himself gunned down in front of a church.

One of the last great gangster movies of the thirties, *The Roaring Twenties* is filled with larger than life talents, including James Cagney and Humphrey Bogart at their best. Raoul Walsh's direction is taut, suspenseful and full of action, thanks to a superb screenplay. In addition, the soundtrack is full of classic songs from the twenties, anticipating the contemporary trend (particularly used by Martin Scorcese) of using pop songs to pinpoint an era and mood, a revolutionary element in the late thirties. *The Roaring Twenties* epitomizes Warner Bros.' style and themes of the thirties, and it was a

perfect cap to the series of classic gangster movies produced by the studio during that decade.

Robards, Jason (b. 1920)

Actor. The son of the respected stage and screen character actor Jason Robards, Sr., Robards has made a name for himself playing eccentrics and intense character roles in movies and on television. In the "B" gangster movie *The St. Valentine's Day Massacre*, he starred as a particularly psychotic Al Capone.

The St. Valentine's Day Massacre (20th Century–Fox, 1967).

Roberts, Florian (1900–1979)

Florian Roberts was the pseudonym of Robert Florey under which he directed a single gangster movie.

Lady Gangster (Warner Bros., 1942).

Robertson, Cliff (b. 1925)

Actor. Born in La Jolla, California, Robertson spent many years on stage before his screen debut at the age of thirty. Handsome, and a good actor, he generally played good guys, and boy next door types. He starred in Samuel Fuller's *Underworld USA* as a petty crook who infiltrates the mob to avenge the gangland murder of his father.

Underworld USA (Columbia, 1961).

Robinson, Edward G. (1893–1973)

Actor. It is perhaps ironic that the man most identified with the gangster genre as its quintessential tough guy was in real life a gentle, cultured man who collected art (his impressionist collection was one of the great private collections of the mid–twentieth century) and was a contributor to human rights and other liberal causes. Born Emmanuel Goldenberg in Bucharest, Romania, Robinson immigrated to the United States at the age of ten. He began acting in his teens and was a major stage actor in New York during the twenties. His film career began in in 1929, but he did not become a full-fledged star until he played the lead in *Little Caesar*. Mervyn LeRoy's gangster melodrama, loosely based on the life of Al Capone, was an enormous box office success, largely due to Robinson's charismatic performance. Unfortunately, it also typecast him as a tough guy. Between the tough guy roles in the genre (which he continued to play sporadically for thirty years, along with many other types of roles), he played a series of interesting variations on his tough guy image. He starred in several gangster satires, including *The Little Giant*, *Brother Orchid* and John Ford's neglected classic *The Whole Town's Talking*. However, it is certainly as a tough guy that he is best remembered, and he followed *Little Caesar* with several similar roles during the thirties in films such as *The Amazing Dr. Clitterhouse*, *Kid Galahad*, *The Last Gangster*. His popularity diminished in the late thirties, but was revitalized during the mid-forties when he starred in two *films noir* directed by Fritz Lang. His renewed popularity was confirmed when he starred in John Huston's *Key Largo* as the psychotic mob boss Johnny Rocco. It was his last important role in the genre, although he continued to play gangsters well into the fifties (in mostly "B" movies) and even in the sixties when he played gang leaders in two minor heist movies, *Grand Slam* and *The Biggest Bundle of Them All*. Without question, Edward G. Robinson remains the genre's greatest icon, and his best performances elevated even the most indifferent material to a higher plane.

The Hole in the Wall (Paramount, 1929). *Outside the Law* (Universal, 1930). *Little Caesar* (First National, 1931). *Smart Money* (Warner Bros., 1931). *The Little Giant* (First National, 1933). *The Whole Town's Talking* (Columbia, 1935). *Kid Galahad* (Warner Bros., 1937). *The Last Gangster*

(MGM, 1937). *The Amazing Dr. Clitterhouse* (Warner Bros., 1938). *I Am the Law* (Columbia, 1938). *A Slight Case of Murder* (Warner Bros., 1938). *Brother Orchid* (Warner Bros., 1940). *Larceny, Inc.* (Warner Bros., 1942). *Key Largo* (Warner Bros., 1948). *Black Tuesday* (United Artists, 1954). *A Bullet for Joey* (United Artists, 1955). *Illegal* (Warner Bros., 1955). *Tight Spot* (Columbia, 1955). *Seven Thieves* (20th Century-Fox, 1960). *The Biggest Bundle of Them All* (MGM, 1968). *Grand Slam* (Paramount, 1968).

Robson, Mark (1913–1978)

Director. Originally an editor, Robson became a director under producer Val Lewton, helming several of the producer's horror films during the mid-forties. He had a strong visual style influenced to some degree by expressionism. His single gangster movie, *The Harder They Fall*, is probably best known as one of Humphrey Bogart's last movies, and is a superior melodrama and exposé of the corrupt boxing world.

The Harder They Fall (Columbia, 1956).

Rocco, Johnny (Fictional character)

Edward G. Robinson's last gangster role in a major film, *Key Largo* (Warner Bros., 1948). Johnny Rocco is a sadistic gangster on the run—he hopes to escape to Cuba before the F.B.I. can find and arrest him—who takes over a small Florida resort hotel with the remainder of his gang to wait out a violent storm. He verbally and physically abuses his mistress, Gaye Dawn (Claire Trevor), as well as his hostages, including Frank McCloud (Humphrey Bogart). McCloud is a veteran who had come to the rundown hotel to visit its proprietors, James and Nora Temple, the father and widow of a war friend killed in action. Rocco and McCloud, symbols of good and evil on several levels, have a conflict of wills which ends, perhaps inevitably, in

Rocco's death at the hands of McCloud, a liberal pacificist who has come to realize, through his confrontation with the mobster, that one must sometimes resort to violence to maintain dignity and freedom. Robinson's performance is typically charismatic, and Johnny Rocco remains one of his best remembered gangster roles.

Roe, Guy
Cinematographer. Roe was most active in the fifties, during which he photographed many "A" and "B" movies. Technically proficient, he did not have a pronounced individual style. He photographed a single gangster movie.
My Six Convicts (Columbia, 1952).

Roemheld, Heinz (1906–1955)
Composer. The German-born Roemheld moved to Hollywood in the early forties, yet another refugee from Hitler's regime. Like Max Steiner, he was long employed by Warner Bros., and he composed the scores for many of their productions during the thirties and forties. He had a typically romantic and dramatic style; and if his music was less melodically memorable than Steiner's, it was no less expressive, and always a welcome addition to any film.
Bullets or Ballots (First National, 1936). *Marked Woman* (Warner Bros., 1937). *San Quentin* (Warner Bros., 1937). *Invisible Stripes* (Warner Bros., 1939). *The Roaring Twenties* (Warner Bros., 1939). *You Can't Get Away with Murder* (Warner Bros., 1939). *Brother Orchid* (Warner Bros., 1940).

Roger Touhy, Gangster (20th Century-Fox, 1944). 65 mins.
Producer: Lee Marcus. *Director*: Robert Florey. *Screenplay*: Crane Wilbur and Jerry Cady. *Director of Photography*: Glen MacWilliams. *Music*: Hugo W. Friedhofer. *Art Directors*: James Basevi and Lewis Creber. *Editor*: Harry Reynolds.

Cast: Preston Foster (Roger Touhy), Victor McLaglen (Owl Banghart), Lois Andrews (Daisy), Kent Taylor (Steve Warren), Anthony Quinn (George Carroll). *With*: William Post, Jr., Henry Morgan, Matt Briggs, Moroni Olsen, Reed Hadley, Trudy Marshall, John Archer.
Set in Chicago, the film tells the story of Roger Touhy, a bootlegger and rival of Al Capone. Touhy's gang is framed on a kidnapping charge when the bootlegger's ex-partner disappears. A witness is murdered, and Touhy, after a failed escape, is sent to prison.
Very loosely based on real events, the real Touhy was indeed a gangster in opposition to Al Capone. In the late twenties, he was sentenced to prison for 99 years, but whether he was framed or not is open to question. He was released in the late fifties, apparently resumed his criminal activities, and was gunned down a number of years later, allegedly by remnants of Capone's old gang. In any case, this film is a lame attempt at the kind of formula that worked so well in the thirties, relying on a second-rate cast to tell its story.

Rogers, Ginger (1911–1995)
Actress. Rogers, a sassy, sexy, sharp-tongued blonde was a great comedienne who longed to do serious, dramatic roles, but achieved immortality as Fred Astaire's dancing partner in a series of incomparable musicals during the thirties. She somehow managed to survive the decade without once appearing in a gangster movie, but late in her career she starred in Phil Karlson's *Tight Spot* as a government witness against the mob — just the sort of role she longed for two decades before. Although not an important film, Rogers' performance is good.
Tight Spot (Columbia, 1955).

Rogue Cop (MGM, 1954). 92 mins.
Producer: Nicholas Nayfack. *Director*: Roy Rowland. *Screenplay*: Sydney Boehm, based on the novel by William

P. McGivern. *Director of Photography*: John Seitz. *Music*: Jeff Alexander. *Art Director*: Cedric Gibbons. *Editor*: James E. Newcom.

Cast: Robert Taylor (Christopher Kelvaney), Janet Leigh (Karen Stephanson), George Raft (Dan Beaumonte), Steve Forrest (Eddie Kelvaney), Anne Francis (Nancy Corlane). *With*: Robert Ellenstein, Robert F. Simon, Anthony Ross, Alan Hale, Jr., Peter Brocco, Vince Edwards.

Christopher Kelvaney, a big-city cop, is on the take, accepting bribes from mob boss Dan Beaumonte. When Kelvaney's younger brother, Eddie, arrests one of Beaumonte's henchmen, he is offered a bribe, but Eddie, an honest cop, refuses, and Beaumonte orders him killed. Angered by his brother's murder, Kelvaney turns in evidence against Beaumonte, and then goes to confront the mobster. In the inevitable shootout, Beaumonte is killed and Kelvaney is arrested for his past crimes.

A superior gangster thriller in the new *noir*-like style of the fifties, *Rogue Cop* was obviously influenced by Fritz Lang's *The Big Heat* (Columbia, 1953). Director Roy Rowland is an underrated director of thrillers, equal in many ways to Raoul Walsh and William Wellman. Like them, his style is unadorned and direct, and relies on violence and action. In other words, he made thrillers in the style of Warner Bros., circa 1935, an unusual kind of filmmaker for MGM in the era of its classic, glossy musicals. Indeed, *Rogue Cop* can be favorably compared to the great gangster movies released by Warner Bros. two decades before. It is also notable for George Raft's excellent performance as the sadistic mob boss.

Roland, Gilbert (1905–1994)

Actor. Born Luis Antonio Damaso de Alonso in Juarez, Mexico, the tall, handsome Roland was one of the most prominent Valentino-like Latin lovers of the late silent era. With the arrival of sound, Roland's popularity was diminished, but he continued to play second leads and character roles in "A" films and leads in "B" movies. He starred in a single "B" gangster movie, as a mobster.

Midnight Taxi (20th Century–Fox, 1937).

Roman, Ruth (b. 1924)

Actress. Born in Boston, Massachusetts, Ruth Roman attended the Bishop Lee Dramatic School before beginning a stage and film career in the early forties. A very capable actress, she did not become a major star. She is probably best known today for her performance in Alfred Hitchcock's *noir* thriller *Strangers on a Train* (Universal, 1951). She costarred with Paul Douglas in *Joe Macbeth*, a curious "B" gangster drama loosely based on the Shakespeare play.

Joe Macbeth (Columbia, 1955).

Romero, Cesar (1907–1994)

Actor. Born in New York City, the dark, handsome Romero was Hollywood's chief Latin lover during the thirties, forties and fifties. He was generally a second lead in "A" productions while also starring in "B" movies. He starred in two gangster pictures, the most important being *Show Them No Mercy* in which he starred as a gangster holding a family hostage. He also played a gangster in the other film.

Show Them No Mercy (20th Century–Fox, 1935). *Public Enemy's Wife* (Warner Bros., 1936).

Rooney, Mickey (b. 1920)

Actor. Born Joe Yule, Jr., Mickey Rooney was probably the most successful juvenile actor in the history of American movies. His film career began in the mid-twenties, when he starred in a series of popular short comedies. He played small roles in many popular movies during the early thirties, including a bit as a street urchin in the classic early gangster movie *City Streets*. An extremely talented actor with an intense style, he was able, better than any other former child actors, to continue his career as an adult. He often starred in high quality "B" movies during the fifties, when he appeared in three gangster movies. Each is distinguished by his strong performance, with the *noir* thriller *Quicksand* standing out as a superior "B" picture.

City Streets (Paramount, 1931). *Quicksand* (United Artists, 1950). *The Big Operative* (MGM, 1959). *The Last Mile* (United Artists, 1959).

Rosi, Francesco (b. 1922)

Director. An Italian director of well made commercial films, Rosi directed a biopic of real life gangster Lucky Luciano, a rather poor attempt to cash in on the success of *The Godfather* (Paramount, 1972).

Lucky Luciano (Avco-Embassy, 1974).

Rossen, Robert (1908–1966)

Writer, producer and director. Originally a journalist, Rossen went to Hollywood in the late thirties and distinguished himself as a screenwriter of superior commercial films. As a staff screenwriter for Warner Bros., he wrote several important gangster movies, including *Marked Woman*, *Racket Busters*, and most importantly, *The Roaring Twenties*, during the latter part of the decade. He joined Paramount in the forties and wrote the classic *film noir The Strange Love of Martha Ivers* (Paramount, 1946) and the lesser known gangster melodrama *Desert Fury*, a variation on *The Petrified Forest* (Warner Bros., 1936). He began directing after this success, making several classics over the next two decades. He had a surprisingly strong visual style (a rarity for screenwriters turned director), and a penchant for themes of corruption. Although he did not write *Body and Soul*, this film is typical: a study of the underworld's corruption of the boxing world, told in

unsentimental style. It is a classic of the genre.

Marked Woman (Warner Bros., 1937; screenplay only). *Racket Busters* (Warner Bros., 1938; screenplay only). *The Roaring Twenties* (Warner Bros., 1939; screenplay only). *Body and Soul* (United Artists, 1947; director only).

Rosson, Hal, aka Harold (1895–1960)

Cinematographer. The British-born Rosson moved to Hollywood in the late teens and later became one of the most important cinematographers of the thirties, forties and fifties. Long employed by MGM, he photographed many of that studio's classics, including the color movies *The Wizard of Oz* (1939), *On the Town* (1949), and *Singing in the Rain* (1952). His black and white work is no less important, and includes Josef von Sternberg's seminal gangster drama *The Docks of New York* and John Huston's gangster *noir The Asphalt Jungle*, his two most important contributions to the genre.

The Docks of New York (Paramount, 1928). *The Dragnet* (Paramount, 1928). *Penthouse* (MGM, 1933). *The Asphalt Jungle* (MGM, 1950). *Pete Kelly's Blues* (Warner Bros., 1955).

Rourke, Mickey (b. 1950)

Actor. Rourke's abrasive, confrontational style and propensity for mumbling has subverted a once promising talent. One of his best performances was in Michael Cimino's controversial and little-seen *The Year of the Dragon* in which he starred as a cop involved with Chinese gangsters.

The Year of the Dragon (MGM/ United Artists, 1985).

Rouse, Russell (b. 1916)

Screenwriter and director. Rouse had a long career as a screenwriter, usually collaborating with Clarence Green. They made a number of films together, with Green producing and Rouse directing. Among these is a passable "B" gangster thriller, *New York Confidential*, his only contribution to the genre.

New York Confidential (Warner Bros., 1955).

Rowland, Roy (b. 1910)
Director. Rowland abandoned a career in law to join MGM as a production assistant during the early thirties. In 1934 he directed a sequence in the compilation *Hollywood Party* for the studio, but did not begin to direct full-time until the early forties. He was technically accomplished, particularly with hard-boiled material. His gangster-police procedural *Rogue Cop* is a superior "B" movie.

Rogue Cop (MGM, 1954).

Rowlands, Gena (b. 1934)
Actress. A cool, beautiful blonde, Rowlands is best known for her performances in her husband John Cassavetes' movies. Among these is *Gloria*, in which she starred in the title role as a gangster's moll who becomes a target of the mob.

Gloria (Columbia, 1980).

Rozsa, Miklos (1907–1995)
Composer. The Hungarian-born Rozsa made a name for himself in the thirties as a serious composer before proving to be a brilliant film composer. He worked in England during the late thirties before moving to Hollywood in 1940. His dramatic, moody sensibilities were particularly well suited to thrillers, and he composed the scores for many classic *films noir*, gangster dramas, and costume epics.

The Killers (Universal, 1946). *Desert Fury* (Paramount, 1947). *The Bribe* (MGM, 1949). *Criss Cross* (Universal, 1949).

Ruddy, Albert S. (b. 1934)
Producer. Extremely active in the seventies, during which he produced a number of commercially successful films, Ruddy's most important contribution to American cinema is *The Godfather*, which remains his most ambitious production.

The Godfather (Paramount, 1972).

Runyon, Damon (1884–1946)
Writer. A journalist and short story writer, Runyon is an important writer of American popular literature, best known for his chronicles of a very imaginative New York City populated by, among others, good-hearted gangsters. His amusing satires were very popular, and many of his stories were adapted for the screen. Each is characterized by a broad sense of humor, gangsters with odd names, and more than a touch of sentimentality.

Lady for a Day (Columbia, 1933). *A Slight Case of Murder* (Warner Bros., 1938). *Guys and Dolls* (MGM, 1955).

Rural gangsters
During the Great Depression, a number of gangs sprang up in the Midwest and Southwest, comprised of mostly rural folk. They wandered from town to town, where they committed their crimes. Unlike the Mafia and the big-city gangs, these gangsters were more like the gangs of the old West, surviving on bank robberies, store thefts, and indiscriminate murders. Most of the rural gangs were made up of three or four individuals, some of whom were often related by blood or marriage. Perhaps the most famous of these rural gangsters were Bonnie and Clyde Barrow and their gang of relatives. Roaming through Texas, Oklahoma, and Louisiana, Bonnie and Clyde left a trail of murder and mayhem through the South, but also became folk heroes to many poor Americans during the early thirties. They inspired a whole rash of novels and films, including *They Live by Night* (RKO, 1948) and *Gun Crazy* (United Artists, 1950) (both of which took liberties with the real story), *The Bonnie Parker Story* (American International, 1953), an excellent "B" biopic (only

loosely based on Bonnie Parker's real life), and the extremely successful *Bonnie and Clyde* (Warner Bros., 1967).

Like Bonnie and Clyde, John Dillinger was a rural native who found crime an easier way to make a living. As murderous as the Barrow gang, John Dillinger's gang covered more territory through many states in the North and Midwest during the same period as the Barrows did in the South (1930–1934). Among the members of Dillinger's gang were Baby Face Nelson and Pretty Boy Floyd, who briefly carried on without him after he was killed in Chicago by the F.B.I. in 1934. Dillinger was brilliantly portrayed by Lawrence Tierney in *Dillinger* (Monogram, 1945) and Warren Oates in *Dillinger* (American International, 1973). Less memorable was *Young Dillinger* (Allied Artists, 1965), a highly fictional account of Dillinger's early life of crime. Dillinger's gang is also the subject of *Baby Face Nelson* (United Artists, 1957) and *Pretty Boy Floyd* (Continental, 1960).

"Ma" Barker and her gang of sons and their wives operated mostly in and around Chicago during the mid-thirties, but were otherwise similar to the Barrow and Dillinger gangs. The Barker gang inspired several films, including *Queen of the Mob* (Paramount, 1940), *Bloody Mama* (American International, 1970) and *Crazy Mama* (New World, 1975).

Martin Scorsese's *Boxcar Bertha* (American International, 1972) was based on the real life adventures of a somewhat less murderous rural gangster, Bertha Thompson, who, with her husband and a friend, committed a series of bank and train robberies during the thirties.

The activities of these gangs also inspired a number of other films about rural gangsters, including Fritz Lang's *You Only Live Once* (United Artists, 1937), the little-known minor classic *Desert Fury* (Paramount, 1947), and, of course, two classics starring Humphrey Bogart, *High Sierra* (Warner Bros., 1941) and *The Petrified Forest* (Warner Bros., 1936).

Russell, Jane (b. 1921)
Actress. Born in Bemidji, Minnesota, Russell got her break in show business when her agent sent her photograph to film producer and multimillionaire Howard Hughes, who cast her in *The Outlaw* (United Artists, 1940). Her considerable physical attributes became the initial focus of attention on her, but she proved to be a good actress, bringing a tongue-in-cheek humor to her performances. Following Hughes to RKO in the late forties, she was cast in several exotic thrillers, including a superior gangster drama, *His Kind of Woman*.

His Kind of Woman (RKO, 1951).

Ruttenberg, Joseph (1889–1983)
Cinematographer. The Russian born Ruttenberg immigrated to the United States in 1915. Beginning in the twenties, he was an important cinematographer for four decades, working in both black and white and color with equally creative results.

The Bribe (MGM, 1949). *Side Street* (MGM, 1949).

Ryan, Robert (1909–1973)
Actor. Ryan was a college athlete who tried professional boxing and modeling before becoming an actor. His strong and immobile features made him a perfect antihero during the cynical forties, and he emerged as a superstar of the era, particularly in *films noir*. He appeared in four gangster movies. In *The Set-Up*, one of several *films noir* based on the corrupt sport of boxing, Ryan was able to draw upon his youthful experiences while playing the boxer compromised by mobsters. He played criminals in his other three gangster movies, most uniquely in *Odds Against Tomorrow* as a racist teamed with a black man in a doomed heist.

The Set-Up (RKO, 1949). *The Racket* (RKO, 1951). *Odds Against Tomorrow* (United Artists, 1951). *The Outfit* (MGM, 1973).

Saint, Eva Marie (b. 1924)
Actress. Born in Newark, New Jersey, this cool, blonde, intelligent actress began her career on Broadway. She made an astonishing screen debut as the widow of a slain union man mixed up with the mob in Elia Kazan's *On the Waterfront*, for which she won an Academy Award as best supporting actress.
On the Waterfront (Columbia, 1954).

St. Clair, Malcolm (1897–1952)
Director. In the twenties it looked as if Malcolm St. Clair was destined for great things when he directed several classic romantic comedies in the manner of Ernst Lubitsch. However, he never lived up to this early promise, and by the mid-thirties was directing "B" movies for 20th Century–Fox. While his silent comedies are often brilliant, polished, and very funny, his later films are mostly uninspired. His single gangster movie is passable entertainment, but little else.
Born Reckless (20th Century–Fox, 1937).

The St. Valentine's Day Massacre (20th Century–Fox, 1967). 100 mins.
Producer and Director: Roger Corman. *Screenplay*: Howard Browne. *Director of Photography*: Milton Krasner. *Music*: Fred Steiner. *Art Directors*: Jack Martin Smith and Philip Jefferies. *Editor*: William B. Murphy.
Cast: Jason Robards (Al Capone), George Segal (Peter Gusenberg), Ralph Meeker (George "Bugs" Moran), Jean Hale (Myrtle Nelson/Koppleman), Clint Ritchie (Machine Gun McGurn), Frank Silvera (Nicholas Sorello). *With*: Joseph Campanella, Richard Bakalyan, David Canary, Bruce Dern, Harold J. Stone, Kurt Krueger.
The film retells the events leading up to February 14, 1929, and the subsequent murder of Bugs Moran and his henchmen by assassins hired by Al Capone. The role of Capone was miscast, and the overall effect is sloppy and poorly made; yet, the film was an enormous success at the time. It is only a minor addition to the genre, made tolerable by its tawdry settings, reliance on violent action, and Ralph Meeker's superb performance as Bugs Moran.

Salkow, Sidney (b. 1909)
Director. Salkow, a native New Yorker, came to the movies via the stage, where he had been a director. His early film career was varied, including stints as a dialogue director, assistant director, and associate producer before he began directing in 1937. Strictly a director of "B" movies, he had some talent and was particularly adept with contemporary thrillers and violent Westerns. He directed two "B" gangster pictures, and, while not anything really special, they are well above average.
Las Vegas Shakedown (Allied Artists, 1955). *Chicago Confidential* (United Artists, 1957).

Le Samourai (CICC-Fida Cinematografica, 1967). 103 mins.
Producer: Eugene Lepicier. *Director*: Jean-Pierre Melville. *Screenplay*: Jean-Pierre Melville, based on the novel *The Ronin* by Joan McLeod. *Director of Photography*: Henri Decae. *Music*: François De Roubaix. *Art Director*: François De Lamothe. *Editors*: Monique Bonnot and Yolande Maurette.
Cast: Alain Delon (Jeff Costello), Nathalie Delon (Jane), François Perier (The Inspector), Cathy Rosier (Valerie), Jacques Leroy (Gunman). *With*: Jean-Pierre Posier, Catherine Jourdan, Michel Boisrond, Robert Favart, Andre Salgues.
Jeff Costello is a professional killer who works for the Paris mob. When he is ordered to kill the owner of a nightclub, he carries out the crime in his usual, ritualistic manner. He later comes to believe his boss has targeted

him, so Jeff kills him. Realizing that he has boxed himself into an inescapable corner, Jeff willingly walks into a police trap and is gunned down.

Owing an enormous debt to both *film noir* and the gangster genre, *Le Samourai* is a typically eccentric, existential underworld thriller directed by Jean-Pierre Melville. It is one of several similar films directed by Melville during the forties, fifties and sixties, and probably the best known. It is in fact superior to any of the movies directed by the New Wave filmmakers, and it has been cited as a major influence on the contemporary American writer-director Quentin Tarantino and Hong Kong director John Woo.

San Quentin (Warner Bros., 1937). 70 mins.
Associate Producer: Samuel Bischoff. *Director*: Lloyd Bacon. *Screenplay*: Peter Milne and Humphrey Cobb. *Director of Photography*: Sid Hickox. *Music*: Heinz Roemheld, Charles Maxwell and David Raksin. *Art Director*: Esdras Hartley. *Editor*: William Holmes.
Cast: Pat O'Brien (Capt. Steve Jameson), Humphrey Bogart (Joe "Red" Kennedy), Ann Sheridan (May Kennedy), Barton MacLane (Lieutenant Druggin), Joseph Sawyer (Sailor Boy Hansen), Veda Ann Borg (Helen). *With*: James Robbins, Joseph King, Gordon Oliver, Garry Owen, Marc Lawrence, Emmett Vogan.

An honest, good-hearted prison guard, Captain Steve Jameson, falls in love with cafe singer May Kennedy. May's brother Joe is a prisoner at San Quentin, the prison where Jameson works. Jameson's attempts to reform prisoners are thwarted by his boss, who plants an informer among the prisoners. The informer, Sailor Boy Hansen, and Joe break out of prison with the help of Joe's moll. Joe goes to May's apartment, surprising Jameson and shooting him. May informs Joe of Jameson's good intentions, convincing

him to return to the penitentiary. However, he is mortally wounded by the police; but before he dies, he expresses his wish that the prisoners go along with Jameson's reforms.

San Quentin has been described as the ultimate Warner Bros.' "B" gangster movie, largely because of its reliance on clichés, a ludicrous plot and, of course, its "B" cast (Bogart was not yet a full-fledged star). Nevertheless, despite the just passable script, it is technically very well made and superbly performed. Its production values are also above average, and all in all, the film succeeds as hard-boiled entertainment.

Sarto, "Little John" (Fictional character)

In real life, Edward G. Robinson was a cultured, quiet man who collected impressionist paintings and was, among his colleagues, also known for his wit. He was not above kidding his own tough guy image, as he demonstrated admirably in at least two notable cases, in John Ford's *The Whole Town's Talking* (Columbia, 1935) and as "Little John" Sarto in *Brother Orchid* (Warner Bros., 1940). After abandoning his criminal milieu to go abroad and acquire culture, Sarto returns home to find his position as mob boss usurped by his former lieutenant. He forms a rival gang, but is captured and taken for a one-way ride. Left for dead, he is rescued by a group of monks who take him to their monastery and nurse him back to health. He becomes the cultivator of the monastery's orchids, and when the gangsters try to take over their flower business, Sarto helps defeat the mobsters and bring them to justice. He decides to remain at the monastery where he has at last found peace and "real class."

Satires and musicals

New York columnist and short story writer Damon Runyon made a specialty of his humorous stories featuring colorful gangsters. Two of his works were made into famous films, the comedy *Lady for a Day* (Columbia, 1933) and the musical *Guys and Dolls* (MGM, 1955). During the heyday of the genre, there were a number of gangster satires, including three starring Edward G. Robinson: *The Whole Town's Talking* (Columbia, 1935), *Brother Orchid* (Warner Bros., 1940) and *Larceny, Inc* (Warner Bros., 1942). However, the most famous gangster satire is Billy Wilder's rollicking *Some Like It Hot* (United Artists, 1959), which had much to say about the genre and America during the twenties. In the seventies, *The Sting* (Universal, 1973) carried on the tradition, while Roger Corman made two satires in the modern, bloody scatological fashion, *Bloody Mama* (American International, 1970) and *Crazy Mama* (New World, 1974). There have been two near contemporary gangster satires, the disappointing *Johnny Dangerously* (20th Century–Fox, 1984), and John Huston's classic *Prizzi's Honor* (20th Century–Fox, 1985), with sterling, hilarious performances by Jack Nicholson and Kathleen Turner as two bumbling mob contract killers. While there have been several classic gangster satires, musicals are less common, perhaps because of the unpleasant occupations of the characters. Besides *Guys and Dolls*, the best of the small group, there are two other gangster musicals, *Casbah* (Universal, 1948) and *Party Girl* (MGM, 1958), both starring pop singer Tony Martin.

Saunders, John Monk (1895–1940)

Screenwriter. A hero of World War I, as a fighter pilot, Saunders began writing short stories in the twenties. Much of his work was based on his experiences as an aviator. He wrote the screenplay for the classic *Wings* (Paramount, 1927), his most important screenplay. He also worked on two gangster pictures, contributing the story for Josef von Sternberg's classic *The Docks of New York* and cowriting

the minor Warner Bros.–First National production, *The Finger Points*.

The Docks of New York (Paramount, 1928; screenplay). *The Finger Points* (First National, 1931; cowriter only).

Savage, Ann (b. 1924)

Actress. An attractive, dark-haired actress, Ann Savage was active in "B" movies throughout the forties. She played the murderous *femme fatale* in the semiclassic *Detour* (PRC, 1945), probably her best known performance. She played a much more sympathetic role in *The Last Crooked Mile*. Although talented, she never escaped "B" movies, and slipped into obscurity during the early fifties.

The Last Crooked Mile (Republic, 1946).

Sawtell, Paul (1906–1971)

Composer. Sawtell was a prolific composer of film scores for mostly minor movies. His scores for two gangster thrillers directed by Anthony Mann are among his best.

T-Men (Eagle-Lion, 1947). *Raw Deal* (Eagle-Lion, 1948).

Saxon, John (b. 1935)

Actor. Born Carmen Orrico in Brooklyn, Saxon was a male model before turning to acting. He was most often seen as a tough guy second lead in minor movies. He starred in the good "B" gangster thriller *Cry Tough* as a street punk who joins a gang and finds the lure of easy money too strong to leave the gang, even under the influence of his beautiful girlfriend.

Cry Tough (United Artists, 1959).

Scarface (Universal, 1983). 170 mins. *Producer*: Martin Bregman. *Director*: Brian De Palma. *Screenplay*: Oliver Stone. *Director of Photography*: John A. Alonzo. *Music*: Giorgio Moroder. *Production Designers*: Blake Russell, Steve Schwartz, Geoff Hubbard. *Editors*: Jerry Greenberg and David Ray.

Paul Muni (center) as the original *Scarface*, here in a temporarily serene moment.

Tony Camonte and his gang pull a heist in *Scarface*. Seconds later, the barely hidden tommy gun erupts.

Cast: Al Pacino (Tony Montana), Steve Bauer (Manny Ray), Michelle Pfeiffer (Elvira), Mary Elizabeth Mastrantonio (Gina), Robert Loggia (Frank Lopez), Miriam Colon (Mama). *With*: F. Murray Abraham, Paul Shenar, Harris Yulen, Pepe Serna, Angel Salazar, Arnaldo Santana.

Retaining much of the plot elements of the original, including the incestuous brother and sister relationship, this version is an update of the 1932 film. Tony Camonte becomes Tony Montana, an immigrant via the Cuban boat lift of 1980. Montana joins a cocaine ring and rises to head the gang, only to be outdone by his jealous overly protective sister, Gina, and greed.

Al Pacino has expressed admiration for this film as one of his favorites. In retrospect, however, his performance, like Paul Muni's in the original, is overblown, and the violence in this version is too explicit and hard to stomach. Director Brian De Palma had reached an artistic zenith shortly before this film, with a series of modestly budgeted thrillers. *Scarface*, because of its extravagant pretensions, is not of the caliber of these films. De Palma would return to this kind of material, more successfully, with *The Untouchables* (Universal, 1988).

Scarface: The Shame of a Nation (United Artists, 1932). 99 mins.
Producer: Howard Hughes. *Director*: Howard Hawks. *Screenplay*: Ben Hecht, S. I. Miller, John Lee Mahin, W. R. Burnett and Fred Palsey, based on the novel by Armitage Trail. *Directors of Photography*: Lee Garmes and L. William O'Connell. *Music*: Adolph Trandler and Gus Arnheim. *Editor*: Edward D. Curtiss.
Cast: Paul Muni (Tony Camonte), Ann Dvorak (Cesca Camonte), Karen Morley (Poppy), Osgood Perkins (Johnny Lovo), Boris Karloff (Gaffney), C. Henry Gordon (Guarino), George Raft (Guido Rinaldo). *With*: Purnell Pratt, Vince Barnett, Inez Palange, Harry J. Vejar, Edwin Maxwell, Tully Marshall.

Tony Camonte, a Sicilian immigrant, joins a small bootlegging operation as a bodyguard, but quickly rises to head the gang. Moving to another city, he eliminates several rivals, including the dapper Gaffney, in his rise to prominence. He falls in love with the sluttish Poppy, but his feelings are confused by his strange relationship with Cesca, his beautiful sister. He is violently jealous of Cesca's interest in other men, and when she begins dating Guido Rinaldo, one of his associates, he can barely contain his anger. When he finds Cesca with Guido in a seedy hotel, he kills him in a violent rage, unaware that he has married Cesca. Cesca forgives him and hides out with Tony while the police search for him. Eventually they discover his hiding place, and both Cesca and Tony Camonte are killed in the shootout.

Coscenarist W. R. Burnett had already published his best seller *Little Caesar* when he was hired to work on *Scarface* in 1931. Like its predecessor, the film was loosely based on the life and character of Al Capone, and the filmmakers even took the risk of using Capone's real life nickname as the title of their film (Capone, it is said, was delighted by the "tribute"). Despite its numerous writers, the film retained a strong, linear plot that, uniquely, introduced a Freudian element in its exploration of the incestuous relationship between Tony Camonte and his sister. The genesis of the film is rather complicated, involving the eccentric producer and entrepreneur Howard Hughes and director Howard Hawks. Hawks fashioned a glossy, innovative movie that was considered a step ahead in the early sound era. In fact, to modern viewers it appears rather slow and stagy, hampered largely by several stilted, moralizing scenes added at the behest of Italian-Americans, and by Paul Muni's occasionally over the top performance. However, the supporting cast is very good, particularly the darkly sensual Ann Dvorak as Camonte's faithful sister. Enormously successful upon its initial release, it remains a classic.

The Scarface Mob (Cari Releasing, 1962). 105 mins.
Producers: Arnoz and Quinn Martin. *Director*: Phil Karlson. *Screenplay*: Paul Monash, based on the novel *The Untouchables* by Eliot Ness and Oscar Fraley. *Director of Photography*: Charles Straumer. *Music*: Wilbur Hatch. *Art Directors*: Ralph Berger and Frank Smith. *Editor*: Robert L. Swanson.

Cast: Robert Stack (Eliot Ness), Keenan Wynn (Joe Fuselli), Barbara Nichols (Brandy La France), Walter Winchell (Narrator), Pat Crowley (Betty Anderson), Neville Brand (Al Capone). *With*: Bill Williams, Joe Mantell, Bruce Gordon, Peter Leeds, Eddie Firestone, Robert Osterloh.

In Chicago during the twenties, the F.B.I. had sent a special agent, Eliot Ness, to help bring order to the lawless city. Against impossible odds, including corrupt officials and violent gangsters led by Al Capone, Ness is able to bring about the downfall of organized crime in the city.

The pilot for the immensely successful television series *The Untouchables* (1959–1962), *The Scarface Mob* was released in England and Europe as a feature. Expertly directed by Phil Karlson, it is as good as any theatrical release and, like the series, has been praised for its portrayal of the real life Eliot Ness and the Chicago underworld of the twenties.

Schnee, Charles (1916–1963)
Screenwriter. A typical professional Hollywood screenwriter, Schnee was proficient but rarely brilliant, without a readily identifiable personal style or set of themes. He was at his best writing melodramas with a gloomy romantic outlook. *I Walk Alone* and *They Live by Night* are among his best and most typical screenplays. The latter, a variation on the Bonnie and Clyde legend, is one of the classics of *film noir*.
I Walk Alone (Paramount, 1948). *They Live by Night* (RKO, 1948).

Schrader, Paul (b. 1946)
Screenwriter. One of the premier American screenwriters to emerge during the seventies, Schrader is probably most famous for his collaborations with director Martin Scorsese, and his Calvinist, moralizing *The Yakuza*. His first screenplay, with its obsessions with mindless violence, organized crime, and explorations of the seamy underbelly of society (uniquely, in this case, Japan and its notorious mafia) shows the way to his later, greater screenplays.
The Yakuza (Warner Bros., 1975).

Schulberg, Budd (b. 1914)
Novelist and screenwriter. The son of Paramount executive and producer B. P. Schulberg, Budd proved a brilliant chronicler of Hollywood in the golden age with his autobiography and great satirical novel *What Makes Sammy Run?* (1949). He also wrote a number of politically engaged screenplays, including the classic underworld melodramas *On the Waterfront* (which won an Academy Award for best original screenplay) and *The Harder They Fall*. Both are distinguished by strong characterizations, liberal political ideals and sharp dialogue.
On the Waterfront (Columbia, 1954). *The Harder They Fall* (Columbia, 1956).

Scorsese, Martin (b. 1942)
Director. Of the so-called "movie brats" who emerged during the seventies (including Steven Spielberg and Brian De Palma), Scorsese has shown the most focused artistic vision and is generally considered by many critics to be the leading American director of his generation. Yet, Scorsese is almost the most erratic of these directors and, while he is less obviously commercial than Spielberg and De Palma, he has

also made terrible movies. Perhaps his greatest faults are his extreme pretensions (particularly in his obsessions with Roman Catholicism) and his tendency to improvise, leaving very little room for character or, most importantly, story development. Still, when Scorsese is at his best, he is an incomparable talent. This is certainly true with *GoodFellas*, a modern classic. It transcends the limits of the gangster genre with several strong performances and a complicated narrative which remains Scorsese's greatest innovation in his films. Also, his propensity to emphasize extravagant technique and camera angles is thankfully suppressed in favor of the story. Scorsese also directed *Mean Streets*, a gritty urban melodrama with gangster themes that first established his reputation as a major American filmmaker during the seventies.

Boxcar Bertha (American International, 1972). *Mean Streets* (Warner Bros., 1973; director and cowriter). *GoodFellas* (Warner Bros., 1990; director and cowriter).

Scott, Adrian (1912–1972)

Screenwriter. Scott was an important figure in the emergence of *film noir* while a producer at RKO during the mid-forties. Before becoming a producer, he spent several years as a screenwriter without particularly distinguishing himself. He did cowrite the classic gangster satire *Mr. Lucky*, one of his last screenplays before turning to production.

Mr. Lucky (RKO, 1943).

Scourby, Alexander (1913–1985)

Character actor. Scourby divided his time between the stage and the screen. Famous for his rich, sonorous voice, he often played elegant yet sinister characters. He was the main villain, the mob boss, in *The Big Heat*.

The Big Heat (Columbia, 1953).

Sears, Fred F. (1913–1957)

Director. Sears was a prolific director of "B" pictures, specializing in action films and Westerns. Despite their low budgets, many of his movies are quite good. His single gangster movie, *The Miami Story*, is a hard-boiled thriller in the *noir* semi-documentary style popular in the fifties.

The Miami Story (Columbia, 1954).

The Secret Six (MGM, 1931). 83 mins.
Director: George Hill. *Screenplay*: Francis Marion. *Director of Photography*: Harold Wenstrom. *Editor*: Blanche Sewell.

Cast: Wallace Beery (Louis Scorpio), Lewis Stone (Newton), John Mack Brown (Hank), Jean Harlow (Anne), Marjorie Rambeau (Peaches), Paul Hurst (Nick the Gouger), Clark Gable (Carl Luckner). *With*: Ralph Bellamy, John Miljan, DeWitt Jennings, Murray Kinnell, Fletcher Norton.

A group of six vigilante businessmen hire two reporters, Carl Luckner and Hank Rogers, to obtain evidence against Scorpio, a gang boss, and Newton, his crooked lawyer. When Scorpio, who is engaged in a war with fellow bootleggers, discovers that he is being investigated by the reporters, he gets his moll, Anne, to seduce one of the reporters, Hank, but she falls for him. After Scorpio is arrested and then acquitted by a fixed jury, he decides to get revenge and kidnaps Anne, but Carl rescues her. The police surround Scorpio's hideout, but Scorpio and his lawyer kill each other in an argument before they can be arrested.

Despite its excellent production values, *The Secret Six* fails on several accounts, not the least of which is a weak screenplay. However, the sexy Jean Harlow and Clark Gable (not yet a star), who plays one of his rare early heroic roles, are quite good.

Segal, George (b. 1934)

Actor. Briefly popular in the seventies, George Segal never became a full-fledged star. He was generally seen supporting the film's nominal star —

generally a female — and usually played comic roles. His rather laconic style is too understated for the kind of charisma needed to really carry a movie, but he is always an entertaining performer. In the low budget exploitation gangster movie *The St. Valentine's Day Massacre*, he played Al Capone's underling Peter Gusenberg, proving more effective than the miscast Jason Robards as Capone.

The St. Valentine's Day Massacre (20th Century-Fox, 1967).

Seiler, Lewis (1891–1964)
Director. For most of his career, which began in the late twenties, Seiler was a contract director for Warner Bros. He was perfectly suited to that studio because of his hard-boiled style, and he directed a number of excellent action features for them. Among these are three superior "B" gangster dramas.

Hell's Kitchen (Warner Bros., 1939). *You Can't Get Away with Murder* (Warner Bros., 1939). *The Big Shot* (Warner Bros., 1942).

Seitz, John (1893–1979)
Cinematographer. Beginning in the early twenties, Seitz was a leading Hollywood cinematographer, an expert at glossy black and white. In the forties he photographed a number of classics directed by Billy Wilder and Preston Sturges. He was the director of photography on five gangster movies, the most important being *This Gun for Hire*.

Hush Money (Fox, 1931). *Lucky Jordan* (Paramount, 1942). *This Gun for Hire* (Paramount, 1942). *Rogue Cop* (MGM, 1954). *Hell on Frisco Bay* (Warner Bros., 1956).

Selznick, David O. (1902–1965)
Producer. The energetic, dynamic Selznick spent time at RKO and MGM during the early thirties before becoming an independent producer in 1936. For MGM he produced the gangster drama *Manhattan Melodrama*, an uncharacteristic movie for Selznick with its male leading character, underworld theme, and pessimistic mood. It is, however, a classic of the genre.

Manhattan Melodrama (MGM, 1934).

Semon, Larry (1889–1928)
Actor. Completely forgotten today except by a handful of film historians, Semon was one of the leading comedians of the silent era, rivaling the popularity of Charlie Chaplin, Buster Keaton, and Harry Langdon. His career went into a sudden, tragic decline during the mid-twenties for a number of reasons, but Semon was on the verge of making a "comeback" as a character actor when he was felled suddenly by a heart attack. His major performance as a character actor was in Josef von Sternberg's *Underworld* as a dapper mob boss.

Underworld (Paramount, 1927).

The Set-Up (RKO, 1949). 72 mins.
Producer: Richard Goldstone. *Director*: Robert Wise. *Screenplay*: Art Cohn. *Director of Photography*: Milton Krasner. *Art Directors*: Albert S. D'Agostino and Jack Okey. *Editor*: Roland Gross.

Cast: Robert Ryan (Stoker Thompson), Audrey Totter (Julie Thompson), George Tobias (Tiny), Alan Baxter (Little Boy), Wallace Ford (Gus), Percy Helton (Red). *With*: James Edwards, Darryl Hickman, Kenny O'Morrison, David Clarke, Phillip Pine, Edwin Max.

While his wife, Julie, waits in a shabby hotel room, Stoker, a thirty-five-year-old boxer past his prime, goes to fight a match. Although Stoker knows he is no longer at his best, he believes he might be able to beat his younger opponent. His manager, however, has arranged for Stoker to take a fall. Stoker refuses to take a dive even after his manager, Tiny, tells him that he will be beaten up if he wins. Indeed, Stoker manages to persevere and beat his young opponent during a tough match. Afterward, the crooks who made the deal with Tiny give Stoker a vicious beating. With broken hands but unbroken spirit, Stoker returns to Julie.

A classic *film noir*, *The Set-Up* has a gritty atmosphere and decor, and, typical of the genre, is set almost entirely at night. It is one of several *noirs* to explore the corrupt sport of boxing, a popular topic of the time. Its gangster elements are at a minimum and, indeed, it just barely qualifies as one of the genre's films; however, the entire background is overshadowed by the influence of gangsters, giving it the ambiance of the genre.

711 Ocean Drive (Columbia, 1950). 102 mins.
Producer: Frank N. Seltzer. *Director*: Joseph M. Newman. *Screenplay*: Richard English and Francis Swan. *Director of Photography*: Franz Planer. *Music*: Sol Kaplan. *Production Designer*: Perry Fergusson. *Editor*: Bert Jordan.
Cast: Edmond O'Brien (Mal Granger), Joanne Dru (Gail Mason), Donald Porter (Larry Mason), Sammy White (Chippie Evans), Dorothy Patric (Trudy), Barry Kelly (Vince Walters). *With*: Otto Kruger, Howard St. John, Robert Osterloh, Bert Freed.

Mal Granger, a hard-working telephone repairman, makes a repair call to a bookie joint run by two businessmen, Larry Mason and Vince Walters. Impressed with Mal's technical acumen, they persuade him to engineer a telephone wire service connecting the racing results of all the West Coast tracks. Mal is successful and, desirous of money and power, eventually takes over Mason's operation, his beautiful wife and has Mason murdered. The operation is so successful that the big mob bosses back east decide to take over the operation and freeze Granger out. Mal is forced to flee to Las Vegas but, cornered at the Hoover Dam by mob assassins, is shot and falls to his death below.

The movie *711 Ocean Drive*, referring to the address of the bookie's joint, is a particularly well made "B" thriller. Edmond O'Brien is very good as the honest man corrupted by money and power. Otto Kruger is superb as the sinister mob boss who takes over Granger's operation.

Seven Thieves (20th Century–Fox, 1960). 100 mins.
Producer: Sydney Boehm. *Director*: Henry Hathaway. *Screenplay*: Sydney Boehm, based on the novel *Lions at the Kill* by Max Catto. *Director of Photography*: Sam Leavitt. *Music*: Dominic Frontiere. *Art Directors*: Lyle Wheeler and John DeCuir. *Editor*: Dorothy Spencer.
Cast: Edward G. Robinson (Theo Wilkins), Rod Steiger (Paul Mason), Joan Collins (Melanie), Eli Wallach (Pancho), Alexander Scourby (Raymond Le May), Michael Dante (Louis). *With*: Berry Kroeger, Sebastian Cabot, Marcel Hillaire, John Berardino, Alphonse Martell.

Theo Wilkins, an American criminal traveling in Europe, arranges a daring scheme to rob a Monte Carlo gambling palace. With six compatriots, Theo plans to impersonate a physician having a heart attack to divert attention while the others carry out the crime. The crime is executed, but typically falls apart during the escape.

The heist drama is a familiar one, having been used successfully in many thrillers. *Seven Thieves* is not one of the classics of this subgenre, but it is highly entertaining thanks to Henry Hathaway's brisk direction and Edward G. Robinson's excellent performance as the aging thief who organizes the final big caper of his career, only to see it collapse and end with his capture by police.

Shane, Maxwell (1905–1983)
Director. Shane, a former publicist, was a screenwriter and director of "B" movies. He cowrote and directed a single minor gangster *noir* distinguished more by an excellent cast than by its rather conventional direction.

The Naked Street (United Artists, 1955).

Sharp, Henry (1892–1966)
Cinematographer. Sharp's career began in the late teens and hit its creative zenith a decade later. He remained a prolific cinematographer for three decades, utilizing a hard-edged, agreeable, simple style. He photographed a few minor gangster movies.
The Big City (MGM, 1928). *Madame Racketeer* (Paramount, 1932). *The Glass Key* (Paramount, 1935). *The Glass Alibi* (Republic, 1946).

Sheridan, Ann (1915–1967)
Actress. Born Clara Lou Sheridan in Denton, Texas, Sheridan planned to be a teacher but went to Hollywood after winning a beauty contest in 1933. After appearing in small roles in over twenty forgettable movies, she joined Warner Bros. as a contract actress in 1936, most often starring as a wise, kindhearted girl in social crime melodramas, including three gangster pictures.
San Quentin (Warner Bros., 1937). *Angels with Dirty Faces* (Warner Bros., 1938). *Castle on the Hudson* (Warner Bros., 1940).

Sherman, George (b. 1908)
Director. An extremely prolific director of "B" movies, Sherman is best known for his action oriented Westerns made for Republic and Universal. However, he also directed some good contemporary crime dramas which include a single "B" gangster movie.
Citadel of Crime (Republic, 1946).

Sherman, Vincent (b. 1906)
Screenwriter and director. Born Abram Orovitz, Sherman first achieved success as a stage actor during the twenties and thirties. In the mid-thirties, he moved to Hollywood, where he became a moderately successful screenwriter and then director of mostly routine movies. For Warner Bros., he cowrote the minor gangster drama *King of the Underworld* and directed a superior gangster *noir*, *The Damned Don't Cry*.
King of the Underworld (Warner Bros., 1939; cowriter only). *The Damned Don't Cry* (Warner Bros., 1950; director only).

Sherwood, Robert E. (1896–1955)
Playwright. The tall (over 6' 5") and gangly Sherwood was an ex-journalist turned playwright who enjoyed his greatest success in the thirties. As a member of the Algonquin Round Table, Sherwood was a well known humorist, but his best plays, like his masterpiece *The Petrified Forest*, are generally dour dramas with a social theme (Sherwood was a notable liberal who later worked as a speech writer for Franklin D. Roosevelt). *The Petrified Forest* was adapted for the screen, retaining much of the original play while changing its more downbeat ending.
The Petrified Forest (Warner Bros., 1936).

Shirley, Anne (1918–1993)
Actress. Born Dawn Paris, Shirley first achieved fame as a child actress during the twenties under the name Dawn O'Day. She later played adult roles in many "B" movies, including a single, minor gangster movie.
Law of the Underworld (RKO, 1938).

Show Them No Mercy (20th Century–Fox, 1935). 76 mins.
Producer: Raymond Griffith. *Director*: George Marshall. *Screenplay*: Kubec Glasmon and Henry Lehrman. *Director of Photography*: Bert Glennon. *Editor*: Jack Murray.
Cast: Rochelle Hudson (Loretta Martin), Cesar Romero (Tobey), Bruce Cabot (Pitch), Edward Norris (Joe Martin), Edward Brophy (Buzz), Warren Hymer (Gimp). *With*: Herbert Rawlinson, Robert Glecker, Charles Wilson, William Davidson, Frank Conroy, Orrin Burke.
While awaiting a ransom in a kid-

napping scheme, a gang's hideout is inadvertently invaded by a stranded couple. The hoodlums — Pitch, Buzz and Gimp, and led by Tobey — debate whether to kill the couple and their sick baby. Tobey, however, decides to send the husband, Joe Martin, to retrieve the ransom, while holding the wife, Loretta, and baby hostage. The F.B.I. discovers the gang's hideout and surround it. In the subsequent shootout, Loretta grabs a machine gun and kills the sadistic Pitch, the gangster who wanted to murder her family.

A taut, suspenseful thriller, *Show Them No Mercy* was coauthored by Kubec Glasmon, who also coauthored *Public Enemy* (Warner Bros., 1931). It is the closest 20th Century–Fox got to the gritty gangster films produced by Warner Bros. in the early thirties — not surprising when one considers that 20th Century's head of production, Darryl F. Zanuck, was largely responsible for the Warner's style of the early thirties. However, this excellent gangster thriller turned out to be a unique production for the company, as Zanuck turned it into a family oriented studio not unlike MGM. Although not well known today, *Show Them No Mercy*, one of the best gangster movies of the mid-thirties, deserves renewed interest.

Shubunka (Fictional character)

Few characters in American cinema have been as cold-blooded and psychotic as this mobster in the classic "B" picture *The Gangster* (Allied Artists, 1947). Played by the veteran character actor Barry Sullivan as an immoral, stone-faced killer, the portrayal is one of the most memorable in all of cinema. In some ways the story of *The Gangster* is conventional — it recounts the downfall of Shubunka after being betrayed by his moll — but its violent action, the tragic almost–Shakesperean theme, and Sullivan's brilliant performance helped raise it above the morass of other "B" gangster melodramas.

The Sicilian Clan (French title: *Le Clan des Siciliens*) (Fox–Europa/Les Films du Siecle, 1968). 120 mins.
Producer: Jacques E. Strauss. *Director*: Henri Verneuil. *Screenplay*: Henri Verneuil, Jose Giovanni, and Pierre Pelegri, based on the novel by Auguste Le Breton. *Director of Photography*: Henri Decae. *Music*: Ennio Morricone. *Art Director*: Jacques Saulnier. *Editor*: Albert Jurgenson.

Cast: Jean Gabin (Vittorio Manalese), Alain Delon (Roger Sartet), Lino Ventura (Inspector Le Goff), Irina Demick (Jeanne Manalese), Amedo Nazzari (Tony Nicosia), Sydney Chaplin (Jack). *With*: Elise Cegani, Karen Blanguernon, March Porel, Yves Lefebvre, Phillippe Baronnet.

Vittorio Manalese, a Mafia chieftain living in exile in France, plans to return to Sicily to pull off one last big job. He enlists the aid of a condemned killer, Roger Sartet, helping him escape from prison. The plot, however, falls apart, resulting in violence and, ultimately, Manalese's death.

A surprising success in the United States (where it grossed over $2 million), *The Sicilian Clan* was an enormous box office success in Europe, and remains one of the all-time moneymakers in France. It is yet another variation on the heist gone bad theme, but in a more violent, action oriented manner than many of its predecessors. It is extremely well written, acted and directed, highlighted by excellent photography in its seaside scenes and the robbery sequence set aboard a private jet in flight!

Side Street (MGM, 1949). 83 mins.
Producer: Sam Zimbalist. *Director*: Anthony Mann. *Screenplay*: Sydney Boehm. *Director of Photography*: Joseph Ruttenberg. *Music*: Lennie Hayton. *Art Directors*: Cedric Gibbons and Daniel B. Ruttenberg. *Editor*: Conrad A. Nervig.

Cast: Farley Granger (Joe Norson), Cathy O'Donnell (Ellen), James Craig (Georgie Garsell), Paul Kelly (Capt.

Walter Anderson), Jean Hagen (Harriet), Paul Harvey (Emil). *With*: Edmon Ryan, Charles McGraw, Ed Max, Adele Jergens, Harry Bellaver, Whit Bissell. Joe Norson, a private mail carrier, steals an envelope filled with cash in a misguided attempt to provide for his pregnant wife. Unknown to Norson, the money is a payoff in an extortion scheme involving several murders. However, when pangs of guilt compel him to return the money, Norson finds himself caught up in a dangerous intrigue involving the police and gangsters. His flight from the gangsters leads him into a nightmare world of sleazy bars and dangerous underworld hangouts. Eventually the mobsters capture and plan to kill Norson. After a high speed chase through the streets of New York City, the police finally catch up with Norson and his captors. In the subsequent shootout, Norson is wounded, but the criminals are captured, and he is reunited with his wife and family.

Trying to capitalize on the success of *They Live by Night* (RKO, 1948), *Side Street* reteamed Farley Granger and Cathy O'Donnell in another crime thriller. The result, directed by Anthony Mann, is a taut thriller shot on location. Its underworld theme is really nothing more than an excuse for a thriller plot, but *Side Street* emerges as an entertaining, minor example of the new breed of gangster dramas that sprang up in the early fifties.

Sidney, Sylvia (1910–1995)
Actress. Born Sophie Kosow in New York City, Sidney was trained as a stage actress and made her Broadway debut at the age of seventeen. Her first film role followed two years later. A major star during the thirties, she became a cultural icon of the Great Depression, almost always seen as the proud but poor girl who suffers at the hands of an indifferent society. This is the character type she played in her three gangster movies.

Dead End (United Artists, 1937).

You Only Live Once (United Artists, 1937). *You and Me* (Paramount, 1938).

Siegel, Benjamin, aka "Bugsy" (1903–1947)
A Jewish gangster in the Italian Mafia, Benjamin Siegel was a notoriously seductive and totally amoral mob flunky whose reputation for indiscriminate violence was well deserved — to call him by his nickname "Bugsy" was to ask for death. When the New York mob discovered that the Chicago mob planned to exploit the as-yet untapped rackets in Hollywood, they sent Siegel to the West Coast to take control of the disparate gangs there. Bugsy the enforcer quickly took control of the Southern California mobs, as well as ingratiating himself in Hollywood. Friends like George Raft introduced him to the Hollywood community, and Siegel not only gained an actress moll (the ultimate status symbol for a New York mobster), but also a screen test. Ultimately, Siegel's relationship was tenuous, as he soon concentrated on starting a gambling community in Las Vegas. When that venture proved unprofitable for the mob, they had him assassinated. A film, *Bugsy* (Tristar, 1992), was made about his life and career in Hollywood and Las Vegas, with Warren Beatty as Siegel.

Siegel, Don (b. 1912)
Director. Originally an editor at RKO, Siegel began directing in the mid-forties. He immediately proved to be a master of visceral, action oriented melodramas with an excess of violence and sexuality. For three decades he was a master filmmaker, but his talents and influence have rarely been acknowledged. Indeed, more than Martin Scorsese (whose themes are similar to Siegel's) his less showy but equally violent style has had an enormous influence on filmmakers throughout the world. In the fifties he directed a number of modestly budgeted crime dramas, including *Riot in Cell Block 11*,

an archetypal prison drama, and *Baby Face Nelson*, a great "B" biopic of the notorious thirties gangster.
Riot in Cell Block 11 (Allied Artists, 1954). *Baby Face Nelson* (United Artists, 1957).

Siegel, Sol C. (1903–1982)
Producer. A prolific, energetic producer of mostly high quality entertainments, Siegel's career began in 1929 and continued successfully until the early seventies. He produced a single, minor gangster movie.
Buy Me That Town (Paramount, 1941).

Silliphant, Stirling (b. 1918)
Screenwriter. For several decades, beginning in the forties, Silliphant was a leading American screenwriter who also created a number of classic television series. He generally wrote contemporary urban melodramas, including the minor gangster movie *Damn Citizen*. He later wrote the screenplays for several popular disaster epics, including *The Poseidon Adventure* (Paramount, 1972) and *The Towering Inferno* (Paramount, 1974).
Damn Citizen (Universal, 1958).

Sinatra, Frank (b. 1915)
Singer and actor. Unquestionably the greatest pop singer of his time, Frank Sinatra is also a competent actor. He costarred in the gangster musical *Guys and Dolls*, which was based on Damon Runyon's colorful characters and stories, and the gangster parody *Robin and the Seven Hoods* (1964), set in twenties Chicago.
Guys and Dolls (MGM, 1956). *Robin and the Seven Hoods* (Warner Bros., 1964).

Siodmak, Robert (1900–1973)
Director. Perhaps the most underrated director of the forties, Siodmak was a master of the cynical, dark, romantic crime melodrama. Born in Germany, he was originally a title writer for silent movies before becoming a

director in 1929. He absorbed the late expressionist style common in that country and only loosely adapted it when he began making movies in Hollywood in 1940. As a contract director for Universal over the course of a decade, he made a number of classic, modestly budgeted movies: *Son of Dracula* (1943), *Cobra Woman* (1944), and the great *films noir*, *Phantom Lady* (1944), *The Suspect* (1945), *The Killers* and *Criss Cross*. The latter two are classic gangster *noirs*, gloomy, romantic and cynical in the extreme, remaining two of the most important crime movies of the forties. Sadly, following the classic minor *noir The File on Thelma Jordan* (Paramount, 1950), Siodmak's career went into decline, and he spent his last years making a number of low budget films in Europe during the fifties and sixties.
The Killers (Universal, 1946). *Criss Cross* (Universal, 1948).

Six Bridges to Cross (Universal, 1955). 96 mins.
Producer: Aaron Rosenberg. *Director*: Joseph Pevney. *Screenplay*: Sydney Boehm, based on the story "They Stole $2,000,000 — And Got Away with It" by Joseph Dineen. *Director of Photography*: William Daniels. *Music Director*: Joseph Gershenson. *Art Directors*: Alexander Golitzen and Robert Clatworthy. *Editors*: Russell Schoengarth and Verna MacCurren.
Cast: Tony Curtis (Jerry Florea), Julie Adams (Ellen Gallagher), George Nader (Edward Gallagher), J. C. Flippen (Vincent), Sal Mineo (Jerry as a boy). *With*: Jan Merlin, William Murphy, Kenny Roberts, Richard Castle, Harry Bartel.

Jerry Florea, a street punk and petty thief, creates a scheme to rob an armored truck. He gathers a gang and they carry out the robbery successfully, but their scheme falters, in part, by their own inadequacy and jealousy.
Based loosely on real events, the plot of *Six Bridges to Cross* is a familiar

one. The heist drama is a subgenre of the gangster genre and is the basis of several classic pictures, including *The Asphalt Jungle* (MGM, 1955). While it is not a classic, *Six Bridges to Cross* is a well made, entertaining thriller.

Skin Deep (Warner Bros., 1929). Approximately 90 mins.
Director: Ray Enright. *Screenplay*: Gordon Rigby, based on the novel *Lucky Damage* by Marc Edmund Jones. *Director of Photography*: Barney McGill. *Editor*: George Marks.
Cast: Monte Blue (Joe Daly), Davey Lee (District Attorney Carlson's son), Betty Compson (Sadie Rogers), Alice Day (Elsa), John Davidson (Blackie Culver). *With*: John Bowers, Georgie Stone, Tully Marshall, Robert Perry.

After a big-city mobster, Joe Daly, marries a pretty gold digger, Sadie Rogers, he decides to go straight. Sadie, however, is really in love with Daly's rival, Blackie Culver, and together they frame Joe on a robbery charge and he is sent to prison. During an escape he is badly injured, but he meets Elsa, a kind girl who takes pity on him. Her father, a surgeon, repairs his damaged face, thus hiding his identity. He discovers his wife's infidelities, and when she is accidently killed, he returns to Elsa and a new life.

A little-known but very interesting early sound gangster melodrama, *Skin Deep* points the way to the classic Warner Bros.' gangster pictures produced only a year or two later. With a stronger director and cast, it might have been a classic. Interestingly, its central plot element (the wanted man with a new face) echoes that of the great *film noir Dark Passage* (Warner Bros., 1947) which starred Humphrey Bogart as a convicted murderer who gets a new identity via plastic surgery and, after the death of his female nemesis, starts life anew with an understanding lover.

Skinner, Frank (1898–1968)
Composer. Skinner was a prolific composer of adequately dramatic scores for mostly minor films, mainly for Universal. His scores, while appropriate, are not particularly innovative.
Forbidden (Universal, 1953).

Skipworth, Alison (1875–1952)
Actress. Born Alison Groom, the chubby, matronly Skipworth was a respected stage actress in her native England and on Broadway before going to Hollywood during the late twenties. She was most often seen in comic roles, particularly as a foil for W. C. Fields, but she also starred in two notable gangster dramas. In *Night After Night* she played a typical role as a high society matron who gets mixed up with gangsters. In *Madame Racketeer*, however, she starred in the title role as a conniving British con woman who becomes the head of a gang in the United States.
Madame Racketeer (Paramount, 1932). *Night After Night* (Paramount, 1932).

A Slight Case of Murder (Warner Bros., 1938). 85 mins.
Producer: Hal B. Wallis. *Director*: Lloyd Bacon. *Screenplay*: Earl Baldwin and Joseph Schrank, based on the play by Damon Runyon and Howard Lindsay. *Director of Photography*: Sid Hickox. *Art Director*: Max Parker. *Editor*: James Gibbons.
Cast: Edward G. Robinson (Remy Marco), Jane Bryan (Mary Marco), Willard Parker (Dick Whitewood), Ruth Donnelly (Mora Marco), Allen Jenkins (Mike), John Litel (Post). *With*: Eric Stanley, Harold Huber, Edward Brophy, Paul Harvey, Margaret Hamilton, George E. Stone.

At the end of Prohibition, gangster Remy Marco decides to go straight and crash respectable society. After he and his wife find a country place, their daughter, Mary, falls for a wealthy young man, but she will not marry him until he gets a job. The only job he can find is with the police department, and he becomes a cop. Meanwhile, one of

Remy's old rivals decides to murder him, but in the subsequent shootout, the assassins kill each other and are also shot by Remy's new son-in-law. Remy starts a successful beer company with $500,000 he has taken from the dead gangster's pockets.

Only Damon Runyon could devise a plot as improbable as this one and get away with it. With Howard Lindsay, he created a hilarious farce based on the conventions of the time, and their play was an enormous success. It was also turned into this rich comedy which manages to poke fun at the genre and its icons, including Edward G. Robinson, who gives an unexpected, hilarious performance.

Stop, You're Killing Me (Warner Bros., 1952) is a color remake of this film. It is directed in high style by Roy Del Ruth, and stars genre icons Broderick Crawford and Claire Trevor. The latter film feels forced and tired, and was not a box office or critical success.

Small, Edward (1891–1977)

Producer. Originally an actor and agent in Hollywood, from 1924, Edward Small found his greatest success as an independent producer, beginning in the mid-thirties. He produced a number of very good, low budget pictures, including two gangster movies, for a variety of studios.

Raw Deal (Eagle-Lion, 1948). *The Naked Street* (United Artists, 1955).

Smart Money (Warner Bros., 1931). 90 mins.

Director: Alfred E. Green. *Screenplay*: Kubec Glasmon, John Bright, Lucien Hubbard, and Joseph Jackson. *Director of Photography*: Robert Kurrie. *Editor*: Jack Killifer.

Cast: Edward G. Robinson (Nick "the Barber" Venizelos), James Cagney (Jack), Evalyn Knapp (Irene), Ralf Harolde (Sleepy Sam), Noel Francis (Marie), Margaret Livingston (The D.A.'s Girl). *With*: Maurice Black,

Boris Karloff, Morgan Wallace, Billy House, Paul Porcasi, Polly Walters.

Nick Venizelos, a small-town barber, operates a small gambling parlor in the rear of his legitimate establishment. Several of his friends raise $10,000 for him to go to the big city to bet against the syndicate. In the city, Marie, a pretty young girl, cons him into a game and he loses the entire fund. Vowing revenge, he returns to the city with his friend Jack and begins betting on the horses. He manages to outmaneuver Sleepy Sam, the man who outwitted him in the con game, and he blackmails Marie into becoming his moll. Eventually Nick establishes a successful gambling house, thus becoming the target of the local district attorney. The D. A. uses a pretty blonde, Irene Graham, to gather evidence against Nick, but they fall in love. After Nick accidentally kills Jack during an argument, he is sent to prison, and Irene agrees to wait for him.

While it is not a major film, *Smart Money* is an entertaining, minor early gangster drama. It is notable for being the only pairing of Edward G. Robinson and James Cagney, who were teamed by the studio immediately following their initial successes in the genre.

Smith, Ted

Art director. Smith was a unit art director at Warner Bros. for many years, specializing in designs for Westerns. However, he also worked on a number of contemporary films, including, most notably, *High Sierra*, his only gangster movie.

High Sierra (Warner Bros., 1941).

Some Like It Hot (United Artists, 1959). 120 mins.

Producer and Director: Billy Wilder. *Screenplay*: Billy Wilder and I. A. L. Diamond, *story by* R. Thoren and M. Logan. *Director of Photography*: Charles Lang, Jr. *Music*: Adolph Deutsch. *Art Director*: Ted Haworth. *Editor*: Arthur Schmidt.

Cast: Marilyn Monroe (Sugar Kane), Tony Curtis (Joe/Josephine), Jack Lemmon (Jerry/Daphne), George Raft (Spats Columbo), Pat O'Brien (Mulligan), Joe E. Brown (Osgood Fielding III). *With*: Nehemiah Persoff, Joan Shawlee, Billy Gray, George E. Stone, Dave Barry, Mike Mazurki, Harry Wilson.

Joe and Jerry are two down on their luck jazz musicians in 1929 Chicago. While retrieving a friend's car in a garage on their way to a gig, they are inadvertent witnesses of the gangland St. Valentine's Day Massacre. Barely escaping with their lives, they hide out with an all girl band, disguising themselves as women when the female troupe travels to Florida for an engagement. While trying to keep their real identities hidden, Joe falls for the sexy singer of the band, Sugar Kane, while Jerry, in his female alter ego, Daphne, finds himself the object of desire of Osgood Fielding III, an eccentric multimillionaire. Meanwhile, Spats Columbo, the gangster from Chicago who had ordered the massacre, arrives in Florida for a gangland conference. He immediately spots Jerry and Joe as the witnesses, but they manage to escape after Spats and his henchmen are gunned down by their colleagues at a dinner party thrown in their honor.

Billy Wilder's freewheeling satire of the Roaring Twenties and the gangster genre has become a kind of icon in its own right and is one of the last representatives of the glamorous Hollywood golden age. Perhaps most famous as one of Marilyn Monroe's last films, *Some Like It Hot* is also a classic romantic comedy and social satire in Wilder's usual caustic style. It made brilliant use of the conventions of the gangster genre, solidified by George Raft's appearance as Spats Columbo. It deserved its enormous box office success and is rightfully regarded as an all-time classic.

Sothern, Ann (1909–1994)
Actress. Born Hariette Lake in Valley City, North Dakota, Sothern was a trained singer who first came to the movies via musicals. Throughout the thirties and forties, the attractive blonde was a popular leading lady in "B" comedies and dramas, and a second lead in "A" productions. She starred opposite Edward G. Robinson in the delightful gangster satire *Brother Orchid*, her only genre film.

Brother Orchid (Warner Bros., 1940).

Sparkuhl, Theodor (1894–1945)
Cinematographer. The German-born Sparkuhl was a leading European cinematographer, working mainly in France before moving to Hollywood in the early thirties. His style was less expressionistic and less interesting than many of his contemporaries in Germany.

Dangerous to Know (Paramount, 1938). *The Tip-Off Girls* (Paramount, 1938). *Queen of the Mob* (Paramount, 1940). *Buy Me That Town* (Paramount, 1940). *The Glass Key* (Paramount, 1942).

Special Agent (Warner Bros., 1935). 76 mins.

Producer: Martin Mooney. *Director*: William Keighley. *Screenplay*: Laird Doyle and Abem Finkle. *Director of Photography*: Sid Hickox. *Music*: Leo F. Forbstein. *Art Director*: Esdras Hartley. *Editor*: Clarence Kilster.

Cast: Bette Davis (Julie), George Brent (Bill Bradford), Ricardo Cortez (Nick Carston), Joseph Sawyer (Rich), Joseph Crehan (Police Chief), Henry O'Neill (District Attorney). *With*: Jack La Rue, Irving Pichel, Robert Strange, Joseph King, William B. Davidson, J. Carrol Naish.

To gather evidence against Nick Carston, an alleged racketeer, the I.R.S. hires Bill Bradford, a newspaperman, to go undercover as a member of the gang. Bradford befriends Julie, the racketeer's bookkeeper, and she agrees to help him gather information. As a result, Carston is arrested. Carston then has his men kidnap Julie, but Bradford trails the gang to their hideout and, with the help of the police, rescues her. Carston is sentenced to prison, and Julie and Bradford plan to get married.

Crisp, fast-moving and entertaining hokum, *Special Agent* is a well made, if minor, gangster melodrama distinguished largely by Bette Davis' hard-boiled performance.

Sperling, Milton (b. 1912)

Producer. Sperling's career began in the mid-forties, and for the next three decades he made many good commercial films, often cowriting them as well. He produced a single minor gangster biopic.

The Rise and Fall of Legs Diamond (Warner Bros., 1960).

Spiegel, Sam (1901–1985)

Producer. A larger than life figure, Spiegel was born in Poland and immigrated to the United States as a young boy. After varied experience in business, he moved to Hollywood in 1941 and immediately became a leading producer (originally under the name S. P. Eagle) of high quality entertainments. He is probably best known for his collaborations with director David Lean, but his career encompassed a variety of genres. One of his most important films was *On the Waterfront*, the classic gangster social drama.

On the Waterfront (Columbia, 1954).

The Squealer (Columbia, 1930). Approximately 75 mins.

Producer: Harry Cohn. *Director*: Harry J. Brown. *Screenplay*: Dorothy Howell, based on the play by Mark Linder. *Director of Photography*: Ted Tetzlaff. *Art Director*: Edward Jewell. *Editor*: Leonard Wheeler.

Cast: Jack Holt (Charles Hart), Dorothy Revier (Margaret Hart), Matt Moore (John Sheridan), Zasu Pitts (Bella), Robert Ellis (Valletti). *With*: Matthew Betz, Arthur Housman, Louis Matheaux, Eddie Kane, Eddie Sturgis, Elmer Ballard.

Charles Hart is a bootlegger who uses a real estate company as a front. A ruthless professional who does not hesitate to kill rivals, he is plagued by problems with his wife, who is in love with his best friend, John Sheridan. Holt is sentenced to prison for murder, but escapes, intent on taking revenge against his wife and her lover. When he realizes his young son is better off with the couple, he decides to leave them alone. He is later killed in a police trap.

The Squealer is a minor early gangster melodrama with the typically poor production values of Columbia's early sound features. Its cast is second rate, but its script, cowritten by the important screenwriter Jo Swerling, is quite good.

Squire, Alan (Fictional character)

In *The Petrified Forest* (Warner Bros., 1936), Squire is the writer held hostage at the Black Mesa Barbeque Cafe and Gas Station by Duke Mantee (Humphrey Bogart) and his gang. Leslie Howard played the role on stage and in the film opposite his friend Humphrey Bogart. Squire is a symbolic figure, representing the cool intellectual of contemporary society who finds himself in conflict with the primitive and instinctual brutality of Mantee. The question of which will ultimately prevail in the near future is left open at the film's end.

Stack, Robert (b. 1919)

Actor. Born Robert Modini to a wealthy family in Los Angeles, Stack began acting in 1939 after a stint at the University of Southern California. For two decades he was a popular second lead in many movies, but he achieved real stardom via the great television series *The Untouchables* in which he played the real life Eliot Ness. *The Scarface Mob* was the theatrical release (in Europe only) of the pilot for the series.

The Scarface Mob (Cari Releasing, 1962).

Stanley, Paul (b. 1919)
Director. Mainly working in television, Paul Stanley has directed a few features, including *Cry Tough*, a routine gangster drama that achieved some notoriety for being one of the earliest American films featuring nudity.
Cry Tough (United Artists, 1959).

The Star Witness (Warner Bros., 1931). 68 mins.
Director: William Wellman. *Screenplay*: Lucien Hubbard. *Director of Photography*: James Van Trees. *Editor*: Hal McLernon.
Cast: Walter Huston (D. A. Whitlock), Charles "Chic" Sale (Grandpa), Frances Starr (Ma Leeds), Sally Blane (Sue Leeds), Tom Dugan (Brown), Ralph Ince (Maxey Campo). *With*: Russell Hopton, Robert Elliott, Fletcher Norton, Guy d'Ennery, Nat Pendleton, Dickie Moore.
While leaving his retirement house to visit his hometown, Grandpa Summerill witnesses a gang war in front of his old home. His family sees the gang members' faces and becomes the target of the mobsters. At the urging of the district attorney, Grandpa bravely agrees to testify before the grand jury.
Chic Sale, a popular twenties stage comedian and actor, enjoyed a brief run of success in the movies during the early thirties. His character in this film is typical, a kindly, brave grandfather who stands up against the bad guys and ends up triumphant.

Stark, Richard (b. 1933)
Richard Stark is the pseudonym of prolific author Donald Westlake under which he wrote several hard-boiled novels, including *The Outfit*, which was adapted for the screen.
The Outfit (MGM, 1973).

Starr, Annie Laurie (Fictional character)
Peggy Cummin's character in *Gun Crazy* (United Artists, 1949), loosely based on Bonnie Parker, is a carnival performer who is erotically obsessed

with gunfire and danger. She leads a fellow gun devotee, Bart Tare (John Dall), into a life of crime and murder, eventually and inevitably leading to their own deaths in a hail of bullets in an overgrown field, not unlike the real Bonnie and Clyde.

Steele, Karen (b. 1937)
Actress. A dark-haired beauty who found her greatest success in "B" movies and on television, Karen Steele starred in *The Rise and Fall of Legs Diamond* as the moll and *femme fatale* who brings about the notorious gangster's death.
The Rise and Fall of Legs Diamond (Warner Bros., 1960).

Steiger, Rod (b. 1925)
Character actor. The burly, dynamic Steiger became one of the most familiar character actors of his generation thanks to several extraordinary performances in important movies. A veteran method actor, he made an early impression in his second movie, *On the Waterfront*, as the corrupted brother of boxer and dock worker, Malloy, played by fellow method actor, Marlon Brando. Less well known is his energetic portrayal of real life gangster *Al Capone* in the low budget biopic of the mobster. He also played a mobster in the Humphrey Bogart vehicle *The Harder They Fall*.
On the Waterfront (Columbia, 1954). *The Harder They Fall* (Columbia, 1956). *Al Capone* (Allied Artists, 1959).

Steiner, Max (1888–1971)
Composer. The Austrian-born Steiner moved to the United States in 1924. He had a varied career as a conductor and arranger, mainly of Broadway musicals, before moving to Hollywood in the early thirties. He became one of Hollywood's most reliable and prolific composers of film music, writing well over a hundred scores. His late romantic and dramatic sensibilities

Robert Stack as he appeared, in a publicity photo, at the beginning of the three year run of television's *The Untouchables*. The show was an enormous success, immensely influential, and Stack achieved stardom as the mob fighting real life Eliot Ness.

were perfectly suited to the medium and many of his scores, including those for *King Kong* (RKO, 1933) and *Gone with the Wind* (MGM, 1939), are not only acknowledged classics of the medium, but also remain popular pieces on classical radio stations. Long employed by Warner Bros., he composed the music for some of their best gangster movies, and his scores are an integral part of these films' overall artistic success.

Kid Galahad (Warner Bros., 1937). *The Amazing Dr. Clitterhouse* (Warner Bros., 1938). *Angels with Dirty Faces* (Warner Bros., 1938). *I Walk Alone* (Paramount, 1948). *Key Largo* (Warner Bros., 1948). *Hell on Frisco Bay* (Warner Bros., 1956). *The F.B.I. Story* (Warner Bros., 1959).

Sterling, Jan (b. 1923)

Actress. Born Jane Sterling Adriance in New York City, Jan Sterling was educated in England and made her Broadway debut at the age of fifteen. An attractive, voluptuous blonde, she was most often seen as a floozy, or an amoral *femme fatale*. She played just such a role in her only gangster movie.

The Harder They Fall (Columbia, 1956).

Sterling, Whit (Fictional character)

Early in his film career, Kirk Douglas played a variety of psychologically weak and morally corrupt characters in several notable *films noir*, including *Out of the Past* (RKO, 1947), in which he played the gangster Whit Sterling. Sterling is a successful gambler and mobster whose relationship with his moll is typical of the forties style: although she is certainly an object of his physical and psychological abuse, she also manipulates and controls him. And eventually his relationship with her leads to his death — another dimension not found in the gangster dramas of the thirties.

Sternard, Rudolph (b. 1905)

Art director. A former architect, Rudolph Sternard was a prominent Hollywood art director, working mainly for 20th Century–Fox and Columbia. He was quite innovative, and for his single gangster movie, the *noir* thriller *Dead Reckoning*, he created appropriately claustrophobic settings.

Dead Reckoning (Columbia, 1947).

Sternberg, Josef von (1894–1969)

Director. The premier Hollywood visual stylist, Josef von Sternberg is best known for directing the series of romantic melodramas starring Marlene Dietrich released during the early thirties. His early life traveling in Europe (he was born in Germany and raised in the United States) was adventurous,

Robert Redford as suave con man Johnny Hooker in *The Sting.*

but he developed a love for cinema while living in England. He partly self financed his first feature (now lost), which brought him to the attention of Charles Chaplin. Chaplin hired Sternberg to direct *The Seagull*. Chaplin refused to release the movie, allegedly because he was jealous of its extraordinary style, and he later destroyed all copies of it. Sternberg then signed with Paramount, a studio that allowed directors a free reign. He inherited a picture in development at the studio and immediately established himself by creating a masterpiece: *Underworld*. Out of the sordid, melodramatic material, Sternberg created a dark, shadowy, visually exciting gangster movie. The film's enormous box office success had a profound influence, both visually and thematically, on American popular cinema, and helped start the initial gangster cycle. Sternberg followed this success with three additional gangster melodramas: *The Dragnet, Docks of New York* and *Thunderbolt*. Like *Underworld, Docks of New York* is generally considered one of the great late silent movies; sadly, the other two have been lost, with only small fragments of both now in existence. Sternberg abandoned this genre during the early thirties in favor of his erotic dramas, but there is no question that he was the genre's greatest early director.

Underworld (Paramount, 1927). *Docks of New York* (Paramount, 1928). *The Dragnet* (Paramount, 1928). *Thunderbolt* (Paramount, 1929).

Stevens, Daisy (Fictional character)

A supporting part in a gangster film as a moll did for Jean Harlow what a similar role in *The Asphalt Jungle* (MGM, 1950) did for Marilyn Monroe — it helped to make her into a star.

In *Beast of the City* (MGM, 1932), Harlow plays the sexy, but avaricious moll in love with Ed Fitzpatrick, a small-time hood mixed up with mob boss Sam Belmonte and his gang. When Ed joins his brother, Captain Jim Fitzpatrick, the chief of police, who is trying to bring Belmonte to justice, Daisy foolishly stays with the Belmonte gang at their hideout. She is killed along with Belmonte and the Fitzpatrick brothers in the climactic shootout between the police and Belmonte's gang.

Stewart, James (b. 1908)

Actor. With his inimitable slow drawl and tall, gangly form, James Stewart became the very ideal of the Midwestern American with a sense of strong morals. For more than three decades, he often played these sorts of characters, but he also played more flawed characters, most notably in Alfred Hitchcock's *Vertigo* (Universal, 1958). However, it was his white bread, all-American image that got him the role in *The F.B.I. Story*, starring as the archetypal and stereotypical F.B.I. agent fighting criminals like John Dillinger.

The F.B.I. Story (Warner Bros., 1958).

Stewart, Paul (1908–1986)

Character actor. Born in New York City, Stewart was a stage actor who made his film debut in Orson Welles' *Citizen Kane* (RKO, 1941). Tall, burly and rather menacing, he was almost always seen in villainous roles, particularly in the gangster genre as a mob henchmen or boss.

Loan Shark (Lippert, 1952). *Chicago Syndicate* (Columbia, 1955). *Hell on Frisco Bay* (Warner Bros., 1956).

The Sting (Universal, 1973). 129 mins.

Producers: Tony Bill, Michael S. Phillips, Julia Phillips. *Director*: George Roy Hill. *Screenplay*: David S. Ward. *Director of Photography*: Robert Surtees. *Music*: Scott Joplin, adapted by Marvin Hamlisch. *Art Director*: Henry Bumstead. *Editor*: William Reynolds.

Cast: Paul Newman (Henry Gondorff), Robert Redford (Johnny Hooker), Robert Shaw (Doyle Lonnegan), Charles Durning (Lieutenant Snyder), Ray Walston (J.J. Singleton), Eileen Brennan (Billie). *With*: Harold Gould, John Heffernan, Dana Elcar, Jack Kehoe, Dimitra Arliss, Robert Earl Jones.

When his partner in crime is killed, con man Johnny Hooker is bent on revenge and goes to Chicago to locate Henry Gondorff, a legendary con man. Johnny wants a crash course in how to get revenge against Doyle Lonnegan, the gangster responsible for his partner's murder. Together, Hooker and Gondorff create an elaborate scheme to trap Doyle into being the fall guy for a large sum of money stolen from mobsters. After a series of complications and double-crosses, the scheme is successfully pulled off. Hooker and Gondorff escape with the stolen money, while Doyle is left to face the wrath of his fellow mobsters.

A rich, colorful satire, *The Sting* was a well deserved success that has become an acknowledged classic. Its greatest virtue is a brilliant, inventive screenplay with more twists and turns and red herrings than an Agatha Christie mystery. The complicated plot is told with great style by George Roy Hill and acted superbly by an expert cast; its best performance, however, is not by the leads, Redford and Newman, but by Robert Shaw as the well dressed, suspicious con man and gangster who ultimately falls victim to his own greed.

The Sting II (Universal, 1982). 103 mins.

Producer: Jennings Lang. *Director*: Jeremy Paul Kagan. *Screenplay*: David S. Ward. *Director of Photography*: Bill Butler. *Music*: Lalo Schifrin. *Production Design*: Edward C. Carfagno. *Editor*: David Garfield.

Cast: Jackie Gleason (Gondorff), Mac Davis (Hooker), Teri Garr (Veronica), Karl Malden (Macalinski), Oliver Reed (Lonnegan), Bert Remsen

(Kid Colors). *With*: Benny Baker, Kathalina Veniero, Frank McCarthy, Jose Perez, Ron Rifkin, Monica Lewis.

Con men Gondorff and Hooker are released from prison. They plan to fleece a gullible nightclub owner. Aiding in the scam is sexy Veronica who also plans to cheat the two con men. After many difficulties, the con is successfully pulled off and Hooker and Veronica fall in love.

Despite its screenplay being written by the same man who wrote the original, *The Sting II* does not live up to the first film. Its cast was second rate or past their prime, but carried out the proceedings with some aplomb. While it is not a classic, *The Sting II* is a mildly diverting entertainment that would have fared better if it had not followed the classic original.

Stockwell, Dean (b. 1938)

Character actor. A former child star of the forties, Stockwell in recent years has become a familiar character actor in films made by trendy directors like David Lynch and Jonathon Demme. In fact, he is a very talented performer; and with his craggy, almost immobile features, he can play a variety of characters from brooding villains to stalwart citizens. In Demme's gangster satire, *Married to the Mob*, Stockwell gave a splendid performance as the eccentric mob boss, Tony the Tiger.

Married to the Mob (Orion, 1988).

Stolen Harmony (Paramount, 1935). 74 mins.

Producer: Albert Lewis. *Director*: Alfred Werker. *Screenplay*: Leon Gordon, Harry Ruskin, Claude Binyon and Lewis Foster. *Director of Photography*: Harry Fischbeck. *Art Directors*: Hans Dreier and Bernard Herzbrun. *Editor*: Otto Lovering.

Cast: George Raft (Ray Angelo/Ray Ferraro), Ben Bernie (Jack Conrad), Grace Bradley (Jean Loring), Goodee Montgomery (Lil Davis), Lloyd Nolan (Chesty Burrage). *With*: Ralf Harolde,

William Cagney, William Pawley, Charles E. Arnt, Cully Richards, Jack Norton.

Band leader Jack Conrad hears inmate Ray Angelo playing the saxophone in a radio broadcast from prison and hires him to play in his band after Angelo's release. Angelo joins Conrad's band in a tour; but when a fellow ex-inmate steals the band's receipts, Angelo is blamed. In the end, however, he manages to prove his innocence and win the love of dancer Jean Loring.

A silly melodrama with musical interludes — mainly to show off Raft's talents as a dancer — *Stolen Harmony* is, at most, unwatchable, a shame when one considers the talents of director Alfred Werker, an expert handler of thrillers.

Stoloff, Benjamin (1895–1960)

Director. Stoloff's career as a film director began in the mid-twenties. In the thirties he became a prolific director of "B" movies, some of which are very good. Among these is *The Lady and the Mob*, a passable "B" gangster picture.

The Lady and the Mob (Columbia, 1939).

Stoloff, Morris W. (1894–1980)

Composer and musical director. No relation to director Ben Stoloff, Morris was a competent if uninspired composer. One of his best scores was for *Blind Alley*, an inventive gangster drama.

Blind Alley (Columbia, 1939).

Stone, Andrew (b. 1902)

Director. Stone is an important director because he was one of the first to make the majority of his pictures on location. He was a good director of action films and thrillers, but few of his movies have stood the test of time. He directed a single, minor low budget gangster picture. While it is not a classic, it is entertaining and very well made.

Highway 301 (Warner Bros., 1950).

Stone, Oliver (b. 1946)

Screenwriter. In the late seventies,

Oliver Stone emerged as an important screenwriter with a strong, visceral style. He wrote or cowrote several important screenplays, including *Scarface* and *The Year of the Dragon*, two modern gangster pictures, over the course of several years. The success of these allowed him to make the move to director in the mid-eighties.

Scarface (Universal, 1983). *The Year of the Dragon* (MGM/United Artists, 1985; cowriter only).

Stone, Vince (Fictional character)

In *The Big Heat* (Columbia, 1953), the number one hit man of mob boss Mike Lagana, a homicidal maniac and sadist, is portrayed by Lee Marvin in one of his best early performances as a tough guy. In a memorable scene, Stone throws scalding coffee into the face of his moll, Debby Marsh (Gloria Grahame), horribly disfiguring her and setting into motion his own downfall. After recovering, Debby sets a trap for him at her apartment and throws coffee into his face. He shoots and kills her but is arrested shortly thereafter by police Sergeant Dave Bannion, his nemesis, who promises to send him to the electric chair for her murder.

The Stone Killer (Columbia, 1973). 95 mins.

Producer and Director: Michael Winner. *Screenplay*: Gerald Wilson, based on the book *A Complete State of Death* by John Gardner. *Director of Photography*: Richard Moore. *Music*: Roy Budd. *Art Director*: Ward Preston. *Editor*: Kelly Emhardt.

Cast: Charles Bronson (Torrey), Martin Balsam (Vescari), David Sheiner (Lorenz), Norman Fell (Daniels), Ralph Waite (Mathews), Eddie Firestone (Armitage). *With*: Walter Burke, David Moody, Charles Tyner, Paul Koslo, Stuart Margolin, John Ritter.

Torrey, an unconventional cop, is suspended from the New York police force after shooting a fleeing teenaged suspect. He moves to Los Angeles and is hired by the L.A.P.D. He subsequently uncovers a scheme by Mafia chief Vescari to take revenge against rival mobsters. Almost single-handedly, Torrey manages to break up the group of assassins hired by Vescari and bring the mob chief to justice.

In the seventies, Charles Bronson was a major box office attraction, mainly as a star of action films and thrillers. Despite their lack of artistic merit, many of these modestly budgeted movies are quite good, and *The Stone Killer* is certainly one of the best. Indeed, with its excessive, almost comic violence and sentimentality, it reminds one of the contemporary crime thrillers of the great Hong Kong director John Woo.

Stradling, Harry (1907–1970)

Cinematographer. The British-born Stradling first made a name for himself in France, photographing several classic films there in the late thirties. He moved to the United States shortly thereafter, becoming a leading cinematographer in Hollywood. He was an expert at both black and white and color photography, the latter brilliantly displayed in the gangster musical *Guys and Dolls*.

Guys and Dolls (MGM, 1958).

Strange Cargo (MGM, 1940). 113 mins.

Producer: Joseph L. Mankiewicz. *Director*: Frank Borzage. *Screenplay*: Lawrence Hazard, based on the novel *Not Too Narrow, Not Too Deep* by Richard Sale. *Director of Photography*: Robert Planck. *Art Director*: Cedric Gibbons. *Editor*: Robert J. Kern.

Cast: Clark Gable (Andre Verne), Joan Crawford (Julie), Ian Hunter (Cambreau), Peter Lorre (Cochon), Paul Lukas (Hessler), Albert Dekker (Moll), J. Edward Bromberg (Flaubert). *With*: John Arledge, Frederic Worlock, Paul Fix, Bernard Nedell, Francis McDonald.

Andre Verne, a prisoner in a French penal colony in New Guinea, plans to escape; but before he can carry out his plans, he has a fight with the evil Moll, a fellow inmate, and is hospitalized. Moll leads his own escape with several other prisoners through the jungle. Later, Andre manages to escape and befriend an entertainer, Julie, who is out of work because she refuses to sleep with the penal colony's dictatorial warden. They join the other escapees aboard a small boat. The conditions are harsh and the prisoners die off one by one, yet because of the kindness of the mysterious Cambreau, the survivors begin to believe he is divine. When only Cambreau, Andre and Julie remain, Andre throws Cambreau overboard, but he has a sudden rebirth of faith and saves the man. Back in port, Andre tell Julie that he loves her, and she agrees to wait while he finishes his sentence.

Based on a superior popular novel by occasional screenwriter Richard Sale, *Strange Cargo* is one of the most bizarre commercial films of Hollywood's golden age. Its semireligious theme is unique among gangster movies, and the story is told in a surprisingly unsentimental, non-patronizing manner. While not a classic, it is certainly one of the most interesting of all gangster pictures.

Street of Chance (Paramount, 1930). 75 mins.
Director: John Cromwell. *Screenplay*: Howard Estabrook, *story by* Oliver H. P. Garrett. *Director of Photography*: Charles Lang. *Editor*: Otto Levering.
Cast: William Powell (John Marsden, aka Natural Davis), Jean Arthur (Judith Marsden), Kay Francis (Alma Marsden), Regis Toomey (Babe Marsden), Stanley Fields (Dorgan). *With*: Brooks Benedict, Betty Francisco, John Risso, Joan Standing, Maurice Black.

In New York City, ace gambler Natural Davis (aka John Marsden) gives his younger brother, Babe, a wedding gift of $10,000 on condition that he not use it to gamble. Marsden's wife wants him to give up gambling, and he almost does until he discovers that his brother has been playing the games and has won big. To teach Babe a lesson, Marsden plans to make him lose his winnings in another card game, but when it is discovered that he is cheating, one of his fellow gamblers shoots and kills him.

A modest success at the time of its release, *Street of Chance*, in retrospect, seems a silly bit of melodrama. Its moralizing dates it terribly, as do its poor production values. However, it is interesting for providing character actor and usual screen bad guy Regis Toomey with one of his few good-guy roles.

Sullivan, Barry (b. 1912)
Actor. Sullivan was born Patrick Barry in New York City and was educated at Temple University. He made his Broadway debut in 1936 and his movie debut in the early forties. He became a dependable leading man, most often appearing in thrillers and gangster movies, usually in heroic roles.
The Gangster (Allied Artists, 1947). *The Miami Story* (Columbia, 1954).

Sullivan, C. Gardner (1885–1965)
Screenwriter. Sullivan's greatest period of success was in the twenties when he was the highest paid scenarist in the world. He cowrote the screenplay for *Alibi*, one of the earliest sound gangster movies.
Alibi (United Artists, 1929).

Sullivan, Rocky (Fictional character)
In *Angels with Dirty Faces* (Warner Bros., 1938), Sullivan, the tough homicidal mobster played with ferocious abandon by James Cagney, rises from petty street thief to become a leading criminal, but is still emotionally attached to his tenement origins. When his childhood friend, Jerry Connelly (Pat O'Brien), now a priest, becomes the target of Rocky's fellow gangsters, including James Frazier (Humphrey Bogart), he kills them to protect his pal. Convicted of the murders, Rocky is sentenced to death. He has, in the

meantime, become the hero of another generation of teenage street toughs — the Dead End Kids — who idolize his bravado. When Father Connelly visits Sullivan in prison to convince his childhood friend to pretend to be frightened by his impending date with the electric chair (in order to show the street toughs that he really is not as tough as his image), the priest is rebuffed. But when he is actually led to the chair, Rocky weeps and screams like a coward. This about-face influences the street kids, who read about the event in the papers and decide they no longer want to emulate their fallen idol.

Interestingly, the climax of the film, brilliantly directed by Michael Curtiz, is shot in such an ambiguous way as to leave the question of Sullivan's demise open to interpretation: has he decided to heed Father Connelly's request, or is he, in fact, a coward?

Surtees, Robert (1906–1985)
Cinematographer. Surtees was one of the great American cinematographers, utilizing a strong, glossy visual style. He worked brilliantly in both color and in black and white. He won Academy Awards for best cinematography for films of both types. His color work is best exemplified in *The Sting*, in which he made excellent use of the colorful settings and costumes.

The Sting (Universal, 1973).

"Swede" (Fictional character)
In *The Killers* (Universal, 1946), Swede is the central character, played by Burt Lancaster. As the film opens, two contract killers arrive in a small town and assassinate the Swede (he has no other name). This first sequence, the only part of the film actually based on Ernest Hemingway's short story which inspired the screenplay, establishes the cynical, dark mood of the film. Through a long flashback which makes up most of the film, the downfall of the Swede is recounted. He was a promising boxer who enters a life of crime when he joins

a gang of thieves, and is later double-crossed by his moll, Kitty Collins (Ava Gardner). Burt Lancaster's strong performance in this, his first film, made him into a star overnight.

Swerling, Jo (1894–1983)
Screenwriter. Swerling was one of the great professional Hollywood screenwriters, working as a scenarist for three decades and cowriting many classic and important movies. He specialized in adventurous stories with romantic themes, but he also wrote more hard-boiled subjects. He cowrote two gangster pictures, the most important being John Ford's classic satire *The Whole Town's Talking*.

The Whole Town's Talking (Columbia, 1935). *I Am the Law* (Columbia, 1938).

Sylos, F. Paul (1900–1979)
Art director. Sylos studied art and design at Yale and painted covers for *Liberty* magazine and others during the twenties and early thirties. He entered movies in 1935, working mainly for Poverty Row studios PRC, Monogram and Republic. He worked on some important "B" movies, creating some imaginative sets despite the minuscule budgets he was often forced to work with. One of the best films he worked on is the superior "B" drama *The Gangster*, in which his designs add to the overall artistic merit.

The Gangster (Allied Artists, 1946).

T-Men (Eagle-Lion, 1947). 96 mins.
Producer: Aubrey Schenck. *Director*: Anthony Mann. *Screenplay*: John C. Higgins, *story by* Virginia Kellogg. *Director of Photography*: John Alton. *Music*: Paul Sawtell. *Art Director*: Edward Jewell. *Editor*: Fred Allen.

Cast: Dennis O'Keefe (Dennis O'Brien), Alfred Ryder (Tony Genaro), Mary Meade (Evangeline), Wallace Ford (Schemer), June Lockhart (Mary Genaro), Charles McGraw (Moxie). *With*: Jane Randolph, Art Smith,

Herbert Heyes, Jack Overman, John Wengraff, Jim Bannon.

Two treasury agents, Dennis O'Brien and Tony Genaro, are assigned to investigate the murder of a fellow agent. They infiltrate the Detroit mob by assuming the identity of small-time hoods. Pretending they are ace counterfeiters, O'Brien and Genaro bargain with the gangsters for a deal on printing plates. The gangsters, including the sadistic henchman Moxie, realize that Genaro is an undercover cop and torture him to death in front of the helpless O'Brien. Genaro, however, had collected enough information to send the crooks to prison. In revenge, O'Brien kills Moxie.

T-Men is a superior "B" police procedural, told in hard-boiled *noir* fashion by Anthony Mann and cinematographer John Alton. It is one of the best of the group of low budget thrillers directed by Mann during the late forties.

Talbot, Lyle (b. 1904)

Character actor. Born Lisle Henderson in Pittsburgh, Talbot began acting in vaudeville as a child. He later appeared on stage in New York City before beginning his film career in 1932. He was a prolific actor, appearing in some 200 movies during the course of his career, playing everything from lawmen to mobsters. He played one of the prisoners in the classic prison drama *20,000 Years in Sing Sing*.

20,000 Years in Sing Sing (First National, 1933).

Tamiroff, Akim (1899–1972)

Actor. Born in Baku, Russia, Tamiroff immigrated to the United States in the twenties and acted in the theater. His screen debut was in *Queen Christina* (Paramount, 1933), and he subsequently became one of the most familiar faces in American movies. With his dark, European good looks, Tamiroff most often played sinister and well mannered rogues. During the thirties and forties he enjoyed popularity as a gangster in several "B" melodramas for Paramount, and later returned to the genre in the great heist drama *Topkapi* as the leader of the gang.

Dangerous to Know (Paramount, 1938). *King of Chinatown* (Paramount, 1938). *The Gangster* (Allied Artists, 1947). *King of Gamblers* (Paramount, 1947). *Topkapi* (United Artists, 1964).

Tare, Bart (Fictional character)

In *Gun Crazy* (United Artists, 1949), the character played by John Dall and loosely based on the real life Clyde Barrow is so obsessed with firearms that, as a teenager, he breaks into a store to steal a coveted rifle. Caught in the act, he is sent away to reform school, and only returns to his hometown, a small town in the Midwest, years later as an adult. He is still obsessed with guns. He meets Annie Laurie Starr, a carnival performer who specializes in gun tricks, and who finds gunplay and danger erotically stimulating. Together, Bart and Annie travel the back roads of the western United States, carrying out a series of robberies and murders until, inevitably, they are gunned down by the authorities in an overgrown field — just like the real Bonnie and Clyde.

Taxi (Warner Bros., 1932). 68 mins.

Director: Roy Del Ruth. *Screenplay*: Kubec Glasmon and John Bright, based on the play *The Blind Spot* by Kenyon Nicholson. *Director of Photography*: James Van Trees. *Music Director*: Leo F. Forbstein. *Art Director*: Esdras Hartley. *Editor*: James Gibbons.

Cast: James Cagney (Matt Nolan), Loretta Young (Sue Riley), George E. Stone (Skeets), Guy Kibbee (Pop Riley), David Landan (Buck Gerard), Ray Cooke (Danny Nolan). *With*: Leila Bennett, Dorothy Burgess, Matt McHugh, George MacFarlane, Polly Walters, Nat Pendleton, George Raft.

A New York City taxi driver, Matt Nolan, is the leader of a group of cabbies who are fighting an organized taxi trust. While his wife tries to tear down his ambitions, a racketeer kills his brother, and Nolan vows revenge. With the help of his fellow taxi drivers, Nolan helps break up the underworld's control of the taxi business and bring his brother's murderer to justice.

Taxi is a decent enough melodrama, remembered chiefly for being James Cagney's first heroic starring role, and also as a demonstration of his considerable abilities as a dancer in one memorable scene. In addition, George Raft makes an early appearance in a small role. A breezy, well made feature, it is also notable as one of Warner Bros.' early attempts to vary the genre; and while not entirely successful, it is a minor classic and an enjoyable, even amusing, entertainment.

Taylor, Robert (1911–1969)

Actor. The blandly handsome Robert Taylor was one of the busiest leading men in Hollywood for three decades, beginning in the early thirties. Born Spangler Arlington Brugh in Filley, Nebraska, Taylor was a music major (a cello virtuoso) who, in the early thirties, followed his cello professor to California, where, while performing with an amateur troupe, he was spotted by an agent for MGM. He was signed to a contract by the company and spent nearly all of his career there. He usually played romantic leads, particularly opposite strong female leads. He varied his roles in costume dramas with occasional hardboiled roles in mysteries and thrillers. He starred in three gangster pictures, playing surprisingly flawed heroes in each.

The Bribe (MGM, 1949). *Rogue Cop* (MGM, 1954). *Party Girl* (MGM, 1958).

Terry, Don (b. 1902)

Actor. Born Donald Locher in Natick, Massachusetts, Terry attended Harvard and was a professional boxer before becoming an actor. He was a popular leading man in "B" movies, playing heroic and un-heroic tough guys. He starred in a single, minor early gangster movie.

Me, Gangster (Fox, 1928).

Tetzlaff, Ted (b. 1903)

Cinematographer and director. In the thirties, Tetzlaff was a leading cinematographer with an elegant, glossy style. As a cinematographer, he worked on one early gangster movie. He became a director in the forties and made a number of interesting "B" movies including one gangster picture.

The Squealer (Columbia, 1930; director of photography). *Johnny Allegro* (Columbia, 1949; director).

They Live by Night (RKO, 1948). 95 mins.

Producer: John Houseman. *Director*: Nicholas Ray. *Screenplay*: Charles Schnee, based on the novel *Thieves Like Us* by Edward Anderson. *Director of Photography*: George E. Diskant. *Music*: Leigh Harline. *Art Directors*: Albert S. D'Agostino and Al Herman. *Editor*: Sherman Todd.

Cast: Cathy O'Donnell (Keechie), Farley Granger (Bowie), Howard da Silva (Chickamaw), J. C. Flippen (T-Dub), Helen Craig (Mattie). *With*: Will Wright, Marie Bryant, Ian Wolfe, William Phipps, Harry Harvey.

Two hardened criminals, Chickamaw and T-Dub, are joined in a prison break by the naive Bowie. After escaping, they rob a bank, but Bowie is injured in the subsequent getaway. Nursed back to health by Keechie, the daughter of a man who helped in their prison break, Bowie falls in love with her, planning to marry her and retire from criminal life. But Chickamaw and T-Dub force Bowie to join them in another bank robbery. Later, after both T-Dub and Chickamaw are killed by the police, Bowie must go on the run when he is turned in by an acquaintance. He is joined by Keechie, but the police catch up with them and Bowie is killed.

For his first film, Nicholas Ray chose a theme familiar to Fritz Lang—lovers, caught in an inescapable web, on the run from the law. The story of *They Live by Night*, based on the best selling novel *Thieves Like Us* by Edward Anderson, is, of course, inspired by the legend of Bonnie and Clyde. However, unlike the real life robbers and murderers, the central characters in *They Live by Night* are victims of circumstance—true *noir* protagonists. A classic gangster movie of forties school, it is also Nicholas Ray's masterpiece.

Thieves Like Us (United Artists, 1974). 120 mins.
Producer: Jerry Bick. *Director*: Robert Altman. *Screenplay*: Calder Willingham and Joan Tewkesbury, based on the novel by Edward Anderson. *Director of Photography*: Jean Boffety. *Editor*: Lou Lombardo.
Cast: Keith Carradine (Bowie), Shelley Duvall (Keechie), John Schuck (Chickamaw), Bert Remsem (T-Dub), Louise Fletcher (Mattie). *With*: Ann Latham, Tom Skerritt, Al Scott, John Roper.

The same story as that of *They Live by Night* (RKO, 1948), and based on the same novel, *Thieves Like Us*, is made in the usual pretentious style of director Robert Altman (long scenes of idyllic beauty and comedy are interrupted by acts of brutal violence). However, Altman does successfully capture the flavor of Mississippi in the late thirties.

This Gun for Hire (Paramount, 1942). 80 mins.
Producer: Richard M. Blumenthal. *Director*: Frank Tuttle. *Screenplay*: Albert Maltz and W. R. Burnett, based on the novel by Graham Greene. *Director of Photography*: John Seitz. *Music*: Frank Loesser. *Art Director*: Hans Dreier. *Editor*: Archie Marshek.
Cast: Veronica Lake (Ellen Graham), Robert Preston (Michael Crane), Laird Cregor (William Gates), Alan Ladd

(Philip Raven), Tully Marshall (Alvin Brewster), Marc Lawrence (Tommy). *With*: Mikhail Rasumny, Harry Shannon, Pamela Blake, Frank Ferguson, Bernadene Hayes.

Philip Raven, a hired assassin, kills a man, but when he tries to collect his fee for the mob, he finds himself caught up in complicated intrigue. By coincidence, a young girl, Ellen Graham, has gone to work as a nightclub singer in a joint owned by the seedy William Gates, the very man who hired Raven but is now trying to avoid paying him. Ellen is the girlfriend of Michael Crane, a Los Angeles policeman investigating a conspiracy to sell poison gas to Japan. She has gone to work at the nightclub as a front to collect information. In her attempts to avoid Gates' advances, Ellen meets and reluctantly teams with Raven. Together they discover that an invalid—wealthy industrialist Alvin Brewster—is behind the schemes. In the final confrontation, Raven kills both Gates and Brewster, but is himself gunned down.

One of the earliest true *films noir*, *This Gun for Hire* can only loosely be described as a gangster movie. It has the usual characters associated with the earlier genre, but its cynicism and relentless paranoia set it apart from the gangster movies of the thirties (as does its topical war and espionage theme). In retrospect, it is only a passable thriller, notable mainly for the palpable charisma of Veronica Lake and Alan Ladd. The latter became a star in this enormously popular movie and was subsequently reteamed with Lake in several other *noir* classics.

Thompson, Steve (Fictional character)
An archetypal gangster antihero of the *noir* era, Steve Thompson (Burt Lancaster) is a basically honest man who, through his own basic weaknesses, falls irrevocably into a life of crime. Thompson returns to his hometown, San Francisco, a year after his divorce from Anna. Still obsessed with Anna,

he visits one of their old hangouts, where he runs into her. She tells him that she is about to marry Slim Dundee, a sleazy mob boss, but is still physically attracted to him. They rekindle their romance, but Anna will not marry the penniless Thompson. As a result, Thompson arranges a meeting with Dundee and suggests that Dundee and his gang rob an armored car owned by the company for which Thompson works as a driver. The robbery is carried out, but two guards are killed in the process. Thompson, with Anna and Dundee, flees to Dundee's rural hideout. When Dundee discovers they are having an affair, he shoots and kills both of them. Anna and Steve die in each other's arms, while outside the screaming of police sirens grow louder, and Dundee's fate is sealed as well.

Thorpe, Richard (1896–1986)

Director. An exceptionally prolific director, Richard Thorpe directed well over 150 features. Born Rollo Smolt Thorpe in Hutchinson, Kansas, he started in vaudeville as an actor and played character roles in silent pictures, beginning in 1921. He began directing a year later. In the early thirties he made features for Poverty Row studios before joining MGM in 1935 to become one of their busiest directors. For that studio he directed two minor gangster movies.

The Earl of Chicago (MGM, 1940).
The Black Hand (MGM, 1950).

Those Who Dance (Warner Bros., 1930). 80 mins.

Director: William Beaudine. *Screenplay*: Joseph Jackson, *story by* George Kibbe Turner. *Director of Photography*: Sid Hickox. *Editor*: George Amy.

Cast: Monte Blue (Dan Hogan), Lila Lee (Nora Brady), William Boyd (Diamond Joe), Betty Compson (Kitty), William Janney (Tim), Wilfred Lucas (Big Ben). *With*: Cornelius Keefe, DeWitt Jennings, Gino Corrado, Bob Perry, Charles McEvoy.

When her boyfriend, Tim, is framed for murder by a tough big-city street gang, Nora Brady persuades the victim's brother, police detective Dan Hogan, to help her prove her lover's innocence. Together they solve the crime and, in the inevitable confrontation, Hogan kills the gang leader.

A minor early gangster melodrama, *Those Who Dance* is notable only as a precursor to the great Warner Bros. gangster movies it only barely preceded.

Three on a Match (First National, 1932). 64 mins.

Associate Producer: Samuel Bischoff. *Director*: Mervyn LeRoy. *Screenplay*: Lucien Hubbard, *story by* Kubec Glasmon and John Bright. *Director of Photography*: Sol Polito. *Art Director*: Robert Haas. *Editor*: Ray Curtis.

Cast: Joan Blondell (Mary Keaton), Warren William (Robert Kirkwood), Ann Dvorak (Vivian Revere), Bette Davis (Ruth Westcoff), Lyle Talbot (Mike), Humphrey Bogart (Harve). *With*: Sheila Terry, Grant Mitchell, Glenda Farrell, Frankie Darro, Clara Blandick.

Three female friends meet a decade after graduating from high school. Mary is a stage actress, Vivian is a society woman who has married a lawyer, and Ruth is an independent businesswoman. Vivian seduces the boyfriend of Mary, setting off a series of events leading to entanglements with gamblers and gangsters, and ultimately leading to Vivian's death.

A silly melodrama, *Three on a Match* manages to transcend its contrived plot largely because of the concise direction of Mervyn LeRoy, its hard-boiled style, and the presence of Ann Dvorak and Bette Davis at their early, sensuous best.

Thunder Road (United Artists, 1958). 94 mins.

Producer: Robert Mitchum. *Director*: Arthur Ripley. *Screenplay*: James

Atley Phillips and Walter Wise. *Directors of Photography*: Alan Stensvold and David Ettinson. *Editor*: Harry Marker.

Cast: Robert Mitchum (Lucas "Luke" Doolin), Gene Barry (Troy Barrett), Jacques Aubuchon (Carl), Keely Smith (Francie), Trevor Bardette (Vernon Doolin), Jim Mitchum (Robin Doolin). *With*: Sandra Knight, Betsy Holt, Frances Koon, Randy Sparks, Mitch Ryan, Peter Breck.

Lucas Doolin's father makes moonshine that Doolin smuggles out of the Tennessee hills in the spare gas tank of his souped up jalopy. Treasury Department agents, however, are closing in on the operation. The operation is further endangered by big-city mobsters who are trying to organize the local moonshiners. Lucas, meanwhile, is in love with a pretty nightclub singer, Francie. The Doolins manage to pit the treasury agents against the big-city mobsters, but they know the respite is only temporary, as their rural way of life is changing around them.

Although not particularly well known today, *Thunder Road* is a very good minor gangster drama. Its screenplay, based on a story by star Robert Mitchum (who also composed two songs for the film), is directed in hard-boiled style by the enigmatic Arthur Ripley. It has several superior chase scenes set in the Tennessee mountains, and is also notable for its truthful portrayal of rural Southern redneck criminals.

Thunderbolt (Paramount, 1929). 95 mins.

Director: Josef von Sternberg. *Screenplay*: Charles Furthman and Herman Mankiewicz, *story by* Charles and Jules Furthman. *Director of Photography*: Henry Gerrard. *Art Director*: Hans Dreier. *Editor*: Helen Lewis.

Cast: George Bancroft (Jim Lange, aka Thunderbolt), Richard Arlen (Bob Moran), Fay Wray (Mary, aka Ritzy), Tully Marshall (Warden), Eugene Besserer (Mrs. Moran). *With*: James Spottswood, Fred Kohler, Mike Donlin, S. S. Stewart, George Irving.

When Mary, mistress of bank robber Thunderbolt, falls in love with Bob Moran, a respectable young banker, she decides to leave the underworld. Not knowing that the police are following her, she meets Thunderbolt in a local nightclub, hoping to persuade him to release her. He refuses and promises to kill any man who comes between them. Bob, meanwhile, has been fired from the bank because of his connections with Mary. When Thunderbolt is arrested for murder and sentenced to death, he is joined on death row by Bob, who has been framed for murder by Thunderbolt's associates. Thunderbolt plans to kill his romantic rival, but when he learns that Bob and Mary were childhood sweethearts, he relents and goes to the electric chair content he has done at least one good thing in his life.

The last of the trilogy of gangster movies made in the late twenties by Josef von Sternberg, *Thunderbolt* was a part talkie. It has been described as a mixture of fantasy and reality about the gangster underworld and is rendered in typically glossy, imaginative style by von Sternberg. The sets are elegant, and the photography is extraordinary, even by today's standards. A fair box office success at the time, only fragments of the film survive today.

Thunderbolt and Lightfoot (United Artists, 1974). 115 mins.

Producer: Robert Daley. *Director and Screenplay*: Michael Cimino. *Director of Photography*: Frank Stanley. *Music*: Dee Burton. *Art Director*: Tambi Larsen. *Editor*: Ferris Webster.

Cast: Clint Eastwood (John "Thunderbolt" Doherty), Jeff Bridges (Lightfoot), George Kennedy (Red Leary), Geoffrey Lewis (Goody), Catherine Bach (Melody), Gary Busey (Curly). *With*: Jack Dodson, Burton Gilliam,

Roy Jenson, Claudia Lennear, Vic Tayback.

John "Thunderbolt" Doherty, an ex-soldier, is a con man masquerading as a preacher. He is also hiding out from his former colleagues in the underworld, Red Leary and Goody, who were captured after a robbery while he escaped with the loot. He joins with fellow con man Lightfoot, and together, partly to appease Red and Goody, they plan to rob the same bank. The robbery is successfully completed, but the thieves, inevitably, turn on each other. Thunderbolt and Lightfoot recover the original loot, but in the end only Thunderbolt survives. He purchases a new Cadillac with the stolen money and drives off alone.

An imaginative heist drama distinguished by a brilliantly executed robbery sequence, *Thunderbolt and Lightfoot* is a precursor to the contemporary buddy picture, but with a decidedly darker outlook. It was the first of two underworld thrillers directed by Michael Cimino and is by far the best; indeed, it is an overlooked classic from an era of many great American movies.

Tidyman, Ernest (1928–1984)

Novelist and screenwriter. Tidyman came to the movies via his best selling series of *Shaft* crime novels. He scripted two of the films based on the series and also wrote the screenplay for the original *The French Connection*.

The French Connection (20th Century–Fox, 1972).

Tierney, Gene (1920–1991)

Actress. The exquisitely beautiful Tierney was born to a wealthy family. She was discovered while modeling and given a Hollywood contract. Her exotic, almost Asian, beauty at first typecast her as a foreigner, but her successful portrayal of the socialite-model title character in *Laura* (20th Century–Fox, 1944) firmly established her as a glamour queen of the forties

and fifties. She was re-teamed with her *Laura* costar Dana Andrews and director Otto Preminger in the minor classic *Where the Sidewalk Ends*, a police procedural with gangster overtones, in which she appears as a socialite in love with a corrupt cop.

Where the Sidewalk Ends (20th Century–Fox, 1950).

Tierney, Lawrence (b. 1919)

Actor. On and off screen, Lawrence Tierney was *the* tough guy actor. For a time in the mid-forties it looked as if he was going to become a major star of the caliber that emerged during that era — Robert Mitchum, Burt Lancaster, and Kirk Douglas are three examples — but Tierney's wild, unpredictable behavior got him into a number of scandals and he never quite escaped "B" movies. He made a striking early appearance in the low budget *Dillinger*, whose enormous box office success made him popular. He also starred as a gangster in the less well known *The Hoodlum* which, like *Dillinger*, was directed by Max Nosseck. His brother Scott Brady costarred in the later film.

Dillinger (Monogram, 1945). *The Hoodlum* (United Artists, 1951).

Tight Spot (Columbia, 1955). 97 mins. *Producer*: Lewis J. Rachmil. *Director*: Phil Karlson. *Screenplay*: William Bowers, based on the novel *Dead Pigeon* by Lenard Kantor. *Director of Photography*: Burnett Guffey. *Musical Director*: Morris Stoloff. *Art Director*: Carl Anderson. *Editor*: Viola Lawrence.

Cast: Ginger Rogers (Sherry Conley), Edward G. Robinson (Lloyd Hallett), Brian Keith (Vince Striker), Lucy Marlowe (Prison Girl), Lorne Greene (Benjamin Costain). *With*: Allen Nourse, Peter Leeds, Doye O'Dell, Eve McVeagh, Helen Wallace.

Sherry Conley, a model, has been sent to prison on a frame up by her underworld friends. A U. S. attorney, Lloyd Hallett, obtains protective custody of her, while the government tries to persuade her to testify against Benjamin Costain, a big-time racketeer. But, partly out of fear, Sherry refuses to comply until a female law enforcement official is killed, and she learns that one of the agents assigned to protect her, Vince Striker, a man to whom she is attracted, turns out to be working for Costain. Realizing how hazardous her situation is, she agrees to testify nevertheless.

A variation on the plot and theme of *The Narrow Margin* (RKO, 1951), *Tight Spot* is a minor gangster melodrama distinguished largely by Phil Karlson's hard-boiled, unsentimental style.

Tiomkin, Dimitri (1894–1979)

Composer. The Russian-born Tiomkin was a reliable composer of very dramatic film music. Many of his scores are classics, and he won several Academy Awards. His scores are very romantic, broad, and soaring, best suited to epics and Westerns.

Dillinger (Monogram 1945). *My Six Convicts* (Columbia, 1952).

The Tip-Off Girls (Paramount, 1938). 61 mins.

Associate Producer: Edward T. Lowe. *Director*: Louis King. *Screenplay*: Maxwell Shane, Robert Yost, Stuart Anthony. *Director of Photography*: Theodor Sparkuhl. *Music*: Boris Morros. *Art Directors*: Hans Dreier and Robert Odell. *Editor*: Ellsworth Hoagland.

Cast: Lloyd Nolan (Bob Anders), Mary Carlisle (Marjorie Rogers), J. Carrol Naish (Joseph Valkus), Harvey Stephens (Jason Baardue), Roscoe Karns (Tom Logan). *With*: Larry "Buster" Crabbe, Evelyn Brent, Anthony Quinn, Benny Barker, Barlowe Borland, Pierre Watkin.

G-men Bob Anders and Tom Logan infiltrate a gang of truck hijackers by pretending to be gangsters. When they discover that the gang uses a group of B–girls for tip-offs about shipments,

the G-men are able to break up the organization and bring its leader, Joseph Valkus, to justice.

A swift moving, entertaining exploitation picture, *Tip-Off Girls* is one of the group of "B" thrillers starring Lloyd Nolan made in the late thirties. Nolan plays a typically heroic role, supported by an excellent cast of bad guys including the ubiquitous J. Carrol Naish as the mob boss and Larry "Buster" Crabbe as one of the mob henchmen.

To Live and Die in L.A. (MGM/United Artists, 1985). 116 mins.

Producers: Samuel Schulman and Bud Smith. *Director*: William Friedkin. *Screenplay*: William Friedkin and Gerald Petievich, based on the novel by Gerald Petievich. *Director of Photography*: Robby Muller. *Art Director*: Buddy Cone. *Editors*: Bud Smith and Scott Smith.

Cast: William L. Peterson (Richard Chance), Willem Dafoe (Eric Masters), John Pankow (John Vulcovich), Debra Feuer (Bianco Torres), John Turturro (Carl Cody). *With*: Darlanne Fluegel, Dean Stockwell, Steve James, Robert Downey, Michael Greene.

After his partner is killed while trailing Eric Masters, a diabolical but talented counterfeiter, Treasury Agent Richard Chance vows revenge. His obsessive quest leads him through the Los Angeles underworld, and he will stop at nothing, even killing an innocent person, in his almost psychotic vendetta. Eventually, however, Chance manages to find and capture the criminal after a lengthy auto chase.

Gerald Petievich, one of the best of the new breed of hard-boiled crime novelists to emerge in the eighties is himself a veteran of both the C.I.A. and the Treasury Department. His novels almost always deal with treasury agents in a typically unsentimental, simple style. *To Live and Die in L.A.* is based on one of his best known novels, and remains truthful to the source.

William Friedkin's direction is adequate, but in the right hands and with a better cast, it could have been one of the great action and crime thrillers of the eighties. Unfortunately, Petievich's work might have the same fate as that of his mentor, Elmore Leonard, whose brilliant novels also have received inadequate film treatments.

Toland, Gregg (1904–1948)
Cinematographer. Influenced by European expressionism and the glossy photography of the glamorous, erotic motion pictures of the late twenties, Toland was one of the great directors of photography of the thirties and forties. He could move effortlessly between glamour and more hard-boiled subjects, bringing a sense of professional beauty to each. He was also a master of trick photography, so well demonstrated in *Citizen Kane* (RKO, 1941), whose innovations can be attributed as much to Toland as to Orson Welles. His work on his single gangster movie, *Dead End*, while less demonstrative, is no less brilliant.
Dead End (United Artists, 1937).

Toler, Sidney (1874–1947)
Character actor. This chubby stage veteran is probably best remembered for his performances as the Oriental detective Charlie Chan in a series of "B" movies during the late thirties and early forties. He also played character roles in dozens of other films, generally cast as bad guys, including a gangster in his only appearance in the genre.
King of Chinatown (Paramount, 1938).

Tolobuff, Alexander (1882–1940)
Art director. The Russian-born Tolobuff studied architecture in St. Petersburg before moving to the United States during the teens. He joined MGM as a unit art director in 1926 and became unit art director for independent producer Walter Wanger in 1935. For Wanger, he designed the exotic sets for the famous gangster romance *Algiers*.
Algiers (United Artists, 1938).

Toomey, Regis (b. 1902)
Character actor. Born in Pittsburgh, Regis Toomey first acted on the screen during the early sound era. He was a mainstay of "B" movies, mainly playing cops and gangsters in over 150 features. He played small parts in three gangster movies, portraying mobsters in each.
Alibi (United Artists, 1929). *The Finger Points* (First National, 1931). *My Six Convicts* (Columbia, 1952).

Topkapi (United Artists, 1964). 120 mins.
Producer and Director: Jules Dassin. *Screenplay*: Monja Danischewsky, based on the novel *The Light of Day* by Eric Ambler. *Director of Photography*: Henri Alekan. *Art Director*: Jacques Douy. *Editor*: Roger Dwyre.
Cast: Melina Mercouri (Elizabeth Lipp), Peter Ustinov (Arthur Simpson), Maximilian Schell (William Walter), Robert Morley (Cedric Page), Akim Tamiroff (Geven). *With*: Gilles Segal, Jess Hahn, Titos Wandis, Ege Ernart, Senih Orkan, Ahmet Topatan.
Elizabeth Lipp and her lover, master criminal William Walter, plan to steal an invaluable, emerald laden dagger from Istanbul's Topkapi museum. They recruit a disparate gang of thieves including Cedric Page, an eccentric English inventor, and a lowlife con artist, Arthur Simpson. Their plans are complicated by Geven, a bizarre old man who believes the group of thieves using his house as headquarters are actually Russian spies. The robbery is eventually executed, but a quirk of fate leads to the group's capture. Undaunted, Elizabeth is already planning her next caper while languishing in prison.
Although most critics prefer the earlier, more hard-boiled *Rififi* (Miracle, 1955), *Topkapi* is a no less entertaining

heist drama also directed by Jules Dassin. Unlike its predecessor, *Topkapi* is leavened with a sense of humor. Famous for its elaborate robbery sequence (shot almost entirely in silence), it was an enormous success also because of a superior cast including Akim Tamiroff, a minor icon of the genre's golden age, in a small role.

Totter, Audrey (b. 1918)
Actress. Totter, born in Joliet, Illinois, came to the screen by way of radio. She was a popular hard-boiled blonde during the forties and fifties, generally cast as a moll or *femme fatale* in "A" and "B" thrillers, and is considered one of *film noir*'s minor female icons.
The Set-Up (RKO, 1949). *A Bullet for Joey* (United Artists, 1955).

Tourneur, Jacques (1904–1977)
Director. Jacques Tourneur was the son of the great silent French director Maurice Tourneur who made films in Hollywood. Jacques began directing features in his native France during the early thirties. When he moved to Hollywood in the late thirties, he befriended Val Lewton who promised to hire Tourneur if he ever became a producer. When the former story editor and pulp novelist joined RKO as a unit producer in the early forties, he immediately hired Tourneur, who directed three great "B" horror movies for Lewton: *Cat People* (RKO, 1942), *I Walked with a Zombie* (RKO, 1943), and *The Leopard Man* (RKO, 1943). It was in these three movies that Tourneur first demonstrated his considerable talents. His style was elegant and moody, influenced by expressionism. He subsequently directed several other important movies of the forties, including *Out of the Past*, his masterpiece. An archetypal *film noir*, it is also an important gangster picture. In the fifties, Tourneur's career went into a sad decline, but he made one last important movie, the minor gangster *noir*, *Nightfall*.

Out of the Past (RKO, 1947). *Nightfall* (Columbia, 1956).

Tover, Leo (1902–1964)
Cinematographer. Best known for his highly expressionist photography for several melodramas of the late forties, Tover also photographed a few gangster movies. He had an imaginative style, relying on creative lighting and shadowy effects.
King of Chinatown (Paramount, 1938). *Dead Reckoning* (Columbia, 1947). *I Walk Alone* (Paramount, 1948).

Tracy, Spencer (1900–1967)
Actor. Tracy was admired by many of his contemporaries for his almost invisible technique and ability to inhabit the characters he played. His low-key style was perfectly suited to film, and he remains one of the great movie actors. His stocky build and uneven features typecast him early in his career as a tough guy, and he was generally cast as a bad guy or gangster. He played criminals in three of his four gangster pictures. His best performance in the genre, however, was in the minor classic *Whipsaw* as a G-man who infiltrates a gang and befriends a lady gangster.
Up the River (Fox, 1930). *Quick Millions* (Fox, 1931). *20,000 Years in Sing Sing* (First National, 1933). *Whipsaw* (MGM, 1935).

Trapped (Eagle-Lion, 1949). 78 mins.
Producer: Bryan Foy. *Director*: Richard Fleischer. *Screenplay*: Earl Felton and George Zuckerman. *Director of Photography*: Guy Roe. *Music*: Sol Kaplan. *Art Director*: Frank Dunlauf. *Editor*: Alfred DeGaetano.
Cast: Lloyd Bridges (Tris Stewart), John Hoyt (John Downey/Hackett), Barbara Payton (Laurie), James Todd (Sylvester), Russ Conway (Gunby). *With*: Bert Conway, Robert Karnes.
John Downey, a treasury agent, is assigned to infiltrate a counterfeiting

ring. He enlists the aid of Tris Stewart, a one-time counterfeiter, whose old plates are being used by the gang. Engineering a scheme to make it look like Stewart has escaped from prison, they manage to infiltrate the gang. Despite certain complications, including Laurie, a gang member's girlfriend, the T-men are able to break up the ring and arrest its leader, Sylvester.

Trapped is one of Richard Fleischer's earliest films as a director and shows the promise of his later and better crime melodramas. It is, in fact, a rather typical "B" thriller of the era, showing the influence of *film noir* in its shadowy style and even, perhaps, the contemporary T-Man gangster movies directed by Anthony Mann. In any case, it is a good, hard-boiled melodrama aided by its small but excellent cast of "B" stars.

With Bette Davis, Claire Trevor was one of the genre's greatest female icons.

Trevor, Claire (b. 1909)

Actress. Born Claire Wemlinger in New York City, Trevor was a highly gifted actress who played second leads in "A" pictures and leads in "B" movies. A deeply sensual actress, the blonde Trevor projected a sense of vulnerability in her hard-boiled roles, and she was at her best as a hooker with a heart of gold, moll, or *femme fatale*. A major female icon of the gangster genre, she appeared in seven gangster movies. Of these, her best known performance is in the classic *Key Largo* in which she played the victimized moll. She won an Academy Award for best supporting actress for this performance.

Human Cargo (20th Century-Fox, 1936). *Dead End* (United Artists, 1937). *King of Gamblers* (Paramount, 1937). *I Stole a Million* (Universal, 1939). *Key Largo* (Warner Bros., 1948). *Raw Deal* (Eagle-Lion, 1948). *Hoodlum Empire* (Empire, 1952).

Turner, Kathleen (b. 1956)

Actress. After experience on the stage and in television soap operas, Kathleen

Turner made a striking big-screen debut as the *femme fatale* in *Body Heat* (Warner Bros., 1981). The role thrust her into stardom, and she was one of the most important film actresses of the eighties. One of her best performances was in *Prizzi's Honor*, John Huston's penultimate film in which she played a mob hit woman.

Prizzi's Honor (20th Century-Fox, 1985).

Tuttle, Frank (1892–1963)

Director. A prolific director whose career began in the mid-twenties and continued until 1959, Tuttle was a studio man who never developed a personal style. However, he was an expert director of solid action oriented pictures who made several classics, including the early *noir This Gun for Hire*, the best of his four gangster movies.

The Glass Key (Paramount, 1935). *I Stole a Million* (Universal, 1939). *This Gun for Hire* (Paramount, 1942). *Hell on Frisco Bay* (Warner Bros., 1955).

20th Century-Fox

Formed in 1935 by a merger between

Darryl F. Zanuck's Twentieth Century Productions, an independent company releasing through United Artists, and Fox Film Corporation, the formerly successful production and distribution company, 20th Century-Fox was financed by the same people who owned Metro-Goldwyn-Mayer. Named Vice President in Charge of Production, a post he held for more than twenty years, Zanuck fashioned the company into a kind of second-string MGM, relying mainly on colorful, family oriented musicals and comedies. Yet, the studio also released its share of hard-boiled melodramas (particularly during the forties), and the classic gangster melodrama *Show Them No Mercy* helped inaugurate the studio's first year of production. With its concentration of musical and comedy talents, and conventional leads, 20th Century-Fox did not have personalities suitable to the genre until the late forties. One of the studio's few early gangster films, *Johnny Apollo*, proved only partly successful, largely due to the unsuitability of its leads, Tyrone Power and Dorothy Lamour. In the late forties, however, the studio signed a new group of actors, including Richard Widmark, Victor Mature and Dana Andrews, who, under the guidance of contract directors Otto Preminger and Henry Hathaway, emerged as the kind of hard-boiled stars who were popular during the early thirties; however, they were complicated by psychological imperfections—in other words, they became the archetypal *film noir* antiheroes. It is from this era, 1945–1955, that the company produced its most important gangster movies. Since the golden age, 20th Century-Fox has continued to produce the occasional genre classic— *The French Connection* pictures in the seventies, for example—and the Coen brothers' *Miller's Crossing* updates the gangster genre in a contemporary style. Zanuck's legacy clearly lives on.

1935: *Show Them No Mercy*. 1936:

Human Cargo. 1937: *Born Reckless*. 1938: *Up the River*. 1940: *Johnny Apollo*. 1941: *Roger Touhy, Gangster*. 1947: *Kiss of Death*. 1950: *Where the Sidewalk Ends*. 1951: *Lucky Nick Cain*. 1955: *Violent Saturday*. 1959: *I, Mobster*. 1960: *Seven Thieves*. 1967: *The St. Valentine's Day Massacre*. 1968: *The Sicilian Clan*. 1971: *The French Connection*. 1975: *The French Connection II*. 1984: *Johnny Dangerously*. 1985: *Prizzi's Honor*. 1990: *Miller's Crossing*.

20,000 Years in Sing Sing (First National, 1933). 77 mins.
Associate Producer: Robert Lord. *Director*: Michael Curtiz. *Screenplay*: Wilson Mizner and Brown Holmes, based on the book by Warden Lewis E. Lawes. *Director of Photography*: Barney McGill. George Amy.
Cast: Spencer Tracy (Tom Connors), Bette Davis (Fay), Lyle Talbot (Bud), Arthur Byron (Warden Long), Grant Mitchell (Dr. Ames), Warren Hymer (Hype). *With*: Louis Calhern, Sheila Terry, Edward McNamara, Spencer Charters, Nella Walker, Harold Huber.

Tom Connors, a tough, streetwise, small-time hood is sent to prison. For the love of his girlfriend, Fay, he tries to go straight. When Fay is injured in a car crash, Connors is given a twenty-four-hour leave, but when she dies from her injuries, he hunts down the man responsible for the crash, ironically the same man responsible for railroading him to prison, and kills him. Tom returns to prison, knowing he will be executed for his crime.

An odd mixture of the prison exposé of the sort explored in *The Big House* (MGM, 1930) and romantic comedy, *20,000 Years in Sing Sing* is a minor classic from Warner Bros.–First National's great period of gangster movies. It is directed with great style by the underrated Michael Curtiz, and acted superbly by Spencer Tracy and Bette Davis.

Udo, Tom (Fictional character)
A supporting role as the deeply psychotic mob hit man Tom Udo in *Kiss of Death* (20th Century-Fox, 1947), made Richard Widmark into an instant star. Udo has been hired to hunt down and kill a mob informer, Nick Bianco (Victor Mature). In one of the most memorable scenes in American cinema, Udo pushes an invalid in a wheelchair down a flight of stairs while laughing maniacally.

Unchained (Warner Bros., 1955). 75 mins.
Producer and Director: Hall Bartlett. *Screenplay*: Hall Bartlett, based on the book *Prisoners Are People* by Kenyon J. Scudder. *Director of Photography*: Virgil E. Miller. *Music*: Alex North. *Art Director*: Stan Fletischer. *Editor*: Cotton Warburton.
Cast: Elroy Hirsh (Steve Davitt), Barbara Hale (Mary Davitt), Chester Morris (Kenyon J. Scudder), Todd Duncan (Bill Howard), Johnny Johnston (Eddie Garrity). *With*: Peggy Knudsen, Jerry Paris, Bill Kennedy, Henry Nakamura, Kathryn Grant.
Steve Davitt, a hardened criminal, is sent to the experimental prison at Chino, California, an unwalled, low-security complex dedicated to reforming criminals. Through the efforts of an understanding warden, Kenyon J. Scudder, and his loyal wife, Mary, Steve is sent on the path of reforming.
Former football star Elroy "Crazylegs" Hirsh starred in this film version of Kenyon J. Scudder's memoirs. While Hirsh was inadequate in the role, film veteran Chester Morris was very good as the sympathetic warden. However, the film is probably best known for its title song, "Unchained Melody," which has become a standard.

The Undercover Man (Columbia, 1949). 85 mins.
Producer: Robert Rossen. *Director*: Joseph H. Lewis. *Screenplay*: Sydney Boehm. *Director of Photography*: Burnett Guffey. *Music Director*: Morris Stoloff. *Art Director*: Walter Holscher. *Editor*: Al Clark.
Cast: Glenn Ford (Frank Warren), Nina Foch (Judith Warren), James Whitmore (George Pappas), Barry Kelley (Edward O'Rourke), David Wolfe (Stanley Weinberg). *With*: Frank Tweddell, John Hamilton, Howard St. John, Leo Penn, Joan Lazer, Anthony Caruso.
When all attempts fail to bring gang boss Edward O'Rourke to justice, the Treasury Department assigns Frank Warren to the case. His job is to uncover evidence of tax evasion, but the powerful gang boss almost halts the operation through acts of intimidation and murder before Warren get the goods on him.
Joseph H. Lewis was a master of style over substance, rarely allowing elements of theme or plot to influence his scenes. Beginning in the late forties, he directed a group of extraordinary *noir* thrillers with underworld themes, including *The Big Combo* (Allied Artists, 1955) and *Gun Crazy* (United Artists, 1949). Although less well known, *The Undercover Man* is no less worthy of praise, one of the few instances where Lewis was able to join style and story in a cohesive manner.

Underworld (Paramount, 1927). Approximately 80 mins.
Presenters: Adolph Zukor and Jesse L. Lasky. *Producer*: Hector Turnbull. *Director*: Josef von Sternberg. *Screenplay*: Robert N. Lee, *story by* Ben Hecht, adapted by Charles Furthman. *Titles*: George Marion, Jr. *Director of Photography*: Bert Glennon. *Art Director*: Hans Dreier.
Cast: George Bancroft (Bull Weed), Clive Brook (Rolls Royce), Evelyn Brent (Feathers), Larry Semon (Slippy Lewis), Fred Kohler (Buck). *With*: Helen Lynch, Jerry Mandy, Karl Morse.
In one of his few acts of kindness,

gangster Bull Weed befriends a derelict whom he dubs Rolls Royce because of his gentlemanly behavior. Rolls becomes a gang member and quickly rises to become the brains of the operation. Bull's moll, Feathers, begins to fall for Royce. Later, at a dance, when a rival makes a pass at her, Bull kills him in a jealous rage. He is arrested, but when a scheme to break him out of jail fails, Bull believes he has been double-crossed, and escapes to exact a revenge against his once trusted lieutenant. When the police corner the duo, they shoot it out. Royce is killed and Bull surrenders, realizing his friend had been loyal.

Based on an original screen story by Ben Hecht (who won an Academy Award for best original story), *Underworld* is a solid gangster melodrama that holds up well. In fact, it was the first great gangster film, and its enormous success launched both Josef von Sternberg's career and the genre. It was the first of a quartet of gangster movies, all box office hits, directed by Sternberg during the late twenties, and it is generally recognized as a peak of elegant style in silent movies. It also established George Bancroft as the genre's first icon.

Underworld U.S.A. (Columbia, 1961). 98 mins.
Producer, Director and Screenplay: Samuel Fuller. *Director of Photography*: Hah Mohr. *Music*: Harry Sukman. *Art Director*: Robert Peterson. *Editor*: Jerome Thoms.
Cast: Cliff Robertson (Tolly Devlin), Dolores Dorn (Cuddles), Beatrice Kay (Sandy), Paul Duboy (Gela), Robert Emhardt (Connors), Larry Gates (Driscoll), Richard Rust (Gus). *With*: Gerald Milton, Allan Gruener, David Kent, Tina Rome, Sally Mills, Robert Lieb.

As a child, Tolly Devlin witnessed the gangland murder of his father. As a young adult, he becomes a petty thief, determined to track down and kill the men responsible for his father's death. While working for the Federal Crime Commission, Tolly infiltrates the local mob, and with the help of a moll, Cuddles, tracks down his father's killers. In the final confrontation, Tolly is killed, and Cuddles, determined to avenge his murder, decides to testify against the mob.

Certainly one of the great directors of crime dramas, Sam Fuller has too long been neglected by American critics (in Europe he is regarded as one of the greatest directors of his generation). His movies, usually written or cowritten by Fuller, present a seedy, sordid vision of America, distorted by greed, corruption, and a lack of values. *Underworld U.S.A.* is a typically bleak, violent melodrama, and its taut, brisk pace has much to teach contemporary directors of thrillers.

United Artists

Founded in 1919 by Mary Pickford, Charles Chaplin, Douglas Fairbanks, and D. W. Griffith, United Artists financed and distributed theirs and others' projects. By the thirties, after an extraordinary decade, all of the founders had been bought out, and the company became purely a financier and distributor of products by independent filmmakers. Among others, the producer Walter Wanger often made movies for the company, but without any real studio or production facilities, United Artists did not develop a house style. Nevertheless, as an outlet for some of the maverick filmmakers during Hollywood's golden age, United Artists released some of the most innovative and risky American movies of the era. This is certainly true for many of Wanger's productions, including the popular gangster romance *Algiers*, all of Samuel Goldwyn's productions, including *Dead End*, one of the most important gangster movies of the thirties, and, of course, *Scarface*, one of the genre's early classics. The independent spirit of the company continued until the early eighties, when it went bankrupt after the *Heaven's Gate* fiasco and was absorbed into the equally troubled MGM. (*Heaven's Gate*, directed by Michael Cimino, was virtually unreleasable despite its $40 million-plus cost.) 1929: *Alibi*. 1932: *Scarface*. 1933: *I Cover the Waterfront*. 1935: *Let 'Em Have It*. 1937: *Dead End, You Only Live Once*. 1938: *Algiers*. 1946: *The Chase*. 1947: *Body and Soul*. 1950: *Gun Crazy, Quicksand*. 1951: *The Hoodlum*. 1952: *Kansas City Confidential*. 1954: *Black Tuesday*. 1955: *A Bullet for Joey, The Naked Street, Rififi*. 1956: *The Killing*. 1957: *Baby Face Nelson, Chicago Confidential*. 1959: *Cry Tough, Inside the Mafia, The Last Mile, Odds Against Tomorrow, Some Like It Hot*. 1964: *Topkapi*. 1972: *Across 110th Street, Hickey and Boggs, The Mechanic*. 1974: *Mr. Majestyk, Thieves Like Us, Thunderbolt and Lightfoot*.

Universal

Founded in 1912 by Carl Laemmle, an exhibitor turned producer, Universal was one of the earliest studios established during the silent era that survived the transition to sound to become one of the leading American studios during Hollywood's golden age. By 1933 the studio was already well established, having produced many classics. Under Carl Laemmle, Jr., who in his early twenties was a true boy wonder, the studio made a bid for the big time (with little resources, it was considered one of the "little two" studios, along with Columbia) and almost succeeded with a series of extraordinary horror films including *Dracula* (1931), *Frankenstein* (1931) and *Bride of Frankenstein* (1935). However, Laemmle, Jr. made some expensive features that lost money, and he, in turn, lost control and retired while still only in his late twenties. Amazingly, the studio only released one gangster movie, *Outside the Law*, during this

period. With its behind the scenes talent and experimental, expressionist style, Universal might well have created a series of interesting gangster movies to rival those of Warner Bros. but perhaps Laemmle, Jr. did not want to compete with his rivals who so dominated the genre during the thirties. In any case, with Laemmle, Jr. gone, the new administration concentrated on more modest, family oriented features, and the few gangster movies that were released by the studio through the late forties were "B" titles or, in the case of *Gang Busters*, a cheaply produced serial. However, in the late forties an extraordinary group of gangster pictures emerged in the new dark, moody, and cynical *noir* style. The genius who created the two greatest of these gangster *noirs* was director Robert Siodmak, who directed the classics *The Killers* and *Criss Cross*. The studio also released *Brute Force*, one of the best prison gangster melodramas, during this period. In the fifties Universal's gangster movies were few and far between and, again, only minor additions to the genre. Don Siegel remade *The Killers* in 1964, but it does not compare favorably with Siodmak's original. *The Sting* was a return to form, but the most important recent gangster movie to be released by Universal is certainly Brian De Palma's *Scarface*.

1930: *Outside the Law*. 1939: *Big Town Czar, Gambling Ship, I Stole a Million*. 1942: *Eyes of the Underworld, Gang Busters* (serial). 1946: *The Killers*. 1947: *Brute Force*. 1948: *Casbah*. 1949: *Criss Cross, Johnny Stool Pigeon*. 1953: *Forbidden*. 1955: *Six Bridges to Cross*. 1958: *Damn Citizen*. 1964: *The Killers*. 1973: *The Don Is Dead, The Sting*. 1974: *Newman's Law*. 1978: *The Brink's Job*. 1983: *Scarface, The Sting II*. 1992: *Mobsters*.

The Untouchables

Inspired by Special F.B.I. agent Eliot Ness' memoirs, *The Untouchables* was a classic 1959–62 television

Brian De Palma (center) directs Robert De Niro (right) as Al Capone in the contemporary gangster classic *The Untouchables.*

Sean Connery (left) and Kevin Costner (right) as the good guys in *The Untouchables.*

series that still holds up well. Largely recounting Ness' attempts to bring Al Capone to justice, it brilliantly recreated twenties Chicago and provided Robert Stack with a great role. Visceral and violent, many episodes were directed by "B" great Phil Karlson, who also helmed the pilot film which was released in Europe as a feature, *The Scarface Mob* (Cari Releasing, 1962).

The Untouchables (Paramount, 1988). 129 mins.
Producer: Art Linson. *Director*: Brian De Palma. *Screenplay*: David Mamet. *Director of Photography*: Stephen H. Burum. *Music*: Ennio Morricone. *Art Director*: William A. Eliott. *Editors*: Jerry Greenberg and Bill Pankow.
Cast: Kevin Costner (Eliot Ness), Sean Connery (Jim Mallone), Charles Martin Smith (Oscar Wallace), Andy Garcia (George Stone), Robert De Niro (Al Capone), Billy Draco (Walter Nitti). *With*: Patricia Clarkson, Vito D'Ambrosio, Brad Sullivan, Steven Goldstein, Don Harvey, Peter Aylward.

In the late twenties, Eliot Ness, a special agent for the F.B.I., is sent to Chicago to help break up Al Capone's criminal organizations financed by illegal liquor sales. With the aid of Jim Mallone, an honest cop, Ness assembles a gang of his own out of honest policemen and government officials. Using extremely questionable techniques, some clearly against the law, Ness begins a bloody campaign against Capone and his gang. When the mob succeeds in killing Mallone, Ness' campaign becomes a personal one, and he targets Capone's psychotic enforcer, Walter Nitti. Ness tracks down Nitti and kills him, but Capone is brought to justice only when the government finds that he has not paid his income taxes.

Brian De Palma's classic modern gangster movie is only very loosely based on the real Eliot Ness' adventures, but it is so wildly entertaining one hardly cares about De Palma and his scenarist's scant adherence to the facts. Extremely popular, the film made Kevin Costner into a star, and helped revitalize Sean Connery's career. Like the television show which inspired it, the film is extremely violent in several extraordinary sequences, including a famous one inspired by Soviet director Sergei Eisenstein's 1925 masterpiece, *Potemkin*.

Up the River (Fox, 1930). 92 mins.
Presenter: William Fox. *Director*: John Ford. *Screenplay*: Maurine Watkins. *Director of Photography*: Joseph August. *Editor*: Frank E. Hull.
Cast: Spencer Tracy (St. Louis), Warren Hymer (Dannemora Dan), Humphrey Bogart (Steve), Claire Luce (Judy), Joan Lawes (Jean), Sharon Lynn (Edith LaVerne). *With*: George MacFarland, Gaylord Pendleton, William Collier, Robert E. O'Connor, Louise MacIntosh.

Two convicts, Dannemora Dan and St. Louis, escape from prison, have a falling out, and are returned to prison. One of their fellow prisoners, Steve, serving time for an accidental manslaughter, falls in love with Judy, a prisoner in the women's section who is serving time for a trumped up theft charge. When the man on the outside who framed Judy learns of her romance with Steve, he plans to ruin Steve's upcoming release. Judy asks St. Louis and Dan for help. They escape from prison again, stop the man before he can act on his threat, and return to prison in time to help win a basketball game.

This ridiculous piece of hokum was described by John Ford as "one of his mortal sins." It is notable for Humphrey Bogart's early performance. Also notable is the appearance of Claire Luce, who became one of the most powerful female publishers and editors of magazines, including *Vanity Fair*, later in the decade.

Up the River (20th Century-Fox, 1938). 75 mins.
Producer: Sol M. Wurtzel. *Director*: Alfred Werker. *Screenplay*: Lou Breslow and John Patrick. *Director of Photography*: Peverell Marley. *Music Director*: Samuel Kaylin. *Art Directors*: Bernard Herzbrun and Chester Gore. *Editor*: Nick DeMaggio.

Cast: Preston Foster (Chipper Morgan), Tony Martin (Tommy Grant), Phyllis Brooks (Helen), Slim Summerville (Slim Nelson), Arthur Treacher (Darby Randall). *With*: Alan Dinehart, Eddie Collins, Jane Darwell, Sidney Toler, Bill Robinson, Edward Gargan.

A "B" remake of the original film, this version is notable only as one of Preston Foster's gangster vehicles. Except for changing of the characters' names, the plot remains identical to the original.

Urban Gangsters

Big cities are a natural breeding ground for crime and criminal organizations because of their closely knit ethnic communities (who generally do not trust the police or report crimes), and because of the many opportunities for criminal exploitation. Likewise, the proximity of legitimate culture and wealth has resulted, in America in particular, in a unique brand of criminal — the urban gangster. A product of the tenement slums, the urban gangster desires assimilation and acceptance from the respectable community. Thus, he is often well dressed and, surrounded by the trappings of a successful legitimate career, has pretensions to sophistication and culture. The real life urban gangsters, Meyer Lansky and Al Capone, were patrons of the arts, contributors to political campaigns, and were often seen at the theater or opera. Such behavior has inspired countless writers' and filmmakers' images of American gangsters — from Bull Weed in *Underworld* (Paramount, 1927) to Don Vito Corleone in *The Godfather* (Paramount, 1972) and beyond.

Ustinov, Peter (b. 1921)
Character actor. Ustinov is a talented actor, screenwriter, director, playwright and novelist. The rotund actor is best known for his comic performances, including the eccentric con man who joins a heist in the classic caper drama, *Topkapi*.

Topkapi (United Artists, 1964).

The Valachi Papers (Columbia, 1972). 127 mins.
Producer: Dino De Laurentiis. *Director*: Terence Young. *Screenplay*: Stephen Geller, based on the book by Peter Maas. *Director of Photography*: Aldo Tonti. *Music*: Riz Ortolani. *Art Director*: Mario Carbuglia. *Editor*: John Dwyre.

Cast: Mario Pilar (Salerno), Charles Bronson ("Joey Cago"/Joseph Valachi), Fred Valleca (Johnny Beck), Giacomino De Michelis (Little Augie), Arny Freeman (Warden). *With*: Lino Ventura, Sylvester Lamont, Gerald S. O'Loughlin, Walter Chiari.

When he learns that the Mafia has put out a contract on his life, former mobster Joseph Valachi agrees to tell the F.B.I. about his experiences in the mob. Via flashbacks, his life in the mob is recounted in vivid, bloody detail. Finished with his tale, he awaits his assassin.

Released shortly after *The Godfather* (Paramount, 1972), *The Valachi Papers*, based on the true story of a Mafia thug, was a poor imitation of the earlier classic, but it was a fair success and helped launch Bronson as a major action star of the seventies.

Van Cleef, Lee (b. 1925)
Character actor. Born in Somerville, New Jersey, Van Cleef returned from Naval service during World War II, joined a little theater group and went straight into films. His sharp features and narrow, steely eyes made him ideal as a villain, and indeed he played psychotic mob henchmen in two notable "B" gangster pictures, *The Big Combo*

and *Kansas City Confidential*. He also played a flashy underworld figure in the lesser known *I Cover the Underworld*.

Kansas City Confidential (United Artists, 1952). *The Big Combo* (Allied Artists, 1955). *I Cover the Underworld* (Republic, 1955).

Van Dyke, W. S. (1899–1943)

Director. W. S. "Woody" Van Dyke was the most efficient and successful contract director at MGM in the thirties and forties. Nicknamed "One-Take" Woody, Van Dyke had a brisk, energetic style best suited to action movies and adventures. He directed several classic movies for MGM including *Tarzan, the Ape Man* (1932), *The Thin Man* (1934), and several of the Jeanette MacDonald and Nelson Eddy operettas. He also directed the classic gangster picture, *Manhattan Melodrama*. His other gangster movie, *Penthouse*, is an entertaining melodrama, if not a classic.

Penthouse (MGM, 1933). *Manhattan Melodrama* (MGM, 1934).

Veiller, Anthony (1903–1965)

Screenwriter. Veiller was a successful screenwriter of good action movies during the forties and fifties. His most important screenplay is *The Killers*, which he brilliantly expanded from Ernest Hemingway's short story.

The Killers (Universal, 1946).

Vidor, Charles (1900–1959)

Director. Vidor was a typical studio director, taking whatever assignments came his way and carrying them out efficiently but with little imagination. The highlight of his three decade career was in the forties when he worked for Columbia, during which he directed the classic *Gilda*. He also directed *Blind Alley*, a superior gangster drama with psychological overtones.

Blind Alley (Columbia, 1939). *Gilda* (Columbia, 1946).

Vinson, Helen (b. 1907)

Actress. Born Helen Rulfs in Beaumont, Texas, Vinson arrived in Hollywood during the early thirties and played cool, aristocratic ladies for two decades in many movies, including two important gangster movies.

I Am a Fugitive from a Chain Gang (Warner Bros., 1932). *The Little Giant* (First National, 1933).

Violent Saturday (20th Century–Fox, 1955). 91 mins.

Producer: Buddy Adler. *Director*: Richard Fleischer. *Screenplay*: Sydney Boehm, based on the novel by William I. Heath. *Director of Photography*: Charles G. Clarke. *Music Director*: Lionel Newman. *Art Directors*: Lyle Wheeler and George W. Davis. *Editor*: Louis Loeffler.

Cast: Victor Mature (Shelley Martin), Richard Egan (Boyd Fairchild), Stephen McNally (Harper), Virginia Leith (Linda), Tommy Noonan (Harry Reeves), Lee Marvin (Bill). *With*: Sylvia Sidney, Margaret Hayes, J. Carrol Naish, Ernest Borgnine, Dorothy Patrick, Billy Chapin.

Three tough crooks plan to rob a bank in a small rural Arizona town. The robbery is successfully carried out but, typically, it begins to fall apart afterward and results in all the participants either dead or apprehended by the law.

Yet another caper drama, *Violent Saturday* is not a classic, but is an extremely well made thriller directed by the underrated Richard Fleischer, a master of violent action. Lee Marvin gives a standout performance as the benzedrine sniffing, sadistic leader of the gang of bank robbers.

Vogel, Paul (1899–1975)

Cinematographer. A distinguished if not particularly individual director of photography, Vogel's extensive filmography is distinguished by a handful of inventive films, of which *The Lady in the Lake* (MGM, 1946) is probably his most important. He also photographed a single minor gangster movie. *The Black Hand* (MGM, 1950).

Vye, Murvyn (1913–1976)
Character actor. Born in Quincy, Massachusetts, Vye acted on Broadway before shifting to films in the late forties. Heavyset, he generally played villains. In *Al Capone*, he made a memorable appearance as Capone's rival Bugs Moran, who became a victim of Capone's wrath in the notorious St. Valentine's Day Massacre.
Al Capone (Allied Artists, 1959).

Wald, Jerry (1911–1962)
Screenwriter and producer. A former New York journalist, the excitable, workaholic Wald is said to have been the inspiration for the live-wire title character of *What Makes Sammy Run?*, Budd Schulberg's novel. After moving to Hollywood in the early thirties, Wald joined Warner Bros. and became an efficient, successful screenwriter. Among the films he cowrote is the classic gangster picture *The Roaring Twenties*. A protégé of producer Hal B. Wallis, Wald began producing features for Warner's in the early forties and became one of the most successful producers of the next twenty years. He produced two important gangster pictures.
The Roaring Twenties (Warner Bros., 1939; cowriter only). *Key Largo* (Warner Bros., 1948; producer). *The Damned Don't Cry* (Warner Bros., 1950; producer).

Walker, Helen (1921–1968)
Actress. Born in Worcester, Massachusetts, Walker was a popular star of the early forties. A pretty blonde, she was most often seen as a no-nonsense working girl, the type she played in the Alan Ladd gangster vehicle *Lucky Jordan*.
Lucky Jordan (Paramount, 1942).

Walker, Joseph (1892–1985)
Cinematographer. Walker is best

known for his collaborations with director Frank Capra during the thirties. His elegant, glittering style was perfectly suited to glossy black and white entertainments, and he photographed a number of important movies including the gangster *noir*, *The Mob*, which showed the influence of expressionism.
The Mob (Columbia, 1951).

Wallach, Eli (b. 1915)
Character actor. Wallach is another of the method actors who emerged during the fifties. He is best known for his intense performances as tortured characters. He played an aging mob boss and rival of Michael Corleone (Al Pacino) in *The Godfather III*.
The Godfather III (Paramount, 1990).

Wallis, Hal (1898–1986)
Producer and executive. After varied experience, including running a movie theater, Wallis joined Warner Bros. in the mid-twenties and quickly rose to an executive position with the studio. For much of the late twenties and early thirties he was in the shadow of Darryl F. Zanuck, but after Zanuck's departure in 1934, Wallis was named production chief and presided over the studio's golden age until forming his own production company in 1944, where, for many years, he released largely through Paramount. As executive producer for Warner Bros. during the thirties and forties, Wallis varied the unsentimental hard-boiled style created by Zanuck with a softer, more romantic approach. The result was a very popular style that was also uniquely American, and many of the films that Wallis helped create as head of production remain some of Hollywood's most beloved and enduring classics: *The Charge of the Light Brigade* (1936), *The Dawn Patrol* (1938), *The Adventures of Robin Hood* (1938), *The Letter* (1940), *Sergeant York* (1941), and *Casablanca* (1942). He also produced many of the best gangster films

of the thirties and forties, and if he is not as well known or as critically acclaimed as some of his contemporaries, he might well be the genre's most important producer.

Little Caesar (Warner Bros., 1930). *Kid Galahad* (Warner Bros., 1937). *A Slight Case of Murder* (Warner Bros., 1938). *The Roaring Twenties* (Warner Bros., 1939). *Brother Orchid* (Warner Bros., 1940). *Invisible Stripes* (Warner Bros., 1940). *High Sierra* (Warner Bros., 1941). *The Maltese Falcon* (Warner Bros., 1941). *Larceny, Inc.* (Warner Bros., 1942). *Desert Fury* (Paramount, 1947). *I Walk Alone* (Paramount, 1947). *Dark City* (Paramount, 1950).

Walsh, Raoul (1887–1981)
Director. Walsh was a master of action and violence with an agreeably visceral style. Beginning in the silent era, Walsh was a leading director, and his career stretched well into the sixties. He did his best work for Warner Bros. during the thirties and forties and was responsible for many of their best hard-boiled melodramas and war films. He directed several excellent gangster movies beginning with *Me, Gangster*, one of the earliest films of the genre, and two of the genre's greatest classics, *High Sierra* and *White Heat*. He also codirected the classic *The Roaring Twenties* (with Anatole Litvak) and, without credit, *The Enforcer*.

Me, Gangster (Fox, 1928). *The Roaring Twenties* (Warner Bros., 1939; codirector only). *High Sierra* (Warner Bros., 1941). *White Heat* (Warner Bros., 1949). *The Enforcer* (Warner Bros., 1951; uncredited codirector).

Wanger, Walter (1894–1968)
Producer. For nearly four decades, beginning in the late twenties, Walter Wanger was one of the most successful independent producers in Hollywood. He specialized in serious action oriented films and thrillers, producing classics directed by John Ford, Alfred Hitchcock and Fritz Lang. He produced the latter's pseudo-gangster melodrama *You Only Live Once*. He also produced the classic gangster romance *Algiers* and Don Siegel's prison drama *Riot in Cell Block 11*.

You Only Live Once (Allied Artists, 1937). *Algiers* (United Artists, 1938). *Riot in Cell Block 11* (Allied Artists, 1954).

Warner Bros. Pictures
Founded in 1923 by the four Warner Bros., Albert, Harry, Sam and Jack, who all had worked as film distributors. Harry and Jack were the two brothers most involved with day to day studio operations, and Jack ran the studio until the late sixties. Because of Jack's notorious thriftiness, the studio's productions developed a gritty, unadorned look, but the man who had the most influence on the studio's developing style in the late twenties was Darryl F. Zanuck. Zanuck, a former screenwriter, proved to be a prolific creator of commercial stories and a rich source of ideas for productions, and he quickly became an invaluable assistant to Jack Warner by 1927. Indeed, Zanuck was directly or indirectly responsible for most of the important Warner Bros. productions between 1927 and 1933, and he also convinced Jack to take a gamble on new sound technologies which would result in the first part talking feature, *The Jazz Singer*, in 1927. With a taste for gritty, hard-boiled subjects, Zanuck developed the early Warner Bros.' gangster movies and took the gamble on signing up New York talent like James Cagney, who made several gangster movies for the studio. *Public Enemy, Jimmy the Gent, Lights of New York, Smart Money, Taxi, I Am a Fugitive from a Chain Gang*, and the group released as First National titles (including Edward G. Robinson in *Little Caesar* in 1930) were all projects developed by Darryl F. Zanuck. Although highly paid—he was making $5,000 a week in 1933 at

the height of the Great Depression — Zanuck felt unappreciated at Warner Bros. where Jack still treated him like a subordinate rather than an equal, and he left at the end of that year to start his own independent production company, Twentieth Century Productions. Warner, however, simply promoted one of Zanuck's assistants, Hal B. Wallis, as the defacto production chief. Under Wallis, the studio entered a golden age. Wallis tempered Zanuck's unsentimental hard-boiled style with a more romantic approach, resulting in the much beloved house style of the late thirties and early forties. During this era, Cagney developed a more palatable image, more heroic than his early villains. Bette Davis became one of the leading female icons of the genre, and a "B" actor, Humphrey Bogart, played endless gangsters while ever so slowly becoming a star. Among the classics of this era are *The Amazing Dr. Clitterhouse*, *Angels with Dirty Faces*, *Invisible Stripes*, *High Sierra*, *The Roaring Twenties*, *Marked Woman*, and *The Petrified Forest*. As the gangster genre lost popularity during the early forties, its stars, including Bogart, began to appear in a greater variety of movies, but Warner and Wallis continued to make the occasional gangster picture. In this age of *film noir*, the Warner gangster *noirs* retained the essential ingredients of the original cycle: good versus evil, the destruction of corruption, and violent action. *White Heat*, *Key Largo* and *The Damned Don't Cry* are the classics of this era. With the departure of Wallis in the early fifties, the company's output became more variable and conventional, and eventually, like all of the studios of the golden age era lost its identifiable style (by 1960). However, it continued to release films which showed the enormous influence of the initial cycle, including, most notably, *The Rise and Fall of Legs Diamond* and *Bonnie and Clyde* during the sixties. Overall, Warner Bros. was the most important contributor to the gangster

genre and, under both Zanuck and Wallis, the creator of the genre's greatest classics.

1928: *Lights of New York*. 1930: *The Doorway to Hell, Those Who Dance*. 1931: *The Maltese Falcon* (Roy Del Ruth, director), *Public Enemy, Smart Money, The Star Witness*. 1932: *I Am a Fugitive from a Chain Gang, The Mouthpiece, Taxi*. 1933: *Lady Killer*. 1934: *Heat Lightning, Jimmy the Gent*. 1935: *The Big Shot, Dr. Socrates, Special Agent*. 1936: *The Petrified Forest, Public Enemy's Wife*. 1937: *Kid Galahad, Marked Woman, San Quentin*. 1938: *The Amazing Dr. Clitterhouse, Angels with Dirty Faces, Racket Busters, A Slight Case of Murder*. 1939: *Each Dawn I Die, Hell's Kitchen, Invisible Stripes, King of the Underworld, The Roaring Twenties, Skin Deep, You Can't Get Away with Murder*. 1940: *Brother Orchid, Castle on the Hudson*. 1941: *High Sierra, The Maltese Falcon* (John Huston, director). 1942: *Lady Gangster, Larceny, Inc.*. 1948: *Key Largo*. 1949: *White Heat*. 1950: *Caged, The Damned Don't Cry, Hell on Frisco Bay, Highway 301, Kiss Tomorrow Goodbye*. 1951: *The Enforcer*. 1953: *Crime Wave*. 1955: *Illegal, New York Confidential, Pete Kelly's Blues*. 1959: *The F.B.I. Story*. 1960: *The Rise and Fall of Legs Diamond*. 1961: *Portrait of a Mobster*. 1967: *Bonnie and Clyde*. 1968: *Bullit*. 1973: *Mean Streets*. 1975: *The Yakuza*. 1983: *City Heat*. 1984: *Once Upon a Time in America*.

Waxman, Franz (1906–1967)

Composer. Born Franz Wachsmann in Germany, Waxman was a concert musician and serious composer before the rise of Hitler induced him to emigrate to the United States in the early thirties. He became one of the most respected film composers of the next three decades, winning two Academy Awards and composing the music for many classic American films. His style was dramatic and melodic. *Strange Cargo* (MGM, 1940).

Webb, Jack (1920–1982)

Character actor and director. Before he achieved fame and immortality as the star and director of *Dragnet*, the television police drama, Jack Webb had a successful career as a character actor in films. He was most often seen, as in his gangster films and *films noir*, as villains and mob henchmen. He also directed and starred in *Pete Kelly's Blues*, an unusual drama about a jazz musician mixed up with gangsters.

Dark City (Paramount, 1950; actor only). *Pete Kelly's Blues* (Warner Bros., 1955; actor and director).

Webb, Roy (1888–1982)

Composer. An important if neglected figure from Hollywood's golden age, Webb was a prolific and successful film composer. Long employed at RKO, he created the music for many of their best movies during the thirties and forties. His melodic style was dramatic and expressive, not unlike the works of French composer Claude Debussy.

Mr. Lucky (RKO, 1943). *Out of the Past* (RKO, 1947).

Weed, Bull (Fictional character)

One of the earliest modern urban gangsters in American cinema, Bull Weed (George Bancroft) rises to prominence in the New York underworld in Josef von Sternberg's *Underworld* (Paramount, 1927), the prototype for all subsequent gangster pictures. Likewise, Weed is an archetype for all cinematic gangsters to come, a dangerous psychopath who is obsessed with culture and is loyal to his friends and mistresses. Unlike later movie gangsters, however, Weed is also remorseful for his actions, and when his best friend is killed in the climactic gun battle with the police, he surrenders willingly, fully aware of his destiny.

Wellman, William (1896–1975)

Director. Like Raoul Walsh, William Wellman was a master of action, at his best when exploring the conflicts of violent men. His style, like Walsh's, was derived from those of D. W. Griffith and John Ford: simple and unobtrusive, letting the camera capture the action in pseudo-documentary fashion. He directed two gangster movies, including the classic *Public Enemy*, which made James Cagney a star and helped popularize the genre during the early thirties.

Public Enemy (Warner Bros., 1931). *The Star Witness* (Warner Bros., 1932).

Werker, Alfred (1896–1975)

Director. Werker began as a runner for Triangle Film Company in 1915 and worked his way up to director over the next ten years. He began directing Westerns in 1925 and was a prolific director of "B" movies well into the fifties. He proved to have a talent for psychological thrillers and made several good films, but few of his movies have stood the test of time.

Stolen Harmony (Paramount, 1935). *Up the River* (20th Century–Fox, 1938).

West, Nathanael (1904–1940)

Novelist and screenwriter. The former Nathan Weinstein of New York City immigrated to Los Angeles like so many others during the thirties, attracted by the weather, glamour and money of Hollywood. Sometimes mentioned as the prime example of Hollywood's deleterious effects on serious novelists, he was, in fact, an extremely well paid screenwriter, making more than four times the average salary of the American worker during his periodic employment at the studios. It is true, however, that West was not wholly successful as a screenwriter; but the craft of novelist and script writer are quite different, and few serious novelists have the talent for screenwriting. Among West's few credits as screenwriter is the minor gangster drama *I Stole a Million*. He is certainly best known for his bitter satire of Hollywood in the thirties, *Day of the Locusts*.

I Stole a Million (Universal, 1939).

West, Roland (1887–1952)

Director. West was most active in the late twenties, during which he directed two classic horror films. He also directed the minor early gangster drama *Alibi*, which was a box office success. He retired, inexplicably, in 1931 after having directed ten features in his twelve-year career.

Alibi (United Artists, 1929).

West Side Story (United Artists, 1961). 155 mins.
Producer: Robert Wise. *Directors*: Robert Wise and Jerome Robbins. *Screenplay*: Ernest Lehmann, based on the musical play by Arthur Laurents. *Director of Photography*: Daniel L. Fapp. *Music*: Leonard Bernstein. *Songs*: Leonard Bernstein and Stephen Sondheim. *Choreography*: Jerome Robbins. *Editors*: Thomas Stanford and Marshall M. Borden.
Cast: Natalie Wood (Maria), Richard Beymer (Tony), Russ Tamblyn (Riff), Rita Moreno (Anita), George Chakiris (Bernardo), Tucker Smith (Ice). *With*: Tony Mordente, David Winters, Bert Michaels, Eliot Feld, Robert Banas, David Bean.

Maria, a beautiful Puerto Rican girl, is in love with Tony, a Polish American. Maria's brother, Bernardo, is the leader of a street gang called the Sharks, whose main rival are the Jets, of which Tony is a member. The starcrossed lover's romance, however, is doomed to tragedy.

Leonard Bernstein and Stephen Sondheim's operatic musical, based loosely on *Romeo and Juliet*, seems contrived today, but at the time had enormous impact. As a Broadway show, it was unique for its tragic theme and story of teenage gangs, then a relatively new phenomenon. The film retains the vigorous score and most of the dances from the stage production, its greatest virtues. However, the vocal performances for Natalie Wood and Richard Beymer were dubbed by others.

Weyl, Carl Jules (1890–1948)

Art director. In the twenties, Weyl had a successful architectural practice in southern California. The Great Depression put an end to his business, and he joined Warner Bros. in 1935 as unit art director, remaining there for the rest of his career. He worked on many classics for the studio, collaborating with director Michael Curtiz on *Yankee Doodle Dandy* (1942), *Casablanca* (1942), *Passage to Marseille* (1944), and many others. He also worked on three gangster films, including the Curtiz-directed *Kid Galahad*.

Bullets or Ballots (First National, 1936). *Kid Galahad* (Warner Bros., 1937). *The Amazing Dr. Clitterhouse* (Warner Bros., 1938).

When Gangland Strikes (Republic, 1956). 70 mins.
Associate Producer: William J. O'Sullivan. *Director*: R. G. Springsteen. *Screenplay*: John K. Butler and Frederic Louis Fox. *Director of Photography*: John L. Russell, Jr. *Music*: Van Alexander. *Editor*: Tony Martinelli.
Cast: Raymond Greenleaf (Luke Ellis), Marjie Millar (June Ellis), John Hudson (Bob Keeler), Anthony Caruso (Duke), Marian Carr (Hazel Worley). *With*: Slim Pickens, Mary Treen, Ralph Dumke, Morris Ankrum, Robert Emmett Keane, Addison Richards.

Luke Ellis, a thoughtful prosecutor in a small town, is forced to throw the case against racketeer Duke Martell because Martell has learned that Ellis' adopted daughter was born in prison and is using that information to blackmail him. Later, when the daughter is arrested for murder, Ellis defends her and proves that the real culprit is Martell.

An unsophisticated, contrived melodrama, *When Gangland Strikes* came at the end of Republic's life. With its small-town setting (Republic mainly targeted small towns and matinee audiences) and lack of sophistication, it is, in fact, a fairly typical film for the studio. Yet, it is well directed by "B" action master R. G. Springsteen.

When G-Men Step In (Columbia, 1938). 60 mins.
Producer: Wallace MacDonald. *Director*: C. C. Coleman, Jr. *Director of Photography*: Henry Freulich. *Editor*: Al Clark.
Cast: Don Terry (Frederick Garth), Jacqueline Wells (Marjorie Drake), Robert Paige (Bruce Garth), Gene Morgan (Neale), Paul Fix (Clip Phillips). *With*: Stanley Andrews, Edward Earle, Horace MacMahon, Huey White.

Frederick Garth, a racketeer, heads a gang involved in various rackets, including charity swindles, gambling, and bogus sweepstakes tickets. When his brother, Bruce, a G-man, discovers Fred is not really an honest businessman, he determines to put him behind bars. With the aid of his partner and girlfriend, Bruce halts his brother's illegal activities and sends him to prison.

When G-Men Step In is one of Columbia better "B" gangster movies of the late thirties, moving at a swift pace, with several good action sequences.

Where the Sidewalk Ends (20th Century-Fox, 1950). 95 mins.
Producer and Director: Otto Preminger. *Screenplay*: Ben Hecht, based on the novel *Night Cry* by Frank Rosenberg. *Director of Photography*: Joseph LaShelle. *Music Director*: Lionel Newman. *Art Directors*: Lyle Wheeler and J. Russell Spencer. *Editor*: Louis Loeffler.
Cast: Dana Andrews (Mark Dixon), Gene Tierney (Morgan Taylor), Gary Merrill (Tommy Scalise), Bert Freed (Paul Klein), Tom Tully (Jiggs Taylor), Karl Malden (Lt. Thomas). *With*: Ruth Donnelly, Craig Stevens, Robert Simon, Harry von Zell, Don Appell, Lou Krugman.

Mark Dixon is a New York City police detective who cannot seem to shake the feeling that he has inherited his father's curse to be a killer. In fact, he accidentally kills a suspect he is following and tries to pin it on Tommy Scalise, a well known gambler and racketeer. However, the police arrest another man for the murder. Dixon is determined to pin the killing on Scalise and begins to gather "evidence" through strong-arm tactics and deceit. But when he falls in love with a beautiful socialite, Morgan Taylor, he decides to confess. She agrees to await his release.

Six years after the enormous success of *Laura* (20th Century–Fox, 1944), Dana Andrews and Gene Tierney were reteamed with director Otto Preminger. Only marginally a gangster movie, *Where the Sidewalk Ends* is a good, solid *noir* thriller, a police procedural which gives insight into the world of petty thieves and small-time gangsters in New York City.

Whipsaw (MGM, 1935). 83 mins.
Director: Sam Wood. *Screenplay*: Howard Emmett Rogers, *story by* James Edward Grant. *Director of Photography*: James Wong Howe. *Art Director*: Cedric Gibbons. *Editor*: Basil Wrangell.
Cast: Myrna Loy (Vivian Palmer), Spencer Tracy (Ross McBryce), Harvey Stephens (Ed Dexter), William Harrigan (Doc), Clay Clement (Harry), Robert Glecker (Steve). *With*: Robert Warwick, Georges Renevant, Paul Stanton, Wade Boteler, Don Rowan, John Qualen.

Vivian Palmer is a young woman mixed up with racketeers involved in the theft of federal funds. G-man Ross McBryce joins the gang undercover and helps Vivian escape with the stolen federal funds. Due to a storm, the couple is forced to take refuge in a farmhouse. They help the farmer's wife deliver a baby. The following morning, as they are about to take their leave from the farmhouse, Ross and Palmer are overtaken by the gangsters and

James Cagney (left) and Steve Cochran (right) threaten John Archer (center) in *White Heat*, one of the genre's finest films.

taken hostage. Vivian insists that she left the money in the city. When Ross tries to escape, he is injured in a shoot-out. The police, however, arrive just in time to rescue the couple. Ross and Palmer admit their mutual love, and he agrees to testify in her behalf at her upcoming trial.

Myrna Loy makes a glamorous, elegant moll, perhaps a bit too elegant, but she was always a charismatic performer, here teamed with the equally charismatic Spencer Tracy, whose gruff style was better suited to the genre. The result is one of MGM's best gangster movies, because it had the right mixture of romance and hard-boiled drama to insure its box office success. It remains one of the genre's most entertaining minor classics.

White Heat (Warner Bros., 1949). 114 mins.
Producer: Louis F. Edelman. *Direc-*

tor: Raoul Walsh. *Screenplay*: Ivan Goff and Ben Roberts, *story by* Virginia Kellogg. *Director of Photography*: Sid Hickox. *Music*: Max Steiner. *Art Director*: Fred M. MacLean. *Editor*: Owen Marks.

Cast: James Cagney (Cody Jarrett), Virginia Mayo (Verna Jarrett), Edmond O'Brien (Vic Pardo), Margaret Wycherly (Ma Jarrett), Steve Cochran (Big Ed), John Archer (Phillip Evans). *With*: Wally Cassell, Fred Clark, Ford Rainey, Fred Coby, G. Pat Collins, Mickey Knox.

After robbing a train, Cody Jarrett and his gang, including his mother, take refuge in a mountain cabin. Cody suffers from blinding headaches, relieved only by the attentions of Ma Jarrett. Big Ed, meanwhile, covets both the gang's leadership and Cody's wife, Verna. When Cody is arrested, he confesses to a lesser crime to avoid being charged for the murder of a railroad

James Cagney (left) as one of his most vicious mobsters, Cody Jarrett in *White Heat*, **one of his last gangster movies.**

man during the robbery. In prison, he befriends Vic Pardo, who is really undercover cop Hank Fallon. When he learns that Big Ed and Verna have killed Ma, the inconsolable Cody breaks out of prison, determined to get revenge. He kills Big Ed, but Verna convinces him that she is innocent and he spares her. Cody plans a payroll robbery, but it is spoiled by Fallon. All of the gangsters except Cody are killed. Mortally wounded, Cody shoots it out from the top of a huge tank at a fuel refinery. The gas is ignited and Cody perishes in the flames, shouting to his dead mother, "Top of the world, Ma!"

James Cagney's return to the gangster genre came in one of his most famous films and one of the classics of the genre. It is directed in high style by Raoul Walsh and expressively photographed by the great cinematographer Sid Hickox. All the performances are good, including a surprising turn by perennial good girl Virginia Mayo as the seductive and wicked moll. But it is James Cagney's dynamic performance as the emotionally crippled Cody Jarrett that makes the film so compelling and ultimately so great.

Whitmore, James (b. 1921)
Character actor. Born in White Plains, New York, Whitmore served in the Marines during World War II and became a stage actor after his discharge in 1945. After establishing himself as an actor on Broadway, he went to Hollywood in 1949 and became one of the busiest character actors of the fifties. His craggy features made him a natural villain, and he played a murderous gang boss in *The Undercover Man*.

The Undercover Man (Columbia, 1949).

The Whole Town's Talking (Columbia, 1935). 93 mins.

Producer: Lester Cowan. *Director*: John Ford. *Screenplay*: Jo Swerling and Robert Riskin, based on the novel by W. R. Burnett. *Director of Photography*: Joseph August. *Editor*: Viola Lawrence.

Cast: Edward G. Robinson (Arthur Jones/Killer Mannion), Jean Arthur ("Bill" Clark), Arthur Hohl (Detective Sergeant Mike Boyle), Wallace Ford (Healy), Arthur Byron (D. A. Spencer), Donald Meek (Hoyt). *With*: Paul Harvey, Edward Brophy, Etienne Girardot, James Donlan, J. Farrell Macdonald.

Arthur Jones, a timid hardware clerk, is arrested when he is mistaken for Public Enemy Number One—Killer Mannion, for whom he is a dead ringer. A go-getter female reporter, Wilhelmina Clark, known as "Bill," proves his innocence and Jones is released. However, he is hunted down by Mannion, who convinces Jones to give him the special I.D. card created by the district attorney. Mannion pulls off a series of crimes before the cops realize what is going on. Jones, meanwhile, emboldened by his contacts with the gangster, tracks Mannion down and, eventually, helps bring him to justice.

Based on W. R. Burnett's best seller, *The Whole Town's Talking* is a curious mixture of satire and melodrama. At times it feels like a Frank Capra film, not surprising when one considers that its screenwriters, Jo Swerling and Robert Riskin, were two of Capra's most important collaborators. John Ford directed in brisk fashion, and both Edward G. Robinson and Jean Arthur are in top form. Indeed, on repeated viewing this great film reveals many interesting layers and it remains perhaps the genre's most neglected classic.

Widmark, Richard (b. 1914)

Actor. Born in Sunrise, Minnesota, Widmark was educated at Lake Forest College in Illinois where he also taught

for a while. He began acting in college and first worked professionally in radio. After Broadway experience, he made a striking film debut as Tommy Udo, the psychotic mob killer in the classic gangster *noir*, *Kiss of Death*. It was a star-making performance, and he subsequently appeared in many other *films noir*, either as a villain or flawed hero.

Kiss of Death (20th Century–Fox, 1947).

Wilbur, Crane (1887–1973)

Screenwriter. After varied experience, including working as a journalist and short story writer, Wilbur moved to Hollywood during the early forties. In his early fifties, he finally found a successful profession as a screenwriter and became one of the masters of hard-boiled melodrama. He worked on several good "B" gangster movies during the forties and fifties.

Hell's Kitchen (Warner Bros., 1939). *Roger Touhy, Gangster* (20th Century–Fox, 1944). *Crime Wave* (Warner Bros., 1953). *The Phenix City Story* (Allied Artists, 1955). *The George Raft Story* (Allied Artists, 1961).

Wild, Harry J.

Cinematographer. Wild was busiest during the forties and fifties, working mainly in "B" movies. A house cinematographer at RKO, he was the director of photography for many excellent "B" films. His expressionist style was more restrained than many of his contemporaries. He photographed two superb gangster movies.

The Big Steal (RKO, 1949). *His Kind of Woman* (RKO, 1951).

The Wild One (Columbia, 1954). 79 mins.

Producer: Stanley Kramer. *Director*: Laslo Benedek. *Screenplay*: John Paxton, *story by* Frank Rooney. *Director of Photography*: Hal Mohr. *Music*: Leith Stevens. *Art Director*: Walter Holscher. *Editor*: Al Clark.

Marlon Brando and Ruth Roman, motorcycle gangster and his moll in *The Wild One*.

Cast: Marlon Brando (Johnny), Mary Murphy (Kathie), Robert Keith (Harry), Lee Marvin (Chino), Jay C. Flippen (Sheriff Singers), Peggy Maley (Mildred), Hugh Sanders (Charlie Thomas). *With*: Ray Teal, John Brown, Will Wright, Robert Osterloh, Robert Brice, William Yedder.

When the Black Rebels are ostra-cized by a larger motorcycle gang, they vent their rage by taking over a small town which has only a token police force. Tensions within the group and within the town grow to a boiling point during which a citizen is accidently killed. Johnny, the leader of the gang, has fallen in love with Kathie, the beau-tiful girlfriend of a cowardly cop. When

Johnny is blamed for the accidental killing, Kathie and her father help prove his innocence and Johnny considers changing his life.

Motorcycle gangs were a new phenomenon in the fifties, but were topical in light of horror stories in the press. In fact, the Hells Angels, created by disillusioned flyers returning from the horrors of World War II, had terrorized several small towns in California during the early fifties. *The Wild One* was the first serious exploration of this new wave of mobile gangsters and like later exploitation biker movies there was an emphasis on violent sex, knife fights, and other unpleasant activities. It is notable chiefly for Marlon Brando's electrifying performance as the leather clad antihero.

Wilde, Cornel (b. 1915)

Actor. Cornelius Louis Wilde was born in New York City. Much of his youth was spent in Europe with his father, who traveled for a New York firm, and he became fluent in several languages. Settling back in the United States in 1932, Wilde studied medicine before drifting into acting. Tall, dark and handsome, he was a popular leading man in the forties and fifties, best known for portraying Frederic Chopin in *A Song to Remember* (Columbia, 1944). He was often seen as a flawed romantic hero, the character type he played in *The Big Combo*. He also had a small role in *High Sierra*.

High Sierra (Warner Bros., 1941). *The Big Combo* (Allied Artists, 1955).

Wilder, Billy (b. 1906)

Screenwriter and director. Wilder always described himself as a screenwriter first and only a reluctant director, but he proved to be one of the finest craftsmen in both professions. Born in Austria, he moved to Berlin as a young man and became a journalist. Turning to screenwriting, he became an important figure in German cinema during the early thirties. Fleeing Germany after the rise of Hitler (his family perished in concentration camps), Wilder worked briefly in France before moving to the United States during the mid-thirties. After a lean year or two, he teamed with Charles Brackett to form what became the greatest of all screenwriting teams. After arguing with director Mitchell Leisen about how to film a script, Wilder began directing the screenplays he and Brackett wrote. After the team broke up in 1949, Wilder worked with many collaborators before teaming with I.A.L. Diamond. Together, they created the great gangster satire *Some Like It Hot*, a rollicking comedy which captured the spirit of the Roaring Twenties. Wilder directed in high style, coaxing fine performances from Marilyn Monroe, Jack Lemmon and Tony Curtis.

Some Like It Hot (United Artists, 1959; director and cowriter).

Wilder, W. Lee (b. 1904)

Director. W. (William) Lee Wilder is the elder brother of the illustrious Billy Wilder. Born to eccentric Austrian parents, both W. Lee and Billy were given American names by parents who were obsessed with the New World. Although he pursued an industrial career in Europe and the United States, he was drawn to a show business career. He first made a name for himself in the early forties as a producer. He began directing in 1946, creating some of the most cynical "B" movies ever made. *The Glass Alibi*, his first film as a director, is an excellent "B" gangster drama.

The Glass Alibi (Republic, 1946).

Wiles, Gordon (1902–1950)

Director. Wiles was originally an art director, working mainly at Fox during the thirties. He began directing in 1936, continuing to work as an art director into the forties. A "B" director, his most important movie is *The Gangster*, generally considered one of the finest "B" *noirs* of the late forties.

The Gangster (Allied Artists, 1947).

William, Warren (1895–1948)

Actor. Nearly forgotten today, the suave, debonair William, born Warren Krech in Minnesota, was a popular leading man in the thirties. He was the romantic lead in two minor gangster movies.

The Mouthpiece (Warner Bros., 1932). *Three on a Match* (First National, 1932).

Williamson, Fred (b. 1938)

Actor. Born in Gary, Indiana, and educated at Northwestern University, Williamson was a professional football player for ten years. He began acting in 1970, appeared in several important features, and became a star in *Black Caesar*. He subsequently starred in several other action oriented crime thrillers, even writing and directing a few.

Black Caesar (American International, 1973).

Willis, Gordon (b. 1938)

Cinematographer. One of the most important American cinematographers to emerge during the seventies, Willis is probably best known for his collaborations with Woody Allen. His updating of thirties glamour in contemporary color is best seen in his three *Godfather* collaborations with director Francis Ford Coppola.

The Godfather (Paramount, 1972). *The Godfather Part II* (Paramount, 1974). *Godfather III* (Paramount, 1991).

Wilson, Richard (b. 1915)

Director. Originally a radio actor, Wilson became a producer in the late forties, and also directed a few movies during the fifties and sixties. Among these is the biopic *Al Capone*, one of the best "B" gangster movies of the fifties.

Al Capone (Allied Artists, 1959).

Windsor, Marie (b. 1922)

Actress. This former Miss Utah was born Emily Marie Bertelson in Marysville, Utah, and was educated at Brigham Young University. Her rather harsh blonde beauty typecast her as a *femme fatale* in the forties and fifties, and she is one of *film noir*'s major female icons. She starred in the gangster *noir*, *The Narrow Margin* playing a variation of her usual type as an undercover cop disguised as a gangster's moll.

The Narrow Margin (RKO, 1951).

Windust, Bretaine (1906–1960)

Director. The Paris-born Windust moved to the United States as a child. After graduating from Princeton University, he became an actor and later a prominent stage director. He made a few films, including the Humphrey Bogart vehicle *The Enforcer*, the action scenes of which were directed by an uncredited Raoul Walsh. Windust was a better handler of actors in a theatrical manner and had greater success as a television director.

The Enforcer (Warner Bros., 1951).

Winner, Michael (b. 1935)

Director. A fashionable director during the sixties and early seventies, the British-born Winner is best known as the director of several successful Charles Bronson vehicles made in the seventies, including two gangster movies. Winner, who always shoots on location, has an agreeably gritty style which relies heavily on violent action.

The Mechanic (United Artists, 1972). *The Stone Killer* (Columbia, 1973).

Winninger, Charles (1887–1969)

Character actor. Born Karl Winninger in Athens, Wisconsin, to show people, Winninger began performing as a child. His Broadway career began in 1912, and he first appeared on screen, in one- and two-reel comedies, in 1915. He continued to act on Broadway until 1930, when he settled permanently in Hollywood. The rotund actor usually appeared as a cheerful eccentric and, indeed, in his only appearance in a gangster movie, played the comic role of a small-town banker on his first gambling spree while vacationing in Las Vegas.

Las Vegas Shakedown (Allied Artists, 1955).

Winters, Shelley (b. 1922)
Actress. Born Shirley Schrift in St. Louis, Shelley Winters grew up in Brooklyn and began acting on Broadway in her late teens. Originally a sexy blonde, she was usually seen as a hard-boiled dame during the forties and fifties. She played a gangster's moll in the minor *Johnny Stool Pigeon*. In her heftier middle age, she starred in *Bloody Mama* as the patriarch of a murderous gang of rural criminals based on the real life Ma Barker and her gang.

Johnny Stool Pigeon (Universal, 1949). *Bloody Mama* (American International, 1970).

Wise, Robert (b. 1914)
Director. Originally an editor, Wise began directing in 1944. A protégé of producer Val Lewton—for whom he directed two excellent horror pictures—Wise became a successful director of commercial features with something to say. *The Set-Up*, one of his earliest films, is an exposé of the mob controlled sport of boxing and its effects on an aging boxer (Robert Ryan). It is a classic of the genre.

The Set-Up (RKO, 1949).

Witney, William (b. 1910)
Director. Born in Lawton, Oklahoma, William Witney had varied experience in the film business before joining Republic as a script supervisor in 1936. He began directing in 1937, becoming one of Republic's most prolific and successful directors. Specializing in action packed serials and Westerns, he later joined American International, for whom he directed a variety of films, including *The Bonnie Parker Story*, an entertaining version of the real life gangster's adventures.

The Bonnie Parker Story (American International, 1958).

Wong, Anna May (1907–1961)
Actress. Born Wong Liu Tsong in the Chinatown section of Los Angeles, Anna May Wong was the first major Chinese-American star. Her film career began in 1924, and during the thirties she was often seen as a mysterious Oriental seductress. She costarred in Josef von Sternberg's *Shanghai Express* (Paramount, 1932) as a prostitute. Although a favorite model of still photographers, she was relegated mainly to "B" movies. She starred in two "B" gangster dramas, playing a moll in *Limehouse Blues*, and in *King of Chinatown*, a pre-feminist heroine, Dr. Mary Ling, who unwittingly becomes entangled with gangsters when she saves a mob boss' life after a shooting.

Limehouse Blues (Paramount, 1934). *King of Chinatown* (Paramount, 1938).

Woo, John (b. 1944)
Director. Hong Kong's most important director of contemporary gangster movies has been thrilling audiences throughout the world with his extremely violent action pictures since the late seventies. Deeply influenced by American gangster movies of the thirties, Martin Scorsese, and French director Jean-Pierre Melville, Woo's films are an exhilarating exercise in bloodletting action sequences and bizarre, almost surrealistic humor. *The Killer* (1989), *A Better Tomorrow* (1986), *A Better Tomorrow II* (1987), *A Bullet in the Head* (1990), and *Hard Boiled* (1992), released in the United States by various independent distributors, are all gangster movies of the modern type, and have been widely praised. They also have a devout following among filmmakers like Quentin Tarantino and Martin Scorsese. Their praise has helped Woo get hired in Hollywood; but whether he will continue to

create gangster movies as vital as his earlier successes, or manage to survive the contemporary Hollywood and American political climates (with strong-arm interest groups on the right and left attacking the ultra violence of films like Woo's) is yet to be seen.

Wood, Sam (1883–1949)
Director. Wood was a moderately successful businessman when he joined Cecil B. DeMille as an assistant in 1915. By 1920 he was directing, and later joined MGM as a staff director. He was a good commercial director, much better in fact than is often acknowledged by contemporary critics. He was a fine handler of action oriented movies, and directed two gangster movies. Of these, the best is *Whipsaw*, a neglected minor classic of the genre.
Let 'Em Have It (United Artists, 1935). *Whipsaw* (MGM, 1935).

Woods, James (b. 1947)
Actor. Originally an engineer, Woods began acting in the early seventies. Lean and craggy faced, he has often played villains. He played one of the gangsters in Sergio Leone's epic *Once Upon a Time in America*, a fine performance in an indifferent film.
Once Upon a Time in America (Warner Bros., 1984). *Against All Odds* (Columbia, 1984).

Wray, Fay (1907–1995)
Actress. Born in Alberta, Canada, and raised in Los Angeles, the diminutive, dark-haired, and beautiful Fay Wray will be forever remembered as the object of the giant ape's amorous interest in *King Kong* (RKO, 1933). She also starred in several other notable horror films during this era. Her film career began in the mid-twenties and she was a major star during the early sound era. She found it difficult, however, to overcome the *King Kong* image, and in the forties, began playing occasional supporting roles. In the late fifties she made a brief but effective

appearance as the aging moll of a murdered mobster.
Hell on Frisco Bay (Warner Bros., 1956).

Wyler, William (1902–1981)
Director. Wyler originally entered the film business as a publicist. He began directing quickie Westerns in 1925 and emerged as a first rank director ten years later with the classic romantic satire *The Good Fairy* (Universal, 1935), scripted by his friend Preston Sturges. He was an adroit handler of literary subjects and tough actresses, particularly his lover, Bette Davis. Backed by an excellent cast, his version of Sidney Kingsley's play *Dead End* is a classic.
Dead End (United Artists, 1937).

Wyman, Jane (b. 1914)
Actress. Born Sarah Jane Fulks in St. Joseph, Missouri, Wyman began as a radio singer before signing with Warner Bros. as a contract actress. She was most often seen as a dumb blonde in romantic comedies, and costarred in the Edward G. Robinson gangster satire *Larceny, Inc.* She proved to be a fine actress during the forties and fifties, appearing mainly as a second lead. Today she is most often remembered as Ronald Reagan's first wife and by her role on television in the nighttime soap opera, *Falcon Crest*.
Larceny, Inc. (Warner Bros., 1942).

The Yakuza (Warner Bros., 1975). 112 mins.
Producers: Sydney Pollack and Michael Hamilburg. *Director*: Sydney Pollack. *Screenplay*: Paul Schrader. *Directors of Photography*: Okazaki Kozo and Duke Callagham. *Music*: Dave Grusin. *Art Director*: Ishida Yoshiyuki. *Editors*: Frederic Steinkamp, Thomas Stanford and Don Guidice.
Cast: Robert Mitchum (Harry Kilmer), Takakura Keo (Tanaka Ken), Brian Keith (George Tanner), Herb

Edelman (Wheat), Richard Jordan (Dusty). *With*: Kishi Keiko, Okada Eiji, James Shigeta, Christina Kokubo, Lee Chirillo.

Harry Kilmer, an old friend from World War II, is hired by George Tanner to locate Tanner's young daughter who has been kidnapped and held for ransom by Japanese gangsters. In Japan, Kilmer meets his one-time mistress, Eiko, who now has an adult daughter, and he enlists the aid of Tanaka Ken, also an old friend who owes him a favor. Tanaka infiltrates the gang. Although he does help liberate the young girl, Kilmer realizes that Tanner is also a hoodlum who has caused several needless murders.

The Yakuza is a moderate thriller, if not quite a classic, that explores the shadowy world of the real Japanese Mafia. It was made in the twilight of Robert Mitchum's career as a star, during which he played in several interesting crime thrillers. *The Yakuza* was not the best of these, but it is passable. It is notable mainly for being director Sydney Pollack's only attempt at this sort of material.

Yates, Peter (b. 1929)

Director. The British-born Yates first made a name for himself as a director of television films and ambitious low budget dramas in his native Great Britain. He came to the United States in the late sixties and immediately made the big time with the gangster police thriller, *Bullitt*. *The Friends of Eddie Coyle*, a more traditional gangster drama, was well received by critics but failed at the box office, perhaps because of its downbeat ending.

Bullitt (Warner Bros., 1968). *The Friends of Eddie Coyle* (Paramount, 1973).

Year of the Dragon (MGM/United Artists, 1985). 136 mins. *Producer*: Dino De Laurentiis. *Director*: Michael Cimino. *Screenplay*: Oliver Stone and Michael Cimino,

based on the novel by Robert Daley. *Director of Photography*: Alex Thomson. *Music*: David Mansfield. *Art Director*: Vicki Paul. *Editor*: Francoise Bonnot.

Cast: Mickey Rourke (Captain Stanley White), John Lone (Go Joey Tai), Ariane (Tracey Tzu), Leonard Termo (Angelo Rizzo), Ray Barry (Louis Bukowski), Caroline Kava (Connie). *With*: Eddie Jones, Joey Chin, Victor Wong, K. Dock Yip, Pao Han Lin, Mark Hammer, Dennis Dun.

Jackie Wong, the unofficial mayor of New York City's Chinatown, is murdered on the eve of celebrations for the Chinese New Year. Stanley White, a bigoted police captain, is assigned to the case, but soon falls in love with Chinese television reporter Tracey Tzu. When the Oriental undercover agent that White hires to help break up the gang responsible for the murder is killed, White uncovers the leader of the gang, Go Joey Tai, and confronts him at the docks. In the subsequent shootout, Tai is wounded and commits suicide rather than be captured.

Attacked as politically incorrect by Chinese Americans, *Year of the Dragon*, is, in fact, a rather obvious attack against racism and racial stereotypes. In any case, Michael Cimino's "comeback" film was poorly adapted from a complex popular thriller, only adequately made, and failed to reestablish him as a viable filmmaker.

Yordan, Philip (b. 1913)

Screenwriter and producer. The prolific Yordan began his career as a screenwriter in the early forties and immediately made a name for himself as a master of hard-boiled subjects. One of his early successes, *Dillinger*, was a low budget gangster picture that became a surprise box office hit. It helped establish Yordan as an important new talent. He subsequently wrote a number of important crime thrillers, including several *films noir* and gangster pictures. He began producing movies in the early fifties (all of which he also wrote), continuing to have success well into the sixties as a screenwriter and producer. Among his successes as writer and producer is *The Harder They Fall*, Humphrey Bogart's last movie.

Dillinger (Monogram, 1945). *The Chase* (United Artists, 1946). *The Big Combo* (Allied Artists, 1955). *Joe Macbeth* (Columbia, 1955). *The Harder They Fall* (Columbia, 1956; producer and writer).

You and Me (Paramount, 1938). 90 mins.

Producer and Director: Fritz Lang. *Screenplay*: Virginia Van Upp, *story by* Norman Krasna. *Director of Photography*: Charles Lang, Jr. *Music*: Kurt Weill and Boris Morros. *Art Directors*: Hans Dreier and Ernst Fegte. *Editor*: Paul Weatherwax.

Cast: Sylvia Sidney (Helen Dennis), George Raft (Joe Dennis), Harry Carey (Mr. Morris), Barton MacLane (Mickey), Warren Hymer (Gimpy), Roscoe Karns (Cuffy). *With*: Robert Cummings, George E. Stone, Adrian Morris, Roger Gray, Cecil Cunningham, Vera Gordon.

Helen and Joe are both ex-convicts employed by Mr. Morris' department store. Joe has been honest about his past but is unaware of Helen's criminal experiences until they are married and she confesses. Disgusted, he rejoins his old gang, who plan to rob Morris' store. When Helen learns of the plans, she convinces store officials to let her handle the situation. She then gives the thieves a stern lecture, and they leave the store, chagrined. Joe is reunited with Helen later, when he discovers that she is pregnant.

With its wildly improbable plot, *You and Me* emerges as the least satisfying of Fritz Lang's gangster movies. Of his American films, it is the closest he came to making a real gangster movie, but it fails to live up to its potential. In fact, Lang inherited the picture shortly before it went into production. Had he developed it from the beginning, there is little doubt it would have been a darker film, and probably a better one as well.

You Can't Get Away with Murder (Warner Bros., 1939). 78 mins.

Associate Producer: Samuel Bischoff. *Director*: Lewis Seiler. *Screenplay*: Robert Buckner, Don Ryan and Kenneth Gamet, based on the play *Chalked Out* by Warden Lewis E. Lawes. *Director of Photography*: Sol Polito. *Music*: Heinz Roemheld. *Art Director*: Hugo Reticker. *Editor*: James Gibbon.

Cast: Humphrey Bogart (Frank Wilson), Billy Halop (Johnnie Stone), Gale Page (Midge Stone), John Litel (Attorney Carey), Henry Travers (Pop). *With*: Harvey Stephens, Harold Huber, Joseph Downing, George E. Stone, Joe Sawyer, Joseph King.

Frank Wilson, a petty thief, takes a young kid, Johnnie Stone, under his wing as a protégé. During a robbery, Frank kills a man with a gun the boy has stolen. Later, the duo are arrested for car theft and sent to jail. In order to keep the boy quiet, Wilson stages a breakout and takes the boy with him, planning to kill the youth later. Trapped in a boxcar, Wilson shoots Johnnie, but the young man lives long enough to tell the police what really happened, ensuring that Frank Wilson will be sent to the chair.

Drawing upon Warner Bros.' stock company of performers, this "B" production emerged as a slick entertainment. It was released a year before Humphrey Bogart, who gave his all in a typical role as a sadistic killer, began his rise to fame.

You Only Live Once (United Artists, 1937). 85 mins.

Producer: Walter Wanger. *Director*: Fritz Lang. *Screenplay*: Gene Towner and Grahame Baker. *Director of Photography*: Leon Shamroy. *Music*: Alfred Newman. *Art Director*: Alexander Toluboff. *Editor*: Daniel Mandell.

Cast: Henry Fonda (Eddie Taylor), Sylvia Sidney (Joan Graham), Barton MacLane (Stephen Witney), Jean Dixon (Bonnie Graham), William Gargan (Father Donlan), Jerome Cowan (Dr. Hill). *With*: Charles "Chic" Sale, Margaret Hamilton, Warren Hymer, John Wray, Jonathan Hale, Ward Bond.

Eddie Taylor is a small-time criminal who is framed for a robbery. Sent to prison, he suffers from a kind of shell shock at the violence around him and then assaults and murders a priest who ironically has brought him news of a pardon. He escapes and with his wife tries to flee to Canada. Barely making it across the border, they are shot by the authorities.

Fritz Lang's second American movie was a dour exploration of society's condemnation of criminals and the poor, and how certain individuals are forced by their surroundings into a life of crime. Familiar themes of repression, guilt and personal honor that Fritz Lang explored in all of his movies, as well as government corruption, were here honed for a Depression-era American audience who could identify with the characters' plights. Although not a gangster movie, per se, *You Only Live Once* is a product of the same era, a socially conscious crime drama that has much in common with the gangster movies of the time, and, stylistically and thematically, presaged *film noir*.

Young, Loretta (b. 1913)

Actress. Without ever becoming a superstar, Loretta Young was one of the most popular stars of the thirties and forties. Born Gretchen Young in Salt Lake City, Loretta began appearing in movies as a child. By the thirties she was a major star. Ethereal, beautiful and gracefully elegant, she was most popular in glamorous roles. However, she was a good actress and starred in a wide variety of films, including some notable *films noir* during the forties. She starred in a single gangster picture, *Taxi!*, one of James Cagney's minor movies in the genre.

Taxi! (Warner Bros., 1932).

Young Dillinger (Allied Artists, 1965). 105 mins.

Producer: Alfred Zimbalist. *Director*: Terry O. Morse. *Screenplay*: Don Zimbalist and Arthur Hoerl. *Editor*: Terry Wallace.

Cast: Nick Adams (John Dillinger), Robert Conrad (Pretty Boy Floyd), Mary Ann Mobley (Elaine), Victor Buono (Professor Hoffman), John Ashley (Baby Face Nelson). *With*: Dan Terranova, John Hoyt.

As a young man during the Great Depression, John Dillinger begins a life of crime to provide "the good life" for his girlfriend, Elaine. After a botched robbery, he is sent to prison where he befriends several criminals including Baby Face Nelson and Pretty Boy Floyd. After release, Dillinger breaks his friends out of jail and they go on a robbery spree. After one of these robberies, Dillinger goes to a hack doctor who messes up his plastic surgery and the doctor tries to rape Elaine. Dillinger kills the doctor. Later, he tries to give up his life of crime, but the F.B.I. surrounds their hideout. Elaine is shot and tells Dillinger to run for his life. He barely escapes.

An extremely romanticized "B" version of John Dillinger's early life as a gangster has little truth in it, but *Young Dillinger* is enjoyable, if violent entertainment. Nick Adams' performance is very good, but the film suffers from poor production values. It achieved some notoriety in 1968 when it was banned from television as too violent.

Yurka, Blanche (1887–1974)

Character actress. Born Blanche Jurka in Czechoslovakia, she moved with her family to the United States while she was still a baby. At fifteen she was given a scholarship to the Metropolitan Opera's School in New York City. Although she had a brief career as an opera singer, Yurka found her greatest success on Broadway, where she reigned as a major star for thirty years. She did not make her film debut until she was nearly fifty. In the "B" gangster movie *Queen of the Mob*, Yurka starred as Ma Webster, the matriarch of a gang based on Ma Barker and her gang.

Queen of the Mob (Paramount, 1940).

Zanuck, Darryl F. (1902–1979)

Studio executive and producer. Zanuck was one of Warner Bros.' most efficient and prolific screenwriters of the mid-twenties. He began producing in the latter part of that decade and immediately proved to be brilliantly successful — so much so that, by thirties, he was Jack Warner's right-hand man, essentially head of production at the studio. Like David O. Selznick, Zanuck often wrote or cowrote his productions and had a hands-on approach to his profession. (Indeed, it would later irk him that John Ford was praised as an artistic genius and an auteur by New York critics, when in fact Zanuck and writer Nunnally Johnson were largely responsible for the artistic vision of many of the director's best films of the thirties and forties.) In the early thirties, Zanuck was almost wholly responsible for the Warner Bros. style that emerged during those years: brash, gritty, realistic, and unsentimental. He developed and personally oversaw all of the key films released by the studio from 1930 to 1934. Zanuck, overworked and under appreciated (although, at $5,000 a week during the height of the Great Depression, hardly underpaid), felt he could no longer work with the dictatorial Jack Warner and left the company. In 1935 his moderately successful independent, Twentieth Century Productions, was merged with Fox to create the powerful 20th Century-Fox, and Zanuck was named Vice President in Charge of Production, a position he held for over twenty years. Zanuck fashioned Twentieth Century-Fox as a kind of alternative MGM. Like that studio, he specialized in glossy family fare, musicals, comedies and costume dramas, the opposite of Warner Bros.' hard-boiled productions. Nevertheless, 20th Century-Fox did produce some important gangster pictures — early on, the neglected classic *Show Them No Mercy* (1935) and, later, becoming important in the development of *film noir*, *Kiss of Death* (1947), one of the most important gangster *noirs*. As the man who helped create such important contributions to the gangster genre as *Little Caesar* (Warner Bros., 1931), *Public Enemy* (Warner Bros., 1931), *I Am a Fugitive from a Chain Gang* (Warner Bros., 1931) and the later productions at 20th Century-Fox, Zanuck is certainly one of the genre's key behind the scenes figures.

The Doorway to Hell (Warner Bros., 1930; executive in charge of production). *Little Caesar* (Warner Bros.-First National, 1931). *Public Enemy* (Warner Bros.-First National, 1931). *Smart Money* (Warner Bros.-First National, 1931). *The Mouthpiece* (Warner Bros.-First National, 1932). *I Am a Fugitive from a Chain Gang* (Warner Bros., 1932). *Show Them No Mercy* (20th Century-Fox, 1935). *Johnny Apollo* (20th Century-Fox, 1941). *Kiss of Death* (20h Century-Fox, 1947).

Appendix:
Films with Peripheral
Gangster Characters

À Bout de Souffle aka *Breathless* (Imperia, 1959)
Ambush (Paramount, 1939)
Angel on My Shoulder (United Artists, 1946)
Arson Racket Squad (Republic, 1938)
Baby Face Morgan PRC, 1942)
Bank Alarm (Grand National, 1937)
The Blonde Bandit (Republic, 1956)
The Brain (Paramount, 1969)
Bunny O'Hare (American International, 1971)
Chicago After Midnight (FBO, 1928)
City for Conquest (Warner Bros., 1940)
City Without Men (Columbia, 1943)
Deported (Universal, 1950)
The Firm (Paramount, 1950)
Gambling Daughters (PRC, 1941)
Gang War (20th Century-Fox, 1958)
The Getaway (Cinerama, 1972)
The Girl from Chicago (Warner Bros., 1927)
Guns Don't Argue (Visual Drama, 1957)
The Happening (Columbia, 1967)
Hard Times (Columbia, 1975)
Hit! (Paramount, 1973)
Hitman (MGM, 1972)

The Hoodlum Saint (MGM, 1946)
The Joker Is Wild (Paramount, 1957)
Juvenile Court (Columbia, 1938)
The Lady Killers (J. Arthur Rank, 1955)
League of Gentlemen (J. Arthur Rank, 1960)
Lepke (Warner Bros., 1975)
Mandalay (Warner Bros., 1934)
Mary Burns, Fugitive (Paramount, 1935)
Missing Daughters (Columbia, 1939)
News Hounds (Monogram, 1947)
Night Whirl (Universal, 1932)
Numbered Men (First National, 1930)
Ocean's 11 (Warner Bros., 1960)
Parole Fixer (Paramount, 1940)
Pulp (United Artists, 1972)
The Ringer (British Lion, 1952)
Robbery (Embassy, 1967)
The Shadow of Silk Lennox (Commodore, 1935)
The Steel Jungle (Warner Bros., 1956)
Stick (Universal, 1985)
That Man Bolt (Universal, 1973)
Tony Rome (20th Century-Fox, 1967)
Unchained (Warner Bros., 1955)
Voice of the City (MGM, 1929)
The Wet Parade (MGM, 1932)
Witness (Paramount, 1985)

Selected Bibliography

Agee, James. *Agee on Film.* 2 vols. New York: Grosset and Dunlap, 1969.
Alloway, Lawrence. *Violent America: The Movies, 1946-1964.* New York: Museum of Modern Art, 1971.
Anderson, Clinton. *Beverly Hills Is My Beat.* Englewood Cliffs, N.J.: Prentice-Hall, 1960.
Aros, Andrew A., ed. *A Title Guide to the Talkies, 1964-1974.* Metuchen, N.J.: Scarecrow, 1977.
Astor, Mary. *A Life on Film.* New York: Delacorte, 1971.
Bacall, Lauren. *Lauren Bacall, By Myself.* New York: Knopf, 1979.
Baer, D. Richard, ed. *Film Buff's Bible.* Hollywood: Hollywood Film Archive, 1979.
Baker, Carlos. *Ernest Hemingway: A Life Story.* New York: Scribners, 1969.
Barbour, Alan G. *Cliffhanger.* Secaucus, N.J.: Citadel Press, 1977.
Bare, Richard L. *The Film Director.* New York: Collier Books, 1971.
Baxter, John. *The Hollywood Exiles.* New York: Taplinger, 1976.
Behlmer, Rudy. *Inside Warner Brothers 1935-1951.* New York: Viking, 1985.
Benchley, Nathaniel. *Humphrey Bogart.* Boston: Little, Brown, 1975.
Berkeley, Busby, and Jim Terry. *The Busby Berkeley Book.* New York: New York Graphic Society, 1973.
Bogdanovich, Peter. *Fritz Lang in America* London: Studio Vista, 1969.
Brenner, Marie. *Going Hollywood.* New York: Delacorte, 1978.
Brownlow, Kevin. *The Parade's Gone By.* New York: Knopf, 1968.
Burch, Noel. *Theory of Film Practice.* New York: Praeger, 1973.
Cagney, James. *Cagney by Cagney.* Garden City, N.J.: Doubleday, 1976.
Cameron, Ian. *A Pictorial History of Crime Films.* London: Hamlyn, 1975.
Clarens, Carlos. *Crime Movies.* New York: W. W. Morrow, 1980.
Clark, Al. *Raymond Chandler in Hollywood.* London: Proteus, 1982.
Cocchi, John. *Second Features.* Secaucus, N.J.: Citadel Books, 1991.
Coffey, Thomas M. *The Long Thirst.* New York: W. W. Norton, 1975.
Cooke, Fred J. *The FBI Nobody Knows.* New York: Macmillan, 1964.
Corliss, Richard. *Talking Pictures.* New York: The Overlook Press, 1974.
Corliss, Richard, ed. *The Hollywood Screenwriters.* New York: Avon, 1972.
Cowie, Peter, ed. *International Film Guide.* Cranbury, N.J.: A. S. Barnes, 1964.
Cross, Robin. *The Big Book of B Movies.* New York: St. Martin's, 1981.
Crowther, Bruce. *Film Noir: Reflections in a Dark Mirror.* New York: Continuum, 1988.
Dardis, Tom. *Some Time in the Sun.* New York: Scribners, 1976.
Davis, Bette. *The Lonely Life: An Autobiography.* New York: Putnam, 1962.

Deming, Barbara. *Running Away from Myself: A Dream Portrait of America Drawn from the Films of the 1940s.* New York: Grossman, 1969.

Eisenberg, Dennis, Dan Uri, and Eli Landau. *Meyer Lansky: Mogul of the Mob.* New York: Paddington, 1979.

Evans, Mark. *Soundtrack: The Music of the Movies.* New York: Hopkinson and Blake, 1975.

Francisco, Charles. *Gentleman: The William Powell Story.* New York: St. Martin's, 1975.

Fraser, John. *Violence in the Arts.* Cambridge, England: Cambridge University Press, 1974.

Fried, Albert. *The Rise and Fall of the Jewish Gangster in America.* New York: Holt, Rhinehart, and Winston, 1980.

Gelman, Howard. *The Films of John Garfield.* Secaucus, N.J.: Citadel, 1975.

Golden, Eve. *Platinum Girl.* New York: Abbeville, 1991.

Goodman, Ezra. *The Fifty-Year Decline and Fall of Hollywood.* New York: Simon and Shuster, 1961.

Gow, Gordon. *Hollywood in the Fifties.* Cranbury, N.J.: A. S. Barnes, 1971.

Halliwell, Leslie. *Halliwell's Film Guide, 7th Edition.* New York: Harper and Row, 1989.

Halliwell, Leslie. *Halliwell's Filmgoer's and Video Watcher's Companion, 9th Edition.* New York: Harper and Row, 1990.

Hamilton, Ian. *Writers in Hollywood, 1915-1951.* New York: Harper and Row, 1990.

Hardy, Phil. *Samuel Fuller.* New York: Praeger, 1970.

Hecht, Ben. *A Child of the Century.* New York: Simon and Shuster, 1954.

Hellman, Lillian. *An Unfinished Woman: A Memoir.* Boston: Little, Brown, 1969.

Highman, Charles. *Hollywood at Sunset.* New York: Saturday Review Press, 1972.

Highman, Charles, and Joel Greenberg. *Hollywood in the 1940s.* New York: A. S. Barnes, 1968.

Hirsch, Foster. *The Dark Side of the Screen: Film Noir.* London: A. S. Barnes, 1981.

Hyams, Joe. *Bogie: The Biography of Humphrey Bogart.* New York: New American Library, 1966.

Jennings, Dean. *We Only Kill Each Other: The Life and Bad Times of Bugsy Siegel.* Englewood Cliffs, N.J.: Prentice-Hall, 1967.

Kaminsky, Stuart. *American Film Genres.* Dayton, Ohio: Pflaum, 1974.

Katz, Ephraim. *The Film Encyclopedia.* New York: Fitzhanry and Whiteside Ltd., 1979.

Johnson, Diane. *Dashiell Hammett: A Life.* New York: Random House, 1983.

Kaminsky, Stuart M. *Don Siegel: Director.* New York: Curtis Books, 1976.

Kaplan, E. Ann, ed. *Women in Film Noir.* London: BFI, 1980.

Lake, Veronica, with Donald Bain. *Veronica.* New York: Citadel, 1971.

LeRoy, Mervyn, as told to Dick Kleiner. *Take One.* New York: Hawthorn, 1974.

Linet, Beverly. *Ladd: The Life, the Legend, the Legacy of Alan Ladd.* New York: Arbor House, 1979.

Luhr, William. *Raymond Chandler and Film.* New York: Ungar, 1982.

McArthur, Colin. *Underworld USA.* London: Secker and Warburg, 1972.

McBride, Joseph. *Orson Welles.* London: Secker and Warburg, 1972.

McCarthy, Todd, and Charles Flynn. *King of the B's.* New York: Dutton, 1975.

McGilligan, Patrick. *Cagney: The Actor as Autuer.* San Diego: A. S. Barnes, 1982.

MacShane, Frank. *The Life of Raymond Chandler.* New York: Dutton, 1976.

Madden, David. *James M. Cain.* New York: Twayne, 1970.

Madden, David, ed. *Tough Guy Writers of the 1930s.* Carbondale, Ill.: Southern Illinois University Press, 1968.

Maltin, Leonard, ed. *TV Movies.* New York: Signet Books, 1978.

Meryman, Richard. *Mank: The Wit, World, and Life of Herman Mankiewicz.* New York: Morrow, 1978.

Messick, Hank. *Lansky.* New York: Putnam, 1971.

Messick, Hank, and Burt Goldblatt. *The Mobs and the Mafia.* New York: Ballantine, 1972.

Miller, Don. *B Movies.* New York: Curtis, 1973.

Monaco, James. *The Encyclopedia of Film.* New York: Perigee/Putnam, 1991.

Mordden, Ethan. *Movie Star: A Look at the Women Who Made Hollywood.* New York: St. Martin's, 1983.

Munden, Kenneth W., ed. *American Film Institute Catalog of Motion Pictures: Feature Films, 1921–1930,* 2 vols. New York: R. R. Bower, 1971.

Nash, Jay Rob. *Bloodletters and Badmen.* New York: Warner, 1973.

Nevins, Francis M., Jr. *The Mystery Writer's Art.* Bowling Green, Ohio: Bowling Green University Popular Press, 1970.

Nichols, Bill, ed. *Movies and Methods.* Berkeley: University of California Press, 1976.

Norman, Barry. *The Story of Hollywood.* New York: Signet, 1987.

Ottoson, Robert. *A Reference Guide to the American Film Noir, 1940–1958.* Metuchen, N.J.: Scarecrow, 1981.

Parrish, James Robert, and Michael Pitts. *Film Directors: A Guide to Their American Films.* Metuchen, N.J.: Scarecrow, 1981.

Phillips, Gene D. *Hemingway and Film.* New York: Ungar, 1980.

Pratley, Gerald. *The Cinema of John Huston.* London: A. S. Barnes, 1977.

Quigley, Martin, ed. *International Motion Picture Almanac.* New York: Quigley Publications, 1929–1977.

Quinn, Anthony. *The Original Sin: A Self-Portrait.* Boston: Little, Brown, 1972.

Robinson, David, and Ann Lloyd. *The Films of the Thirties.* London: Orbis, 1982.

Robinson, David, and Ann Lloyd. *The Films of the Forties.* London: Orbis, 1982.

Robinson, David, and Ann Lloyd. *The Films of the Fifties.* London: Orbis, 1982.

Robinson, Edward G., and Leonard Spigelglass. *All My Yesterdays.* New York: Hawthorn, 1973.

Rosten, Leo C. *Hollywood: The Movie Colony, the Movie Makers.* New York: Harcourt, Brace, 1941.

Russell, Jane. *My Path and My Detours: An Autobiography.* New York: Franklin Watts, 1985.

Sarris, Andrew. *The American Cinema: Directors and Directions.* New York: E. P. Dutton, 1968.

Schary, Dore. *Heyday.* Boston: Little, Brown, 1979.

Schatz, Thomas. *The Genius of the System.* New York: Patheum, 1988.

Selby, Spencer. *Dark City: The Film Noir.* Jefferson, N.C.: McFarland, 1984.

Sennet, Ted. *Great Hollywood Movies.* New York: Abrams, 1986.

Shadoian, Jack. *Dreams and Dead Ends: The American Gangster/Crime Film.* Cambridge, Mass.: MIT Press, 1977.

Silver, Alain, and Elizabeth Ward, eds. *Film Noir: An Encyclopedic Reference to the American Style.* New York: Overlook, 1979.

Sklar, Robert. *Movie-Made America: A Cultural History of American Movies.* New York: Random House, 1975.

Swindell, Larry. *Body and Soul: The Story of John Garfield.* New York: Morrow, 1975.

Thomson, David. *America in the Dark: Hollywood and the Gift of Unreality*. London: Hutchinson, 1978.
Tierney, Gene, with Mickey Herskowitz. *Self-Portrait*. New York: Wyden, 1979.
Turner, Lana. *The Lady, the Legend, the Truth*. New York: Dutton, 1982.
Tyler, Parker. *Classics of the Foreign Film*. London: Spring, 1966.
Vermilye, Jerry. *The Films of the Thirties*. Secaucus, N.J.: Citadel, 1992.
Walsh, Raoul. *Each Man in His Time*. New York: Farrar, Straus, and Giroux, 1974.
Weaver, John T., ed. *Forty Years of Screen Credits*. Metuchen, N.J.: Scarecrow, 1973.
Wolfenstein, Martha, and Nathan Leites. *Movies: A Psychological Study*. Glencoe, Ill.: The Free Press, 1950.
Yablonsky, Lewis. *George Raft*. New York: McGraw-Hill, 1974.
Zierold, Norman. *The Moguls* New York: Coward, McCann, 1969.

Periodicals consulted include: *Bright Lights, Cahiers du Cinema, Film Comment, Film Threat, Films and Filming, Films in Review, Movieline, The New York Times, Photoplay, Premier, Sight and Sound, Time, Variety.*

Index

337